MINITAB
User's Guide 2:
Data Analysis
and Quality Tools

Release 13

for Windows®

Windows® 95, Windows® 98, and Windows NT™

February 2000

D0897457

ISBN 0-925636-44-4

Printed in the USA

1st Printing, 11/99

Text and cover printed on recycled paper.

Table of Contents

part IV: Design of Experiments

Welcome

How to Use this Guide

This guide is not designed to be read from cover to cover. It is designed to provide you with quick access to the information you need to complete tasks. If it fails to meet that objective, please let us know in any way you find convenient, including using the Info form at the back of this book, or sending e-mail to doc_comments@minitab.com.

This guide is half of a two-book set and provides reference information on the following topics:

– statistics
– quality control
– reliability and survival analysis
– design of experiments

We provide task-oriented documentation based on using the menus and dialog boxes. We hope you can now easily learn how to complete the specific task you need to accomplish. We welcome your comments.

See *Documentation for MINITAB for Windows, Release 13* on page xv for information about the entire documentation set for this product.

Assumptions

This guide assumes that you know the basics of using your operating system (such as Windows 95, Windows 98, or Windows NT). This includes using menus, dialog boxes, a mouse, and moving and resizing windows. If you are not familiar with these operations, see your operating system documentation.

Register as a MINITAB User

Please send us your MINITAB registration card. If you have lost or misplaced your registration card, contact your distributor, Minitab Ltd., Minitab SARL, or Minitab Inc. Please refer to the back cover of this guide or the *International Partners Card* included in your software product box for contact information. You can also register via the world wide web at http://www.minitab.com.

Registered MINITAB users are eligible to receive free technical support (subject to the terms and conditions of their License Agreement), new product announcements, maintenance updates, and MINITAB newsletters containing useful articles, tips, and macro information.

Global Support

Minitab Inc. and its international subsidiaries and partners provide sales and support services to Minitab customers throughout the world. Please refer to the *International Partners Card* included in your software product box. You can also access the most up-to-date international partner information via our web site at http://www.minitab.com.

Customer Support

For technical help, contact your central computing support group if one exists. You may also be eligible to receive customer support from your distributor, or from Minitab Inc., Minitab Ltd., or Minitab SARL directly, subject to the terms and conditions of your License Agreement. Eligible users may contact their distributor, Minitab Ltd., Minitab SARL, or Minitab Inc. (phone 814-231-2MTB (2682), fax 814-238-4383, or send e-mail through our web site at http://www.minitab.com/contacts). Technical support at Minitab Inc. is available Monday through Friday, between the hours of 9:00 a.m. and 5:00 p.m. Eastern time. When you are calling for technical support, it is helpful if you can be at your computer when you call. Please have your serial and software version numbers handy (from the **Help ➤ About MINITAB** screen), along with a detailed description of the problem.

Troubleshooting information is provided in a file called ReadMe.txt, installed in the main MINITAB directory, and in Help under the topics *Troubleshooting* and *How Do I....* You can also visit the Support section of our web site at http://www.minitab.com/support.

MINITAB on the Internet

Visit our web site at http://www.minitab.com. You can download demos, macros, and maintenance updates, get the latest information about our company and its products, get help from our technical support specialists, and more.

About the Documentation

Printed MINITAB documentation provides menu and dialog box documentation only. You'll find step-by-step "how-to's" throughout the books. (You'll find complete session command documentation available via online Help.)

MINITAB's new StatGuide provides you with statistical guideance for many analyses, so you get the most from your data analysis. Chapter overviews, particularly in *User's Guide 2*, provide additional statistical guidance to help determine suitability of a particular method. Many examples in both printed documentation and online Help include *Interpreting your output*.

The software itself provides online Help, a convenient, comprehensive, and useful source of information. To help you use MINITAB most effectively, Minitab Inc. and other publishers offer a variety of helpful texts and documents.

To order from Minitab Inc. from within the U.S. or Canada call: 800-448-3555. Additional contact information for Minitab Inc., Minitab Ltd., and Minitab SARL is given on the back cover of this book.

Documentation for MINITAB for Windows, Release 13

MINITAB Help, ©2000, Minitab Inc. This comprehensive, convenient source of information is available at the touch of a key or the click of the mouse. In addition to complete menu and dialog box documentation, you can find overviews, examples, guidance for setting up your data, information on calculations and methods, and a glossary. A separate online Help file is available for session commands.

MINITAB StatGuide, ©2000, Minitab Inc. Statistical guidance for many of MINITAB's text-based and graphical analyses—from basic statistics, to quality assurance, to design of experiments—so you get the most from your data analysis efforts. The MINITAB StatGuide uses preselected examples to help you understand and interpret output.

Meet MINITAB, ©2000, Minitab Inc. Rather than fully document all features, this book explains the fundamentals of using MINITAB—how to use the menus and dialog boxes, how to manage and manipulate data and files, how to produce graphs, and more. This guide includes five step-by-step sample sessions to help you learn MINITAB quickly.

MINITAB User's Guide 1: Data, Graphics, and Macros, ©2000, Minitab Inc. This guide includes how to use MINITAB's input, output, and data manipulation capabilities; how to work with data and graphs; and how to write macros.

MINITAB User's Guide 2: Data Analysis and Quality Tools, ©2000, Minitab Inc. This guide includes how to use MINITAB's statistics, quality control, reliability and survival analysis, and design of experiments tools.

Online tutorials. The same tutorials available in *Meet MINITAB*, designed to help new users learn MINITAB, are now available in the Help menu.

Session Command Quick Reference, ©2000, Minitab Inc. A Portable Document Format (PDF) file, to be read with Acrobat Reader, that lists all MINITAB commands and subcommands.

The CD-ROM distribution of MINITAB Release 13 includes our printed documentation—*Meet MINITAB, MINITAB User's Guide 1*, and *MINITAB User's Guide 2*—in Portable Document Format (PDF) files along with the Acrobat Reader for you to use these publications electronically. You may view them online with the Reader, or print portions of particular interest to you.

Related Documentation

Companion Text List, 1996, Minitab Inc., State College, PA. More than 300 textbooks, textbook supplements, and other related teaching materials that include MINITAB are featured in the *Companion Text List*. For a complete bibliography, the *Companion Text List* is available online at http://www.minitab.com.

MINITAB Handbook, Third Edition, 1994, Barbara F. Ryan, and Brian L. Joiner, Duxbury Press, Belmont, CA. A supplementary text that teaches basic statistics using MINITAB. The Handbook features the creative use of plots, application of standard statistical methods to real data, in-depth exploration of data, simulation as a learning tool, screening data for errors, manipulating data, transformation of data, and performing multiple regressions. Please contact your bookstore, Minitab Inc., or Duxbury Press to order this book.

Typographical Conventions Used in this Book

C	denotes a column, such as C12 or 'Height'.
K	denotes a constant, such as 8.3 or K14.
M	denotes a matrix, such as M5.
Enter	denotes a key, such as the Enter key.
Alt + D	denotes pressing the second key while holding down the first key. For example, while holding down the Alt key, press the D key.
File ➤ Exit	denotes a menu command, such as choose Exit from the File menu. Here is another example: **Stat ➤ Tables ➤ Tally** means open the Stat menu, then open the Tables submenu, then choose Tally.
Click **OK**.	Bold text also clarifies dialog box items and buttons.
Enter *Pulse1*.	Italic text specifies text to be entered by you.

Examples

Note the
special symbol
for examples.

We have designed the examples in the guides so you can follow along and duplicate the results. Here is an example with both Session window and Graph window output:

➤ Example of displaying descriptive statistics

You want to examine characteristic of the height (in inches) of male (Sex = 1) and female (Sex = 2) students who participated in the pulse study. You choose to display descriptive statistics with the option of a boxplot of the data.

1 Open the worksheet PULSE.MTW.

2 Choose **Stat ➤ Basic Statistics ➤ Display Descriptive Statistics**.

3 In **Variables**, enter *Height*. Check **By variable** and enter *Sex* in the text box.

4 Click **Graphs**. Check **Boxplot of data**. Click **OK** in each dialog box.

Session window output

Descriptive Statistics: Height by Sex

Variable	Sex	N	Mean	Median	TrMean	StDev
Height	1	57	70.754	71.000	70.784	2.583
	2	35	65.400	65.500	65.395	2.563

Variable	Sex	SE Mean	Minimum	Maximum	Q1	Q3
Height	1	0.342	66.000	75.000	69.000	73.000
	2	0.433	61.000	70.000	63.000	68.000

Graph window output

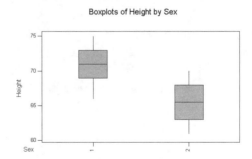

Boxplots of Height by Sex

Interpreting the results

The means shown in the Session window and the boxplots indicate that males are approximately 5.3 inches taller than females, and the spread of the data is about the same.

Sample Data Sets

For some examples you need to type data into columns. But for most examples, you can use data already stored in sample data set files in the DATA subdirectory of the main MINITAB directory.

MINITAB comes with a number of sample data sets that are stored in the DATA, STUDENT1, STUDENT8, STUDENT9, and STUDNT12 subdirectories (folders). For complete descriptions of most of these data sets, see the Help topic *sample data sets*.

part I

Statistics

1

Basic Statistics

Basic Statistics Overview

Use MINITAB's basic statistics capabilities for calculating basic statistics and for simple estimation and hypothesis testing with one or two samples. The basic statistics capabilities include procedures for

- calculating or storing descriptive statistics

- hypothesis tests and confidence intervals of the mean or difference in means

- hypothesis tests and confidence intervals for a proportion or the difference in proportions

- hypothesis test for equality of variance

- measuring association

- testing for normality of a distribution

Calculating and storing descriptive statistics

- **Display Descriptive Statistics** produces descriptive statistics for each column or subset within a column. You can print the statistics in the Session window and/or display them in a graph.

- **Store Descriptive Statistics** stores descriptive statistics for each column or subset within a column.

For a list of descriptive statistics available for display or storage see page 1-4. To calculate descriptive statistics individually and store them as constants, see the *Calculations* chapter in MINITAB *User's Guide 1*.

Confidence intervals and hypothesis tests of means

The four procedures for hypothesis tests and confidence intervals for population means or the difference between means are based upon the distribution of the sample mean following a normal distribution. According to the Central Limit Theorem, the normal distribution becomes an increasingly better approximation for the distribution of the sample mean drawn from any distribution as the sample size increases.

- **1-Sample Z** computes a confidence interval or performs a hypothesis test of the mean when the population standard deviation, σ, is known. This procedure is based upon the normal distribution, so for small samples, this procedure works best if your data were drawn from a normal distribution or one that is close to normal. From the Central Limit Theorem, you may use this procedure if you have a large sample, substituting the sample standard deviation for σ. A common rule of thumb is to consider samples of size 30 or higher to be large samples. Many analysts choose the t-procedure over the Z-procedure whenever σ is unknown.

- **1-Sample t** computes a confidence interval or performs a hypothesis test of the mean when σ is unknown. This procedure is based upon the t-distribution, which is derived from a normal distribution with unknown σ. For small samples, this procedure works best if your data were drawn from a distribution that is normal or close to normal. This procedure is more conservative than the Z-procedure and should always be chosen over the Z-procedure with small sample sizes and an unknown σ. Many analysts choose the t-procedure over the Z-procedure anytime σ is unknown. According to the Central Limit Theorem, you can have increasing confidence in the results of this procedure as sample size increases, because the distribution of the sample mean becomes more like a normal distribution.

- **2-Sample t** computes a confidence interval and performs a hypothesis test of the difference between two population means when σ's are unknown and samples are drawn independently from each other. This procedure is based upon the t-distribution, and for small samples it works best if data were drawn from distributions that are normal or close to normal. You can have increasing confidence in the results as the sample sizes increase.

- **Paired t** computes a confidence interval and performs a hypothesis test of the difference between two population means when observations are paired. When data are paired, as with before-and-after measurements, the paired t-procedure results in a smaller variance and greater power of detecting differences than would the above 2-sample t-procedure, which assumes that the samples were independently drawn.

Confidence intervals and hypothesis tests of proportions

- **1 Proportion** computes a confidence interval and performs a hypothesis test of a population proportion.

- **2 Proportions** computes a confidence interval and performs a hypothesis test of the difference between two population proportions.

Confidence intervals and hypothesis tests of equality of variance

- **2 Variances** computes a confidence interval and performs a hypothesis test for the equality, or homogeneity, of variance of two samples.

Measures of association

- **Correlation** calculates the Pearson product moment coefficient of correlation (also called the correlation coefficient or correlation) for pairs of variables. The correlation coefficient is a measure of the degree of linear relationship between two variables. You can obtain a p-value to test if there is sufficient evidence that the correlation coefficient is not zero.

By using a combination of MINITAB commands, you can also compute Spearman's correlation and a partial correlation coefficient. Spearman's correlation is simply the correlation computed on the ranks of the two samples. A partial correlation coefficient is the correlation coefficient between two variables while adjusting for the effects of other variables.

- **Covariance** calculates the covariance for pairs of variables. The covariance is a measure of the relationship between two variables but it has not been standardized, as is done with the correlation coefficient, by dividing by the standard deviation of both variables.

Distribution test

- **Normality Test** generates a normal probability plot and performs a hypothesis test to examine whether or not the observations follow a normal distribution. Some statistical procedures, such as a Z- or t-test, assume that the samples were drawn from a normal distribution. Use this procedure to test the normality assumption.

Descriptive Statistics Available for Display or Storage

The following table shows the descriptive statistics that you can display in the Session window, in a graphical summary, or that you can store. When you display statistics, you get all of the indicated statistics (see *Display Descriptive Statistics* on page 1-6); when you store statistics, you can choose which ones to store (see *Store Descriptive Statistics* on page 1-9).

Statistic	Session window	Graphical summary	Store
Number of nonmissing values	✗	✗	✗
Number of missing values	✗		✗
Total number			✗
Cumulative number			✗
Percent			✗
Cumulative percent			✗
Mean	✗	✗	✗

Statistic	Session window	Graphical summary	Store
Trimmed mean	✗		
Confidence interval for μ		✗	
Standard error of mean	✗		✗
Standard deviation	✗	✗	✗
Confidence interval for σ		✗	
Variance		✗	✗
Sum			✗
Minimum	✗	✗	✗
Maximum	✗	✗	✗
Range			✗
Median	✗	✗	✗
Confidence interval for median		✗	
First and third quartiles	✗	✗	✗
Interquartile range			✗
Sums of squares			✗
Skewness		✗	✗
Kurtosis		✗	✗
MSSD			✗
Normality test statistic, p-value		✗	

Calculations

Trimmed Mean. To calculate the trimmed mean (TrMean), MINITAB removes the smallest 5% and the largest 5% of the values (rounded to the nearest integer), and then averages the remaining data.

Standard Error of Mean. Calculated by $\text{StDev}/\sqrt{N}$.

Standard Deviation. If the column contains $x_1, x_2, \ldots, x_n$, with mean $\bar{x}$, then

$$\text{standard deviation} = \sqrt{\Sigma(x - \bar{x})^2/(n - 1)}$$

Confidence Interval for σ. The confidence interval for σ is

$$\sqrt{\frac{(n-1)s^2}{\chi^2_{n-1,\,1-\alpha/2}}} \quad to \quad \sqrt{\frac{(n-1)s^2}{\chi^2_{n-1,\,\alpha/2}}}$$

Variance. The standard deviation squared or $\Sigma(x-\bar{x})^2/(n-1)$.

Median. If sample size is odd, the median is the $(n+1)/2$th ordered value. If sample size is even, the median is the mean of the two middle ordered values.

Confidence Interval for Median. Uses one-sample sign confidence interval described on page 5-3.

Quartiles. To calculate quartiles, MINITAB orders the data from smallest to largest. The first quartile (Q1) is the observation at position $(n+1)/4$, and the third quartile (Q3) is the observation at position $3(n+1)/4$, where n is the number of observations. If the position is not an integer, interpolation is used.

Sums of Squares. This is the uncorrected sum of squares, or the sum of squared data values.

Skewness. This is a measure of distribution asymmetry or the tendency of one tail to be heavier than the other. A negative value indicates skewness to the left and a positive values indicates skewness to the right, though a value of zero does not necessarily indicate symmetry. Skewness is calculated as

$$n/(n-1)(n-2)\ \Sigma(x-\bar{x})^3/s^3$$

Kurtosis. This is a measure of how different a distribution is from the normal distribution. A positive value typically indicates that the distribution has a sharper peak, thinner shoulders, and fatter tails than the normal distribution. A negative value means that a distribution has a flatter peak, fatter shoulders, and thinner tails than the normal distribution. Kurtosis is calculated as

$$n(n+1)/(n-1)(n-2)(n-3)\Sigma(x-\bar{x})^4/s^4 - 3(n-1)^2/(n-2)(n-3)$$

MSSD. This is half the Mean of Successive Squared Differences. For example, if the data are 1, 2, 4, 10, successive differences are 1, 2, 6, and the MSSD is

(mean of $1^2, 2^2, 6^2$) / 2, or 6.833

Display Descriptive Statistics

Use Display Descriptive Statistics to produce statistics for each column or for subsets within a column. You can display these statistics in the Session window and optionally in a graph (see *Descriptive Statistics Available for Display or Storage* on page 1-4).

Data

The data columns must be numeric. The optional grouping column (also called a By column) can be numeric, text, or date/time and must be the same length as the data columns. If you wish to change the order in which text categories are processed from their default alphabetical order, you can define your own order (see *Ordering Text Categories* in the *Manipulating Data* chapter in MINITAB *User's Guide 1*).

MINITAB automatically omits missing data from the calculations.

▶ To calculate descriptive statistics

1 Choose Stat ➤ Basic Statistics ➤ Display Descriptive Statistics.

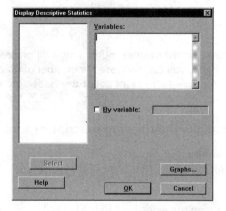

2 In **Variables**, enter the column(s) containing the data you want to describe.

3 If you like, use one or more of the options listed below, then click **OK**.

Options

Display Descriptive Statistics dialog box

■ display separate statistics for each unique value in a By column.

Graphs subdialog box

■ generate a histogram, a histogram with a normal curve, a dotplot, or a boxplot of the data in separate Graph windows.

■ display statistics in a single graphical summary. You can specify the confidence level for the displayed confidence intervals. The default level is 95%.

See *Descriptive statistics graphs* on page 1-8.

Descriptive statistics graphs

You can display your data in a histogram, a histogram with normal curve, a dotplot, or a boxplot, or display a graphical summary. The displayed statistics are listed in *Descriptive Statistics Available for Display or Storage* on page 1-4.

The graphical summary includes a table of descriptive statistics, a histogram with normal curve, a boxplot, a confidence interval for the population mean, μ, and a confidence interval for the population median. MINITAB can display a maximum of 100 graphs at a time. Therefore, the graphical summary will not work when there are more than 100 columns, 100 distinct levels or groups in a By column, or the combination of columns and By levels is more than 100.

There is no restriction on the number of columns or levels when producing output in the Session window.

Tip | If you exceed the maximum number of graphs because of the number of levels of your By variable, you can decrease the number of graphs by unstacking your data and displaying descriptive statistics for data subsets. See the *Manipulating Data* chapter in MINITAB *User's Guide 1* for more information.

▷ Example of displaying descriptive statistics

You want to compare the height (in inches) of male (Sex = 1) and female (Sex = 2) students who participated in the pulse study. You choose to display a boxplot of the data.

1 Open the worksheet PULSE.MTW.

2 Choose **Stat ➤ Basic Statistics ➤ Display Descriptive Statistics**.

3 In **Variables**, enter *Height*. Check **By variable** and enter *Sex* in the text box.

4 Click **Graphs**. Check **Boxplot of data**. Click **OK** in each dialog box.

Session window output

Descriptive Statistics: Height by Sex

Variable	Sex	N	Mean	Median	TrMean	StDev
Height	1	57	70.754	71.000	70.784	2.583
	2	35	65.400	65.500	65.395	2.563

Variable	Sex	SE Mean	Minimum	Maximum	Q1	Q3
Height	1	0.342	66.000	75.000	69.000	73.000
	2	0.433	61.000	70.000	63.000	68.000

*Graph
window
output*

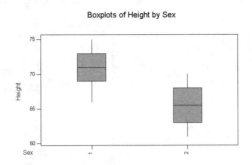

Interpreting the results

The means shown in the Session window and the boxplots indicate that males are approximately 5.3 inches taller than females, and the spread of the data is about the same.

Store Descriptive Statistics

You can store descriptive statistics for each column or for subsets within a column (see *Descriptive Statistics Available for Display or Storage* on page 1-4).

Data

The data columns must be numeric. The optional grouping column (also called a By column) can be numeric, text, or date/time and must be the same length as the data columns. If you wish to change the order in which text categories are processed from their default alphabetical order, you can define your own order (see *Ordering Text Categories* in the *Manipulating Data* chapter in MINITAB *User's Guide 1*).

MINITAB automatically omits missing data from the calculations.

▶ **To store descriptive statistics**

   1 Choose Stat ➤ Basic Statistics ➤ Store Descriptive Statistics.

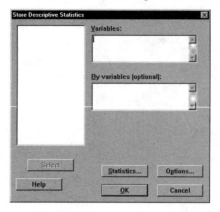

   2 In **Variables**, enter the column(s) containing the data you want to describe.

   3 If you like, use one or more of the options listed below, then click **OK**.

Options

Store Descriptive Statistics dialog box

- calculate statistics corresponding to values in one or more By columns

Statistics subdialog box

- select the statistics that you wish to store. The defaults are sample mean and sample size (nonmissing).

Options subdialog box

- store a row of output for each row of input. By default, MINITAB stores the requested statistics at the top of the worksheet only. If you check **Store a row of output for each row of input**, MINITAB will append the appropriate statistics to each row of input data.

When you use a By variable, you can also:

- store statistics for empty cells (default)—see *Storing Descriptive Statistics* on page 1-11

- include missing data as a valid By variable classification—see *Storing Descriptive Statistics* on page 1-11

- store the distinct values of the By variables (default)—see *Storing Descriptive Statistics* on page 1-11

Storing Descriptive Statistics

The worksheet below shows descriptive statistics that have been stored. The four columns on the right were stored by entering *Width* in **Variables**, and *Supplier Material* in **By variables** in the Store Descriptive Statistics dialog box.

Supplier	Material	Width	ByVar1	ByVar2	Mean1	N1
1	A	3.04	1	A	3.05667	3
1	A	3.06	1	B	*	0
1	A	3.07	2	A	2.97667	3
2	A	3.01	2	B	3.01500	2
2	A	2.94	3	A	*	0
2	A	2.98	3	B	3.01667	3
*	B	3.02				
2	B	3.00				
2	B	3.03				
3	B	3.02				
3	B	3.02				
3	B	3.01				
*	B	3.04				

Include empty cells

If you choose more than one By variable, MINITAB generates and stores summary data for each cell in the cross-classification. That is, MINITAB includes summary statistics for all combinations of the By variable levels, including combinations for which there are no data (called *empty cells*). Notice in the above example, that MINITAB included a column of stored data for the Supplier 1/Material B and Supplier 3/Material A cells, which are empty. If you do not want to store empty cells, uncheck **Include empty cells** in the Options subdialog box.

Include missing as a By level

By default, MINITAB ignores data from rows with missing values in a By column. To include missing values as a distinct level of the By variable, check **Include missing as a By level** in the Options subdialog box. If you check this option, MINITAB will add the following two rows to the stored data illustrated above:

ByVar1	ByVar2	Mean1	N1
:	:	:	:
:	:	:	:
*	A	*	0
*	B	3.03000	2

Store distinct values of By variables

By default, MINITAB includes columns in the summary data that indicate the levels of the By variables. Notice for example, the *ByVar1* and *ByVar2* columns above. If you do not want to store these columns, uncheck **Store distinct values of By variables** in the Options subdialog box.

Naming stored columns

MINITAB automatically names the storage columns with the name of the stored statistic and a sequential integer starting at 1. For example, suppose you enter two columns in **Variables** and choose to store the default mean and sample size. MINITAB will name the storage columns Mean1 and N1 for the first variable and Mean2 and N2 for the second variable. If you use two By variables, MINITAB will store the distinct levels (subscripts) of the By variables in columns named ByVar1 and ByVar2, with the appended integer cycling as with the stored statistics.

If you erase the storage columns or rename them, the integers will start over at 1. If you store statistics for many columns, you may want to rename the corresponding stored columns so that you can keep track of their origin.

One-Sample Z-Test and Confidence Interval

Use 1-Sample Z to compute a confidence interval or perform a hypothesis test of the mean when σ is known. For a two-tailed one-sample Z

$H_0: \mu = \mu_0$ versus $H_1: \mu \neq \mu_0$

where μ is the population mean and μ_0 is the hypothesized population mean.

Data

Enter each sample in a single numeric column. You can generate a hypothesis test or confidence interval for more than one column at a time.

MINITAB automatically omits missing data from the calculations.

▶ To do a Z-test and confidence interval of the mean

1 Choose Stat ➤ Basic Statistics ➤ 1-Sample Z.

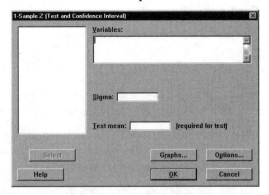

2 In **Variables**, enter the column(s) containing the samples.

3 In **Sigma**, enter a value for σ.

4 If you like, use one or more of the options listed below, then click **OK**.

Options

1-Sample Z dialog box

- to perform a hypothesis test, specify a null hypothesized test value in **Test mean**.

Options subdialog box

- specify a confidence level for the confidence interval. The default is 95%.

- define the alternative hypothesis by choosing less than (lower-tailed), not equal (two-tailed), or greater than (upper-tailed). The default is a two-tailed test.

Note that if you choose a lower-tailed or an upper-tailed hypothesis test, an upper or lower confidence bound will be constructed, respectively, rather than a confidence interval.

Graphs subdialog box

- display a histogram, dotplot, and boxplot for each column. The graphs show the sample mean and a confidence interval (or bound) for the mean. When you do a hypothesis test, the graphs also show the null hypothesis test value.

Method

Confidence interval

The confidence interval is calculated as

$$\bar{x} - z_{\alpha/2}(\sigma/\sqrt{n}) \text{ to } \bar{x} + z_{\alpha/2}(\sigma/\sqrt{n})$$

where $\bar{x}$ is the mean of the data, σ is the population standard deviation, n is the sample size, and $z_{\alpha/2}$ is the value from the normal table where α is 1 − confidence level / 100.

Note that the appropriate confidence bound is constructed in a similar fashion with $\alpha/2$ replaced by α. Then the lower bound is the sample mean minus the error margin and the upper bound is the sample mean plus the error margin.

You can specify a confidence level by entering any number between 1 and 100 in **Level**. The confidence level is 95% by default.

Hypothesis test

MINITAB calculates the test statistic by

$$Z = \frac{\bar{x} - \mu_0}{\sigma/\sqrt{n}}$$

where $\bar{x}$ is the mean of the data, μ is the hypothesized population mean, σ is the population standard deviation, and n is the sample size.

MINITAB performs a two-tailed test unless you specify a one-tailed test.

➤ Example of one-sample Z-test and confidence interval

Measurements were made on nine widgets. You know that the distribution of measurements has historically been close to normal with $\sigma = 0.2$. Since you know σ, and you wish to test if the population mean is 5 and obtain a 90% confidence interval for the mean, you use the Z-procedure.

1   Open the worksheet EXH_STAT.MTW.

2   Choose **Stat ➤ Basic Statistics ➤ 1-Sample Z**.

3   In **Variables**, enter *Values*.

4   In **Sigma**, enter *0.2*.

5   In **Test mean**, enter *5*.

6   Click **Options**. In **Confidence level**, enter 90. Click **OK**.

7   Click **Graphs**. Check **Dotplot of data**. Click **OK** in each dialog box.

Session window output

One-Sample Z: Values

```
Test of mu = 5 vs mu not = 5
The assumed sigma = 0.2

Variable          N      Mean     StDev    SE Mean
Values            9     4.7889    0.2472    0.0667

Variable            90.0% CI              Z       P
Values        (  4.6792,  4.8985)    -3.17   0.002
```

Graph window output

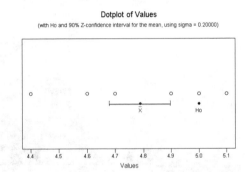

Dotplot of Values
(with Ho and 90% Z-confidence interval for the mean, using sigma = 0.20000)

Interpreting the results

The test statistic, Z, for testing if the population mean equals 5 is –3.17. The p-value of the test, or the probability of obtaining a more extreme value of the test statistic by chance if the null hypothesis was true, is 0.002. This is called the attained significance level, p-value, or attained α of the test. Since the p-value of 0.002 is smaller than commonly choosen α-levels, there is significant evidence that μ is not equal to 5, so we reject H_0 in favor of μ not being 5.

A hypothesis test at $\alpha = 0.1$ could also be performed by viewing the dotplot. The hypothesized value falls outside the 90% confidence interval for the population mean (4.6792, 4.8985), and so the null hypothesis can be rejected.

One-Sample t-Test and Confidence Interval

Use 1-Sample t to compute a confidence interval and perform a hypothesis test of the mean when the population standard deviation, σ, is unknown. For a two-tailed one-sample t,

$H_0: \mu = \mu_0$ versus $H_1: \mu \neq \mu_0$

where μ is the population mean and μ_0 is the hypothesized population mean.

Data

Enter each sample in a single numeric column. You can generate a hypothesis test or confidence interval for more than one column at a time.

MINITAB automatically omits missing data from the calculations.

▶ To compute a t-test and confidence interval of the mean

1   Choose **Stat ➤ Basic Statistics ➤ 1-Sample t**.

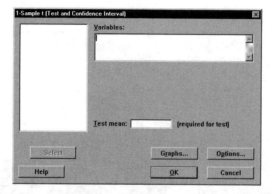

2   In **Variables**, enter the column(s) containing the samples.

3   If you like, use one or more of the options listed below, then click **OK**.

Options

1-Sample t dialog box

■   perform a hypothesis test by specifying a null hypothesized test value in **Test mean**.

Options subdialog box

■   specify a confidence level for the confidence interval. The default is 95%.

■   define the alternative hypothesis by choosing less than (lower-tailed), not equal (two-tailed), or greater than (upper-tailed). The default is a two-tailed test.

Note that if you choose a lower-tailed or an upper-tailed hypothesis test, an upper or lower confidence bound will be constructed, respectively, rather than a confidence interval.

Graphs subdialog box

■   display a histogram, dotplot, and boxplot for each column. The graphs show the sample mean and a confidence interval (or bound) for the mean. In addition, the null hypothesis test value is displayed when you do a hypothesis test.

Method

Confidence interval

The confidence interval is calculated as

$$\bar{x} - t_{\alpha/2}(s/\sqrt{n}) \quad \text{to} \quad \bar{x} + t_{\alpha/2}(s/\sqrt{n})$$

where $\bar{x}$ is the mean of the data, s is the sample standard deviation, n is the sample size, and $t_{\alpha/2}$ is the value from a t-distribution table where α is 1 − confidence level / 100 and degrees of freedom are $(n - 1)$.

Note that the appropriate confidence bound is constructed in a similar fashion with $\alpha/2$ replaced by α. Then the lower bound is the sample mean minus the error margin and the upper bound is the sample mean plus the error margin.

You can specify a confidence level by entering any number between 1 and 100 in **Confidence level**. The confidence level is 95% by default.

Hypothesis test

MINITAB calculates the test statistic by

$$t = \frac{\bar{x} - \mu_0}{s/\sqrt{n}}$$

where $\bar{x}$ is the mean of the data, μ_0 is the hypothesized population mean, s is the sample standard deviation, and n is the sample size.

MINITAB performs a two-tailed test unless you specify a one-tailed test.

⯈ Example of a one-sample t-test and confidence interval

Measurements were made on nine widgets. You know that the distribution of widget measurements has historically been close to normal, but suppose that you do not know σ. To test if the population mean is 5 and to obtain a 90% confidence interval for the mean, you use a t-procedure.

1 Open the worksheet EXH_STAT.MTW.

2 Choose **Stat ➤ Basic Statistics ➤ 1-Sample t**.

3 In **Variables**, enter *Values*.

4 In **Test mean**, enter 5.

5 Click **Options**. In **Confidence level** enter 90. Click **OK** in each dialog box.

*Session
window
output*

One-Sample T: Values

```
Test of mu = 5 vs mu not = 5

Variable          N      Mean    StDev   SE Mean
Values            9    4.7889   0.2472    0.0824

Variable            90.0% CI             T      P
Values       (  4.6357,  4.9421)     -2.56  0.034
```

Interpreting the results

The test statistic, T, for H_0: $\mu = 5$ is calculated as -2.56.

The p-value of this test, or the probability of obtaining more extreme value of the test statistic by chance if the null hypothesis was true, is 0.034. This is called the attained significance level, or p-value. Therefore, reject H_0 if your acceptable α level is greater than the p-value, or 0.034.

A 90% confidence interval for the population mean, μ, is (4.6356, 4.9421). This interval is slightly wider than the corresponding Z-interval shown in *Example of one-sample Z-test and confidence interval* on page 1-14.

Two-Sample t-Test and Confidence Interval

Use 2-Sample t to perform a hypothesis test and compute a confidence interval of the difference between two population means when the population standard deviations, σ's, are unknown. For a two-tailed two-sample t

$$H_0: \mu_1 - \mu_2 = \delta_0 \quad \text{versus} \quad H_1: \mu_1 - \mu_2 \neq \delta_0$$

where μ_1 and μ_2 are the population means and δ_0 is the hypothesized difference between the two population means.

Data

Data can be entered in one of two ways:

- both samples in a single numeric column with another grouping column (called subscripts) to identify the population. The grouping column may be numeric, text, or date/time.

- each sample in a separate numeric column.

The sample sizes do not need to be equal. MINITAB automatically omits missing data from the calculations.

► **To do a two-sample test and confidence interval**

1 Choose Stat ➤ Basic Statistics ➤ 2-Sample t.

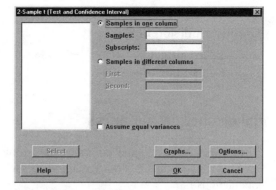

2 Choose one of the following:

- If your data are stacked in a single column:
  - choose **Samples in one column**
  - in **Samples**, enter the column containing the numeric data
  - in **Subscripts**, enter the column containing the group or population codes

- If your data are unstacked, that is each sample is in a separate column:
  - choose **Samples in different columns**
  - in **First**, enter the column containing the first sample
  - in **Second**, enter the column containing the other sample

3 If you like, use one or more of the options listed below, and click **OK**.

Options

2-Sample t dialog box

- assume that the populations have equal variances. The default is to assume unequal variances—see *Equal or unequal variances* on page 1-20.

Options subdialog box

- specify a confidence level for the confidence interval. The default is 95%.

- specify a null hypothesized test value in **Test mean** to perform a hypothesis test. The default is zero, or that the two population means are equal.

- define the alternative hypothesis by choosing less than (lower-tailed), not equal (two-tailed), or greater than (upper-tailed). The default is a two-tailed test.

Note that if you choose a lower-tailed or an upper-tailed hypothesis test, an upper or lower confidence bound will be constructed, respectively, rather than a confidence interval.

Graphs subdialog box

■ display a dotplot or boxplot of each sample in the same graph. The graphs also display the sample means.

Equal or unequal variances

If you check **Assume equal variances**, the sample standard deviations are pooled to obtain a single estimate of σ. (See *Standard deviations* under *Method* below for calculations.)

The two-sample t-test with a pooled variance is slightly more powerful than the two-sample t-test with unequal variances, but serious error can result if the variances are not equal. Therefore, the pooled variance estimate should not be used in many cases. Use *Test for Equal Variances* on page 3-60 to test the equal variance assumption.

Method

Confidence interval

The confidence interval is calculated as

$$(\bar{x}_1 - \bar{x}_2) - t_{\alpha/2}s \quad \text{to} \quad (\bar{x}_1 - \bar{x}_2) + t_{\alpha/2}s$$

where $t_{\alpha/2}$ is the value from a t-distribution table where α is 1 - confidence level/100. The sample standard deviation, s, of $\bar{x}_1 - \bar{x}_2$ and the degrees of freedom depend upon the variance assumption.

When a one-tailed test is specified, the appropriate confidence bound is constructed in a similar fashion with $\alpha/2$ replaced by α. Then the lower bound is the sample mean minus the error margin and the upper bound is the sample mean plus the error margin.

You can specify a confidence level of any number between 1 and 100 in **Confidence level**. The confidence level is 95% by default.

Hypothesis test

MINITAB calculates the test statistic, t, by

$$t = ((\bar{x}_1 - \bar{x}_2) - \delta_0)/s$$

The sample standard deviation, s, of $\bar{x}_1 - \bar{x}_2$ depends upon the variance assumption. Recall that δ_0 is the hypothesized difference between the two population means.

Standard deviations

When you assume *unequal variances*, the sample standard deviation of $\bar{x}_1 - \bar{x}_2$ is

$$s = \sqrt{\frac{s_1^2}{n_1} + \frac{s_2^2}{n_2}}$$

The test statistic degrees of freedom are

$$df = \frac{(VAR_1 + VAR_2)^2}{[(VAR_1)^2/(n_1 - 1)] + [(VAR_2)^2/(n_2 - 1)]}$$

where $VAR_1 = s_1^2/n_1$, and $VAR_2 = s_2^2/n_2$. MINITAB truncates the degrees of freedom to an integer, if necessary. This is a more conservative approach than rounding.

When you assume *equal variances*, the pooled sample standard deviation is

$$s_p = \sqrt{\frac{(n_1 - 1)s_1^2 + (n_2 - 1)s_2^2}{n_1 + n_2 - 2}}$$

The standard deviation of $(\bar{x}_1 - \bar{x}_2)$ is estimated by

$$s = s_p \sqrt{\frac{1}{n_1} + \frac{1}{n_2}}$$

The test statistic degrees of freedom are $(n_1 + n_2 - 2)$.

☞ Example of a two-sample t-test and confidence interval

A study was performed in order to evaluate the effectiveness of two devices for improving the efficiency of gas home-heating systems. Energy consumption in houses was measured after one of the two devices was installed. The two devices were an electric vent damper (Damper = 1) and a thermally activated vent damper (Damper = 2). The energy consumption data (BTU.In) are stacked in one column with a grouping column (Damper) containing identifiers or subscripts to denote the population. Previously, you performed a variance test and found no evidence for variances being unequal (see *Example of a test for equal variances* on page 1-36). Now you want to compare the effectiveness of these two devices by determining whether or not there is any evidence that the difference between the devices is different from zero.

1 Open the worksheet FURNACE.MTW.

2 Choose **Stat ➤ Basic Statistics ➤ 2-Sample T**.

3 Choose **Samples in one column**.

4 In **Samples**, enter *'BTU.In'*.

5 In **Subscripts**, enter *Damper*.

6 Check **Assume equal variances**. Click **OK**.

Session
window
output

Two-Sample T-Test and CI: BTU.In, Damper

```
Two-sample T for BTU.In

Damper      N      Mean     StDev    SE Mean
1          40      9.91      3.02      0.48
2          50     10.14      2.77      0.39


Difference = mu (1) - mu (2)
Estimate for difference:  -0.235
95% CI for difference: (-1.450, 0.980)
T-Test of difference = 0 (vs not =): T-Value = -0.38  P-Value = 0.701  DF = 88
Both use Pooled StDev = 2.88
```

Interpreting the result

MINITAB displays a table of the sample sizes, sample means, standard deviations, and standard errors for the two samples.

Since we previously found no evidence for variances being unequal, we chose to use the pooled standard deviation by choosing **Assume equal variances**. The pooled standard deviation, 2.88, is used to calculate the test statistic and the confidence intervals.

A second table gives a confidence interval for the difference in population means. For this example, a 95% confidence interval is (−1.45, 0.98), which includes zero, thus suggesting that there is no difference. Next is the hypothesis test result. The test statistic is −0.38, with p-value of 0.70, and 88 degrees of freedom.

Since the p-value is greater than commonly choosen α-levels, there is no evidence for a difference in energy use when using an electric vent damper versus a thermally activated vent damper.

Paired t-Test and Confidence Interval

Use the Paired t command to compute a confidence interval and perform a hypothesis test of the difference between population means when observations are paired. A paired t-procedure matches responses that are dependent or related in a pairwise manner. This matching allows you to account for variability between the pairs usually resulting in a smaller error term, thus increasing the sensitivity of the hypothesis test or confidence interval.

Typical examples of paired data include measurements on twins or before-and-after measurements. For a paired t-test:

$H_0: \mu_d = \mu_0$ versus $H_1: \mu_d \neq \mu_0$ where μ_d is the population mean of the differences and μ_0 is the hypothesized mean of the differences.

When the samples are drawn independently from two populations, use the two-sample t-procedure (page 1-18).

Data

The data from each sample must be in separate numeric columns of equal length. Each row contains the paired measurements for an observation. If either measurement in a row is missing, MINITAB automatically omits that row from the calculations.

▶ To compute a paired t-test and confidence interval

1 Choose **Stat ➤ Basic Statistics ➤ Paired t**.

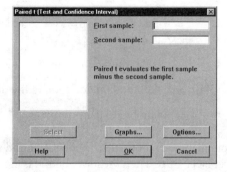

2 In **First Sample**, enter the column containing the first sample.

3 In **Second Sample**, enter the column containing the second sample.

4 If you like, use one or more of the options listed below, and click **OK**.

Options

Graphs subdialog box

■ display a histogram, dotplot, and boxplot of the paired differences. The graphs show the sample mean of the differences and a confidence interval (or bound) for the mean of the differences. In addition, the null hypothesis test value is displayed when you do a hypothesis test.

Options subdialog box

■ specify a confidence level for the confidence interval. The default is 95%.

■ specify a null hypothesis test value. The default is 0.

■ define the alternative hypothesis by choosing less than (lower-tailed), not equal (two-tailed), or greater than (upper-tailed). The default is a two-tailed test.

Note that if you choose a lower-tailed or an upper-tailed hypothesis test, an upper or lower confidence bound will be constructed, respectively, rather than a confidence interval.

Method

Confidence interval

For a two-tailed test, the confidence interval is calculated as

$$\bar{d} - t_{\alpha/2}(s_d/\sqrt{n}) \quad \text{to} \quad \bar{d} + t_{\alpha/2}(s_d/\sqrt{n})$$

where:

$\bar{d}$	$=$	$\Sigma d/n$, where $d = x_1 - x_2$ and x_1 and x_2 are paired observations from populations 1 and 2, respectively
$t_{\alpha/2}$		is the value from a t-distribution where α is $1 -$ confidence level $/ 100$
s_d	$=$	the standard deviation of the differences
n	$=$	number of pairs of values

Note that the appropriate confidence bound is constructed in a similar fashion with $\alpha/2$ replaced by α. Then the lower bound is the sample mean minus the error margin and the upper bound is the sample mean plus the error margin.

The standard deviation of the differences is calculated by:

$$s_d = \sqrt{\frac{\Sigma(d - \bar{d})^2}{(n-1)}}$$

You can specify a confidence level of any number between 1 and 100. The confidence level is 95% by default.

Hypothesis test

MINITAB calculates the test statistic, t, by:

$$t = \frac{\bar{d} - \mu_0}{(s_d/\sqrt{n})} \qquad \text{where } \mu_0 \text{ is the hypothesized mean of the differences.}$$

When μ_0 is not specified in **Test mean**, $\mu_0 = 0$ is used. MINITAB performs a two-tailed test unless you specify a one-tailed test.

► Example of a test and confidence interval for paired data

A shoe company wants to compare two materials, A and B, for use on the soles of boys' shoes. In this example, each of ten boys in a study wore a special pair of shoes with the sole of one shoe made from Material A and the sole on the other shoe made from Material B. The sole types were randomly assigned to account for systematic differences in wear between the left and right foot. After three months, the shoes are measured for wear.

For these data, you would use a paired design rather than an unpaired design. A paired t-procedure would probably have a smaller error term than the corresponding unpaired procedure because it removes variability that is due to differences between the pairs. For example, one boy may live in the city and walk on pavement most of the day, while another boy may live in the country and spend much of his day on unpaved surfaces.

1 Open the worksheet EXH_STAT.MTW.

2 Choose **Stat ➤ Basic Statistics ➤ Paired t**.

3 In **First Sample**, enter *Mat-A*. In **Second Sample**, enter *Mat-B*. Click **OK**.

Session window output

Paired T-Test and CI: Mat-A, Mat-B

```
Paired T for Mat-A - Mat-B

                   N       Mean     StDev    SE Mean
Mat-A             10     10.630     2.451      0.775
Mat-B             10     11.040     2.518      0.796
Difference        10     -0.410     0.387      0.122


95% CI for mean difference: (-0.687, -0.133)
T-Test of mean difference = 0 (vs not = 0): T-Value = -3.35  P-Value = 0.009
```

Interpreting the results

The confidence interval for the mean difference between the two materials does not include zero, which suggests a difference between the two materials. The small p-value ($p = 0.009$) further suggests that the data are inconsistent with H_0: $\mu_d = 0$, that is, the two materials do not perform equally. Specifically, Material B ($\overline{X} = 11.04$) performed better than Material A ($\overline{X} = 10.63$) in terms of wear over the three-month test period.

Compare the results from the paired procedure with those from an unpaired, two-sample t-test (**Stat ➤ Basic Statistics ➤ 2-Sample t**). The results of the paired procedure led us to believe that the data are not consistent with H_0 ($t = -3.35$; $p = 0.009$). The results of the unpaired procedure (not shown) are quite different, however. An unpaired t-test results in a t-value of -0.37, and a p-value of 0.72. Based on such results, we would fail to reject the null hypothesis and would conclude that there is no difference in the performance of the two materials.

In the unpaired procedure, the large amount of variance in shoe wear between boys (average wear for one boy was 6.50 and for another 14.25) obscures the somewhat less dramatic difference in wear between the left and right shoes (the largest difference between shoes was 1.10). This is why a paired experimental design and subsequent analysis with a paired t-test, where appropriate, is often much more powerful than an unpaired approach.

Test and Confidence Interval of a Proportion

Use 1 Proportion to compute a confidence interval and perform a hypothesis test of the proportion. For example, an automotive parts manufacturer claims that his spark plugs are less than 2% defective. You could take a random sample of spark plugs and determine whether or not the actual proportion defective is consistent with the claim. For a two-tailed test of a proportion:

$H_0: p = p_0$ versus $H_1: p \neq p_0$ where p is the population proportion
and p_0 is the hypothesized value

To compare two proportions, use **Stat ➤ Basic Statistics ➤ 2 Proportions** described on page 1-30.

Data

You can have data in two forms: raw or summarized.

Raw data

Enter each sample in a numeric, text, or date/time column in your worksheet. Columns must be all of the same type. Each column contains both the success and failure data for that sample. Successes and failures are determined by numeric or alphabetical order. MINITAB defines the lowest value as the failure; the highest value as the success. For example:

- for the numeric column entries of "20" and "40," observations of 20 are considered failures; observations of 40 are considered successes.

- for the text column entries of "alpha" and "omega," observations of alpha are considered failures; observations of omega are considered successes. If the data entries are "red" and "yellow," observations of red are considered failures; observations of yellow are considered successes.

  You can reverse the definition of success and failure in a text column by applying a value order (see *Ordering Text Categories* in the *Manipulating Data* chapter of *MINITAB User's Guide 1*).

With raw data, you can generate a hypothesis test or confidence interval for more than one column at a time. When you enter more than one column, MINITAB performs a separate analysis for each column.

MINITAB omits missing data from the calculations.

Summarized data

Enter the number of trials and one or more values for the number of successes directly in the 1 Proportion dialog box. When you enter more than one success value, MINITAB performs a separate analysis for each one.

▶ **To calculate a test and confidence interval of a proportion**

1 Choose Stat ➤ Basic Statistics ➤ 1 Proportion.

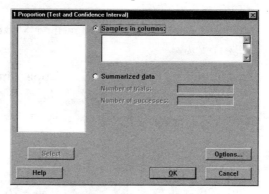

2 Do one of the following:

- If you have raw data, choose **Samples in columns**, and enter the columns containing the raw data.

- If you have summarized data:
    1 Choose **Summarized data**.
    2 In **Number of trials**, enter a whole number.
    3 In **Number of successes**, enter one or more whole numbers.

4 If you like, use one or more of the options listed below, and click **OK**.

Options

Options subdialog box

- specify a confidence level for the confidence interval. The default is 95%.

- specify a null hypothesis test value. The default is 0.5.

- define the alternative hypothesis by choosing less than (lower-tailed), not equal (two-tailed), or greater than (upper-tailed). The default is a two-tailed test.

Note that if you choose a lower-tailed or an upper-tailed hypothesis test, an upper or lower confidence bound will be constructed, respectively, rather than a confidence interval.

- use a normal approximation rather than the exact test for both the hypothesis test and confidence interval—see *Method* on page 1-28.

Method

Confidence interval

By default, MINITAB uses an exact method [5] to calculate the confidence interval limits (p_L, p_U):

Lower limit (p_L)	Upper limit (p_U)

$$p_L = \frac{v_1 F}{v_2 + v_1 F}$$

$$p_U = \frac{v_1 F}{v_2 + v_1 F}$$

where:

$v_1 = 2x$
$v_2 = 2(n - x + 1)$
x = number of successes
n = number of trials
F = lower $\alpha/2$ point of F with v_1 and v_2 degrees of freedom

where:

$v_1 = 2(x + 1)$
$v_2 = 2(n - x)$
x = number of successes
n = number of trials
F = upper $\alpha/2$ point of F with v_1 and v_2 degrees of freedom

If you choose to use a normal approximation, MINITAB calculates the confidence interval as:

$$\hat{p} \pm z_{\alpha/2} \sqrt{\frac{\hat{p}(1 - \hat{p})}{n}}$$

where:

$\hat{p}$ is the observed probability, $\hat{p} = x / n$, where x is the observed number of successes in n trials

$z_{\alpha/2}$ is the value from the z-distribution where α is $1 -$ confidence level / 100

n is the number of trials

Note that the appropriate confidence bound is constructed in a similar fashion with $\alpha/2$ replaced by α. Then the lower bound is the sample mean minus the error margin and the upper bound is the sample mean plus the error margin.

You can specify a confidence level of any number between 1 and 100 in **Confidence level**. The confidence level is 95% by default.

Hypothesis test

By default, MINITAB uses an exact method to calculate the test probability. If you choose to use a normal approximation, MINITAB calculates the test statistic (Z) as:

$$Z = \frac{\hat{p} - p_0}{\sqrt{\dfrac{p_0(1 - p_0)}{n}}}$$

where:

$\hat{p}$ is the observed probability, $\hat{p} = x / n$, where x is the observed number of successes in n trials

p_0 is the hypothesized probability

n is the number of trials

The probabilities are obtained from a standard normal distribution table (Z table).

When p_0 is not specified in **Test proportion**, $p_0 = 0.5$ is used. MINITAB performs a two-tailed test unless you specify a one-tailed test.

▷ Example of a test and confidence interval for a proportion

A county district attorney would like to run for the office of state district attorney. She has decided that she will give up her county office and run for state office if more than 65% of her party constituents support her. You need to test H_0: p = 0.65 versus H_1: p > .65.

As her campaign manager, you collected data on 950 randomly selected party members and find that 560 party members support the candidate. A test of proportion was performed to determine whether or not the proportion of supporters was greater than the required proportion of 0.65. In addition, a 95% confidence bound was constructed to determine the lower bound for the proportion of supporters.

1 Choose **Stat ► Basic Statistics ► 1 Proportion**.

2 Choose **Summarized data**.

3 In **Number of trials**, enter 950. In **Number of successes**, enter 560.

4 Click **Options**.

5 In **Test proportion**, enter 0.65.

6 From **Alternative**, choose **greater than**. Click **OK** in each dialog box.

Session window output

Test and CI for One Proportion

Test of p = 0.65 vs p > 0.65

Sample	X	N	Sample p	95.0% Lower Bound	Exact P-Value
1	560	950	0.589474	0.562515	1.000

Interpreting the Results

The p-value of 1.0 suggests that the data are consistent with the null hypothesis (H_0: $p = .65$), that is, the proportion of party members that support the candidate is not greater than the required proportion of 0.65. As her campaign manager, you would advise her not to run for the office of state district attorney.

Test and Confidence Interval of Two Proportions

Use the 2 Proportions command to compute a confidence interval and perform a hypothesis test of the difference between two proportions. For example, suppose you wanted to know whether the proportion of consumers who return a survey could be increased by providing an incentive such as a product sample. You might include the product sample with half of your mailings and see if you have more responses from the group that received the sample than from those who did not. For a two-tailed test of two proportions:

H_0: $p_1 - p_2 = p_0$ versus H_1: $p_1 - p_2 \neq p_0$

where p_1 and p_2 are the proportions of success in populations 1 and 2, respectively, and p_0 is the hypothesized difference between the two proportions.

To test one proportion, use **Stat ➤ Basic Statistics ➤ 1 Proportion** described on page 1-26.

Data

Data can be in two forms: raw or summarized.

Raw data

Raw data can be entered in two ways: stacked and unstacked.

- enter both samples in a single column (stacked) with a group column to identify the population. Columns may be numeric, text, or date/time. Successes and failures are determined by numeric or alphabetical order. MINITAB defines the lowest value as the failure; the highest value as the success. For example:
  - for the numeric column entries of "5" and "10," observations of 5 are considered failures; observations of 10 are considered successes.
  - for the text column entries of "agree" and "disagree," observations of agree are considered failures; observations of disagree are considered successes. If the data entries are "yes" and "no," observations of no are considered failures; observations of yes are considered successes.

- enter each sample (unstacked) in separate numeric or text columns. Both columns must be the same type — numeric or text. Successes and failures are defined as above for stacked data.

You can reverse the definition of success and failure in a text column by applying a value order (see *Ordering Text Categories* in the *Manipulating Data* chapter of MINITAB *User's Guide 1*).

The sample sizes do not need to be equal. MINITAB automatically omits missing data from the calculations.

Summarized data

Enter the number of trials and the number of successes for each sample directly in the 2 Proportions dialog box.

▶ **To calculate a test and confidence interval for the difference in proportions**

1 Choose Stat ➤ Basic Statistics ➤ 2 Proportions.

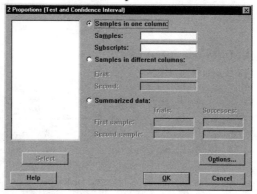

2 Do one of the following:

- If your raw data are stacked in a single column:
  1 Choose **Samples in one column**.
  2 In **Samples**, enter the column containing the raw data.
  3 In **Subscripts**, enter the column containing the group or population codes.
- If your raw data are unstacked, that is, each sample is in a separate column:
  1 Choose **Samples in different columns**.
  2 In **First**, enter the column containing the first sample.
  3 In **Second**, enter the column containing the other sample.
- If you have summarized data:
  1 Choose **Summarized data**.
  2 In **First sample**, enter numeric values under **Trials** and under **Successes**.
  3 In **Second sample**, enter numeric values under **Trials** and under **Successes**.

3 If you like, use one or more of the options listed below, and click **OK**.

Options

Options subdialog box

- specify a confidence level for the confidence interval. The default is 95%.

- specify a null hypothesis test difference. The default is 0.

- define the alternative hypothesis by choosing less than (lower-tailed), not equal (two-tailed), or greater than (upper-tailed). The default is a two-tailed test.

Note that if you choose a lower-tailed or an upper-tailed hypothesis test, an upper or lower confidence bound will be constructed, respectively, rather than a confidence interval.

- use a pooled estimate of p to calculate the test statistic. See *Hypothesis test* on page 1-33.

Method

Confidence interval

The confidence interval is calculated as

$$\hat{p}_1 - \hat{p}_2 \pm z_{\alpha/2}\sqrt{\frac{\hat{p}_1(1 - \hat{p}_1)}{n_1} + \frac{\hat{p}_2(1 - \hat{p}_2)}{n_2}}$$

where:

$\hat{p}_1$ and $\hat{p}_2$ are the observed probabilities of sample one and sample two respectively, $\hat{p} = x / n$, where x is the observed success in n trials

$z_{\alpha/2}$ is the value from a Z-distribution where α is 1 − confidence level / 100

Note that the appropriate confidence bound is constructed in a similar fashion with $\alpha/2$ replaced by α. Then the lower bound is the sample mean minus the error margin and the upper bound is the sample mean plus the error margin.

You can specify a confidence level of any number between 1 and 100 in **Confidence level**. The confidence level is 95% by default.

Hypothesis test

The calculation of the test statistic, Z, depends on the method used to estimate p.

- By default, MINITAB uses separate estimates of p for each population and calculates Z by:

$$Z = \frac{(\hat{p}_1 - \hat{p}_2) - d_o}{\sqrt{\dfrac{\hat{p}_1(1 - \hat{p}_1)}{n_1} + \dfrac{\hat{p}_2(1 - \hat{p}_2)}{n_2}}}$$

where d_0 is the hypothesized difference. When d_0 is not specified in **Test difference**, $d_0 = 0$ is used.

- If you choose to use a pooled estimate of p for the test, MINITAB calculates Z by:

$$Z = \frac{\hat{p}_1 - \hat{p}_2}{\sqrt{\hat{p}_c(1 - \hat{p}_c)\left(\dfrac{1}{n_1} + \dfrac{1}{n_2}\right)}}$$

where $\hat{p}_c$ is the pooled estimate of p (pooled observed probability).

$$\hat{p}_c = \frac{x_1 + x_2}{n_1 + n_2}$$

Note   It is only appropriate to use a pooled estimate when the hypothesized difference is zero ($d_0 = 0$).

MINITAB performs a two-tailed test unless you specify a one-tailed test.

➤ Example of a test and confidence interval of two proportions

As your corporation's purchasing manager, you need to authorize the purchase of twenty new photocopy machines. After comparing many brands in terms of price, copy quality, warranty, and features, you have narrowed the choice to two: Brand X and Brand Y. You decide that the determining factor will be the reliability of the brands as defined by the proportion requiring service within one year of purchase.

Because your corporation already uses both of these brands, you were able to obtain information on the service history of 50 randomly selected machines of each brand. Records indicate that six Brand X machines and eight Brand Y machines needed service. Use this information to guide your choice of brand for purchase.

1 Choose **Stat ➤ Basic Statistics ➤ 2 Proportions**.

2 Choose **Summarized data**.

3 In **First sample**, under **Trials**, enter 50. Under **Successes**, enter 44.

4 In **Second sample**, under **Trials**, enter 50. Under **Successes**, enter 42. Click **OK**.

Session window output

Test and CI for Two Proportions

```
Sample       X       N  Sample p
1           44      50  0.880000
2           42      50  0.840000
```

```
Estimate for p(1) - p(2):  0.04
95% CI for p(1) - p(2):  (-0.0957903, 0.175790)
Test for p(1) - p(2) = 0 (vs not = 0):  Z = 0.58  P-Value = 0.564
```

Interpreting the results

Since the p-value of 0.564 is larger than commonly choosen α-levels, the data are consistent with the null hypothesis (H_0: $p_1 - p_2 = 0$). That is, the proportion of photocopy machines that needed service in the first year did *not* differ depending on brand. As the purchasing manager, you need to find a different criterion to guide your decision on which brand to purchase.

You can make the same decision using the 95% confidence interval. Because zero falls in the confidence interval (−0.096, 0.176), you can conclude that the data are consistent with the null hypothesis. If you think that the confidence interval is too wide and does not provide precise information as to the value of $p_1 - p_2$, you may want to collect more data in order to obtain a better estimate of the difference.

Test for Equal Variances

You can use the variance test to perform hypothesis tests for equality, or homogeneity, of variance among two populations using an F-test and Levene's test. Many statistical procedures, including the two sample t-procedures, assume that the two samples are from populations with equal variance. The variance test procedure will test the validity of this assumption.

Data

Data can be entered in one of two ways:

- both samples in a single numeric column with another grouping column (called subscripts) to identify the population. The grouping column may be numeric, text, or date/time.

- each sample in a separate numeric column.

The sample sizes do not need to be equal. MINITAB automatically omits missing data from the calculations.

▶ **To perform a variance test**

1 Choose **Stat ➤ Basic Statistics ➤ 2 Variances**.

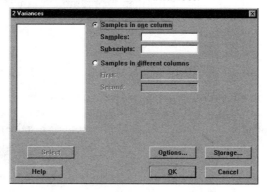

2 Choose one of the following:
   - If your data are stacked in a single column:
     1 choose **Samples in one column**
     2 in **Samples**, enter the column containing the numeric data
     3 in **Subscripts**, enter the column containing the group or population codes
   - If your data are unstacked, that is each sample is in a separate column:
     1 choose **Samples in different columns**
     2 in **First**, enter the column containing the first sample
     3 in **Second**, enter the column containing the other sample

3 If you like, use one or more of the options listed below, and click **OK**.

Options

Options subdialog box

- specify a confidence level for the confidence interval (the default is 95%)
- replace the default graph title with your own title

Storage subdialog box

- store standard deviations, variances, and upper and lower confidence limits for σ by factor levels

F-test versus Levene's test

MINITAB calculates and displays a test statistic and p-value for both an F-test and Levene's test where the null hypothesis is of equal variances versus the alternative of unequal variances. Use the F-test when the data come from a normal distribution and Levene's test when the data come from a continuous, but not necessarily normal, distribution.

The computational method for Levene's Test is a modification of Levene's procedure [6] developed by [2]. This method considers the distances of the observations from their sample median rather than their sample mean. Using the sample median rather than the sample mean makes the test more robust for smaller samples.

See Help for the computational form of these tests.

▶ Example of a test for equal variances

A study was performed in order to evaluate the effectiveness of two devices for improving the efficiency of gas home-heating systems. Energy consumption in houses was measured after one of the two devices was installed. The two devices were an electric vent damper (Damper = 1) and a thermally activated vent damper (Damper = 2). The energy consumption data (BTU.In) are stacked in one column with a grouping column (Damper) containing identifiers or subscripts to denote the population. You are interested in comparing the variances of the two populations so that you can construct a two-sample t-test and confidence interval to compare the two dampers. (See *Example of a two-sample t-test and confidence interval* on page 1-21.)

1 Open the worksheet FURNACE.MTW.

2 Choose **Stat ➤ Basic Statistics ➤ 2 Variances**.

3 Choose **Samples in one column**.

4 In **Samples**, enter *'BTU.In'*.

5 In **Subscripts**, enter *Damper*. Click **OK**.

Session window output

```
Test for Equal Variances
Response    BTU.In
Factors     Damper
ConfLvl     95.0000


Bonferroni confidence intervals for standard deviations

    Lower      Sigma      Upper    N  Factor Levels


  2.40655    3.01987    4.02726   40   1
  2.25447    2.76702    3.56416   50   2


F-Test (normal distribution)


Test Statistic: 1.191
P-Value        : 0.558


Levene's Test (any continuous distribution)


Test Statistic: 0.000
P-Value        : 0.996
```

*Graph
window
output*

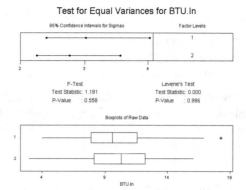

Interpreting the results

The variance test generates a plot that displays Bonferroni 95% confidence intervals for the population standard deviation at both factor levels. The graph also displays the side-by-side boxplots of the raw data for the two samples. Finally, the results of the F-test and Levene's test are given in both the Session window and the graph. Note that the 95% confidence level applies to the family of intervals and the asymmetry of the intervals is due to the skewness of the chi-square distribution.

For the energy consumption example, the p-values of 0.558 and 0.996 are greater than reasonable choices of α, so you fail to reject the null hypothesis of the variances being equal. That is, these data do not provide enough evidence to claim that the two populations have unequal variances. Thus, it is reasonable to assume equal variances when using a two-sample t-procedure.

Correlation

You can use the Pearson product moment correlation coefficient to measure the degree of linear relationship between two variables. The correlation coefficient assumes a value between −1 and +1. If one variable tends to increase as the other decreases, the correlation coefficient is negative. Conversely, if the two variables tend to increase together the correlation coefficient is positive. For a two-tailed test of the correlation:

$H_0: \rho = 0$ versus $H_1: \rho \neq 0$ where ρ is the correlation between a pair of variables.

Data

Data must be in numeric columns of equal length.

MINITAB omits missing data from calculations using a method that is often called *pairwise deletion*. MINITAB omits from the calculations for each column pair only those rows that contain a missing value for that pair.

If you are calculating correlations between multiple columns at the same time, pairwise deletion may result in different observations being included in the various correlations. Although this method is the best for each individual correlation, the correlation matrix as a whole may not be well behaved (for example, it may not be positive definite).

▶ **To calculate the Pearson product moment correlation**

1 Choose **Stat ➤ Basic Statistics ➤ Correlation**.

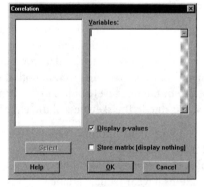

2 In **Variables**, enter the columns containing the measurement data.

3 If you like, use either of the options listed below, then click **OK**.

Options

- display the p-value for individual hypothesis tests. This is the default.
- store the correlation matrix. MINITAB does not display the correlation matrix when you store the matrix. To display the matrix, choose **Manip ➤ Display Data**.

Method

For the two variables x and y,

$$r = \frac{\sum (x - \bar{x})(y - \bar{y})}{(n-1)s_x s_y}$$

where $\bar{x}$ and s_x are the sample mean and standard deviation for the first sample, and $\bar{y}$ and s_y are the sample mean and standard deviation for the second sample.

Example of Pearson correlations

We have verbal and math SAT scores and first-year college grade-point averages for 200 students and we wish to investigate the relatedness of these variables. We use correlation with the default choice for displaying p-values.

1 Open the worksheet GRADES.MTW.

2 Choose **Stat ➤ Basic Statistics ➤ Correlation**.

3 In **Variables**, enter *Verbal Math GPA*. Click **OK**.

Session window output

Correlations: Verbal, Math, GPA

```
           Verbal      Math
Math        0.275
            0.000

GPA         0.322     0.194
            0.000     0.006

Cell Contents: Pearson correlation
               P-Value
```

Interpreting the results

MINITAB displays the lower triangle of the correlation matrix when there are more than two variables. The Pearson correlation between Math and Verbal is 0.275, between GPA and Verbal is 0.322, and between GPA and Math is 0.194. MINITAB prints the p-values for the individual hypothesis tests of the correlations being zero below the correlations. Since all the p-values are smaller than 0.01, there is sufficient evidence at $\alpha = 0.01$ that the correlations are not zero, in part reflecting the large sample size of 200.

Spearman's ρ

You can also use Correlation to obtain Spearman's ρ (rank correlation coefficient). Like the Pearson product moment correlation coefficient, Spearman's ρ is a measure of the relationship between two variables. However, Spearman's ρ is calculated on ranked data.

▶ To calculate Spearman's ρ

1 Delete any rows that contain missing values.

2 If the data are not already ranked, use **Manip ➤ Rank** to rank them. See the *Manipulating Data* chapter in MINITAB *User's Guide 1*.

3 Compute the Pearson's correlation on the columns of ranked data. See *To calculate the Pearson product moment correlation* on page 1-38.

Partial correlation coefficients

By using a combination of MINITAB commands, you can also compute a partial correlation coefficient. This is the correlation coefficient between two variables while adjusting for the effects of other variables. Partial correlation coefficients can be used when you have multiple potential predictors, and you wish to examine the individual effect of predictors upon the response variable after taking into account the other predictors.

▶ To calculate a partial correlation coefficient between two variables

1 Regress the first variable on the other variables and store the residuals—see *Regression* on page 2-3.

2 Regress the second variable on the other variables and store the residuals.

3 Calculate the correlation between the two columns of residuals.

▶ Example of computing a partial correlation coefficient

A survey was conducted in restaurants in 19 Wisconsin counties. Variables measured include: Sales, the gross sales; Newcap, new capital invested; and Value, estimated market value of the business. All variables are measured in thousands of dollars.

We want to look at the relationship between sales and new capital invested removing the influence of market value of the business. First we calculate the regular Pearson correlation coefficient for comparison. Then we demonstrate calculating the partial correlation coefficient between sales and new capital.

Step 1: Calculate unadjusted correlation coefficients

1 Open the worksheet RESTRNT.MTW.

2 Choose **Stat ➤ Basic Statistics ➤ Correlation**.

3 In **Variables**, enter *Sales Newcap Value*. Click **OK**.

The remaining steps calculate partial correlation between Sales and Newcap.

Step 2: Regress Sales on Value and store the residuals (Resi1)

1 Choose **Stat ➤ Regression ➤ Regression**.

2 In **Response**, enter *Sales*. In **Predictors**, enter *Value*.

3 Click **Storage**, and check **Residuals**. Click **OK** in each dialog box.

Step 3: Regress Newcap on Value and store the residuals (Resi2)

1 Choose **Stat ➤ Regression ➤ Regression**.

2 In **Response**, enter *Newcap*. In **Predictors**, enter *Value*.

3 Click **OK**.

Step 4: Calculate correlations of the residual columns

1 Choose **Stat ➤ Basic Statistics ➤ Correlation**.

2 In **Variables**, enter *Resi1* and *Resi2*. Click **OK**.

Session window output

Correlations: Sales, Newcap, Value

```
              Sales    Newcap
Newcap       0.615
             0.000

Value        0.803    0.734
             0.000    0.000

Cell Contents: Pearson correlation
               P-Value
```

Session window output

Correlations: RESI1, RESI2

```
Pearson correlation of RESI1 and RESI2 = 0.078
P-Value = 0.261
```

Interpreting the results

The correlation between the residual columns is 0.078. In other words, after adjusting for the linear effect of Value, the correlation between Sales and Newcap is 0.078—a value that is quite different from the uncorrected 0.615 value. In addition, the p-value of 0.261 indicates that there is no evidence that the correlation between Sales and Newcap—after accounting for the Value effect—is different from zero.

You can repeat this example to obtain the partial correlation coefficients between other variables. The partial correlation between Sales and Value is 0.654; the partial correlation between Newcap and Value is 0.502.

Covariance

You can calculate the covariance for all pairs of columns. Like the Pearson correlation coefficient, the covariance is a measure of the relationship between two variables. However, the covariance has not been standardized, as is done with the correlation coefficient. The correlation coefficient is standardized by dividing by the standard deviation of both variables.

Data

Data must be in numeric columns of equal length.

MINITAB omits missing data from calculations using a method that is often called *pairwise deletion*. MINITAB omits from the calculations for each column pair only those rows that contain a missing value for that pair.

If you are calculating covariances between multiple columns at the same time, pairwise deletion may result in different observations being included in the various covariances. Although this method is the best for each individual covariance, the covariance matrix as a whole may not be well behaved (for example, it may not be positive definite).

▶ To calculate the covariance

1   Choose **Stat ➤ Basic Statistics ➤ Covariance**.

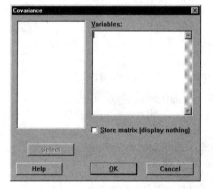

2   In **Variables**, enter the columns containing the measurement data.

3   If you like, use the option listed below, then click **OK**.

Options

You can store the covariance matrix. MINITAB does not display the covariance matrix when you store the matrix. To display the matrix, choose **Manip ➤ Display Data**.

Method

The covariance between each pair of columns is calculated, using the formula

$$S_{xy} = \frac{\sum (x - \bar{x})(y - \bar{y})}{n - 1}$$

where $\bar{x}$ is the sample mean for the first sample and $\bar{y}$ is the sample mean for the second sample.

Normality Test

Normality test generates a normal probability plot and performs a hypothesis test to examine whether or not the observations follow a normal distribution. For the normality test, the hypotheses are,

H_0: data follow a normal distribution vs. H_1: data do not follow a normal distribution

Data

You need one numeric column. MINITAB automatically omits missing data from the calculations.

▶ To perform a normality test

1 Choose **Stat ➤ Basic Statistics ➤ Normality Test**.

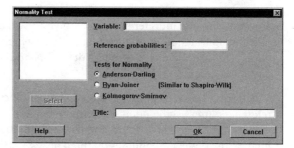

2 In **Variable**, enter the column containing the measurement data.

3 If you like, use one or more of the options listed below, and click **OK**.

Options

- mark reference probabilities and corresponding data values on the plot—see *Method* on page 1-44

- perform an Anderson-Darling, Ryan-Joiner, or Kolmogorov-Smirnov test for normality—see *Choosing a normality test* below

- replace the default graph title with your own title

Choosing a normality test

You have a choice of hypothesis tests for testing normality:

- Anderson-Darling test (the default), which is an ECDF (empirical cumulative distribution function) based test

- Ryan-Joiner test [4], [7] (similar to the Shapiro-Wilk test [8], [9]) which is a correlation based test

- Kolmogorov-Smirnov test, an ECDF based test

The Anderson-Darling and Ryan-Joiner tests have similar power for detecting non-normality. The Kolmogorov-Smirnov test has lesser power—see [3] and [7] for discussions of these tests for normality.

The common null hypothesis for these three tests is H_0: data follow a normal distribution. If the p-value of the test is less than your α level, reject H_0.

Method

The input data are plotted as the x-values. MINITAB calculates the probability of occurrence, assuming a normal distribution, and plots the calculated probabilities as y-values. The grid on the graph resembles the grids found on normal probability paper, with a log scale for the probabilities. A least-squares line is fit to the plotted points and drawn on the plot for reference. The line forms an estimate of the cumulative distribution function for the population from which data are drawn. MINITAB also displays the sample mean, standard deviation, and sample size of the input data on the plot.

When you enter the optional reference probabilities, they are marked with horizontal references lines. At the point where the reference line intersects the least-squares fit, a vertical reference line is drawn and labeled with the corresponding data value. To include reference probabilities on the plot:

- In **Reference probabilities**, enter a column containing the reference probabilities, which must be values between 0 and 1.

▷ Example of an Anderson-Darling normality test

In an operating engine, parts of the crankshaft move up and down. AtoBDist is the distance (in mm) from the actual (A) position of a point on the crankshaft to a baseline (B) position. To ensure production quality, a manager took five measurements each working day in a car assembly plant, from September 28 through October 15, and then ten per day from the 18th through the 25th.

You wish to see if these data follow a normal distribution, so you use Normality test.

1 Open the worksheet CRANKSH.MTW.

2 Choose **Stat ➤ Basic Statistics ➤ Normality Test**.

3 In **Variable**, enter *AtoBDist*. Click **OK**.

*Graph
window
output*

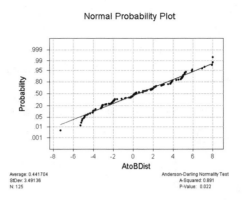

Interpreting the results

The graphical output is a plot of normal probabilities versus the data. The data depart from the fitted line most evidently in the extremes, or distribution tails. The Anderson-Darling test's p-value indicates that, at α levels greater than 0.022, there is evidence that the data do not follow a normal distribution. There is a slight tendency for these data to be lighter in the tails than a normal distribution because the smallest points are below the line and the largest point is just above the line. A distribution with heavy tails would show the opposite pattern at the extremes.

References

[1] S.F. Arnold (1990). *Mathematical Statistics*, Prentice-Hall, pp.383-384.

[2] M.B. Brown and A.B. Forsythe (1974). *Journal of the American Statistical Association*, 69, 364-367.

[3] R.B. D'Augostino and M.A. Stevens, Eds. (1986). *Goodness-of-Fit Techniques*, Marcel Dekker.

[4] J.J. Filliben (1975). "The Probability Plot Correlation Coefficient Test for Normality," *Technometrics*, Vol 17, p.111.

[5] N.L. Johnson and S. Kotz (1969). *Discrete Distributions*, John Wiley & Sons, pp.58-61.

[6] H. Levene (1960). *Contributions to Probability and Statistics*, pp.278-292. Stanford University Press, CA.

[7] T.A. Ryan, Jr. and B.L. Joiner (1976). *"Normal Probability Plots and Tests for Normality,"* Technical Report, Statistics Department, The Pennsylvania State University. (Available from MINITAB Inc.)

[8] S.S. Shapiro and R.S. Francia (1972). "An Approximate Analysis of Variance Test for Normality," *Journal of the American Statistical Association*, Vol 67, p.215.

[9] S.S. Shapiro and M.B. Wilk. "An Analysis of Variance Test for Normality (Complete Samples)," *Biometrika*, Vol 52, p. 591.

2

Regression

Regression Overview

Regression analysis is used to investigate and model the relationship between a response variable and one or more predictors. MINITAB provides various least-squares and logistic regression procedures.

- Use least squares regression when your response variable is continuous.

- Use logistic regression when your response variable is categorical.

Both least squares and logistic regression methods estimate parameters in the model so that the fit of the model is optimized. Least squares minimizes the sum of squared errors to obtain parameter estimates, whereas MINITAB's logistic regression commands obtain maximum likelihood estimates of the parameters. See *Logistic Regression Overview* on page 2-29 for more information about logistic regression.

Use the table below to assist in selecting a procedure:

Use...	to...	response type	estimation method
Regression (page 2-3)	perform simple or multiple regression: fit a model, store regression statistics, examine residual diagnostics, generate point estimates, generate prediction and confidence intervals, and perform lack-of-fit tests	continuous	least squares
Stepwise (page 2-14)	perform stepwise, forward selection, or backward elimination which add or remove variables from a model in order to identify a useful subset of predictors	continuous	least squares
Best Subsets (page 2-20)	identify subsets the predictors based on the maximum R^2 criterion	continuous	least squares
Fitted Line Plot (page 2-24)	perform linear and polynomial regression with a single predictor and plot a regression line through the data; on the actual or $\log_{10}$ scale	continuous	least squares
Residual Plots (page 2-27)	generate a set of residual plots to use for residual analysis: normal score plot, a chart of individual residuals, a histogram of residuals, and a plot of fits versus residuals	continuous	least squares
Binary Logistic (page 2-33)	perform logistic regression on a response with only two possible values, such as presence or absence	categorical	maximum likelihood
Ordinal Logistic (page 2-44)	perform logistic regression on a response with three or more possible values that have a natural order, such as none, mild, or severe	categorical	maximum likelihood
Nominal Logistic (page 2-51)	perform logistic regression on a response with three or more possible values that have no natural order, such as sweet, salty, or sour	categorical	maximum likelihood

Regression

You can use Regression to perform simple and multiple regression using the method of least squares. Use this procedure for fitting general least squares models, storing regression statistics, examining residual diagnostics, generating point estimates, generating prediction and confidence intervals, and performing lack-of-fit tests.

You can also use this command to fit polynomial regression models. However, if you want to fit a polynomial regression model with a single predictor, you may find it more advantageous to use *Fitted Line Plot* (page 2-24).

Data

Enter response and predictor variables in numeric columns of equal length so that each row in your worksheet contains measurements on one observation or subject.

MINITAB omits all observations that contain missing values in the response or in the predictors, from calculations of the regression equation and the ANOVA table items.

▶ To do a linear regression

1 Choose **Stat ➤ Regression ➤ Regression**.

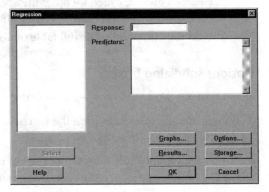

2 In **Response**, enter the column containing the response (Y) variable.

3 In **Predictors**, enter the columns containing the predictor (X) variables.

4 If you like, use one or more of the options listed below, then click **OK**.

Options

Graphs subdialog box

- draw five different residual plots for regular, standardized, or deleted residuals—see *Choosing a residual type* on page 2-5. Available residual plots include a:
  - histogram.
  - normal probability plot.
  - plot of residuals versus the fitted values ($\hat{Y}$).
  - plot of residuals versus data order. The row number for each data point is shown on the x-axis (for example, 1 2 3 4... *n*).
  - separate plot for the residuals versus each specified column.

  For a discussion, see *Residual plots* on page 2-6.

Results subdialog box

- display the following in the Session window:
  - no output
  - the estimated regression equation, table of coefficients, s, R^2, and the analysis of variance table
  - the default output, which includes the above output plus the sequential sums of squares and the fits and residuals of unusual observations
  - the default output, plus the full table of fits and residuals

Options subdialog box

- perform weighted regression—see *Weighted regression* on page 2-6
- exclude the intercept term from the regression by unchecking **Fit Intercept**—see *Regression through the origin* on page 2-7
- display the variance inflation factor (VIF—a measure of multicollinearity effect) associated with each predictor—see *Variance inflation factor* on page 2-7
- display the Durbin-Watson statistic which detects autocorrelation in the residuals— see *Detecting autocorrelation in residuals* on page 2-8
- display the PRESS statistic and adjusted R-squared
- perform a pure error lack-of-fit test for testing model adequacy when there are predictor replicates—see *Testing lack-of-fit* on page 2-8
- perform a data subsetting lack-of-fit test to test the model adequacy—see *Testing lack-of-fit* on page 2-8
- predict the response, confidence interval, and prediction interval for new observations—see *Prediction of new observations* on page 2-9

Storage subdialog box

- store the coefficients, fits, and regular, standardized, and deleted residuals—see *Choosing a residual type* on page 2-5.

- store the leverages, Cook's distances, and DFITS, for identifying outliers—see *Identifying outliers* on page 2-9.

- store the mean square error, the $(\mathbf{X'X})^{-1}$ matrix, and the $\mathbf{R}$ matrix of the $\mathbf{QR}$ or Cholesky decomposition. (The variance-covariance matrix of the coefficients is $MSE^*(\mathbf{XX})^{-1}$.) See Help for information on these matrices.

Residual analysis and regression diagnostics

Regression analysis usually does not end when a regression model has been fit. You also can examine residual plots and other regression diagnostics to assess if the residuals appear random and normally distributed. MINITAB provides a number of residual plots through the Graphs subdialog box. Alternatively, after fits and residuals are stored, you can use **Stat ➤ Regression ➤ Residual Plots** to obtain four plots within a single graph window.

MINITAB also produces regression diagnostics for identifying outliers or unusual observations. These observations may have a significant influence upon the regression results. See *Identifying outliers* on page 2-9. You might check unusual observations to see if they are correct. If so, you can try to determine why they are unusual and consider what effect they have on the regression equation. You might wish to examine how sensitive the regression results are to the outliers being present. Outliers can suggest inadequacies in the model or a need for additional information.

Choosing a residual type

You can calculate three types of residuals. Use the table below to help you choose which type you would like to plot:

Residual type...	Choose when you want to...	Calculation
regular	examine residuals in the original scale of the data	response – fit
standardized	use a rule of thumb for identifying observations that are not fit well by the model. A standardized residual greater than 2, in absolute value, might be considered to be large. MINITAB displays these observations in a table of unusual observations, labeled with an R.	(residual) / (standard deviation of the residual)

Residual type...	Choose when you want to...	Calculation
Studentized	identify observations that are not fit well by the model. Removing observations can affect the variance estimate and also can affect parameter estimates. A large absolute Studentized residual may indicate that including the observation in the model increases the error variance or that it has a large affect upon the parameter estimates, or both.	(residual) / (standard deviation of the residual). The ith studentized residual is computed with the ith observation removed.

Residual plots

MINITAB generates residual plots that you can use to examine the goodness of model fit. You can choose the following residual plots:

- **Normal plot of residuals.** The points in this plot should generally form a straight line if the residuals are normally distributed. If the points on the plot depart from a straight line, the normality assumption may be invalid. To perform a statistical test for normality, use **Stat ➤ Basic Statistics ➤ Normality Test** (page 1-43).

- **Histogram of residuals.** This plot should resemble a normal (bell-shaped) distribution with a mean of zero. Substantial clusters of points away from zero may indicate that factors other than those in the model may be influencing your results.

- **Residuals versus fits.** This plot should show a random pattern of residuals on both sides of 0. There should not be any recognizable patterns in the residual plot. The following may indicate error that is not random:
    - a series of increasing or decreasing points
    - a predominance of positive residuals, or a predominance of negative residuals
    - patterns such as increasing residuals with increasing fits

- **Residuals versus order.** This is a plot of all residuals in the order that the data was collected and can be used to find non-random error, especially of time-related effects.

- **Residuals versus other variables.** This is a plot of all residuals versus another variable. Commonly, you might use a predictor or a variable left out of the model and see if there is a pattern that you may wish to fit.

If certain residual values are of concern, you can brush your graph to identify these values. See the *Brushing Graphs* chapter in MINITAB *User's Guide 1* for more information.

Weighted regression

Weighted least squares regression is a method for dealing with observations that have nonconstant variances. If the variances are not constant, observations with

- large variances should be given relatively small weights
- small variances should be given relatively large weights

The usual choice of weights is the inverse of pure error variance in the response.

▶ **To perform weighted regression**

1 Choose **Stat ➤ Regression ➤ Regression ➤ Options**.

2 In **Weights**, enter the column containing the weights. The weights must be greater than or equal to zero. Click **OK** in each dialog box.

If there are n observations in the data set, MINITAB forms an n × n matrix **W** with the column of weights as its diagonal and zeros elsewhere. MINITAB calculates the regression coefficients by $(\mathbf{X'WX})^{-1}(\mathbf{X'WY})$. This is equivalent to minimizing a weighted error sum of squares,

$$\sum [w_i(y - \text{fit})^2] , \text{ where } w_i \text{ is the weight.}$$

Regression through the origin

By default, the y-intercept term (also called the constant) is included in equation. Thus, MINITAB fits the model

$$Y = \beta_0 + \beta_1 X_1 + \beta_2 X_2 + ... + \beta_k X_k + \varepsilon$$

However, if the response at X = 0 is naturally zero, a model without an intercept can make sense. If so, Uncheck Fit Intercept in the Options subdialog box, and the β_0 term will be omitted. Thus, MINITAB fits the model

$$Y = \beta_1 X_1 + \beta_2 X_2 + ... + \beta_k X_k + \varepsilon$$

Because it is difficult to interpret the R^2 when the constant is omitted, the R^2 is not printed. If you wish to compare fits of models with and without intercepts, compare mean square errors and examine residual plots.

Variance inflation factor

The variance inflation factor (VIF) is used to detect whether one predictor has a strong linear association with the remaining predictors (the presence of multicollinearity among the predictors). VIF measures how much the variance of an estimated regression coefficient increases if your predictors are correlated (multicollinear).

VIF = 1 indicates no relation; VIF > 1, otherwise. The largest VIF among all predictors is often used as an indicator of severe multicollinearity. Montgomery and Peck [21] suggest that when VIF is greater than 5-10, then the regression coefficients are poorly estimated. You should consider the options to break up the multicollinearity: collecting additional data, deleting predictors, using different predictors, or an alternative to least square regression. For additional information, see [3], [21].

Detecting autocorrelation in residuals

In linear regression, it is assumed that the residuals are independent (that is, they are not autocorrelated) of each other. If the independence assumption were violated, some model fitting results would be questionable. For example, positive correlation between error terms tends to inflate the t-values for coefficients. Because of that, checking model assumptions after fitting a model is an important part of regression analysis.

MINITAB provides two methods to check this assumption:

- A graph of residuals versus data order (1 2 3 4... n) can provide a means to visually inspect residuals for autocorrelation.

- The Durbin-Watson statistic tests for the presence of autocorrelation in regression residuals by determining whether or not the correlation between two adjacent error terms is zero. The test is based upon an assumption that errors are generated by a first-order autoregressive process. If there are missing observations, these are omitted from the calculations, and only the nonmissing observations are used.

  To reach a conclusion from the test, you will need to compare the displayed statistic with lower and upper bounds in a table. If D > upper bound, no correlation; if D < lower bound, positive correlation; if D is in between the two bounds, the test is inconclusive. For additional information, see [4], [22].

Testing lack-of-fit

MINITAB provides two lack-of-fit tests so you can determine whether or not the regression model adequately fits your data. The pure error lack-of-fit test requires replicates; the data subsetting lack-of-fit test does not require replicates.

- **Pure error lack-of-fit test**—If your predictors contain replicates (repeated x values with one predictor or repeated combinations of x values with multiple predictors), MINITAB can calculate a pure error test for lack-of-fit. The error term will be partitioned into pure error (error within replicates) and a lack-of-fit error. The F-test can be used to test if you have chosen an adequate regression model. For additional information, see [9], [22], [29].

- **Data subsetting lack-of-fit test**—MINITAB also performs a lack-of-fit test that does not require replicates but involves subsetting the data, and attempts to identify the nature of any lack-of-fit. This test is nonstandard, but it can provide information about the lack-of-fit relative to each variable. See [6] and Help for more information.

MINITAB performs 2k+1 hypothesis tests, where k is the number of predictors, and then combines them using Bonferroni inequalities to give an overall significance level of 0.1. A message is printed out for each test for which there is evidence of lack-of-fit. For each predictor, a curvature test and an interaction test are performed by comparing the fit above and below the predictor mean using indicator variables. A test can also be performed by fitting the model to the "central" portion of the data and then comparing the error sums of squares of that central data portion to the error sums of squares of all the data.

Prediction of new observations

If you have new predictor (X) values and you wish to know what the response would be using the regression equation, then use **Prediction intervals for new observations** in the Options subdialog box. Enter constants or columns containing the new x values, one for each predictor. Columns must be of equal length. If you enter a constant and a column(s), MINITAB will assume that you want predicted values for all combinations of constant and column values. You can change the confidence level from the default 95%, and you can also store the printed values: fits, standard errors of fits, confidence limits, and prediction limits. If you use prediction with weights, see Help for obtaining correct results.

Identifying outliers

In addition to graphs, you can store three additional measures for the purpose of identifying outliers, or unusual observations that can have a significant influence upon the regression. The measures are leverages, Cook's distance, and DFITS:

- **Leverages** are the diagonals of the "hat" matrix, $\mathbf{H} = \mathbf{X}(\mathbf{X'X})^{-1}\mathbf{X'}$, where $\mathbf{X}$ is the design matrix. Note that h_i depends only on the predictors; it does not involve the response Y. Many people consider h_i to be large enough to merit checking if it is more than $2p/n$ or $3p/n$, where p is the number of predictors (including one for the constant). MINITAB displays these in a table of unusual observations with high leverage. Those with leverage over $3p/n$ or 0.99, whichever is smallest, are marked with an X and those with leverage greater than $5p/n$ are marked with XX.

- **Cook's distance** combines leverages and Studentized residuals into one overall measure of how unusual the predictor values and response are for each observation. Large values signify unusual observations. Geometrically, Cook's distance is a measure of the distance between coefficients calculated with and without the ith observation. Cook [7] and Weisberg [29] suggest checking observations with Cook's distance > F (.50, p, n–p), where F is a value from an F-distribution.

- **DFITS**, like Cook's distance, combines the leverage and the Studentized residual into one overall measure of how unusual an observation is. DFITS (also called DFFITS) is the difference between the fitted values calculated with and without the ith observation, and scaled by stdev ($\hat{Y}_i$). Belseley, Kuh, and Welsch [3] suggest that observations with DFITS > $2\sqrt{p/n}$ should be considered as unusual. See Help for more details on these measures.

► Example of performing a simple linear regression

You are a manufacturer who wishes to easily obtain a quality measure on a product, but the procedure is expensive. However, there is a quick-and-dirty way of doing the same thing that is much less expensive but also is slightly less precise. You examine the relationship between the two scores to see if you can predict the desired score (Score2) from the score that is easy to obtain (Score1). You also obtain a prediction interval for an observation with Score1 being 8.2.

1 Open the worksheet EXH_REGR.MTW.

2 Choose **Stat ► Regression ► Regression**.

3 In **Response**, enter *Score2*. In **Predictors**, enter *Score1*.

4 Click **Options**.

5 In **Predict intervals for new observations**, type 8.2. Click **OK** in each dialog box.

Session window output

Regression Analysis: Score2 versus Score1

```
The regression equation is
Score2 = 1.12 + 0.218 Score1
```

Predictor	Coef	SE Coef	T	P
Constant	1.1177	0.1093	10.23	0.000
Score1	0.21767	0.01740	12.51	0.000

```
S = 0.1274    R-Sq = 95.7%    R-Sq(adj) = 95.1%
```

Analysis of Variance

Source	DF	SS	MS	F	P
Regression	1	2.5419	2.5419	156.56	0.000
Residual Error	7	0.1136	0.0162		
Total	8	2.6556			

Unusual Observations

Obs	Score1	Score2	Fit	SE Fit	Residual	St Resid
9	7.50	2.5000	2.7502	0.0519	-0.2502	-2.15R

R denotes an observation with a large standardized residual

Predicted Values for New Observations

New Obs	Fit	SE Fit	95.0% CI	95.0% PI
1	2.9026	0.0597	(2.7614, 3.0439)	(2.5697, 3.2356)

Values of Predictors for New Observations

New Obs	Score1
1	8.20

Interpreting the results

The regression procedure fits the model

$$Y = \beta_0 + \beta_1 X + \varepsilon$$

where Y is the response, X is the predictor, β_0 and β_1 are the regression coefficients, and ε is an error term having a normal distribution with mean of zero and standard deviation σ. MINITAB estimates β_0 by b_0, β_1 by b_1, and σ by s. The fitted equation is then

$$\hat{Y} = b_0 + b_1 X$$

where $\hat{Y}$ is called the predicted or fitted value. In this example, b_0 is 1.12 and b_1 is 0.218.

Table of Coefficients. The first table in the output gives the estimated coefficients, b_0 and b_1, along with their standard errors. In addition, a t-value that tests whether the null hypothesis of the coefficient is equal to zero and the corresponding p-value is given. In this example, the p-values that are used to test whether the constant and slope are equal to zero are printed as 0.000, because MINITAB rounds these values to three decimal points. These p-values are actually less than 0.0005. These values indicate that there is sufficient evidence that the coefficients are not zero for likely Type I error rates (α levels).

S = 0.1274. This is an estimate of σ, the estimated standard deviation about the regression line. Note that

$$s^2 = MSError$$

R-Sq = 95.7%. This is R^2, also called the coefficient of determination. Note that $R^2 = $ Correlation $(Y, \hat{Y})^2$. Also,

$$R^2 = (SS\ Regression) / (SS\ Total)$$

The R^2 value is the proportion of variability in the Y variable (in this example, Score2) accounted for by the predictors (in this example, Score1).

R-Sq(adj) = 95.1%. This is R^2 adjusted for degrees of freedom. If a variable is added to an equation, R^2 will get larger even if the added variable is of no real value. To compensate for this, MINITAB also prints R-Sq (adj), which is an approximately unbiased estimate of the population R^2 that is calculated by the formula

$$R^2(adj) = 1 - \frac{SS\ Error\ /(n-p)}{SS\ Total\ /(n-1)}$$

converted to a percent, where p is the number of coefficients fit in the regression equation (2 in our example). In the same notation, the usual R^2 is

$$R^2 = 1 - \frac{SS\ Error}{SS\ Total}$$

Analysis of Variance. This table contains sums of squares (abbreviated SS). SS Regression is sometimes written SS (Regression | b_0) and sometimes called SS Model. SS Error is sometimes written as SS Residual, SSE, or RSS. MS Error is often written as MSE. SS Total is the total sum of squares corrected for the mean. Use the analysis of variance table to assess the overall fit. The F-test is a test of the hypothesis H_0: All regression coefficients, excepting β_0, are zero.

Unusual Observations. Unusual observations are marked with an X if the predictor is unusual (large leverage), and they are marked with an R if the response is unusual (large standardized residual). See *Choosing a residual type* on page 2-5 and *Identifying outliers* on page 2-9. The default is to print only unusual observations. You can choose to print a full table of fitted values by selecting this option in the Results subdialog box.

The Fit or fitted Y value is sometimes called predicted Y value or $\hat{Y}$. SE Fit is the (estimated) standard error of the fitted value. St Resid is the standardized residual.

Predicted Values. The interval displayed under 95% CI is the confidence interval for the population mean of all responses (Score2) that correspond to the given value of the predictor (Score1 = 8.2). The interval displayed under 95% PI is the prediction interval for an individual observation taken at Score1 = 8.2. The confidence interval is appropriate for the data used in the regression. If you have new observations, use the prediction interval. See *Prediction of new observations* on page 2-9.

Regression analysis would not be complete without examining residual patterns. The following multiple regression example and residual plots procedure provide additional information about regression analysis.

▷ Example of a multiple regression

As part of a test of solar thermal energy, you measure the total heat flux from homes. You wish to examine whether total heat flux (Heatflux) can be predicted by insulation, by the position of the focal points in the east, south, and north directions, and by the time of day. Data are from [21], page 486. You found, using best subsets regression on page 2-23, that the best two-predictor model included the variables North and South and the best three-predictor added the variable East. You would like to evaluate the three-predictor model using multiple regression.

1 Open the worksheet EXH_REGR.MTW.

2 Choose **Stat ➤ Regression ➤ Regression**.

3 In **Response**, enter *Heatflux*.

4 In **Predictors**, enter *North South East*. Click **OK**.

*Session
window
output*

Regression Analysis: HeatFlux versus North, South, East

The regression equation is
HeatFlux = 389 - 24.1 North + 5.32 South + 2.12 East

Predictor	Coef	SE Coef	T	P
Constant	389.17	66.09	5.89	0.000
North	-24.132	1.869	-12.92	0.000
South	5.3185	0.9629	5.52	0.000
East	2.125	1.214	1.75	0.092

S = 8.598   R-Sq = 87.4%   R-Sq(adj) = 85.9%

Analysis of Variance

Source	DF	SS	MS	F	P
Regression	3	12833.9	4278.0	57.87	0.000
Residual Error	25	1848.1	73.9		
Total	28	14681.9			

Source	DF	Seq SS
North	1	10578.7
South	1	2028.9
East	1	226.3

Unusual Observations

Obs	North	HeatFlux	Fit	SE Fit	Residual	St Resid
4	17.5	230.70	210.20	5.03	20.50	2.94R
22	17.6	254.50	237.16	4.24	17.34	2.32R

R denotes an observation with a large standardized residual

Interpreting the results

MINITAB fits the regression model

$$Y = \beta_0 + \beta_1 X_1 + \beta_2 X_2 + \beta_3 X_3 + e$$

where Y is the response, X_1, X_2, and X_3 are the predictors, β_0, β_1, β_2, and β_3 are the regression coefficients, and ε is an error term having a normal distribution with mean of 0 and standard deviation σ.

The multiple regression output is similar to the simple regression output, but it also includes the sequential sums of squares. Sequential sums of squares differ from t-statistics. T-statistics test the null hypothesis that each coefficient is zero, given that all other variables are present in the model. The sequential sums of squares are the unique sums of squares of the current variable, given the sums of squares of any previously entered variables.

For example, in the sequential sums of squares column of the Analysis of Variance table, the value for North (10578.7) is the sums of squares for North; the value for South (2028.9) is the unique sums of squares for South given the sums of squares for

North; and the value for East (226.3) is the unique sums of squares for East given the sums of squares of North and South.

The first line in the sequential sums of squares table gives SS ($b_1 \mid b_0$), or the reduction in SS Error due to fitting the b_1 term (an equivalent is to use X1 as a predictor), assuming that you have already fit b_0. The next line gives SS ($b_2 \mid b_0, b_1$), or the reduction in SS Error due to fitting the b_2 term, assuming that you have already fit the terms b_0 and b_1. The next line is SS ($b_3 \mid b_0, b_1, b_2$), and so on. If you want a different sequence, say SS ($b_2 \mid b_0, b_3$), then repeat the regression procedure and enter X3 first, then X2. MINITAB does not print p-values for the sequential sums of squares. Except for the last sequential sums of squares, the mean square error should not be used to test the significance of these terms.

In this example, t-test p-values of less than 0.0005 indicate that there is significant evidence that the coefficients of variables North and South are not zero. The coefficient of the variable East, however, has an t-test p-value of 0.092. If the evidence for the coefficient not being zero appears insufficient and if it adds little to the prediction, you may choose the more parsimonious model with predictors North and South. Make this decision only after examining the residuals. In the residual plots example on page 2-28, you examine the residuals from the model with predictors North and South. (Alternatively, you could have used the graphs available in the Graphs subdialog box.)

Stepwise Regression

Stepwise regression removes and adds variables to the regression model for the purpose of identifying a useful subset of the predictors. MINITAB provides three commonly used procedures: standard stepwise regression (adds and removes variables), forward selection (adds variables), and backward elimination (removes variables).

Data

Enter response and predictor variables in the worksheet in numeric columns of equal length so that each row in your worksheet contains measurements on one observation or subject. MINITAB automatically omits rows with missing values from the calculations.

▶ **To do a stepwise regression**

1 Choose Stat ➤ Regression ➤ Stepwise.

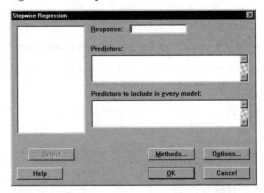

2 In **Response**, enter the numeric column containing the response (Y) data.

3 In **Predictors**, enter the numeric columns containing the predictor (X) variables.

4 If you like, use one or more of the options listed below, then click **OK**.

Options

Stepwise dialog box

■ By entering variables in **Predictors to include in every model**, you can designate a set of predictor variables that *cannot* be removed from the model, even when their p-values are less than the **Alpha to enter** value.

Method subdialog box

■ perform standard stepwise regression (adds and removes variables), forward selection (adds variables), or backward elimination (removes variables).

■ when you choose the stepwise method, you can enter a starting set of predictor variables in **Predictors in initial model**. These variables *are* removed if their p-values are greater than the **Alpha to enter** value. If you want keep variables in the model regardless of their p-values, enter them in **Predictors to include in every model** in the main dialog box. See *Stepwise regression (default)* on page 2-16.

■ when you choose the stepwise or forward selection method, you can set the value of the α for entering a new variable in the model in **Alpha to enter**. See *Stepwise regression (default)* and *Forward selection* on page 2-17.

■ when you choose the stepwise or backward elimination method, you can set the value of α for removing a variable from the model in **Alpha to remove**. See *Stepwise regression (default)* and *Backward elimination* on page 2-17.

Options subdialog box

- display the next best alternate predictors up to the number requested. If a new predictor is entered into the model, MINITAB displays the predictor which was the second best choice, the third best choice, and so on, up to the requested number.

- set the number of steps between pauses. See *User intervention* on page 2-17.

- exclude the intercept term from the regression by unchecking **Fit Intercept**. See *Regression through the origin* on page 2-7.

- display PRESS statistic and predicted R-square.

Method

MINITAB provides three commonly used procedures: standard stepwise regression (page 2-16), forward selection (page 2-17), and backward elimination (page 2-17)

Stepwise regression (default)

The first step in stepwise regression is to calculate an F-statistic and p-value for each variable in the model. If the model contains j variables, then F for any variable, Xr, is

$$F_{(1, n-j-1)} = \frac{SSE_{\{j-Xr\}} - SSE_j}{MSE_j}$$

where n is the number of observations, $SSE_{\{j-Xr\}}$ is the error sum of squares for the model after Xr is removed, and SSE_j and MSE_j are the error sums of squares and mean squared errors (respectively) for the model before Xr is removed.

If the p-value for any variable is greater than **Alpha to remove**, then the variable with the largest p-value is removed from the model, the regression equation is calculated, the results are printed, and the next step is initiated.

If no variable can be removed, the procedure attempts to add a variable. An F-statistic and p-value are calculated for each variable that is not in the model. If the model contains j variables, then F for any variable, Xa, is

$$F_{(1, n-j)} = \frac{SSE_j - SSE_{\{j+Xa\}}}{MSE_{\{j+Xa\}}}$$

where n is the number of observations, SSE_j is calculated before Xa is added to the model, and $SSE_{\{j+Xa\}}$ and $MSE_{\{j+Xa\}}$ are calculated after Xa is added to the model.

If the p-value corresponding to the F-value for any variable is smaller than **Alpha to enter**, the variable with the smallest p-value is then added to the model. The regression equation is then calculated, results are displayed, and the procedure goes to a new step. When no more variables can be entered into or removed from the model, the stepwise procedure ends.

Forward selection

This procedure adds variables to the model using the same method as the stepwise procedure. Once added, however, a variable is never removed. The forward selection procedure ends when none of the candidate variables have a p-value smaller than **Alpha to enter**.

Backward elimination

This procedure starts with the model that contains all the predictors and then removes variables, one at a time, using the same method as the stepwise procedure. No variable, however, can re-enter the model. The backward elimination procedure ends when none of the variables included the model have a p-value greater than **Alpha to remove**.

User intervention

Stepwise proceeds automatically by steps and then pauses. You can set the number of steps between pauses in the Options subdialog box.

The number of steps can start at one with the default and maximum determined by the output width. Set a smaller value if you wish to intervene more often. You must check **Editor ➤ Enable Commands** in order to intervene and use the procedure interactively. If you do not, the procedure will run to completion without pausing.

At the pause, MINITAB displays a MORE? prompt. At this prompt, you can continue the display of steps, terminate the procedure, or intervene by typing a subcommand.

To ...	Type
display another "page" of steps (or until no more predictors can enter or leave the model)	YES
terminate the procedure	NO
enter a set of variables	ENTER C...C
remove a set of variables	REMOVE C...C
force a set of variables to be in model	FORCE C...C
display the next best alternate predictors	BEST K
set the number of steps between pauses	STEPS K
change F to enter	FENTER K
change F to remove	FREMOVE K
change α to enter	AENTER K
change α to remove	AREMOVE K

Use of variable selection procedures

Variable selection procedures can be a valuable tool in data analysis, particularly in the early stages of building a model. At the same time, these procedures present certain dangers. Here are some considerations:

- Since the procedures automatically "snoop" through many models, the model selected may fit the data "too well." That is, the procedure can look at many variables and select ones which, by pure chance, happen to fit well.

- The three automatic procedures are heuristic algorithms, which often work very well but which may not select the model with the highest R^2 value (for a given number of predictors).

- Automatic procedures cannot take into account special knowledge the analyst may have about the data. Therefore, the model selected may not be the best from a practical point of view.

▷ Example of a stepwise regression

Students in an introductory statistics course participated in a simple experiment. Each student recorded his or her height, weight, gender, smoking preference, usual activity level, and resting pulse. They all flipped coins, and those whose coins came up heads ran in place for one minute. Afterward, the entire class recorded their pulses once more. You wish to find the best predictors for the second pulse rate.

1 Open the worksheet PULSE.MTW.

2 Press (Ctrl)+(M) to make the Session window active.

3 Check **Editor ➤ Enable Commands**.

4 Choose **Stat ➤ Regression ➤ Stepwise**.

5 In **Response**, enter *Pulse2*.

6 In **Predictors**, enter *Pulse1 Ran–Weight*.

7 Click **Options**.

8 In **Number of steps between pauses**, enter 2. Click **OK** in each dialog box.

9 At the first **More?** prompt, type *Yes*.

10 At the second **More?** prompt, type *No*.

*Session
window
output*

Stepwise Regression: Pulse2 versus Pulse1, Ran, ...

```
F-to-Enter: 4  F-to-Remove: 4

  Response is  Pulse2  on  6 predictors, with N =    92


           Step           1        2
        Constant       10.28    44.48

        Pulse1         0.957    0.912
        T-Value         7.42     9.74
        P-Value        0.000    0.000

        Ran                    -19.1
        T-Value                -9.05
        P-Value                0.000

        S               13.5     9.82
        R-Sq           37.97    67.71
        R-Sq(adj)      37.28    66.98
        C-p            103.2     13.5
         More? (Yes, No, Subcommand, or Help)


           Step           3
        Constant       42.62

        Pulse1         0.812
        T-Value         8.88
        P-Value        0.000

        Ran           -20.1
        T-Value      -10.09
        P-Value       0.000

        Sex             7.8
        T-Value        3.74
        P-Value       0.000

        S              9.18
        R-Sq          72.14
        R-Sq(adj)     71.19
        C-p             1.9
         More? (Yes, No, Subcommand, or Help)
```

Interpreting the results

This example uses six predictors. You requested that MINITAB do two steps of the automatic stepwise procedure, display the results, and allow you to intervene.

The first "page" of output gives results for the first two steps. In step 1, the variable Pulse1 entered the model; in step 2, the variable Ran entered. No variables were removed on either of the first two steps. For each model, MINITAB displays the constant term, the coefficient and its t-value for each variable in the model, S (square root of MSE), and R^2.

Because you answered YES at the MORE? prompt, the automatic procedure continued for one more step, adding the variable Sex. At this point, no more variables could enter or leave, so the automatic procedure stopped and again allowed you to intervene. Because you do not want to intervene, you typed NO.

The stepwise output is designed to present a concise summary of a number of fitted models. If you want more information on any of the models, you can use the regression procedure (page 2-3).

Best Subsets Regression

Best subsets regression identifies the best fitting regression models that can be constructed with the predictor variables that you specify. By default, all possible subsets of the predictors are evaluated, beginning with all models containing one predictor, and then all models containing two predictors, and so on. By default, Minitab reports the two best models that can be constructed with each number of predictors.

For example, suppose you conduct a best subsets regression with three predictors. Minitab will report the best and second best one-predictor models, followed by the best and second best two-predictor models, followed by the full model containing all three predictors.

Models are evaluated based on R^2, however, adjusted R^2, C_p, and s are also reported.

Best subsets regression is an efficient way to identify models that achieve your goals with as few predictors as possible. Subset models may actually estimate the regression coefficients and predict future responses with smaller variance than the full model using all predictors [15].

Data

Enter response and predictor variables in the worksheet in numeric columns of equal length so that each row in your worksheet contains measurements on one unit or subject. Minitab automatically omits rows with missing values from all models.

You can use as many as 31 free predictors. However, the analysis can take a long time when 15 or more free predictors are used. When analyzing a very large data set, forcing certain predictors to be in the model by entering them in Predictors in all models can decrease the length of time required to run the analysis. The total number of predictors (forced and free) in the analysis can not be more than 100.

▶ **To do a best subsets regression**

1 Choose Stat ➤ Regression ➤ Best Subsets.

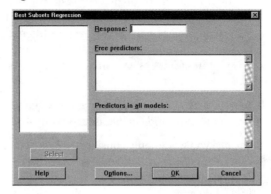

2 In **Response**, enter the numeric column containing the response (Y) data.

3 In **Free predictors**, enter from 1 to 31 numeric columns containing the candidate predictor (X) variables.

4 If you like, use one or more of the options listed below, then click **OK**.

Options

Best Subsets Regression dialog box

- specify a set of predictors to be included in all models by entering these variables in **Predictors in all models**. The maximum number of variables which can be entered is equal to 100 minus the number of variables entered in **Free predictors**.

Options subdialog box

- specify the minimum and maximum number of free predictors to include under **Free Predictor(s) In Each Model**. For example, if you specify a minimum of 3 and a maximum of 6 free predictors, MINITAB will determine the best models that contain 3, 4, 5, and 6 free predictors. (Note, in addition to the specified number of free predictors, these models will also contain any variables entered in **Predictors in all models**.)

- specify the number of models to display for each number of variables by entering the desired value in **Models of each size to print**. For example, if you enter 3, MINITAB will display the best, second best, and third best models for each number of free predictors. You can enter a value from 1 to 5 (the default is 2).

- exclude the intercept term from the regression by unchecking **Fit Intercept**—see *Regression through the origin* on page 2-7.

Using the best subsets regression procedure

The best subsets regression procedure can be used to select a group of likely models for further analysis. The general method is to select the smallest subset that fulfills certain statistical criteria. The reason that you would use a subset of variables rather than a full set is because the subset model may actually estimate the regression coefficients and predict future responses with smaller variance than the full model using all predictors [15].

The statistics R^2, adjusted R^2, C_p, and s (square root of MSE) are calculated by the best subsets procedure and can be used as comparison criteria.

Typically, you would only consider subsets that provide the largest R^2 value. However, R^2 always increases with the size of the subset. For example, the best 5-predictor model will always have a higher R^2 than the best 4-predictor model. Therefore, R^2 is most useful when comparing models of the same size. When comparing models with the same number of predictors, choosing the model with the highest R^2 is equivalent to choosing the model with the smallest SSE.

Use adjusted R^2 and C_p to compare models with different numbers of predictors. In this case, choosing the model with the highest adjusted R^2 is equivalent to choosing the model with the smallest mean square error (MSE). If adjusted R^2 is negative (usually when there is a large number of predictors and small R^2) then MINITAB sets the adjusted R^2 to zero.

The C_p statistic is given by the formula

$$C_p = \frac{SSE_p}{MSE_m} - (n - 2p)$$

where SSE_p is SSE for the best model with p parameters (including the intercept, if it is in the equation), and MSE_m is the mean square error for the model with all m predictors.

In general, look for models where C_p is small and close to p. If the model is adequate (i.e., fits the data well), then the expected value of C_p is approximately equal to p (the number of parameters in the model). A small value of C_p indicates that the model is relatively precise (has small variance) in estimating the true regression coefficients and predicting future responses. This precision will not improve much by adding more predictors. Models with considerable lack-of-fit have values of C_p larger than p. See [15] for additional information on C_p.

Exercise caution when using variable selection procedures such as best subsets (and stepwise regression). These procedures are automatic and therefore do not consider the practical importance of any of the predictors. In addition, anytime you fit a model to data, the goodness of the fit comes from two basic sources:

- fitting the underlying structure of the data (a structure that will appear in other data sets gathered in the same way)
- fitting the peculiarities of the one particular data set you analyze

Unfortunately, when you search through many models to find the "best," as you do in best subsets regression, a good fit is often chosen largely for the second reason. There are two ways that you can verify a model obtained by a variable selection procedure. You can

- verify the model using a new set of data.

- take the original data set and randomly divide it into two parts. Then use the variable selection procedure on one part to select a model and verify the fit using the second part.

► Example of best subsets regression

Total heat flux is measured as part of a solar thermal energy test. You wish to see how total heat flux is predicted by other variables: insolation, the position of the focal points in the east, south, and north directions, and the time of day. Data are from Montgomery and Peck [21], page 486.

1 Open the worksheet EXH_REGR.

2 Choose **Stat ► Regression ► Best Subsets.**

3 In **Response**, enter *Heatflux*.

4 In **Free Predictors**, enter *Insolation-Time*. Click **OK**.

Session window output

Best Subsets Regression: HeatFlux versus Insolation, East, ...

Response is HeatFlux

Vars	R-Sq	R-Sq(adj)	C-p	S	Insolation	East	South	North	Time
1	72.1	71.0	38.5	12.328				X	
1	39.4	37.1	112.7	18.154	X				
2	85.9	84.8	9.1	8.9321		X	X		
2	82.0	80.6	17.8	10.076			X	X	
3	87.4	85.9	7.6	8.5978		X	X	X	
3	86.5	84.9	9.7	8.9110	X		X	X	
4	89.1	87.3	5.8	8.1698	X	X	X	X	
4	88.0	86.0	8.2	8.5550	X		X	X	X
5	89.9	87.7	6.0	8.0390	X	X	X	X	X

Interpreting the results

Each line of the output represents a different model. Vars is the number of variables or predictors in the model. The statistics R^2, adjusted R^2, C_p, and s are displayed next (R^2

and adjusted R^2 are converted to percentages). Predictors that are present in the model are indicated by an X.

In this example, the best one-predictor model uses North (R^2 adj = 71.0) and the second-best one-predictor model uses Insolation (R^2 adj = 37.1). Moving from the best one-predictor model to the best two-predictor model increased the adjusted R^2 from 71.0 to 84.8. R^2 usually increases slightly as more predictors are added even when the new predictors do not improve the model. The best two-predictor model might be considered as the minimum fit. The multiple regression example on page 2-12 and the residual plots example on page 2-28 indicate that adding the variable East does not improve the fit of the model.

Fitted Line Plot

This procedure performs regression with linear and polynomial (second or third order) terms, if requested, of a single predictor variable and plots a regression line through the data, on the actual or $\log_{10}$ scale. Polynomial regression is one method for modeling curvature in the relationship between a response variable (Y) and a predictor variable (X) by extending the simple linear regression model to include X^2 and X^3 as predictors.

Data

Enter your response and single predictor variables in the worksheet in numeric columns of equal length so that each row in your worksheet contains measurements on one unit or subject. MINITAB automatically omits rows with missing values from the calculations.

▶ **To do a fitted line plot**

1   Choose **Stat ➤ Regression ➤ Fitted Line Plot**.

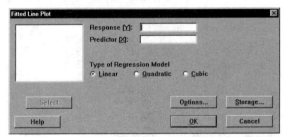

2   In **Response (Y)**, enter the numeric column containing the response data.

3   In **Predictor (X)**, enter the numeric column containing the predictor variable.

4   If you like, use one or more of the options listed below, then click **OK**.

Options

Fitted Line Plot dialog box

- choose a linear (default), quadratic, or cubic regression model to automatically include all lower order terms. See *Polynomial regression model choices* on page 2-25.

Options subdialog box

- transform the y-variable by $\log_{10}Y$. You can also choose to display the y-scale in the $\log_{10}$ scale.

- transform the x-variable by $\log_{10}X$. You can also choose to display the plot x scale in the $\log_{10}$ scale. If you use this option with polynomials of order greater than one, then the polynomial regression will be based on powers of the $\log_{10}X$.

- display confidence bands and prediction bands about the regression line. You can also change the confidence level from the default of 95%.

- replace the default title with your own title.

Storage subdialog box

- store the residuals, fits, and regression model coefficients (b_0, b_1, b_2, up to b_3 down the column, where b_i is the coefficient of the ith power of the predictor or transformed predictor).

- store the scaled residuals and scaled fits when using the y-variable transformation, $\log_{10}Y$.

Polynomial regression model choices

You can fit the following linear, quadratic, or cubic regression models:

Model type	Order	Statistical model
linear	first	$Y = \beta_0 + \beta_1 X + \varepsilon$
quadratic	second	$Y = \beta_0 + \beta_1 X + \beta_2 X^2 + \varepsilon$
cubic	third	$Y = \beta_0 + \beta_1 X + \beta_2 X^2 + \beta_3 X^3 + \varepsilon$

Another way of modeling curvature is to generate additional models by using the $\log_{10}$ of X and/or Y for linear, quadratic, and cubic models. In addition, taking the $\log_{10}$ of Y may be used to reduce right-skewness or nonconstant variance of residuals.

☞ Example of plotting a fitted regression line

You are studying the relationship between a particular machine setting and the amount of energy consumed. This relationship is known to have considerable curvature, and you believe that a log transformation of the response variable will produce a more symmetric error distribution. You choose to model the relationship between the machine setting and the amount of energy consumed with a quadratic model.

1 Open the worksheet EXH_REGR.MTW.

2 Choose **Stat ➤ Regression ➤ Fitted Line Plot**.

3 In **Response (Y)**, enter *EnergyConsumption*.

4 In **Predictor (X)**, enter *MachineSetting*.

5 Under **Type of Regression Model**, choose **Quadratic**.

6 Click **Options**. Check **Logten of Y, Display logscale for Y variable, Display confidence bands**, and **Display prediction bands**. Click **OK** in each dialog box.

Session window output

Polynomial Regression Analysis: EnergyConsum versus MachineSetti

```
The regression equation is
log(EnergyConsum) = 7.06962 - 0.698628 MachineSetti
 + 0.0173974 MachineSetti**2


S = 0.167696      R-Sq = 93.1 %      R-Sq(adj) = 91.1 %

Analysis of Variance

Source            DF        SS        MS        F        P
Regression         2   2.65326   1.32663  47.1743   0.000
Error              7   0.19685   0.02812
Total              9   2.85012


Source       DF    Seq SS        F       P
Linear        1   0.03688   0.1049   0.754
Quadratic     1   2.61638  93.0370   0.000
```

Graph window output

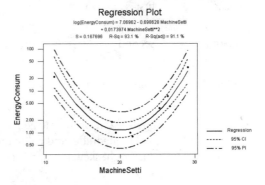

Regression Plot

Interpreting the results

The quadratic model (p-value = 0.000, or actually p-value < 0.0005) appears to provide a good fit to the data. The R^2 indicates that machine setting accounts for 93.1% of the variation in $\log_{10}$ of the energy consumed. A visual inspection of the plot reveals that the data are evenly spread about the regression line, implying no systematic lack-of-fit. The lines labeled CI are the 95% confidence limits for the $\log_{10}$ of energy consumed. The lines labeled PI are the 95% prediction limits for new observations.

Residual Plots

You can generate a set of plots to use for residual analysis by storing fits and residuals using another procedure, such as regression, and then using the Residual Plots procedure to produce a normal score plot, a chart of individual residuals, a histogram of residuals, and a plot of fits versus residuals, all on the same graph.

Data

You must save a column of residuals and a column of fits from another MINITAB procedure. MINITAB automatically omits rows with missing values from the calculations.

▶ **To display the residual plots**

1 Choose **Stat ➤ Regression ➤ Residual Plots**.

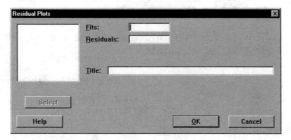

2 In **Fits**, enter the column containing stored fits.

3 In **Residuals**, enter the column containing the stored residuals.

4 If you like, use the option listed below, then click **OK**.

Options

You can replace the default title with your own title.

Example of residual plots

You examine the residuals from the best two-predictor model of the best subsets regression example on page 2-23. You determined in the multiple regression example on page 2-12 that adding the third variable from the best three-predictor model may not add appreciably to the fit. You now examine residual patterns from the best two-predictor model to further examine goodness-of-fit.

Step 1: Store the residuals and fits from a regression analysis

1 Open the worksheet EXH_REGR.MTW.

2 Choose **Stat ➤ Regression ➤ Regression**.

3 In **Response**, enter *Heatflux*.

4 In **Predictors**, enter *South North*.

5 Click **Storage**. Check **Fits** and **Standardized residuals**.

6 Click **OK** in each dialog box.

Step 2: Generate the residual plots

1 Choose **Stat ➤ Regression ➤ Residual Plots**.

2 In **Fits**, enter the column containing the stored fits.

3 In **Residuals**, enter the column containing the stored residuals. Click **OK**.

Session window output

Residual Plots

```
TEST 1. One point more than 3.00 sigmas from center line.
Test Failed at points: 22

TEST 2. 9 points in a row on same side of center line.
Test Failed at points: 16
```

Graph window output

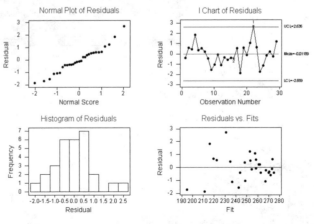

Interpreting the results

The residuals plots procedure generates four plots in one graph window. The normal plot shows an approximately linear pattern that is consistent with a normal distribution. Similarly, the histogram exhibits a pattern that is consistent with a sample from a normal distribution. However, the I Chart (a control chart of individual observations) reveals that one point labeled with a 1—the twenty-second value—is outside the three sigma limits, and another point labeled with a 2 is flagged because it is the ninth in a row on the same side of the mean.

Tip | You can identify points in the plots using the brushing capabilities. See the *Brushing Graphs* chapter in MINITAB *User's Guide 1*.

The plot of residuals versus fits shows that the fit tends to be better for higher predicted values. Investigation shows that the highest residual coincides with the highest value of the variable East. Including East in the model and repeating the residual plots procedure showed that no points are flagged as unusual (not shown). The contribution to the fit by the variable East may warrant further investigation.

Logistic Regression Overview

Both logistic regression and least squares regression investigate the relationship between a response variable and one or more predictors. A practical difference between them is that logistic regression techniques are used with *categorical* response variables, and linear regression techniques are used with *continuous* response variables.

MINITAB provides three logistic regression procedures that you can use to assess the relationship between one or more predictor variables and a categorical response variable of the following types:

Variable type	Number of categories	Characteristics	Examples
Binary	2	two levels	success, failure yes, no
Ordinal	3 or more	natural ordering of the levels	none, mild, severe fine, medium, coarse
Nominal	3 or more	no natural ordering of the levels	blue, black, red, yellow sunny, rainy, cloudy

Both logistic and least squares regression methods estimate parameters in the model so that the fit of the model is optimized. Least squares minimizes the sum of squared errors to obtain parameter estimates, whereas logistic regression obtains maximum likelihood estimates of the parameters using an iterative-reweighted least squares algorithm [19].

How to specify the model terms

The logistic regression procedures can fit models with:

- up to 9 factors and up to 50 covariates
- crossed or nested factors—see *Crossed vs. nested factors* on page 3-19
- covariates that are crossed with each other or with factors, or nested within factors

Model continuous predictors as covariates and categorical predictors as factors. Here are some examples. A is a factor and X is a covariate.

Model terms

A X A*X	fits a full model with a covariate crossed with a factor
A | X	an alternative way to specify the previous model
A X X*X	fits a model with a covariate crossed with itself making a squared term
A X(A)	fits a model with a covariate nested within a factor

The model for logistic regression is a generalization of the model used in MINITAB's general linear model (GLM) procedure. Any model fit by GLM can also be fit by the logistic regression procedures. For a discussion of specifying models in general, see *Specifying the model terms* on page 3-21 and *Specifying reduced models* on page 3-22. In the logistic regression commands, MINITAB assumes any variable in the model is a covariate unless the variable is specified as a factor. In contrast, GLM assumes that any variable in the model is a factor unless the variable is specified as a covariate.

Model restrictions

Logistic regression models in MINITAB have the restrictions as GLM models:

- There must be enough data to estimate all the terms in your model, so that the model is *full rank*. MINITAB will automatically determine if your model is full rank and display a message. In most cases, eliminating some unimportant high order interactions in your model should solve your problem.

- The model must be hierarchical. In a hierarchical model, if an interaction term is included, all lower order interactions and main effects that comprise the interaction term must appear in the model.

Reference levels for factors

MINITAB needs to assign one factor level as the *reference level*, meaning that the interpretation of the estimated coefficients is relative to this level. MINITAB designates the reference level based on the data type:

- For numeric factors, the reference level is the level with the *least* numeric value.
- For date/time factors, the reference level is the level with the *earliest* date/time.
- For text factors, the reference level is the level that is *first* in alphabetical order.

You can change the default reference level in the Options subdialog box.

Note | If you have defined a value order for a text factor, the default rule above does not apply. MINITAB designates the first value in the defined order as the reference value. See *Ordering Text Categories* in the *Manipulating Data* chapter in MINITAB *User's Guide 1*.

For more information, *Interpreting the parameter estimates relative to the event and the reference levels* on page 2-39.

Logistic regression creates a set of design variables for each factor in the model. If there are k levels, there will be k–1 design variables and the reference level will be coded as 0. Here are two examples of the default coding scheme:

Factor A with 4 levels (1 2 3 4)				Factor B with 3 levels (Temp Pressure Humidity)		
reference level	A1	A2	A3	reference level	B1	B2
1	0	0	0	Humidity	0	0
2	1	0	0	Pressure	1	0
3	0	1	0	Temp	0	1
4	0	0	1			

Reference event for the response variable

MINITAB needs to designate one of the response values as the *reference event*. MINITAB defines the reference event based on the data type:

- For numeric factors, the reference event is the *greatest* numeric value.
- For date/time factors, the reference event is the *most recent* date/time.
- For text factors, the reference event is the *last* in alphabetical order.

You can change the default reference event in the Options subdialog box.

For more information, *Interpreting the parameter estimates relative to the event and the reference levels* on page 2-39.

Note | If you have defined a value order for a text factor, the default rule above does not apply. MINITAB designates the last value in the defined order as the reference event. See *Ordering Text Categories* in the *Manipulating Data* chapter in MINITAB *User's Guide 1*.

Worksheet structure

Data used for input to the logistic regression procedures may be arranged in two different ways in your worksheet: as raw (categorical) data, or as frequency (collapsed) data. For binary logistic regression, there are three additional ways to arrange the data in your worksheet: as successes and trials, as successes and failures, or as failures and trials. These ways are illustrated here for the same data.

The response entered as raw data or as frequency data

Raw Data: one row for each observation

Frequency Data: one row for each combination of factor and covariate

C1	C2	C3	C4		C1	C2	C3	C4
Response		Factor	Covar		Response	Count	Factor	Covar
0		1	12 —— 1		0	1	1	12
1		1	12		1	19	1	12
1		1	12		0	1	2	12
.		.	. ⎱ 19		1	19	2	12
.		.	.		0	5	1	24
1		1	12 ⎰		1	15	1	24
0		2	12 —— 1		0	4	2	24
1		2	12		1	16	2	24
.		.	. ⎱ 19		0	7	1	50
.		.	.		1	13	1	50
1		2	12 ⎰		0	8	2	50
.		.	.		1	12	2	50
.		.	.		0	11	1	125
					1	2	1	125
					0	9	2	125
					1	11	2	125
					0	19	1	200
					1	1	1	200
					0	18	2	200
					1	2	2	200

The binary response entered as the number of successes, failures, or trials

Enter one row for each combination of factor and covariate.

Successes and Trials				Successes and Failures				Failures and Trials			
C1	C2	C3	C4	C1	C2	C3	C4	C1	C2	C3	C4
S	T	Factor	Covar	S	F	Factor	Covar	F	T	Factor	Covar
19	20	1	12	19	1	1	12	1	20	1	12
19	20	2	12	19	1	2	12	1	20	2	12
15	20	1	24	15	5	1	24	5	20	1	24
16	20	2	24	16	4	2	24	4	20	2	24
13	20	1	50	13	7	1	50	7	20	1	50
12	20	2	50	12	8	2	50	8	20	2	50
9	20	1	125	9	11	1	125	11	20	1	125
11	20	2	125	11	9	2	125	9	20	2	125
1	20	1	200	1	19	1	200	19	20	1	200
2	20	2	200	2	18	2	200	18	20	2	200

Use caution when viewing large regression coefficients

If the absolute value of the regression coefficient is large, exercise caution in judging the p-value of the test. When the absolute regression coefficients are large, their calculated standard errors can be too large, leading you to conclude that they are not significant [13]. If you have one or more large absolute regression coefficients for the factor(s) and/or covariate(s), the best test is to perform logistic regression both with and without these terms and make a conclusion based upon the change in the log-likelihood.

If you do test the significance of model terms in this way, your test statistic will be −2*(log-likelihood from reduced model − log-likelihood from full model). To compute the p-value for this test, choose **Calc ➤ Probability Distributions ➤ Chi-square**. In **Degrees of freedom**, enter the model degrees of freedom from full model − model degrees of freedom from reduced model, where the model degrees of freedom are the number of estimated coefficients. Check **Input constant**, and enter the test statistic from above. Store the answer in a constant, say k1, and then calculate the p-value as 1 − k1 using **Calc ➤ Calculator**.

Binary Logistic Regression

Use binary logistic regression to perform logistic regression on a binary response variable. A binary variable only has two possible values, such as presence or absence of a particular disease. A model with one or more predictors is fit using an iterative-reweighted least squares algorithm to obtain maximum likelihood estimates of the parameters [19].

Binary logistic regression has also been used to classify observations into one of two categories, and it may give fewer classification errors than discriminant analysis for some cases [10], [23].

Data

Your data must be arranged in your worksheet in one of five ways: as raw data, as frequency data, as successes and trials, as successes and failures, or as failures and trials. See *Worksheet structure* on page 2-32.

Factors, covariates, and response data can be numeric, text, or date/time. The *reference level* and the *reference event* depend on the data type. See *Reference levels for factors* on page 2-31 and *Reference event for the response variable* on page 2-31 for details.

The predictors may either be factors (nominal variables) or covariates (continuous variables). Factors may be crossed or nested. Covariates may be crossed with each other or with factors, or nested within factors.

The model can include up to 9 factors and 50 covariates. Unless you specify a predictor in the model as a factor, the predictor is assumed to be a covariate. Model continuous predictors as covariates and categorical predictors as factors. See *How to specify the model terms* on page 2-30 for more information.

MINITAB automatically omits observations with missing values from all calculations.

▶ To do a binary logistic regression

1 Choose **Stat ➤ Regression ➤ Binary Logistic Regression**.

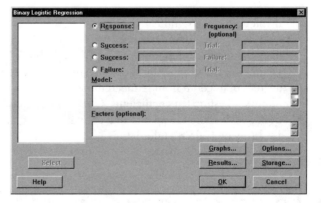

2 Do one of the following:

- If your data is in raw form, choose **Response** and enter the column containing the response variable.

- If your data is in frequency form, choose **Response** and enter the column containing the response variable. In **Frequency**, enter the column containing the count or frequency variable.

- If your data is in success-trial, success-failure, or failure-trial form, choose **Success** with **Trial**, **Success** with **Failure**, or **Failure** with **Trial**, and enter the respective columns in the accompanying boxes.

See *Worksheet structure* on page 2-32.

3 In **Model**, enter the model terms. See *How to specify the model terms* on page 2-30.

4 If you like, use one or more of the options listed below, then click **OK**.

Options

Binary Logistic Regression dialog box

- include categorical variables (factors) in the model

Graphics subdialog box

- plot delta Pearson χ^2, delta deviance, delta β based on standardized Pearson residuals, and delta β based on Pearson residuals versus:
  - the estimated event probability for each distinct factor/covariate pattern
  - the leverage for each distinct factor/covariate pattern

See *Regression diagnostics and residual analysis* on page 2-38.

Options subdialog box

- specify the link function: logit (the default), normit (also called probit), or gompit (also called complementary log-log)—see *Link functions* on page 2-46

- change the reference event of the response or the reference levels for the factors— see *Interpreting the parameter estimates relative to the event and the reference levels* on page 2-39

- specify initial values for model parameters or parameter estimates for a validation model—see *Entering initial values for parameter estimates* on page 2-37

- change the maximum number of iterations for reaching convergence (the default is 20)

- change the number of groups for the Hosmer-Lemeshow goodness-of-fit test from the default of 10—see *Groups for the Hosmer-Lemeshow goodness-of-fit test* on page 2-38

Results subdialog box

- display the following in the Session window:
  - no output.
  - basic information on response, parameter estimates, the log-likelihood, and the test for all slopes being zero.
  - the default output, which includes the above output plus three goodness-of-fit tests (Pearson, deviance, and Hosmer-Lemeshow), a table of observed and expected frequencies, and measures of association.
  - the default, along with factor level values, and tests for terms with more than 1 degree of freedom. If you choose the logit link function, MINITAB also prints two Brown goodness-of-fit tests.
- display the log-likelihood at each iteration of the parameter estimation process.

Storage subdialog box

- store the following diagnostic measures:
  - Pearson, standardized Pearson, and deviance residuals
  - changes (delta) in: Pearson χ^2, the deviance statistic, and the estimated regression coefficients based on either standardized Pearson or Pearson residuals when the respective factor/covariate patterns are removed
  - leverages, the diagonals of the hat matrix

  See *Regression diagnostics and residual analysis* on page 2-38.

- store the following characteristics of the estimated regression equation:
  - predicted probabilities of success
  - estimated model coefficients, their standard errors, and the variance-covariance matrix of the estimated coefficients
  - the log-likelihood for the last maximum likelihood iteration
- store the following aggregated data:
  - the number of occurrences for each factor/covariate pattern
  - the number of trials for each factor/covariate pattern

Link functions

MINITAB provides three link functions—logit (the default), normit (also called probit), and gompit (also called complementary log-log)—allowing you to fit a broad class of binary response models. These are the inverse of the cumulative logistic distribution function (logit), the inverse of the cumulative standard normal distribution function (normit), and the inverse of the Gompertz distribution function (gompit). This class of models is defined by:

$$g(\pi_j) = \beta_0 + x'_j\beta \text{ , where}$$

π_j = the probability of a response for the jth factor/covariate pattern

$g(\pi_j)$ = the link function (described below)

β_0 = the intercept

x'_j = a vector of predictor variables associated with the jth factor/covariate pattern

β = a vector of unknown coefficients associated with the predictors

The link function is the inverse of a distribution function. The link functions and their corresponding distributions are summarized below (pi in the variance is 3.14159):

Name	Link function	Distribution	Mean	Variance
logit	$g(\pi_j) = \log_e(\pi_j / (1-\pi_j))$	logistic	0	$pi^2 / 3$
normit	$g(\pi_j) = \Phi^{-1}(\pi_j)$	normal	0	1
gompit	$g(\pi_j) = \log_e(-\log_e(1-\pi_j))$	Gompertz	$-\gamma$ (Euler constant)	$pi^2 / 6$

You want to choose a link function that results in a good fit to your data. Goodness-of-fit statistics can be used to compare fits using different link functions. Certain link functions may be used for historical reasons or because they have a special meaning in a discipline.

An advantage of the logit link function is that it provides an estimate of the odds ratios. For a comparison of link functions, see [19].

Entering initial values for parameter estimates

There are several scenarios for which you might enter values for parameter estimates. For example, you may wish to give starting estimates so that the algorithm converges to a solution, or you may wish to validate a model with an independent sample.

- **Convergence**—The maximum likelihood solution may not converge if the starting estimates are not in the neighborhood of the true solution. If the algorithm does not converge to a solution, you can specify what you think are good starting values for parameter estimates in **Starting estimates for algorithm** in the Options subdialog box.

- **Validation**—You may also wish to validate the model with an independent sample. Typically, this is done by splitting the data into two subsets. Use the first set to estimate and store the coefficients. If you enter these estimates in **Estimates for validation model** in the Options subdialog box, MINITAB will use these values as the parameter estimates rather than calculating new parameter estimates. Then, you can assess the model fit for the independent sample.

In both cases, enter a column with the first entry being the constant estimate, and the remaining entries corresponding to the model terms in the order in which they appear in the **Model** box or the output.

Groups for the Hosmer-Lemeshow goodness-of-fit test

The Hosmer-Lemeshow statistic is the chi-square goodness-of-fit statistic from a $2 \times$ (the number of groups) table. The default number of groups is 10. This may work for a large number of problems but if the number of distinct factor/covariate patterns is small or large you may wish to adjust the number of groups. Hosmer and Lemeshow suggest using a minimum of six groups. See [16] for details.

Regression diagnostics and residual analysis

Following any modeling procedure, it is a good idea to assess the validity of your model. Logistic regression has a collection of diagnostic plots, goodness-of-fits tests, and other diagnostic measures to do this. These residuals and diagnostic statistics allow you to identify factor/covariate patterns that are either poorly fit by the model, have a strong influence upon the estimated parameters, or which have a high leverage. MINITAB provides different options for each of these, as listed in the following table (See Help for computational details). Hosmer and Lemeshow [16] suggest that you interpret these diagnostics jointly to understand any potential problems with the model.

To identify...	Use...	Which measures...
poorly fit factor/ covariate patterns	Pearson residual	the difference between the actual and predicted observation
	standardized Pearson residual	the difference between the actual and predicted observation, but standardized to have $\sigma = 1$
	deviance residual	deviance residuals, a component of deviance χ^2
	delta chi-square	changes in the Pearson χ^2 when the jth factor/ covariate pattern is removed
	delta deviance	changes in the deviance when the jth factor/ covariate pattern is removed
factor/covariate patterns with a strong influence on parameter estimates	delta beta	changes in the coefficients when the jth factor/ covariate pattern is removed—based on Pearson residuals
	delta beta based on standardized Pearson residuals	changes in the coefficients when the jth factor/ covariate pattern is removed—based on standardized Pearson residuals
factor/covariate patterns with a large leverage	leverage (Hi)	leverages of the jth factor/covariate pattern, a measure of how unusual predictor values are

The graphs available in the Graphs subdialog box allow you to visualize some of these diagnostics jointly; you can plot a measure useful for identifying poorly fit factor/covariate patterns (delta chi-square or delta deviance) or a measure useful for identifying a factor/covariate pattern with a strong influence on parameter estimates (one of the delta beta statistics) versus either the estimated event probability or leverage. The estimated event probability is the probability of the event, given the data and model. Leverages are used to assess how unusual the predictor values are (see *Identifying outliers* on page 2-9). See [16] for a further discussion of diagnostic plots. You can use MINITAB's graph brushing capabilities to identify points. See the *Brushing Graphs* chapter in MINITAB *User's Guide 1* for more information.

Interpreting the parameter estimates relative to the event and the reference levels

The interpretation of the parameter estimates depends on: the link function (see *Link functions* on page 2-36), reference event (see *Reference event for the response variable* on page 2-31), and reference factor levels (see *Reference levels for factors* on page 2-31). A parameter estimate associated with a predictor (factor or covariate) represents the change in the link function for each unit change in the predictor, while all other predictors are held constant. A unit change in a factor refers to a comparison of a certain level to the reference level.

The logit link provides the most natural interpretation of the parameter estimates and is therefore the default link in MINITAB. A summary of the interpretation follows:

■ The odds of a reference event is the ratio of P(event) to P(not event). The parameter estimate of a predictor (factor or covariate) is the estimated change in the log of P(event)/P(not event) for each unit change in the predictor, assuming the other predictors remain constant.

■ The parameter estimates can also be used to calculate the odds ratio, or the ratio between two odds. Exponentiating the parameter estimate of a factor yields the ratio of P(event)/P(not event) for a certain factor level compared to the reference level. The odds ratios at different values of the covariate can be constructed relative to zero. In the covariate case, it may be more meaningful to interpret the odds and not the odds ratio. Note that a parameter estimate of zero or an odds ratio of one both imply the same thing—the factor or covariate has no effect.

You can change the event or reference levels in the Options subdialog box if you wish to change how you view the parameter estimates. To change the event, specify the new event value in the **Event** box. To change the reference level for a factor, specify the factor variable followed by the new reference level in the **Reference factor level** box. You can specify reference levels for more than one factor at the same time. If the levels are text or date/time, enclose them in double quotes.

⯈ Example of a binary logistic regression

You are a researcher who is interested in understanding the effect of smoking and weight upon resting pulse rate. Because you have categorized the response—pulse rate—into low and high, a binary logistic regression analysis is appropriate to investigate the effects of smoking and weight upon pulse rate.

1 Open the worksheet EXH_REGR.MTW.

2 Choose **Stat ➤ Regression ➤ Binary Logistic Regression**.

3 In **Response**, enter *RestingPulse*. In **Model**, enter *Smokes Weight*. In **Factors (optional)**, enter *Smokes*.

4 Click **Graphs**. Check **Delta chi-square vs probability** and **Delta chi-square vs leverage**. Click **OK**.

5 Click **Results**. Choose **In addition, list of factor level values, tests for terms with more than 1 degree of freedom, and 2 additional goodness-of-fit tests**. Click **OK** in each dialog box.

Binary Logistic Regression: RestingPulse versus Smokes, Weight

Session window output

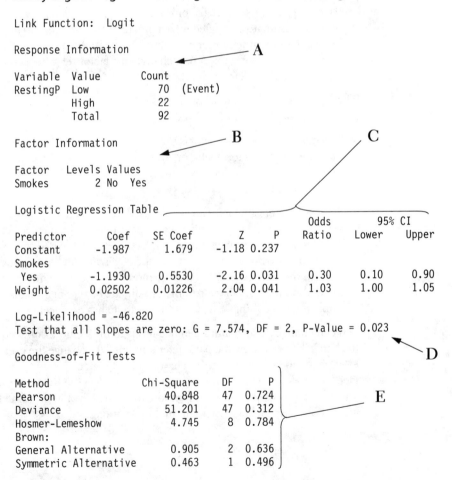

```
Link Function:  Logit

Response Information                        ◀────  A

Variable  Value      Count
RestingP  Low           70   (Event)
          High          22
          Total         92


Factor Information                    ──  B              C

Factor    Levels Values
Smokes        2 No   Yes

Logistic Regression Table
                                                    Odds        95% CI
Predictor       Coef    SE Coef        Z     P     Ratio    Lower   Upper
Constant      -1.987      1.679    -1.18 0.237
Smokes
  Yes         -1.1930     0.5530    -2.16 0.031     0.30     0.10    0.90
Weight        0.02502     0.01226    2.04 0.041     1.03     1.00    1.05


Log-Likelihood = -46.820
Test that all slopes are zero: G = 7.574, DF = 2, P-Value = 0.023
                                                                      ◀  D

Goodness-of-Fit Tests

Method                  Chi-Square    DF     P
Pearson                    40.848     47   0.724                      E
Deviance                   51.201     47   0.312
Hosmer-Lemeshow             4.745      8   0.784
Brown:
General Alternative         0.905      2   0.636
Symmetric Alternative       0.463      1   0.496
```

Table of Observed and Expected Frequencies:
(See Hosmer-Lemeshow Test for the Pearson Chi-Square Statistic)   **F**

Value	1	2	3	4	5	6	7	8	9	10	Total
					Group						
Low											
Obs	4	6	6	8	8	6	8	12	10	2	70
Exp	4.4	6.4	6.3	6.6	6.9	7.2	8.3	12.9	9.1	1.9	
High											
Obs	5	4	3	1	1	3	2	3	0	0	22
Exp	4.6	3.6	2.7	2.4	2.1	1.8	1.7	2.1	0.9	0.1	
Total	9	10	9	9	9	9	10	15	10	2	92

Measures of Association:
(Between the Response Variable and Predicted Probabilities)

Pairs	Number	Percent	Summary Measures	
Concordant	1045	67.9%	Somers' D	0.38
Discordant	461	29.9%	Goodman-Kruskal Gamma	0.39
Ties	34	2.2%	Kendall's Tau-a	0.14
Total	1540	100.0%		

G

Graph window output

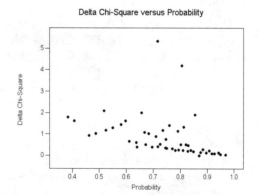

Delta Chi-Square versus Probability

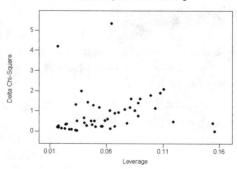

Delta Chi-Square versus Leverage

Interpretation of results

The Session window output contains the following seven parts:

A **Response Information** — displays the number of missing observations and the number of observations that fall into each of the two response categories. The response value that has been designated as the *reference event* is the first entry under Value and labeled as the event. In this case, the reference event is low pulse rate (see *Reference event for the response variable* on page 2-31).

B **Factor Information** — displays all the factors in the model, the number of levels for each factor, and the factor level values. The factor level that has been designated as the *reference level* is first entry under Values, the subject does not smoke (see *Reference levels for factors* on page 2-31).

C **Logistic Regression Table** — shows the estimated coefficients (parameter estimates), standard error of the coefficients, z-values, and p-values. When you use the logit link function, you also see the odds ratio and a 95% confidence interval for the odds ratio.

   ▪ From the output, you can see that both Smokes (z = −2.16, p = 0.031) and Weight (z = 2.04, p = 0.041) have p-values less than 0.05, indicating that there is sufficient evidence that the parameters are not zero using a significance level of α = 0.05.

   ▪ The coefficient of -1.193 for Smokes represents the estimated change in the log of P(low pulse)/P(high pulse) when the subject smokes compared to when he/she does not smoke, with the covariate Weight held constant. The coefficient of 0.0250 for Weight is the estimated change in the log of P(low pulse)/P(high pulse) with a 1 unit (lb) increase in Weight, with the factor Smokes held constant.

   ▪ Although there is evidence that the parameter of Weight is not zero, the odds ratio is very close to one (1.03), indicating that a one pound increase in weight minimally effects a person's resting pulse rate. A more meaningful difference would be found if you compared subjects with a larger weight difference (for example, if the weight unit is 10 pounds, the odds ratio becomes 1.28, indicating that the odds of a subject having a low pulse increases by 1.28 times with each 10 pound increase in weight).

   ▪ For Smokes, the negative coefficient of -1.193 and the odds ratio of 0.30 indicate that subjects who smoke tend to have a higher resting pulse rate than subjects who do not smoke. Given that subjects have the same weight, the odds ratio can be interpreted as the odds of non-smokers in the sample having a low pulse being 30% of the odds of smokers having a low pulse.

D Next, the last Log-Likelihood from the maximum likelihood iterations is displayed along with the statistic G. This statistic tests the null hypothesis that all the coefficients associated with predictors equal zero versus these coefficients not all being equal to zero. In this example, G = 7.574, with a p-value of 0.023, indicating that there is sufficient evidence that at least one of the coefficients is different from zero, given that your accepted α level is greater than 0.023.

- Note that for factors with more than 1 degree of freedom, MINITAB performs a multiple degrees of freedom test with a null hypothesis that all the coefficients associated with the factor are equal to 0 versus them not all being equal to 0. This example does not have a factor with more than 1 degree of freedom.

E **Goodness-of-Fit Tests**—displays Pearson, deviance, and Hosmer-Lemeshow goodness-of-fit tests. In addition, two Brown tests—general alternative and symmetric alternative—are displayed because you have chosen the logit link function and the selected option in the Results subdialog box. The goodness-of-fit tests, with p-values ranging from 0.312 to 0.724, indicate that there is insufficient evidence to claim that the model does not fit the data adequately. If the p-value is less than your accepted α level, the test would reject the null hypothesis of an adequate fit.

F **Table of Observed and Expected Frequencies**—allows you to see how well the model fits the data by comparing the observed and expected frequencies. There is insufficient evidence that the model does not fit the data well, as the observed and expected frequencies are similar. This supports the conclusions made by the **Goodness of Fit Tests**.

G **Measures of Association**—display a table of the number and percentage of concordant, discordant, and tied pairs, as well as common rank correlation statistics. These values measure the association between the observed responses and the predicted probabilities.

- The table of concordant, discordant, and tied pairs is calculated by pairing the observations with different response values. Here, you have 70 individuals with a low pulse and 22 with a high pulse, resulting in $70 * 22 = 1540$ pairs with different response values. Based on the model, a pair is concordant if the individual with a low pulse rate has a higher probability of having a low pulse, discordant if the opposite is true, and tied if the probabilities are equal. In this example, 67.9% of pairs are concordant and 29.9% are discordant. You can use these values as a comparative measure of prediction, for example in comparing fits with different sets of predictors or with different link functions.

- Somers' D, Goodman-Kruskal Gamma, and Kendall's Tau-a are summaries of the table of concordant and discordant pairs. These measures most likely lie between 0 and 1 where larger values indicate that the model has a better predictive ability. In this example, the measure range from 0.14 to 0.39 which implies less than desirable predictive ability.

Plots—In the example, you chose two diagnostic plots—delta Pearson χ^2 versus the estimated event probability and delta Pearson χ^2 versus the leverage. Delta Pearson χ^2 for the jth factor/covariate pattern is the change in the Pearson χ^2 when all observations with that factor/covariate pattern are omitted. These two graphs indicate that two observations are not well fit by the model (high delta χ^2). A high delta χ^2 can be caused by a high leverage and/or a high Pearson residual. In this case, a high Pearson residual caused the large delta χ^2, because the leverages are less than 0.1. Hosmer and Lemeshow indicate that delta χ^2 or delta deviance greater than 3.84 is large.

If you choose **Editor ➤ Brush,** brush these points, and then click on them, they will be identified as data values 31 and 66. These are individuals with a high resting pulse, who do not smoke, and who have smaller than average weights (Weight = 116, 136 pounds). You might further investigate these cases to see why the model did not fit them well.

Ordinal Logistic Regression

Use ordinal logistic regression to perform logistic regression on an ordinal response variable. Ordinal variables are categorical variables that have three or more possible levels with a natural ordering, such as strongly disagree, disagree, neutral, agree, and strongly agree. A model with one or more predictors is fit using an iterative-reweighted least squares algorithm to obtain maximum likelihood estimates of the parameters [19].

Parallel regression lines are assumed, and therefore, a single slope is calculated for each covariate. In situations where this assumption is not valid, nominal logistic regression, which generates separate logit functions, is more appropriate.

Data

Your data may be arranged in one of two ways: as raw data or as frequency data. See *Worksheet structure* on page 2-32.

Factors, covariates, and response data can be numeric, text, or date/time. The *reference level* and the *reference event* depend on the data type. See *Reference levels for factors* on page 2-31 and *Reference event for the response variable* on page 2-31 for details.

The predictors may either be factors (nominal variables) or covariates (continuous variables). Factors may be crossed or nested. Covariates may be crossed with each other or with factors, or nested within factors.

The model can include up to 9 factors and 50 covariates. Unless you specify a predictor in the model as a factor, the predictor is assumed to be a covariate. Model continuous predictors as covariates and categorical predictors as factors. See *How to specify the model terms* on page 2-30 for more information.

MINITAB automatically omits observations with missing values from all calculations.

▶ To do an ordinal logistic regression

1 Choose Stat ➤ Regression ➤ Ordinal Logistic Regression.

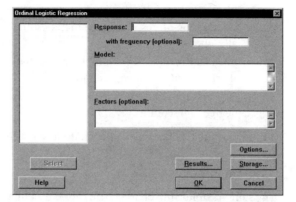

2 Do one of the following:

   ■ If you have raw response data, in **Response**, enter the numeric column containing the response data.

   ■ If you have frequency data, in **Response**, enter the numeric column containing the response values. Then, in **Frequency**, enter the variable containing the counts.

   See *Worksheet structure* on page 2-32.

3 In **Model**, enter the model terms. See *How to specify the model terms* on page 2-30.

4 If you like, use one or more of the options listed below, then click **OK**.

Options

Ordinal Logistic Regression dialog box

   ■ include categorical variables (factors) in the model

Options subdialog box

   ■ specify the link function: logit (the default), normit (also called probit), or gompit (also called complementary log-log)—see *Link functions* on page 2-46

   ■ specify the order of the response values or change the reference levels for the factors—see *Interpreting the parameter estimates relative to the order of response values and the reference levels* on page 2-47

   ■ specify initial values for model parameters or parameter estimates for a validation model—see *Entering initial values for parameter estimates* on page 2-37

   ■ change the maximum number of iterations for reaching convergence (default is 20)

Results subdialog box

- display the following in the Session window:
  - no output
  - information on response, parameter estimates, the log-likelihood, and the test for all slopes being zero
  - the default output, which includes the above output plus two goodness-of-fit tests (Pearson and deviance), and measures of association
  - the default output plus factor level values, and tests for terms with more than one degree of freedom
- display the log-likelihood at each iteration of the parameter estimation process

Storage subdialog box

- store the following characteristics of the estimated regression equation:
  - estimated model coefficients, their standard errors, and the variance-covariance matrix of the estimated coefficients.
  - the log-likelihood for the last maximum likelihood iteration.
- store the following event probabilities and/or aggregated data:
  - the number of trials for each factor/covariate pattern.
  - event probabilities, cumulative event probabilities, and number of occurrences for each factor/covariate pattern. Note that the number of events (distinct response values) must be specified to store these values.

Link functions

MINITAB provides three link functions—logit (the default), normit (also called probit), and gompit (also called complementary log-log)—allowing you to fit a broad class of ordinal response models. These are the inverse of the cumulative logistic distribution function (logit), the inverse of the cumulative standard normal distribution function (normit), and the inverse of the Gompertz distribution function (gompit). This class of models is defined by:

$$g(\gamma_{ij}) = \theta_i + x'_j\beta, \quad i=1, ..., k-1$$

where

k = the number of distinct values of the response or the number of possible events

γ_{ij} = the cumulative probability up to and including event i for the jth factor/covariate pattern

$g(\gamma_{ij})$ = the link function (described below)

θ_i = the constant associated with the ith event

x'_j = a vector of predictor variables associated with the jth factor/covariate pattern

β = a vector of coefficients associated with the predictors

The link function is the inverse of a distribution function. The link functions and their corresponding distributions are summarized below (π in the variance is 3.14159):

Name	Link function	Distribution	Mean	Variance
logit	$g(\gamma_{ij}) = \log_e(\gamma_{ij} / (1 - \gamma_{ij}))$	logistic	0	$pi^2 / 3$
normit	$g(\gamma_{ij}) = \Phi^{-1}(\gamma_{ij})$	normal	0	1
gompit	$g(\gamma_{ij}) = \log_e(-\log_e(1 - \gamma_{ij}))$	Gompertz	$-\gamma$ (Euler constant)	$pi^2 / 6$

You want to choose a link function that results in a good fit to your data. Goodness-of-fit statistics can be used to compare the fits using different link functions. Certain link functions may be used for historical reasons or because they have a special meaning in a discipline.

An advantage of the logit link function is that it provides an estimate of the odds ratios. The logit link function is the default. For a comparison of link functions, see [19].

Interpreting the parameter estimates relative to the order of response values and the reference levels

The interpretation of the parameter estimates depends on: the link function (see *Link functions* on page 2-36), reference event (see *Reference event for the response variable* on page 2-31), and reference factor levels (see *Reference levels for factors* on page 2-31). A parameter estimate associated with a predictor (factor or covariate) represents the change in the link function for each unit change in the predictor, while all other predictors are held constant. A unit change in a factor refers to a comparison of a certain level to the reference level.

The logit link provides the most natural interpretation of the estimated coefficients and is therefore the default link in MINITAB. A summary of the interpretation follows:

- The odds of a reference event is the ratio of P(event) to P(not event). The estimated coefficient of a predictor (factor or covariate) is the estimated change in the log of P(event)/P(not event) for each unit change in the predictor, assuming the other predictors remain constant.

- The estimated coefficient can also be used to calculate the odds ratio, or the ratio between two odds. Exponentiating the parameter estimate of a factor yields the ratio of P(event)/P(not event) for a certain factor level compared to the reference level. The odds ratios at different values of the covariate can be constructed relative to zero. In the covariate case, it may be more meaningful to interpret the odds and not the odds ratio. Note that a coefficient of zero or an odds ratio of one both imply the same thing—the factor or covariate has no effect.

You can change the order of response values or the reference level in the Options subdialog box if you wish to change how you view the parameter estimates. If your responses were coded Low, Medium, and High, rather than 1, 2, 3, the default alphabetical ordering of the responses would be improper. To change the order of response values, specify the new order in the **Order of the response values** box. To order as Low, Medium, and High, enter these values in this order, each enclosed in double quotes. To change the reference level for a factor, specify the factor variable and the new reference level in the **Reference factor level** box. You can specify reference levels for more than one factor at the same time. If the levels are text or date/time, enclose them in double quotes.

▷ Example of an ordinal logistic regression

Suppose you are a field biologist and you believe that the adult population of salamanders in the Northeast has gotten smaller over the past few years. You would like to determine whether any association exists between the length of time a hatched salamander survives and level of water toxicity, as well as whether there is a regional effect. Survival time is coded as 1 if it is less than 10 days, 2 if it is equal to 10 to 30 days, and 3 if it is equal to 31 to 60 days.

1 Open the worksheet EXH_REGR.MTW.

2 Choose **Stat ➤ Regression ➤ Ordinal Logistic Regression**.

3 In **Response**, enter *Survival*. In **Model**, enter *Region ToxicLevel*. In **Factors (optional)**, enter *Region*.

4 Click **Results**. Choose **In addition, list of factor level values, and tests for terms with more than 1 degree of freedom**. Click **OK** in each dialog box.

*Session
window
output*

Ordinal Logistic Regression: Survival versus Region, ToxicLevel

```
Link Function:  Logit                           A

Response Information

Variable  Value        Count
Survival  1               15
          2               46
          3               12
          Total           73

Factor Information                    B              C

Factor    Levels Values
Region      2  1 2

Logistic Regression Table
                                                Odds        95% CI
Predictor       Coef     SE Coef      Z     P    Ratio   Lower   Upper
Const(1)       -7.043      1.680   -4.19 0.000
Const(2)       -3.523      1.471   -2.39 0.017
Region
 2              0.2015     0.4962    0.41 0.685   1.22    0.46    3.23
ToxicLev        0.12129    0.03405   3.56 0.000   1.13    1.06    1.21

Log-likelihood = -59.290
Test that all slopes are zero: G = 14.713, DF = 2, P-Value = 0.001

Goodness-of-Fit Tests

Method      Chi-Square   DF     P             D
Pearson       122.799   122  0.463
Deviance      100.898   122  0.918

Measures of Association:
(Between the Response Variable and Predicted Probabilities)

Pairs         Number  Percent    Summary Measures
Concordant      1127    79.3%    Somers' D               0.59      E
Discordant       288    20.3%    Goodman-Kruskal Gamma   0.59
Ties               7     0.5%    Kendall's Tau-a         0.32
Total           1422   100.0%
```

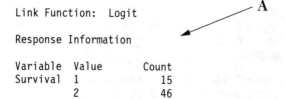

Interpreting the results

The Session window contains the following five parts:

A Response Information—displays the number of observations that fall into each of the response categories and the number of missing observations. The ordered response values, from lowest to highest, are shown. Here, you use the default coding scheme, which orders the values from lowest to highest: 1 is less than 10 days, 2 is equal to 10 to 30 days, and 3 is equal to 31 to 60 days (see *Reference event for the response variable* on page 2-31).

B **Factor Information**—displays all the factors in the model, the number of levels for each factor, and the factor level values. The factor level that has been designated as the *reference level* is the first entry under Values, region 1 (see *Reference levels for factors* on page 2-31).

C **Logistic Regression Table**—shows the estimated coefficients (parameter estimates), standard error of the coefficients, z-values, and p-values. When you use the logit link function, MINITAB displays the calculated odds ratio and a 95% confidence interval for the odds ratio.

- The values labeled Const(1) and Const(2) are estimated intercepts for the logits of the cumulative probabilities of survival for less than 10 days, and for 10 to 30 days, respectively. Because the cumulative probability for the last response value is 1, there is no need to estimate an intercept for 31 to 60 days.

- The coefficient of 0.2015 for Region is the estimated change in the logit of the cumulative survival time probability when the region is 2 compared to region being 1, with the covariate ToxicLevel held constant. Because the p-value for this parameter estimate is 0.685, there is insufficient evidence to conclude that Region has an effect upon survival time.

- There is one parameter estimated for each covariate, which gives parallel lines for the factor levels. Here, the estimated coefficient for the single covariate, ToxicLevel, is 0.121, with a p-value of less than 0.0005. The p-value indicates that there is sufficient evidence to conclude that the toxic level affects survival. The positive coefficient, and an odds ratio that is greater than one, indicates that higher toxic levels tend to be associated with lower values of survival.

- Next, MINITAB displays the last **Log-Likelihood** from the maximum likelihood iterations along with the statistic **G**. This statistics tests the null hypothesis that all the coefficients associated with predictors equal to 0 versus them not all being equal to 0. In this example, G = 14.713 with a p-value of 0.001, indicating that there is sufficient evidence to conclude that at least one of the coefficients is different from zero.

D **Goodness-of-Fit Tests**—displays both Pearson and deviance goodness-of-fit tests. In our example, the p-value for the Pearson test is 0.463, and the p-value for the deviance test is 0.918, indicating that there is insufficient evidence to claim that the model does not fit the data adequately. If the p-value is less than your selected α level, the tests rejects the null hypothesis of an adequate fit.

E **Measures of Association**—displays a table of the number and percentage of concordant, discordant, and tied pairs, as well as common rank correlation statistics. These values measure the association between the observed responses and the predicted probabilities.

- The table of concordant, discordant, and tied pairs is calculated by pairing the observations with different response values. Here, you have fifteen 1's, forty-six 2's, and twelve 3's, resulting in $(15 * 46) + (15 * 12) + (46 * 12) = 1422$ pairs of different response values. Pairs involving the lowest coded response value (the 1-2 and 1-3 value pairs in the example) are concordant if the cumulative probability up to the lowest response value (here 1) is greater for the observation with the lowest value. This pattern applies to other value pairs. Pairs involving responses coded as 2 and 3 in this example are concordant if the cumulative probability up to 2 is greater for the observation coded as 2. The pair is discordant if the opposite is true and tied if the cumulative probabilities are equal. In this example, 79.3% of pairs are concordant, 20.3% are discordant, and 0.5% are ties. You can use these values as a comparative measure of prediction (for example, when evaluating predictors and different link functions).

- Somers' D, Goodman-Kruskal Gamma, and Kendall's Tau-a are summaries of the table of concordant and discordant pairs. The numbers have the same numerator (the number of concordant pairs minus the number of discordant pairs). The denominators are the total number of pairs with Somers' D, the total number of pairs excepting ties with Goodman-Kruskal Gamma, and the number of all possible observation pairs for Kendall's Tau-a. These measures most likely lie between 0 and 1, where larger values indicate that the model has a better predictive ability.

Nominal Logistic Regression

Use nominal logistic regression to perform logistic regression on a nominal response variable using an iterative-reweighted least squares algorithm to obtain maximum likelihood estimates of the parameters [19]. Nominal variables are categorical variables that have three or more possible levels with no natural ordering. For example, the levels in a food tasting study may include crunchy, mushy, and crispy.

Data

Your data may be arranged in one of two ways: as raw data or as frequency data. See *Worksheet structure* on page 2-32.

Factors, covariates, and response data can be numeric, text, or date/time. The *reference level* and the *reference event* depend on the data type. See *Reference levels for factors* on page 2-31 and *Reference event for the response variable* on page 2-31 for details.

The predictors may either be factors (nominal variables) or covariates (continuous variables). Factors may be crossed or nested. Covariates may be crossed with each other or with factors, or nested within factors.

The model can include up to 9 factors and 50 covariates. Unless you specify a predictor in the model as a factor, the predictor is assumed to be a covariate. Model continuous predictors as covariates and categorical predictors as factors. See *How to specify the model terms* on page 2-30 for more information.

MINITAB automatically omits observations with missing values from all calculations.

▶ **To do a nominal logistic regression**

1 Choose **Stat** ➤ **Regression** ➤ **Nominal Logistic Regression**.

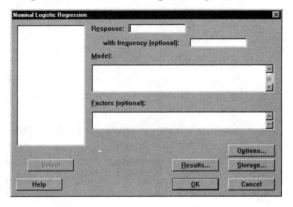

2 Do one of the following:

■ If you have raw response data, in **Response**, enter the numeric column containing the response data.

■ If you have frequency data, in **Response**, enter the numeric column containing the response values. Then, in **Frequency**, enter the variable containing the counts.

See *Worksheet structure* on page 2-32.

3 In **Model**, enter the model terms. See *How to specify the model terms* on page 2-30.

4 If you like, use one or more of the options listed below, then click **OK**.

Options

Nominal Logistic Regression dialog box

■ define the factors (categorical variables) in the model

Options subdialog box

- change the reference event of the response or the reference levels for the factors—see *Interpreting the parameter estimates relative to the reference event and reference levels* on page 2-54

- specify initial values for model parameters or parameter estimates for a validation model—see *Entering initial values for parameter estimates* on page 2-37

- change the maximum number of iterations for reaching convergence from the default of 20

Results subdialog box

- display the following in the Session window:
  - no output
  - basic information on response, parameter estimates, the log-likelihood, and the test for all slopes being zero
  - the default output, which includes the above output plus two goodness-of-fit tests (Pearson and deviance)
  - the default output, plus factor level values and tests for terms with more than one degree of freedom

- display the log-likelihood at each iteration of the parameter estimation process

Storage subdialog box

- store characteristics of the estimated regression equation:
  - estimated model coefficients, their standard errors, and the variance-covariance matrix of the estimated coefficients.
  - the log-likelihood for the last maximum likelihood iteration.

- store event probabilities and/or aggregated data:
  - the number of trials for each factor/covariate pattern.
  - event probabilities and number of occurrences for each factor/covariate pattern. Note that the number of events (distinct response values) must be specified to store these values.

Nominal logistic regression model

The model fit by nominal logistic regression is defined by:

$$\log_e\left(\frac{\pi_{ij}}{\pi_{1j}}\right) = \beta_{i0} + x'_j\beta_i \text{ , i=2, ..., k , where}$$

k   = the number of distinct values of the response or the number of possible events

π_{ij} = the probability of the ith event for the jth factor/covariate pattern
(π_{1j} is the probability of the reference event for the jth factor/covariate pattern)

b_{i0} = the intercept for the $(i-1)^{st}$ logit function

x'_j = a vector of predictor variables for the jth factor/covariate pattern

b_i = a vector of unknown coefficients associated with the predictors for the $(i-1)^{st}$ logit function

See [16] for additional discussion.

Interpreting the parameter estimates relative to the reference event and reference levels

The interpretation of the parameter estimates depends upon the designated reference event (see *Reference event for the response variable* on page 2-31) and reference factor levels (see *Reference levels for factors* on page 2-31). A parameter estimate associated with a predictor represents the change in the particular logit for each unit change in the predictor, assuming that all other factors and covariates are held constant. A one unit change in a factor refers to a comparison of a certain level to the reference level.

If there are k distinct response values, MINITAB estimates k−1 sets of parameter estimates. These are the estimated differences in log odds or logits of levels of the response variable relative to the reference event. Each set contains a constant and coefficients for the factors and the covariates. Note that these sets of parameter estimates give nonparallel lines for the response value. The interpretation of the parameter estimates is as follows:

■ The coefficient of a predictor (factor or covariate) is the estimated change in the log of P(response level)/P(reference event) for each unit change in the predictor, assuming the other predictors remain constant.

■ The coefficient can also be used to calculate the odds ratio, or the ratio between two odds. Exponentiating the parameter estimate of a factor yields the ratio of P(response level)/P(reference event) for a certain factor level compared to the reference level. The odds ratios at different values of the covariate can be constructed relative to zero. In the covariate case, it may be more meaningful to interpret the odds and not the odds ratio. Note that a coefficient of zero or an odds ratio of one both imply the same thing—the factor or covariate has no effect.

You can change the reference event or reference levels in the Options subdialog box if you wish to change how you view the parameter estimates. To change the event, specify the new event value in the **Reference event** box. To change the reference event, give the new level. To change the reference level for a factor, specify the factor variable followed by the new reference level in the **Reference factor level** box. You can specify reference levels for more than one factor at the same time. If the levels are text or date/time, enclose them in double quotes.

▷ **Example of a nominal logistic regression**

Suppose you are a grade school curriculum director interested in what children identify as their favorite subject and how this subject is associated with their age or the teaching method employed. Thirty children, 10 to 13 years old, had classroom instruction in science, math, and language arts that employed either lecture or discussion techniques. At the end of the school year, they were asked to identify their favorite subject. You use nominal logistic regression because the response is categorical but possesses no implicit categorical ordering.

1 Open the worksheet EXH_REGR.MTW.

2 Choose **Stat ➤ Regression ➤ Nominal Logistic Regression**.

3 In **Response**, enter *Subject*. In **Model**, enter *TeachingMethod Age*. In **Factors (optional)**, enter *TeachingMethod*.

4 Click **Results**. Choose **In addition, list of factor level values, tests for terms with more than 1 degree of freedom**. Click **OK** in each dialog box.

Session window output

Nominal Logistic Regression: Subject versus TeachingMethod, Age

```
Response Information
                                                      ─── A
Variable  Value         Count
Subject   science          10   (Reference Event)
          math             11
          arts              9
          Total            30
                                    ─ B
Factor Information
                                            C
Factor    Levels Values
Teaching       2 discuss lecture

Logistic Regression Table _____
                                               Odds        95% CI
Predictor         Coef    SE Coef       Z    P    Ratio   Lower   Upper
Logit 1: (math/science)
Constant        -1.123     4.564   -0.25 0.806
Teaching
  lecture       -0.5631   0.9376   -0.60 0.548    0.57    0.09    3.58
Age              0.1247   0.4011    0.31 0.756    1.13    0.52    2.49


Logit 2: (arts/science)
Constant       -13.848     7.243   -1.91 0.056
Teaching
  lecture        2.770     1.372    2.02 0.044   15.96    1.08  234.91
Age              1.0135    0.5845   1.73 0.083    2.76    0.88    8.66


Log-likelihood = -26.446
Test that all slopes are zero: G = 12.825, DF = 4, P-Value = 0.012
                                                              ↘ D
Goodness-of-Fit Tests
                                          ─── E
Method     Chi-Square   DF      P
Pearson         6.953   10  0.730
Deviance        7.886   10  0.640
```

Interpreting the results

The Session window output contains the following five parts:

A Response Information—displays the number of observations that fall into each of the response categories (science, math, and language arts), as well as the number of missing observations. The response value that has been designated as the *reference event* is the first entry under Value and labeled as the reference event. Here, the default coding scheme defines the reference event as science using reverse alphabetical order.

B **Factor Information** — displays all the factors in the model, the number of levels for each factor, and the factor level values. The factor level that has been designated as the *reference level* is the first entry under Values. Here, the default coding scheme defines the reference level as "discussion" using alphabetical order.

C **Logistic Regression Table** — shows the estimated coefficients (parameter estimates), standard error of the coefficients, z-values, and p-values. MINITAB also displays the odds ratio and a 95% confidence interval for the odds ratio. The coefficient associated with a predictor is the estimated change in the logit with a one unit change in the predictor, assuming that all other factors and covariates are the same.

- If there are k distinct response values, MINITAB estimates k–1 sets of parameter estimates, here labeled as Logit(1) and Logit(2). These are the estimated differences in log odds or logits of math and language arts, respectively, compared to science as the reference event. Each set contains a constant and coefficients for the factors (here, teaching method) and the covariates (here, age). The TeachingMethod coefficient is the estimated change in the logit when TeachingMethod is lecture compared to the teaching method being discussion, with Age held constant. The Age coefficient is the estimated change in the logit with a one year increase in age with teaching method held constant. These sets of parameter estimates give nonparallel lines for the response values.

- The first set of estimated logits, labeled Logit(1), are the parameter estimates of the change in logits of math relative to the reference event, science. The p-values of 0.548 and 0.756 for TeachingMethod and Age, respectively, indicate that there is insufficient evidence to conclude that a change in teaching method from discussion to lecture or a change in age affected the choice of math as favorite subject compared to science.

- The second set of estimated logits, labeled Logit(2), are the parameter estimates of the change in logits of language arts relative to the reference event, science. The p-values of 0.044 and 0.083 for TeachingMethod and Age, respectively, indicate that there is sufficient evidence, if the p-values are less than your acceptable α level, to conclude that a change in teaching method from discussion to lecture or a change in age affected the choice of language arts as the favorite subject compared to science. The positive coefficient for teaching method indicates students given a lecture style of teaching tend to prefer language arts over science compared to students given a discussion style of teaching. The estimated odds ratio of 15.96 implies that the odds of choosing language arts over science is about 16 times higher for these students when the teaching method changes from discussion to lecture. The positive coefficient associated with age indicates that students tend to like language arts over science as they become older.

D Next, MINITAB displays the last Log-Likelihood from the maximum likelihood iterations along with the statistic G. G is the difference in −2 log-likelihood for a model that only has the constant terms and the fitted model shown in the **Logistic Regression Table**. G is the test statistic for testing the null hypothesis that all the coefficients associated with predictors being equal to 0 versus them not all being equal to 0. G = 12.825 with a p-value of 0.012, which indicates that at α = 0.05 there is sufficient evidence for at least one coefficient being different from 0.

E **Goodness-of-Fit Tests**—displays Pearson and deviance goodness-of-fit tests. The p-value for the Pearson test is 0.730 and the p-value for the deviance test is 0.640, indicating that there is insufficient evidence for the model not fitting the data adequately. If the p-value is less than your selected α level, the test would indicate sufficient evidence for an inadequate fit.

References

[1] A. Agresti (1984). *Analysis of Ordinal Categorical Data*, John Wiley & Sons, Inc.

[2] A. Agresti (1990). *Categorical Data Analysis*, John Wiley & Sons, Inc.

[3] D.A. Belsley, E. Kuh, and R.E. Welsch (1980). *Regression Diagnostics*, John Wiley & Sons, Inc.

[4] A. Bhargava (1989). "Missing Observations and the Use of the Durbin-Watson Statistic," *Biometrika* 76, 4, pp.828–831.

[5] C.C. Brown (1982). "On a Goodness of fit Test for the Logistic Model Based on Score Statistics," *Communications in Statistics*, 11, pp.1087–1105.

[6] D.A. Burn and T.A. Ryan, Jr. (1983). "A Diagnostic Test for Lack of Fit in Regression Models," ASA 1983 *Proceedings of the Statistical Computing Section*, pp.286–290.

[7] R.D. Cook (1977). "Detection of Influential Observations in Linear Regression," *Technometrics* 19, pp.15–18.

[8] R.D. Cook and S. Weisberg (1982). *Residuals and Influence in Regression*, Chapman and Hall.

[9] N.R. Draper and H. Smith (1981). *Applied Regression Analysis*, Second Edition, John Wiley & Sons, Inc.

[10] S.E. Fienberg (1987). *The Analysis of Cross-Classified Categorical Data*. The MIT Press.

[11] M.J. Garside (1971). "Some Computational Procedures for the Best Subset Problem," *Applied Statistics* 20, pp.8–15.

[12] James H. Goodnight (1979). "A Tutorial on the Sweep Operator," *The American Statistician* 33, pp.149–158.

[13] W.W. Hauck and A. Donner (1977). "Wald's test as applied to hypotheses in logit analysis. *Journal of the American Statistical Association* 72, 851-853.

[14] D.C. Hoaglin and R.E. Welsch (1978). "The Hat Matrix in Regression and ANOVA," *The American Statistician* 32, pp.17–22, and Corrigenda 32, p.146.

[15] R.R. Hocking (1976). "A Biometrics Invited Paper: The Analysis and Selection of Variables in Linear Regression," *Biometrics* 32, pp.1–49.

[16] D.W. Hosmer and S. Lemeshow (1989). *Applied Logistic Regression*, John Wiley & Sons, Inc.

[17] LINPACK (1979). *Linpack User's Guide* by J.J. Dongarra, J.R. Bunch, C.B. Moler, and G.W. Stewart, Society for Industrial and Applied Mathematics, Philadelphia, PA.

[18] J.H. Maindonald (1984). *Statistical Computation*, John Wiley & Sons, Inc.

[19] P. McCullagh and J.A. Nelder (1992). *Generalized Linear Models*, Chapman & Hall.

[20] W. Miller (1978). "Performing Armchair Roundoff Analysis of Statistical Algorithms," *Communications in Statistics*, pp.243–255.

[21] D.C. Montgomery and E.A. Peck (1982). *Introduction to Linear Regression Analysis*. John Wiley & Sons.

[22] J. Neter, W. Wasserman, and M. Kutner (1985). *Applied Linear Statistical Models*, Richard D. Irwin, Inc.

[23] S.J. Press and S. Wilson (1978). "Choosing Between Logistic Regression and Discriminant Analysis," *Journal of the American Statistical Association* 73, 699-705.

[24] M. Schatzoff, R. Tsao, and S. Fienberg (1968). "Efficient Calculation of All Possible Regressions," *Technometrics* 10, pp.769–779.

[25] G.W. Stewart (1973). *Introduction to Matrix Computations*, Academic Press.

[26] R.A. Thisted (1988). *Elements of Statistical Computing: Numerical Computation*, Chapman & Hall.

[27] P. Velleman and R. Welsch (1981). "Efficient Computation of Regression Diagnostics," *The American Statistician* 35, pp.234–242.

[28] P.F. Velleman, J. Seaman, and I.E. Allen (1977). "Evaluating Package Regression Routines," *ASA 1977 Proceedings of the Statistical Computing Section.*

[29] S. Weisberg (1980). *Applied Linear Regression*, John Wiley & Sons, Inc.

Acknowledgments

We are very grateful for help in the design of the regression algorithm from W. Miller and from G.W. Stewart and for useful suggestions from. P.F. Velleman and S. Weisberg and many others.

3

Analysis of Variance

Analysis of Variance Overview

Analysis of variance (ANOVA) is similar to regression in that it is used to investigate and model the relationship between a response variable and one or more independent variables. However, analysis of variance differs from regression in two ways: the independent variables are qualitative (categorical), and no assumption is made about the nature of the relationship (that is, the model does not include coefficients for variables). In effect, analysis of variance extends the two-sample t-test for testing the equality of two population means to a more general null hypothesis of comparing the equality of more than two means, versus them not all being equal. Several of MINITAB's ANOVA procedures, however, allow models with both qualitative and quantitative variables.

MINITAB's ANOVA capabilities include procedures for fitting ANOVA models to data collected from a number of different designs, for fitting MANOVA models to designs with multiple responses, for fitting ANOM (analysis of means) models, and specialty graphs for testing equal variances, for error bar or confidence interval plots, and graphs of main effects and interactions.

One-way and two-way ANOVA models

- **One-way analysis of variance** tests the equality of population means when classification is by one variable. The classification variable, or factor, usually has three or more levels (one-way ANOVA with two levels is equivalent to a t-test), where the *level* represents the treatment applied. For example, if you conduct an experiment where you measure durability of a product made by one of three methods, these methods constitute the levels. The one-way procedure also allows you to examine differences among means using multiple comparisons.

- **Two-way analysis of variance** performs an analysis of variance for testing the equality of populations means when classification of treatments is by two variables or factors. In two-way ANOVA, the data must be balanced (all cells must have the same number of observations) and factors must be fixed.

  If you wish to specify certain factors to be random, use **Balanced ANOVA** if your data are balanced; use **General Linear Models** if your data are unbalanced or if you wish to compare means using multiple comparisons.

Analysis of Means

Analysis of Means (ANOM) is a graphical analog to ANOVA for the testing of the equality of population means. ANOM [15] was developed to test main effects from a designed experiment in which all factors are fixed. This procedure is used for one-way designs. MINITAB uses an extension of ANOM or Analysis of Mean treatment Effects (ANOME) [23] to test the significance of mean treatment effects for two-way designs.

ANOM can be used if you assume that the response follows a normal distribution (similar to ANOVA) and the design is one-way or two-way. You can also use ANOM when the response follows either a binomial or Poisson distribution.

More complex ANOVA models

MINITAB offers a choice of three procedures for fitting models based upon designs more complicated than one- or two-way designs. Balanced ANOVA and General Linear Model are general procedures for fitting ANOVA models that are discussed more completely in *Overview of Balanced ANOVA and GLM* on page 3-18.

■ **Balanced ANOVA** performs univariate (one response) analysis of variance when you have a balanced design (though one-way designs can be unbalanced). Balanced designs are ones in which all cells have the same number of observations. Factors can be crossed or nested, fixed or random. You can also use **General Linear Models** to analyze balanced, as well as unbalanced, designs.

■ **General linear model (GLM)** fits the general linear model for univariate responses. In matrix form, this model is $Y = XB + E$, where Y is the response vector, X contains the predictors, B contains parameters to be estimated, and E represents errors assumed to be normally distributed with mean vector 0 and variance Σ. Using the general linear model, you can perform a univariate analysis of variance with balanced and unbalanced designs, analysis of covariance, and regression. GLM also allows you to examine differences among means using multiple comparisons.

■ **Fully nested ANOVA** fits a fully nested (hierarchical) analysis of variance and estimates variance components. All factors are implicitly assumed to be random.

Testing the equality of means from multiple response

Balanced MANOVA and general MANOVA are procedures for testing the equality of vectors of means from multiple responses. Your choice between these two procedures depends upon the experimental design and the available options. Both procedures can fit MANOVA models to balanced data with up to 31 factors.

■ **Balanced MANOVA** is used to perform multivariate analysis of variance with balanced designs. See *Balanced designs* on page 3-19. You can also specify factors to be random and obtain expected means squares. Use general MANOVA with unbalanced designs.

■ **General MANOVA** is used to perform multivariate analysis of variance with either balanced or unbalanced designs that can also include covariates. You cannot specify factors to be random as you can for balanced MANOVA, although you can work around this restriction by specifying the error term for testing different model terms.

The table below summarizes the differences between Balanced and General MANOVA:

	Balanced MANOVA	General MANOVA
Can fit unbalanced data	no	yes
Can specify factors as random and obtain expected means squares	yes	no
Can fit covariates	no	yes
Can fit restricted and unrestricted forms of a mixed model	yes	no; unrestricted only

Special analytical graphs

- **Test for equal variances** performs Bartlett's (or F-test if 2 levels) and Levene's hypothesis tests for testing the equality or homogeneity of variance. Many statistical procedures, including ANOVA, are based upon the assumption that samples from different populations have the same variance.

- **Interval plot for mean** creates a plot of means with either error bars or confidence intervals when you have a one-way design.

- **Main effects plot** creates a main effects plot for either raw response data or fitted values from a model-fitting procedure. The points in the plot are the means at the various levels of each factor with a reference line drawn at the grand mean of the response data. Use the main effects plot to compare magnitudes of marginal means.

- **Interactions plot** creates a single interaction plot if two factors are entered, or a matrix of interaction plots if 3 to 9 factors are entered. An interactions plot is a plot of means for each level of a factor with the level of a second factor held constant. Interactions plots are useful for judging the presence of interaction, which means that the difference in the response at two levels of one factor depends upon the level of another factor. Parallel lines in an interactions plot indicate no interaction. The greater the departure of the lines from being parallel, the higher the degree of interaction. To use an interactions plot, data must be available from all combinations of levels.

Use the main effects plot and the interactions plot in Chapter 19 to generate main effects plots and interaction plots specifically for 2-level factorial designs, such as those generated by Create Factorial Design and Create RS Design.

One-Way Analysis of Variance

One-way analysis of variance tests the equality of population means when classification is by one variable. There are two ways to organize your data in the worksheet. You can enter the response in one column (stacked) or in different columns (unstacked). If your response is in one column, you can examine differences among means using multiple comparisons.

Data

The response variable must be numeric. You can enter the sample data from each population into separate columns of your worksheet (*unstacked* case), or you can stack the response data in one column with another column of level values identifying the population (*stacked* case). In the stacked case, the factor level column can be numeric, text, or date/time. If you wish to change the order in which text levels are processed from their default alphabetical order, you can define your own order. See *Ordering Text Categories* in the *Manipulating Data* chapter of MINITAB *User's Guide 1*. You do not need to have the same number of observations in each level. You can use **Calc ➤ Make Patterned Data** to enter repeated factor levels. See the *Generating Patterned Data* chapter in MINITAB *User's Guide 1*.

▶ To perform a one-way analysis of variance with stacked data

1 Choose **Stat ➤ ANOVA ➤ One-way**.

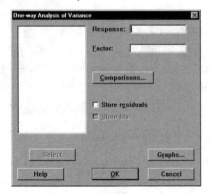

2 In **Response**, enter the column containing the responses.

3 In **Factor**, enter the column containing the factor levels.

4 If you like, use one or more of the options described below, then click **OK**.

▶ **To perform a one-way analysis of variance with unstacked data**

1 Choose Stat ➤ ANOVA ➤ One-way (Unstacked).

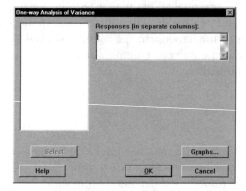

2 In **Responses (in separate columns)**, enter the columns containing the separate response variables.

3 If you like, use one or more of the options described below, then click **OK**.

Options with stacked data

One-way dialog box

■ store residuals and fitted values (the means for each level).

Comparisons subdialog box

■ display confidence intervals for the differences between means, using four different multiple comparison methods: Fisher's LSD, Tukey's, Dunnett's, and Hsu's MCB (multiple comparisons with the best). See *Multiple comparisons of means* on page 3-7.

Graphs subdialog box

■ draw boxplots, dotplots, and residual plots. You can draw five different residual plots:
  – histogram.
  – normal probability plot.
  – plot of residuals versus the fitted values ($\hat{Y}$).
  – plot of residuals versus data order. The row number for each data point is shown on the x-axis—for example, 1 2 3 4... *n*.
  – separate plot for the residuals versus each specified column.

For a discussion of the residual plots, see *Residual plots* on page 2-6.

Options with unstacked data

Graphs subdialog box

■ draw boxplots and dotplots that display the sample mean for each sample.

Multiple comparisons of means

Multiple comparisons of means allow you to examine which means are different and to estimate by how much they are different. When you have a single factor and your data are stacked, you can obtain multiple comparisons of means by choosing the **Stat ➤ ANOVA ➤ One-way** and then clicking the Comparisons subdialog box.

The choice of method

The multiple comparison methods compare different means and use different error rates. If you wish to examine all pairwise comparisons of means, use either Fisher's least significant difference (LSD) or Tukey's (also called Tukey-Kramer in the unbalanced case) method. The choice depends on whether you wish to control the individual (comparison-wise) error rate or the family (experiment-wise) error rate. The danger in using the individual error rate with Fisher's method is having an unexpectedly high probability of making at least one Type I error (declaring a difference when there is none) among all the comparisons. MINITAB displays both error rates. In most cases, the Tukey method is probably the choice that you should make when you want to judge all pairwise differences, because you can control the family error rate.

Choose the Dunnett method if you are comparing treatments to a control. When this method is suitable, it is inefficient to use the Tukey all-pairwise approach, because the Tukey confidence intervals will be wider and the hypothesis tests less powerful for a given family error rate. You will need to specify which level represents the control. If this level is text or date/time, enclose it with double quotes.

Choose Hsu's MCB (multiple comparison with the best) method if it makes sense to compare each mean only with the "best" among all of the other ones. This procedure allows you to judge how much worse a level might be if it is not the best or how much better it might be than its closest competitor. You will need to specify if the "best" is smallest or largest. If you are mainly interested in comparing each level to the "best" it is inefficient to use the Tukey all-pairwise approach because you will waste your error rate comparing pairs of level means which do not include the best mean.

Your choice among them may depend on their properties. Some properties of the multiple comparison methods are summarized below:

Comparison method	Purpose	Error rate
Fisher's LSD	all pairwise differences	individual
Tukey	all pairwise differences	family
Dunnett	comparison to a control	family
Hsu's MCB	comparison with the best	family

Interpreting confidence intervals

MINITAB presents results in confidence interval form to allow you to assess the practical significance of differences among means, in addition to statistical significance. As usual, the null hypothesis of no difference between means is rejected if and only if zero is not contained in the confidence interval.

Specify error rates as percents between 0.1 and 50%. The default error rate of 5% is the family error rate for the Tukey, Dunnett, and MCB methods and the individual error rate for the Fisher method. Individual error rates are exact in all cases, meaning that they can be calculated by an explicit formula. Family error rates are exact for equal group sizes. If group sizes are unequal, the true family error rate for the Tukey, Fisher, and MCB methods will be slightly smaller than stated, resulting in conservative confidence intervals [4], [21]. The Dunnett family error rates are exact for unequal sample sizes.

The F-test and multiple comparisons

The results of the F-test and multiple comparisons can conflict. For example, it is possible for the F-test to reject the null hypothesis of no differences among the level means, and yet all the Tukey pairwise confidence intervals may contain zero. Conversely, it is possible for the F-test to fail to reject the null hypothesis, and yet have one or more of the Tukey pairwise confidence intervals not include zero. The F-test has been used to protect against the occurrence of false positive differences in means. However, the Tukey, Dunnett, and MCB methods have protection against false positives built in, while the Fisher method only benefits from this protection when all means are equal. If the use of multiple comparisons is conditioned upon the significance of the F-test, the error rate can be higher than the error rate in the unconditioned application of multiple comparisons [14].

See Help for computational details of the multiple comparison methods.

▷ Example of a one-way ANOVA with multiple comparisons

You design an experiment to assess the durability of four experimental carpet products. You place a sample of each of the carpet products in four homes and you measure durability after 60 days. Because you wish to test the equality of means and to assess the differences in means, you use the one-way ANOVA procedure (data in stacked form) with multiple comparisons. Generally, you would choose one multiple comparison method as appropriate for your data. However, two methods are selected here to demonstrate MINITAB's capabilities.

1 Open the worksheet EXH_AOV.MTW.

2 Choose **Stat ➤ ANOVA ➤ One-way**.

3 In **Response**, enter *Durability*. In **Factor**, enter *Carpet*.

4 Click **Comparisons**. Check **Tukey's, family error rate** and enter *10* in the text box. Check **Hsu's MCB, family error rate** and enter *10* in the text box. Click **OK** in each dialog box.

Session window output

One-way ANOVA: Durability versus Carpet

```
Analysis of Variance for Durabili
Source     DF        SS        MS        F        P
Carpet      3     111.6      37.2     2.60    0.101
Error      12     172.0      14.3
Total      15     283.6
                                     Individual 95% CIs For Mean
                                     Based on Pooled StDev
Level       N      Mean     StDev  ---------+---------+---------+-------
1           4    14.483     3.157                (-------*-------)
2           4     9.735     3.566   (-------*--------)
3           4    12.808     1.506       (--------*-------)
4           4    17.005     5.691                  (-------*-------)
                                     ---------+---------+---------+-------
Pooled StDev =     3.786              10.0      15.0      20.0


Hsu's MCB (Multiple Comparisons with the Best)

     Family error rate = 0.100

Critical value = 1.87

Intervals for level mean minus largest of other level means

Level       Lower    Center    Upper  -+---------+---------+---------+------
1          -7.527    -2.522    2.482              (--------*-------)
2         -12.274    -7.270    0.000   (-------*-----------)
3          -9.202    -4.198    0.807       (-------*-------)
4          -2.482     2.522    7.527                   (-------*--------)
                                        -+---------+---------+---------+------
                                      -12.0      -6.0       0.0       6.0
```

```
Tukey's pairwise comparisons

    Family error rate = 0.100
Individual error rate = 0.0250

Critical value = 3.62

Intervals for (column level mean) - (row level mean)

                  1              2            3

        2     -2.106
              11.601

        3     -5.178         -9.926
               8.528          3.781

        4     -9.376        -14.123       -11.051
               4.331         -0.417         2.656
```

Interpreting the results

The default one-way output contains an analysis of variance table, a table of level means, individual 95% confidence intervals, and the pooled standard deviation. The F-test p-value of 0.101 indicates that there is not quite sufficient evidence (at $\alpha = 0.10$ or less) to claim that not all the means are equal. However, you should examine the multiple comparison results, which use family error rates of 0.10, because the methods used (Tukey, MCB) have built in protection against false positive results.

The output labeled "Hsu's MCB" compares each mean with the best of the other means. Here, "best" is the default or largest of the others. The means of carpets 1, 2, and 3 were compared to the level 4 mean because the carpet 4 mean is the largest of the rest. The level 4 mean was compared to the carpet 1 mean. Carpets 1, 3, or 4 may be best, since the corresponding confidence intervals contain positive values. There is no evidence that carpet 2 is the best because the upper interval endpoint is 0, the smallest it can be.

In addition, it is possible to describe the potential advantage or disadvantage of any of the contenders for the best. For example, if carpet 3 is best, it is no more than 0.809 better than its closest competitor, and it may be as much as 9.204 worse than the best of the other level means. If carpet 1 is not the best, it is no more than 2.484 worse than the best of the other means, and it may be as much as 7.529 better than the best of the others.

The first pair of numbers in the Tukey output table, (−2.106, 11.601), gives the confidence interval for the mean of carpet 1 minus the mean of carpet 2. Confidence intervals for entries not in the table can be found from entries in the table. For example, the confidence interval for the mean of level 2 minus the mean of carpet 1 is (−11.601, 2.106). Carpets 2 and 4 are the only ones for which the means can be declared as different, since the confidence interval for this combination of means is the only one that excludes zero.

By not conditioning upon the F-test, differences in treatment means appear to have occurred at family error rates of 0.10. If the MCB method is a good choice for these data, carpet 2 might be eliminated as a choice for the "best". By the Tukey method, the mean durability from carpets 2 and 4 appears to be different.

Two-Way Analysis of Variance

A two-way analysis of variance tests the equality of populations means when classification of treatments is by two variables or factors. For this procedure, the data must be balanced (all cells must have the same number of observations) and factors must be fixed.

If you wish to specify certain factors to be random, use **Balanced ANOVA** if your data are balanced, and use **General Linear Model** if your data are unbalanced or if you wish to compare means using multiple comparisons.

Data

The response variable must be numeric and in one worksheet column. You must have a single factor level column for each of the two factors. These can be numeric, text, or date/time. If you wish to change the order in which text categories are processed from their default alphabetical order, you can define your own order. See *Ordering Text Categories* in the *Manipulating Data* chapter of MINITAB *User's Guide 1*. You must have a balanced design (same number of observations in each treatment combination) with fixed and crossed factors. See *Balanced designs* on page 3-19, *Fixed vs. random factors* on page 3-20, and *Crossed vs. nested factors* on page 3-19. You can use **Calc ➤ Make Patterned Data** to enter repeated factor levels. See the *Generating Patterned Data* chapter in MINITAB *User's Guide 1*.

▶ **To perform a two-way analysis of variance**

1 Choose Stat ➤ ANOVA ➤ Two-way.

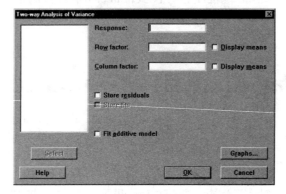

2 In **Response**, enter the column containing the response.

3 In **Row Factor**, enter one of the factor level columns.

4 In **Column Factor**, enter the other factor level column.

5 If you like, use one or more of the options described below, then click **OK**.

Options

Two-way dialog box

- print sample means and 95% confidence intervals for factor levels means.

- store residuals and fits.

- fit an additive model, that is, a model without the interaction term. In this case, the fitted value for cell (i, j) is (mean of observations in row i) + (mean of observations in row j) − (mean of all observations).

Graphs subdialog box

- draw five different residual plots. You can display the following plots:
  - histogram.
  - normal probability plot.
  - plot of residuals versus the fitted values ($\hat{Y}$).
  - plot of residuals versus data order. The row number for each data point is shown on the x-axis—for example, 1 2 3 4... *n*.
  - separate plot for the residuals versus each specified column.

  For a discussion of the residual plots, see *Residual plots* on page 2-6.

▷ **Example of two-way analysis of variance**

You are a biologist who is studying how zooplankton live in two lakes. You set up twelve tanks in your laboratory, six each with water from a different lake. You add one of three nutrient supplements to each tank and after 30 days you count the zooplankton in a unit volume of water. You use two-way ANOVA to test if the population means are equal, or equivalently, to test whether there is significant evidence of interactions and main effects.

1 Open the worksheet EXH_AOV.MTW.

2 Choose **Stat ➤ ANOVA ➤ Two-way**.

3 In **Response**, enter *Zooplankton*.

4 In **Row factor**, enter *Supplement*. Check **Display means**.

5 In **Column factor**, enter *Lake*. Check **Display means**. Click **OK**.

*Session
window
output*

Two-way ANOVA: Zooplankton versus Supplement, Lake

```
Analysis of Variance for Zooplank
Source       DF      SS     MS      F       P
Suppleme      2    1919    959    9.25   0.015
Lake          1      21     21    0.21   0.666
Interaction   2     561    281    2.71   0.145
Error         6     622    104
Total        11    3123


                    Individual 95% CI
Suppleme     Mean    --+---------+---------+---------+---------
1            43.5        (-------*-------)
2            68.3                           (--------*-------)
3            39.8    (--------*-------)
                    --+---------+---------+---------+---------
                    30.0      45.0      60.0      75.0


                    Individual 95% CI
Lake         Mean    ------+---------+---------+---------+-----
Dennison     51.8        (----------------*----------------)
Rose         49.2    (----------------*----------------)
                    ------+---------+---------+---------+-----
                        42.0      48.0      54.0      60.0
```

Interpreting the results

The default output for two-way ANOVA is the analysis of variance table. For the zooplankton data, there is no significant evidence for a supplement*lake interaction effect or a lake main effect if your acceptable α value is less than 0.145 (the p-value for the interaction F-test). There is significant evidence for supplement main effects, as the F-test p-value is 0.015.

As requested, the means are displayed with individual 95% confidence intervals. Supplement 2 appears to have provided superior plankton growth in this experiment. These are t-distribution confidence intervals calculated using the error degrees of freedom and the pooled standard deviation (square root of the mean square error). If you want to examine simultaneous differences among means using multiple comparisons, use General Linear Model (page 3-37).

Analysis of Means

Analysis of Means (ANOM), a graphical analog to ANOVA, tests the equality of population means. ANOM [15] was developed to test main effects from a designed experiment in which all factors are fixed. This procedure is used for one-factor designs. MINITAB uses an extension of ANOM or ANalysis Of Mean treatment Effects (ANOME) [23] to test the significance of mean treatment effects for two-factor designs.

An ANOM chart can be described in two ways: by its appearance and by its function. In appearance, it resembles a Shewhart control chart. In function, it is similar to ANOVA for detecting differences in population means [12]. There are some important differences between ANOM and ANOVA, however. The hypotheses they test are not identical [16]. ANOVA tests whether the treatment means are different from each other; ANOM tests whether the treatment means differ from the grand mean.

For most cases, ANOVA and ANOM will likely give similar results. However, there are some scenarios where the two methods might be expected to differ: 1) if one group of means is above the grand mean and another group of means is below the grand mean, ANOVA's F-test might indicate evidence for differences where ANOM might not; 2) if the mean of one group is separated from the other means, the ANOVA F-test might not indicate evidence for differences whereas ANOM might flag this group as being different from the grand mean. Refer to [20], [21], [22], and [23] for an introduction to the analysis of means.

ANOM can be used if you assume that the response follows a normal distribution, similar to ANOVA, and the design is one-way or two-way. You can also use ANOM when the response follows either a binomial distribution or a Poisson distribution.

Data

Response data from a normal distribution

Your response data must be numeric and entered into one column. Factor columns may be numeric, text, or date/time and may contain any values. MINITAB's capability to enter patterned data can be helpful in entering numeric factor levels. If you wish to change the order in which text categories are processed from their default alphabetical order, you can define your own order. See *Ordering Text Categories* in the

Manipulating Data chapter of MINITAB *User's Guide 1*. You can use **Calc ➤ Make Patterned Data** to enter repeated factor levels. See the *Generating Patterned Data* chapter in MINITAB *User's Guide 1*.

One-way designs may be balanced or unbalanced and can have up to 100 levels. Two-way designs must be balanced and can have up to 50 levels for each factor. All factors must be fixed. See *Fixed vs. random factors* on page 3-20.

Rows with missing data are automatically omitted from calculations. If you have two factors, the design must be balanced after omitting rows with missing values.

Response data from a binomial distribution

The response data are the numbers of defectives (or defects) found in each sample, with a maximum of 500 samples. These data must be entered into one column.

Since the decision limits in the ANOM chart are based upon the normal distribution, one of the assumptions that must be met when the response data are binomial is that the sample size must be large enough to ensure that the normal approximation to the binomial is valid. A general rule of thumb is to only use ANOM if $np > 5$ and $n(1 - p) > 5$, where n is the sample size and p is the proportion of defectives. The second assumption is that all of the samples are the same size. See [23] for more details.

A sample with a missing response value ($*$) is automatically omitted from the analysis.

Response data from a Poisson distribution

The response data are the numbers of defects found in each sample. You can have up to 500 samples.

The Poisson distribution can be adequately approximated by a normal distribution if the mean of the Poisson distribution is at least 5. Hence, when the Poisson mean is large enough, analysis of means can be applied to data from a Poisson distribution to test if the population means are equal to the grand mean.

A sample with a missing response value ($*$) is automatically omitted from the analysis.

▶ **To perform an analysis of means**

1   Choose **Stat ➤ ANOVA ➤ Analysis of Means**.

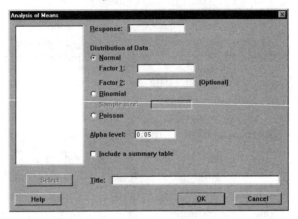

2   In **Response**, enter a numeric column containing the response variable.

3   Under **Distribution of Data**, choose **Normal**, **Binomial**, or **Poisson**.

   ■ If you choose **Normal**, do one of the following:
      – for a one-way design, enter the column containing the factor levels in **Factor 1**
      – for a two-way design, enter the columns containing the factor levels in **Factor 1** and **Factor 2**

   ■ If you choose **Binomial**, enter a number in **Sample size**.

4   If you like, use one or more of the options described below, then click **OK**.

Options

   ■ change the experiment wide error rate, or alpha level (default is 0.05). This will change the location of the decision lines on the graph.

   ■ print a summary table of level statistics for normal (prints means, standard errors, sample size) or binomial data (prints number, proportion of defectives).

   ■ replace the default graph title with your own title.

▷ **Example of a two-way analysis of means (ANOM)**

You perform an experiment to assess the effect of three process time levels and three strength levels on density. You use analysis of means for normal data and a two-way design to identify any significant interactions or main effects.

1   Open the worksheet EXH_AOV.MTW.

2   Choose **Stat ➤ ANOVA ➤ Analysis of Means**.

3 In **Response**, enter *Density*.

4 Choose **Normal**.

5 In **Factor 1**, enter *Minutes*. In **Factor 2**, enter *Strength*. Click **OK**.

*Graph
window
output*

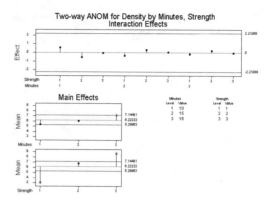

Interpreting the results

Three plots are displayed in one graph with a two-way ANOM: one showing the interaction effects, one showing the means for the first factor, and one showing the means for the second factor. Control charts have a center line and control limits. If a point falls outside the control limits, then there is significant evidence that the mean represented by that point is different from the grand mean. With a two-way ANOM, look at the interaction effects first. If there is significant evidence for interaction, it usually does not make sense to consider main effects, because the effect of one factor depends upon the level of the other.

In our example, the interaction effects are well within the control limits, signifying no evidence of interaction. Now you can look at the main effects. The lower two plots show the means for the levels of the two factors, with the main effect being the difference between the mean and the center line. The point representing the level 3 mean of the factor Minutes is displayed by a red asterisk, which indicates that there is significant evidence for the level 3 mean being different from the grand mean at $\alpha = 0.05$. You may wish to investigate any point near or above the control limits. The main effects for levels 1 and 3 of factor Strength are well outside the control limits of the lower left plot, signifying that there is evidence for these means being different from the grand mean at $\alpha = 0.05$.

▷ Example of an ANOM for binomial response data

You count the number of rejected welds from samples of size 80 in order to identify samples whose proportions of rejects are out of line with the other samples. Because the data are binomial (two possible outcomes, constant proportion of success, and independent samples) you use analysis of means for binomial data.

1 Open the worksheet EXH_AOV.MTW.

2 Choose **Stat ➤ ANOVA ➤ Analysis of Means**.

3 In **Response**, enter *WeldRejects*.

4 Choose **Binomial** and enter *80* in **Sample size**. Click **OK**.

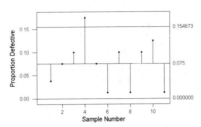

One-Way Binomial Analysis of Means for WeldRejects

Interpreting the results

A single plot displays the proportion of defects, a center line representing the average proportion, and upper and lower decision limits. A similar plot is displayed for one-way normal data or for Poisson data. As with the two-way ANOM plot, you can judge if there is significant evidence for a sample mean being different from the average if the point representing that sample falls outside the control limits.

In this example, the proportion of defective welds in sample four is identified as being unusually high because the point representing this sample falls outside the control limits.

Overview of Balanced ANOVA and GLM

Balanced ANOVA and general linear model (GLM) are ANOVA procedures for analyzing data collected with many different experimental designs. Your choice between these procedures depends upon the experimental design and the available options. The experimental design refers to the selection of units or subjects to measure, the assignment of treatments to these units or subjects, and the sequence of

measurements taken on the units or subjects. Both procedures can fit univariate
models to balanced data with up to 31 factors. Here are some of the other options:

	Balanced ANOVA	GLM
Can fit unbalanced data	no	yes
Can specify factors as random and obtain expected means squares	yes	yes
Fits covariates	no	yes
Performs multiple comparisons	no	yes
Fits restricted/unrestricted forms of mixed model	yes	unrestricted only

You can use balanced ANOVA to analyze data from balanced designs—see *Balanced
designs* on page 3-19. You can use GLM to analyze data from any balanced design,
though you cannot choose to fit the restricted case of the mixed model, which only
balanced ANOVA can fit—see *Restricted and unrestricted form of mixed models* on page
3-28.

To determine how to classify your variables, see *Crossed vs. nested factors* on page 3-19,
Fixed vs. random factors on page 3-20, and *Covariates* on page 3-20.

For information on how to specify the model, see *Specifying the model terms* on page
3-21, *Specifying terms involving covariates* on page 3-22, *Specifying reduced models* on
page 3-22, and *Specifying models for some specialized designs* on page 3-23.

For easy entering of repeated factor levels into your worksheet, see *Using patterned data
to set up factor levels* on page 3-25.

Balanced designs

Your design must be balanced to use balanced ANOVA, with the exception of a
one-way design. A *balanced* design is one with equal numbers of observations at each
combination of your treatment levels. A quick test to see whether or not you have a
balanced design is to use **Stat ➤ Tables ➤ Cross Tabulation**. Enter your classification
variables and see if you have equal numbers of observations in each cell, indicating
balanced data.

Crossed vs. nested factors

When two or more factors are present in a design, they may be *crossed* or *nested*,
depending upon how the levels of one factor appear with the levels of the other factor.
This concept can be demonstrated by the following example. Suppose that there are

two factors: plant and operator. If observations are made with each operator at each plant, then these are *crossed* factors. If observations are made with different operators at each plant, then operator is *nested* within plant. In general, if each level of factor A occurs with each level of factor B, factors A and B are *crossed*. If each level of factor B occurs within only one level of factor A, then factor B is *nested* within factor A. The designation of whether a factor is crossed or nested within MINITAB occurs with the specification of the model. See *Specifying the model terms* on page 3-21. It is important make the correct designation in order to obtain the correct error term for factors.

Fixed vs. random factors

In addition to the crossed or nested designation for pairs of factors, a factor can be either *fixed* or *random*. Designating a factor as fixed or random depends upon how you view that factor in a larger context. Suppose that one factor is machine operator. If one is truly interested in each operator and may, for example, initiate a training procedure for specific operators depending upon the tests results, then the operator factor is *fixed*. If the operators are considered to be drawn at random from a population of all operators and interest is in the population and not the individuals, then the factor is *random*. In MINITAB, factors are assumed to be fixed unless specified otherwise. It is important to make the correct designation in order to obtain the correct error term for factors.

The terms *fixed* and *random* often modify the word *effect*. What is usually meant by *effect* for a fixed factor is the difference between the mean corresponding to a factor level and the overall mean. The testing of fixed effects being zero is equivalent to the testing of treatment means being equal. An effect for a random factor is not defined as the difference in means because the interest is in estimation and testing of variance components. An effect is *mixed* if it is the interaction effect of fixed and random factors. With balanced ANOVA, you can choose whether to restrict the sum of mixed effects. See *Restricted and unrestricted form of mixed models* on page 3-28.

Covariates

A *covariate* is a quantitative variable included in an ANOVA model. A covariate may be a variable for which the level is not controlled as part of the design, but has been measured and it is entered into the model to reduce the error variance. A covariate may also be a quantitative variable for which the levels have been controlled as part of the experiment. Regardless of the origin, the statistical model contains a coefficient for the covariate as if the covariate was a predictor in a regression model.

Specifying the model terms

You must specify the model terms in the **Model** box. This is an abbreviated form of the statistical model that you may see in textbooks. Because you enter the response variable(s) in **Responses,** in **Model** you enter only the variables or products of variables that correspond to terms in the statistical model. MINITAB uses a simplified version of a statistical model as it appears in many textbooks. Here are some examples of statistical models and the terms to enter in **Model**. A, B, and C represent factors.

Case	Statistical model	Terms in model
Factors A, B crossed	$y_{ijk} = \mu + a_i + b_j + ab_{ij} + e_{k(ij)}$	A B A*B
Factors A, B, C crossed	$y_{ijkl} = \mu + a_i + b_j + c_k + ab_{ij} + ac_{ik} + bc_{jk} + abc_{ijk} + e_{l(ijk)}$	A B C A*B A*C B*C A*B*C
3 factors nested (B within A, C within A and B)	$y_{ijkl} = \mu + a_i + b_{j(i)} + c_{k(ij)} + e_{l(ijk)}$	A B(A) C(AB)
Crossed and nested (B nested within A, both crossed with C)	$y_{ijkl} = \mu + a_i + b_{j(i)} + c_k + ac_{ik} + bc_{jk(i)} + e_{l(ijk)}$	A B(A) C A*C B*C

In MINITAB's models you omit the subscripts, μ, e, and +'s that appear in textbook models. An * is used for an interaction term and parentheses are used for nesting. For example, when B is nested within A, you enter B (A), and when C is nested within both A and B, you enter C (A B). Enter B(A) C(B) for the case of 3 sequentially nested factors. Terms in parentheses are always factors in the model and are listed with blanks between them. Thus, D*F (A B E) is correct but D*F (A*B E) and D (A*B*C) are not. Also, one set of parentheses cannot be used inside another set. Thus, C (A B) is correct but C (A B (A)) is not. An interaction term between a nested factor and the factor it is nested within is invalid.

See *Specifying terms involving covariates* on page 3-22 for details on specifying models with covariates.

Several special rules apply to naming columns. You may omit the quotes around variable names. Because of this, variable names must start with a letter and contain only letters and numbers. Alternatively, you can use C notation (C1, C2, etc.) to denote data columns. You can use special symbols in a variable name, but then you must enclose the name in single quotes.

You can specify multiple responses. In this case, a separate analysis of variance will be performed for each response.

Specifying terms involving covariates

You can specify variables to be covariates in GLM. You must specify the covariates in **Covariates**, but you can enter the covariates in **Model,** though this is not necessary unless you cross or nest the covariates (see below table).

In an unbalanced design or a design involving covariates, GLM's sequential sums of squares (the additional model sums of squares explained by a variable) will depend upon the order in which variables enter the model. If you do not enter the covariates in **Model** when using GLM, they will be fit first, which is what you usually want when a covariate contributes background variability. The subsequent order of fitting is the order of terms in **Model**. The sequential sums of squares for unbalanced terms A B will be different depending upon the order that you enter them in the model. The default adjusted sums of squares (sums of squares with all other terms in the model), however, will be the same, regardless of model order.

GLM allows terms containing covariates crossed with each other and with factors, and covariates nested within factors. Here are some examples of these models, where A is a factor.

Case	Covariates	Terms in model
test homogeneity of slopes (covariate crossed with factor)	X	A X A*X
same as previous	X	A | X
quadratic in covariate (covariate crossed with itself)	X	A X X*X
full quadratic in two covariates (covariates crossed)	X Z	A X Z X*X Z*Z X*Z
separate slopes for each level of A (covariate nested within a factor)	X	A X(A)

Specifying reduced models

You can fit *reduced* models. For example, suppose you have a three factor design, with factors, A, B, and C. The *full* model would include all one factor terms: A, B, C, all two-factor interactions: A*B, A*C, B*C, and the three-factor interaction: A*B*C. It becomes a reduced model by omitting terms. You might reduce a model if terms are not significant or if you need additional error degrees of freedom and you can assume that certain terms are zero. For this example, the model with terms A B C A*B is a reduced three-factor model.

One rule about specifying reduced models is that they must be hierarchical. That is, for a term to be in the model, all lower order terms contained in it must also be in the model. For example, suppose there is a model with four factors: A, B, C, and D. If the term A∗B∗C is in the model, then the terms A B C A∗B A∗C B∗C must also be in the model, though any terms involving D do not have to be in the model. The hierarchical structure applies to nesting as well. If B(A) is in the model, then A must be also.

Because models can be quite long and tedious to type, two shortcuts have been provided. A vertical bar indicates crossed factors, and a minus sign removes terms.

Long form	Short form
A B C A∗B A∗C B∗C A∗B∗C	A|B|C
A B C A∗B A∗C B∗C	A|B|C – A∗B∗C
A B C B∗C E	A B|C E
A B C D A∗B A∗C A∗D B∗C B∗D C∗D A∗B∗D A∗C∗D B∗C∗D	A|B|C|D – A∗B∗C – A∗B∗C∗D
A B(A) C A∗C B∗C	A|B(A)|C

In general, all crossings are done for factors separated by bars unless the cross results in an illegal term. For example, in the last example, the potential term A∗B(A) is illegal and MINITAB automatically omits it. If a factor is nested, you must indicate this when using the vertical bar, as in the last example with the term B(A).

Specifying models for some specialized designs

Some experimental designs can effectively provide information when measurements are difficult or expensive to make or can minimize the effect of unwanted variability on treatment inference. The following is a brief discussion of three commonly used designs that will show you how to specify the model terms in MINITAB. To illustrate these designs, two treatment factors (A and B) and their interaction (A∗B) are considered. These designs are not restricted to two factors, however. If your design is balanced, you can use balanced ANOVA to analyze your data. Otherwise, use GLM.

Randomized block design

A *randomized block* design is a commonly used design for minimizing the effect of variability when it is associated with discrete units (e.g. location, operator, plant, batch, time). The usual case is to randomize one replication of each treatment combination within each block. There is usually no intrinsic interest in the blocks and these are considered to be random factors. The usual assumption is that the block by treatment interaction is zero and this interaction becomes the error term for testing treatment effects. If you name the block variable as Block, enter *Block A B A∗B* in **Model** and enter *Block* in **Random Factors**.

Split-plot design

A *split-plot* design is another blocking design, which you can use if you have two or more factors. You might use this design when it is more difficult to randomize one of the factors compared to the other(s). For example, in an agricultural experiment with the factors variety and harvest date, it may be easier to plant each variety in contiguous rows and to randomly assign the harvest dates to smaller sections of the rows. The block, which can be replicated, is termed the *main plot* and within these the smaller plots (variety strips in example) are called *subplots*.

This design is frequently used in industry when it is difficult to randomize the settings on machines. For example, suppose that factors are temperature and material amount, but it is difficult to change the temperature setting. If the blocking factor is operator, observations will be made at different temperatures with each operator, but the temperature setting is held constant until the experiment is run for all material amounts. In this example, the plots under operator constitute the main plots and temperatures constitute the subplots.

There is no single error term for testing all factor effects in a split-plot design. If the levels of factor A form the subplots, then the mean square for Block*A will be the error term for testing factor A. There are two schools of thought for what should be the error term to use for testing B and A*B. If you enter the term Block*B, the expected mean squares show that the mean square for Block*B is the proper term for testing factor B and that the remaining error (which is Block*A*B) will be used for testing A*B. However, it is often assumed that the Block*B and Block*A*B interactions do not exist and these are then lumped together into error [6]. You might also pool the two terms if the mean square for Block*B is small relative to Block*A*B. In you don't pool, enter *Block A Block*A B Block*B A*B* in **Model** and what is labeled as Error is really Block*A*B. If you do pool terms, enter *Block A Block*A B A*B* in **Model** and what is labeled as Error is the set of pooled terms. In both cases enter *Block* in **Random Factors**.

Latin square with repeated measures design

A *repeated measures* design is a design where repeated measurements are made on the same subject. There are a number of ways in which treatments can be assigned to subjects. With living subjects especially, systematic differences (due to learning, acclimation, resistance, etc.) between successive observations may be suspected. One common way to assign treatments to subjects is to use a Latin square design. An advantage of this design for a repeated measures experiment is that it ensures a balanced fraction of a complete factorial (i.e. all treatment combinations represented) when subjects are limited and the sequence effect of treatment can be considered to be negligible.

A *Latin square* design is a blocking design with two orthogonal blocking variables. In an agricultural experiment there might be perpendicular gradients that might lead you to choose this design. For a repeated measures experiment, one blocking variable is the group of subjects and the other is time. If the treatment factor B has three levels, b_1, b_2, and b_3, then one of twelve possible Latin square randomizations of the levels of B to subjects groups over time is:

	Time 1	Time 2	Time 3
Group 1	b_2	b_3	b_1
Group 2	b_3	b_1	b_2
Group 3	b_1	b_2	b_3

The subjects receive the treatment levels in the order specified across the row. In this example, group 1 subjects would receive the treatments levels in order b_2, b_3, b_1. The interval between administering treatments should be chosen to minimize carryover effect of the previous treatment.

This design is commonly modified to provide information on one or more additional factors. If each group was assigned a different level of factor A, then information on the A and A*B effects could be made available with minimal effort if an assumption about the sequence effect given to the groups can be made. If the sequence effects are negligible compared to the effects of factor A, then the group effect could be attributed to factor A. If interactions with time are negligible, then partial information on the A*B interaction may be obtained [27]. In the language of repeated measures designs, factor A is called a *between-subjects* factor and factor B a *within-subjects* factor.

Let's consider how to enter the model terms into MINITAB. If the group or A factor, subject, and time variables were named A, Subject, and Time, respectively, enter A Subject(A) Time B A*B in **Model** and enter Subject in **Random Factors**.

It is not necessary to randomize a repeated measures experiments according to a Latin square design. See *Example of a repeated measures design* on page 3-31 for a repeated measures experiment where the fixed factors are arranged in a complete factorial design.

Using patterned data to set up factor levels

MINITAB's set patterned data capability can be helpful when entering numeric factor levels. For example, to enter the level values for a three-way crossed design with a, b, and c (a, b, and c represent numbers) levels of factors A, B, C, and n observations per cell, fill out the **Calc ➤ Make Patterned Data ➤ Simple Set of Numbers** dialog box and execute 3 times, once for each factor, as shown: (See the *Generating Patterned Data* chapter in MINITAB *User's Guide 1*.)

	Factor		
Dialog item	A	B	C
From first value	1	1	1
From last value	a	b	c
List each value	bcn	cn	n
List the whole sequence	1	a	ab

Balanced ANOVA

Use Balanced ANOVA to perform univariate analysis of variance for each response variable.

Your design must be balanced, with the exception of one-way designs. *Balanced* means that all treatment combinations (cells) must have the same number of observations. See *Balanced designs* on page 3-19. Use General Linear Model (page 3-37) to analyze balanced and unbalanced designs.

Factors may be crossed or nested, fixed or random. See *Crossed vs. nested factors* on page 3-19 and *Fixed vs. random factors* on page 3-20. You may include up to 50 response variables and up to 31 factors at one time.

Data

You need one column for each response variable and one column for each factor, with each row representing an observation. Regardless of whether factors are crossed or nested, use the same form for the data. Factor columns may be numeric, text, or date/time. If you wish to change the order in which text categories are processed from their default alphabetical order, you can define your own order. See *Ordering Text Categories* in the *Manipulating Data* chapter in MINITAB *User's Guide 1*.

Balanced data are required except for one-way designs. The requirement for balanced data extends to nested factors as well. Suppose A has 3 levels, and B is nested within A. If B has 4 levels within the first level of A, B must have 4 levels within the second and third levels of A. MINITAB will tell you if you have unbalanced nesting. In addition, the subscripts used to indicate the 4 levels of B within each level of A must be the same. Thus, the four levels of B cannot be (1 2 3 4) in level 1 of A, (5 6 7 8) in level 2 of A, and (9 10 11 12) in level 3 of A. However, you can use GLM to analyze data coded in this way.

If any response or factor column specified contains missing data, that entire observation (row) is excluded from all computations. The requirement that data be balanced must be preserved after missing data are omitted. If an observation is missing for one response variable, that row is eliminated for all responses. If you want to eliminate missing rows separately for each response, perform balanced ANOVA separately for each response.

▶ **To perform a balanced ANOVA**

  1 Choose Stat ➤ ANOVA ➤ Balanced ANOVA.

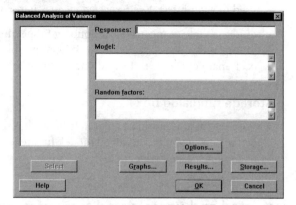

  2 In **Responses**, enter up to 50 numeric columns containing the response variables.

  3 In **Model**, type the model terms you want to fit. See *Specifying the model terms* on page 3-21.

  4 If you like, use one or more of the options described below, then click **OK**.

Options

Balanced Analysis of Variance dialog box

  ■ specify which factors are random factors—see *Fixed vs. random factors* on page 3-20.

Options subdialog box

  ■ use the restricted form of the mixed models (both fixed and random effects). The restricted model forces mixed interaction effects to sum to zero over the fixed effects. By default, MINITAB fits the unrestricted model. See *Restricted and unrestricted form of mixed models* on page 3-28.

Graphs subdialog box

  ■ draw five different residual plots. You can display the following plots:
    – histogram.
    – normal probability plot.
    – plot of residuals versus the fitted values ($\hat{Y}$).
    – plot of residuals versus data order. The row number for each data point is shown on the x-axis—for example, 1 2 3 4... n.
    – separate plot for the residuals versus each specified column.

  For a discussion of the residual plots, see *Residual plots* on page 2-6.

Results subdialog box

- display expected means squares, estimated variance components, and error terms used in each F-test. See *Expected mean squares* on page 3-28.

- display a table of means corresponding to specified terms from the model. For example, if you specify A B D A∗B∗D, four tables of means will be printed, one for each main effect, A, B, D, and one for the three-way interaction, A∗B∗D.

Storage subdialog box

- store the fits and residuals separately for each response. If you fit a full model, fits are cell means. If you fit a reduced model, fits are least squares estimates. See *Specifying reduced models* on page 3-22.

Restricted and unrestricted form of mixed models

A mixed model is one with both fixed and random factors. There are two forms of this model: one requires the crossed, mixed terms to sum to zero over subscripts corresponding to fixed effects (this is called the restricted model), and the other does not. See *Example of both restricted and unrestricted forms of the mixed model* on page 3-33. Many textbooks use the restricted model. Most statistics programs (e.g., SAS, JMP, and SPSS) use the unrestricted model. MINITAB fits the unrestricted model by default, but you can choose to fit the restricted form. The reasons to choose one form over the other have not been clearly defined in the statistical literature. Searle et al. [24] say "that question really has no definitive, universally acceptable answer," but also say that one "can decide which is more appropriate to the data at hand," without giving guidance on how to do so.

Your choice of model form does not affect the sums of squares, degrees of freedom, mean squares, or marginal and cell means. It does affect the expected mean squares, error terms for F-tests, and the estimated variance components. See *Example of both restricted and unrestricted forms of the mixed model* on page 3-33.

Expected mean squares

If you do not specify any factors to be random, MINITAB will assume that they are fixed. In this case, the denominator for F-statistics will be the MSE. However, for models which include random terms, the MSE is not always the correct error term. You can examine the expected means squares to determine the error term that was used in the F-test.

When you select **Display expected mean squares and variance components** in the Results subdialog box, MINITAB will print a table of expected mean squares, estimated variance components, and the error term (the denominator mean squares) used in each F-test. The *expected mean squares* are the expected values of these terms with the specified model. If there is no exact F-test for a term, MINITAB solves for the appropriate error term in order to construct an approximate F-test. This test is called a *synthesized test*.

The estimates of variance components are the usual unbiased analysis of variance estimates. They are obtained by setting each calculated mean square equal to its expected mean square, which gives a system of linear equations in the unknown variance components that is then solved. Unfortunately, this method can result in negative estimates, which should be set to zero. MINITAB, however, prints the negative estimates because they sometimes indicate that the model being fit is inappropriate for the data. Variance components are not estimated for fixed terms.

▶ Example of ANOVA with two crossed factors

An experiment was conducted to test how long it takes to use a new and an older model of calculator. Six engineers each work on both a statistical problem and an engineering problem using each calculator model; the time in minutes to solve the problem is recorded. The engineers can be considered as blocks in the experimental design. There are two factors—type of problem, and calculator model—each with two levels. Because each level of one factor occurs in combination with each level of the other factor, these factors are crossed. The example and data are from Neter, Wasserman, and Kutner [18], page 936.

1 Open the worksheet EXH_AOV.MTW.

2 Choose **Stat ➤ ANOVA ➤ Balanced ANOVA**.

3 In **Responses**, enter *SolveTime*.

4 In **Model**, type *Engineer ProbType | Calculator*.

5 In **Random Factors**, enter *Engineer*.

6 Click **Results**. In **Display means corresponding to the terms**, type *ProbType | Calculator*. Click **OK** in each dialog box.

*Session
window
output*
ANOVA: SolveTime versus Engineer, ProbType, Calculator

```
Factor        Type Levels Values
Engineer   random    6   Adams    Dixon Erickson    Jones    Maynes
                          Williams
ProbType   fixed     2   Eng  Stat
Calculat   fixed     2   New   Old
```

Analysis of Variance for SolveTim

Source	DF	SS	MS	F	P
Engineer	5	1.053	0.211	3.13	0.039
ProbType	1	16.667	16.667	247.52	0.000
Calculat	1	72.107	72.107	1070.89	0.000
ProbType*Calculat	1	3.682	3.682	54.68	0.000
Error	15	1.010	0.067		
Total	23	94.518			

Means

ProbType	N	SolveTim
Eng	12	3.8250
Stat	12	5.4917

Calculat	N	SolveTim
New	12	2.9250
Old	12	6.3917

ProbType	Calculat	N	SolveTim
Eng	New	6	2.4833
Eng	Old	6	5.1667
Stat	New	6	3.3667
Stat	Old	6	7.6167

Interpreting the results

MINITAB displays a list of factors, with their type (fixed or random), number of levels, and values. Next displayed is the analysis of variance table. The analysis of variance indicates that there is a significant calculator by problem type interaction, which implies that the decrease in mean compilation time in switching from the old to the new calculator depends upon the problem type.

Because you requested means for all factors and their combinations, the means of each factor level and factor level combinations are also displayed. These show that the mean compilation time decreased in switching from the old to new calculator type.

▷ Example of a repeated measures design

The following example contains data from Winer [27], p. 546, to illustrate a complex repeated measures model. An experiment was run to see how several factors affect subject accuracy in adjusting dials. Three subjects perform tests conducted at one of two noise levels. At each of three time periods, the subjects monitored three different dials and made adjustments as needed. The response is an accuracy score. The noise, time, and dial factors are crossed, fixed factors. Subject is a random factor, nested within noise. Noise is a between-subjects factor, time (variable ETime) and dial are within-subjects factors.

The model terms are entered in a certain order so that the error terms used for the fixed factors are just below the terms for whose effects they test. (With a single random factor, the interaction of a fixed factor with the random factor becomes the error term for that fixed effect.) Because Subject was specified as Subject(Noise) the first time, you do not need to repeat "(Noise)" in the interactions involving Subject. The interaction ETime*Dial*Subject, the error term for ETime*Dial, is not entered in the model because there would be zero degrees of freedom left over for error. By not entering ETime*Dial*Subject in the model, it is labeled as Error and you have the error term that is needed.

1 Open the worksheet EXH_AOV.MTW.

2 Choose **Stat ➤ ANOVA ➤ Balanced ANOVA**.

3 In **Responses**, enter *Score*.

4 In **Model**, enter *Noise Subject(Noise) ETime Noise*ETime ETime*Subject Dial Noise*Dial Dial*Subject ETime*Dial Noise*ETime*Dial*.

5 In **Random Factors**, enter *Subject*.

6 Click **Options**.

7 Check **Use the restricted form of the model**. Click **OK**.

8 Click **Results**.

9 Check **Display expected mean squares and variance components**. Click **OK** in each dialog box.

*Session
window
output*

ANOVA: Score versus Noise, ETime, Dial, Subject

```
Factor              Type Levels Values
Noise              fixed     2    1    2
Subject(Noise)    random     3    1    2    3
ETime              fixed     3    1    2    3
Dial               fixed     3    1    2    3
```

Analysis of Variance for Score

Source	DF	SS	MS	F	P
Noise	1	468.17	468.17	0.75	0.435
Subject(Noise)	4	2491.11	622.78	78.39	0.000
ETime	2	3722.33	1861.17	63.39	0.000
Noise*ETime	2	333.00	166.50	5.67	0.029
ETime*Subject(Noise)	8	234.89	29.36	3.70	0.013
Dial	2	2370.33	1185.17	89.82	0.000
Noise*Dial	2	50.33	25.17	1.91	0.210
Dial*Subject(Noise)	8	105.56	13.19	1.66	0.184
ETime*Dial	4	10.67	2.67	0.34	0.850
Noise*ETime*Dial	4	11.33	2.83	0.36	0.836
Error	16	127.11	7.94		
Total	53	9924.83			

Source	Variance component	Error term	Expected Mean Square for Each Term (using restricted model)
1 Noise		2	(11) + 9(2) + 27Q[1]
2 Subject(Noise)	68.315	11	(11) + 9(2)
3 ETime		5	(11) + 3(5) + 18Q[3]
4 Noise*ETime		5	(11) + 3(5) + 9Q[4]
5 ETime*Subject(Noise)	7.139	11	(11) + 3(5)
6 Dial		8	(11) + 3(8) + 18Q[6]
7 Noise*Dial		8	(11) + 3(8) + 9Q[7]
8 Dial*Subject(Noise)	1.750	11	(11) + 3(8)
9 ETime*Dial		11	(11) + 6Q[9]
10 Noise*ETime*Dial		11	(11) + 3Q[10]
11 Error	7.944		(11)

Interpreting the results

MINITAB displays the table of factor levels, the analysis of variance table, and the expected mean squares. Important information to gain from the expected means squares are the estimated variance components and discovering which error term is used for testing the different model terms.

The term labeled Error is in row 11 of the expected mean squares table. The column labeled "Error term" indicates that term 11 was used to test terms 2, 5, and 8 to 10. Dial*Subject is numbered 8 and was used to test the sixth and seventh terms. You can follow the pattern for other terms.

You can gain some idea about how the design affected the sensitivity of F-tests by viewing the variance components. The variance components used in testing within-subjects factors are smaller (7.139, 1.750, 7.944) than the between-subjects variance (68.315). It is typical that a repeated measures model can detect smaller differences in means within subjects as compared to between subjects.

Of the four interactions among fixed factors, the noise by time interaction was the only one with a low p-value (0.029). This implies that there is significant evidence for judging that a subjects' sensitivity to noise changed over time. Because this interaction is significant, at least at $\alpha = 0.05$, the noise and time main effects are not examined. There is also significant evidence for a dial effect (p-value < 0.0005). Among random terms, there is significant evidence for time by subject (p-value $= 0.013$) and subject (p-value < 0.0005) effects.

▷ Example of both restricted and unrestricted forms of the mixed model

A company ran an experiment to see how several conditions affect the thickness of a coating substance that it manufactures. The experiment was run at two different times, in the morning and in the afternoon. Three operators were chosen from a large pool of operators employed by the company. The manufacturing process was run at three settings, 35, 44, and 52. Two determinations of thickness were made by each operator at each time and setting. Thus, the three factors are crossed. One factor, operator, is random; the other two, time and setting, are fixed.

The statistical model is

$$Y_{ijkl} = \mu + T_i + O_j + S_k + TO_{ij} + TS_{ik} + OS_{jk} + TOS_{ijk} + e_{ijkl},$$

where T_i is the time effect, O_j is the operator effect, and S_k is the setting effect, and TO_{ij}, TS_{ik}, OS_{jk}, and TOS_{ijk} are the interaction effects.

Operator, all interactions with operator, and error are random. The random terms are:

$$O_j \quad TO_{ij} \quad OS_{jk} \quad TOS_{ijk} \quad e_{ijkl}$$

These terms are all assumed to be normally distributed random variables with mean zero and variances given by

var $(O_j) = V(O)$	var $(TO_{ij}) = V(TO)$	var $(OS_{jk}) = V(OS)$
var $(TOS_{jkl}) = V(TOS)$	var $(e_{ijkl}) = V(e) = \sigma^2$	

These variances are called variance components. The output from expected means squares contains estimates of these variances.

In the unrestricted model, all these random variables are independent. The remaining terms in this model are fixed.

In the restricted model, any term which contains one or more subscripts corresponding to fixed factors is required to sum to zero over each fixed subscript. In the example, this means

$$\sum_i (T_i) = 0 \qquad\qquad \sum_k (S_k) = 0 \qquad\qquad \sum_i (TO_{ij}) = 0$$

$$\sum_k (TS_{ik}) = 0 \qquad\qquad \sum_k (OS_{jk}) = 0 \qquad\qquad \sum_i (TOS_{ijk}) = 0$$

Your choice of model does not affect the sums of squares, degrees of freedom, mean squares, or marginal and cell means. However, it does affect the expected mean squares, error term for the F-tests, and the estimated variance components.

Step 1: Fit the restricted form of the model

1 Open the worksheet EXH_AOV.MTW.

2 Choose Stat ➤ ANOVA ➤ Balanced ANOVA.

3 In **Responses**, enter *Thickness*.

4 In **Model**, type *Time | Operator | Setting*.

5 In **Random Factors**, enter *Operator*.

6 Click **Options**. Check **Use the restricted form of the model**. Click **OK**.

7 Click **Results**. Check **Display expected mean squares and variance components**.

8 Click **OK** in each dialog box.

Step 2: Fit the unrestricted form of the model

1 Repeat steps 1-8 above except that in 6), uncheck **Use the restricted form of the model**.

Output for restricted case

*Session
window
output*

ANOVA: Thickness versus Time, Operator, Setting

```
Factor      Type Levels Values
Time        fixed     2    1    2
Operator    random    3    1    2    3
Setting     fixed     3   35   44   52
```

Analysis of Variance for Thicknes

Source	DF	SS	MS	F	P
Time	1	9.0	9.0	0.29	0.644
Operator	2	1120.9	560.4	165.38	0.000
Setting	2	15676.4	7838.2	73.18	0.001
Time*Operator	2	62.0	31.0	9.15	0.002
Time*Setting	2	114.5	57.3	2.39	0.208
Operator*Setting	4	428.4	107.1	31.61	0.000
Time*Operator*Setting	4	96.0	24.0	7.08	0.001
Error	18	61.0	3.4		
Total	35	17568.2			

Source	Variance component	Error term	Expected Mean Square for Each Term (using restricted model)
1 Time		4	(8) + 6(4) + 18Q[1]
2 Operator	46.421	8	(8) + 12(2)
3 Setting		6	(8) + 4(6) + 12Q[3]
4 Time*Operator	4.602	8	(8) + 6(4)
5 Time*Setting		7	(8) + 2(7) + 6Q[5]
6 Operator*Setting	25.931	8	(8) + 4(6)
7 Time*Operator*Setting	10.306	8	(8) + 2(7)
8 Error	3.389		(8)

Output for unrestricted case

Session
window
output

ANOVA: Thickness versus Time, Operator, Setting

```
Factor      Type Levels Values
Time        fixed     2   1    2
Operator    random    3   1    2    3
Setting     fixed     3  35   44   52
```

Analysis of Variance for Thicknes

Source	DF	SS	MS	F	P
Time	1	9.0	9.0	0.29	0.644
Operator	2	1120.9	560.4	4.91	0.090 x
Setting	2	15676.4	7838.2	73.18	0.001
Time*Operator	2	62.0	31.0	1.29	0.369
Time*Setting	2	114.5	57.3	2.39	0.208
Operator*Setting	4	428.4	107.1	4.46	0.088
Time*Operator*Setting	4	96.0	24.0	7.08	0.001
Error	18	61.0	3.4		
Total	35	17568.2			

x Not an exact F-test.

Source	Variance component	Error term	Expected Mean Square for Each Term (using unrestricted model)
1 Time		4	(8) + 2(7) + 6(4) + Q[1,5]
2 Operator	37.194	*	(8) + 2(7) + 4(6) + 6(4) + 12(2)
3 Setting		6	(8) + 2(7) + 4(6) + Q[3,5]
4 Time*Operator	1.167	7	(8) + 2(7) + 6(4)
5 Time*Setting		7	(8) + 2(7) + Q[5]
6 Operator*Setting	20.778	7	(8) + 2(7) + 4(6)
7 Time*Operator*Setting	10.306	8	(8) + 2(7)
8 Error	3.389		(8)

* Synthesized Test.

Error Terms for Synthesized Tests

Source	Error DF	Error MS	Synthesis of Error MS
2 Operator	3.73	114.1	(4) + (6) - (7)

Interpreting the results

The organization of the output is the same for restricted and unrestricted models: a table of factor levels, the analysis of variance table, and as requested, the expected mean squares. The differences in the output are in the expected means squares and the F-tests for some model terms. In this example, the F-test for Operator is synthesized for the unrestricted model because it could not be calculated exactly.

Examine the 3 factor interaction, Time*Operator*Setting. The F-test is the same for both forms of the mixed model, giving a p-value of 0.001. This implies that the coating thickness depends upon the combination of time, operator, and setting. Many analysts would go no further than this test. If an interaction is significant, any lower order interactions and main effects involving terms of the significant interaction are not considered meaningful.

Let's examine where these models give different output. The Operator*Setting F-test is different, because the error terms are Error in the restricted case and Time*Operator*Setting in the unrestricted case, giving p-values of < 0.0005 and 0.088, respectively. Likewise, the Time*Operator differs for the same reason, giving p-values of 0.002 and 0.369, for the restricted and unrestricted cases, respectively. The estimated variance components for Operator, Time*Operator, and Operator*Setting also differ.

General Linear Model

Use General Linear Model (GLM) to perform univariate analysis of variance with balanced and unbalanced designs, analysis of covariance, and regression, for each response variable.

Calculations are done using a regression approach. A "full rank" design matrix is formed from the factors and covariates and each response variable is regressed on the columns of the design matrix.

Factors may be crossed or nested, fixed or random. Covariates may be crossed with each other or with factors, or nested within factors. You can analyze up to 50 response variables with up to 31 factors and 50 covariates at one time.

Data

Set up your worksheet in the same manner as with balanced ANOVA: one column for each response variable, one column for each factor, and one column for each covariate, so that there is one row for each observation. The factor columns may be numeric, text, or date/time. If you wish to change the order in which text categories are processed from their default alphabetical order, you can define your own order. See *Ordering Text Categories* in the *Manipulating Data* chapter in MINITAB *User's Guide 1*.

Although models can be unbalanced in GLM, they must be "full rank," that is, there must be enough data to estimate all the terms in your model. For example, suppose you have a two-factor crossed model with one empty cell. Then you can fit the model with terms A B, but not A B A*B. MINITAB will tell you if your model is not full rank. In most cases, eliminating some of the high order interactions in your model (assuming, of course, they are not important) can solve this problem.

Nesting does not need to be balanced. A nested factor must have at least 2 levels at some level of the nesting factor. If factor B is nested within factor A, there can be unequal levels of B within each level of A. In addition, the subscripts used to identify the B levels can differ within each level of A. This means, for example, that the B levels can be (1 2 3 4) in level 1 of A, (5 6 7 8) in level 2 of A, and (9 10 11 12) in level 3 of A.

If any response, factor, or covariate column contains missing data, that entire observation (row) is excluded from all computations. If you want to eliminate missing rows separately for each response, perform GLM separately for each response.

▶ **To perform an analysis using general linear model**

1   Choose **Stat ➤ ANOVA ➤ General Linear Model**.

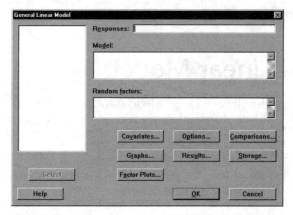

2   In **Responses**, enter up to 50 numeric columns containing the response variables.

3   In **Model**, type the model terms you want to fit. See *Specifying the model terms* on page 3-21.

4   If you like, use one or more of the options described below, then click **OK**.

Options

General Linear Model dialog box

■   specify which factors are random factors—see *Fixed vs. random factors* on page 3-20.

Covariates subdialog box

■   include up to 50 covariates in the model.

Options subdialog box

■   enter a column containing weights to perform weighted regression—see *Weighted regression* on page 2-6.

■   select adjusted (Type III) or sequential (Type I) sums of squares for calculations. See *Adjusted vs. sequential sums of squares* on page 3-43.

Comparisons subdialog box

- perform multiple comparison of treatment means with the mean of a control level. You can also choose
  - pairwise comparisons or comparisons with a control
  - the term(s) you wish to compare the means
  - from among three methods (Tukey, Bonferroni, and/or Sidak for pairwise comparisons or Dunnett, Bonferroni, and/or Sidak for comparisons with a control)
  - the alternative (less than, equal to, greater than) when you choose comparisons with a control. *Equal to* is the default.
  - whether to display the comparisons by confidence intervals or hypothesis tests (both are given by default). You can specify the family confidence level of intervals (the default is 95%).

  For a discussion of multiple comparisons, see *Multiple comparisons of means* on page 3-40.

Graphs subdialog box

- draw five different residual plots for regular, standardized, or deleted residuals—see *Choosing a residual type* on page 2-5. Available residual plots include a
  - histogram.
  - normal probability plot.
  - plot of residuals versus the fitted values ($\hat{Y}$).
  - plot of residuals versus data order. The row number for each data point is shown on the x-axis—for example, 1 2 3 4... *n*.
  - separate plot for the residuals versus each specified column.

  For a discussion of the residual plots, see *Residual plots* on page 2-6.

Results subdialog box

- display the following in the Session window:
  - no output.
  - the table of factor levels and the analysis of variance table.
  - the default output, which includes the above plus estimated coefficients for covariate terms and a table of unusual observations
  - the above plus estimated coefficients for all terms
- display expected means squares, estimated variance components, and error terms used in each F-test—see *Expected mean squares* on page 3-28.
- display the adjusted or least squares means (fitted values) corresponding to specified terms from the model.

Storage subdialog box

- store coefficients for the model, in separate columns for each response.

- store fits and regular, standardized, and deleted residuals separately for each response—see *Choosing a residual type* on page 2-5.

- store leverages, Cook's distances, and DFITS, for identifying outliers—see *Identifying outliers* on page 2-9.

- store the design matrix. The design matrix multiplied by the coefficients will yield the fitted values. See *Design matrix used by General Linear Model* on page 3-43.

Factor Plots subdialog box

- enter factors to construct a main effects plot—see *Main Effects Plot* on page 3-66.

- enter factors to construct an interactions plot—see *Interactions Plot* on page 3-68.

Multiple comparisons of means

Multiple comparisons of means allow you to examine which means are different and to estimate by how much they are different. When you have multiple factors, you can obtain multiple comparisons of means through GLM's Comparisons subdialog box.

There are some common pitfalls to the use of multiple comparisons. If you have a quantitative factor you should probably examine linear and higher order effects rather than performing multiple comparisons (see [12] and *Example of using GLM to fit linear and quadratic effects* on page 3-44). In addition, performing multiple comparisons for those factors which appear to have the greatest effect or only those with a significant F-test can result in erroneous conclusions (see *Which means to compare?* on page 3-41).

You have the following choices when using multiple comparisons:

- pairwise comparisons or comparisons with a control
- which means to compare
- the method of comparison
- display comparisons in confidence interval or hypothesis test form
- the confidence level, if you choose to display confidence intervals
- the alternative, if you choose comparisons with a control

Following are some guidelines for making these choices.

Pairwise comparisons or comparison with a control

Choose **Pairwise Comparisons** when you do not have a control level but you would like to examine which pairs of means are different.

Choose **Comparisons with a Control** when you are comparing treatments to a control. When this method is suitable, it is inefficient to use the all-pairwise approach, because the all-pairwise confidence intervals will be wider and the hypothesis tests less powerful for a given family error rate. If you do not specify a level that represents the control, MINITAB will assume that the lowest level of the factors is the control. If you wish to change which level is the control, specify a level that represents the control for each term that you are comparing the means of. If these levels are text or date/time, enclose each with double quotes.

Which means to compare?

Choosing which means to compare is an important consideration when using multiple comparisons; a poor choice can result in confidence levels that are not what you think. Issues that should be considered when making this choice might include: 1) should you compare the means for only those terms with a significant F-test or for those sets of means for which differences appear to be large? 2) how deep into the design should you compare means—only within each factor, within each combination of first-level interactions, or across combinations of higher level interactions?

It is probably a good idea to decide which means you will compare before collecting your data. If you compare only those means with differences that appear to be large, which is called data snooping, then you are increasing the likelihood that the results suggest a real difference where no difference exists [9], [18]. Similarly, if you condition the application of multiple comparisons upon achieving a significant F-test, then the error rate of the multiple comparisons can be higher than the error rate in the unconditioned application of multiple comparisons [9], [14]. The multiple comparison methods have protection against false positives already built in.

In practice, however, many people commonly use F-tests to guide the choice of which means to compare. The ANOVA F-tests and multiple comparisons are not entirely separate assessments. For example, if the p-value of an F-test is 0.9, you probably will not find statistically significant differences among means by multiple comparisons.

How deep within the design should you compare means? There is a trade-off: if you compare means at all two-factor combinations and higher orders turn out to be significant, then the means that you compare might be a mix of effects; if you compare means at too deep a level, you lose power because the sample sizes become smaller and the number of comparisons become larger. In practice, you might decide to compare means for factor level combinations for which you believe the interactions are meaningful.

MINITAB restricts the terms that you can compare means for to fixed terms or interactions among fixed terms. Nesting is considered to be a form of interaction.

To specify which means to compare, enter terms from the model in the **Terms** box. If you have 2 factors named A and B, entering **A B** will result in multiple comparisons within each factor. Entering **A∗B** will result in multiple comparisons for all level combination of factors A and B. You can use the notation **A|B** to indicate interaction for pairwise comparisons but not for comparisons with a control.

The multiple comparison method

You can choose from among three methods for both pairwise comparisons and comparisons with a control. Each method provides simultaneous or joint confidence intervals, meaning that the confidence level applies to the set of intervals computed by each method and not to each one individual interval. By protecting against false positives with multiple comparisons, the intervals are wider than if there were no protection.

The Tukey (also called Tukey-Kramer in the unbalanced case) and Dunnett methods are extensions of the methods used by one-way ANOVA. The Tukey approximation has been proven to be conservative when comparing three means. "Conservative" means that the true error rate is less than the stated one. In comparing larger numbers of means, there is no proof that the Tukey method is conservative for the general linear model. The Dunnett method uses a factor analytic method to approximate the probabilities of the comparisons. Because it uses the factor analytic approximation, the Dunnett method is not generally conservative. The Bonferroni and Sidak methods are conservative methods based upon probability inequalities. The Sidak method is slightly less conservative than the Bonferroni method.

Some characteristics of the multiple comparison methods are summarized below:

Comparison method	Properties
Dunnett	comparison to a control only, not proven to be conservative
Tukey	all pairwise differences only, not proven to be conservative
Bonferroni	most conservative
Sidak	conservative, but slightly less so than Bonferroni

Display of comparisons in confidence interval or hypothesis test form

MINITAB presents multiple comparison results in confidence interval and/or hypothesis test form. Both are given by default.

When viewing confidence intervals, you can assess the practical significance of differences among means, in addition to statistical significance. As usual, the null hypothesis of no difference between means is rejected if and only if zero is not contained in the confidence interval. When you request confidence intervals, you can specify family confidence levels for the confidence intervals. The default level is 95%.

MINITAB calculates adjusted p-values for hypothesis test statistics. The adjusted p-value for a particular hypothesis within a collection of hypotheses is the smallest family wise α level at which the particular hypothesis would be rejected.

See Help for computational details of the multiple comparison methods.

Adjusted vs. sequential sums of squares

MINITAB by default uses adjusted (Type III) sums of squares for all GLM calculations. Adjusted sums of squares are the additional sums of squares determined by adding each particular term to the model given the other terms are already in the model. You also have the choice of using sequential (Type I) sums of squares in all GLM calculations. Sequential sums of squares are the sums of squares added by a term with only the previous terms entered in the model. These sums of squares can differ when your design is unbalanced or if you have covariates. Usually, you would probably use adjusted sums of squares. However, there may be cases where you might want to use sequential sums of squares.

Design matrix used by General Linear Model

General Linear Model uses a regression approach to fit the model that you specify. First MINITAB creates a design matrix, from the factors and covariates, and the model that you specify. The columns of this matrix are the predictors for the regression.

The design matrix has n rows, where n = number of observations, and one block of columns, often called dummy variables, for each term in the model. There are as many columns in a block as there are degrees of freedom for the term. The first block is for the constant and contains just one column, a column of all ones. The block for a covariate also contains just one column, the covariate column itself.

Suppose A is a factor with 4 levels. Then it has 3 degrees of freedom and its block contains 3 columns, call them A1, A2, A3. Each row is coded as one of the following:

level of A	A1	A2	A3
1	1	0	0
2	0	1	0
3	0	0	1
4	−1	−1	−1

Suppose factor B has 3 levels nested within each level of A. Then its block contains $(3 - 1) \times 4 = 8$ columns, call them B11, B12, B21, B22, B31, B32, B41, B42, coded as follows:

level of A	level of B	B11	B12	B21	B22	B31	B32	B41	B42
1	1	1	0	0	0	0	0	0	0
1	2	0	1	0	0	0	0	0	0
1	3	−1	−1	0	0	0	0	0	0
2	1	0	0	1	0	0	0	0	0
2	2	0	0	0	1	0	0	0	0
2	3	0	0	−1	−1	0	0	0	0
3	1	0	0	0	0	1	0	0	0
3	2	0	0	0	0	0	1	0	0
3	3	0	0	0	0	−1	−1	0	0
4	1	0	0	0	0	0	0	1	0
4	2	0	0	0	0	0	0	0	1
4	3	0	0	0	0	0	0	−1	−1

To calculate the dummy variables for an interaction term, just multiply all the corresponding dummy variables for the factors and/or covariates in the interaction. For example, suppose factor A has 6 levels, C has 3 levels, D has 4 levels, and Z and W are covariates. Then the term A*C*D*Z*W*W has $5 \times 2 \times 3 \times 1 \times 1 \times 1 = 30$ dummy variables. To obtain them, multiply each dummy variable for A by each for C, by each for D, by the covariates Z once and W twice.

▶ Example of using GLM to fit linear and quadratic effects

An experiment is conducted to test the effect of temperature and glass type upon the light output of an oscilloscope. There are three glass types and three temperature levels: 100, 125, and 150 degrees Fahrenheit. These factors are fixed because we are interested in examining the response at those levels. The example and data are from Montgomery [14], page 252.

When a factor is quantitative with three or more levels it is appropriate to partition the sums of squares from that factor into effects of polynomial orders [12]. If there are k levels to the factor, you can partition the sums of squares into k-1 polynomial orders. In this example, the effect due to the quantitative variable temperature can be partitioned into linear and quadratic effects. Similarly, you can partition the interaction. To do this, you must code the quantitative variable with the actual treatment values (that is, code Temperature levels as 100, 125, and 150), use GLM to analyze your data, and declare the quantitative variable to be a covariate.

1 Open the worksheet EXH_AOV.MTW.

2 Choose **Stat ▶ ANOVA ▶ General Linear Model**.

3 In **Responses**, enter *LightOutput*.

4 In **Model**, type *Temperature Temperature * Temperature GlassType GlassType * Temperature GlassType *Temperature *Temperature*.

5 Click **Covariates**. In **Covariates**, enter *Temperature*.

6 Click **OK** in each dialog box.

General Linear Model: LightOutput versus GlassType

```
Factor      Type Levels Values
GlassTyp    fixed      3 1 2 3
```

Analysis of Variance for LightOut, using Adjusted SS for Tests

Source	DF	Seq SS	Adj SS	Adj MS	F	P
Temperat	1	1779756	262884	262884	719.21	0.000
Temperat*Temperat	1	190579	190579	190579	521.39	0.000
GlassTyp	2	150865	41416	20708	56.65	0.000
GlassTyp*Temperat	2	226178	51126	25563	69.94	0.000
GlassTyp*Temperat*						
Temperat	2	64374	64374	32187	88.06	0.000
Error	18	6579	6579	366		
Total	26	2418330				

Term	Coef	SE Coef	T	P
Constant	-4968.8	191.3	-25.97	0.000
Temperat	83.867	3.127	26.82	0.000
Temperat*Temperat	-0.28516	0.01249	-22.83	0.000
Temperat*GlassTyp				
1	-24.400	4.423	-5.52	0.000
2	-27.867	4.423	-6.30	0.000
Temperat*Temperat*GlassTyp				
1	0.11236	0.01766	6.36	0.000
2	0.12196	0.01766	6.91	0.000

Unusual Observations for LightOut

Obs	LightOut	Fit	SE Fit	Residual	St Resid
11	1070.00	1035.00	11.04	35.00	2.24R
17	1000.00	1035.00	11.04	-35.00	-2.24R

R denotes an observation with a large standardized residual.

Interpreting the results

MINITAB first displays a table of factors, with their number of levels, and the level values. The second table gives an analysis of variance table. This is followed by a table of coefficients, and then a table of unusual observations.

The Analysis of Variance table gives, for each term in the model, the degrees of freedom, the sequential sums of squares (Seq SS), the adjusted (partial) sums of squares (Adj SS), the adjusted means squares (Adj MS), the F-statistic from the adjusted means squares, and its p-value. The sequential sums of squares is the added sums of squares given that prior terms are in the model. These values depend upon the model order. The adjusted sums of squares are the sums of squares given that all other terms are in the model. These values do not depend upon the model order. If you had selected sequential sums of squares in the Options subdialog box, MINITAB would use these values for mean squares and F-tests.

In the example, all p-values were printed as 0.000, meaning that they are less than 0.0005. This indicates significant evidence of effects if your level of significance, α, is greater than 0.0005. The significant interaction effects of glass type with both linear and quadratic temperature terms implies that the coefficients of second order regression models of the effect of temperature upon light output depends upon the glass type.

The next table gives the estimated coefficients for the covariate, Temperature, and the interactions of Temperature with GlassType, their standard errors, t-statistics, and p-values. Following the table of coefficients is a table of unusual values. Observations with large standardized residuals or large leverage values are flagged. In our example, two values have standardized residuals whose absolute values are greater than 2.

▷ Example of using GLM and multiple comparisons with an unbalanced nested design

Four chemical companies produce insecticides that can be used to kill mosquitoes, but the composition of the insecticides differs from company to company. An experiment is conducted to test the efficacy of the insecticides by placing 400 mosquitoes inside a glass container treated with a single insecticide and counting the live mosquitoes 4 hours later. Three replications are performed for each product. The goal is to compare the product effectiveness of the different companies. The factors are fixed because you are interested in comparing the particular brands. The factors are nested because each insecticide for each company is unique. The example and data are from Milliken and Johnson [13], page 414. You use GLM to analyze your data because the design is unbalanced and you will use multiple comparisons to compare the mean response for the company brands.

1 Open the worksheet EXH_AOV.MTW.

2 Choose **Stat ➤ ANOVA ➤ General Linear Model**.

3 In **Responses**, enter *NMosquito*.

4 In **Model**, enter *Company Product(Company)*.

5 Click **Comparisons**. Under **Pairwise Comparisons**, enter *Company* in **Terms**. Click **OK** in each dialog box.

*Session
window
output*

General Linear Model: NMosquito versus Company, Product

```
Factor             Type Levels Values
Company            fixed      4 A B C D
Product(Company)   fixed     11 A1 A2 A3 B1 B2 C1 C2 D1 D2 D3 D4

Analysis of Variance for NMosquit, using Adjusted SS for Tests

Source             DF    Seq SS    Adj SS    Adj MS      F      P
Company             3   22813.3   22813.3    7604.4 132.78  0.000
Product(Company)    7    1500.6    1500.6     214.4   3.74  0.008
Error              22    1260.0    1260.0      57.3
Total              32   25573.9

Tukey 95.0% Simultaneous Confidence Intervals
Response Variable NMosquit
All Pairwise Comparisons among Levels of Company

Company = A subtracted from:

Company    Lower    Center    Upper  ---------+---------+---------+-------
B          -2.92      8.17    19.25                                 (---*----)
C         -52.25    -41.17   -30.08            (----*---)
D         -61.69    -52.42   -43.14         (---*---)
                                       ---------+---------+---------+-------
                                             -50       -25         0

Company = B subtracted from:

Company    Lower    Center    Upper  ---------+---------+---------+-------
C         -61.48    -49.33   -37.19           (----*----)
D         -71.10    -60.58   -50.07      (---*---)
                                       ---------+---------+---------+-------
                                             -50       -25         0

Company = C subtracted from:

Company    Lower    Center     Upper ---------+---------+---------+-------
D         -21.77    -11.25   -0.7347                       (----*---)
                                       ---------+---------+---------+-------
                                             -50       -25         0

Tukey Simultaneous Tests
Response Variable NMosquit
All Pairwise Comparisons among Levels of Company

Company = A subtracted from:

Level      Difference      SE of            Adjusted
Company     of Means   Difference  T-Value   P-Value
B               8.17        3.989     2.05    0.2016
C             -41.17        3.989   -10.32    0.0000
D             -52.42        3.337   -15.71    0.0000

Company = B subtracted from:
```

```
Level        Difference      SE of                    Adjusted
Company       of Means   Difference   T-Value     P-Value
C               -49.33        4.369    -11.29      0.0000
D               -60.58        3.784    -16.01      0.0000

Company = C subtracted from:

Level        Difference      SE of                    Adjusted
Company       of Means   Difference   T-Value     P-Value
D               -11.25        3.784     -2.973     0.0329
```

Interpreting the results

MINITAB displays a factor level table, an ANOVA table, multiple comparison confidence intervals for pairwise differences between companies, and the corresponding multiple comparison hypothesis tests. The ANOVA F-tests indicate that there is significant evidence for company effects.

Examine the multiple comparison confidence intervals. There are three sets: 1) for the company A mean subtracted from the company B, C, and D means; 2) for the company B mean subtracted from the company C and D means; and 3) for the company C mean subtracted from the company D mean. The first interval, for the company B mean minus the company A mean, contains zero is in the confidence interval. Thus, there is no significant evidence at $\alpha = 0.05$ for differences in means. However, there is evidence that all other pairs of means are different, because the confidence intervals for the differences in means do not contain zero. An advantage of confidence intervals is that you can see the magnitude of the differences between the means.

Examine the multiple comparison hypothesis tests. These are laid out in the same way as the confidence intervals. You can see at a glance the mean pairs for which there is significant evidence of differences. The adjusted p-values are small for all but one comparison, that of company A to company B. An advantage of hypothesis tests is that you can see what α level would be required for significant evidence of differences.

Fully Nested ANOVA

Use Fully Nested ANOVA to perform fully nested (hierarchical) analysis of variance and to estimate variance components for each response variable. All factors are implicitly assumed to be random. MINITAB uses sequential (Type I) sums of squares for all calculations.

You can analyze up to 50 response variables with up to 9 factors at one time.

If your design is not hierarchically nested or if you have fixed factors, use either Balanced ANOVA or GLM. Use GLM if you want to use adjusted sums of squares for a fully nested model.

Data

Set up your worksheet in the same manner as with Balanced ANOVA or GLM: one column for each response variable and one column for each factor, so that there is one row for each observation. The factor columns may be numeric, text, or date/time. If you wish to change the order in which text categories are processed from their default alphabetical order, you can define your own order. See *Ordering Text Categories* in the *Manipulating Data* chapter in MINITAB *User's Guide 1*.

Nesting does not need to be balanced. A nested factor must have at least 2 levels at some level of the nesting factor. If factor B is nested within factor A, there can be unequal levels of B within each level of A. In addition, the subscripts used to identify the B levels can differ within each level of A.

If any response or factor column contains missing data, that entire observation (row) is excluded from all computations. If an observation is missing for one response variable, that row is eliminated for all responses. If you want to eliminate missing rows separately for each response, perform a fully nested ANOVA separately for each response.

▶ **To perform an analysis using fully nested ANOVA**

1 Choose **Stat ➤ ANOVA ➤ Fully Nested ANOVA**.

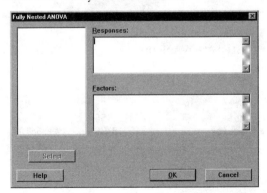

2 In **Responses**, enter up to 50 numeric columns containing the response variables.

3 In **Factors**, type in the factors in hierarchical order. See *The fully nested or hierarchical model* below.

The fully nested or hierarchical model

MINITAB fits a fully nested or hierarchical model with the nesting performed according to the order of factors in the **Factors** box. If you enter factors **A B C**, then the model terms will be **A B(A) C(B)**. You do not need to specify these terms in model form as you would for Balanced ANOVA or GLM.

MINITAB uses sequential (Type I) sums of squares for all calculations of fully nested ANOVA. This usually makes sense for a hierarchical model. GLM offers the choice of sequential or adjusted (Type III) sums of squares and uses the adjusted sums of squares by default. These sums of squares can differ when your design is unbalanced. Use GLM if you want to use adjusted sums of squares for calculations.

▷ Example of a fully nested ANOVA

You are an engineer trying to understand the sources of variability in the manufacture of glass jars. The process of making the glass requires mixing materials in small furnaces for which the temperature setting is to be 475 degrees F. Your company has a number of plants where the jars are made, so you select four as a random sample. You conduct an experiment and measure furnace temperature three times during a work shift for each of four operators from each plant over four different shifts. Because your design is fully nested, you use Fully Nested ANOVA to analyze your data.

1 Open the worksheet FURNTEMP.MTW.

2 Choose **Stat ➤ ANOVA ➤ Fully Nested ANOVA**.

3 In **Responses**, enter *Temp*.

4 In **Factors**, enter *Plant-Batch*. Click **OK**.

Session window output

Nested ANOVA: Temp versus Plant, Operator, Shift, Batch

Analysis of Variance for Temp

Source	DF	SS	MS	F	P
Plant	3	731.5156	243.8385	5.854	0.011
Operator	12	499.8125	41.6510	1.303	0.248
Shift	48	1534.9167	31.9774	2.578	0.000
Batch	128	1588.0000	12.4062		
Total	191	4354.2448			

Variance Components

Source	Var Comp.	% of Total	StDev
Plant	4.212	17.59	2.052
Operator	0.806	3.37	0.898
Shift	6.524	27.24	2.554
Batch	12.406	51.80	3.522
Total	23.948		4.894

```
Expected Mean Squares

 1 Plant      1.00(4) +  3.00(3) + 12.00(2) + 48.00(1)
 2 Operator   1.00(4) +  3.00(3) + 12.00(2)
 3 Shift      1.00(4) +  3.00(3)
 4 Batch      1.00(4)
```

Interpreting the results

MINITAB displays three tables of output: 1) the ANOVA table, 2) the estimated variance components, and 3) the expected means squares. There are four sequentially nested sources of variability in this experiment: plant, operator, shift, and batch. The ANOVA table indicates that there is significant evidence for plant and shift effects at $\alpha = 0.05$ (F-test p-values < 0.05). There is no significant evidence for an operator effect. The variance component estimates indicate that the variability attributable to batches, shifts, and plants was 52, 27, and 18 percent, respectively, of the total variability.

If a variance component estimate is less than zero, MINITAB displays what the estimate is, but sets the estimate to zero in calculating the percent of total variability.

Balanced MANOVA

Use Balanced MANOVA to perform multivariate analysis of variance (MANOVA) for balanced designs. You can take advantage of the data covariance structure to simultaneously test the equality of means from different responses.

Your design must be balanced, with the exception of one-way designs. *Balanced* means that all treatment combinations (cells) must have the same number of observations. Use General MANOVA (page 3-57) to analyze either balanced and unbalanced MANOVA designs or if you have covariates. You cannot designate factors to be random with general MANOVA, unlike for balanced ANOVA, though you can work around this restriction by supplying error terms to test the model terms.

Factors may be crossed or nested, fixed or random. See *Crossed vs. nested factors* on page 3-19 and *Fixed vs. random factors* on page 3-20.

Data

You need one column for each response variable and one column for each factor, with each row representing an observation. Regardless of whether factors are crossed or nested, use the same form for the data. Factor columns may be numeric, text, or date/ time. If you wish to change the order in which text categories are processed from their default alphabetical order, you can define your own order. See *Ordering Text Categories* in the *Manipulating Data* chapter in MINITAB *User's Guide 1*. You may include up to 50 response variables and up to 31 factors at one time.

Balanced data are required except for one-way designs. The requirement for balanced data extends to nested factors as well. Suppose A has 3 levels, and B is nested within A. If B has 4 levels within the first level of A, B must have 4 levels within the second and third levels of A. MINITAB will tell you if you have unbalanced nesting. In addition, the subscripts used to indicate the 4 levels of B within each level of A must be the same. Thus, the four levels of B cannot be (1 2 3 4) in level 1 of A, (5 6 7 8) in level 2 of A, and (9 10 11 12) in level 3 of A. You can use general MANOVA if you have different levels of B within the levels of A.

If any response or factor column specified contains missing data, that entire observation (row) is excluded from all computations. The requirement that data be balanced must be preserved after missing data are omitted.

▶ **To perform a balanced MANOVA**

1 Choose Stat ➤ ANOVA ➤ Balanced MANOVA.

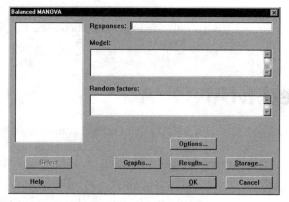

2 In **Responses**, enter up to 50 numeric columns containing the response variables.

3 In **Model**, type the model terms that you want to fit. See *Overview of Balanced ANOVA and GLM* on page 3-18.

4 If you like, use one or more of the options described below, then click **OK**.

Options

Balanced MANOVA dialog box

■ specify which factors are random factors—see *Fixed vs. random factors* on page 3-20

Options subdialog box

■ use the restricted form of the mixed models (both fixed and random effects). The restricted model forces mixed interaction effects to sum to zero over the fixed effects. By default, MINITAB fits the unrestricted model. See *Restricted and unrestricted form of mixed models* on page 3-28.

Graphs subdialog box

- draw five different residual plots. You can display the following plots:
  - histogram
  - normal probability plot
  - plot of residuals versus the fitted values ($\hat{Y}$)
  - plot of residuals versus data order. The row number for each data point is shown on the x-axis—for example, 1 2 3 4... n
  - separate plot for the residuals versus each specified column

  For a discussion of the residual plots, see *Residual plots* on page 2-6.

Results subdialog box

- display different MANOVA output. You can request the display of the hypothesis matrix H, the error matrix E, and a matrix of partial correlations (see *MANOVA tests* on page 3-54), the eigenvalues and eigenvalues for the matrix E^{-1} H, univariate analysis of variance for each response, and when you have requested univariate analyses of variance, the expected means squares.

- display a table of means corresponding to specified terms from the model. For example, if you specify A B D A*B*D, four tables of means will be printed, one for each main effect, A, B, D, and one for the three-way interaction, A*B*D.

- perform four multivariate tests for model terms that you specify. See *Specifying terms to test* on page 3-53. Default tests are performed for all model terms.

Storage subdialog box

- store the fits and residuals separately for each response. If you fit a full model, fits are cell means. If you fit a reduced model, fits are least squares estimates. See *Specifying reduced models* on page 3-22.

Specifying terms to test

In the Results subdialog box, you can specify model terms in **Custom multivariate test for the following terms** and designate an error term in **Error** and MINITAB will perform four multivariate tests (see below) for those terms. This option is probably less useful for balanced MANOVA than it is for general MANOVA; because you can specify factors to be random with balanced MANOVA, MINITAB will use the correct error terms. This option exists for special purpose tests.

If you specify an error term, it must be a single term that is in the model. This error term is used for all requested tests. If you do not specify an error term, MINITAB determines an appropriate error term.

MANOVA tests

MINITAB automatically performs four multivariate tests—Wilk's test, Lawley-Hotelling test, Pillai's test, and Roy's largest root test—for each term in the model and for specially requested terms (see above). All four tests are based on two SSCP (sums of squares and cross products) matrices: H, the hypothesis matrix and E, the error matrix. There is one H associated with each term. E is the matrix associated with the error for the test. These matrices are printed when you request the hypothesis matrices and are labeled by SSCP Matrix.

The test statistics can be expressed in terms of either H and/or E or the eigenvalues of $E^{-1} H$. You can request to have these eigenvalues printed. (If the eigenvalues are repeated, corresponding eigenvectors are not unique and in this case, the eigenvectors MINITAB prints and those in books or other software may not agree. The MANOVA tests, however, are always unique.) See Help for computational details on the tests.

You can also print the matrix of partial correlations, which are the correlations among the residuals, or alternatively, the correlations among the responses conditioned on the model. The formula for this matrix is $W^{-.5} E W^{-.5}$, where E is the error matrix and W has the diagonal of E as its diagonal and 0's off the diagonal.

Hotelling's T^2 Test

Hotelling's T^2 test to compare the mean vectors of two groups is a special case of MANOVA, using one factor that has two levels. MINITAB's MANOVA option can be used to do this test. The usual T^2 test statistic can be calculated from MINITAB's output using the relationship $T^2=(N-2)U$, where N is the total number of observations and U is the Lawley-Hotelling trace. See Help for calculations.

▷ Example of balanced MANOVA

You perform a study in order to determine optimum conditions for extruding plastic film. You measure three responses—tear resistance, gloss, and opacity—five times at each combination of two factors—rate of extrusion and amount of an additive—each set at low and high levels. The data and example are from Johnson and Wichern [10], page 266. You use Balanced MANOVA to test the equality of means because the design is balanced.

1 Open the worksheet EXH_MVAR.MTW.

2 Choose **Stat ➤ ANOVA ➤ Balanced MANOVA**.

3 In **Responses**, enter *Tear Gloss Opacity*.

4 In **Model**, enter *Extrusion | Additive*.

5 Click **Results**. Under **Display of Results**, check **Matrices (hypothesis, error, partial correlations)** and **Eigen analysis**. Click **OK** in each dialog box.

*Session
window
output*

ANOVA: Tear, Gloss, Opacity versus Extrusion, Additive

```
MANOVA for Extrusio          s = 1    m = 0.5   n =      6.0

Criterion        Test Statistic            F         DF        P
Wilk's                 0.38186          7.554   ( 3,   14)   0.003
Lawley-Hotelling       1.61877          7.554   ( 3,   14)   0.003
Pillai's               0.61814          7.554   ( 3,   14)   0.003
Roy's                  1.61877

SSCP Matrix for Extrusio

                Tear     Gloss    Opacity
Tear           1.740    -1.504     0.8555
Gloss         -1.504     1.301    -0.7395
Opacity        0.855    -0.739     0.4205

SSCP Matrix for Error

                Tear     Gloss    Opacity
Tear           1.764     0.0200    -3.070
Gloss          0.020     2.6280    -0.552
Opacity       -3.070    -0.5520    64.924

Partial Correlations for the Error SSCP Matrix

                Tear      Gloss    Opacity
Tear         1.00000    0.00929   -0.28687
Gloss        0.00929    1.00000   -0.04226
Opacity     -0.28687   -0.04226    1.00000

EIGEN Analysis for Extrusio

Eigenvalue     1.619    0.00000   0.00000
Proportion     1.000    0.00000   0.00000
Cumulative     1.000    1.00000   1.00000

Eigenvector        1          2          3
Tear          0.6541     0.4315     0.0604
Gloss        -0.3385     0.5163     0.0012
Opacity       0.0359     0.0302    -0.1209
```

---multivariate output for Additive and Extrusion*Additive would follow---

Interpreting the results

By default, MINITAB displays a table of the four multivariate tests (Wilk's, Lawley-Hotelling, Pillai's, and Roy's) for each term in the model. The values s, m, and n are used in the calculations of the F-statistics for Wilk's, Lawley-Hotelling, and Pillai's tests. The F-statistic is exact if s = 1 or 2, otherwise it is approximate [10]. Because you requested the display of additional matrices (hypothesis, error, and partial correlations) and an eigen analysis, this information is also displayed. The output is shown only for one model term, Extrusion, and not for the terms Additive or Extrusion*Additive.

Examine the p-values for the Wilk's, Lawley-Hotelling, and Pillai's test statistic to judge whether there is significant evidence for model effects. These values are 0.003 for the model term Extrusion, indicating that there is significant evidence for Extrusion main effects at α levels greater than 0.003. The corresponding p-values for Additive and for Additive*Extrusion are 0.025 and 0.302, respectively (not shown), indicating that there is no significant evidence for interaction, but there is significant evidence for Extrusion and Additive main effects at α levels of 0.05 or 0.10.

You can use the SSCP matrices to assess the partitioning of variability in a similar way as you would look at univariate sums of squares. The matrix labeled as SSCP Matrix for Extrusn is the hypothesis sums of squares and cross-products matrix, or H, for the three response with model term Extrusion. The diagonal elements of this matrix, 1.740, 1.301, and 0.4205, are the univariate ANOVA sums of squares for the model term Extrusion when the response variables are Tear, Gloss, and Opacity, respectfully. The off-diagonal elements of this matrix are the cross products.

The matrix labeled as SSCP Matrix for Error is the error sums of squares and cross-products matrix, or E. The diagonal elements of this matrix, 1.764, 2.6280, and 64.924, are the univariate ANOVA error sums of squares when the response variables are Tear, Gloss, and Opacity, respectfully. The off-diagonal elements of this matrix are the cross products. This matrix is printed once, after the SSCP matrix for the first model term.

You can use the matrix of partial correlations, labeled as Partial Correlations for the Error SSCP Matrix, to assess how related the response variables are. These are the correlations among the residuals or, equivalently, the correlations among the responses conditioned on the model. Examine the off-diagonal elements. The partial correlations between Tear and Gloss of 0.00929 and between Gloss and Opacity of -0.04226 are small. The partial correlation of -0.28687 between Tear and Opacity is not large. Because the correlation structure is weak, you might be satisfied with performing univariate ANOVA for these three responses. This matrix is printed once, after the SSCP matrix for error.

You can use the eigen analysis to assess how the response means differ among the levels of the different model terms. The eigen analysis is of E^{-1} H, where E is the error SCCP matrix and H is the response variable SCCP matrix. These are the eigenvalues that are used to calculate the four MANOVA tests.

Place the highest importance on the eigenvectors that correspond to high eigenvalues. In the example, the second and third eigenvalues are zero and therefore the corresponding eigenvectors are meaningless. For both factors, Extrusion and Additive, the first eigenvectors contain similar information The first eigen vector for Extrusion is 0.6541, -0.3385, 0.0359 and for Additive it is -0.6630, -0.3214, -0.0684 (not shown). The highest absolute value within these eigenvectors is for the response Tear, the second highest is for Gloss, and the value for Opacity is small. This implies that the Tear means have the largest differences between the two factor levels of either Extrusion or Additive, the Gloss means have the next largest differences, and the Opacity means have small differences.

General MANOVA

Use general MANOVA to perform multivariate analysis of variance (MANOVA) with balanced and unbalanced designs or if you have covariates. This procedure takes advantage of the data covariance structure to simultaneously test the equality of means from different responses.

Calculations are done using a regression approach. A "full rank" design matrix is formed from the factors and covariates and each response variable is regressed on the columns of the design matrix.

Factors may be crossed or nested, but they cannot be declared as random; it is possible to work around this restriction by specifying the error term to test model terms (see *Specifying terms to test* on page 3-59). Covariates may be crossed with each other or with factors, or nested within factors. You can analyze up to 50 response variables with up to 31 factors and 50 covariates at one time.

Data

Set up your worksheet in the same manner as with balanced MANOVA: one column for each response variable, one column for each factor, and one column for each covariate, so that there is one row of the worksheet for each observation. The factor columns may be numeric, text, or date/time. If you wish to change the order in which text categories are processed from their default alphabetical order, you can define your own order. See *Ordering Text Categories* in the *Manipulating Data* chapter in MINITAB *User's Guide 1*.

Although models can be unbalanced in general MANOVA, they must be "full rank." That is, there must be enough data to estimate all the terms in your model. For example, suppose you have a two-factor crossed model with one empty cell. Then you can fit the model with terms A B, but not A B A*B. MINITAB will tell you if your model is not full rank. In most cases, eliminating some of the high order interactions in your model (assuming, of course, they are not important) can solve non-full rank problems.

Nesting does not need to be balanced. If factor B is nested within factor A, there can be unequal levels of B within each level of A. In addition, the subscripts used to identify the B levels can differ within each level of A.

If any response, factor, or covariate column contains missing data, that entire observation (row) is excluded from all computations.

▶ **To perform an analysis using general MANOVA**

1 Choose Stat ➤ ANOVA ➤ General MANOVA.

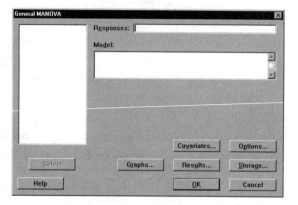

2 In **Responses**, enter up to 50 numeric columns containing the response variables.

3 In **Model**, type the model terms you want to fit. See *Overview of Balanced ANOVA and GLM* on page 3-18.

4 If you like, use one or more of the options described below, then click **OK**.

Options

Covariates subdialog box

■ include up to 50 covariates in the model

Options subdialog box

■ enter a column containing weights to perform weighted regression—see *Weighted regression* on page 2-6

Graphs subdialog box

■ draw five different residual plots for regular, standardized, or deleted residuals—see *Choosing a residual type* on page 2-5. Available residual plots include a
  – histogram
  – normal probability plot
  – plot of residuals versus the fitted values ($\hat{Y}$)
  – plot of residuals versus data order. The row number for each data point is shown on the x-axis—for example, 1 2 3 4... n
  – separate plot for the residuals versus each specified column

For a discussion of the residual plots, see *Residual plots* on page 2-6.

Results subdialog box

- display different MANOVA output. You can request the display of the hypothesis matrix H, the error matrix E, and a matrix of partial correlations (see *MANOVA tests* on page 3-59), the eigenvalues and eigenvalues for the matrix E^{-1} H, and univariate analysis of variance for each response.

- display a table of means corresponding to specified terms from the model. For example, if you specify A B D A*B*D, four tables of means will be printed, one for each main effect, A, B, D, and one for the three-way interaction, A*B*D.

- perform 4 multivariate tests for model terms that you specify. See *Specifying terms to test* on page 3-59. Default tests are performed for all model terms.

Storage subdialog box

- store model coefficients and fits in separate columns for each response.

- regular, standardized, and deleted residuals separately for each response—see *Choosing a residual type* on page 2-5.

- store leverages, Cook's distances, and DFITS, for identifying outliers—see *Identifying outliers* on page 2-9.

- store the design matrix. The design matrix multiplied by the coefficients will yield the fitted values. See *Design matrix used by General Linear Model* on page 3-43.

Specifying terms to test

In the Results subdialog box, you can specify model terms in **Custom multivariate test for the following terms** and designate the error term in **Error**. MINITAB will perform four multivariate tests (see below) for those terms. This option is most useful when you have factors that you consider as random factors. Model terms that are random or that are interactions with random terms may need a different error term than general MANOVA supplies. You can determine the appropriate error term by entering one response variable with General Linear Model (page 3-37), choose to display the expected mean squares, and determine which error term was used for each model terms (see *Expected mean squares* on page 3-28).

If you specify an error term, it must be a single term that is in the model. This error term is used for all requested tests. If you have different error terms for certain model terms, enter each separately and exercise the general MANOVA dialog for each one. If you do not specify an error term, MINITAB uses MSE.

MANOVA tests

The MANOVA tests with general MANOVA are similar to those performed for balanced MANOVA. See *MANOVA tests* on page 3-54 for details.

However, with general MANOVA, there are two SSCP matrices associated with each term in the model, the sequential SSCP matrix and the adjusted SSCP matrix. These matrices are analogous to the sequential SS and adjusted SS in univariate General Linear Model (see page 3-37). In fact, the univariate SS's are along the diagonal of the corresponding SSCP matrix. If you do not specify an error term in **Error** when you enter terms in **Custom multivariate tests for the following terms**, then the adjusted SSCP matrix is used for H and the SSCP matrix associated with MSE is used for E. If you do specify an error term, the sequential SSCP matrices associated with H and E are used. Using sequential SSCP matrices guarantees that H and E are statistically independent. See Help for details on these tests.

You can also perform Hotelling's T^2 test to compare the mean vectors of two groups (see *Hotelling's T^2 Test* on page 3-54). Refer to *Example of balanced MANOVA* on page 3-54 for an example of MANOVA. The dialog operation of general MANOVA is similar to that of balanced MANOVA.

Test for Equal Variances

Use the test for equal variances to perform hypothesis tests for equality or homogeneity of variance using Bartlett's and Levene's tests. An F-test replaces Bartlett's test when you have just two levels.

Many statistical procedures, including analysis of variance, assume that although different samples may come from populations with different means, they have the same variance. The effect of unequal variances upon inferences depends upon whether your model includes fixed or random effects, disparities in sample sizes, and the choice of multiple comparison procedure. The ANOVA F-test is only slightly affected by inequality of variance if the model only contains fixed factors and has equal or nearly equal sample sizes. F-tests involving random effects may be substantially affected, however [18]. Use the variance test procedure to test the validity of the equal variance assumption.

Data

Set up your worksheet with one column for the response variable and one column for each factor, so that there is one row for each observation. Your response data must be in one column. You may have up to 9 factors. Factor columns may be numeric, text, or date/time, and may contain any value. If there are many cells (factors and levels), the print in the output chart can get very small.

Rows where the response column contains missing data (*) are automatically omitted from the calculations. When one or more factor columns contain missing data, MINITAB displays the chart and Bartlett's test results, but not the Levene's test results.

Data limitations include: (1) if none of the cells have multiple observations, nothing is calculated. In addition, there must be at least one nonzero standard deviation; (2) the F-test for 2 levels requires both cells to have multiple observations; (3) Bartlett's test requires two or more cells to have multiple observations; (4) Levene's test requires two or more cells to have multiple observations, but one cell must have three or more.

▶ **To perform a test for equal variances**

1 Choose Stat ➤ ANOVA ➤ Test for Equal Variances.

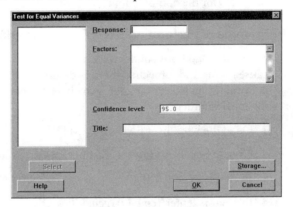

2 In **Response**, enter the column containing the response.

3 In **Factors**, enter up to nine columns containing the factor levels.

4 If you like, use one or more of the options described below, then click **OK**.

Options

Test for Equal Variances dialog box

- specify a confidence level for the confidence interval (the default is 95%)

- replace the default graph title with your own title

Storage subdialog box

- store standard deviations, variances, and/or upper and lower confidence limits for σ by factor levels

Bartlett's versus Levene's tests

MINITAB calculates and displays a test statistic and p-value for both Bartlett's test and Levene's test where the null hypothesis is of equal variances versus the alternative of not all variances being equal. (When there are only two levels, an F-test is performed in place of Bartlett's test.) Use Bartlett's test when the data come from a normal distribution and Levene's test when the data come from a continuous, but not necessarily normal, distribution. Bartlett's test is not robust to departures from normality.

The computational method for Levene's Test is a modification of Levene's procedure [11] developed by [2]. This method considers the distances of the observations from their sample median rather than their sample mean. Using the sample median rather than the sample mean makes the test more robust for smaller samples.

See Help for the computational form of these tests.

⊳ Example of performing a test for equal variances

You study conditions conducive to potato rot by injecting potatoes with bacteria that cause rotting and subjecting them to different temperature and oxygen regimes. Before performing analysis of variance, you check the equal variance assumption using the test for equal variances.

1 Open the worksheet EXH_AOV.MTW.

2 Choose **Stat ➤ ANOVA ➤ Test for Equal Variances**.

3 In **Response**, enter *Rot*.

4 In **Factors**, enter *Temp Oxygen*. Click **OK**.

Session window output

Test for Equal Variances

```
Response     Rot
Factors      Temp  Oxygen
ConfLvl      95.0000
```

Bonferroni confidence intervals for standard deviations

Lower	Sigma	Upper	N	Factor Levels	
2.26029	5.29150	81.890	3	10	2
1.28146	3.00000	46.427	3	10	6
2.80104	6.55744	101.481	3	10	10
1.54013	3.60555	55.799	3	16	2
1.50012	3.51188	54.349	3	16	6
3.55677	8.32666	128.862	3	16	10

Bartlett's Test (normal distribution)

```
Test Statistic: 2.712
P-Value       : 0.744
```

Levene's Test (any continuous distribution)

```
Test Statistic: 0.372
P-Value       : 0.858
```

*Graph
window
output*

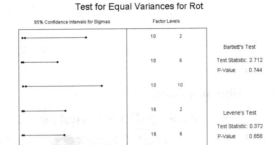

Interpreting the results

The test for equal variances generates a plot that displays Bonferroni 95% confidence intervals for the response standard deviation at each level. Bartlett's and Levene's test results are displayed in both the Session window and in the graph. Note that the 95% confidence level applies to the the family of intervals and the asymmetry of the intervals is due to the skewness of the chi-square distribution.

For the potato rot example, the p-values of 0.744 and 0.858 are greater than reasonable choices of α, so you fail to reject the null hypothesis of the variances being equal. That is, these data do not provide enough evidence to claim that the populations have unequal variances

Interval Plot for Mean

Use Interval Plot to produce a plot of group means and standard error bars or confidence intervals about the means. This plot illustrates both a measure of central tendency and variability of the data.

Data

The response (Y variable) data must be stacked in one numeric column. You must also have a column that contains the group identifiers. The grouping column can be numeric, text, or date/time. If you wish to change the order in which text levels are processed, you can define your own order. See *Ordering Text Categories* in the *Manipulating Data* chapter in MINITAB *User's Guide 1*.

Special cases include one observation in a group or a standard deviation of 0 (such as when all observations are the same). In the first case, the mean is plotted, but not the interval bar. In the second case, you see a symbol for the mean *and* a horizontal interval bar.

MINITAB automatically omits rows with missing responses or factor levels from the calculations.

▶ **To display an interval plot for the mean**

1 Choose **Stat ➤ ANOVA ➤ Interval Plot**.

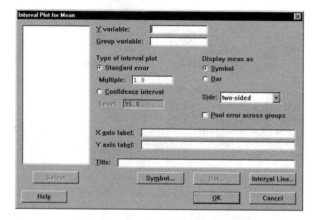

2 In **Y variable**, enter the column containing the response data.

3 In **Group variable**, enter the column containing the grouping variable or subscripts.

4 If you like, use any of the options listed below, then click **OK**.

Options

Interval Plot for Mean dialog box

- determine the type of interval displayed on the plot. You can display
  - the default plot which uses standard error bars. That is, the error bars are $(s)/\sqrt{n}$ away from the mean. You also can specify a multiplier for the standard error bars. For example, specifying the multiplier allows you to display error bars that are two times the standard error away from the mean.
  - display error bars that show a normal distribution confidence interval for the mean (rather than using the standard error). You can change the confidence level from the default 95%.

- display a symbol at the mean position or a bar that extends from the x-axis (or a specified base) to the mean.

- display error bars (or confidence intervals) above the mean (upper one-sided), below the mean (lower one-sided), or both above and below the mean (two-sided).

- pool the standard error across all subgroups instead of calculating the standard error for each subgroup separately.

- replace the default x- and y-axis labels with your own labels.

- replace the default graph title with your own title.

Symbol subdialog box

- set the type, color, and size of symbols at each subgroup mean.

Bar subdialog box

- set the fill type, foreground color, background color, edge size, and base (y-value to which bars extend to from the mean) of the bars.

Interval Line subdialog box

- specify the type, color, and size of the error bar lines at each subgroup mean.

☞ Example of an interval plot

Six varieties of alfalfa were grown on plots within four different fields. You are interested in comparing yields of the different varieties. After harvest, you wish to examine means with their standard errors using an error bar plot.

1 Open the worksheet ALFALFA.MTW.

2 Choose **Stat ➤ ANOVA ➤ Interval Plot**.

3 In **Y variable**, enter *Yield*.

4 In **Group variable**, enter *Variety*. Click **OK**.

Graph window output

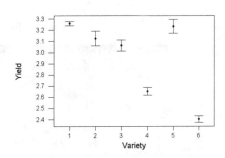

Interpreting the results

The error bar plot plots the means of each alfalfa variety at the symbols with lines extending one standard error above and below the means. The variability between varieties appears to be large relative to the variability within varieties, as there is some distance between some of the error bars for the different varieties.

Main Effects Plot

Use Main Effects Plot to plot data means when you have multiple factors. The points in the plot are the means of the response variable at the various levels of each factor, with a reference line drawn at the grand mean of the response data. Use the main effects plot for comparing magnitudes of main effects.

Use the main effects plot described on page 19-53 to generate main effects plots specifically for two-level factorial designs.

Data

Set up your worksheet with one column for the response variable and one column for each factor, so that each row in the response and factor columns represents one observation. It is not required that your data be balanced.

The factor columns may be numeric, text, or date/time and may contain any values. If you wish to change the order in which text levels are processed, you can define your own order. See *Ordering Text Categories* in the *Manipulating Data* chapter in MINITAB *User's Guide 1*. You may have up to 9 factors.

Missing values are automatically omitted from calculations.

▶ To perform a main effects plot

1 Choose Stat ➤ ANOVA ➤ Main Effects Plot.

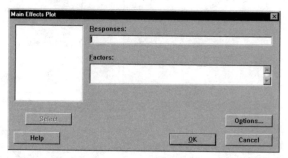

2 In **Responses**, enter the column(s) containing the response data.

3 In **Factors**, enter the columns containing the factor levels. You can enter up to 9 factors.

4 If you like, use any of the options listed below, then click **OK**.

Options

Options subdialog box

- specify the y-value(s) to use for the minimum and/or the maximum of the graph scale.

- you can replace the default graph title with your own title.

▷ Example of a main effects plot

You grow six varieties of alfalfa on plots within four different fields and you weigh the yield of the cuttings. You are interested in comparing yields from the different varieties and consider the fields to be blocks. You want to preview the data and examine yield by variety and field using the main effects plot.

1 Open the worksheet ALFALFA.MTW.

2 Choose **Stat ➤ ANOVA ➤ Main Effects Plot**.

3 In **Responses**, enter *Yield*.

4 In **Factors**, enter *Variety Field*. Click **OK**.

Graph window output

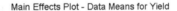
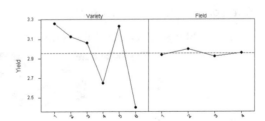

Main Effects Plot - Data Means for Yield

Interpreting the results

The main effects plot displays the response means for each factor level in sorted order if the factors are numeric or date/time or in alphabetical order if text, unless value ordering has been assigned (see *Ordering Text Categories* in the *Manipulating Data* chapter in MINITAB *User's Guide 1*). A horizontal line is drawn at the grand mean. The effects are the differences between the means and the reference line. In the example, the variety effects upon yield are large compared to the effects of field (the blocking variable).

Interactions Plot

Interactions Plot creates a single interaction plot for two factors, or a matrix of interaction plots for three to nine factors. An interactions plot is a plot of means for each level of a factor with the level of a second factor held constant. Interactions plots are useful for judging the presence of interaction.

Interaction is present when the response at a factor level depends upon the level(s) of other factors. Parallel lines in an interactions plot indicate no interaction. The greater the departure of the lines from the parallel state, the higher the degree of interaction. To use interactions plot, data must be available from all combinations of levels.

Use the Interactions Plot in Chapter 19 to generate interaction plots specifically for 2-level factorial designs, such as those generated by Fractional Factorial Design, Central Composite Design, and Box-Behnken Design.

Data

Set up your worksheet with one column for the response variable and one column for each factor, so that each row in the response and factor columns represents one observation. Your data is not required to be balanced.

The factor columns may be numeric, text, or date/time and may contain any values. If you wish to change the order in which text levels are processed, you can define your own order. See *Ordering Text Categories* in the *Manipulating Data* chapter in MINITAB *User's Guide 1*. You may have from 2 through 9 factors.

Missing data are automatically omitted from calculations.

▶ To display an interactions plot

1   Choose **Stat ➤ ANOVA ➤ Interactions Plot**.

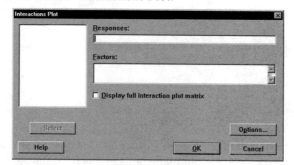

2   In **Responses**, enter the column(s) containing the response data.

3   In **Factors**, enter from 2 to 9 columns containing the factor levels. If you have two factors, the x-variable will be the second factor that you enter.

4   If you like, use any of the options listed below, then click **OK**.

Options

Main Effects Plot dialog box

- display the full interaction matrix for more than two factors, rather than the default upper right portion of the matrix.

Options subdialog box

- specify the y-value(s) to use for the minimum of the graph scale. You can enter one value to be used for all plots or one value for each response.

- specify the y-value(s) to use for the maximum of the graph scale. You can enter one value to be used for all plots or one value for each response.

- replace the default graph title with your own title.

▷ Example of an interaction plot with two factors

You conduct an experiment to test the effect of temperature and glass type upon the light output of an oscilloscope (example and data from [14], page 252). There are three glass types and three temperatures, 100, 125, and 150 degrees Fahrenheit. You choose interactions plot to visually assess interaction in the data. You enter the quantitative variable second because you want this variable as the x variable in the plot.

1 Open the worksheet EXH_AOV.MTW.

2 Choose **Stat ➤ ANOVA ➤ Interactions Plot**.

3 In **Responses**, enter *LightOutput*.

4 In **Factors**, enter *GlassType Temperature*. Click **OK**.

Graph window output

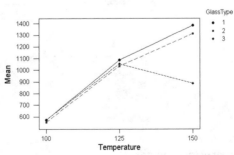

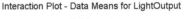

Interpreting the results

This interaction plot shows the mean light output versus the temperature for each of the three glass types. The legend shows which symbols are assigned to the glass types. The means of the factor levels are plotted in sorted order if numeric or date/time or in alphabetical order if text, unless value ordering has been assigned (see *Ordering Text Categories* in the *Manipulating Data* chapter in MINITAB *User's Guide 1*).

This plot shows apparent interaction because the lines are not parallel, implying that the effect of temperature upon light output depends upon the glass type. You test this using GLM on page 3-44.

▶ Example of an interaction plot with more than two factors

Plywood is made by cutting a thin layer of wood from logs as they are spun on their axis. Considerable force is required to turn a log hard enough so that a sharp blade can cut off a layer. Chucks are inserted into the ends of the log to apply the torque necessary to turn the log. You conduct an experiment to study factors that affect torque. These factors are diameter of the logs, penetration distance of the chuck into the log, and the temperature of the log. You wish to preview the data to check for the presence of interaction.

1   Open the worksheet PLYWOOD.MTW.

2   Choose **Stat ➤ ANOVA ➤ Interactions Plot**.

3   In **Responses,** enter *Torque.*

4   In **Factors,** enter *Diameter-Temp.* Click **OK**.

*Graph
window
output*

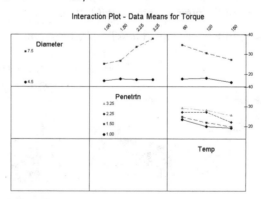

Interpreting the results

An interaction plot with three or more factors show separate two-way interaction plots for all two-factor combinations. In this example, the plot in the middle of the top row shows the mean torque versus the penetration levels for both levels of diameter, 4.5 and 7.5, averaged over all levels of temperature. There are analogous interactions plots for diameter by temperature (upper right) and penetration by temperature (second row).

For this example, the diameter by penetration and the diameter by temperature plots show nonparallel lines, indicating interaction. The presence of penetration by temperature interaction is not so easy to judge. This interaction might best be judged in conjunction with a model-fitting procedure, such as GLM.

References

[1] R.E. Bechhofer and C.W. Dunnett (1988). "Percentage points of multivariate Student t distributions," *Selected Tables in Mathematical Studies*, Vol.11. American Mathematical Society, Providence, R.I.

[2] M.B. Brown and A.B. Forsythe (1974). *Journal of the American Statistical Association*, 69, 364–367.

[3] H.L. Harter (1970). *Order Statistics and Their Uses in Testing and Estimation*, Vol.1. U.S. Government Printing Office, Washington, D.C.

[4] A.J. Hayter (1984). "A proof of the conjecture that the Tukey-Kramer multiple comparisons procedure is conservative," *Annals of Statistics*, 12, pp.61–75.

[5] D.L. Heck (1960). "Charts of Some Upper Percentage Points of the Distribution of the Largest Characteristic Root," *The Annals of Statistics*, pp.625–642.

[6] C.R. Hicks (1982). *Fundamental Concepts in the Design of Experiments*, Third Edition, CBC College Publishing.

[7] Y. Hochberg and A.C. Tamhane (1987). *Multiple Comparison Procedures*. John Wiley & Sons, New York.

[8] J.C. Hsu (1984). "Constrained Two-Sided Simultaneous Confidence Intervals for Multiple Comparisons with the Best," *Annals of Statistics*, 12, pp.1136–1144.

[9] J.C. Hsu (1996). *Multiple Comparisons, Theory and methods*, Chapman & Hall, New York.

[10] R. Johnson and D. Wichern (1992). *Applied Multivariate Statistical Methods*, Third Edition, Prentice Hall.

[11] H. Levene (1960). *Contributions to Probability and Statistics*, pp.278–292. Stanford University Press, CA.

[12] T.M. Little (1981). "Interpretation and Presentation of Result," *HortScience*, 19, pp.637-640.

[13] G.A. Milliken and D.E. Johnson (1984). *Analysis of Messy Data. Volume I: Designed Experiments*, Van Nostrand Reinhold.

[14] D.C. Montgomery (1991). *Design and Analysis of Experiments*, Third Edition, John Wiley & Sons.

[15] D. Morrison (1967). *Multivariate Statistical Methods*, McGraw-Hill.

[16] L.S. Nelson (1974). "Factors for the Analysis of Means," *Journal of Quality Technology*, 6, pp.175–181.

[17] P.R. Nelson (1983). "A Comparison of Sample Sizes for the Analysis of Means and the Analysis of Variance," *Journal of Quality Technology*, 15, pp.33–39.

[18] J. Neter, W. Wasserman and M.H. Kutner (1985). *Applied Linear Statistical Models*, Second Edition, Irwin, Inc.

[19] R.A. Olshen (1973). "The conditional level of the F-test," *Journal of the American Statistical Association*, 68, pp.692–698.

[20] E.R. Ott (1983). "Analysis of Means—A Graphical Procedure," *Journal of Quality Technology*, 15, pp.10–18.

[21] E.R. Ott and E.G. Schilling (1990). *Process Quality Control—Troubleshooting and Interpretation of Data*, 2nd Edition, McGraw-Hill.

[22] P.R. Ramig (1983). "Applications of the Analysis of Means," *Journal of Quality Technology*, 15, pp.19–25.

[23] E.G. Schilling (1973). "A Systematic Approach to the Analysis of Means," *Journal of Quality Technology*, 5, pp.93–108, 147–159.

[24] S.R. Searle, G. Casella, and C.E. McCulloch (1992). *Variance Components*, John Wiley & Sons.

[25] N.R. Ullman (1989). "The Analysis of Means (ANOM) for Signal and Noise," *Journal of Quality Technology*, 21, pp.111–127.

[26] E. Uusipaikka (1985). "Exact simultaneous confidence intervals for multiple comparisons among three or four mean values," *Journal of the American Statistical Association*, 80, pp.196–201.

[27] B.J. Winer (1971). *Statistical Principals in Experimental Design*, Second Edition, McGraw-Hill.

Acknowledgment

We are grateful for assistance in the design and implementation of multiple comparisons from Jason C. Hsu, Department of Statistics, Ohio State University and for the guidance of James L. Rosenberger, Statistics Department, The Pennsylvania State University, in developing the Balanced ANOVA, Analysis of Covariance, and General Linear Models procedures.

4

Multivariate Analysis

Multivariate Analysis Overview

Use MINITAB's multivariate analysis procedures to analyze your data when you have made multiple measurements on items or subjects. You can choose a method depending on whether you want to

- analyze the data covariance structure for the sake of understanding it or to reduce the data dimension

- assign observations to groups

Analyzing the data covariance structure and assigning observations to groups are characterized by their non-inferential nature, that is, tests of significance are not computed. There may be no single answer but what may work best for your data may require knowledge of the situation.

Analysis of the data structure

MINITAB offers two procedures that you can use to analyze the data covariance structure:

- **Principal Components Analysis** is used to help you to understand the covariance structure in the original variables and/or to create a smaller number of variables using this structure.

- **Factor Analysis**, like principal components, is used to summarize the data covariance structure in a smaller number of dimensions. The emphasis in factor analysis, however, is the identification of underlying "factors" that might explain the dimensions associated with large data variability.

Grouping observations

MINITAB offers discriminant analysis and three-cluster analysis methods for grouping observations:

- **Discriminant Analysis** is used for classifying observations into two or more groups if you have a sample with known groups. Discriminant analysis can also used to investigate how the predictors contribute to the groupings.

- **Cluster Observations** is used to group or cluster observations that are "close" to each other, when the groups are initially unknown. This method is a good choice when there is no outside information about grouping. The choice of final grouping is usually made according to what makes sense for your data after viewing clustering statistics.

- **Cluster Variables** is used to group or cluster variables that are "close" to each other, when the groups are initially unknown. The procedure is similar to clustering of observations. One reason to cluster variables may be to reduce their number.

- **K-means clustering**, like clustering of observations, is used to group observations that are "close" to each other. K-means clustering works best when sufficient information is available to make good starting cluster designations.

Principal Components Analysis

Use principal component analysis to help you to understand the underlying data structure and/or form a smaller number of uncorrelated variables (for example, to avoid multicollinearity in regression).

Data

Set up your worksheet so that each row contains measurements on a single item or subject. You must have two or more numeric columns, with each column representing a different measurement (response).

MINITAB automatically omits rows with missing data from the analysis.

▶ To perform principal component analysis

1 Choose **Stat ➤ Multivariate ➤ Principal Components**.

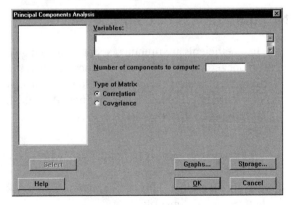

2 In **Variables**, enter the columns containing the measurement data.

3 If you like, use one or more of the options listed below, then click **OK**.

Options

Principal Components dialog box

- specify the number of principal components to calculate (the default number is the number of variables).

- use the correlation or covariance matrix to calculate the principal components. Use the correlation matrix if it makes sense to standardize variables (the usual choice when variables are measured by different scales); use the covariance matrix if you do not wish to standardize.

Graphs subdialog box

- display an eigenvalue profile plot (also called a scree plot). Scree plots display the eigenvalues versus their order. Use this plot to judge the relative magnitude of eigenvalues.

- plot second principal component scores (y-axis) versus the first principal component scores (x-axis). You can also create plots for other components, by storing the scores and using **Graph ➤ Plot**.

Storage subdialog box

- store the coefficients and scores of the principal components. Coefficients are eigenvector coefficients and scores are the linear combinations of your data using the coefficients.

Nonuniqueness of coefficients

The coefficients are unique (except for a change in sign) if the eigenvalues are distinct and not zero. If an eigenvalue is repeated, then the "space spanned" by all the principal component vectors corresponding to the same eigenvalue is unique, but the individual vectors are not. Therefore, the coefficients that MINITAB prints and those in a book or another program may not agree, though the eigenvalues (variances) will always be the same.

If the covariance matrix has rank r < p, where p is the number of variables, then there will be p − r eigenvalues equal to zero. Eigenvectors corresponding to these eigenvalues may not be unique. This can happen if the number of observations is less than p or if there is multicollinearity.

➤ Example of principal components analysis

You record the following characteristics for 14 census tracts: total population (Pop), median years of schooling (School), total employment (Employ), employment in health services (Health), and median home value (Home). The data were obtained from [5], Table 8.2.

You wish to understand the underlying data structure so you perform principal components analysis. You use the correlation matrix to standardize the measurements because they are not measured with the same scale.

1 Open the worksheet EXH_MVAR.MTW.

2 Choose **Stat ➤ Multivariate ➤ Principal Components**.

3 In **Variables**, enter *Pop-Home*.

4 Under **Type of Matrix**, choose **Correlation**.

5 Click **Graphs**. Check **Eigenvalue (Scree) plot**. Click **OK** in each dialog box.

Session window output

Principal Component Analysis: Pop, School, Employ, Health, Home

Eigenanalysis of the Correlation Matrix

Eigenvalue	3.0289	1.2911	0.5725	0.0954	0.0121
Proportion	0.606	0.258	0.114	0.019	0.002
Cumulative	0.606	0.864	0.978	0.998	1.000

Variable	PC1	PC2	PC3	PC4	PC5
Pop	-0.558	-0.131	0.008	0.551	-0.606
School	-0.313	-0.629	-0.549	-0.453	0.007
Employ	-0.568	-0.004	0.117	0.268	0.769
Health	-0.487	0.310	0.455	-0.648	-0.201
Home	0.174	-0.701	0.691	0.015	0.014

Graph window output

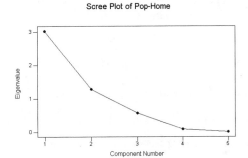

Interpreting the results

The first principal component has variance (eigenvalue) 3.0289 and accounts for 60.6% of the total variance. The coefficients listed under PC1 show how to calculate the principal component scores:

PC1 = −.558 Pop − .313 School − .568 Employ − .487 Health + .174 Home

It should be noted that the interpretation of the principal components is subjective, however, obvious patterns emerge quite often. For instance, one could think of the first principal component as representing an overall population size, level of schooling, employment level, and employment in health services effect. We say this because the coefficients of these terms have the same sign and are not close to zero.

The second principal component has variance 1.2911 and accounts for 25.8% of the data variability. It is calculated from the original data using the coefficients listed under PC2. This component could be thought of as contrasting level of schooling and home value with health employment to some extent.

Together, the first two and the first three principal components represent 86.4% and 97.8%, respectfully, of the total variability. Thus, most of the data structure can be captured in two or three underlying dimensions. The remaining principal components account for a very small proportion of the variability and are probably unimportant. The eigenvalue (scree) plot provides this information visually.

Factor Analysis

Use factor analysis, like principal components analysis, to summarize the data covariance structure in a few dimensions of the data. However, the emphasis in factor analysis is the identification of underlying "factors" that might explain the dimensions associated with large data variability.

Data

You can have three types of input data:

- columns of raw data
- a matrix of correlations or covariances
- columns containing factor loadings

The typical case is to use raw data. Set up your worksheet so that a row contains measurements on a single item or subject. You must have two or more numeric columns, with each column representing a different measurement (response). MINITAB automatically omits rows with missing data from the analysis.

Note | If you want to store coefficients, factor scores, or the residual matrix, or view an eigenvalue or scores plot, you must enter raw data.

Usually the factor analysis procedure calculates the correlation or covariance matrix from which the loadings are calculated. However, you can enter a matrix as input data. You can also enter both raw data and a matrix of correlations or covariances. If you do, MINITAB uses the matrix to calculate the loadings. MINITAB then uses these loadings and the raw data to calculate storage values and generate graphs. See *Using a matrix as input data* on page 4-10.

If you store initial factor loadings, you can later input these initial loadings to examine the effect of different rotations. You can also use stored loadings to predict factor scores of new data. See *Using stored loadings as input data* on page 4-11.

▶ **To perform factor analysis with raw data**

1 Choose **Stat ➤ Multivariate ➤ Factor Analysis**.

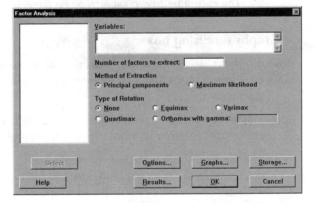

2 In **Variables**, enter the columns containing the measurement data.

3 If you like, use one or more of the options listed below, then click **OK**.

Options

Factor Analysis dialog box

- specify the number of factors to extract (required if you use maximum likelihood as your method of extraction). With principal components extraction, the default number is the number of variables.

- use maximum likelihood rather than principal components for the initial solution — see *The maximum likelihood method* on page 4-9.

- perform an equimax, varimax, quartimax, or orthomax rotation of the initial factor loadings—see *Rotating the factor loadings* on page 4-10.

Options subdialog box

- use a correlation or covariance matrix. Use the correlation matrix if it makes sense to standardize variables (the usual choice when variables are measured by different scales); use the covariance matrix if you do not wish to standardize.

- enter a covariance or correlation matrix as input data—see *Using a matrix as input data* on page 4-10.

- use stored loadings for the initial solution—see *Using stored loadings as input data* on page 4-11.

- when using maximum likelihood extraction, you can specify
  - initial values for the communalities.
  - maximum number of iterations allowed for a solution (default is 25).
  - criterion for convergence (default is 0.005).

  See *The maximum likelihood method* on page 4-9.

Graphs subdialog box

- display an eigenvalue profile plot (also called a scree plot). Scree plots display the eigenvalues versus their order. Use this plot to judge the relative magnitude of eigenvalues.

- plot the second factor scores (y-axis) versus the first factor scores (x-axis). You can create plots for other factors, by storing the scores and using **Graph ➤ Plot**.

- plot the second factor loadings (y-axis) versus the first factor loadings (x-axis). You can create loadings plots for other factors, by storing the loadings and using **Graph ➤ Plot**.

Storage subdialog box

- store the loadings, factor score coefficients, factor or standard scores, the rotation matrix, residual matrix, eigenvalues, and matrix of eigenvectors—see *Factor analysis storage* on page 4-12.

Results subdialog box

- display the following in the Session window:
  - no results.
  - loadings (and sorted loadings) for the final solution.
  - the default results, which includes loadings (and sorted loadings) for the final solution, and factor score coefficients.

- the default results, plus information on each iteration when you use maximum likelihood extraction.

■ sort the loadings in the Session window display (within a factor if the maximum absolute loading occurs there). You can also display all loadings less than a given value as zero.

Factor analysis in practice

The goal of factor analysis is to find a small number of factors, or unobservable variables, that explains most of the data variability and yet makes contextual sense. You need to decide how many factors to use and find loadings that make the most sense for your data.

Number of factors

The choice of the number of factors is often based upon the proportion of variance explained by the factors, subject matter knowledge, and reasonableness of the solution [5]. Initially, try using the principal components extraction method without specifying the number of components. Examine the proportion of variability explained by different factors and narrow down your choice of how many factors to use. An eigenvalue (scree) plot may be useful here in visually assessing the importance of factors. Once you have narrowed this choice, examine the fits of the different factor analyses. Communality values, the proportion of variability of each variable explained by the factors, may be especially useful in comparing fits. You may decide to add a factor if it contributes to the fit of certain variables. Try the maximum likelihood method of extraction as well.

Rotation

Once you have selected the number of factors, you will probably want to try different rotations. Johnson and Wichern [5] suggest the varimax rotation. A similar result from different methods can lend credence to the solution you have selected. At this point you may wish to interpret the factors using your knowledge of the data. For more information, see *Rotating the factor loadings* on page 4-10.

The maximum likelihood method

The maximum likelihood method estimates the factor loadings, assuming the data follows a multivariate normal distribution. As its name implies, this method finds a solution by maximizing the likelihood function. Equivalently, this is done by minimizing an expression involving the variances of the residuals. The algorithm iterates until a minimum is found or until the maximum specified number of iterations (the default is 25) is reached. MINITAB uses an algorithm based on [6], with some adjustments to improve convergence. See Help, [5], or [6] for details.

When minimizing the variance expression, it is possible to find residual variances that are 0 or negative. To prevent this, MINITAB's algorithm bounds these values away from 0. Specifically, if a unique variance is less than the value specified for convergence, it is set equal to this convergence value. Once the algorithm converges, a final check is done on the unique variances. If any unique values are less than the convergence value (default is 0.005), they are set equal to 0. The corresponding communality is then equal to 1. This condition is called a Heywood case and a message is printed to this effect. Optimization algorithms, such as the one used for maximum likelihood factor analysis, can give different answers with minor changes in the input. For example, if you change a few data values, change the starting communality estimates, or change the convergence value, you may see differences in estimated loadings, especially if the solution lies in a relatively flat place on the maximum likelihood surface.

Rotating the factor loadings

There are four methods to orthogonally rotate the initial factor loadings found by either principal components or maximum likelihood extraction. An orthogonal rotation simply rotates the axes to give you a different perspective. The methods are equimax, varimax, quartimax, and orthomax. MINITAB rotates the loadings in order to minimize a simplicity criterion [4]. A parameter, γ, within this criterion is determined by the rotation method. If you use a method with a low value of γ, the rotation will tend to simplify the rows of the loadings; if you use a method with a high value of γ, the rotation will tend to simplify the columns of the loadings. The table below summarizes the rotation methods.

Rotation method	Goal is ...	γ
equimax	to rotate the loadings so that a variable loads high on one factor but low on others	number of factors / 2
varimax	to maximize the variance of the squared loadings	1
quartimax	simple loadings	0
orthomax	user determined, based on the given value of γ	0–1

Using a matrix as input data

You can calculate the factor loadings from a correlation or covariance matrix. If it makes sense to standardize variables (usual choice when variables are measured by different scales), enter a correlation matrix; if you do not wish to standardize, enter a covariance matrix.

You can use both raw data and a matrix of correlations or covariances as input data. If you do, MINITAB uses the matrix to calculate the factor loadings. MINITAB then uses these loadings and the raw data to calculate storage values and generate graphs.

▶ **To perform factor analysis with a correlation or covariance matrix**

1 Choose **Stat ▶ Multivariate ▶ Factor Analysis**.

2 Optionally, in **Variables**, enter the columns containing raw data.

3 Click **Options**.

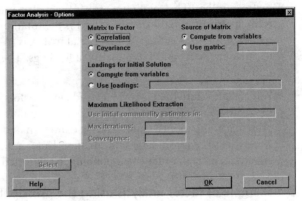

4 Under **Matrix to Factor**, choose **Correlation** or **Covariance**.

5 Under **Source of Matrix**, choose **Use matrix** and enter the matrix. Click **OK**.

Using stored loadings as input data

If you store initial factor loadings from an earlier analysis, you can input these initial loadings to examine the effect of different rotations. You can also use stored loadings to predict factor scores of new data.

▶ **To perform factor analysis with stored loadings**

1 In the Factor Analysis dialog box, click **Options**.

2 Under **Loadings for Initial Solution**, choose **Use loadings**. Enter the columns containing the loadings. Click **OK**.

3 Do one of the following, and then click **OK**:

   ■ To examine the effect of a different rotation method, choose an option under **Type of Rotation**. See *Rotating the factor loadings* on page 4-10 for a discussion of the various rotations.

   ■ To predict factor scores with new data, in **Variables**, enter the columns containing the new data.

Factor analysis storage

To store loadings, factor score coefficients, or factor scores, enter a column name or column number for each factor that has been extracted. The number of storage columns specified must be equal in number to the number of factors calculated. If a rotation was specified, MINITAB stores the values of the rotated solution. MINITAB calculates factor scores by multiplying factor score coefficients and your data after they have been centered by subtracting means.

You can also store the rotation matrix and residual matrix. Enter a matrix name or matrix number. The rotation matrix is the matrix used to rotate the initial loadings. If L is the matrix of initial loadings and M is the rotation matrix that you store, LM is the matrix of rotated loadings. The residual matrix is (A-LL′), where A is the correlation or covariance matrix and L is a matrix of loadings. The residual matrix is the same for initial and rotated solutions.

You can also store the eigenvalues and eigenvectors of the correlation or covariance matrix (depending on which is factored) if you chose the initial factor extraction via principal components. Enter a single column name or number for storing eigenvalues, which are stored from largest to smallest. Enter a matrix name or number to store the eigenvectors in an order corresponding to the sorted eigenvalues.

▷ Example of factor analysis using the principal components method

You record the following characteristics of 14 census tracts (see also *Example of principal components analysis* on page 4-4): total population (Pop), median years of schooling (School), total employment (Employ), employment in health services (Health), and median home value (Home) (data from [5], Table 8.2). You would like to investigate what "factors" might explain most of the variability. As the first step in your factor analysis, you use the principal components extraction method and examine an eigenvalues (scree) plot in order to help you to decide upon the number of factors.

1 Open the worksheet EXH_MVAR.MTW.

2 Choose **Stat ➤ Multivariate ➤ Factor Analysis**.

3 In **Variables**, enter *Pop-Home*.

4 Click **Graphs**. Check **Eigenvalue (Scree) plot**. Click **OK** in each dialog box.

*Session
window
output*

Factor Analysis: Pop, School, Employ, Health, Home

Principal Component Factor Analysis of the Correlation Matrix

Unrotated Factor Loadings and Communalities

Variable	Factor1	Factor2	Factor3	Factor4	Factor5	Communality
Pop	-0.972	-0.149	0.006	0.170	-0.067	1.000
School	-0.545	-0.715	-0.415	-0.140	0.001	1.000
Employ	-0.989	-0.005	0.089	0.083	0.085	1.000
Health	-0.847	0.352	0.344	-0.200	-0.022	1.000
Home	0.303	-0.797	0.523	0.005	0.002	1.000
Variance	3.0289	1.2911	0.5725	0.0954	0.0121	5.0000
% Var	0.606	0.258	0.114	0.019	0.002	1.000

Factor Score Coefficients

Variable	Factor1	Factor2	Factor3	Factor4	Factor5
Pop	-0.321	-0.116	0.011	1.782	-5.511
School	-0.180	-0.553	-0.726	-1.466	0.060
Employ	-0.327	-0.004	0.155	0.868	6.988
Health	-0.280	0.272	0.601	-2.098	-1.829
Home	0.100	-0.617	0.914	0.049	0.129

*Graph
window
output*

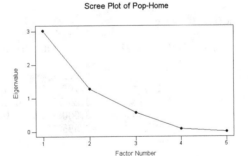

Scree Plot of Pop-Home

Interpreting the results

Five factors describe these data perfectly, but the goal is to reduce the number of factors needed to explain the variability in the data. Examine the Session window results line of % Var or the eigenvalues plot. The proportion of variability explained by the last two factors is minimal (0.019 and 0.002, respectively) and they can be eliminated as being important. The first two factors together represent 86% of the variability while three factors explain 98% of the variability. The question is whether to use two or three factors. The next step might be to perform separate factor analyses with two and three factors and examine the communalities to see how individual variables are represented. If there were one or more variables not well represented by the more parsimonious two factor model, you might select a model with three or more factors.

See the example below for a rotation of loadings extracted by the maximum likelihood method with a selection of two factors.

▷ Example of factor analysis using maximum likelihood and a rotation

You decide to examine the factor analysis fit with two factors in the above census tract example. You perform a maximum likelihood extraction with varimax rotation.

1 Open the worksheet EXH_MVAR.MTW.

2 Choose **Stat ➤ Multivariate ➤ Factor Analysis**.

3 In **Variables**, enter *Pop-Home*.

4 **Number of factors to extract**, enter *2*.

5 Under **Method of Extraction**, choose **Maximum likelihood**.

6 Under **Type of Rotation**, choose **Varimax**.

7 Click **Graphs**. Check **Loading plot for first 2 factors**. Uncheck **Eigenvalue (Scree) plot**. Click **OK**.
Click **Results**. Check **Sort loadings**. Click **OK** in each dialog box.

Session window output

Factor Analysis: Pop, School, Employ, Health, Home

Maximum Likelihood Factor Analysis of the Correlation Matrix

* NOTE * Heywood case

Unrotated Factor Loadings and Communalities

Variable	Factor1	Factor2	Communality
Pop	0.971	0.160	0.968
School	0.494	0.833	0.938
Employ	1.000	0.000	1.000
Health	0.848	-0.395	0.875
Home	-0.249	0.375	0.202
Variance	2.9678	1.0159	3.9837
% Var	0.594	0.203	0.797

Rotated Factor Loadings and Communalities
Varimax Rotation

Variable	Factor1	Factor2	Communality
Pop	0.718	0.673	0.968
School	-0.052	0.967	0.938
Employ	0.831	0.556	1.000
Health	0.924	0.143	0.875
Home	-0.415	0.173	0.202
Variance	2.2354	1.7483	3.9837
% Var	0.447	0.350	0.797

Sorted Rotated Factor Loadings and Communalities

Variable	Factor1	Factor2	Communality
Health	0.924	0.143	0.875
Employ	0.831	0.556	1.000
Pop	0.718	0.673	0.968
Home	-0.415	0.173	0.202
School	-0.052	0.967	0.938
Variance	2.2354	1.7483	3.9837
% Var	0.447	0.350	0.797

Factor Score Coefficients

Variable	Factor1	Factor2
Pop	-0.165	0.246
School	-0.528	0.789
Employ	1.150	0.080
Health	0.116	-0.173
Home	-0.018	0.027

Graph window output

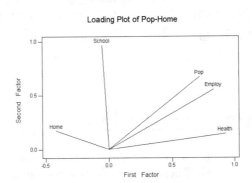

Loading Plot of Pop-Home

Interpreting the results

The results indicates that this is a Heywood case. For a description of this condition, see *The maximum likelihood method* on page 4-9. There are three tables of loadings and communalities: unrotated, rotated, and sorted and rotated. The unrotated factors explain 79.7% of the data variability (see last line under Communality) and the communality values indicate that all variables but Home are well represented by these two factors (communalities are 0.202 for Home, 0.875-1.0 for other variables). The percent of total variability represented by the factors does not change with rotation, but after rotating, these factors are more evenly balanced in the percent of variability that they represent, being 44.7% and 35.0%, respectfully.

Sorting is done by the maximum absolute loading for any factor. Variables that have their highest absolute loading on factor 1 are printed first, in sorted order. Variables with their highest absolute loadings on factor 2 are printed next, in sorted order, and so on. Factor 1 has large positive loadings on Health (0.924), Employ (0.831), and Pop (0.718), and a −0.415 loading on Home while the loading on School is small. Factor 2 has a large positive loading on School of 0.967 and loadings of 0.556 and 0.673, respectively, on Employ and Pop, and small loadings on Health and Home.

You can view the rotated loadings graphically in the loadings plot. What stands out for factor 1 are the high loadings on the variables Pop, Employ, and Health and the negative loading on Home. School has a high positive loading for factor 2 and somewhat lower values for Pop and Employ.

Let's give a possible interpretation to the factors. The first factor positively loads on population size and on two variables, Employ and Health, that generally increase with population size. It negatively loads on home value, but this may be largely influenced by one point. We might consider factor 1 to be a "health care - population size" factor. The second factor might be considered to be a "education - population size" factor. Both Health and School are correlated with Pop and Employ, but not much with each other.

In addition, MINITAB displays a table of factor score coefficients. These show you how the factors are calculated. MINITAB calculates factor scores by multiplying factor score coefficients and your data after they have been centered by subtracting means.

You might repeat this factor analysis with three factors to see if it makes more sense for your data.

Discriminant Analysis

Use discriminant analysis to classify observations into two or more groups if you have a sample with known groups. Discriminant analysis can also used to investigate how variables contribute to group separation.

MINITAB offers both linear and quadratic discriminant analysis. With linear discriminant analysis, all groups are assumed to have the same covariance matrix. Quadratic discrimination does not make this assumption but its properties are not as well understood.

In the case of classifying new observations into one of two categories, logistic regression may be superior to discriminant analysis [3], [9]. See *Logistic Regression Overview* on page 2-29.

Data

Set up your worksheet so that a row of data contains information about a single item or subject. You must have one or more numeric columns containing measurement data, or predictors, and a single grouping column containing up to 20 groups. The column of group codes may be numeric, text, or date/time. If you wish to change the order in which text groups are processed from their default alphabetized order, you can define your own order. See *Ordering Text Categories* in the *Manipulating Data* chapter in MINITAB *User's Guide 1*. MINITAB automatically omits observations with missing measurements or group codes from the calculations.

If a high degree of multicollinearity exists (i.e., if one or more predictors is highly correlated with another) or one or more of the predictors is essential constant, discriminant analysis calculations cannot be done and MINITAB displays a message to that effect.

▶ **To perform linear discriminant analysis**

1 Choose **Stat ➤ Multivariate ➤ Discriminant Analysis**.

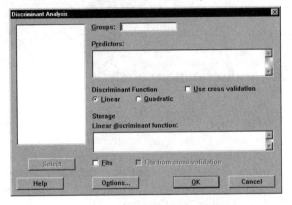

2 In **Groups**, enter the column containing the group codes.

3 In **Predictors**, enter the column(s) containing the measurement data.

4 If you like, use one or more of the options listed below, then click **OK**.

Options

Discriminant Analysis dialog box

- perform linear (default) or quadratic discrimination—see *Quadratic discriminant analysis* on page 4-18.

- perform cross-validation—see *Cross-Validation* on page 4-20. You can store the fitted values from cross-validation.

- store the coefficients from the linear discriminant function.

- store the fitted values. The fitted value for an observation is the group into which it is classified.

Options subdialog box

- specify prior probabilities—see *Prior probabilities* on page 4-19.

- predict group membership for new observations—see *Predicting group membership for new observations* on page 4-19.

- display the following in the Session window:
  - no results.
  - the classification matrix.
  - the default results, which includes the classification matrix, distance between all pairs of group centers (i.e., group means), the linear discriminant function, and a summary of misclassified observations.
  - the default results, plus the means, standard deviations, and covariance matrices (for each group and pooled).
  - the results described above, plus display a summary of how all observations were classified. MINITAB marks misclassified observations with two asterisks.

Linear discriminant analysis

An observation is classified into a group if the squared distance (also called the Mahalanobis distance) of observation to the group center (mean) is the minimum. An assumption is made that covariance matrices are equal for all groups. There is a unique part of the squared distance formula for each group and that is called the linear discriminant function for that group. For any observation, the group with the smallest squared distance has the largest linear discriminant function and the observation is then classified into this group.

Linear discriminant analysis has the property of symmetric squared distance: the linear discriminant function of group i evaluated with the mean of group j is equal to the linear discriminant function of group j evaluated with the mean of group i.

We have described the simplest case, no priors and equal covariance matrices. If you consider Mahalanobis distance a reasonable way to measure the distance of an observation to a group, then you do not need to make any assumptions about the underlying distribution of your data. See Help for more information.

Quadratic discriminant analysis

There is no assumption with quadratic discriminant analysis that the groups have equal covariance matrices. As with linear discriminant analysis, an observation is classified into the group that has the smallest squared distance. However, the squared distance does not simplify into a linear function, hence the name quadratic discriminant analysis.

Unlike linear distance, quadratic distance is not symmetric. In other words, the quadratic discriminant function of group i evaluated with the mean of group j is not equal to the quadratic discriminant function of group j evaluated with the mean of group i. On the results, quadratic distance is called the generalized squared distance. If the determinant of the sample group covariance matrix is less than one, the generalized squared distance can be negative.

Prior probabilities

Sometimes items or subjects from different groups are encountered according to different probabilities. If you know or can estimate these probabilities a priori, discriminant analysis can use these so-called prior probabilities in calculating the posterior probabilities, or probabilities of assigning observations to groups given the data. With the assumption that the data have a normal distribution, the linear discriminant function is increased by $\ln(p_i)$, where p_i is the prior probability of group i. Because observations are assigned to groups according to the smallest generalized distance, or equivalently the largest linear discriminant function. The effect is to increase the posterior probabilities for a group with a high prior probability.

Predicting group membership for new observations

Generally, discriminant analysis is used to calculate the discriminant functions from observations with known groups. When new observations are made, you can use the discriminant function to predict which group that they belong to. You can do this by either calculating (using **Calc ➤ Calculator**) the values of the discriminant function for the observation(s) and then assigning it to the group with the highest function value or by using MINITAB's discriminant procedure:

▶ **To predict group membership for new observations**

1 Choose **Stat ➤ Multivariate ➤ Discriminant Analysis**.

2 In **Groups**, enter the column containing the group codes from the original sample.

3 In **Predictors**, enter the column(s) containing the measurement data of the original sample.

4 Click **Options**. In **Predict group membership for**, enter constants or columns representing one or more observations. The number of constants or columns must be equivalent to the number of predictors.

Cross-Validation

Cross-validation is one technique that is used to compensate for an optimistic apparent error rate. The apparent error rate is the percent of misclassified observations. This number tends to be optimistic because the data being classified are the same data used to build the classification function.

The cross-validation routine works by omitting each observation one at a time, recalculating the classification function using the remaining data, and then classifying the omitted observation. The computation time takes approximately four times longer with this procedure. When cross-validation is performed, MINITAB prints an additional summary table.

Another technique that you can use to calculate a more realistic error rate is to split your data into two parts. Use one part to create the discriminant function, and the other part as a validation set. Predict group membership for the validation set and calculate the error rate as the percent of these data that are misclassified.

▷ Example of discriminant analysis

In order to regulate catches of salmon stocks, it is desirable to identify fish as being of Alaskan or Canadian origin. Fifty fish from each place of origin were caught and growth ring diameters of scales were measured for the time when they lived in freshwater and for the subsequent time when they lived in saltwater. The goal is to be able to identify newly-caught fish as being from Alaskan or Canadian stocks. The example and data are from [5], pages 519-520.

1 Open the worksheet EXH_MVAR.MTW.

2 Choose **Stat ➤ Multivariate ➤ Discriminant Analysis**.

3 In **Groups**, enter *SalmonOrigin*. In **Predictors**, enter *Freshwater Marine*. Click **OK**.

Session window output

Discriminant Analysis: SalmonOrigin versus Freshwater, Marine

```
Linear Method for Response:   SalmonOr
Predictors:  Freshwat  Marine

Group    Alaska   Canada
Count       50       50

Summary of Classification

Put into    ....True Group....
Group      Alaska   Canada
Alaska         44        1
Canada          6       49
Total N        50       50
N Correct      44       49
Proportion  0.880    0.980

N =  100    N Correct =   93     Proportion Correct = 0.930
```

```
Squared Distance Between Groups
            Alaska   Canada
Alaska     0.00000  8.29187
Canada     8.29187  0.00000

Linear Discriminant Function for Group
            Alaska   Canada
Constant  -100.68   -95.14
Freshwat     0.37     0.50
Marine       0.38     0.33
```

Summary of Misclassified Observations

Observation	True Group	Pred Group	Group	Squared Distance	Probability
1 **	Alaska	Canada	Alaska	3.544	0.428
			Canada	2.960	0.572
2 **	Alaska	Canada	Alaska	8.1131	0.019
			Canada	0.2729	0.981
12 **	Alaska	Canada	Alaska	4.7470	0.118
			Canada	0.7270	0.882
13 **	Alaska	Canada	Alaska	4.7470	0.118
			Canada	0.7270	0.882
30 **	Alaska	Canada	Alaska	3.230	0.289
			Canada	1.429	0.711
32 **	Alaska	Canada	Alaska	2.271	0.464
			Canada	1.985	0.536
71 **	Canada	Alaska	Alaska	2.045	0.948
			Canada	7.849	0.052

Interpreting the results

As shown in the Summary of Classification table, the discriminant analysis correctly identified 93 of 100 fish, though the probability of correctly classifying an Alaskan fish was lower (44/50 or 88%) than was the probability of correctly classifying a Canadian fish (49/50 or 98%). To identify newly-caught fish, you could compute the linear discriminant functions associated with Alaskan and Canadian fish and identify the new fish as being of a particular origin depending upon which discriminant function value is higher. You can either do this by using **Calc ➤ Calculator**, or by performing discriminant analysis again and predicting group membership for new observations.

The Summary of Misclassified Observations table shows the squared distances from each misclassified point to group centroids and the posterior probabilities. The squared distance value is the squared distance from the observation to the group centroid, or mean vector. The probability value is the posterior probability, or the probability of a group given the data. Observations are assigned to the group with the highest posterior probability.

Clustering of Observations

Use clustering of observations to classify observations into groups when the groups are initially not known.

This procedure uses an agglomerative hierarchical method that begins with all observations being separate, each forming its own cluster. In the first step, the two observations closest together are joined. In the next step, either a third observation joins the first two, or two other observations join together into a different cluster. This process will continue until all clusters are joined into one, however this single cluster is not useful for classification purposes. Therefore you must decide how many groups are logical for your data and classify accordingly. See *Determining the final cluster grouping* on page 4-25.

Data

You can have two types of input data: columns of raw data or a matrix of distances.

Typically, you would use raw data. Each row contains measurements on a single item or subject. You must have two or more numeric columns, with each column representing a different measurement. You must delete rows with missing data from the worksheet before using this procedure.

If you store an n × n distance matrix, where n is the number of observations, you can use this matrix as input data. The (i, j) entry in this matrix is the distance between observations i and j. If you use the distance matrix as input, statistics on the final partition are not available.

▶ To perform clustering of observations

1   Choose **Stat ➤ Multivariate ➤ Cluster Observations**.

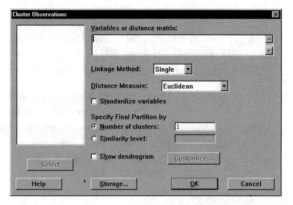

2   In **Variables or distance matrix,** enter either columns containing the raw (measurement) data or a matrix of distances.

3   If you like, use one or more of the options listed below, then click **OK**.

Options

Cluster Observations dialog box

- specify the method to measure distance between observations if you enter raw data. Available methods are Euclidean (default), Squared Euclidean, Pearson, Squared Pearson, or Manhattan. See *Distance measures for observations* on page 4-23.

- choose the linkage method—single (default), average, centroid, complete, McQuitty, median, or Ward's—that will determine how the distance between two clusters is defined. See *Linkage methods* on page 4-24.

- standardize all variables by subtracting the means and dividing by the standard deviation before the distance matrix is calculated—a good idea if variables are in different units and you wish to minimize the effect of scale differences. If you standardize, cluster centroids and distance measures are in standardized variable space.

- determine the final partition by the specified number of clusters (default is 1) or by the similarity level. See *Determining the final cluster grouping* on page 4-25.

- display the dendrogram (tree diagram) showing the amalgamation steps.

Customize subdialog box

- customize the dendrogram:
  - add a title
  - display similarities (the default) or distances on the y-axis
  - show the dendrogram in one window (default) or in separate windows for each cluster
  - specify the line type, line color, and line size used to represent each cluster—see *Specifying dendrogram attributes* on page 4-26

Storage subdialog box

- store cluster membership

- store distances between observations and cluster centroids for each cluster group

- store the n × n distance matrix, where n is the number of observations

Distance measures for observations

If you do not supply a distance matrix, MINITAB's first step is to calculate an n × n distance matrix, **D**, where n is the number of observations. The matrix entries, d(i, j), in row i and column j, is the distance between observations i and j.

MINITAB provides five different methods to measure distance. You might choose the distance measure according to properties of your data.

- The Euclidean method is a standard mathematical measure of distance (square root of the sum of squared differences).

- The Pearson method is a square root of the sum of square distances divided by variances. This method is for standardizing.

- Manhattan distance is the sum of absolute distances, so that outliers receive less weight than they would if the Euclidean method were used.

- The squared Euclidean and squared Pearson methods use the square of the Euclidean and Pearson methods, respectfully. Therefore, the distances that are large under the Euclidean and Pearson methods will be even larger under the squared Euclidean and squared Pearson methods.

Tip | If you choose average, centroid, median, or Ward as the linkage method, it is generally recommended [7] that you use one of the squared distance measures.

Linkage methods

The linkage method that you choose determines how the distance between two clusters is defined. At each amalgamation stage, the two closest clusters are joined. At the beginning, when each observation constitutes a cluster, the distance between clusters is simply the inter-observation distance. Subsequently, after observations are joined together, a linkage rule is necessary for calculating inter-cluster distances when there are multiple observations in a cluster.

You may wish to try several linkage methods and compare results. Depending on the characteristics of your data, some methods may provide "better" results than others.

- With *single linkage*, or "nearest neighbor," the distance between two clusters is the minimum distance between an observation in one cluster and an observation in the other cluster. Single linkage is a good choice when clusters are clearly separated. When observations lie close together, single linkage tends to identify long chain-like clusters that can have a relatively large distance separating observations at either end of the chain [5].

- With *average linkage*, the distance between two clusters is the mean distance between an observation in one cluster and an observation in the other cluster. Whereas the single or complete linkage methods group clusters based upon single pair distances, average linkage uses a more central measure of location.

- With *centroid linkage*, the distance between two clusters is the distance between the cluster centroids or means. Like average linkage, this method is another averaging technique.

- With *complete linkage*, or "furthest neighbor," the distance between two clusters is the maximum distance between an observation in one cluster and an observation in the other cluster. This method ensures that all observations in a cluster are within a maximum distance and tends to produce clusters with similar diameters. The results can be sensitive to outliers [8].

- With *median linkage*, the distance between two clusters is the median distance between an observation in one cluster and an observation in the other cluster. This is another averaging technique, but uses the median rather than the mean, thus downweighting the influence of outliers.

- With *McQuitty's linkage*, when two clusters are joined, the distance of the new cluster to any other cluster is calculated as the average of the distances of the soon to be joined clusters to that other cluster. For example, if clusters 1 and 3 are to be joined into a new cluster, say 1∗, then the distance from 1∗ to cluster 4 is the average of the distances from 1 to 4 and 3 to 4. Here, distance depends on a combination of clusters rather than individual observations in the clusters.

- With *Ward's linkage*, the distance between two clusters is the sum of squared deviations from points to centroids. The objective of Ward's linkage is to minimize the within-cluster sum of squares. It tends to produce clusters with similar numbers of observations, but it is sensitive to outliers [8]. In Ward's linkage, it is possible for the distance between two clusters to be larger than d_{max}, the maximum value in the original distance matrix. If this happens, the similarity will be negative.

Determining the final cluster grouping

The final grouping of clusters (also called the final partition) is the grouping of clusters which will, hopefully, identify groups whose observations share common characteristics. The decision about final grouping is also called *cutting the dendrogram*. The complete dendrogram (tree diagram) is a graphical depiction of the amalgamation of observations into one cluster. Cutting the dendrogram is akin to drawing a line across the dendrogram to specify the final grouping.

How do you know where to cut the dendrogram? You might first execute cluster analysis without specifying a final partition. Examine the similarity and distance levels in the Session window results and in the dendrogram. The similarity level at any step is the percent of the minimum distance at that step relative to the maximum inter-observation distance in the data. The pattern of how similarity or distance values change from step to step can help you to choose the final grouping. The step where the values change abruptly may identify a good point for cutting the dendrogram, if this makes sense for your data.

After choosing where you wish to make your partition, rerun the clustering procedure, using either **Number of clusters** or **Similarity level** to give you either a set number of groups or a similarity level for cutting the dendrogram. Examine the resulting clusters in the final partition to see if the grouping seems logical. Looking at dendrograms for different final groupings can also help you to decide which one makes the most sense for your data.

Note	For some data sets, average, centroid, median and Ward's methods may not produce a hierarchical dendrogram. That is, the amalgamation distances do not always increase with each step. In the dendrogram, such a step will produce a join that goes downward rather than upward.

Specifying dendrogram attributes

You can specify the line type, line color, and line size used to draw the portion of the dendrogram corresponding to each cluster in the final partition. If there are k clusters, you can give up to k values for each of these attributes. If you give less than k values, the ones that you enter will cycle until one is assigned to each cluster. For line type and line color, enter numbers that correspond to the types and colors below.

	Line types			**Line colors**			
	0	null (invisible)		0	white	8	dark red
(default)	1	solid	(default)	1	black	9	dark green
	2	dashes		2	red	10	dark blue
	3	dots		3	green	11	dark cyan
	4	dash 1-dot		4	blue	12	dark magenta
	5	dash 2-dots		5	cyan	13	dark yellow
	6	dash 3-dots		6	magenta	14	dark gray
	7	long dashes		7	yellow	15	light gray

You can specify any positive real number for the line sizes. Larger values yield wider lines. The default size is 1.

▷ Example of cluster observations

You make measurements on five nutritional characteristics (protein, carbohydrate, and fat content, calories, and percent of the daily allowance of Vitamin A) of 12 breakfast cereal brands. The example and data are from p. 623 of [5]. The goal is to group cereal brands with similar characteristics. You use clustering of observations with the complete linkage method, squared Euclidean distance, and you choose standardization because the variables have different units. You also request a dendrogram and assign different line types and colors to each cluster.

1 Open the worksheet CEREAL.MTW.

2 Choose **Stat ➤ Multivariate ➤ Cluster Observations**.

3 In **Variables or distance matrix**, enter *Protein-VitaminA*.

4 For **Linkage Method**, choose **Complete**. For **Distance Measure** choose **Squared Euclidean**.

5 Check **Standardize variables**.

6   Under **Specify Final Partition by**, choose **Number of clusters** and enter *4*.

7   Check **Show dendrogram**.

8   Click **Customize**. In **Title**, enter *Dendrogram for Cereal Data*. In **Type**, enter *1 2 1*.
    In **Color**, enter *2 3 4*. Click **OK** in each dialog box.

Session
window
output

Cluster Analysis of Observations: Protein, Carbo, Fat, Calories, VitaminA

Standardized Variables, Squared Euclidean Distance, Complete Linkage

Amalgamation Steps

Step	Number of clusters	Similarity level	Distance level	Clusters joined		New cluster	Number of obs. in new cluster
1	11	100.00	0.000	5	12	5	2
2	10	99.82	0.064	3	5	3	3
3	9	98.79	0.435	3	11	3	4
4	8	94.68	1.913	6	8	6	2
5	7	93.41	2.373	2	3	2	5
6	6	87.33	4.560	7	9	7	2
7	5	86.19	4.970	1	4	1	2
8	4	80.60	6.981	2	6	2	7
9	3	68.08	11.487	2	7	2	9
10	2	41.41	21.085	1	2	1	11
11	1	0.00	35.987	1	10	1	12

Final Partition

Number of clusters: 4

	Number of observations	Within cluster sum of squares	Average distance from centroid	Maximum distance from centroid
Cluster1	2	2.485	1.115	1.115
Cluster2	7	8.999	1.043	1.769
Cluster3	2	2.280	1.068	1.068
Cluster4	1	0.000	0.000	0.000

Cluster Centroids

Variable	Cluster1	Cluster2	Cluster3	Cluster4	Grand centrd
Protein	1.9283	-0.3335	-0.2030	-1.1164	0.0000
Carbo	-0.7587	0.5419	0.1264	-2.5289	-0.0000
Fat	0.3385	-0.0967	0.3385	-0.6770	0.0000
Calories	0.2803	0.2803	0.2803	-3.0834	-0.0000
VitaminA	-0.6397	-0.2559	2.0471	-1.0235	-0.0000

Distances Between Cluster Centroids

	Cluster1	Cluster2	Cluster3	Cluster4
Cluster1	0.0000	2.6727	3.5418	4.9896
Cluster2	2.6727	0.0000	2.3838	4.7205
Cluster3	3.5418	2.3838	0.0000	5.4460
Cluster4	4.9896	4.7205	5.4460	0.0000

*Graph
window
output*

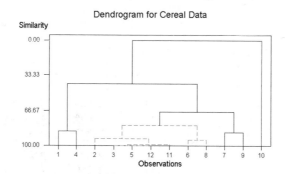

Interpreting the results

MINITAB displays the amalgamation steps in the Session window. At each step, two clusters are joined. The table shows which clusters were joined, the distance between them, the corresponding similarity level, the identification number of the new cluster (this number is always the smaller of the two numbers of the clusters joined), the number of observations in the new cluster, and the number of clusters. Amalgamation continues until there is just one cluster.

The amalgamation steps show that the similarity level decreases by increments of about 6 or less until it decreases by about 13 at the step from four clusters to three. This indicates that four clusters are reasonably sufficient for the final partition. If this grouping makes intuitive sense for the data, then it is probably a good choice.

When you specify the final partition, MINITAB displays three additional tables. The first table summarizes each cluster by the number of observations, the within cluster sum of squares, the average distance from observation to the cluster centroid, and the maximum distance of observation to the cluster centroid. In general, a cluster with a small sum of squares is more compact than one with a large sum of squares. The centroid is the vector of variable means for the observations in that cluster and is used as a cluster midpoint. The second table displays the centroids for the individual clusters while the third table gives distances between cluster centroids.

The dendrogram displays the information printed in the amalgamation table in the form of a tree diagram. Because this book is in black and white, you cannot see the assigned cluster colors. Using color can make it easier to discriminate between the clusters. In our example, cereals 1 and 4 make up the first cluster; cereals 2, 3, 5, 12, 11, 6, and 8 make up the second; cereals 7 and 9 make up the third; cereal 10 makes up the fourth.

Clustering of Variables

Use Clustering of Variables to classify variables into groups when the groups are initially not known. One reason to cluster variables may be to reduce their number. This technique may give new variables that are more intuitively understood than those found using principal components.

This procedure is an agglomerative hierarchical method that begins with all variables separate, each forming its own cluster. In the first step, the two variables closest together are joined. In the next step, either a third variable joins the first two, or two other variables join together into a different cluster. This process will continue until all clusters are joined into one, but you must decide how many groups are logical for your data. See *Determining the final cluster grouping* on page 4-25.

Data

You can have two types of input data to cluster observations: columns of raw data or a matrix of distances.

Typically, you would use raw data. Each row contains measurements on a single item or subject. You must have two or more numeric columns, with each column representing a different measurement. You must delete rows with missing data from the worksheet before using this procedure.

If you store a p × p distance matrix, where p is the number of variables, you can use this matrix as input data. The (i, j) entry in this matrix is the distance between observations i and j. If you use the distance matrix as input, statistics on the final partition are not available.

▶ To perform clustering of variables

1 Choose **Stat ➤ Multivariate ➤ Cluster Variables**.

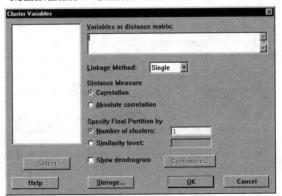

2 In **Variables or distance matrix,** enter either columns containing the raw (measurement) data or a matrix of distances.

3 If you like, use one or more of the options listed below, then click **OK**.

Options

Cluster Variables dialog box

- choose the linkage method—single (default), average, centroid, complete, McQuitty, median, or Ward's—that will determine how the distance between two clusters is defined. See *Linkage methods* on page 4-24.

- choose correlation or absolute correlation as a distance measure if you use raw data—see *Distance measures for variables* on page 4-30.

- determine the final partition by the specified number of clusters or the specified level of similarity—see *Determining the final cluster grouping* on page 4-25.

- display the dendrogram (tree diagram) showing the amalgamation steps.

Customize subdialog box

- customize the dendrogram:
  - add a title.
  - display similarities (the default) or distances on the y-axis.
  - show dendrogram in one window (default) or separate windows for each cluster .
  - specify the line type, line color, and line size used to represent each cluster in the final partition—see *Specifying dendrogram attributes* on page 4-26.

Storage subdialog box

- store the $p \times p$ distance matrix, where p is the number of variables.

Distance measures for variables

You can use correlations or absolute correlations for distance measures. With the correlation method, the (i,j) entry of the distance matrix is $d_{ij} = 1 - \rho_{ij}$ and for the absolute correlation method, $d_{ij} = 1 - |\rho_{ij}|$, where ρ_{ij} is the (Pearson product moment) correlation between variables i and j. Thus, the correlation method will give distances between 0 and 1 for positive correlations, and between 1 and 2 for negative correlations. The absolute correlation method will always give distances between 0 and 1.

- If it makes sense to consider negatively correlated data to be farther apart than postively correlated data, then use the correlation method.

- If you think that the strength of the relationship is important in considering distance and not the sign, then use the absolute correlation method.

Clustering variables in practice

You must make similar decisions to cluster variables as you would to cluster observations. Follow the guidelines in *Determining the final cluster grouping* on page 4-25 to help you determine groupings. However, if the purpose behind clustering of variables is data reduction, you may decide to use your knowledge of the data to a greater degree in determining the final clusters of variables. See the following example.

▷ Example of clustering variables

You conduct a study to determine the long-term effect of a change in environment on blood pressure. The subjects are 39 Peruvian males over 21 years of age who had migrated from the Andes mountains to larger towns at lower elevations. You recorded their age (Age), years since migration (Years), weight in kg (Weight), height in mm (Height), skin fold of the chin, forearm, and calf in mm (Chin, Forearm, Calf), pulse rate in beats per minute (Pulse), and systolic and diastolic blood pressure (Systol, Diastol).

Your goal is to reduce the number of variables by combining variables with similar characteristics. You use clustering of variables with the default correlation distance measure, average linkage and a dendrogram.

1 Open the worksheet PERU.MTW.

2 Choose **Stat ➤ Multivariate ➤ Cluster Variables**.

3 In **Variables or distance matrix**, enter *Age-Diastol*.

4 For **Linkage Method**, choose **Average**.

5 Check **Show dendrogram**. Click **OK**.

Session window output

Cluster Analysis of Variables: Age, Years, Weight, Height, Chin, Forearm, Calf,

Correlation Coefficient Distance, Average Linkage

Amalgamation Steps

Step	Number of clusters	Similarity level	Distance level	Clusters joined		New cluster	Number of obs. in new cluster
1	9	86.78	0.264	6	7	6	2
2	8	79.41	0.412	1	2	1	2
3	7	78.85	0.423	5	6	5	3
4	6	76.07	0.479	3	9	3	2
5	5	71.74	0.565	3	10	3	3
6	4	65.55	0.689	3	5	3	6
7	3	61.34	0.773	3	8	3	7
8	2	56.60	0.868	1	3	1	9
9	1	55.44	0.891	1	4	1	10

Graph window output

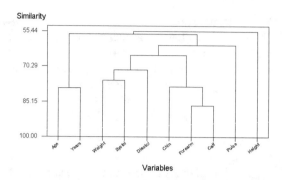

Interpreting the results

MINITAB displays shows the amalgamation steps in the Session window. At each step, two clusters are joined. The table shows which clusters were joined, the distance between them, the corresponding similarity level, the identification number of the new cluster (this is always the smaller of the two numbers of the clusters joined), the number of variables in the new cluster and the number of clusters. Amalgamation continues until there is just one cluster.

If you had requested a final partition you would also receive a list of which variables are in each cluster.

The dendrogram displays the information printed in the amalgamation table in the form of a tree diagram. Dendrogram suggest variables which might be combined, perhaps by averaging or totaling. In this example, the chin, forearm, and calf skin fold measurements are similar and you decide to combine those. The age and year since migration variables are similar, but you will investigate this relationship. If subjects tend to migrate at a certain age, then these variables could contain similar information and be combined. Weight and the two blood pressure measurements are similar. You decide to keep weight as a separate variable but you will combine the blood pressure measurements into one.

K-Means Clustering of Observations

Use K-means clustering of observations, like clustering of observations on page 4-22, to classify observations into groups when the groups are initially unknown. This procedure uses non-hierarchical clustering of observations according to MacQueen's algorithm [5]. K-means clustering works best when sufficient information is available to make good starting cluster designations. See *Initializing the K-means clustering process* on page 4-34.

Data

You must use raw data as input to K-means clustering of observations. Each row contains measurements on a single item or subject. You must have two or more numeric columns, with each column representing a different measurement. You must delete rows with missing data from the worksheet before using this procedure.

To initialize the clustering process using a data column, you must have a column that contains a cluster membership value for each observation. The initialization column must contain positive, consecutive integers or zeros (it should not contain all zeros). Initially, each observation is assigned to the cluster identified by the corresponding value in this column. An initialization of zero means that an observation is initially unassigned to a group. The number of distinct positive integers in the initial partition column equals the number of clusters in the final partition.

▶ To perform K-means clustering of observations

1 Choose **Stat ➤ Multivariate ➤ Cluster K-Means**.

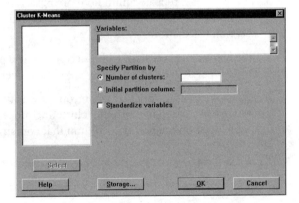

2 In **Variables**, enter the columns containing the measurement data.

3 If you like, use one or more of the options listed below, then click **OK**.

Options

Cluster K-Means dialog box

- specify the number of clusters to form or specify a column containing cluster membership to begin the partition process—see *Initializing the K-means clustering process* on page 4-34.

- standardize all variables by subtracting the means and dividing by the standard deviation before the distance matrix is calculated. This is a good idea if the variables are in different units and you wish to minimize the effect of scale differences. If you standardize, cluster centroids and distance measures are in standardized variable space.

Storage subdialog box

- store the final cluster membership for each observation

- store the distance between each observation and each cluster centroid

Initializing the K-means clustering process

K-means clustering begins with a grouping of observations into a predefined number of clusters.

1 MINITAB evaluates each observation, moving it into the nearest cluster. The nearest cluster is the one which has the smallest Euclidean distance between the observation and the centroid of the cluster.

2 When a cluster changes, by losing or gaining an observation, MINITAB recalculates the cluster centroid.

3 This process is repeated until no more observations can be moved into a different cluster. At this point, all observations are in their nearest cluster according to the criterion listed above.

Unlike hierarchical clustering of observations, it is possible for two observations to be split into separate clusters after they are joined together.

K-means procedures work best when you provide good starting points for clusters [8]. There are two ways to initialize the clustering process: specifying a number of clusters or supplying an initial partition column that contains group codes.

▶ **To initialize the process by specifying the number of clusters**

1 Choose **Stat ➤ Multivariate ➤ Cluster K-Means**.

2 In **Variables**, enter the columns containing the measurement data.

3 Under **Specify Partition by**, choose **Number of clusters** and enter a number, k, in the box. MINITAB will use the first k observations as initial cluster seeds, or starting locations. Click **OK**.

For guidance in setting up your worksheet, see below.

▶ **To initialize the process using a data column**

1 Choose **Stat ➤ Multivariate ➤ Cluster K-Means**.

2 In **Variables**, enter the columns containing the measurement data.

3 Under **Specify Partition by**, choose **Initial partition column**. Enter the column containing the initial cluster membership for each observation. Click **OK**.

You may be able to initialize the process when you do not have complete information to initially partition the data. Suppose you know that the final partition should consist of three groups, and that observations 2, 5, and 9 belong in each of those groups, respectively. Proceeding from here depends upon whether you specify the number of clusters or supply an initial partition column.

- If you specify the number of clusters, you must rearrange your data in the Data window to move observations 2, 5 and 9 to the top of the worksheet, and then specify 3 for **Number of clusters**.

- If you enter an initial partition column, you do not need to rearrange your data in the Data window. In the initial partition worksheet column, enter group numbers 1, 2, and 3, for observations 2, 5, and 9, respectively, and enter 0 for the other observations. See the following example.

The final partition will depend to some extent on the initial partition that MINITAB uses. You might try different initial partitions.

▷ Example of K-means clustering

You live-trap, anesthetize, and measure one hundred forty-three black bears. The measurements are total length and head length (Length, Head.L), total weight and head weight (Weight, Weight.H), and neck girth and chest girth (Neck.G, Chest.G). You wish to classify these 143 bears as small, medium-sized, or large bears. You know that the second, seventy-eighth, and fifteenth bears in the sample are typical of the three respective categories. First, you create an initial partition column with the three seed bears designated as 1 = small, 2 = medium-sized, 3 = large, and with the remaining bears as 0 (unknown) to indicate initial cluster membership. Then you perform K-means clustering and store the cluster membership in a column named BearSize.

1 Open the worksheet BEARS.MTW.

2 To create the initial partition column, choose **Calc ➤ Make Patterned Data ➤ Simple Set of Numbers**.

3 In **Store patterned data in**, type *Initial* for the storage column name. In both **From first value** and **To last value**, enter *0*. In **List each value**, type *143*. Click **OK**.

4 Go to the Data window and type 1, 2, and 3 in the second, seventy-eighth, and fifteenth rows, respectively, of the column named Initial.

5 Choose **Stat ➤ Multivariate ➤ Cluster K-Means**.

6 In **Variables**, enter *'Head.L' –Weight*.

7 Under **Specify Partition by**, choose **Initial partition column** and enter *Initial*.

8 Check **Standardize variables**.

9 Click **Storage**. In **Cluster membership column**, type *BearSize*. Click **OK** in each dialog box.

Session window output

K-means Cluster Analysis: Head.L, Head.W, Neck.G, Length, Chest.G, Weight

Standardized Variables

Final Partition

Number of clusters: 3

	Number of observations	Within cluster sum of squares	Average distance from centroid	Maximum distance from centroid
Cluster1	41	63.075	1.125	2.488
Cluster2	67	78.947	0.997	2.048
Cluster3	35	65.149	1.311	2.449

Cluster Centroids

Variable	Cluster1	Cluster2	Cluster3	Grand centrd
Head.L	-1.0673	0.0126	1.2261	-0.0000
Head.W	-0.9943	-0.0155	1.1943	0.0000
Neck.G	-1.0244	-0.1293	1.4476	-0.0000
Length	-1.1399	0.0614	1.2177	0.0000
Chest.G	-1.0570	-0.0810	1.3932	-0.0000
Weight	-0.9460	-0.2033	1.4974	-0.0000

Distances Between Cluster Centroids

	Cluster1	Cluster2	Cluster3
Cluster1	0.0000	2.4233	5.8045
Cluster2	2.4233	0.0000	3.4388
Cluster3	5.8045	3.4388	0.0000

Interpreting the results

K-means clustering classified the 143 bears as 41 small bears, 67 medium-size bears, and 35 large bears. MINITAB displays, in the first table, the number of observations in each cluster, the within cluster sum of squares, the average distance from observation to the cluster centroid, and the maximum distance of observation to the cluster centroid. In general, a cluster with a small sum of squares is more compact than one with a large sum of squares. The centroid is the vector of variable means for the observations in that cluster and is used as a cluster midpoint.

The centroids for the individual clusters are printed in the second table while the third table gives distances between cluster centroids.

The column BearSize contains the cluster designations.

References

[1] T.W. Anderson (1984). *An Introduction to Multivariate Statistical Analysis*, Second Edition, John Wiley & Sons.

[2] W. Dillon and M. Goldstein (1984). *Multivariate Analysis, Methods and Applications*, John Wiley & Sons.

[3] S.E. Fienberg (1987). *The Analysis of Cross-Classified Categorical Data*. The MIT Press.

[4] H. Harmon (1976). *Modern Factor Analysis*, Third Edition, University of Chicago Press.

[5] R. Johnson and D. Wichern (1992). *Applied Multivariate Statistical Methods*, Third Edition, Prentice Hall.

[6] K. Joreskog (1977). "Factor Analysis by Least Squares and Maximum Likelihood Methods," *Statistical Methods for Digital Computers*, ed. K. Enslein, A. Ralston and H. Wilf, John Wiley & Sons.

[7] G.N. Lance and W.T. Williams (1967), "A General Theory of Classificatory Sorting Strategies, I. Hierarchical systems," *Computer Journal*, 9, 373–380

[8] G. W. Milligan (1980). "An Examination of the Effect of Six Types of Error Pertubation on Fifteen Clustering Algorithms," Psychometrika, 45, 325-342.

[9] S.J. Press and S. Wilson (1978). "Choosing Between Logistic Regression and Discriminant Analysis," *Journal of the American Statistical Association* 73, 699-705.

5

Nonparametrics

Nonparametrics Overview

MINITAB provides the following types of nonparametric procedures:

- tests of the population location (sign test, Wilcoxon test, Mann-Whitney test, Kruskal-Wallis test, Mood's median test, and Friedman test)

- a test of randomness (runs test)

- procedures for calculating pairwise statistics (pairwise averages, pairwise differences, and pairwise slopes)

Parametric implies that a distribution is assumed for the population. Often, an assumption is made when performing a hypothesis test that the data are a sample from a certain distribution, commonly the normal distribution. *Nonparametric* implies that there is no assumption of a specific distribution for the population.

An advantage of a parametric test is that if the assumptions hold, the power, or the probability of rejecting H_0 when it is false, is higher than is the power of a corresponding nonparametric test with equal sample sizes. An advantage of nonparametric tests is that the test results are more robust against violation of the assumptions. Therefore, if assumptions are violated for a test based upon a parametric model, the conclusions based on parametric test p-values may be more misleading than conclusions based upon nonparametric test p-values. See [1] for comparing the power of some of these nonparametric tests to their parametric equivalent.

Tests of population location

These nonparametric tests are analogous to the parametric t-tests and analysis of variance procedures in that they are used to perform tests about population location or center value. The center value is the mean for parametric tests and the median for nonparametric tests.

- **1-Sample Sign** performs a one-sample sign test of the median and calculates the corresponding point estimate and confidence interval. Use this test as a nonparametric alternative to one-sample Z and one-sample t-tests.

- **1-Sample Wilcoxon** performs a one-sample Wilcoxon signed rank test of the median and calculates the corresponding point estimate and confidence interval. Use this test as a nonparametric alternative to one-sample Z and one-sample t-tests.

- **Mann-Whitney** performs a hypothesis test of the equality of two population medians and calculates the corresponding point estimate and confidence interval. Use this test as a nonparametric alternative to the two-sample t-test.

- **Kruskal-Wallis** performs a hypothesis test of the equality of population medians for a one-way design (two or more populations). This test is a generalization of the procedure used by the Mann-Whitney test and, like Mood's median test, offers a nonparametric alternative to the one-way analysis of variance. The Kruskal-Wallis test looks for differences among the populations medians.

The Kruskal-Wallis test is more powerful (the confidence interval is narrower, on average) than Mood's median test for analyzing data from many distributions, including data from the normal distribution, but is less robust against outliers.

- **Mood's Median** performs a hypothesis test of the equality of population medians in a one-way design. Mood's median test, like the Kruskal-Wallis test, provides a nonparametric alternative to the usual one-way analysis of variance. Mood's median test is sometimes called a median test or sign scores test.

  Mood's median test is robust against outliers and errors in data, and is particularly appropriate in the preliminary stages of analysis. Mood's median test is more robust against outliers than the Kruskal-Wallis test, but is less powerful (the confidence interval is wider, on the average) for analyzing data from many distributions, including data from the normal distribution.

- **Friedman** performs a nonparametric analysis of a randomized block experiment and thus provides an alternative to the two-way analysis of variance.

  Randomized block experiments are a generalization of paired experiments. The Friedman test is a generalization of the paired sign test with a null hypothesis of treatments having no effect. This test requires exactly one observation per treatment-block combination.

Tests for randomness

Runs Test tests whether or not the data order is random. No assumptions are made about population distribution parameters. Use **Stat ➤ Quality Tools ➤ Run Chart** to generate a run chart and perform additional tests for randomness. See *Run Chart* on page 10-2 for more information.

Procedures for calculating pairwise statistics

Pairwise Averages, **Pairwise Differences**, and **Pairwise Slopes** compute averages, differences, and slopes, respectively, for all possible pairs of values. These statistics are sometimes used in nonparametric statistical calculations.

One-Sample Sign Test

You can perform a one-sample sign test of the median or calculate the corresponding point estimate and confidence interval. For the one-sample sign test, the hypotheses are

H_0: median = hypothesized median   versus H_1: median ≠ hypothesized median

Use the sign test as a nonparametric alternative to one-sample Z (page 1-12) and one-sample t-tests (page 1-15), which use the mean rather than the median.

Data

You need at least one column of numeric data. If you enter more than one column of data, MINITAB performs a one-sample sign test separately for each column. MINITAB automatically omits missing data from the calculations.

▶ **To calculate a sign confidence interval and test for the median**

1 Choose **Stat ➤ Nonparametrics ➤ 1-Sample Sign**.

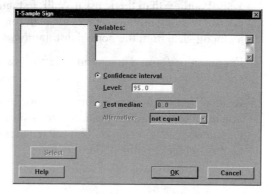

2 In **Variables**, enter the column(s) containing the data.

3 Choose one of the following:

- to calculate a sign confidence interval for the median, choose **Confidence interval**

- to perform a sign test, choose **Test median**

4 If you like, use one or more of the options listed below, then click **OK**.

Options

- specify a level of confidence for the confidence interval. The default is 95%.

- specify the null hypothesis test value. The default is 0.

- define the alternative hypothesis by choosing less than (lower-tailed), not equal (two-tailed), or greater than (upper-tailed). The default is a two-tailed test.

Method

Sign test for the median

The sign hypothesis test is based upon the binomial distribution. You can choose an alternative hypothesis that is one-tailed or two-tailed.

- If the alternative hypothesis is one-tailed (in **Alternative** you chose **less than** or **greater than**), MINITAB tallies the number of observations less than the hypothesized value (for a lower-tailed test) or greater than the hypothesized value (for an upper-tailed test). For each test, the p-value is the binomial probability of observing:
  - the number of tallied observations or fewer for a lower-tailed test
  - the number of tallied observations or more for an upper-tailed test

  using the observed sample size (n) and a probability of occurrence (p) of 0.5.

- If you perform a two-tailed test (in **Alternative** you choose **not equal**), the procedure uses the larger number of tallied values above or below the hypothesized one. The p-value of the sign test is two times the binomial probability of observing the tallied number of observations or fewer with the observed n and p = 0.5.

MINITAB omits observations (for both alternative hypotheses) equal to the hypothesized value from the calculations, and n is reduced by one for each omitted value. When n ≤ 50, the probability calculations are exact. When n > 50, MINITAB uses a normal approximation to the binomial.

Sign confidence interval for the median

MINITAB calculates three sign confidence intervals. The output below illustrates the three intervals:

	N	Median	Achieved Confidence	Confidence interval	Position
Chemical	70	51.50	0.9270	(49.00, 55.00)	28
			0.9500	(48.35, 55.00)	NLI
			0.9578	(48.00, 55.00)	27

The first row gives the achievable confidence level (0.9270) just below the requested confidence level (0.95); the third row gives the achievable confidence level (0.9578) just above the requested level (0.95).

The calculation of the first and third intervals uses a method similar to the sign method used when doing a hypothesis test of the median. Observations are first ordered. The interval that goes from the dth smallest observation to the dth largest observation has confidence $1 - 2P (X < d)$ using the binomial distribution with p = 0.5. The intervals with confidence coefficients just above and below the requested level are those selected. Only rarely can you achieve the requested confidence with these intervals.

MINITAB finds the middle confidence interval by a nonlinear interpolation procedure developed by Hettmansperger and Sheather [2]. The confidence coefficient of this interval will be as close to the requested level as possible. This method has the following properties:

- the actual confidence level is between the confidence levels for the bounding intervals

- the interpolation is a very good approximation for a wide variety of symmetric distributions, including the normal distribution, the Cauchy distribution, and the uniform distribution

- the interpolation tends to be not quite as good for asymmetric distributions as for symmetric distributions but it is much more accurate than linear interpolation [2]

Boxplot (in the *Core Graphs* chapter in MINITAB *User's Guide 1*) also uses this interpolation procedure to calculate the confidence interval for the median.

⊳ Example of a one-sample sign test of the median

Price index values for 29 homes in a suburban area in the Northeast were determined. Real estate records indicate the population median for similar homes the previous year was 115. This test will determine if there is sufficient evidence for judging if the median price index for the homes was greater than 115 using $\alpha = 0.10$.

1 Open the worksheet EXH_STAT.MTW.

2 Choose **Stat ➤ Nonparametrics ➤ 1-Sample Sign**.

3 In **Variables**, enter *PriceIndex*.

4 Choose **Test median** and enter *115* in the text box.

5 In **Alternative**, choose **greater than**. Click **OK**.

Session window output

Sign Test for Median: PriceIndex

```
Sign test of median = 115.0 versus  >  115.0

               N  Below  Equal  Above       P    Median
PriceInd      29     12      0     17  0.2291     144.0
```

Interpreting the results

Of the 29 price index data, 12 are below and 17 are above the hypothesize value, 115. Because an upper one-sided test was chosen, the p-value is the binomial probability of observing 17 or more observations greater than 115 if p is 0.5. If your α level was less than a p-value of 0.2291, you would fail to conclude that the population median was greater than 115, which seems likely for most situations.

If you had performed a two-sided test using the same sample (H_0: median = 115 versus H_1: median $\neq$ 115), there would be 12 observations below 115 and 17 above. Since you would be performing a two-sided test, you would look at the number of observations below and above 115, and take the larger of these, 17. The binomial probability of observing this many observations or more is 0.2291, and the p-value of the two-sided test is twice this value, or 2 (0.2291) = 0.4582. If n had been > 50, MINITAB would have used a normal approximation to the binomial in calculating the p-value.

▷ **Example of a one-sample sign confidence interval**

Using data for the 29 houses in the previous example, you also want to obtain a 95% confidence interval for the population median.

1 Open the worksheet EXH_STAT.MTW.

2 Choose **Stat ➤ Nonparametrics ➤ 1-Sample Sign**.

3 In **Variables**, enter *PriceIndex*. Choose **Confidence interval**. Click **OK**.

Session window output

Sign CI: PriceIndex

```
Sign confidence interval for median

                          Achieved
            N   Median   Confidence    Confidence interval    Position
PriceInd    29   144.0     0.9386      (  110.0,   210.0)        10
                           0.9500      (  108.5,   211.7)        NLI
                           0.9759      (  101.0,   220.0)         9
```

Interpreting the results

MINITAB calculates three intervals. The first and third intervals have confidence levels below and above the requested level, respectively. The confidence levels are calculated according to binomial probabilities. For example, the interval that goes from the 9th smallest observation to the 9th largest observation has a confidence of $1 - 2P(X < 9) = 0.9759$, where X has a binomial distribution with n = 29 and p = 0.5. The middle confidence interval of (110.0, 211.7) is found by a nonlinear interpolation procedure [2], and has a confidence level equal to the requested level or the default of 95%.

One-Sample Wilcoxon Test

You can perform a one-sample Wilcoxon signed rank test of the median or calculate the corresponding point estimate and confidence interval. The Wilcoxon signed rank test hypotheses are

H_0: median = hypothesized median   versus H_1: median ≠ hypothesized median

An assumption for the one-sample Wilcoxon test and confidence interval is that the data are a random sample from a continuous, symmetric population. When the population is normally distributed, this test is slightly less powerful (the confidence interval is wider, on the average) than the t-test. It may be considerably more powerful (the confidence interval is narrower, on the average) for other populations.

Data

You need at least one column of numeric data. If you enter more than one column of data, MINITAB performs a one-sample Wilcoxon test separately for each column. MINITAB automatically omits missing data from the calculations.

▶ **To calculate a one-sample Wilcoxon confidence interval and test for the median**

1 Choose **Stat ➤ Nonparametrics ➤ 1-Sample Wilcoxon**.

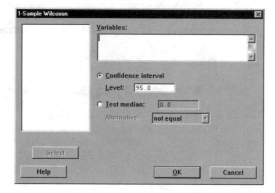

2 In **Variables**, enter the column(s) containing the variable(s).

3 Choose one of the following:

- to calculate a Wilcoxon confidence interval for the median, choose **Confidence interval**

- to perform a Wilcoxon signed rank test, choose **Test median**

4 If you like, use one or more of the options listed below, then click **OK**.

Note | If you do not specify a hypothesized median, a one-sample Wilcoxon test tests whether the sample median is different from zero.

Options

- specify a level of confidence for the confidence interval. The default is 95%.

- specify the null hypothesis test value. The default is 0.

- define the alternative hypothesis by choosing less than (lower-tailed), not equal (two-tailed), or greater than (upper-tailed). The default is a two-tailed test.

Method

Test for the median

MINITAB first eliminates any observations equal to the hypothesized median. Then the pairwise (Walsh) averages, $(Y_i + Y_j) / 2$ for $i \leq j$, are formed. The Wilcoxon statistic is the number of Walsh averages exceeding the hypothesized median, plus one half the number of Walsh averages equal to the hypothesized median. This statistic is approximately normally distributed. Under H_0, the distribution mean for the Wilcoxon is $N(N + 1) / 4$, where N is the number of observations for the test. The attained p-value is calculated using a normal approximation with a continuity correction.

An algebraically equivalent form of the test is based on ranks. Subtract the hypothesized median from each observation, discard any zeros, and rank the absolute values of these differences. The number of differences is the sample size reduced by one for each observation equal to the median. If two or more absolute differences are tied, assign the average rank to each. The Wilcoxon statistic is the sum of ranks corresponding to positive differences.

The Wilcoxon point estimate of the population median is the median of the Walsh averages. MINITAB obtains the test statistic and point estimate of the population median using an algorithm based on Johnson and Mizoguchi [4].

Confidence interval

The confidence interval is the set of values (d) for which the test of H_0: median = d is not rejected in favor of H_1: median $\neq$ d, using $\alpha = 1 - $ (percent confidence) / 100. Because of the discreteness of the Wilcoxon test statistic, it will seldom be possible to achieve the specified confidence. The procedure prints the closest value, which is computed using a normal approximation with a continuity correction.

▷ Example of a one-sample Wilcoxon test for the median

Achievement test scores in science were recorded for 9 students. This test enables you to judge if there is sufficient evidence for the population median being different than 77 using $\alpha = 0.05$.

1   Open the worksheet EXH_STAT.MTW.

2   Choose **Stat ➤ Nonparametrics ➤ 1-Sample Wilcoxon.**

3   In **Variables**, enter *Achievement*.

4   Choose **Test median**, and enter 77 in the box. Click **OK**.

*Session
window
output*

Wilcoxon Signed Rank Test: Achievement

Test of median = 77.00 versus median not = 77.00

```
                    N for   Wilcoxon                  Estimated
              N     Test   Statistic         P         Median
Achievem      9       8        19.5      0.889          77.50
```

Interpreting the results

The Wilcoxon test statistic of 19.5 is the number of Walsh averages exceeding 77. Because one test score was equal to the hypothesized value, the sample size used for the test was reduced by one to 8, as indicated under "N for Test". There is insufficient evidence to reject the hypothesis that the population median was different from 77 because the p-value of the test is not less than $\alpha = .05$. The estimated median, here 77.5, is the median of the Walsh averages. This median may be different from the median of the data, which is 77 in this example.

▷ Example of a one-sample Wilcoxon confidence interval

A 95% confidence interval for the population median can be calculated by the one-sample Wilcoxon method.

1 Open the worksheet EXH_STAT.MTW.

2 Choose **Stat ➤ Nonparametrics ➤ 1-Sample Wilcoxon**.

3 In **Variables**, enter *Achievement*.

4 Choose **Confidence interval**. Click **OK**.

*Session
window
output*

Wilcoxon Signed Rank CI: Achievement

```
          Estimated    Achieved
              N     Median  Confidence  Confidence Interval
Achievem      9       77.5        95.6  (    70.0,    84.0)
```

Interpreting the results

The computed confidence interval (70, 84) has a confidence level of 95.6%. You can also perform the above two-sided hypothesis test at $\alpha = 1 - 0.956 = 0.044$ by noting that 77 is within the confidence interval, and thus fail to reject H_0. The estimated median is the median of the Walsh averages.

Two-Sample Mann-Whitney Test

You can perform a two-sample rank test (also called the Mann-Whitney test, or the two-sample Wilcoxon rank sum test) of the equality of two population medians, and calculate the corresponding point estimate and confidence interval. The hypotheses are

$H_0: \eta_1 = \eta_2$ versus $H_1: \eta_1 \neq \eta_2$

where η is the population median.

An assumption for the Mann-Whitney test is that the data are independent random samples from two populations that have the same shape (hence the same variance) and a scale that is continuous or ordinal (possesses natural ordering) if discrete. The two-sample rank test is slightly less powerful (the confidence interval is wider on the average) than the two-sample test with pooled sample variance when the populations are normal, and considerably more powerful (confidence interval is narrower, on the average) for many other populations. If the populations have different shapes or different standard deviations, a two-sample t-test without pooling variances (see page 1-18 for two-sample t-test) may be more appropriate.

Data

You will need two columns containing numeric data drawn from two populations. The columns do not need to be the same length. MINITAB automatically omits missing data from the calculations.

▶ **To calculate a Mann-Whitney test**

1 Choose **Stat ➤ Nonparametrics ➤ Mann-Whitney**.

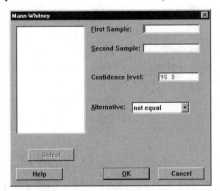

2 In **First Sample**, enter the column containing the sample data from one population.

3 In **Second Sample**, enter the column containing the other sample data.

4 If you like, use one or more of the options listed below, then click **OK**.

Options

- specify a level of confidence for the confidence interval. The default is 95%.

- define the alternative hypothesis by choosing less than (lower-tailed), not equal (two-tailed), or greater than (upper-tailed). The default is a two-tailed test.

Method

To calculate the test statistic, W:

1 MINITAB ranks the two combined samples, with the smallest observation given rank 1, the second smallest, rank 2, etc.

2 If two or more observations are tied, the average rank is assigned to each.

3 Then, MINITAB calculates the sum of the ranks of the first sample. This sum is the test statistic, W.

The point estimate of the population median is the median of all the pairwise differences between observations in the first sample and the second sample.

Mann-Whitney determines the attained significance level of the test using a normal approximation with a continuity correction factor. If there are ties in the data, MINITAB adjusts the significance level. The unadjusted significance level is conservative if ties are present; the adjusted significance level is usually closer to the correct values, but is not always conservative.

The confidence interval is the set of values d for which the test of $H_0: \eta_1 - \eta_2 = d$ versus $H_1: \eta_1 \neq \eta_2$ is not rejected, at $\alpha = 1 - $ (percent confidence) / 100. The method used to calculate the confidence interval is described in [6].

▶ Example of two-sample Mann-Whitney test

Samples were drawn from two populations and diastolic blood pressure was measured. You will want to determine if there is evidence of a difference in the population locations without assuming a parametric model for the distributions. Therefore, you choose to test the equality of population medians using the Mann-Whitney test with $\alpha = 0.05$ rather than using a two-sample t-test, which tests the equality of population means.

1 Open the worksheet EXH_STAT.MTW.

2 Choose **Stat ➤ Nonparametrics ➤ Mann-Whitney**.

3 In **First Sample**, enter *DBP1*. In **Second Sample**, enter *DBP2*. Click **OK**.

*Session
window
output*

Mann-Whitney Test and CI: DBP1, DBP2

```
DBP1       N =    8     Median =        69.50
DBP2       N =    9     Median =        78.00
Point estimate for ETA1-ETA2 is         -7.50
95.1 Percent CI for ETA1-ETA2 is (-18.00,4.00)
W = 60.0
Test of ETA1 = ETA2  vs  ETA1 not = ETA2 is significant at 0.2685
The test is significant at 0.2679 (adjusted for ties)

Cannot reject at alpha = 0.05
```

Interpreting the results

MINITAB calculates the sample medians of the ordered data as 69.5 and 78. The 95.1% confidence interval for the difference in population medians (ETA1–ETA2) is [−18 to 4]. The test statistic W = 60 has a p-value of 0.2685 or 0.2679 when adjusted for ties. Since the p-value is not less than the chosen α level of 0.05, you conclude that there is insufficient evidence to reject H$_0$. Therefore, the data does not support the hypothesis that there is a difference between the population medians.

Kruskal-Wallis Test for a One-Way Design

You can perform a Kruskal-Wallis test of the equality of medians for two or more populations.

This test is a generalization of the procedure used by the Mann-Whitney test and, like Mood's Median test, offers a nonparametric alternative to the one-way analysis of variance. The Kruskal-Wallis hypotheses are:

H$_0$: the population medians are all equal versus H$_1$: the medians are not all equal

An assumption for this test is that the samples from the different populations are independent random samples from continuous distributions, with the distributions having the same shape. The Kruskal-Wallis test is more powerful than Mood's median test for data from many distributions, including data from the normal distribution, but is less robust against outliers.

Data

The response (measurement) data must be stacked in one numeric column. You must also have a column that contains the factor levels or population identifiers. Factor levels can be numeric, text, or date/time data. If you wish to change the order in which text levels are processed, you can define your own order. See *Ordering Text Categories* in the *Manipulating Data* chapter in MINITAB *User's Guide 1*. **Calc ➤ Make Patterned**

Data can be helpful in entering the level values of a factor. See the *Generating Patterned Data* chapter in MINITAB *User's Guide 1*.

MINITAB automatically omits rows with missing responses or factor levels from the calculations.

▶ **To do a Kruskal-Wallis test**

1 Choose **Stat ➤ Nonparametrics ➤ Kruskal-Wallis**.

2 In **Response**, enter the column containing the measurement data.

3 In **Factor**, enter the column containing the factor levels. Click **OK**.

Method

To calculate the test statistic, H:

1 First, MINITAB ranks the combined samples, with the smallest observation given rank 1, the second smallest, rank 2, etc.

2 If two or more observations are tied, the average rank is assigned to each.

3 Then, MINITAB calculates the test statistic:

$$H = \frac{12 \sum n_i [\bar{R}_i - \bar{R}]^2}{N(N+1)}$$

where n_i is the number of observations in group i, N is the total sample size, $\bar{R}_i$ is the average of the ranks in group i, and $\bar{R}$ is the average of all the ranks.

Under the null hypothesis, the distribution of H can be approximated by a χ^2 distribution with $k - 1$ degrees of freedom. The approximation is reasonably accurate if no group has fewer than five observations. Large values of H suggest that there are some differences in location among the populations.

Some authors (such as, Lehmann [5]) suggest adjusting H when there are ties in the data. Suppose there are J distinct values among the N observations, and for the jth distinct value, there are d_j tied observations ($d_j = 1$ if there are no ties). Then the adjusted test statistic is:

$$H(adj) = \frac{H}{1 - [\sum (d_j^3 - d_j)/(N^3 - N)]}$$

When there are no ties, $H(adj) = H$. Under the null hypothesis, the distribution of $H(adj)$ is also approximately a χ^2 with $k - 1$ degrees of freedom. For small samples, the use of exact tables is suggested (such as, Hollander and Wolfe [3]). MINITAB displays $H(adj)$ if there are ties.

MINITAB also displays z-value for each group. The value of z_i indicates how the mean rank ($\bar{R}_i$) for group i differs from the mean rank ($\bar{R}$) for all N observations. For group i:

$$z_i = \frac{\bar{R}_i - (N + 1)/2}{\sqrt{(N + 1)(N/n_i - 1)/12}}$$

Under the null hypothesis, z_i is approximately normal with mean 0 and variance 1.

⮞ Example of a Kruskal-Wallis test

Measurements in growth were made on samples that were each given one of three treatments. Rather than assuming a data distribution and testing the equality of population means with one-way ANOVA, you decide to select the Kruskal-Wallis procedure to test H_0: $\eta_1 = \eta_2 = \eta_3$, versus H_1: not all η's are equal, where the η's are the population medians.

1 Open the worksheet EXH_STAT.MTW.

2 Choose **Stat ➤ Nonparametrics ➤ Kruskal-Wallis**.

3 In **Response**, enter *Growth*.

4 In **Factor**, enter *Treatment*. Click **OK**.

Session window output

Kruskal-Wallis Test: Growth versus Treatment

```
Kruskal-Wallis Test on Growth

Treatmen    N    Median    Ave Rank        Z
1           5     13.20         7.7    -0.45
2           5     12.90         4.3    -2.38
3           6     15.60        12.7     2.71
Overall    16                   8.5

H = 8.63   DF = 2   P = 0.013
H = 8.64   DF = 2   P = 0.013 (adjusted for ties)
```

Interpreting the results

The sample medians for the three treatments were calculated 13.2, 12.9, and 15.6. The z-value for level 1 is −0.45, the smallest absolute z-value. This size indicates that the mean rank for treatment 1 differed least from the mean rank for all observations. The mean rank for treatment 2 was lower than the mean rank for all observations, as the z-value is negative (z = −2.38). The mean rank for treatment 3 is higher than the mean rank for all observations, as the z-value is positive (z = 2.71).

The test statistic (H) had a p-value of 0.014, both unadjusted and adjusted for ties, indicating that the null hypothesis can be rejected at α levels higher than 0.014 in favor of the alternative hypothesis of at least one difference among the treatment groups.

Mood's Median Test for a One-Way Design

Mood's median test can be used to test the equality of medians from two or more populations and, like the Kruskal-Wallis Test, provides an nonparametric alternative to the one-way analysis of variance. Mood's median test is sometimes called a median test or sign scores test. Mood's median test tests:

H_0: the population medians are all equal   versus H_1: the medians are not all equal

An assumption of Mood's median test is that the data from each population are independent random samples and the population distributions have the same shape. Mood's median test is robust against outliers and errors in data and is particularly appropriate in the preliminary stages of analysis. Mood's median test is more robust than is the Kruskal-Wallis test against outliers, but is less powerful for data from many distributions, including the normal.

Data

The response (measurement) data must be stacked in one numeric column. You must also have a column that contains the factor levels or population identifiers. Factor levels can be numeric, text, or date/time data. If you wish to change the order in which text levels are processed, you can define your own order. See *Ordering Text Categories* in the *Manipulating Data* chapter in MINITAB *User's Guide 1*. **Calc ➤ Make Patterned Data** can be helpful in entering the level values of a factor. See the *Generating Patterned Data* chapter in MINITAB *User's Guide 1*.

MINITAB automatically omits rows with missing responses or factor levels from the calculations.

▶ **To do a Mood's median test**

1 Choose Stat ➤ Nonparametrics ➤ Mood's Median Test.

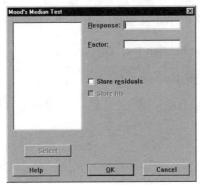

2 In **Response**, enter the column containing the measurement data.

3 In **Factor**, enter the column containing the factor levels.

4 If you like, use any of the options listed below, then click **OK**.

Options

- store the residuals
- store the fitted values, which are the group medians

Method

The overall median is the median of all the data. For each level, Mood's median test prints the number of observations less than or equal to the overall median, and the number of observations greater than the overall median. If there are k different levels, Mood's median test gives a $2 \times k$ table of counts. A χ^2 test for association is done on this table. Large values of χ^2 indicate that the null hypothesis may be false. Only groups containing two or more observations are included in the analysis.

If there are relatively few observations above the median due to ties with the median, then observations equal to the median may be counted with those above the median.

▷ **Example of Mood's median test**

One hundred seventy-nine participants were given a lecture with cartoons to illustrate the subject matter. Subsequently, they were given the OTIS test, which measures general intellectual ability. Participants were rated by educational level: 0 = preprofessional, 1 = professional, 2 = college student. The Mood's median test was selected to test H_0: $\eta_1 = \eta_2 = \eta_3$, versus H_1: not all η's are equal, where the η's are the median population OTIS scores for the three education levels.

1 Open the worksheet CARTOON.MTW.

2 Choose **Stat** ➤ **Nonparametrics** ➤ **Mood's Median Test**.

3 In **Response**, enter *Otis*. In **Factor**, enter *Ed*. Click **OK**.

Session
window
output

Mood Median Test: Otis versus ED

```
Mood median test for Otis

Chi-Square = 49.08   DF = 2    P = 0.000

                                         Individual 95.0% CIs
ED        N<=    N>   Median   Q3-Q1    ----+---------+---------+---------+--
0          47     9     97.5    17.3    (-----+-----)
1          29    24    106.0    21.5              (------+------)
2          15    55    116.5    16.3                                (----+----)
                                         ----+---------+---------+---------+--
                                         96.0      104.0     112.0     120.0
Overall median = 107.0
```

Interpreting the results

The participant scores are classified as being below or above the overall median, and a chi-square test for association is performed. The χ^2 value of 49.08 with a p-value of < 0.0005 indicates that there is sufficient evidence to reject H_0 in favor of H_1 at commonly used α levels.

For each factor level, MINITAB prints the median, interquartile range, and a sign confidence interval for the population median. The confidence interval is the nonlinear interpolation interval done by the one-sample sign procedure (see *Method* on page 5-5). Test scores are highest for college students. (You might conjecture that it is the college student whose intellect is most stimulated by cartoons.)

If a level has less than six observations, the confidence level would be less than 95%. When there are only two factor levels, MINITAB displays a 95% two-sample confidence interval for the difference between the two population medians.

Friedman Test for a Randomized Block Design

A Friedman test is a nonparametric analysis of a randomized block experiment, and thus provides an alternative to the two-way analysis of variance. The hypotheses are:

H_0: all treatment effects are zero   versus H_1: not all treatment effects are zero

Randomized block experiments are a generalization of paired experiments, and the Friedman test is a generalization of the paired sign test. Additivity (fit is sum of treatment and block effect) is not required for the test, but is required for the estimate of the treatment effects.

Data

The response (measurement) data must be stacked in one numeric column. You must also have a column that contains the treatment levels and a column that contains the block levels. Treatment and block levels can be numeric, text, or date/time data. If you wish to change the order in which text levels are processed, you can define your own order. See *Ordering Text Categories* in the *Manipulating Data* chapter in MINITAB *User's Guide 1*. **Calc ➤ Make Patterned Data** can be helpful in entering the level values of a factor. See the *Generating Patterned Data* chapter in MINITAB *User's Guide 1*.

You must have exactly one nonmissing observation per treatment–block combination. MINITAB automatically omits rows with missing responses, treatment levels, or block levels from the calculations.

▶ **To do a Friedman test**

1   Choose **Stat ➤ Nonparametrics ➤ Friedman**.

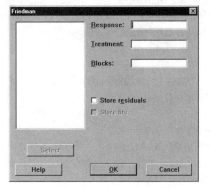

2   In **Response**, enter the column containing the measurement data.

3   In **Treatment**, enter the column containing the treatment levels.

4   In **Blocks**, enter the column that contains the block levels.

5   If you like, use any of the options listed below, then click **OK**.

Options

■   store the residuals. The residuals are the (observation adjusted for treatment effect) – (adjusted block median).

■   store the fitted values. The fits are the (treatment effect) + (adjusted block median) or observation – residual.

Method

To calculate the test statistic, S:

1 MINITAB first ranks the data separately within each block.

2 Next, sum the ranks for each treatment.

3 Calculate the test statistic (S) which is a constant times

$$\sum [(R_j - \bar{R})^2]$$

where R_j is the sum of ranks for treatment j and $\bar{R}$ is the average of the R_j's. See standard nonparametric texts (such as [3]) for details on computing S adjusted for ties.

The test statistic has an approximately χ^2 distribution, with associated degrees of freedom of (number of treatments – one). If there are ties within one or more blocks, MINITAB uses the average rank and prints a test statistic that has been corrected for ties. If there are many ties, the uncorrected test statistic is conservative; the corrected version is usually closer, but may be either conservative or liberal. For details of the method used, see [3].

Calculating treatment effects, adjusted block medians, and the grand median

To calculate adjusted block medians, adjust each observation by subtracting the appropriate treatment effect from the observation. Adjusted block medians are simply the medians of these adjusted data, calculated within each block. The grand median is the median of the adjusted block medians. The estimated median for each treatment level is the treatment effect plus the grand median.

To calculate the treatment effects, the block medians, and the grand median, use the following data:

Treatment	Block 1	2	3	4
1	0.15	0.26	0.23	0.99
2	0.55	0.26	–0.22	0.99
3	0.55	0.66	0.77	0.99

To calculate treatment effects (Doksum method, [3] pages 158–161), first find the median difference between pairs of treatment. The pairwise differences for treatment 1 minus treatment 2 are $0.15 - 0.55 = -0.4$, $0.26 - 0.26 = 0$, $0.23 - (-0.22) = 0.45$, and $0.99 - 0.99 = 0$. The median of the differences is 0. Doing this for the other two pairs gives –0.4 for treatment 1 minus treatment 3, and –0.2 for treatment 2 minus treatment 3.

The effect for each treatment is the average of the median differences of that treatment with all other treatments (including itself). For the data in this example, effect(2) = [median (2 − 1) + median (2 − 2) + median (2 − 3)]/3 = (0.00 + 0.00 − 0.20)/3 = −0.0667. Similarly, effect(1) = −0.1333 and effect(3) = 0.20.

▷ Example of a Friedman test

A randomized block experiment was conducted to evaluate the effect of a drug treatment on enzyme activity. Three different drug therapies were given to four animals, with each animal belonging to a different litter. The Friedman test provides the desired test of H_0: all treatment effects are zero vs. H_1: not all treatment effects are zero.

1 Open the worksheet EXH_STAT.MTW.

2 Choose **Stat ➤ Nonparametrics ➤ Friedman**.

3 In **Response**, enter *EnzymeActivity*.

4 In **Treatment**, enter *Therapy*. In **Blocks**, enter *Litter*. Click **OK**.

Session window output

```
Friedman Test: EnzymeActivity versus Therapy, Litter

Friedman test for EnzymeAc by Therapy blocked by Litter

S = 2.38  DF = 2  P = 0.305
S = 3.80  DF = 2  P = 0.150 (adjusted for ties)

                     Est      Sum of
Therapy      N     Median     Ranks
1            4     0.2450      6.5
2            4     0.3117      7.0
3            4     0.5783     10.5

Grand median  =    0.3783
```

Interpreting the results

The test statistic, S, has a p-value of 0.305, unadjusted for ties, and 0.150, adjusted for ties. For α levels 0.05 or 0.10, there is insufficient evidence to reject H_0 because the p-value is greater than the α level. You therefore conclude that the data do not support the hypothesis that any of the treatment effects are different from zero.

The sum of ranks value is the sum of the treatment ranks, when ranked within each block. These values can serve as a measure of the relative size of treatment medians and are used in calculating the test statistic.

Runs Test

Use Runs Test to see if the data order is random. This is a nonparametric test because no assumption is made about population distribution parameters. Use this test when you want to determine if the order of responses above or below a specified value is random. A run is a set of consecutive observations either all less than or all greater than some value.

Stat ➤ Quality Tools ➤ Run Chart generates a run chart and performs other tests for randomness. See *Run Chart* on page 10-2 for more information.

Data

You need at least one column of numeric data. If you have more than one column of data, MINITAB performs a runs test separately for each column.

You may have missing data at the beginning or end of a data column, but not in the middle. You must omit missing data from the middle of a worksheet column before using this procedure.

▶ To do a runs test

1 Choose **Stat ➤ Nonparametrics ➤ Runs Test**.

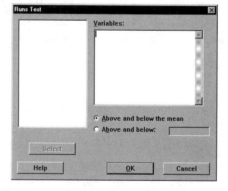

2 In **Variables**, enter the column(s) containing the data you want to test for randomness.

3 If you like, use the option listed below, and click **OK**.

Options

You can specify a value other than the mean as the value for defining the runs.

▷ Example of a runs test

Suppose an interviewer selects 30 people at random and asks them each a question for which there are four possible answers. Their responses are coded 0, 1, 2, and 3. You wish to perform a runs test in order to check the randomness of answers. Answers that are not in random order may indicate that there is a gradual bias in the phrasing of the questions or that subjects are not being selected at random.

1 Open the worksheet EXH_STAT.MTW.

2 Choose **Stat ➤ Nonparametrics ➤ Runs Test**.

3 In **Variables**, enter *Response*. Click **OK**.

Session window output

Runs Test: Response

Response

```
    K =      1.2333


    The observed number of runs =    8
    The expected number of runs =   14.9333
    11 Observations above K     19 below
              The test is significant at   0.0054
```

Interpreting the results

Since the option of a value other than the mean was not specified as the comparison criterion, the mean, 1.233, was used. There are 8 observed runs:

(0, 0, 1, 0, 1, 1, 1, 1) (2, 3, 3, 2) (0, 0, 0) (2) (1, 1, 1, 1) (2, 3, 3) (0, 0, 1, 0) (2, 2, 3)

The first run consists of the eight consecutive observations of 0 or 1; the second run is the set of the next four observations of 2 or 3, and so on. Is 8 an unusual number of runs? To determine this, Runs Test first calculates the number of observations above 1.233, or 11, and the number below 1.233, or 19. Then Runs Test calculates the expected number of runs, conditioned on these values. In the example, the expected number of runs is 14.9333. The probability of getting as extreme a number of runs or more extreme is found using a normal approximation. The approximation is quite good if at least 10 observations are greater than the comparison criterion and at least 10 are less than or equal to the comparison criterion. The probability is the attained significance level or p-value, which in this case is 0.0055. This p-value indicates that for α levels above 0.0055, there is sufficient evidence to conclude that the data are not in random order.

If there are too few observations greater than the comparison criterion or too few observations less than or equal to the comparison criterion for the normal approximation to be valid, a message is printed. Exact tables are widely available in texts on nonparametric tests if you wish to calculate the exact p-value. See [1] for example.

Pairwise Averages

Pairwise Averages calculates and stores the average for each possible pair of values in a single column, including each value with itself. Pairwise averages are also called Walsh averages. Pairwise averages are used, for example, for the Wilcoxon method.

Data

You must have one numeric data column. If you have missing data, the pairwise averages involving the missing values are set to missing.

▶ To calculate pairwise averages

1   Choose Stat ➤ Nonparametrics ➤ Pairwise Averages.

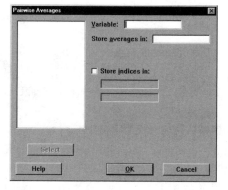

2   In **Variable**, enter the column for which you want to obtain averages.

3   In **Store averages in**, enter a column name or number to store the pairwise (Walsh) averages. For n data values, MINITAB stores n (n + 1) / 2 pairwise averages.

4   If you like, use the option listed below, then click **OK**.

Options

You can store the indices for each average (in two columns). The Walsh average, $(x_i + x_j) / 2$, has indices i and j. The value of i is put in the first storage column and the value of j is put in the second storage column.

Pairwise Differences

Pairwise Differences calculates and stores the differences between all possible pairs of values formed from two columns. These differences are useful for nonparametric tests and confidence intervals. For example, the point estimate given by Mann-Whitney (page 5-11) can be computed as the median of the differences.

Data

You must have two numeric data columns. If you have missing data, the pairwise differences involving the missing values are set to missing.

▶ To calculate pairwise differences

1 Choose **Stat ➤ Nonparametrics ➤ Pairwise Differences**.

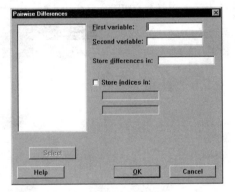

2 In **First variable**, enter a column. The column you enter in **Second variable** will be subtracted from this column.

3 In **Second variable**, enter a column. This column will be subtracted from the column you entered in **First variable**.

4 In **Store differences in**, enter a column name or number to store the differences. For n data values, MINITAB stores $n (n + 1) / 2$ pairwise differences.

5 If you like, use the option listed below, then click **OK**.

Options

You can store the indices for each difference (in two columns). The difference, $(x_i - y_j)$, has indices i and j. The value of i is put in the first storage column and the value of j is put in the second storage column.

Pairwise Slopes

Pairwise Slopes calculates and stores the slope between all possible pairs of points, where a row in y–x columns defines a point in the plane. This procedure is useful for finding robust estimates of the slope of a line through the data.

Data

You must have two numeric data columns, one that contains the response variable (y) and one that contains the predictor variable (x). If you have missing data or the slope is not defined (e.g. slope of a line parallel to the y axis), the slope will be stored as missing.

▶ **To calculate pairwise slopes**

1 Choose **Stat ➤ Nonparametrics ➤ Pairwise Slopes**.

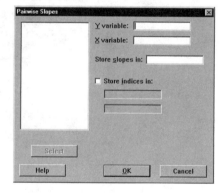

2 In **Y variable**, enter the column containing the response data.

3 In **X variable**, enter the column containing the predictor data.

4 In **Store slopes in**, enter a column name or number to store the pairwise slopes. For n pairs, MINITAB stores (n–1) / 2 slopes.

5 If you like, use the option listed below, then click **OK**.

Options

You can store the indices for each slope in two columns. The slope, $(x_i - y_j)$, has indices i and j. The value of i is put in the first storage column and the value of j is put in the second storage column.

References

[1] Gibbons, J.D. (1976). *Nonparametric Methods for Quantitative Analysis*. Holt, Rhinehart, and Winston.

[2] T.P. Hettmansperger and S.J. Sheather (1986). "Confidence Intervals Based on Interpolated Order Statistics," *Statistics and Probability Letters*, 4, pp.75–79.

[3] M. Hollander and D.A. Wolfe (1973). *Nonparametric Statistical Methods*, John Wiley & Sons.

[4] D.B. Johnson and T. Mizoguchi (1978). "Selecting the Kth Element in X + Y and X1 + X2 + … + Xm," *SIAM Journal of Computing* 7, pp.147–153.

[5] E.L. Lehmann (1975). *Nonparametrics: Statistical Methods Based on Ranks*, Holden–Day.

[6] J.W. McKean and T.A. Ryan, Jr. (1977). "An Algorithm for Obtaining Confidence Intervals and Point Estimates Based on Ranks in the Two Sample Location Problem," *Transactions on Mathematical Software*, pp.183–185.

[7] G. Noether (1971). *Statistics—A Non–Parametric Approach*, Houghton-Mifflin.

6

Tables

Tables Overview

Table procedures summarize data into table form or perform a further analysis of a tabled summary. Your data needs to be arranged in the worksheet in certain way in order to do these procedures. The different possibilities of arranging your data can be seen in *Arrangement of Input Data* on page 6-3. The Tables procedures are described below.

- **Cross Tabulation** displays one-way, two-way, and multi-way tables containing counts, percents, and summary statistics, such as means, standard deviations, and maximums, for associated variables. To use this procedure, your data must be in raw form, or they can be in frequency form if summary statistics for associated variables are not desired.

- **Tally Unique Values** displays counts, cumulative counts, percents, and cumulative percents for each unique value of a variable when input data are in raw form.

Chi-Square tests

- **Chi-Square Test for Association** tests for non-independence in a two-way classification. Use this procedure to test if the probabilities of items or subjects being classified for one variable depend upon the classification of the other variable. Your data can be in raw, collapsed, or contingency table form.

- **Chi-Square Test for Goodness-of-Fit** tests if the sample outcomes result from a known discrete probability model.

Correspondence analysis

- **Simple Correspondence Analysis** helps you to explore relationships in a two-way classification. Because three-way and four-way tables can be collapsed into two-way tables, simple correspondence analysis can also operate on them. Simple correspondence analysis decomposes a contingency table in a manner similar to how principal components analysis decomposes multivariate continuous data. Simple correspondence analysis performs an eigen analysis of the data, and variability is broken down into underlying dimensions and associated with rows and/or columns.

- **Multiple Correspondence Analysis** extends simple correspondence analysis to the case of three or more categorical variables. Multiple correspondence analysis performs a simple correspondence analysis on a matrix of indicator variables where each column of the matrix corresponds to a level of a categorical variable. Rather than having the two-way table of simple correspondence analysis, here the multi-way table is collapsed into one dimension.

Arrangement of Input Data

Data used for input to the Tables procedures can be arranged in four different ways in your worksheet: as raw or categorical data, as frequency or collapsed data, as a contingency table, or as indicator variables. These four ways to arrange your data are illustrated below in the following example.

Suppose you are interested in the connection between gender and political party preference. You query 100 people about their political affiliation and record group codes for gender (1 = male, 2 = female) and political party (1 = Democrat, 2 = Republican, 3 = Other).

Raw data	Frequency data	Contingency table	Indicator variables
One row for each observation:	Each row represents a unique combination of group codes:	Each cell contains counts:	One row for each observation:
C1 = gender	C1 = gender	C1 = males	C1 = 1 if male
C2 = politics	C2 = politics	C2 = females	= 0 if female
	C3 = the number of obser-vations at that level	Rows 1-3 represent the three levels for politics, respectively	C2 = 1 if female
			= 0 if male
			C3 = 1 if Democrat
			= 0 otherwise
			C4 = 1 if Republican
			= 0 otherwise
			C5 = 1 if Other
			= 0 otherwise

C1	C2		C1	C2	C3		C1	C2		C1	C2	C3	C4	C5
1	1		1	1	17		17	18		1	0	1	0	0
2	1		1	2	10		10	19		0	1	1	0	0
2	3		1	3	19		19	17		0	1	0	0	1
1	2		2	1	18					1	0	0	1	0
.	.		2	2	19					.	.			
.	.		2	3	17					.	.			
.	.													

To obtain frequency data from raw data, see *Store Descriptive Statistics* on page 1-9. To create a contingency table from raw data or frequency data, see *Cross Tabulation* on page 6-3, and copy and paste the table output into your worksheet. To create indicator variables from raw data, use **Calc ➤ Make Indicator Variables**.

Cross Tabulation

Cross tabulation prints one-way, two-way, and multi-way tables containing counts, percents, and summary statistics, such as means, standard deviations, and maximums, for associated variables. To use this procedure, your data must be in raw form, or they can be in collapsed form if summary statistics for associated variables are not desired. See the *Chi-Square Test for Association* on page 6-14 for performing a chi-square test for association.

Data

You can arrange your data in the worksheet in raw or frequency form. See *Arrangement of Input Data* on page 6-3. The data must be in raw form to display summary statistics for associated variables.

If your data are in *raw form*, you can have between two and ten classification columns with each row representing one observation. The classification or category data may be numeric, text, or date/time. If you wish to change the order in which text categories are processed from their default alphabetized order, you can define your own order. See *Ordering Text Categories* in the *Manipulating Data* chapter in MINITAB *User's Guide 1*. Associated variables must be numeric and can contain any numeric values. By default, Cross Tabulation omits rows with missing classification values. Optionally, you can include these rows.

If your data are in *frequency or collapsed form*, you can have between two and ten columns containing your categories and another column containing the frequencies for the category combinations. The category data may be numeric, text, or date/time, and may contain any values. The frequency data must be integers. By default, Cross Tabulation omits rows with frequency data. Optionally, you can include these rows.

If you have two-category columns, a two-way table will be tabulated. Otherwise you can obtain multiple two-way tables (the default) or multi-way tables.

▶ To cross tabulate data

1   Choose **Stat ➤ Tables ➤ Cross Tabulation**.

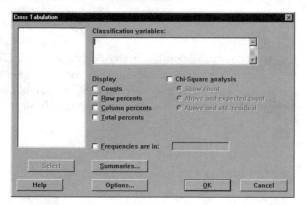

2 Do one of the following:

- To enter raw data, enter the columns containing the raw data in **Classification variables.**

- To enter frequency or collapsed data:
  - in **Classification variables**, enter the columns containing the category data
  - check **Frequencies are in** and enter the column containing the frequencies

3 If you like, use one or more of the options listed below, then click **OK**.

Options

Cross Tabulation dialog box

- display the percent of each cell within its row, its column, or the total two-way table. If you do not choose a percent option, MINITAB displays counts by default. If you choose a percent option and want counts, you must check **Counts**.

- perform a chi-square test for association for each two-way table. See *Chi-Square Test for Association* on page 6-14.

Summaries subdialog box

- calculate and display the mean, median, minimum, maximum, sum, and standard deviation for associated variables

- display the data, the number of nonmissing data, the number of missing data, the proportion of observations equal to a specified value, and the proportion of observations between specified values for associated variables

Options subdialog box

- adjust the table layout. See *Changing the table layout* below.

- use missing values as a level accepted by MINITAB. However, MINITAB does not include missing levels in calculations of marginal statistics, percents, or the chi-square test for association.

- specify the values to display marginal statistics for. By default, marginal statistics are printed for all rows and columns. Marginal statistics are summaries for rows and columns of a table.

Changing the table layout

You can adjust the table layout by assigning variables to rows and columns. You may want to organize variables to emphasize a relationship, or create a more compact display for a report. See *Example of changing the table layout* on page 6-10.

To perform a chi-square test for association, you must use the default layout.

▶ **To assign row and column variables**

1 In the Cross Tabulation dialog box, click **Options**.

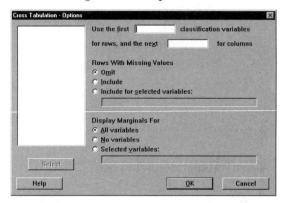

2 To assign the row variables, enter a number in **Use the first ___ classification variables for rows**. MINITAB will assign the specified number of variables to rows using the order in which they were entered in the main dialog box.

3 To assign the column variables, enter a 0, 1, or 2 in **and the next ___ for columns**. MINITAB will assign the specified number of variables to columns using the order in which they were entered in the main dialog box.

MINITAB uses category variables that are not assigned to define the combination of categories at a higher level. For default two-way and higher tables, the first category variable is the row variable and the second is the column variable.

Some simple tables

Tips on doing the examples

Because the default alphabetized order of text levels is A lot, Moderate, and Slight for the variable Activity used in the examples, we will use value ordering to set the more natural order of Slight, Moderate, and A lot. To do this:

1 Open the worksheet EXH_TABL.MTW.

2 Click on any cell in the variable *Activity* of the worksheet.

3 Choose **Editor ▶ Column ▶ Value Order**.

4 Choose **User-specified order**.

5 In the right box change the order A *lot, Moderate, Slight* to be *Slight, Moderate, A lot*. You can use the right-mouse button to cut and paste. Click **OK**.

You will not see the order of levels changed in the worksheet but commands will process these levels in the new order.

Tip | Between examples, set the dialog box settings to their default state by pressing (F3). Resetting the dialog boxes to their default settings eliminates unwanted dialog box changes made previously. Value ordering will not be affected by resetting dialogs to their default state.

▷ Example of cross tabulation

The following example illustrates output for a two-way table with summary statistics for associated variables.

1 Open the worksheet EXH_TABL.MTW. Set the value order for the variable *Activity* as shown in *Tips on doing the examples* on page 6-6, if you have not already done so.

2 Choose **Stat ➤ Tables ➤ Cross Tabulation**.

3 In **Classification variables**, enter *Gender Activity*. Under **Display**, check **Counts**.

4 Click **Summaries**. In **Associated variables**, enter *Height Weight*. Under **Display**, check **Means**. Click **OK** in each dialog box.

Session window output

Tabulated Statistics: Gender, Activity

```
Rows: Gender     Columns: Activity

           Slight Moderate   A lot     All

Female        4       26        5      35
          65.000   65.615   64.600   65.400
          123.00   124.46   121.00   123.80

Male          5       35       16      56
          72.400   70.429   71.125   70.804
          170.00   158.09   155.50   158.41

All           9       61       21      91
          69.111   68.377   69.571   68.725
          149.11   143.75   147.29   145.10

Cell Contents --
                Count
           Height:Mean
           Weight:Mean
```

Interpreting the results

The first classification variable, Gender, is the row variable, and the second classification variable, Activity, is the column variable. Each cell contains the requested statistics: the count, the sample mean for Height, and the sample mean for the Weight for each Gender–Activity combination. For example, the upper left cell in the table, women with a slight activity level, contains four observations. These four women have a mean height of 65 inches and a mean weight of 123 pounds.

The column headed All contains the row margins. For example, the first number in this column, 35, is the total number of observations in row one, and the second number, 65.400, is the mean height for these 35 women. The row headed All contains the corresponding column margins.

➤ Example of using cross tabulation to display data

This example shows how to display data values for a variable associated with the classification variables.

1 Open the worksheet EXH_TABL.MTW.

2 Choose **Stat ➤ Tables ➤ Cross Tabulation**.

3 In **Classification variables**, enter *Gender Smokes*.

4 Click **Summaries**. In **Associated variables**, enter *Pulse*.

5 Under **Display**, check **Data**. Click **OK** in each dialog box.

Session window output

Tabulated Statistics: Gender, Smokes

Rows: Gender   Columns: Smokes

```
                 No       Yes

Female  96.000    78.000
        62.000   100.000
        82.000    88.000
        68.000    62.000
        96.000    94.000
        78.000    88.000
        80.000    76.000
        84.000    90.000
        61.000
        64.000
        60.000
        72.000
        58.000
        66.000
        84.000
        62.000
        66.000
        80.000
        78.000
        68.000
        72.000
        82.000
        87.000
        78.000
```

```
                        68.000
                        86.000
                        76.000

                          No       Yes

          Male          64.000    62.000
                        58.000    66.000
                        64.000    90.000
                        74.000    92.000
                        84.000    66.000
                        68.000    70.000
                        62.000    68.000
                        76.000    70.000
                        80.000    72.000
                        68.000    68.000
                        60.000    54.000
                        62.000    72.000
                        72.000    82.000
                        70.000    70.000
                        74.000    62.000
                        66.000    90.000
                        62.000    70.000
                        60.000    92.000
                        62.000    60.000
                        76.000
                        74.000
                        74.000
                        68.000
                        68.000
                        64.000
                        58.000
                        54.000
                        76.000
                        88.000
                        70.000
                        78.000
                        90.000
                        72.000
                        68.000
                        84.000
                        74.000
                        68.000

          Cell Contents --
                    Pulse:Data
```

Interpreting the results

The numbers in the table are the Pulse data corresponding to the levels of Gender and Smokes.

▷ Example of cross tabulation with three classification variables

This example illustrates a three-way table.

1 Open the worksheet EXH_TABL.MTW. Set the value order for the variable *Activity* as shown in *Some simple tables* on page 6-6, if you have not already done so.

2 Choose **Stat ➤ Tables ➤ Cross Tabulation**.

3 In **Classification variables**, enter *Gender Activity Smokes*. Click **OK**.

Session window output

Tabulated Statistics: Gender, Activity, Smokes

```
Control: Smokes = No
  Rows: Gender      Columns: Activity

            Slight Moderate   A lot     All

  Female        3       20       4      27
  Male          3       22      12      37
  All           6       42      16      64

Control: Smokes = Yes
  Rows: Gender      Columns: Activity

            Slight Moderate   A lot     All

  Female        1        6       1       8
  Male          2       13       4      19
  All           3       19       5      27

  Cell Contents --
            Count
```

Interpreting the results

MINITAB displays three-way tables as separate two-way tables for each level of the third variable. By default, the first classification variable, Gender, is used for the rows, the second variable, Activity, for the columns, and the remaining variable, Smokes, as a control. You can change the table layout, as shown in the next example.

Since no statistics were requested, by default the cells contain only the counts.

▷ Example of changing the table layout

This example uses the same data in a three-way table as in the example above, but the table layout is different.

1 Open the worksheet EXH_TABL.MTW. Set the value order for the variable *Activity* as shown in *Some simple tables* on page 6-6, if you have not already done so.

2 Choose **Stat ➤ Tables ➤ Cross Tabulation**.

3 In **Classification variables**, enter *Gender Activity Smokes*.

4 Click **Options**. In **Use the first ___ classification variables for rows** enter *1*. In **and the next ___ for columns**, enter *2*. Click **OK** in each dialog box.

Tabulated Statistics: Gender, Activity, Smokes

```
Rows: Gender     Columns: Activity / Smokes

                 Slight              Moderate             A lot
             --------------       --------------       --------------
                No      Yes          No      Yes          No      Yes

  Female        3        1          20        6           4        1
  Male          3        2          22       13          12        4
  All           6        3          42       19          16        5

                 All
              -----
                 All

  Female        35
  Male          56
  All           91

   Cell Contents --
                  Count
```

Interpreting the results

MINITAB displays three-way tables as separate two-way tables for each level of the third variable. The row variable is Smokes, the uppermost column variable is Gender, and innermost column variable is Activity. It may be easier to compare across tables using a layout such as this rather than the default. The row margins with this layout are now the sums of Smokes.

▷ Example of a summary of associated data using a layout

This example displays a table of descriptive statistics for two measurement variables classified in two ways.

1 Open the worksheet EXH_TABL.MTW. Set the value order for the variable *Activity* as shown in *Some simple tables* on page 6-6, if you have not already done so.

2 Choose **Stat ➤ Tables ➤ Cross Tabulation**.

3 In **Classification variables**, enter *Gender Activity*.

4 Click **Options**. In **Use the first ___ classification variables for rows** enter *2*. In **and the next ___ for columns**, enter *0*. Click **OK**.

5 Click **Summaries**. In **Associated Variables**, enter *Height Weight*. Under **Display**, check **Means**, **Standard deviations**, and **N nonmissing**. Click **OK** in each dialog box.

Session window output

Tabulated Statistics: Gender, Activity

Rows: Gender / Activity

		Height Mean	Weight Mean	Height StDev	Weight StDev	Height N	Weight N
Female							
	Slight	65.000	123.00	2.160	7.70	4	4
	Moderate	65.615	124.46	2.735	12.78	26	26
	A lot	64.600	121.00	2.074	21.02	5	5
Male							
	Slight	72.400	170.00	2.510	19.69	5	5
	Moderate	70.429	158.09	2.521	20.58	35	35
	A lot	71.125	155.50	2.649	13.21	16	16
All							
	All	68.725	145.10	3.679	23.87	91	91

Interpreting the results

This example shows a table of descriptive statistics that might be useful in a report. MINITAB displays the mean, standard deviation, and sample size of Height and Weight, classified by Gender, the outermost variable, and by Activity. The column margins are the statistics for all the data.

Tally Unique Values

Use Tally to display counts, cumulative counts, percents, and cumulative percents for each unique value of a variable or variables.

Data

Your data must be arranged in your worksheet as columns of raw data. See *Arrangement of Input Data* on page 6-3. Data may be numeric, text, or date/time. If you wish to change the order in which text data are processed from their default alphabetized order, you can define your own order. See *Ordering Text Categories* in the *Manipulating Data* chapter in MINITAB *User's Guide 1*. Column lengths do not need to be equal.

▶ **To tally**

1 Choose Stat ➤ Tables ➤ Tally.

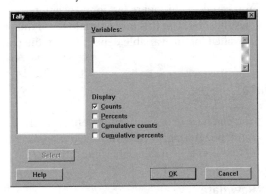

2 In **Variables**, enter the column(s) for tallying.

3 If you like, use the option listed below, then click **OK**.

Options

You can display the counts, percents, cumulative counts, and cumulative percents of each nonmissing value.

▶ Example of tally with all four statistics

This example generates frequency counts, cumulative counts, percents, and cumulative percents.

1 Open the worksheet EXH_TABL.MTW. Set the value order for the variable *Activity* as shown in *Some simple tables* on page 6-6, if you have not already done so.

2 Choose Stat ➤ Tables ➤ Tally.

3 In **Variables**, enter *Activity*. Under **Display**, check **Counts**, **Percents**, **Cumulative counts**, and **Cumulative percents**. Click **OK**.

Session window output

Tally for Discrete Variables: Activity

Activity	Count	CumCnt	Percent	CumPct
Slight	9	9	9.89	9.89
Moderate	61	70	67.03	76.92
A lot	21	91	23.08	100.00
N=	91			

Interpreting the results

The count, cumulative count, percent of the total count, and cumulative percent are given for the variable Activity.

Chi-Square Test for Association

You can do a chi-square test for association (non-independence) in a two-way classification. Use this procedure to test if the probabilities of items or subjects being classified for one variable depends upon the classification of the other variable.

Data

You can have data arranged in your worksheet in raw, frequency, or contingency table form. See *Arrangement of Input Data* on page 6-3. The form of the worksheet data determines acceptable data values.

Raw data

If your data are in *raw form*, you can have between two and ten columns with each row representing one observation. The data represent categories and can be numeric, text, or date/time, and can contain any values. If you wish to change the order in which text categories are processed from their default alphabetized order, you can define your own order. See *Ordering Text Categories* in the *Manipulating Data* chapter in MINITAB *User's Guide 1*. When you enter:

- two columns, MINITAB tabulates a two-way table

- more than two columns, MINITAB tabulates multiple two-way tables and performs a chi-square test for association on each table

  MINITAB automatically omits rows with missing data.

Frequency data

If your data are in *frequency or collapsed form*, you can have between two and ten columns containing your categories with another column containing the frequencies for the category combinations. The category data may be numeric, text, or date/time, and may contain any values. If you wish to change the order in which text categories are processed from their default alphabetized order, you can define your own order. See *Ordering Text Categories* in the *Manipulating Data* chapter in MINITAB *User's Guide 1*. The frequency data must be integer. When you enter:

- two category columns, MINITAB tabulates a two-way table

- more than two category columns, MINITAB tabulates multiple two-way tables and performs a chi-square test for association on each table

MINITAB automatically omits rows with missing category or frequency data.

Contingency table data

If your data are in *contingency table form*, consider the table to have dimension r × c, where r is the number of row categories and c is the number of the column categories. You must have c columns, with a maximum of seven, each with r rows, containing integer frequencies of your category combination. You must delete rows with missing data from the worksheet before using this procedure.

More | To calculate a $\chi 2$ statistic for a contingency table with more than seven columns allowed with Cross Tabulation, you can use Simple Correspondence Analysis (page 6-21).

▶ **To perform a χ^2 test with raw data or frequency data**

1 Choose **Stat ➤ Tables ➤ Cross Tabulation**.

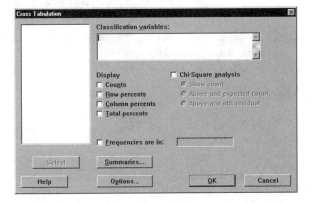

2 To input your data, do one of the following:

■ For raw data, enter the columns containing the raw data in **Classification variables**

■ For frequency or collapsed data,
   – enter the columns containing the category data in **Classification variables**
   – check **Frequencies are in** and enter the column containing the frequencies

3 Check **Chi-Square analysis**.

4 If you like, use one or more of the options listed below, then click **OK**.

Options

■ display the expected count for each cell. By default, MINITAB displays the expected count with contingency table data.

■ display the standardized residual, which is the contribution to χ^2 from each cell. By default, MINITAB displays the standardized residual with contingency table data.

▶ **To perform a χ^2 test for association with contingency table data**

1 Choose **Stat ▶ Tables ▶ Chi-Square Test**.

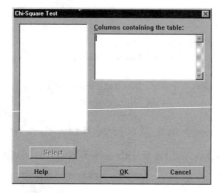

2 In **Columns containing the table**, enter the columns containing the contingency table data. Click **OK**.

Method

Under the null hypothesis of no association, expected frequencies for each (i, j) cell of the r × c table are:

$$E_{ij} = \frac{(\text{total of row i}) \times (\text{total of column j})}{\text{total number of observations}}$$

The total χ^2 is calculated by

$$\sum_i \sum_i \frac{(O_{ij} - E_{ij})^2}{E_{ij}}$$

where O_{ij} = observed frequency in cell (i, j) and E_{ij} = expected frequency for cell (i, j). The degrees of freedom associated with a contingency table possessing r rows and c columns equals $(r - 1)(c - 1)$.

The contribution to the χ^2 statistic from each cell is:

$$\text{Standardized residual} = \frac{\text{observed count} - \text{expected}}{\sqrt{\text{expected count}}}$$

Use the χ^2 contribution from each cell to see how different cells contribute to a judgement about the degree of association.

Exercise caution when there are small expected counts. MINITAB will give a count of the number of cells that have expected frequencies less than five. Some statisticians hesitate to use the chi-square test if more than 20% of the cells have expected frequencies below five, especially if the p-value is small and these cells give a large contribution to the total χ^2 value.

If, in addition, some cells have expected frequencies less than one, the total χ^2 is not printed, since most statisticians would not use the chi-square test in this case. If some cells have small expected frequencies, combining or omitting row and/or column categories can often help.

Yates' correction for 2×2 tables is not used.

▷ Example of χ^2 test with raw data

This example illustrates a chi-square test for association using raw data.

1 Open the worksheet EXH_TABL.MTW. Set the value order for the variable *Activity* as shown in *Some simple tables* on page 6-6 if you have not already done so.

2 Choose **Stat ➤ Tables ➤ Cross Tabulation**.

3 In **Classification variables**, enter *Gender Activity*. Check **Chi-Square analysis** and then choose **Above and std. residual**. Click **OK**.

Session window output

Tabulated Statistics: Gender, Activity

Rows: Gender   Columns: Activity

	Slight	Moderate	A lot	All
Female	4	26	5	35
	3.46	23.46	8.08	35.00
	0.29	0.52	-1.08	--
Male	5	35	16	56
	5.54	37.54	12.92	56.00
	-0.23	-0.41	0.86	--
All	9	61	21	91
	9.00	61.00	21.00	91.00
	--	--	--	--

Chi-Square = 2.487, DF = 2, P-Value = 0.288
1 cells with expected counts less than 5.0

Cell Contents --
                  Count
                  Exp Freq
                  St Resid

Interpreting the results

The cells in the table contain the counts, the expected frequencies, and the standardized residual or contribution to the χ^2 statistic. The p-value of the test, 0.288, indicates that there is no evidence for association between these variables, Gender and Activity. One of six cells showed an expected frequency of less than five, but this number is slightly less than the 20% threshold that indicates you may want to interpret the results with caution.

▷ Example of a χ^2 test with contingency data

Suppose you are interested in the connection between gender and political party preference. You query 100 people about their political affiliation and record the number of males (row 1) and females (row 2) for each political party. The worksheet data appears as follows:

C1	C2	C3
Democrat	Republican	Other
28	18	4
22	27	1

1 Open the worksheet EXH_TABL.MTW.

2 Choose **Stat ▸ Tables ▸ Chi-Square Test**.

3 In **Columns containing the table**, enter *Democrat – Other*. Click **OK**.

Session window output

Chi-Square Test: Democrat, Republican, Other

Expected counts are printed below observed counts

	Democrat	Republic	Other	Total
1	28	18	4	50
	25.00	22.50	2.50	
2	22	27	1	50
	25.00	22.50	2.50	
Total	50	45	5	100

```
Chi-Sq = 0.360 + 0.900 + 0.900 +
         0.360 + 0.900 + 0.900 = 4.320
DF = 2, P-Value = 0.115
2 cells with expected counts less than 5.0
```

Interpreting the results

The p-value of 0.116 indicates that there is not strong evidence that gender and political party choice are related. Note that there are two of six cells with expected counts less than five. Therefore, even if you had a significant p-value for these data, you might interpret the results with skepticism. To be more confident of the results, you may want to repeat the test omitting the Other category.

Chi-Square Goodness-of-Fit Test

You can do a chi-square goodness-of-fit test for testing if sample outcomes result from a given probability model. There are several examples that illustrate how to compute the expected number of outcomes, the chi-square test statistic, and its p-value. You can use this same procedure for other cases where the number of outcomes is discrete and you can compute the expected number of outcomes.

Calculating expected number of outcomes

The first step in performing a chi-square goodness-of-fit test is to calculate the expected number of outcomes. To calculate the expected number of outcomes, multiply the probability of each outcome by the sample size. Consider the following common probability models.

The *equal probability of outcomes* case occurs if the k attributes are equally likely (probability = 1 / k). Then the expected number of outcomes for each category is n / k. For example, you might assume an equal probability of outcomes model if you wish to test if there are differences in consumer preferences.

The *discrete distribution* occurs if there are k possible categories with unequal probabilities, p1, p2, ..., pk. Then the expected numbers of outcomes are np1, np2, ..., npk.

The *binomial distribution* occurs if there are two possible outcomes for any subject or item, say "success" and "failure," with a constant probability of success (p) and with repeated draws or encounters of subjects, with independent results in each encounter. For example, the number of females in a family of three children, or the number of defectives in a batch of ten widgets, can follow a binomial probability model. To calculate the expected number of outcomes in n such experiments, multiply the binomial probabilities by n.

The *Poisson distribution* is often used as a probability model for events that occur randomly in time, such as arrival times.

You can use MINITAB to compute the expected number of outcomes for the binomial, discrete, integer (equal probability of outcomes case), and Poisson distributions.

Calculating the expected number of outcomes for a binomial case

The following example illustrates how to calculate the expected number of outcomes for a binomial case.

Suppose you count how many times heads appears in five tosses of a coin, and you repeat the set of five tosses 1,000 times. There can be from zero to five heads in any set of tosses. If you wish to test whether the coin toss is fair (gives heads half the time), you need to calculate the expected number of outcomes.

1   Enter the possible outcomes *0, 1, 2, 3, 4,* and *5* in a worksheet column. Name the
    column by typing *Outcomes* in the name cell. This column is already present in the
    worksheet EXH_TABL.MTW

2   Choose **Calc ➤ Probability Distributions ➤ Binomial**.

3   In **Number of trials**, enter 5. In **Probability of success**, enter .5.

4   Choose **Input column**, then enter *Outcomes*. In **Optional storage**, enter *Probs* to
    name the storage column. Click **OK**.

5   Choose **Calc ➤ Calculator**.

6   In **Store result in variable**, enter *Expected* to name the storage column.

7   In **Expression**, enter *Probs ∗ 1000*. Click **OK**.

Computing a test statistic and p-value

After you calculate the expected number of outcomes, you can calculate the χ^2 statistic
and associated p-value. This example illustrates the binomial case, but you would
follow the same procedure for the other discrete probability models.

Suppose you performed the binomial experiment described above: five tosses of a coin
1000 times. You observed the following outcomes:

Number of Heads	0	1	2	3	4	5
Count	39	166	298	305	144	48

▶ **To calculate the χ^2 statistic and p-value**

1   Enter the observed values in a worksheet column. Name the column by typing
    Observed in the name cell. This column is already present in the worksheet
    EXH_TABL.MTW

2   Choose **Calc ➤ Calculator**.

3   In **Store result in variable**, enter *Chisquare* to name the storage column.

4   In **Expression**, enter *SUM((Observed – Expected)∗∗2 / Expected)*. Click **OK**.

5   Choose **Calc ➤ Probability Distributions ➤ Chi-Square**.

6   Choose **Cumulative probability**, and in **Degrees of freedom**, enter 5. The degrees
    of freedom value is equal to the number of outcomes minus one (6 – 1 = 5).

7   Choose **Input column**, and enter *Chisquare*. In **Optional storage**, enter *CumProb*
    to name the storage column. Click **OK**.

8   Choose **Calc ➤ Calculator**.

9   In **Store result in variable**, enter *Pvalue* to name the storage column.

10 In **Expression**, enter *1 – CumProb*. Click **OK**.

View the calculated p-value in the Data window, or use **Manip ➤ Display Data** and display the p-value in the Session window. The p-value of 0.0205 associated with the χ^2 statistic of 13.3216 indicates the binomial probability model with p = 0.5 is probably not a good model for this experiment. That is, the observed number of outcomes are not consistent with expected number of outcomes using a binomial model.

Simple Correspondence Analysis

Simple correspondence analysis helps you to explore relationships in a two-way classification. Simple correspondence analysis can also operate on three-way and four-way tables because they can be collapsed into two-way tables. This procedure decomposes a contingency table in a manner similar to how principal components analysis decomposes multivariate continuous data. An eigen analysis of the data is performed, and the variability is broken down into underlying dimensions and associated with rows and/or columns.

Data

Worksheet data may be arranged in two ways: raw or contingency table form. See *Arrangement of Input Data* on page 6-3. Worksheet data arrangement determines acceptable data values.

- If your data are in *raw form*, you can have two, three, or four classification columns with each row representing one observation. The data represent categories and may be numeric, text, or date/time. If you wish to change the order in which text categories are processed from their default alphabetized order, you can define your own order. See *Ordering Text Categories* in the *Manipulating Data* chapter in MINITAB *User's Guide 1*. You must delete missing data before using this procedure. Because simple correspondence analysis works with a two-way classification, the standard approach is to use two worksheet columns. However, you can obtain a two-way classification with three or four variables by crossing variables within the simple correspondence analysis procedure. See *Crossing variables to create a two-way table* on page 6-25.

- If your data are in *contingency table form*, worksheet columns must contain integer frequencies of your category combinations. You must delete any rows or columns with missing data or combine them with other rows or columns. Unlike the χ^2 test for association procedure, there is no set limit on the number of contingency table columns. You could use simple correspondence analysis to obtain χ^2 statistics for large tables.

Supplementary data

When performing a simple correspondence analysis, you have a main classification set of data on which you perform your analysis. However, you may also have additional or *supplementary data* in the same form as the main set, because you can see how these supplementary data are "scored" using the results from the main set. These supplementary data may be further information from the same study, information from other studies, or target profiles [2]. MINITAB does not include these data when calculating the components, but you can obtain a profile and display supplementary data in graphs.

You can have row supplementary data or column supplementary data. Row supplementary data constitutes an additional row(s) of the contingency table, while column supplementary data constitutes an additional column(s) of the contingency table. Supplementary data must be entered in contingency table form. Therefore, each worksheet column of these data must contain c entries (where c is the number of contingency table columns) or r entries (where r is the number of contingency table rows).

▶ **To perform a simple correspondence analysis**

   1 Choose **Stat ➤ Tables ➤ Simple Correspondence Analysis**.

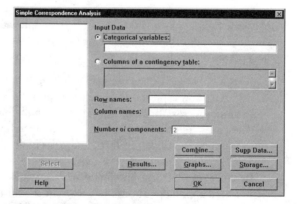

   2 How you enter your data depends on the form of the data and the number of categorical variables.

      ■ If you have two categorical variables, do one of the following:
        – for raw data, enter the columns containing the raw data in **Categorical variables**
        – for contingency table data, enter the columns containing the data in **Columns of a contingency table**

      ■ If you have three or four categorical variables, you must cross some variables before entering data as shown above. See *Crossing variables to create a two-way table* on page 6-25.

   3 If you like, use one or more of the options listed below, then click **OK**.

Options

Simple Correspondence Analysis dialog box

- name the rows and/or columns by entering a text column that contains an entry for each row and/or column of the contingency table. MINITAB prints the first eight characters of names in tables, but prints all characters on graphs.

- specify the number of components to calculate. The default is two, the minimum number is one, and the maximum number for a contingency table with r rows and c columns is the smaller of $(r - 1)$ or $(c - 1)$.

Results subdialog box

- print the contingency table.

- print row and/or column profiles. See *Interpreting the results* on page 6-29.

- print expected frequencies, observed minus expected frequencies, χ^2 values, or relative inertias in each cell of the contingency table. The expected frequencies, observed frequencies, and χ^2 values are the values you would obtain by doing χ^2 test for association. The relative inertia is the χ^2 value divided by the total frequency.

Combine subdialog box

- cross two category variables to create a single variable. See *Crossing variables to create a two-way table* on page 6-25.

Supp Data subdialog box

- use supplementary rows or columns.

- name the supplementary rows and/or columns by entering a text column that contains an entry for each supplementary row and/or column of the contingency table. MINITAB prints the first eight characters of names in tables, but prints all characters on graphs.

Graphs subdialog box

- generate symmetric and asymmetric plots. You can display
  - a symmetric plot with rows only, with columns only, or with rows and columns
  - an asymmetric row plot showing rows and columns
  - an asymmetric column plot showing rows and columns

- specify the component pairs and their axes for plotting.

- plot supplementary points.

See *Simple correspondence analysis graphs* on page 6-26.

Storage subdialog box

- store the contingency table. MINITAB stores each column of the contingency table in a separate worksheet column.

- store principal and standardized coordinates for rows and columns. See *Method* below for definitions. If you enter names for k columns, MINITAB stores the coordinates for the first k components. When you have supplementary data, MINITAB stores their coordinates at the end of the column.

Method

Simple correspondence analysis performs a weighted principal components analysis of a contingency table. If the contingency table has r rows and c columns, the number of underlying dimensions is the smaller of $(r - 1)$ or $(c - 1)$. As with principal components, variability is partitioned, but rather than partitioning the total variance, simple correspondence analysis partitions the Pearson χ^2 statistic (the same statistic calculated in the chi-square test for association). Traditionally, correspondence analysis uses χ^2 / n, which is termed inertia or total inertia, rather than χ^2.

Principal axes

Lower dimensional subspaces are spanned by principal components, also called principal axes. The first principal axis is chosen so that it accounts for the maximum amount of the total inertia; the second principal axis is chosen so that it accounts for the maximum amount of the remaining inertia; and so on. The first principal axis spans the best (i.e., closest to the profiles using an appropriate metric) one-dimensional subspace; the first two principal axes span the best two-dimensional subspace; and so on. These subspaces are nested, i.e., the best one-dimensional subspace is a subspace of the best two-dimensional subspace, and so on.

Principal and standardized coordinates

The principal coordinate for row profile i and component (axis) k is the coordinate of the projection of row profile i onto component k. The row standardized coordinates for component k are the principal coordinates for component k divided by the square root of the kth inertia.

Likewise, the principal coordinate for column profile j and component k is the coordinate of the projection of column profile j onto component k. The column standardized coordinates for component k are the column principal coordinates for component k divided by the square root of the kth inertia.

Row and column profiles

The contingency table can be analyzed in terms of row profiles or column profiles. A row profile is a list of row proportions that are calculated from the counts in the contingency table. Specifically, the profile for row i is $(n_{i1} / n_{i.}, n_{i2} / n_{i.}, \ldots, n_{ic} / n_{i.})$. A column profile is a list of column proportions, where n_{ij}, is the frequency in row i and column j of the table and $n_{i.}$, is the sum of the frequencies in row i. Specifically, the profile for column j is $(n_{1j} /n_{.j}, n_{2j} / n_{.j}, \ldots, n_{rj} / n_{.j})$, where $n_{.j}$, is the sum of the frequencies in column j.

The two analyses are mathematically equivalent. The one that you choose will depend on which is more natural for a given analysis. Most of the time, a researcher is interested in studying either how the row profiles differ from each other or how the column profiles differ from each other.

Row profiles are vectors of length c and therefore lie in a c-dimensional space (similarly, column profiles lie in an r-dimensional space). Since this dimension is usually too high to allow easy interpretation, you will want to try to find a subspace of lower dimension (preferably not more than two or three) that lies close to all the row profile points (or column profile points). You can then project the profile points onto this subspace and study the projections. If the projections are close to the profiles, we do not lose much information. Working in two or three dimensions allows you to study the data more easily and, in particular, allows you to examine plots. This process is analogous to choosing a small number of principal components to summarize the variability of continuous data.

If d = the smaller of (r−1) and (c−1), then the row profiles (or equivalently the column profiles) will lie in a d-dimensional subspace of the full c-dimensional space (or equivalently the full r-dimensional space). Thus, there are at most d principal components.

Inertia

MINITAB prints the inertia associated with each component, and also displays these in a histogram. The inertias associated with all of the principal components add up to the total inertia. Ideally, the first one, two, or three components account for most of the total inertia for the table.

See *Simple Correspondence Analysis* in Help for additional definitions and calculations.

Crossing variables to create a two-way table

Crossing variables allows you to use simple correspondence analysis to analyze three-way and four-way contingency tables. You can cross the first two variables to form rows and/or the last two variables to form columns. You must enter three categorical variables to perform one cross, and four categorical variables to perform two crosses.

The following example illustrates row crossing. Column crossing is similar. Suppose you have two variables. The row variable, Sex, has two levels: male and female; the column variable, Age, has three levels; young, middle aged, old.

Crossing Sex with Age will create $2 \times 3 = 6$ rows, ordered as follows:

    male / young
    male / middle aged
    male / old
    female / young
    female / middle aged
    female / old

Simple correspondence analysis graphs

You can display the following simple correspondence-analysis plots:

- a row plot or a column plot

- a symmetric plot

- an asymmetric row plot or an asymmetric column plot

A *row plot* is a plot of row principal coordinates. A *column plot* is a plot of column principal coordinates. See *Method* on page 6-24 for definitions.

A *symmetric plot* is a plot of row and column principal coordinates in a joint display. An advantage of this plot is that the profiles are spread out for better viewing of distances between them. The row-to-row and column-to-column distances are approximate χ^2 distances between the respective profiles. However, this same interpretation cannot be made for row-to-column distances. Because these distances are two different mappings, you must interpret these plots carefully [2].

An *asymmetric row plot* is a plot of row principal coordinates and of column standardized coordinates in the same plot. Distances between row points are approximate χ^2 distances between the row profiles. Choose the asymmetric row plot over the asymmetric column plot if rows are of primary interest.

An *asymmetric column plot* is a plot of column principal coordinates and row standardized coordinates. Distances between column points are approximate χ^2 distances between the column profiles. Choose an asymmetric column plot over an asymmetric row plot if columns are of primary interest.

An advantage of asymmetric plots is that there can be an intuitive interpretation of the distances between row points and column points, especially if the two displayed components represent a large proportion of the total inertia [2]. Suppose you have an asymmetric row plot, as shown in *Example of simple correspondence analysis* on page 6-27. This graph plots both the row profiles and the column vertices for components 1 and 2. The closer a row profile is to a column vertex, the higher the row profile is with respect to the column category. In this example, of the row points, Biochemistry is closest to column category E, implying that biochemistry as a discipline has the highest percentage of unfunded researchers in this study. A disadvantage of asymmetric plots is that the profiles of interest are often bunched in the middle of the graph [2], as happens with the asymmetric plot of this example.

▶ To display simple correspondence analysis plots

1 Perform steps 1–2 of *To perform a simple correspondence analysis* on page 6-22.

2 Click **Graphs**.

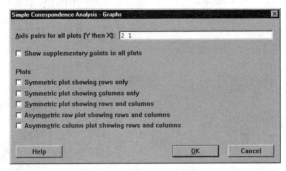

3 Check all of the plots that you would like to display.

4 If you like, you can specify the component pairs and their axes for plotting. Enter between 1 and 15 component pairs in **Axis pairs for all plots (Y then X)**. MINITAB plots the first component in each pair on the vertical or y-axis of the plot; the second component in the pair on the horizontal or x-axis of the plot.

5 If you have supplementary data and would like to include this data in the plot(s), check **Show supplementary points in all plots**. Click **OK** in each dialog box.

In all plots, row points are plotted with red circles—solid circles for regular points, and open circles for supplementary points. Column points are plotted with blue squares—blue squares for regular points, and open squares for supplementary points.

▷ Example of simple correspondence analysis

The following example is from *Correspondence Analysis in Practice*, by M. J. Greenacre, p.75. Seven hundred ninety-six researchers were cross-classified into ten academic disciplines and five funding categories, where A is the highest funding category, D is the lowest, and category E is unfunded. Here, disciplines are rows and funding categories are columns. You wish to see how the disciplines compare to each other relative to the funding categories so you perform correspondence analysis from a row orientation. Supplementary data include: a row for museum researchers not included in the study and a row for mathematical sciences, which is the sum of Mathematics and Statistics.

1 Open the worksheet EXH_TABL.MTW.

2 Choose **Stat ➤ Tables ➤ Simple Correspondence Analysis**.

3 Choose **Columns of a contingency table**, and enter *CT1-CT5* in the box. Enter *RowNames* in **Row names** and *ColNames* in **Column names**.

4 Click **Results**. Check **Row profiles**. Click **OK**.

5 Click **Supp Data**. In **Supplementary Rows**, enter *RowSupp1* and *RowSupp2*. In **Row names**, enter *RSNames*. Click **OK**.

6 Click **Graphs**. Check **Show supplementary points in all plots**. Check **Symmetric plot showing rows only** and **Asymmetric row plot showing rows and columns**. Click **OK** in each dialog box.

Session window output

Simple Correspondence Analysis: CT1, CT2, CT3, CT4, CT5

Row Profiles

	A	B	C	D	E	Mass
Geology	0.035	0.224	0.459	0.165	0.118	0.107
Biochemi	0.034	0.069	0.448	0.034	0.414	0.036
Chemistr	0.046	0.192	0.377	0.162	0.223	0.163
Zoology	0.025	0.125	0.342	0.292	0.217	0.151
Physics	0.088	0.193	0.412	0.079	0.228	0.143
Engineer	0.034	0.125	0.284	0.170	0.386	0.111
Microbio	0.027	0.162	0.378	0.135	0.297	0.046
Botany	0.000	0.140	0.395	0.198	0.267	0.108
Statisti	0.069	0.172	0.379	0.138	0.241	0.036
Mathemat	0.026	0.141	0.474	0.103	0.256	0.098
Mass	0.039	0.161	0.389	0.162	0.249	

Analysis of Contingency Table

Axis	Inertia	Proportion	Cumulative	Histogram
1	0.0391	0.4720	0.4720	******************************
2	0.0304	0.3666	0.8385	***********************
3	0.0109	0.1311	0.9697	********
4	0.0025	0.0303	1.0000	*
Total	0.0829			

Row Contributions

					----Component 1----			----Component 2----		
ID	Name	Qual	Mass	Inert	Coord	Corr	Contr	Coord	Corr	Contr
1	Geology	0.916	0.107	0.137	-0.076	0.055	0.016	-0.303	0.861	0.322
2	Biochemi	0.881	0.036	0.119	-0.180	0.119	0.030	0.455	0.762	0.248
3	Chemistr	0.644	0.163	0.021	-0.038	0.134	0.006	-0.073	0.510	0.029
4	Zoology	0.929	0.151	0.230	0.327	0.846	0.413	-0.102	0.083	0.052
5	Physics	0.886	0.143	0.196	-0.316	0.880	0.365	-0.027	0.006	0.003
6	Engineer	0.870	0.111	0.152	0.117	0.121	0.039	0.292	0.749	0.310
7	Microbio	0.680	0.046	0.010	-0.013	0.009	0.000	0.110	0.671	0.018
8	Botany	0.654	0.108	0.067	0.179	0.625	0.088	0.039	0.029	0.005
9	Statisti	0.561	0.036	0.012	-0.125	0.554	0.014	-0.014	0.007	0.000
10	Mathemat	0.319	0.098	0.056	-0.107	0.240	0.029	0.061	0.079	0.012

Supplementary Rows

				----Component 1----			----Component 2----		
ID	Name	Qual	Mass	Inert	Coord	Corr	Contr	Coord	Corr	Contr
1	Museums	0.556	0.067	0.353	0.314	0.225	0.168	-0.381	0.331	0.318
2	MathSci	0.559	0.134	0.041	-0.112	0.493	0.043	0.041	0.066	0.007

Column Contributions

					----Component 1----			----Component 2----		
ID	Name	Qual	Mass	Inert	Coord	Corr	Contr	Coord	Corr	Contr
1	A	0.587	0.039	0.187	-0.478	0.574	0.228	-0.072	0.013	0.007
2	B	0.816	0.161	0.110	-0.127	0.286	0.067	-0.173	0.531	0.159
3	C	0.465	0.389	0.094	-0.083	0.341	0.068	-0.050	0.124	0.032
4	D	0.968	0.162	0.347	0.390	0.859	0.632	-0.139	0.109	0.103
5	E	0.990	0.249	0.262	0.032	0.012	0.006	0.292	0.978	0.699

Graph window output

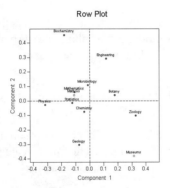

Row Plot

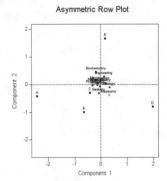

Asymmetric Row Plot

Interpreting the results

Row Profiles. The first table gives the proportions of each row category by column. Thus, of the class Geology, 3.5% are in column A, 22.4% are column B, etc. The mass of the Geology row, 0.107, is the proportion of all Geology subjects in the data set.

Analysis of Contingency Table. The second table shows the decomposition of the total inertia. For this example, the table gives a summary of the decomposition of the 10×5 contingency table into 4 components. The column labeled Inertia contains the χ^2 / n value accounted for by each component. Of the total inertia, 65.972 / 796 or 0.0829, 47.2% is accounted for by the first component, 36.66% by the second component, and so on. Here, 65.972 is the χ^2 statistic you would obtain if you performed a χ^2 test of association with this contingency table.

Row Contributions. You can use the third table to interpret the different components. Since the number of components was not specified, MINITAB calculates 2 components.

- The column labeled Qual, or quality, is the proportion of the row inertia represented by the two components. The rows Zoology and Geology, with quality = 0.928 and 0.916, respectively, are best represented among the rows by the two component breakdown, while Math has the poorest representation, with a quality value of 0.319.

■ The column labeled Mass has the same meaning as in the Row Profiles table—the proportion of the class in the whole data set.

■ The column labeled Inert is the proportion of the total inertia contributed by each row. Thus, Geology contributes 13.7% to the total χ^2 statistic.

Next, MINITAB displays information for each of the two components (axes).

■ The column labeled Coord gives the principal coordinates of the rows.

■ The column labeled Corr represents the contribution of the component to the inertia of the row. Thus, Component 1 accounts for most of the inertia of Zoology and Physics (Coor = 0.846 and 0.880, respectively), but explains little of the inertia of Microbiology (Coor = 0.009).

■ Contr, the contribution of each row to the axis inertia, shows that Zoology and Physics contribute the most, with Botany contributing to a smaller degree, to Component 1. Geology, Biochemistry, and Engineering contribute the most to Component 2.

Supplementary rows. You can interpret this table in a similar fashion as the row contributions table.

Column Contributions. The fifth table shows that two components explain most of the variability in funding categories B, D, and E. The funded categories A, B, C, and D contribute most to component 1, while the unfunded category, E, contributes most to component 2.

Row Plot. This plot displays the row principal coordinates. Component 1, which best explains Zoology and Physics, shows these two classes well removed from the origin, but with opposite sign. Component 1 might be thought of as contrasting the biological sciences Zoology and Botany with Physics. Component 2 might be thought of as contrasting Biochemistry and Engineering with Geology.

Asymmetric Row Plot. Here, the rows are scaled in principal coordinates and the columns are scaled in standard coordinates. Among funding classes, Component 1 contrasts levels of funding, while Component 2 contrasts being funded (A to D) with not being funded (E). Among the disciplines, Physics tends to have the highest funding level and Zoology has the lowest. Biochemistry tends to be in the middle of the funding level, but highest among unfunded researchers. Museums tend to be funded, but at a lower level than academic researchers.

Multiple Correspondence Analysis

Multiple correspondence analysis extends simple correspondence analysis to the case of three or more categorical variables. Multiple correspondence analysis performs a simple correspondence analysis on a matrix of indicator variables where each column of the matrix corresponds to a level of categorical variable. Rather than having the two-way table of simple correspondence analysis, here the multi-way table is collapsed into one dimension. By moving from the simple to multiple procedure, you gain information on a potentially larger number of variables, but you may lose information on how rows and columns relate to each other.

Data

Worksheet data may be arranged in two ways: raw or indicator variable form. See *Arrangement of Input Data* on page 6-3. Worksheet data arrangement determines acceptable data values.

- If your data are in *raw form*, you can have one or more classification columns with each row representing one observation. The data represent categories and may be numeric, text, or date/time. If you wish to change the order in which text categories are processed from their default alphabetized order, you can define your own order. See *Ordering Text Categories* in the *Manipulating Data* chapter in MINITAB *User's Guide 1*. You must delete missing data before using this procedure.

- If your data are in *indicator variable form*, each row will also represent one observation. There will be one indicator column for each category level. You can use **Calc ➤ Make Indicator Variables** to create indicator variables from raw data. You must delete missing data before using this procedure.

Supplementary data

When performing a multiple correspondence analysis, you have a main classification set of data on which you perform your analysis. However, you may also have additional or *supplementary data* in the same form as the main set, and you might want to see how this supplementary data are "scored" using the results from the main set. These supplementary data are typically a classification of your variables that can help you to interpret the results. MINITAB does not include these data when calculating the components, but you can obtain a profile and display supplementary data in graphs.

Set up your supplementary data in your worksheet using the same form, either raw data or indicator variables, as you did for the input data. Because your supplementary data will provide additional information about your observations, your supplementary data column(s) must be the same length as your input data.

▶ **To perform a multiple correspondence analysis**

1 Choose Stat ➤ Tables ➤ Multiple Correspondence Analysis.

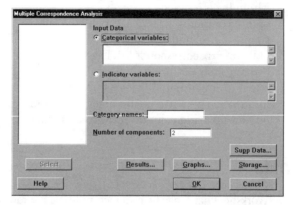

2 To enter your data, do one of the following:

■ For raw data, enter the columns containing the raw data in **Categorical variables**

■ For indicator variable data, enter the columns containing the indicator variable data in **Indicator variables**

3 If you like, use one or more of the options listed below, then click **OK**.

Options

Multiple Correspondence Analysis dialog box

■ name the categories by entering a text column that has one row for each category of all input variables. For example, suppose there are 3 categorical variables: Gender (male, female), Hair color (blond, brown, black), and Age (under 20, from 20 to 50, over 50), and no supplementary variables. You would assign eight category names (2 + 3 + 3), and enter the names in a column. MINITAB prints the first eight characters of names in tables, but prints all characters on graphs.

■ specify the number of components to calculate. The default is two, the minimum number is one, and the maximum is the number of underlying dimensions. If the number of categories in the j categorical columns are c_1, c_2, ..., c_j, the number of underlying dimensions is the sum of $(c_i - 1)$, where $i = 1, 2, ..., j$.

Results subdialog box

■ print a table of the indicator variables.

■ print a Burt table. The Burt table is a symmetric matrix with one column and one row for each level (category) of a categorical variable that contains the frequencies.

Supp Data subdialog box

- use supplementary data.

- name the supplementary data categories by entering a text column that contains an entry for each category of all supplementary variables. MINITAB prints the first eight characters of names in tables, but prints all characters on graphs.

Graphs subdialog box

- display a column plot

- specify the component pairs and their axes for plotting

- plot supplementary points

See *Simple correspondence analysis graphs* on page 6-26 for instructions.

Storage subdialog box

- store component coordinates. See *Method* on page 6-34 for definitions. If you enter names for k columns, MINITAB stores the coordinates for the first k components. When you have supplementary data, MINITAB stores their coordinates at the end of the column.

Method

Multiple correspondence analysis decomposes a matrix of indicator variables formed from all entered variables. Unlike simple correspondence analysis, where all row classes are from one variable and all column classes are from another variable, here all variable classes are column contributors.

Multiple correspondence analysis performs a weighted principal-components analysis of the matrix of indicator variables. If the number of categories in the j categorical columns are c_1, c_2, ..., c_j, the number of underlying dimensions is the sum of $(c_i - 1)$, where i = 1, 2, ..., j. As with simple correspondence analysis, multiple correspondence analysis partitions the Pearson χ^2 statistic. Unlike simple correspondence analysis, there is no choice of examining either row or column profiles—there are only column profiles. See *Method* under simple correspondence analysis on page 6-24 for additional information and definitions. Because there are no rows, multiple correspondence analysis offers only one graph—a plot of column coordinates.

▷ Example of multiple correspondence analysis

Automobile accidents are classified [3] (data from [1]) according to the type of accident (collision or rollover), severity of accident (not severe or severe), whether or not the driver was ejected, and the size of the car (small or standard). Multiple correspondence analysis was used to examine how the categories in this four-way table are related to each other.

1   Open the worksheet EXH_TABL.MTW.

2   Choose **Stat ➤ Tables ➤ Multiple Correspondence Analysis**.

3   Choose **Categorical variables**, and enter *CarWt DrEject AccType AccSever* in the box.

4   In **Category names**, enter *AccNames*.

5   Click **Graphs**. Check **Display column plot**. Click **OK** in each dialog box.

Session window output

Multiple Correspondence Analysis: CarWt, DrEject, AccType, AccSever

Analysis of Indicator Matrix

Axis	Inertia	Proportion	Cumulative	Histogram
1	0.4032	0.4032	0.4032	******************************
2	0.2520	0.2520	0.6552	******************
3	0.1899	0.1899	0.8451	**************
4	0.1549	0.1549	1.0000	***********
Total	1.0000			

Column Contributions

					----Component 1----			----Component 2----		
ID	Name	Qual	Mass	Inert	Coord	Corr	Contr	Coord	Corr	Contr
1	Small	0.965	0.042	0.208	0.381	0.030	0.015	-2.139	0.936	0.771
2	Standard	0.965	0.208	0.042	-0.078	0.030	0.003	0.437	0.936	0.158
3	NoEject	0.474	0.213	0.037	-0.284	0.472	0.043	-0.020	0.002	0.000
4	Eject	0.474	0.037	0.213	1.659	0.472	0.250	0.115	0.002	0.002
5	Collis	0.613	0.193	0.057	-0.426	0.610	0.087	0.034	0.004	0.001
6	Rollover	0.613	0.057	0.193	1.429	0.610	0.291	-0.113	0.004	0.003
7	NoSevere	0.568	0.135	0.115	-0.652	0.502	0.143	-0.237	0.066	0.030
8	Severe	0.568	0.115	0.135	0.769	0.502	0.168	0.280	0.066	0.036

Graph window output

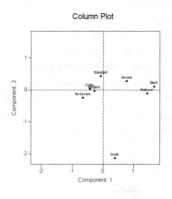

Interpreting the results

Analysis of Indicator Matrix. This table gives a summary of the decomposition of variables. The column labeled Inertia is the χ^2 / n value accounted for by each component. Of the total inertia of 1, 40.3%, 25.2%, 19.0%, and, 15.5% are accounted for by the first through fourth components, respectively.

Column Contributions. Use the column contributions to interpret the different components. Since we did not specify the number of components, MINITAB calculates 2 components.

- The column labeled Qual, or quality, is the proportion of the column inertia represented by the all calculated components. The car-size categories (Small, Standard) are best represented by the two component breakdown with Qual = 0.965, while the ejection categories are the least represented with Qual = 0.474. When there are only two categories for each class, each is represented equally well by any component, but this rule would not necessarily be true for more than two categories.

- The column labeled Mass is the proportion of the class in the whole data set. In this example, the CarWt, DrEject, AccType, and AccSever classes combine for a proportion of 0.25.

- The column labeled Inert is the proportion of Inertia contributed by each column. The categories small cars, ejections, and collisions have the highest inertia, summing 61.4%, which indicates that these categories are more dissociated from the others.

Next, MINITAB displays information for each of the two components (axes).

- The column labeled Coord gives the column coordinates. Eject and Rollover have the largest absolute coordinates for component 1 and Small has the largest absolute coordinate for component 2. The sign and relative size of the coordinates are useful in interpreting components.

- The column labeled Corr represents the contribution of the respective component to the inertia of the row. Here, Component 1 accounts for 47 to 61% of the inertia of the ejection, collision type, and accident severity categories, but explains only 3.0% of the inertia of car size.

- Contr, the contribution of the row to the axis inertia, shows Eject and Rollover contributing the most to Component 1 (Contr = 0.250 and 0.291, respectively). Component 2, on the other hand accounts for 93.6% of the inertia of the car size categories, with Small contributing 77.1% of the axis inertia.

Column Plot. As the contribution values for Component 1 indicate, Eject and Rollover are most distant from the origin. This component contrasts Eject and Rollover and to some extent Severe with NoSevere. Component 2 separates Small with the other categories. Two components may not adequately explain the variability of these data, however.

References

[1] S. E. Fienberg. (1987). *The Analysis of Cross-Classified Categorical Data*. The MIT Press, Cambridge, Massachusetts.

[2] M. J. Greenacre (1993). *Correspondence Analysis in Practice*, Academic Press, Harcourt, Brace & Company, New York.

[3] J. K. Kihlberg, E. A. Narragon, and B. J. Campbell. (1964). Automobile crash injury in relation to car size. Cornell Aero. Lab. Report No. VJ-1823-R11.

Acknowledgment

We are grateful for the collaboration of James R. Allen of Allen Data Systems, Cross Plains, Wisconsin in the development of the cross tabulation procedure.

7

Time Series

Time Series Overview

MINITAB's time series procedures can be used to analyze data collected over time, commonly called a time series. These procedures include simple forecasting and smoothing methods, correlation analysis methods, and ARIMA modeling. Although correlation analysis may be performed separately from ARIMA modeling, we present the correlation methods as part of ARIMA modeling.

Simple forecasting and smoothing methods are based on the idea that reliable forecasts can be achieved by modeling patterns in the data that are usually visible in a time series plot, and then extrapolating those patterns to the future. Your choice of method should be based upon whether the patterns are *static* (constant in time) or *dynamic* (changes in time), the nature of the trend and seasonal components, and how far ahead that you wish to forecast. These methods are generally easy and quick to apply.

ARIMA modeling also makes use of patterns in the data, but these patterns may not be easily visible in a plot of the data. Instead, ARIMA modeling uses differencing and the autocorrelation and partial autocorrelation functions to help identify an acceptable model. ARIMA stands for Autoregressive Integrated Moving Average, which represent the filtering steps taken in constructing the ARIMA model until only random noise remains. While ARIMA models are valuable for modeling temporal processes and are also used for forecasting, fitting a model is an iterative approach that may not lend itself to application speed and volume.

Simple forecasting and smoothing methods

The simple forecasting and smoothing methods model components in a series that are usually easy to see in a time series plot of the data. This approach decomposes the data into its component parts, and then extends the estimates of the components into the future to provide forecasts. You can choose from the static methods of trend analysis and decomposition, or the dynamic methods of moving average, single and double exponential smoothing, and Winters' method. *Static* methods have components that do not change over time; *dynamic* methods have components that do change over time and estimates are updated using neighboring values.

You may use two methods in combination. That is, you may choose a static method to model one component and a dynamic method to model another component. For example, you may fit a static trend using trend analysis and dynamically model the seasonal component in the residuals using Winters' method. Or, you may fit a static seasonal model using decomposition and dynamically model the trend component in the residuals using double exponential smoothing. You might also apply a trend analysis and decomposition together so that you can use the wider selection of trend models offered by trend analysis (see examples on pages 7-8 and 7-13). A disadvantage of combining methods is that the confidence intervals for forecasts are not valid.

For each of the methods, the following table provides a summary and a graph of fits and forecasts of typical data.

Command	Forecast	Example
Trend Analysis Fits a general trend model to time series data. Choose among the linear, quadratic, exponential growth or decay, and S-curve models. Use this procedure to fit trend when there is no seasonal component to your series.	Length: long Profile: extension of trend line	
Decomposition Separates the times series into linear trend and seasonal components, as well as error. Choose whether the seasonal component is additive or multiplicative with the trend. Use this procedure to forecast when there is a seasonal component to your series or if you simply want to examine the nature of the component parts.	Length: long Profile: trend with seasonal pattern	
Moving Average Smooths your data by averaging consecutive observations in a series. This procedure can be a likely choice when your data do not have a trend or seasonal component. There are ways, however, to use moving averages when your data possess trend and/or seasonality.	Length: short Profile: flat line	
Single Exponential Smoothing Smooths your data by computing exponentially weighted averages. This procedure works best without a trend or seasonal component. The single dynamic component in a moving average model is the level, or the exponentially weighted average of all data up to time t. Single exponential smoothing fits an ARIMA (0,1,1) model.	Length: short Profile: flat line	
Double Exponential Smoothing Smooths your data by Holt (and Brown as a special case) double exponential smoothing. This procedure can work well when trend is present but it can also serve as a general smoothing method. Double Exponential Smoothing calculates dynamic estimates for two components: level and trend. Double exponential smoothing fits an ARIMA (0,2,2) model.	Length: short Profile: straight line with slope equal to last trend estimate	
Winters' Method Smooths your data by Holt-Winters exponential smoothing. Use this procedure when trend and seasonality are present, with these two components being either additive or multiplicative. Winters' Method calculates dynamic estimates for three components: level, trend, and seasonal.	Length: short to medium Profile: trend with seasonal pattern	

The left margin labels "Static" for the first two commands (Trend Analysis and Decomposition) and "Dynamic" for the remaining commands (Moving Average, Single Exponential Smoothing, Double Exponential Smoothing, Winters' Method).

Correlation analysis and ARIMA modeling

Examining correlation patterns within a time series or between two time series is an important step in many statistical analyses. The correlation analysis tools of differencing, autocorrelation, and partial autocorrelation are often used in ARIMA modeling to help identify an appropriate model.

ARIMA modeling can be used to model many different time series, with or without trend or seasonal components, and to provide forecasts. The forecast profile depends upon the model that is fit. The advantage of ARIMA modeling compared to the simple forecasting and smoothing methods is that it is more flexible in fitting the data. However, identifying and fitting a model may be time-consuming, and ARIMA modeling is not easily automated.

- **Differences** computes and stores the differences between data values of a time series. If you wish to fit an ARIMA model but there is trend or seasonality present in your data, differencing data is a common step in assessing likely ARIMA models. Differencing is used to simplify the correlation structure and to reveal any underlying pattern.

- **Lag** computes and stores the lags of a time series. When you lag a time series, MINITAB moves the original values down the column and inserts missing values at the top of the column. The number of missing values inserted depends on the length of the lag.

- **Autocorrelation** computes and plots the autocorrelations of a time series. Autocorrelation is the correlation between observations of a time series separated by k time units. The plot of autocorrelations is called the autocorrelation function or acf. View the acf to guide your choice of terms to include in an ARIMA model.

- **Partial Autocorrelation** computes and plots the partial autocorrelations of a time series. Partial autocorrelations, like autocorrelations, are correlations between sets of ordered data pairs of a time series. As with partial correlations in the regression case, partial autocorrelations measure the strength of relationship with other terms being accounted for. The partial autocorrelation at a lag of k is the correlation between residuals at time t from an autoregressive model and observations at lag k with terms for all intervening lags present in the autoregressive model. The plot of partial autocorrelations is called the partial autocorrelation function or pacf. View the pacf to guide your choice of terms to include in an ARIMA model.

- **Cross Correlation** computes and graphs correlations between two time series.

- **ARIMA** fits a Box-Jenkins ARIMA model to a time series. ARIMA stands for Autoregressive Integrated Moving Average. The terms in the name—Autoregressive, Integrated, and Moving Average—represent filtering steps taken in constructing the ARIMA model until only random noise remains. Use ARIMA to model time series behavior and to generate forecasts.

Trend Analysis

Trend analysis fits a general trend model to time series data and provides forecasts. Choose among the linear, quadratic, exponential growth or decay, and S-curve models. Use this procedure to fit trend when there is no seasonal component to your series.

Data

The time series must be in one numeric column. If you choose the S-curve trend model, you must delete missing data from the worksheet before performing the trend analysis. MINITAB automatically omits missing values from the calculations when you use one of the other three trend models.

► To do a trend analysis

1 Choose Stat ➤ Time Series ➤ Trend Analysis.

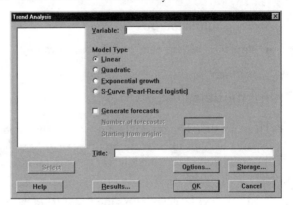

2 In **Variable**, enter the column containing the series.

3 If you like, use one or more of the options listed below, then click **OK**.

Options

Trend Analysis dialog box

- fit a linear (default), quadratic, exponential growth curve, or S-curve (Pearl-Reed logistic) trend model. See *Trend models* on page 7-6.

- specify the number of time units (leads) to forecast.

- specify the origin of forecasts (time unit before first forecast). The default is the end of the data.

- replace the default title with your own title.

Results subdialog box

- suppress display of the trend analysis plot
- control the amount of output. You can display
  - the default Session window output, which includes the length of the series, number of missing values, the fitted trend equation, and three measures to help you determine the accuracy of the fitted values: MAPE, MAD, and MSD
  - the default Session window output, plus the data, fits, and residuals (the detrended data)

Options Subdialog box

- apply coefficients (weights) from fitting other data to obtain weighted average fit. See *Weighted average trend analysis* on page 7-7.
- enter weights of coefficients of current data when obtaining weighted average fit. See *Weighted average trend analysis* on page 7-7.

Storage subdialog box

- store the fits, residuals, and forecasted values

Trend models

There are four different trend models you can choose from: linear (default), quadratic, exponential growth curve, or S-curve (Pearl-Reed logistic). Use care when interpreting the coefficients from the different models, as they have different meanings. See [4] for details.

Trend analysis by default uses the *linear trend model*:

$$y_t = \beta_0 + \beta_1 t + e_t$$

In this model, β_1 represents the average change from one period to the next.

The *quadratic trend model* which can account for simple curvature in the data, is:

$$y_t = \beta_0 + \beta_1 t + \beta_2 t^2 + e_t$$

The *exponential growth trend model* accounts for exponential growth or decay. For example, a savings account might exhibit exponential growth. The model is:

$$y_t = \beta_0 \beta_1^t + e_t$$

The *S-curve model* fits the Pearl-Reed logistic trend model. This accounts for the case where the series follows an S-shaped curve. The model is:

$$y_t = \frac{10^a}{\beta_0 + \beta_1(\beta_2^{\,t-1})}$$

Weighted average trend analysis

You can perform a weighted average trend analysis to incorporate knowledge learned from fitting the same trend model to prior data in order to obtain an "improved" fit to the present data. The smoothed trend line combines prior and new information in much the same way that exponential smoothing works. In a sense, this smoothing of the coefficients filters out some of the noise from the model parameters estimated in successive cycles.

If you supply coefficients from a prior trend analysis fit, MINITAB performs a weighted trend analysis. If the weight for a particular coefficient is α, MINITAB estimates the new coefficient by

$\alpha p_1 + (1 - \alpha)p_2$, where p_1 is the coefficient estimated from the current data and p_2 is the prior coefficient.

▶ To perform a weighted average trend analysis

1 In the Trend Analysis dialog box, click **Options**.

2 Enter the coefficient estimates from the prior trend analysis in the order in which they are given in the Session window or the graph.

3 Optionally enter weights between 0 and 1 for each new coefficient, in the same order as for coefficients. Default weights of 0.2 will be used for each coefficient if you don't enter any. If you do enter weights, the number that you enter must be equal to the number of coefficients.

MINITAB generates a time series plot of the data, plus a second time series plot that shows trend lines for three models. The Session window displays the coefficients and accuracy measures for all three models.

Measures of accuracy

MINITAB computes three measures of accuracy of the fitted model: MAPE, MAD, and MSD for each of the simple forecasting and smoothing methods. For all three measures, the smaller the value, the better the fit of the model. Use these statistics to compare the fits of the different methods.

MAPE, or Mean Absolute Percentage Error, measures the accuracy of fitted time series values. It expresses accuracy as a percentage.

$$\text{MAPE} = \frac{\Sigma \left| (y_t - \hat{y}_t) / y_t \right|}{n} \times 100 \qquad (y_t \neq 0)$$

where y_t equals the actual value, $\hat{y}_t$ equals the forecast value, and n equals the number of forecasts.

MAD, which stands for Mean Absolute Deviation, measures the accuracy of fitted time series values. It expresses accuracy in the same units as the data, which helps conceptualize the amount of error.

$$\text{MAD} = \frac{\displaystyle\sum_{t=1}^{n} \left| y_t - \hat{y}_t \right|}{n}$$

where y_t equals the actual value, $\hat{y}_t$ equals the forecast value, and n equals the number of forecasts.

MSD stands for Mean Squared Deviation. It is very similar to MSE, mean squared error, a commonly-used measure of accuracy of fitted time series values. MSD is always computed using the same denominator, n, regardless of the model, so you can compare MSD values across models. MSE's are computed with different degrees of freedom for different models, so you cannot always compare MSE values across models.

$$\text{MSD} = \frac{\displaystyle\sum_{t=1}^{n} (y_t - \hat{y}_t)^2}{n}$$

where y_t equals the actual value, $\hat{y}_t$ equals the forecast value, and n equals the number of forecasts.

Forecasting

Forecasts are extrapolations of the trend model fits. Data prior to the forecast origin are used to fit the trend.

▷ Example of a trend analysis

You collect employment in a trade business over 60 months and wish to predict employment for the next 12 months. Because there is an overall curvilinear pattern to the data, you use trend analysis and fit a quadratic trend model. Because there is also a seasonal component, you save the fits and residuals to perform decomposition of the residuals (see *Example of decomposition* on page 7-13).

1 Open the worksheet EMPLOY.MTW.

2 Choose **Stat ➤ Time Series ➤ Trend Analysis**.

3 In **Variable**, enter *Trade*.

4 Under **Model Type**, choose **Quadratic**.

5 Check **Generate forecasts** and enter *12* in **Number of forecasts**.

6 Click **Storage**.

7 Check **Fits (trend line)**, **Residuals (detrended data)**, and **Forecasts**. Click **OK** in each dialog box.

Session wIndow output

Trend Analysis

```
Data        Trade
Length      60.0000
NMissing    0
```

Fitted Trend Equation

$$Yt = 320.762 + 0.509373*t + 1.07E\text{-}02*t**2$$

Accuracy Measures

```
MAPE:       1.70760
MAD:        5.95655
MSD:        59.1305
```

Row	Period	FORE1
1	61	391.818
2	62	393.649
3	63	395.502
4	64	397.376
5	65	399.271
6	66	401.188
7	67	403.127
8	68	405.087
9	69	407.068
10	70	409.071
11	71	411.096
12	72	413.142

*Graph
window
output*

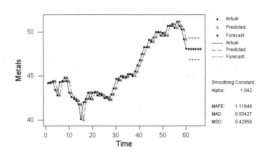

Interpreting the results

The trend plot that shows the original data, the fitted trend line, and forecasts. The Session window output also displays the fitted trend equation and three measures to help you determine the accuracy of the fitted values: MAPE, MAD, and MSD. The trade employment data show a general upward trend, though with an evident seasonal component. The trend model appears to fit well to the overall trend, but the seasonal pattern is not well fit. To better fit these data, you also use decomposition on the stored residuals and add the trend analysis and decomposition fits and forecasts (see *Example of decomposition* on page 7-13).

Decomposition

You can use decomposition to separate the time series into linear trend and seasonal components, as well as error, and provide forecasts. You can choose whether the seasonal component is additive or multiplicative with the trend. Use this procedure when you wish to forecast and there is a seasonal component to your series, or if you simply want to examine the nature of the component parts. See [6] for a discussion of decomposition methods.

Data

The time series must be in one numeric column. MINITAB automatically omits missing data from the calculations.

The data that you enter depends upon how you use this procedure. Usually, decomposition is performed in one step by simply entering the time series. Alternatively, you can perform a decomposition of the trend model residuals. This process may improve the fit of the model by combining the information from the trend analysis and the decomposition. See *Decomposition of trend model residuals* on page 7-13.

▶ **To do a decomposition**

1 Choose Stat ➤ Time Series ➤ Decomposition.

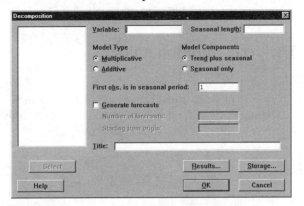

2 In **Variable**, enter the column containing the series.

3 In **Seasonal length**, enter the seasonal length or period.

4 If you like, use one or more of the options listed below, then click **OK**.

Options

Decomposition dialog box

- specify if the trend and seasonal components should be additive rather than multiplicative, or if you wish to omit trend from the model. See *The decomposition model* on page 7-12.

- specify where the first observation is in the seasonal period (default is 1). For example, if you have an annual cycle starting in January with monthly data (seasonal length is 12) and your first observation is in June, specify 6.

- specify the number of time units (leads) to forecast.

- specify the origin of forecasts (time unit before first forecast). The default is the end of the data.

- replace the default title with your own title.

Results subdialog box

- suppress display of the trend analysis plot

- display a summary of the fit

- display a summary of the fits, plus a table of the data, the trend, the seasonal component, the detrended data (seasonal plus residual), the seasonally adjusted data (trend plus residual), fits (trend plus seasonal), and residuals

Storage subdialog box

■ store the trend line, detrended data, the seasonal component, the seasonally adjusted data, forecasts, residuals, and fits

The decomposition model

By default, MINITAB uses a *multiplicative model*. Use the multiplicative model when the size of the seasonal pattern in the data depends on the level of the data. This model assumes that as the data increase, so does the seasonal pattern. Most time series exhibit such a pattern. The multiplicative model is

Y_t = Trend * Seasonal + Error

where Y_t is the observation at time t.

The *additive model* is

Y_t = Trend + Seasonal + Error

where Y_t is the observation at time t.

You can also omit the trend component from the decomposition. You will probably choose this if you have already detrended your data with the trend analysis procedure. If the data contain a trend component but you omit it from the decomposition, this can influence the estimates of the seasonal indices.

Method

Decomposition involves the following steps:

1 MINITAB fits a trend line to the data, using least squares regression.

2 Next, the data are detrended by either dividing the data by the trend component (multiplicative model) or subtracting the trend component from the data (additive model).

3 Then, the detrended data are smoothed using a centered moving average with a length equal to the length of the seasonal cycle. When the seasonal cycle length is an even number, a two-step moving average is required to synchronize the moving average correctly.

4 Once the moving average is obtained, it is either divided into (multiplicative model) or subtracted from (additive model) the detrended data to obtain what are often referred to as raw seasonals.

5 Within each seasonal period, the median value of the raw seasonals is found. The medians are also adjusted so that their mean is one (multiplicative model) or their sum is zero (additive model). These adjusted medians constitute the seasonal indices.

6 The seasonal indices are used in turn to seasonally adjust the data.

Decomposition of trend model residuals

You can use trend analysis and decomposition in combination when your data have a trend that is fit well by the quadratic, exponential growth curve, or S-curve models of trend analysis and possess seasonality that can be fit well by decomposition.

▶ **To combine trend analysis and decomposition:**

1 Perform a Trend Analysis and store the fits, residuals, and forecasts (see *Example of a trend analysis* on page 7-8).

2 Choose **Stat ➤ Time Series ➤ Decomposition**.

3 In **Variable**, enter the column containing trend analysis residuals.

4 Under **Model Type**, choose **Additive**.

5 Under **Model Components**, choose **Seasonal only**.

6 Click **Storage** and check **Fits**. Click **OK** in each dialog box.

7 Next, you need to calculate the fits from the combined procedure:

   ▪ If you want these components to be additive, add the respective fits together.

Note | The MAPE, MAD, MSD accuracy measures from decomposition used in this manner are not comparable to these statistics calculated from other procedures, but you can calculate the comparable values fairly easily. We demonstrate this with MSD in the decomposition example.

Forecasts

Decomposition calculates the forecast as the linear regression line multiplied by (multiplicative model) or added to (additive model) the seasonal indices. Data prior to the forecast origin are used for the decomposition.

▷ **Example of decomposition**

You wish to predict trade employment for the next 12 months using data collected over 60 months. Because the data have a trend that is fit well by trend analysis' quadratic trend model and possess a seasonal component, you use the residuals from trend analysis example (see *Example of a trend analysis* on page 7-8) to combine both trend analysis and decomposition for forecasting.

1 Do the trend analysis example on page 7-8.

2 Choose **Stat ➤ Time Series ➤ Decomposition**.

3 In **Variable**, enter the name of the residual column you stored in from trend analysis.

4 In **Seasonal length**, enter *12*.

5 Under **Model Type**, choose **Additive**. Under **Model Components**, choose **Seasonal only**.

6 Check **Generate forecasts** and enter *12* in **Number of forecasts**.

7 Click **Storage**.

8 Check **Forecasts** and **Fits**. Click **OK** in each dialog box.

Session window output

Time Series Decomposition

Data   RESI1
Length   60.0000
NMissing   0

Seasonal Indices

Period	Index
1	-8.48264
2	-13.3368
3	-11.4410
4	-5.81597
5	0.559028
6	3.55903
7	1.76736
8	3.47569
9	3.26736
10	5.39236
11	8.49653
12	12.5590

Accuracy of Model

MAPE: 881.582
MAD: 2.802
MSD: 11.899

Forecasts

Row	Period	FORE2
1	61	-8.4826
2	62	-13.3368
3	63	-11.4410
4	64	-5.8160
5	65	0.5590
6	66	3.5590
7	67	1.7674
8	68	3.4757
9	69	3.2674
10	70	5.3924
11	71	8.4965
12	72	12.5590

*Graph
window
output*

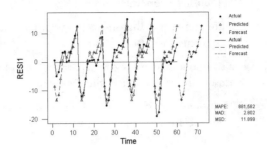

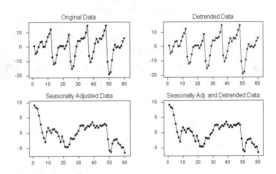

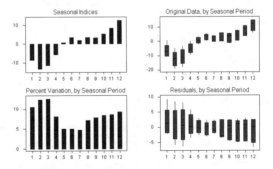

Interpreting the results

Decomposition generates three sets of plots:

- a time series plot that shows the original series with the fitted trend line, predicted values, and forecasts

- a component analysis—in separate plots are the series, the detrended data, the seasonally adjusted data, the seasonally adjusted and detrended data (the residuals)

- a seasonal analysis—charts of seasonal indices and percent variation within each season relative to the sum of variation by season and boxplots of the data and of the residuals by seasonal period

In addition, MINITAB displays the fitted trend line, the seasonal indices, the three accuracy measures—MAPE, MAD, and MSD (see *Measures of accuracy* on page 7-7)—and forecasts in the Session window.

In the example, the first graph shows that the detrended residuals from trend analysis are fit fairly well by decomposition, except that part of the first annual cycle is underpredicted and the last annual cycle is overpredicted. This is also evident in the lower right plot of the second graph; the residuals are highest in the beginning of the series and lowest at the end.

► Example of fits and forecasts of combined trend analysis and decomposition

Now, let's look at the combined trend analysis and decomposition results:

Step 1: Calculate the fits and forecasts of the combined trend analysis and decomposition

1 Choose **Calc ➤ Calculator**.

2 In **Store result in variable**, enter *NewFits*.

3 In **Expression**, add the fits from trend analysis to the fits from decomposition. Click **OK**.

4 Choose **Calc ➤ Calculator**. Clear the **Expression** box by selecting the contents and pressing the delete key.

5 In **Store result in variable**, enter *NewFore*.

6 In **Expression**, add the fits from trend analysis to the fits from decomposition. Click **OK**.

Step 2: Plot the fits and forecasts of the combined trend analysis and decomposition

1 Choose **Stat ➤ Time Series ➤ Time Series Plot**.

2 In **Graph variables**, enter *Trade*, *NewFits*, and *NewFore* in rows 1–3, respectively.

3 Choose **Frame** ➤ **Multiple Graphs**.

4 Under **Generation of Multiple Graphs**, choose **Overlay graphs on the same page**. Click **OK**.

5 Click **Options**. In **Start time**, enter *1 1 61* in rows 1–3, respectively. Click **OK** in each dialog box.

Step 3: Calculate MSD

1 Choose **Calc** ➤ **Calculator**.

2 In **Store result in variable**, enter *MSD*.

3 Clear the **Expression** box by selecting the contents and pressing the delete key.

4 In **Functions**, double-click **Sum**. Within the parentheses in **Expression**, enter *((Trade − NewFits)**2) / 60*. Click **OK**.

5 Choose **Manip** ➤ **Display Data**.

6 In **Columns, Constants, and Matrices to display**, enter MSD. Click **OK**.

Graph window output

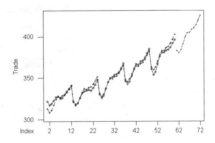

Session window output

Data Display

MSD
    11.8989

Interpreting the results

In the time series plot, the circles are the data, the pluses are the fits, and the crosses are the forecasts.

You can compare fits of different models using MSD. MSD for the quadratic trend model was 59.13. Additive and multiplicative decomposition models with a linear trend (not shown) give MSD values of 20.39 and 18.54, respectively. The MSD value of 11.90 for the combined quadratic trend and decomposition of residuals indicates a better fit using the additive trend analysis and decomposition models. You might also check the fit to these data of the multiplicative trend analysis and decomposition models.

Moving Average

Moving Average smooths your data by averaging consecutive observations in a series and provides short-term forecasts. This procedure can be a likely choice when your data do not have a trend or seasonal component. There are ways, however, to use moving averages when your data possess trend and/or seasonality.

Data

The time series must be in one numeric column. MINITAB automatically omits missing data from the calculations.

▶ To do a moving average

1 Choose **Stat ➤ Time Series ➤ Moving Average**.

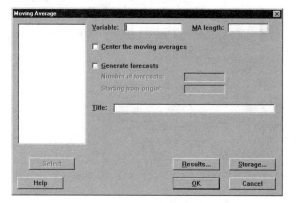

2 In **Variable**, enter the column containing the time series.

3 In **MA length**, enter a number to indicate the moving average length. See *Determining the moving average length* on page 7-19.

4 If you like, use one or more of the options listed below, then click **OK**.

Options

Moving Average dialog box

- center the moving averages. See *Centering moving average values* on page 7-19.
- specify the number of time units (leads) to forecast.
- specify the origin of forecasts (time unit before first forecast). The default is the end of the data.
- replace the default title with your own title.

Results subdialog box

- control the Graph window output. You can display
  - a plot of the fits or predicted values versus the actual data (the default)
  - a plot of the smoothed values versus the actual data
  - no plot
- control the Session window output. You can display
  - the default output, which includes a summary table.
  - the default output, a table of the data, the moving averages (smoothed values), the fits or predicted values (uncentered moving average from time $t-1$), and residuals. If you choose to forecast, the table also includes the forecasts with upper and lower 95% prediction limits.

Storage subdialog box

- store the moving averages, fits or predicted values (uncentered moving average from time $t-1$), residuals, forecasts, and upper and lower 95% prediction limits

Method

To calculate a moving average, MINITAB averages consecutive groups of observations in a series. For example, suppose a series begins with the numbers 4, 5, 8, 9, 10 and you use a moving average length of 3. The first two values of the moving average are missing. The third value of the moving average is the average of 4, 5, 8; the fourth value is the average of 5, 8, 9; the fifth value is the average of 8, 9, 10.

Determining the moving average length

With non-seasonal time series, it is common to use short moving averages to smooth the series, although the length you select may depend on the amount of noise in the series. A longer moving average filters out more noise, but is also less sensitive to changes in the series. With seasonal series, it is common to use a moving average of length equal to the length of the period. For example, you might choose a moving average length of 12 for monthly data with an annual cycle.

Centering moving average values

By default, moving average values are placed at the end of the period for which they are calculated. For example, for a moving average of length 3, the first two moving averages are missing (*), the first numeric moving average value is placed at time 3, the next at time 4, and so on.

When you center the moving averages, they are placed at the center of the range rather than at the end of the range. This is done to position the moving average values at their central positions in time.

If the moving average length is odd: Suppose the moving average length is 3. In this case, MINITAB places the first numeric moving average value at time 2, the next at time 3, and so on, with missing moving average values for the first and last times.

If the moving average length is even: Suppose the moving average length is 4. The center of that range is 2.5, but you cannot place a moving average value at time 2.5. Instead, data values 1–4 and 2–5 are averaged separately, then averaged together and placed at time 3. This process is repeated throughout the series, with missing values placed at the first two and the last two positions.

Forecasting

The fitted value at time t is the uncentered moving average at time t −1. The forecasts are the fitted values at the forecast origin. If you forecast 10 time units ahead, the forecasted value for each time will be the fitted value at the origin. Data up to the origin are used for calculating the moving averages.

You can use the *linear moving average method* by performing consecutive moving averages. This is often done when there is a trend in the data. First, compute and store the moving average of the original series. Then compute and store the moving average of the previously stored column to obtain a second moving average.

In *naive forecasting*, the forecast for time t is the data value at time t −1. Using moving average procedure with a moving average of length one gives naive forecasting.

See [1], [4], and [6] for a discussion of forecasting.

➤ Example of moving average

You wish to predict employment over the next 6 months in a segment of the metals industry using data collected over 60 months. You use the moving average method as there is no well-defined trend or seasonal pattern in the data.

1 Open the worksheet EMPLOY.MTW.

2 Choose **Stat ➤ Time Series ➤ Moving Average**.

3 In **Variable**, enter *Metals*. In **MA length**, enter 3.

4 Check **Center the moving averages**.

5 Check **Generate forecasts**, and enter 6 in **Number of forecasts**. Click **OK**.

Session window output

Moving average
```
Data        Metals
Length      60.0000
NMissing    0

Moving Average
Length: 3

Accuracy Measures
MAPE: 1.55036
MAD:  0.70292
MSD:  0.76433
```

Row	Period	Forecast	Lower	Upper
1	61	49.2	47.4865	50.9135
2	62	49.2	47.4865	50.9135
3	63	49.2	47.4865	50.9135
4	64	49.2	47.4865	50.9135
5	65	49.2	47.4865	50.9135
6	66	49.2	47.4865	50.9135

Graph window output

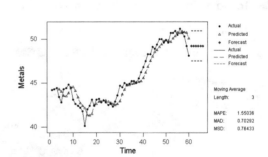

Interpreting the results

MINITAB generated the default time series plot which displays the series and fitted values (one-period-ahead forecasts), along with the six forecasts. Notice that the fitted value pattern lags behind the data pattern. This is because the fitted values are the moving averages from the previous time unit. If you wish to visually inspect how moving averages fit your data, plot the smoothed values rather than the predicted values.

To see exponential smoothing methods applied to the same data, see *Example of single exponential smoothing* on page 7-25 and *Example of double exponential smoothing* on page 7-29.

In the Session window, MINITAB displays three measures to help you determine the accuracy of the fitted values: MAPE, MAD, and MSD. See *Measures of accuracy* on page 7-7. MINITAB also displays the forecasts along with the corresponding lower and upper 95% prediction limits.

Single Exponential Smoothing

Single exponential smoothing smooths your data by computing exponentially weighted averages and provides short-term forecasts. This procedure works best for data without a trend or seasonal component. See [1], [4], and [6] for a discussion of exponential smoothing methods.

Data

Your time series must be in a numeric column.

The time series **cannot** include any missing values. If you have missing values, you may want to provide estimates of the missing values. If you

- have seasonal data, estimate the missing values as the fitted values from the decomposition procedure on page 7-10

- do not have seasonal data, estimate the missing values as the fitted values from the moving average procedure on page 7-18

▶ **To do a single exponential smoothing**

1 Choose **Stat** ➤ **Time Series** ➤ **Single Exp Smoothing**.

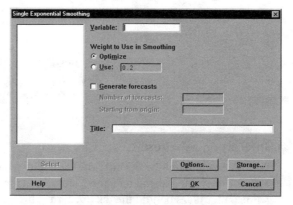

2 In **Variable**, enter the column containing the time series.

3 If you like, use one or more of the options listed below, then click **OK**.

Options

Single Exponential Smoothing dialog box

- specify a smoothing weight between 0 and 1 rather than using the calculated optimal weight. See *Choosing a weight* on page 7-23.

- specify the number of time units (leads) to forecast.
- specify the origin of forecasts (time unit before first forecast). The default is the end of the data.
- replace the default title with your own title.

Options subdialog box

- control the Graph window output. You can display
    - a plot of the fits or predicted values versus the actual data (the default)
    - a plot of the smoothed values versus the actual data
    - no plot
- control the Session window output. You can display
    - the default output, which includes a summary table.
    - the default output, a table of the data, the smoothed values, the fits or predicted values (smoothed value at time t −1), and residuals (data − fits). If you choose to forecast, the table also includes the forecasts with upper and lower 95% prediction limits.
- set the initial smoothed value to be the average of the first k observations when you specify the weight. You can specify k, which is 6 by default.

Storage subdialog box

- store the smoothed values, the fits or predicted values (smoothed value at time t −1), the residuals (data − fits), forecasts, and upper and lower 95% prediction limits

Choosing a weight

The weight is the smoothing parameter. You can have MINITAB supply the optimal weight (the default) or you can specify the weight. See *Method* on page 7-24 for more information.

Large weights result in more rapid changes in the fitted line; small weights result in less rapid changes in the fitted line. Therefore, the larger the weights the more the smoothed values follow the data; the smaller the weights the smoother the pattern in the smoothed values. Thus, small weights are usually recommended for a series with a high noise level around the signal or pattern. Large weights are usually recommended for a series with a small noise level around the pattern.

Among single exponential smoothing fits, the MSD accuracy measure will be smallest with optimal weights, but it is possible to obtain smaller MAPE and MAD values with non-optimal weights. See *Measures of accuracy* on page 7-7.

▶ **To specify your own weight**

In the main Single Exponential Smoothing dialog box, choose **Use** under **Weight to use in smoothing**, and enter a value between 0 and 2, although the usual choices are between 0 and 1.

You can use a rule of thumb for choosing a weight.

- A weight α will give smoothing that is approximately equivalent to an unweighted moving average of length $(2 - \alpha) / \alpha$.

- Conversely, if you want a weight to give a moving average of approximate length l, specify the weight to be $2 / (l + 1)$.

Method

The smoothed (predicted) values are obtained in one of two ways: with an optimal weight or with a specified weight.

- Optimal weight
  1. MINITAB fits the ARIMA $(0,1,1)$ model and stores the fits.
  2. The smoothed values are the ARIMA model fits, but lagged one time unit.
  3. Initial smoothed value (at time zero) by backcasting:

     initial smoothed value = [smoothed in period two $- \alpha$(data in period 1)] $/ (1 - \alpha)$

     where α is the weight.

- Specified weight
  1. MINITAB uses the average of the first six (or N, if N < 6) observations for the initial smoothed value (at time zero).
  2. Subsequent smoothed values are calculated from the formula:

     smoothed value at time t = (α)(data at t) $+ (1 - \alpha)$(smoothed at t − 1)

     where α is the weight.

Forecasting

The fitted value at time t is the smoothed value at time t − 1. The forecasts are the fitted value at the forecast origin. If you forecast 10 time units ahead, the forecasted value for each time will be the fitted value at the origin. Data up to the origin are used for the smoothing.

In *naive forecasting*, the forecast for time t is the data value at time t − 1. Perform single exponential smoothing with a weight of one to give naive forecasting.

➤ Example of single exponential smoothing

You wish to predict employment over 6 months in a segment of the metals industry using data collected over 60 months. You use single exponential smoothing because there is no clear trend or seasonal pattern in the data.

1 Open the worksheet EMPLOY.MTW.

2 Choose **Stat ➤ Time Series ➤ Single Exp Smoothing**.

3 In **Variable**, enter *Metals*.

4 Check **Generate forecasts**, and enter 6 in **Number of forecasts**. Click **OK**.

*Graph
window
output*

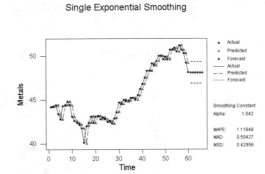

Interpreting the results

MINITAB generated the default time series plot which displays the series and fitted values (one-period-ahead forecasts), along with the six forecasts.

In both the Session and Graph windows, MINITAB displays the smoothing constant (weight) used and three measures to help you to determine the accuracy of the fitted values: MAPE, MAD, and MSD (see *Measures of accuracy* on page 7-7). The three accuracy measures, MAPE, MAD, and MSD, were 1.12, 0.50, and 0.43, respectively for the single exponential smoothing model, compared to 1.55, 0.70, and 0.76, respectively, for the moving average fit (see *Example of moving average* on page 7-20). Because these values are smaller for single exponential smoothing, you can judge that this method provides a better fit to these data.

Double Exponential Smoothing

Double exponential smoothing smooths your data by Holt (and Brown as a special case) double exponential smoothing and provides short-term forecasts. This procedure can work well when a trend is present but it can also serve as a general smoothing method. Dynamic estimates are calculated for two components: level and trend.

Data

Your time series must be in a numeric column.

The time series **cannot** include any missing values. If you have missing values, you may want to provide estimates of the missing values. If you

- have seasonal data, estimate the missing values as the fitted values from the decomposition procedure on page 7-10

- do not have seasonal data, estimate the missing values as the fitted values from the moving average procedure on page 7-18

▶ **To do a double exponential smoothing**

1 Choose **Stat ➤ Time Series ➤ Double Exp Smoothing**.

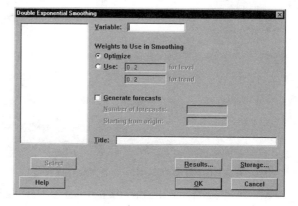

2 In **Variable**, enter the column containing the time series.

3 If you like, use one or more of the options listed below, then click **OK**.

Options

Double Exponential Smoothing dialog box

- specify smoothing weights for the level and trend components rather than using the calculated optimal weight. See *Choosing weights* on page 7-27.

- specify the number of time units (leads) to forecast.

- specify the origin of forecasts (time unit before first forecast). The default is the end of the data.

- replace the default title with your own title.

Results subdialog box

- control the Graph window output. You can display
  - a plot of the fits or predicted values versus the actual data (the default)
  - a plot of the smoothed values versus the actual data
  - no plot
- control the Session window output. You can display
  - the default output, which includes a summary table.
  - the default output, plus a table of the data, the smoothed values, the fits or predicted values (smoothed value at time t −1), and residuals (data − fits). If you choose to forecast, the table also includes the forecasts with upper and lower 95% prediction limits.

Storage subdialog box

You can store the smoothed values, the level (same as smoothed) and trend components, the fits or one-period-ahead forecasts, residuals, forecasts, and upper and lower 95% prediction limits. The fits at time t are the sum of level and trend from time t−1.

Choosing weights

The weights are the smoothing parameters. You can have MINITAB supply the optimal weights (the default) or you can specify weights between 0 and 1 for the trend and level components. See *Method* on page 7-28 for more information.

Regardless of the component, large weights result in more rapid changes in that component; small weights result in less rapid changes. Therefore, the larger the weights the more the smoothed values follow the data; the smaller the weights the smoother the pattern in the smoothed values. The components in turn affect the smoothed values and the predicted values. Thus, small weights are usually recommended for a series with a high noise level around the signal or pattern. Large weights are usually recommended for a series with a small noise level around the signal.

Among double exponential smoothing fits, the MSD accuracy measure will be smallest with optimal weights, but it is possible to obtain smaller MAPE and MAD values with nonoptimal weights. See *Measures of accuracy* on page 7-7.

▶ To specify your own weights

In the main Double Exponential Smoothing dialog box, choose **Use** under **Weight to use in smoothing**, and enter a value between 0 and 1 in the boxes for the level and/or the trend.

Method

Double exponential smoothing employs a level component and a trend component at each period. It uses two weights, or smoothing parameters, to update the components at each period. The double exponential smoothing equations are:

$$L_t = \alpha Y_t + (1 - \alpha)[L_{t-1} + T_{t-1}]$$

$$T_t = \gamma[L_t - L_{t-1}] + (1 - \gamma)T_{t-1}$$

$$\hat{Y}_t = L_{t-1} + T_{t-1}$$

where L_t is the level at time t, α is the weight for the level, T_t is the trend at time t, γ is the weight for the trend, Y_t is the data value at time t, and $\hat{Y}_t$ is the fitted value, or one-period-ahead forecast, at time t.

If the first observation is numbered one, then level and trend estimates at time zero must be initialized in order to proceed. The initialization method used to determine how the smoothed values are obtained in one of two ways: with optimal weights or with specified weights.

- Optimal weights
  1 MINITAB fits an ARIMA (0,2,2) model to the data, in order to minimize the sum of squared errors.
  2 The trend and level components are then initialized by backcasting.

- Specified weights
  1 MINITAB fits a linear regression model to time series data (y variable) versus time (x variable).
  2 The constant from this regression is the initial estimate of the level component, the slope coefficient is the initial estimate of the trend component.

When you specify weights that do not correspond to an equal-root ARIMA (0,2,2) model, MINITAB employs Holt's method. If you specify weights that do correspond to an equal-root ARIMA (0,2,2) model, MINITAB employs Brown's method.

Forecasting

Double exponential smoothing uses the level and trend components to generate forecasts. The forecast for m periods ahead from a point at time t is

$L_t + mT_t$, where L_t is the level and T_t is the trend at time t.

Data up to the forecast origin time will be used for the smoothing.

☞ **Example of double exponential smoothing**

You wish to predict employment over six months in a segment of the metals industry. You use double exponential smoothing as there is no clear trend or seasonal pattern in the data, and you want to compare the fit by this method with that from single exponential smoothing (see *Example of single exponential smoothing* on page 7-25).

1 Open the worksheet EMPLOY.MTW.

2 Choose **Stat ➤ Time Series ➤ Double Exp Smoothing**.

3 In **Variable**, enter *Metals*.

4 Check **Generate forecasts** and enter 6 in **Number of forecasts**. Click **OK**.

Session window output

Double Exponential Smoothing

```
Data       Metals
Length     60.0000
NMissing   0

Smoothing Constants
Alpha (level): 1.03840
Gamma (trend): 0.02997

Accuracy Measures
MAPE: 1.19684
MAD:  0.54058
MSD:  0.46794
```

Row	Period	Forecast	Lower	Upper
1	61	48.0961	46.7717	49.4206
2	62	48.1357	46.0599	50.2114
3	63	48.1752	45.3134	51.0369
4	64	48.2147	44.5545	51.8748
5	65	48.2542	43.7898	52.7185
6	66	48.2937	43.0220	53.5653

Graph window output

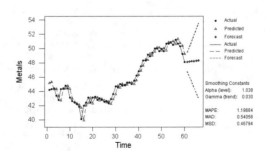

Double Exponential Smoothing for Metals

Interpreting the results

MINITAB generated the default time series plot which displays the series and fitted values (one-period-ahead forecasts), along with the six forecasts.

In both the Session and Graph windows, MINITAB displays the smoothing constants (weights) for the level and trend components and three measures to help you determine the accuracy of the fitted values: MAPE, MAD, and MSD (see *Measures of accuracy* on page 7-7).

The three accuracy measures, MAPE, MAD, and MSD, were 1.30, 0.54, and 0.47, respectively, for double exponential smoothing fit, compared to 1.12, 0.50, and 0.43, respectively, for the single exponential smoothing fit (see *Example of single exponential smoothing* on page 7-25). Because these values are smaller for single exponential smoothing, you can judge that this method provides a slightly better fit to these data when optimal weights are used.

Because the difference in accuracy measures for the two exponential smoothing methods are small, you might consider the type of forecast (horizontal line versus line with slope) in selecting between methods. Double exponential smoothing forecasts an employment pattern that is slightly increasing though the last four observations are decreasing. A higher weight on the trend component can result in a prediction in the same direction as the data, which may be more realistic, but the measured fit will not be as good as with the optimal weights.

Winters' Method

Winters' Method smooths your data by Holt-Winters exponential smoothing and provides short to medium-range forecasting. You can use this procedure when both trend and seasonality are present, with these two components being either additive or multiplicative. Winters' Method calculates dynamic estimates for three components: level, trend, and seasonal.

Data

Your time series must be in one numeric column.

The time series **cannot** include any missing values. If you have missing values, you may want to provide estimates of the missing values. If you

- have seasonal data, estimate the missing values as the fitted values from the decomposition procedure on page 7-10

- do not have seasonal data, estimate the missing values as the fitted values from the moving average procedure on page 7-18

▶ **To do an exponential smoothing by Winters' method**

1 Choose Stat ➤ Time Series ➤ Winters' Method.

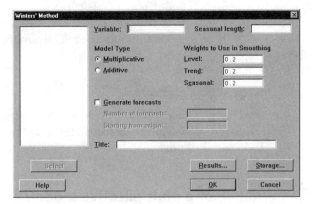

2 In **Variable**, enter the column containing the time series.

3 In **Seasonal length**, enter a number ≥ 2 for the period or seasonal length.

4 If you like, use one or more of the options listed below, then click **OK**.

Options

Winters' Method dialog box

- specify that the level and seasonal components should be additive rather than multiplicative. See *An additive or a multiplicative model?* on page 7-32.

- specify weights for the level, trend, and seasonal components. The defaults are 0.2. See *Choosing weights* on page 7-32.

- specify the number of time units (leads) to forecast.

- specify the origin of forecasts (time unit before first forecast). The default is the end of the data.

- replace the default title with your own title.

Results subdialog box

- control the Graph window output. You can display
  - a plot of the fits or predicted values versus the actual data (the default)
  - a plot of the smoothed values versus the actual data
  - no plot

- control the Session window output. You can display
  - the default output, which includes a summary table.
  - the default output, plus a table of the data, the smoothed values, the fits or predicted values (one-period-ahead forecasts), and residuals (data – fits). If you choose to forecast, the table also includes the forecasts with upper and lower 95% prediction limits.

Storage subdialog box

- store the smoothed values, level, trend, and seasonal estimates, the fits or predicted values (one-period-ahead forecasts), the residuals (data – fits), forecasts, and upper and lower 95% prediction limits

An additive or a multiplicative model?

The Holt-Winters' model is multiplicative when the level and seasonal components are multiplied together and it is additive when they are added together. Choose the multiplicative model when the magnitude of the seasonal pattern in the data depends on the magnitude of the data. In other words, the magnitude of the seasonal pattern increases as the data values increase, and decreases as the data values decrease.

Choose the additive model when the magnitude of the seasonal pattern in the data does not depend on the magnitude of the data. In other words, the magnitude of the seasonal pattern does not change as the series goes up or down.

Choosing weights

You can enter weights, or smoothing parameters, for the level, trend, and seasonal components. The default weights are 0.2 and you can enter values between 0 and 1. Since an equivalent ARIMA model exists only for a very restricted form of the Holt-Winters model, MINITAB does not compute optimal parameters for Winters' method as it does for single and double exponential smoothing.

Regardless of the component, large weights result in more rapid changes in that component; small weights result in less rapid changes. The components in turn affect the smoothed values and the predicted values. Thus, small weights are usually recommended for a series with a high noise level around the signal or pattern. Large weights are usually recommended for a series with a small noise level around the signal.

Method

Winters' method employs a level component, a trend component, and a seasonal component at each period. It uses three weights, or smoothing parameters, to update the components at each period. Initial values for the level and trend components are obtained from a linear regression on time. Initial values for the seasonal component are obtained from a dummy-variable regression using detrended data. The Winters' method smoothing equations are:

- Additive model:

$$L_t = \alpha(Y_t - S_{t-p}) + (1-\alpha)[L_{t-1} + T_{t-1}]$$

$$T_t = \gamma[L_t - L_{t-1}] + (1-\gamma)T_{t-1}$$

$$S_t = \delta(Y_t - L_t) + (1-\delta)S_{t-p}$$

$$\hat{Y}_t = L_{t-1} + T_{t-1} + S_{t-p}$$

- Multiplicative model:

$$L_t = \alpha(Y_t / S_{t-p}) + (1-\alpha)[L_{t-1} + T_{t-1}]$$

$$T_t = \gamma[L_t - L_{t-1}] + (1-\gamma)T_{t-1}$$

$$S_t = \delta(Y_t / L_t) + (1-\delta)S_{t-p}$$

$$\hat{Y}_t = (L_{t-1} + T_{t-1}) \times (S_{t-p})$$

where L_t is the level at time t, α is the weight for the level, T_t is the trend at time t, γ is the weight for the trend, S_t is the seasonal component at time t, δ is the weight for the seasonal component, p is the seasonal period, Y_t is the data value at time t, and $\hat{Y}_t$ is the fitted value, or one-period-ahead forecast, at time t.

Forecasting

Winters' method uses the level, trend, and seasonal components to generate forecasts. The forecast for m periods ahead from a point at time t is

$L_t + mT_t$, where L_t is the level and T_t is the trend at time t, multiplied by (or added to for an additive model) the seasonal component for the same period from the previous year.

Winters' Method uses data up to the forecast origin time to generate the forecasts.

> **Example of Winters' method**

You wish to predict employment for the next six months in a food preparation industry using data collected over the last 60 months. You use Winters' method with the default multiplicative model, because there is a seasonal component, and possibly trend, apparent in the data.

1 Open the worksheet EMPLOY.MTW.

2 Choose **Stat ➤ Time Series ➤ Winters' Method**.

3 In **Variable**, enter *Food*, and *12* in **Seasonal length**.

4 Under **Model Type**, choose **Multiplicative**.

5 Check **Generate forecasts** and enter 6 in **Number of forecasts**. Click **OK**.

Session window output

Winters' multiplicative model

```
Data        Food
Length      60.0000
NMissing    0

Smoothing Constants
Alpha (level):   0.2
Gamma (trend):   0.2
Delta (seasonal): 0.2

Accuracy Measures
MAPE: 1.88377
MAD:  1.12068
MSD:  2.86696
```

Row	Period	Forecast	Lower	Upper
1	61	57.8102	55.0645	60.5558
2	62	57.3892	54.5864	60.1921
3	63	57.8332	54.9687	60.6977
4	64	57.9307	55.0005	60.8609
5	65	58.8311	55.8313	61.8309
6	66	62.7415	59.6686	65.8145

Graph window output

Winters' Multiplicative Model for Food

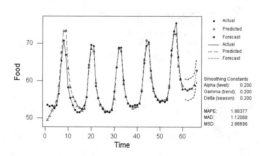

Interpreting the results

MINITAB generated the default time series plot which displays the series and fitted values (one-period-ahead forecasts), along with the six forecasts.

In both the Session and Graph windows, MINITAB displays the smoothing constants (weights) used for level, trend, and seasonal components used and three measures to help you determine the accuracy of the fitted values: MAPE, MAD, and MSD (see *Measures of accuracy* on page 7-7).

For these data, MAPE, MAD, and MSD were 1.88, 1.12, and 2.87, respectively, with the multiplicative model. MAPE, MAD, and MSD were 1.95, 1.15, and 2.67, respectively (output not shown) with the additive model, indicating that the multiplicative model provided a slightly better fit according to two of the three accuracy measures.

Differences

Differences computes the differences between data values of a time series. If you wish to fit an ARIMA model but there is trend or seasonality present in your data, differencing data is a common step in assessing likely ARIMA models. Differencing is used to simplify the correlation structure and to help reveal any underlying pattern.

Data

Your time series must be in one numeric column. MINITAB stores the difference for missing data as missing (*).

▶ **To do differencing**

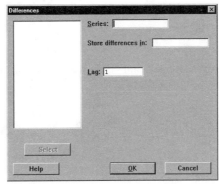

1 Choose **Stat ➤ Time Series ➤ Differences**.

2 In **Series** enter a column containing the series you wish to difference.

3 In **Store differences in**, enter a name for the storage column.

4 If you like, use the option listed below, then click **OK**.

Options

You can change the lag period from the default of one.

Method

MINITAB calculates the differences between data values. The values that are differenced depend on the length of the lag. If you request a lag of k, the entries in the stored column are the data values in the original column minus the data value k rows above. For example, suppose you difference a column using a lag of two:

```
Input        Stored
  1             *
  3             *
  8     →       7
 12             9
  7            -1
```

Since the lag = 2, MINITAB stores asterisks (*) in rows 1 and 2 of Stored. Row 3 of Stored contains 8 − 1, row 4 contains 12 − 3, row 5 contains 7 − 8.

Lag

Lag computes lags of a column and stores them in a new column. To lag a time series, MINITAB moves the data down the column and inserts missing values at the top of the column. The number of missing values inserted depends on the length of the lag.

Data

Your time series must be in one numeric column. MINITAB stores the lag for missing data as missing.

▶ **To lag a time series**

  1 Choose **Stat ➤ Time Series ➤ Lag**.

  2 In **Series**, enter a column containing the series you wish to lag.

  3 In **Store lags in**, enter a name for the storage column.

  4 If you like, use the option listed below, then click **OK**.

Options

You can change the lag period from the default of one.

Method

To lag a time series, MINITAB moves the data down the column and inserts missing
values at the top of the column. The number of missing values inserted depends on the
length of the lag. If you request lag of k time units, the entries in the stored column are
the same as units of the original column shifted down k cells, with k missing values
inserted at the top. For example, suppose you lag a column using a lag of three:

```
Input        Stored
   5            *
   3            *
  18     →      *
   7            5
  10            3
   2            18
```

Since the lag = 3, MINITAB stores asterisks (*) in rows 1, 2, and 3 of Stored. Beginning
with row 4, the original data is stored down the column until the column of lagged data
is the same length as the original time series data.

Autocorrelation

Autocorrelation computes and plots the autocorrelations of a time series. Autocorrelation is the correlation between observations of a time series separated by k time units. The plot of autocorrelations is called the autocorrelation function or acf. View the acf to guide your choice of terms to include in an ARIMA model. See *Fitting an ARIMA model* on page 7-46.

More | See Help for calculations.

Data

Your time series must be entered in one numeric column. You must either estimate or delete missing data before using this procedure.

▶ **To do an autocorrelation function**

1 Choose **Stat ➤ Time Series ➤ Autocorrelation**.

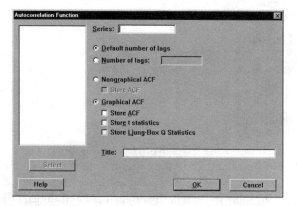

2 In **Series**, enter the column containing the time series.

3 If you like, use one or more of the options listed below, then click **OK**.

Options

- change the number of lags for which to display autocorrelations. The default is n / 4 for a series with less than or equal to 240 observations or $\sqrt{n} + 45$ for a series with more than 240 observations, where n is the number of observations in the series.

- display the acf in the Session window or in a Graph window.

- when you display the acf in the Session window:
  - the maximum number of lags is n − 1.
  - you can store the acf.
- when you display the acf in a Graph window:
  - the maximum number of lags is n − 1, however, only the first 75 lags will be displayed in the table beneath the graph. (Note, if you specify more than n − 1 lags, MINITAB will use the default number of lags instead.)
  - you can store the acf, the t-statistics, and the Ljung-Box Q statistics.
  - you can replace the default title with your own title.

▷ Example of autocorrelation

You wish to predict employment in a food preparation industry using past employment data. You want to use ARIMA to do this but first you use autocorrelation in order to help identify a likely model. Because the data exhibit a strong 12 month seasonal component, you take a difference at lag 12 in order to induce stationarity and look at the autocorrelation of the differenced series. There may be some long-term trend in these data, but the magnitude of it appears to be small compared to the seasonal component. If the trend was larger, you might consider taking another difference at lag 1 to induce stationarity.

1 Open the worksheet EMPLOY.MTW.

2 Choose **Stat ➤ Time Series ➤ Differences**.

3 In **Series**, enter *Food*.

4 In **Store differences in**, enter *Food2*.

5 In **Lag**, enter *12*. Click **OK**.

6 Choose **Stat ➤ Time Series ➤ Autocorrelation**.

7 In **Series**, enter *Food2*. Click **OK**.

Graph window output

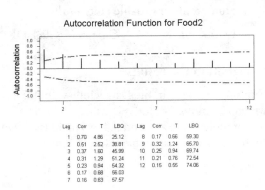

Autocorrelation Function for Food2

Lag	Corr	T	LBQ	Lag	Corr	T	LBQ
1	0.70	4.86	25.12	8	0.17	0.66	59.30
2	0.51	2.52	38.81	9	0.32	1.24	65.70
3	0.37	1.60	45.99	10	0.25	0.94	69.74
4	0.31	1.29	51.24	11	0.21	0.76	72.54
5	0.23	0.94	54.32	12	0.15	0.55	74.06
6	0.17	0.68	56.03				
7	0.16	0.63	57.57				

Interpreting the results

MINITAB generates an autocorrelation function with confidence limits for the correlations in a Graph window. Below the acf, MINITAB displays the autocorrelations, associated Ljung-Box Q statistics, and t-statistics. Since you did not specify the lag length, autocorrelation uses the default length of n / 4 for a series with less than or equal to 240 observations.

The acf for these data shows large positive, significant spikes at lags 1 and 2 with subsequent positive autocorrelations that do not die off quickly. This pattern is typical of an autoregressive process.

The following example tests the null hypothesis that the autocorrelations for all lags up to a lag of 6 are zero.

▷ Example of testing the autocorrelations

You can use the Ljung-Box Q (LBQ) statistic to test the null hypothesis that the autocorrelations for all lags up to lag k equal zero. Let's test that all autocorrelations up to a lag of 6 are zero. The LBQ statistic is 56.03.

To compute the cumulative probability function:

1 Choose **Calc ➤ Probability Distributions ➤ Chi-Square**.

2 Check **Cumulative Probability**.

3 In **Degrees of freedom**, enter 6 (the lag of your test).

4 Choose **Input constant** and enter 56.03 (the LBQ value).

5 In **Optional storage**, enter *Cumprob*. This stores the cumulative probability function in a constant named *Cumprob*. Click **OK**.

To compute the p-value

6 Choose **Calc ➤ Calculator**.

7 In **Store result in variable** enter *pvalue*.

8 In **Expression**, enter *1 − 'Cumprob'*. Click **OK**.

Interpreting the results

Examine the value in the Data window. In this example, the p-value is 0.000000, which means the p-value is less than 0.0000005. The very small p-value implies that one or more of the autocorrelations up to lag 6 can be judged as significantly different from zero at any reasonable α level.

Partial Autocorrelation

Partial Autocorrelation computes and plots the partial autocorrelations of a time series. Partial autocorrelations, like autocorrelations, are correlations between sets of ordered data pairs of a time series. As with partial correlations in the regression case, partial autocorrelations measure the strength of relationship with other terms being accounted for. The partial autocorrelation at a lag of k is the correlation between residuals at time t from an autoregressive model and observations at lag k with terms for all intervening lags present in the autoregressive model. The plot of partial autocorrelations is called the partial autocorrelation function or pacf. View the pacf to guide your choice of terms to include in an ARIMA model.

Data

Your time series must be entered in one numeric column. You must either estimate or delete missing data before using this procedure.

▶ To do a partial autocorrelation function

1 Choose **Stat ➤ Time Series ➤ Partial Autocorrelation**.

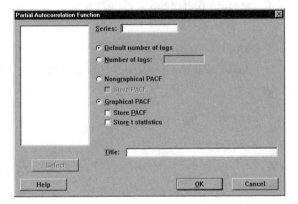

2 In **Series**, enter the column containing the time series.

3 If you like, use one or more of the options listed below, then click **OK**.

Options

- change the number of lags for which to display partial autocorrelations. The default is n / 4 for a series with less than or equal to 240 observations or $\sqrt{n} + 45$ for a series with more than 240 observations, where n is the number of observations in the series.

- display the pacf in the Session window or in a Graph window.

- when you display the pacf in the Session window:
  - the maximum number of lags is n − 1.
  - you can store the pacf.

- when you display the pacf in a Graph window:
  - the maximum number of lags is n − 1, however, only the first 75 lags will be displayed in the table beneath the graph. (Note, if you specify more than n − 1 lags, MINITAB will use the default number of lags instead.)
  - you can store the pacf and the t-statistics.
  - you can replace the default title with your own title.

▷ Example of partial autocorrelation

You obtain a pacf of the food industry employment data, after taking a difference of lag 12, in order to help determine a likely ARIMA model.

1 Open the worksheet EMPLOY.MTW.

2 Choose **Stat ➤ Time Series ➤ Differences**.

3 In **Series**, enter *Food*.

4 In **Store differences in**, enter *Food2*.

5 In **Lag**, enter *12*. Click **OK**.

6 Choose **Stat ➤ Time Series ➤ Partial Autocorrelation**.

7 In **Series**, enter *Food2*. Click **OK**.

Graph window output

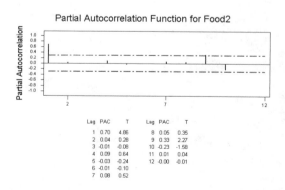

Partial Autocorrelation Function for Food2

Lag	PAC	T	Lag	PAC	T
1	0.70	4.86	8	0.05	0.35
2	0.04	0.28	9	0.33	2.27
3	-0.01	-0.08	10	-0.23	-1.58
4	0.09	0.64	11	0.01	0.04
5	-0.03	-0.24	12	-0.00	-0.01
6	-0.01	-0.10			
7	0.08	0.52			

Interpreting the results

MINITAB generates a partial autocorrelation function with confidence limits for the correlations in a Graph window. Below the graph, MINITAB displays the partial autocorrelations and associated t-statistics.

In the food data example, there is a single large spike of 0.7 at lag 1, which is typical of an autoregressive process of order one. There is also a significant spike at lag 9, but you have no evidence of a nonrandom process occurring there.

Cross Correlation

Cross correlation computes and graphs correlations between two time series.

Data

You must have two time series in separate numeric columns of equal length. You must either estimate or delete missing data before using this procedure.

▶ To do a cross correlation

1 Choose Stat ➤ Time Series ➤ Cross Correlation.

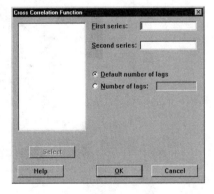

2 In **First Series**, enter the column containing one time series.

3 In **Second Series**, enter the column containing other time series.

4 If you like, use the option listed below, then click **OK**.

Options

You can specify the number of lags for which to display cross correlations. The default is $-(\sqrt{n} + 10)$ to $(\sqrt{n} + 10)$ lags.

ARIMA

ARIMA fits a Box-Jenkins ARIMA model to a time series. ARIMA stands for Autoregressive Integrated Moving Average with each term representing steps taken in the model construction until only random noise remains. Use ARIMA to model time series behavior and to generate forecasts. ARIMA modeling differs from the other time series methods discussed in this chapter in the fact that ARIMA modeling uses correlational techniques. ARIMA can be used to model patterns that may not be visible in plotted data. The concepts used in this procedure follow Box and Jenkins [2]. For an elementary introduction to time series, see [3], [11].

Data

Your time series must be in a numeric column. Missing data in the middle of your series are not allowed. If you have missing values, you may want to provide estimates of the missing values.

▶ To fit an ARIMA model

1 Choose **Stat ➤ Time Series ➤ ARIMA**.

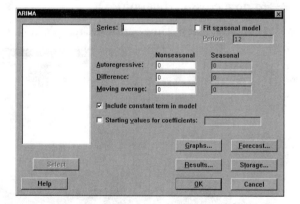

2 In **Series**, enter the column containing the time series.

3 For at least one of **Autoregressive** or **Moving Average** under either **Nonseasonal** or **Seasonal**, enter the number of parameters. See *Entering the ARIMA model* on page 7-47.

4 If you like, use one or more the options listed below, then click **OK**.

Options

ARIMA dialog box

- fit a seasonal model and specify the period. The default period is 12.

- specify the number of autoregressive and moving average parameters to include in nonseasonal or seasonal ARIMA models. You must specify a number for one of these. See *Entering the ARIMA model* on page 7-47.

- specify the number of nonseasonal or seasonal differences to take. See *Entering the ARIMA model* on page 7-47.

- exclude a constant term from the model.

- specify starting values for the parameter estimates. Default starting values are 0.1 except for the constant. See *Entering the ARIMA model* on page 7-47.

Graphs subdialog box

- display a time series plot with forecasts and 95% confidence limits of the raw data

- display an acf, a pacf, a histogram, or a normal plot of the residuals

- display scatter plots of the residuals vs. fits, the residuals vs. data order (1 2 3 4... *n*), or the residuals vs. specified columns

Results subdialog box

- display the following in the Session window:
  - no output
  - final parameter estimates, differencing information, residual sums of squares, and the number of observations
  - the default output, which includes the output described above, plus parameter estimates at each iteration, and back forecasts if they are not dying out rapidly
  - the default output, plus a correlation matrix of the parameter estimates
  - all the output described above, plus the back forecasts

Forecast subdialog box

- specify the number of time units (leads) to forecast.

- specify the origin of forecasts (time unit before first forecast). The default is the end of the data.

- store forecasts, and upper and lower limits.

Storage subdialog box

- store residuals, fits, or coefficients

Fitting an ARIMA model

Box and Jenkins [2] present an interactive approach for fitting ARIMA models to time series. This iterative approach involves identifying the model, estimating the parameters, checking model adequacy, and forecasting, if desired. The model identification step generally requires judgement from the analyst.

1 First, decide if the data are stationary.- That is, do the data possess constant mean and variance.

   ■ Examine a time series plot to see if a transformation is required to give constant variance.

   ■ Examine the acf to see if large autocorrelations do not die out, indicating that differencing may be required to give a constant mean.

   A seasonal pattern that repeats every k^{th} time interval suggests taking the kth difference to remove a portion of the pattern. Most series should not require more than two difference operations or orders. Be careful not to overdifference. If spikes in the acf die out rapidly, there is no need for further differencing. A sign of an overdifferenced series is the first autocorrelation close to -0.5 and small values elsewhere [11].

   Use **Stat ➤ Time Series ➤ Differences** to take and store differences. Then, to examine the acf and pacf of the differenced series, use **Stat ➤ Time Series ➤ Autocorrelation** and **Stat ➤ Time Series ➤ Partial Autocorrelation**.

2 Next, examine the acf and pacf of your stationary data in order to identify what autoregressive or moving average models terms are suggested.

   ■ An acf with large spikes at initial lags that decay to zero or a pacf with a large spike at the first and possibly at the second lag indicates an autoregressive process.

   ■ An acf with a large spike at the first and possibly at the second lag and a pacf with large spikes at initial lags that decay to zero indicates a moving average process.

   ■ The acf and the pacf both exhibiting large spikes that gradually die out indicates that both autoregressive and moving averages processes are present.

   For most data, no more than two autoregressive parameters or two moving average parameters are required in ARIMA models. See [11] for more details on identifying ARIMA models.

3 Once you have identified one or more likely models, you are ready to use the ARIMA procedure.

   ■ Fit the likely models and examine the significance of parameters and select one model that gives the best fit. See *Entering the ARIMA model* on page 7-47.

   ■ Check that the acf and pacf of residuals indicate a random process, signified when there are no large spikes. You can easily obtain an acf and a pacf of residual using ARIMA's Graphs subdialog box. If large spikes remain, consider changing the model.

■ You may perform several iterations in finding the best model. When you are satisfied with the fit, go ahead and make forecasts.

The ARIMA algorithm will perform up to 25 iterations to fit a given model. If the solution does not converge, store the estimated parameters and use them as starting values for a second fit. You can store the estimated parameters and use them as starting values for a subsequent fit as often as necessary.

Entering the ARIMA model

After you have identified one or more likely models, you need to specify the model in the main ARIMA dialog box.

■ If you want to fit a seasonal model, check **Fit seasonal model** and enter a number to specify the period. The period is the span of the seasonality or the interval at which the pattern is repeated. The default period is 12.

You must check **Fit seasonal model** before you can enter the seasonal autoregressive and moving average parameters or the number of seasonal differences to take.

■ To specify autoregressive and moving average parameters to include in nonseasonal or seasonal ARIMA models, enter a value from 0 to 5. The maximum is 5. At least one of these parameters must be nonzero. The total for all parameters must not exceed 10. For most data, no more than two autoregressive parameters or two moving average parameters are required in ARIMA models.

Suppose you enter 2 in the box for **Moving Average** under **Seasonal**, the model will include first and second order moving average terms.

■ To specify the number of nonseasonal and/or seasonal differences to take, enter a number in the appropriate box. If you request one seasonal difference with k as the seasonal period, the kth difference will be taken.

■ To include the constant in the model, check **Include constant term in model**.

■ You may want to specify starting values for the parameter estimates. You must first enter the starting values in a worksheet column in the following order: AR's (autoregressive parameters), seasonal AR's, MA's (moving average parameters), seasonal MA's, and if you checked **Include constant term in model** enter the starting value for the constant in the last row of the column. This is the same order in which the parameters appear on the output. Check **Starting values for coefficients**, and enter the column containing the starting values for each parameter included in the model. Default starting values are 0.1 except for the constant.

▷ Example of fitting an ARIMA model

The acf and pacf of the food employment data (see *Example of autocorrelation* on page 7-39 and *Example of partial autocorrelation* on page 7-42) suggest an autoregressive model of order 1, or AR(1), after taking a difference of order 12. You fit that model here, examine diagnostic plots, and examine the goodness of fit. To take a seasonal difference of order 12, you specify the seasonal period to be 12, and the order of the difference to be 1. In the subsequent example, you perform forecasting.

1 Open the worksheet EMPLOY.MTW.

2 Choose **Stat ➤ Time Series ➤ ARIMA**.

3 In **Series**, enter *Food*.

4 Check **Fit seasonal model**. In **Period**, enter *12*. Under **Nonseasonal**, enter *1* in **Autoregressive**. Under **Seasonal**, enter *1* in **Difference**.

5 Click **Graphs**.

6 Check **ACF of residuals** and **PACF of residuals**. Click **OK** in each dialog box.

Session window output

ARIMA Model: Food

```
ARIMA model for Food

Estimates at each iteration
Iteration       SSE     Parameters
       0     95.2343    0.100    0.847
       1     77.5568    0.250    0.702
       2     64.5317    0.400    0.556
       3     56.1578    0.550    0.410
       4     52.4345    0.700    0.261
       5     52.2226    0.733    0.216
       6     52.2100    0.741    0.203
       7     52.2092    0.743    0.201
       8     52.2092    0.743    0.200
       9     52.2092    0.743    0.200
Relative change in each estimate less than  0.0010

Final Estimates of Parameters
Type        Coef     SE Coef        T        P
AR   1     0.7434     0.1001     7.42    0.000
Constant   0.1996     0.1520     1.31    0.196

Differencing: 0 regular, 1 seasonal of order 12
Number of observations:  Original series 60, after differencing 48
Residuals:    SS =  51.0364  (backforecasts excluded)
              MS =   1.1095  DF = 46

Modified Box-Pierce (Ljung-Box) Chi-Square statistic
Lag              12       24       36       48
Chi-Square     11.3     19.1     27.7        *
DF               10       22       34        *
P-Value       0.338    0.641    0.768        *
```

Graph window output

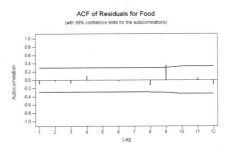

ACF of Residuals for Food
(with 95% confidence limits for the autocorrelations)

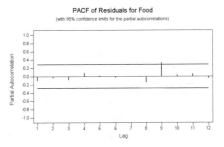

PACF of Residuals for Food
(with 95% confidence limits for the partial autocorrelations)

Interpreting the results

The ARIMA model converged after nine iterations. The AR(1) parameter had a t-value of 7.42. As a rule of thumb, you can consider values over two as indicating that the associated parameter can be judged as significantly different from zero. The MSE, here 1.1095, can be used to compare fits of different ARIMA models.

The Ljung-Box statistics give nonsignificant p-values, indicating that the residuals appeared to uncorrelated. The acf and pacf of the residuals corroborate this. You assume that the spikes in the acf and pacf at lag 8 are the result of random events. The AR(1) model appears to fit well so you use it to forecast employment in the next example.

⏵ Example of forecasting with an ARIMA model

In the previous example, you found that an AR(1) model with a twelfth seasonal difference gave a good fit to the food sector employment data. You now use this fit to predict employment for the next 12 months. The Session window output is not shown; you can see this output on page 7-48.

Step 1: Refit the ARIMA model without displaying the acf and pacf of the residuals:

1 Perform steps 1–5 of *Example of fitting an ARIMA model* on page 7-48.

2 Uncheck **ACF of residuals** and **PACF of residuals**.

To display a time series plot:

3 Check **Time series plot**. Click **OK**.

Step 2: Generate the forecasts:

4 Click **Forecast**. In **Lead,** enter *12*. Click **OK** in each dialog box.

*Graph
window
output*

Interpreting the results

ARIMA gives forecasts, with 95% confidence limits, using the AR(1) model in both the Session window (not shown) and a Graph window. The seasonality dominates the forecast profile for the next 12 months with the forecast values being slightly higher than for the previous 12 months.

References

[1] B.L. Bowerman and O'Connell (1987). *Time Series Forecasting: Unified Concepts and Computer Implementation*, Duxbury, Boston.

[2] G.E.P. Box and G.M. Jenkins (1976). *Time Series Analysis: Forecasting and Control*, Revised Edition, Holden Day.

[3] J.D. Cryer (1986). *Time Series Analysis*, Duxbury Press.

[4] N.R. Farnum and L.W. Stanton (1989). *Quantitative Forecasting Methods*. PWS-Kent, Boston.

[5] G.M. Ljung and G.E.P. Box (1978). "On a Measure of Lack of Fit in Time Series Models," *Biometrika* 65, pp.67–72.

[6] S. Makridakis, S.C. Wheelwright, and V.E. McGee (1983). *Forecasting: Methods and Applications*. Wiley, New York.

[7] D.W. Marquardt (1963). "An Algorithm for Least Squares Estimation of Nonlinear Parameters," *Journal Soc. Ind. Applied Mathematics* 11, pp.431–441.

[8] W.Q. Meeker, Jr. (1977). "TSERIES—A User-oriented Computer Program for Identifying, Fitting and Forecasting ARIMA Time Series Models," *ASA 1977 Proceedings of the Statistical Computing Section*.

[9] W.Q. Meeker, Jr. (1977). *TSERIES User's Manual*, Statistical Laboratory, Iowa State University.

[10] R.B. Miller and D.W. Wichern (1977). *Intermediate Business Statistics*, Holt, Rinehart and Winston.

[11] W. Vandaele (1983). *Applied Time Series and Box-Jenkins Models*. Academic Press, Inc, New York.

Acknowledgment

The ARIMA algorithm is based on the fitting routine in the TSERIES package written by Professor William Q. Meeker, Jr., of Iowa State University [8], [9]. We are grateful to Professor Meeker for his help in the adaptation of his routine to MINITAB.

8

Exploratory Data Analysis

Exploratory Data Analysis Overview

Exploratory data analysis (EDA) methods are used primarily to explore data before using more traditional methods, or to examine residuals from a model. These methods are particularly useful for identifying extraordinary observations and noting violations of traditional assumptions, such as nonlinearity or nonconstant variance.

- **Letter Values** generates a letter-value display. Use this procedure to describe the location and spread of sample distributions.

- **Median Polish** fits an additive model to a two-way design and identifies data patterns not explained by row and column effects. This procedure is similar to analysis of variance except medians are used instead of means, thus adding robustness against the effect of outliers.

- **Resistant Line** uses a method that is resistant to outliers to fit a straight line to your data. You can fit a resistant line before using a least squares regression to see if the relationship is linear, to find re-expressions to linearize the relationship if necessary, and to identify outliers.

- **Resistant Smooth** smooths an ordered sequence of data, usually collected over time, to remove random fluctuations. Smoothing is useful for discovering and summarizing both data trends and outliers.

- **Rootogram** displays a suspended rootogram for your data. A suspended rootogram is a histogram with a normal distribution fit to it, which displays the deviations from the fitted normal distribution.

Letter Values

Use letter-value displays to describe the location and spread of sample distributions. The statistics given depend on the sample size, and include median, hinges, eighths, and more.

Data

You need one column that contains numeric or date/time data, but no missing values. Delete any missing values from the worksheet before displaying letter values.

▶ **To display letter values**

1 Choose Stat ➤ EDA ➤ Letter Values.

2 In **Variable**, enter the column that contains the data for which you want to obtain letter values.

3 If you like, use the option listed below, then click **OK**.

Options

You can store the letter values, middle values, and spreads.

Method

Letter values are defined by their depth. We use n for the number of observations.

depth of median:	d(M)	=	(n + 1) / 2
depth of hinges:	d(H)	=	([d(M)] + 1) / 2
depth of eighths:	d(E)	=	([d(H)] + 1) / 2
depth of sixteenths:	d(D)	=	([d(E)] + 1) / 2

Remaining depths are found by continuing the pattern (depth of thirty-seconds, sixty-fourths, etc.). The depth is determined by the amount of data in the column. Remaining depths are labeled sequentially C, B, A, Z, Y, X, W, V, U...

To find the letter values, MINITAB first orders the data. The lower hinge is the observation at a distance d(H) from the smallest observation; the upper hinge is the observation at a distance d(H) from the largest observation. Similarly, the lower and upper eighths are the observations at a depth d(E), and so on. If the depth for the data does not coincide with a data value, the average of the nearest neighbors is taken.

The middle value for a given depth is the average of the upper and lower letter values at that depth. The spread is (upper – lower).

When you store the letter values, the column will contain all the numbers on the output listed under Lower (starting from the bottom and going up), then the median, and then the numbers listed under Upper (starting from the top and going down).

▷ Example of letter values

Students in an introductory statistics course participated in a simple experiment. Before beginning the experiment each student recorded their resting pulse rate. We will use a letter-value display to describe the location and spread of the resting pulse rate data.

1 Open the worksheet PULSE.MTW.

2 Choose **Stat ➤ EDA ➤ Letter Values**.

3 In **Variable**, enter *Pulse1*. Click **OK**.

Session window output

Letter Value Display: Pulse1

	Depth	Lower	Upper	Mid	Spread
N=	92				
M	46.5	71.000		71.000	
H	23.5	64.000	80.000	72.000	16.000
E	12.0	62.000	88.000	75.000	26.000
D	6.5	59.000	91.000	75.000	32.000
C	3.5	56.000	95.000	75.500	39.000
B	2.0	54.000	96.000	75.000	42.000
	1	48.000	100.000	74.000	52.000

Interpreting the results

Pulse1 contains 92 observations (N = 92). The letter values displayed are found by moving in from each end of the ordered observations to a given depth as shown under *Method* on page 8-3.

If the depth does not coincide with a data value, the average of the nearest neighbors is taken.

- The median for this data is the average of the forty-sixth and forty-seventh ordered observations and is 71.

- The hinges are the average of the twenty-second and twenty-third observations from either end, with values of 64 and 80, the average of these being the Mid, or 72. The difference between the upper and lower hinges is the Spread, or 16.

- The eighths (E), sixteenths (D), and other letter values are calculated in a similar fashion.

Median Polish

Median Polish fits an additive model to a two-way design and identifies data patterns not explained by row and column effects. This procedure is similar to analysis of variance except medians are used instead of means, thus adding robustness against the effect of outliers. For a complete discussion, see [1] and [2].

Median Polish does not print results. Use **Stat ➤ Tables ➤ Cross Tabulation** to display the data, stored fits, or residuals.

Data

Arrange your data in three numeric columns in the worksheet—a response, a row factor, and a column factor. Each row represents one observation. Row levels and column levels must be consecutive integers starting at one. The table may be unbalanced and may have empty cells, but you cannot have any missing values. Delete any missing values from the worksheet before performing a median polish.

▶ To perform a median polish

1 Choose **Stat ➤ EDA ➤ Median Polish**.

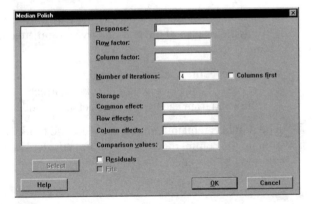

2 In **Response**, enter the column that contains the measurement data.

3 In **Row factor**, enter the column that contains the row factor levels.

4 In **Column factor**, enter the column that contains the column factor levels.

5 If you like, use one or more of the options listed below, then click **OK**.

Options

- specify the number of iterations to find the solution. The default is four. See *Method* on page 8-6.

- use column medians rather than row medians for the first iteration. Starting with rows and starting with columns does not necessarily yield the same fits, even if many iterations are done.

- store the common, row, and column effects.

- store the comparison values. See *Improving the fit of an additive model* on page 8-6.

- store the residuals and fitted values.

Method

Median Polish uses an iterative algorithm.

1 On the first iteration, MINITAB finds the median for each row of the table, subtracts these from the numbers in the corresponding rows, and uses them as preliminary values for the row effects. This gives a column of row medians and a new table from which the row medians have been subtracted.

2 On the second iteration, it finds the median for each column of the new table, subtracts these from the numbers in the columns, and uses them as preliminary values for the column effects. In addition, it finds the median of the row effects, subtracts it from each row effect, and uses it as the preliminary common value.

3 Median Polish now goes back to rows. This time when it finds row medians, it also finds the median of the preliminary column effects, subtracts it from the row effects, and adds it to the common value.

4 This procedure continues, working on rows and columns alternately. After the last iteration, the row of column effects is corrected by itself: the median of this row is subtracted from each column effect and is added to the common.

The numbers remaining in the table are the residuals. The margins of the table contain the common, row, and column effects. The fitted value for row i, column j is common + (row effect i) + (column effect j). As in analysis of variance, data = fit + residual.

Improving the fit of an additive model

Data that is not well described by an additive model may be made more additive by re-expressing or transforming the data. You can use comparison values to help you choose an appropriate data transformation.

1 Calculate the comparison values for each observation. For an observation in row i and column j:

$$\text{comparison value} = \frac{(\text{row effect i}) \times (\text{column effect j})}{\text{common effect}}$$

2 Plot each residual against its comparison value for visual inspection of the data.

3 Fit a straight line to the data using the Resistant Line procedure on page 8-9.

4 Determine whether or not a transformation will improve the fit of the additive model. Let p = 1 − (slope of the resistant line).

- If p = 1 (the line is horizontal), no simple transformation will improve the model.

- If p = ½, $\sqrt{Y}$, where Y is the data, is likely to be more nearly additive (and thus better analyzed by median polish).

- If p = 0, log Y will be more nearly additive.

- If p is between 0 and 1, then Y^p will be more nearly additive.

The exploratory technique described above is similar to Tukey's one degree of freedom for non-additivity method.

▷ Example of median polish

Suppose you want to fit a model to experimental data in a two-way design. The experiment involved three types of helmets where a force was applied to the front and the back of the helmet. The two factors of interest are helmet type and location of force applied; whereas, the response measure is impact. The impact was measured to determine whether or not any identifiable data patterns exist that would indicate a difference between the three helmet types and the front and back portion of the helmet, with the level of protection (as measured by Impact) provided. Here, we fit an additive model to a two-way design using a median polish.

Since Median Polish does not display any results, use Display Data and Cross Tabulation to display results in the Session window.

Step 1: Perform the median polish

1 Open the worksheet EXH_STAT.MTW. Choose **Stat ➤ EDA ➤ Median Polish**.

2 In **Response**, enter *Impact*.

3 In **Row factor**, enter *HelmetType*. In **Column factor**, enter *Location*.

4 In **Common effect**, enter *CommonEffect*. In **Row effects**, enter *RowEffect*. In **Column effects**, enter *ColumnEffect*.

5 Check **Residuals**. Click **OK**.

Session window output

```
This version of MPOLISH does not display any results.
Store the results and use Display Data and Cross Tabulation.
```

Step 2: Display the common, row, and column effects

1 Choose **Manip ➤ Display Data**.

2 In **Columns, constants, and matrices to display**, enter *CommonEffect, RowEffect,* and *ColumnEffect*. Click **OK**.

Session window output

Data Display

```
CommonEffect    44.5000

 Row  RowEffect  ColumnEffect

  1        0          -1
  2       23           1
  3       -3
```

Step 3: Display the data and residuals

1 Choose **Stat ➤ Tables ➤ Cross Tabulation**.

2 In **Classification variables**, enter *HelmetType* and *Location*.

3 Click **Summaries**. In **Associated variables**, enter *Resi1*. Check **Data**. Click **OK** in each dialog box.

Session window output

Tabulated Statistics: HelmetType, Location

```
Rows: HelmetTy   Columns: Location

             1         2

  1     3.5000    0.5000
       -0.5000   -5.5000

  2    -4.5000   -1.5000
        1.5000    2.5000

  3     0.5000   -0.5000
       -1.5000    3.5000

  Cell Contents --
          RESI1:Data
```

Interpreting the results

This section is based on the output from both steps 2 and 3. The common effect, which summarizes the general level of Impact, is 44.5.

The row effects account for changes in Impact from row to row relative to the common value. The row effects are 0, 23, −3 for helmet type 1, 2, and 3, respectively, indicating that the impact for helmet type 2 was much higher than the common level; whereas, helmet type 3 was slightly lower.

The column effects account for changes in Impact from column to column relative to the common value. The column effects are −1, 1 for locations 1 and 2, respectively, indicating that the impact was slightly lower than the common effect for the front of the helmet and slightly higher for the back of the helmet.

The residuals for the two observations per cell are shown in the printed table. These are 3.5 and −0.5 for cell 1,1, and so on. You can use the residuals to identify extraordinary values.

Resistant Line

Resistant line fits a straight line to your data using a method that is resistant to outliers. Velleman and Hoaglin [2] suggest fitting a resistant line before using least squares regression to see if the relationship is linear, to find re-experiences to linearize the relationship if necessary, and to identify outliers.

Data

You must have two numeric columns—a response variable column and predictor variable column—with at least six, but preferably nine or more, observations.

MINITAB automatically omits missing data from the calculations.

▶ **To fit a resistant line**

1 Choose **Stat ➤ EDA ➤ Resistant Line**.

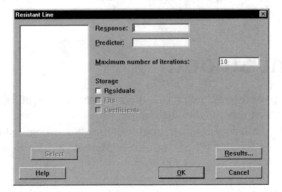

2 In **Response**, enter the column that contains the measurement data (Y).

3 In **Predictor**, enter the column that contains the predictor variable data (X).

4 If you like, use one or more of the options listed below, then click **OK**.

Options

Resistant Line dialog box

■ specify the maximum number of iterations used to find a solution. The default is 10. This procedure will stop before the specified number of iterations if the value of the slope does not change very much.

■ store the residuals, fitted values, and coefficients.

Results subdialog box

■ display the following in the session window:
  – no output
  – the default output, which includes the slope, level, and half-slope ratio
  – the default output, plus the slope for each iteration

Method

First the data are partitioned into three groups: data with low x-values, middle x-values, and high x-values. The resistant line is fit so that the median residual in the left (low – x) partition is equal to the median residual in the right partition.

Resistant Line uses an iterative method to find this solution. It will usually reach a solution in fewer than the default 10 iterations but, for some data sets, it may not converge at all. Failure to converge is especially likely to happen if the data have extraordinary x-values. If you wish to print the slope for each iteration, choose **In addition, the slope for each iteration** in the Results subdialog box.

Resistant Smooth

Resistant Smooth smooths an ordered series of data, usually collected over time, to remove random fluctuations. Smoothing is useful for discovering and summarizing both data trends and outliers. Resistant Smooth offers two smoothing methods: *4253H, twice* and *3RSSH, twice*. See *Method* on page 8-11.

Data

You must have a numeric column with at least seven observations. You can have missing data at the beginning and end of the column, but not in the middle.

▶ **To perform a resistant smoothing**

1 Choose **Stat ➤ EDA ➤ Resistant Smooth**.

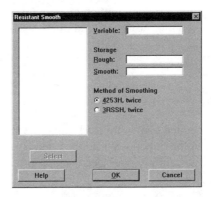

2 In **Variable**, enter the column that contains the raw data to be smoothed.

3 In **Rough**, enter a column to store the rough data (rough data = raw data − smoothed data).

4 In **Smooth**, enter a column to store the smoothed data.

5 If you like, use the option below, then click **OK**.

Options

You can choose to use the *3RSSH, twice* smoother. The default method is to use the *4253H, twice* smoother.

Method

The smoothers are built up by successive applications of simple smoothers, such as running medians and hanning. Running medians replace each observation by the median of the observations immediately before and after it. Medians of 2, 3, 4, and 5 consecutive observations are used by Resistant Smooth. Hanning replaces y_t by the running average, $0.25y_{t-1} + 0.5y_t + 0.25y_{t+1}$. Special methods are used at the ends of the sequence. MINITAB provides two smoothing methods: *4253H, twice* and *3RSSH, twice*.

- *4253H, twice* (the default) consists of a running median of 4, then 2, then 5, then 3, followed by hanning (H). Each residual, or rough, is then smoothed by the same smoother. The smooth of the residual is then added to the smooth of the first pass to produce the full smoother, *4253H, twice*.

- *3RSSH, twice* is made up of three simple smoothers: 3R, followed by SS, followed by H. 3R says to repeatedly use running medians of length 3 until there are no changes. SS, or splitting, uses a special method to remove flat spots that often appear after 3R. H is hanning.

See [2] for a full description of these methods. Detailed analyses of the properties of these smoothers can be found in [1].

Rootogram

A suspended rootogram is a histogram with a normal distribution fit to it, which displays the deviations from the fitted normal distribution. Since a rootogram is fit using percentiles, it protects against outliers and extraordinary bin counts. For further details see [2].

Data

Your data can be in one of two forms: raw or frequency. To use

- raw data, you need one column of numeric or date/time data. By default, the rootogram procedure will determine the bin boundaries.

- frequency data, you need one numeric column that contains the count (frequency) of observations for each bin. The frequencies need to be ordered down the column from the upper-most bin to the lower-most bin (equivalent to the left-most and right-most bins in a histogram, respectively). By default, the bins have a width of 1.

Optionally, you can specify the bin boundaries for both raw and frequency data in another column. In the bin boundary column, enter the bin boundaries down the column from the smallest to largest.

If you are using bin boundaries with frequency data, the first row of the frequency data column is the count for the number of observations that fall below the smallest bin boundary. If no observations fall below the first bin boundary, the count in the first row is zero. Similarly, the last row of the frequency data column contains the count for the number of observations that fall above the largest bin boundary. The frequency data column will have one more entry than the column of bin boundaries.

MINITAB automatically omits missing data from the calculations.

▶ **To display a suspended rootogram**

1 Choose Stat ➤ EDA ➤ Rootogram.

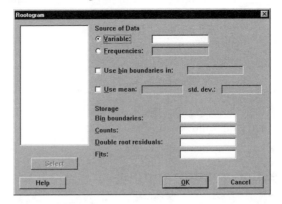

2 Do one of the following:

- under **Source of Data**, choose **Variable**, and enter the column that contains the raw data, or

- choose **Frequencies**, and enter the column that contains the counts

3 If you like, use one or more of the options listed below, then click **OK**.

Options

- specify bin boundaries. Enter a column that contains bin boundaries ordered from smallest to largest. If no bin boundaries are given and you enter frequency data, the bins are set to a width of 1.

- enter known values for μ and σ, overriding the automatic estimation of the mean and standard deviation used in fitting the Gaussian comparison curve. If you enter a value for one parameter, you must enter a value for the other parameter.

- store bin boundaries, counts, double root residuals, and fitted counts.

Method

Let $x_1, \ldots, x_k$ be the bin boundaries (the same as class boundaries for a histogram). These determine $k + 1$ bins. Let b_i = bin from x_{i-1} to x_i. Let b_1 = half-open bin below x_1, and b_{k+1} = half-open bin above x_k. Let n_i = (number observations in b_i). If an observation falls on x_i, it is put in b_{i+1}. If a mean and standard deviation are not specified, they are calculated as $m = (1/2) (H_L + H_U)$ and $s = (H_U - H_L) / 1.349$, where H_L and H_U are the lower and upper hinges. See *Method* for Letter Values on page 8-3 for definitions of hinges.

The fitting of the normal distribution is based upon square roots of the counts in each bin to stabilize variance. The fitted count, f_i, is N × (area under normal curve with the specified mean and stdev, in bin i), where N = total number of observations. The raw residuals, RawRes, are $(n_i - f_i)$. The double root residuals, DRRes, are

$$\sqrt{2 + 4n_i} - \sqrt{1 + 4f_i} \quad \text{if } n_i \text{ is not zero}$$

$$1 - \sqrt{1 + 4n_i} \quad \text{if } n_i \text{ is zero}$$

Double root residuals are essentially $2(\sqrt{n_i} - \sqrt{f_i})$, with a minor modification to avoid some difficulties with small counts.

Session window output

The suspended rootogram plots the DRRes, using the sign (− or +) of the DRRes for the plotting symbol. The double root residuals indicate how closely the data follow the comparison (normal) distribution. An * indicates that a DRRes goes beyond −3 or +3. A vertical line of dots is plotted at −2 and +2. These give approximate 95% confidence limits for the DRRes. As an aid in drawing a vertical line at zero, the "R" in the label "Suspended Rootogram" (above the display) lies where a line can pass to the left of the R. "OO" is in the same position below the display; the line can pass between the O's.

Rootogram output includes for each bin: the count, fitted count minus count (RawRes), the double root residuals (DRRes), and the suspended rootogram.

▷ Example of a rootogram

Here, we use a rootogram to determine whether or not the weight measurements from 92 students follow a normal distribution.

1 Open the worksheet PULSE.MTW.

2 Choose **Stat ➤ EDA ➤ Rootogram**.

3 In **Variable**, enter *Weight*. Click **OK**.

Session window output

Rootogram: Weight

Bin	Count	RawRes	DRRes	Suspended Rootogram
1	0.0	-0.7	-0.90	. ----- .
2	0.0	-1.2	-1.44	. -------- .
3	2.0	-0.8	-0.35	. -- .
4	5.0	-0.5	-0.10	. - .
5	12.0	3.0	0.99	. +++++ .
6	12.0	-0.5	-0.06	. - .
7	11.0	-3.7	-0.94	. ----- .
8	17.0	2.4	0.66	. ++++ .
9	16.0	3.7	1.03	. ++++++ .
10	5.0	-3.8	-1.34	. ------- .
11	5.0	-0.4	-0.04	. - .
12	5.0	2.2	1.23	. +++++++ .
13	1.0	-0.2	0.04	. + .
14	0.0	-0.4	-0.66	. ---- .
15	1.0	0.9	1.20	. +++++++ .
16	0.0	-0.0	-0.09	. - .

In display, value of one character is .2   00

Interpreting the results

The suspended rootogram plots the double root residuals (DRRes) using the sign of the DRRes as the plotting symbol. The DRRes indicate how closely the data follow the comparison (normal) distribution.

For the Weight variable, there is a slight concentration of negative signs in the lower bins, and the highest concentration of positive signs in the middle and higher bins, indicating where the sample distribution tends to depart from normal. However, there is no strong evidence that a normal distribution could not be used to describe these data because the double root residuals are all within the confidence limits.

References

[1] P.F. Velleman (1980). "Definition and Comparison of Robust Nonlinear Data Smoothing Algorithms," *Journal of the American Statistical Association*, Volume 75, Number 371, pp. 609–615.

[2] P.F. Velleman and D.C. Hoaglin (1981). *ABC's of EDA*, Duxbury Press.

Acknowledgments

MINITAB's EDA commands use the programs in the book *ABC's of EDA* by P. Velleman and D. Hoaglin [2]. See this book for a full explanation of these commands and guidance on how to use them. We thank Paul Velleman and David Hoaglin for permission to use their routines and for assistance in adapting them to MINITAB.

9

Power and Sample Size

Power and Sample Size Overview

Use MINITAB's power and sample size capabilities to evaluate power and sample size before you design and run an experiment (prospective) or after you perform an experiment (retrospective).

- A prospective study is used before collecting data to consider design sensitivity. You want to be sure that you have enough power to detect differences (effects) that you have determined to be important. For example, you can increase the design sensitivity by increasing the sample size or by taking measures to decrease the error variance.

- A retrospective study is used after collecting data to help understand the power of the tests that you have performed. For example, suppose you conduct an experiment and the data analysis does not reveal any statistically significant results. You can then calculate power based on the minimum difference (effect) you wish to detect. If the power to detect this difference is low, you may want to modify your experimental design to increase the power and continue to evaluate the same problem. However, if the power is high, you may want to conclude that there is no meaningful difference (effect) and discontinue experimentation.

MINITAB provides power, sample size, and difference (effect) calculations (also the number of center points for factorial and Plackett-Burman designs) for the following procedures:

- one-sample Z
- one-sample t
- two-sample t
- one-sample proportion
- two-sample proportion
- one-way analysis of variance
- two-level factorial designs
- Plackett-Burman designs

What is power?

There are four possible outcomes for a hypothesis test. The outcomes depend on whether the null hypothesis (H_0) is true or false and whether you decide to "reject" or "fail to reject" H_0. The *power* of a test is the probability of correctly rejecting H_0 when it is false. In other words, power is the likelihood that you will identify a significant difference (effect) when one exists.

The four possible outcomes are summarized below:

| | Null hypothesis | |
Decision	True	False
fail to reject H_0	correct decision $p = 1 - \alpha$	Type II error $p = \beta$
reject H_0	Type I error $p = \alpha$	correct decision $p = 1 - \beta$

power

- When H_0 is true and you reject it, you make a type I error. The probability (p) of making a type I error is called *alpha* (α) and is sometimes referred to as the *level of significance* for the test.

- When H_0 is false and you fail to reject it, you make a type II error. The probability (p) of making a type II error is called *beta* (β).

Choosing probability levels

When you are determining the α and β values for your test, you should consider the

- **severity of making an error**—The more serious the error, the less often you should be willing to allow it to occur. Therefore, you should assign smaller probability values to more serious errors.

- **magnitude of effect you want to detect**—*Power* is the probability (p = 1 − β) of correctly rejecting H_0 when it is false. Ideally, you want to have high power to detect a difference that you care about, and low power for a meaningless difference.

  For example, suppose you want to claim that children in your school scored higher than the general population on a standardized achievement test. You need to decide how much higher than the general population your test scores need to be so you are not making claims that are misleading. If your mean test score is only .7 points higher than the general population on a 100 point test, do you really want to detect a difference? Probably not. Therefore, you should choose your sample size so that you only have power to detect differences that you consider meaningful.

Factors that influence power

A number of factors influence power:

- α, the probability of a type I error (level of significance). As the probability of a type I error (α) increases, the probability of a type II error (β) decreases. Hence, as α increases, power = 1 − β also increases.

- σ, the variability in the population. As σ increases, power decreases.

- the size of the population difference (effect). As the size of population difference (effect) decreases, power decreases.

- sample size. As sample size increases, power increases.

Z-Test and t-Tests

Z- and t-tests are used to perform hypothesis tests of the mean (one-sample) or the difference in means (two-sample). For these tests, you can calculate the

- power
- sample size
- minimum difference (effect)

You need to determine what are acceptable values for any two of these parameters and MINITAB will solve for the third.

For example, to calculate the sample size, you need to determine the power and the minimum difference that you consider to be acceptable. Then, MINITAB solves for the sample size you need to be able to reject the null hypothesis when the true value differs from the hypothesized value by this minimum difference. See *Defining the minimum difference* on page 9-5.

▶ **To calculate power, sample size, or minimum difference**

1 Choose **Stat ▶ Power and Sample Size ▶ 1-Sample Z, 1-Sample t, or 2-Sample t.**

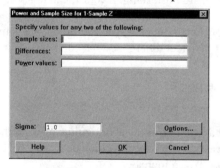

This dialog box is for a one-sample Z-test. The dialog boxes for the 1- and 2-Sample t are identical.

2 Do one of the following:

- Solve for power
    1 In **Sample sizes**, enter one or more numbers. For a two-sample test, the number you enter is considered the sample size for each group. For example, if you want to determine power for an analysis with 10 observations in each group for a total of 20, you would enter 10.
    2 In **Differences**, enter one or more numbers.

- Solve for sample size
    1 In **Differences**, enter one or more numbers.
    2 In **Power values**, enter one or more numbers.

■ Solve for the minimum difference

1 In **Sample sizes**, enter one or more numbers. For a two-sample test, the number you enter is considered the sample size for each group.

2 In **Power values**, enter one or more numbers.

MINITAB will solve for all combinations of the specified values. For example, if you enter 3 values in **Sample sizes** and 2 values in **Differences**, MINITAB will compute the power for all 6 combinations of sample sizes and differences.

For a discussion of the value needed in **Differences**, see *Defining the minimum difference* on page 9-5.

3 In **Sigma**, enter an estimate of the population standard deviation (σ) for your data. See *Estimating σ* on page 9-6.

4 If you like, use one or more of the options listed below, then click **OK**.

Options

Options subdialog box

■ define the alternative hypothesis by choosing less than (lower-tailed), not equal (two-tailed), or greater than (upper-tailed). The default is a two-tailed test.

■ specify the significance level (α). The default is 0.05.

■ store the sample sizes, differences (effects), and power values. When calculating sample size, MINITAB stores the power value that will generate the nearest integer sample size.

Defining the minimum difference

When calculating sample size or power, you need to specify the minimum *difference* you are interested in detecting. The manner in which you express this difference depends on whether you are performing a one- or two-sample test:

■ For a one-sample Z- or t-test, express the difference in terms of the null hypothesis.

For example, suppose you are testing whether or not your students' mean test score is different from the population mean. You would like to detect a difference of three points. In the dialog box, you would enter 3 in **Differences**.

■ For a two-sample t-test, express the difference as the difference between the population means that you would like to be able to detect.

For example, suppose you are investigating the effects of water acidity on the growth of two groups of tadpoles. You decide that any difference in growth between the two groups that is smaller than 4 mm is not important. In the dialog box, you would enter 4 in **Differences**.

Estimating σ

For power or minimum difference calculations, the estimate of σ depends on whether or not you have already collected data.

- Prospective studies are done before collecting data so σ has to be estimated. You can use related research, pilot studies, or subject-matter knowledge to estimate σ.

- Retrospective studies are done after data have been collected so you can use the sample standard deviation to estimate σ. You could also use related research, pilot studies, or subject-matter knowledge. Use Display Descriptive Statistics (page 1-6) to calculate the sample standard deviation.

For sample size calculations, the data have not been collected yet so the population standard deviation (σ) has to be estimated. You can use related research, pilot studies, or subject-matter knowledge to estimate σ.

Note | By default, MINITAB sets σ to 1.0. This is fine if the differences (effects) are standardized, but will present erroneous results if they are not. When the differences (effects) are not standardized, be sure to enter an estimate of σ.

▷ Example of calculating sample size for a one-sample t-test

Suppose you are the production manager at a dairy plant. In order to meet state requirements, you must maintain strict control over the packaging of ice cream. The volume cannot vary more than 3 oz for a half gallon (64 oz) container. The packaging machine tolerances are set so the process σ is 1. How many samples must be taken to estimate the mean package volume at a confidence level of 99% ($\alpha = .01$) for power values of 0.7, 0.8, and 0.9?

1 Choose **Stat ➤ Power and Sample Size ➤ 1-Sample t**.

2 In **Differences**, enter 3. In **Power values**, enter *0.7 0.8 0.9*.

3 In **Sigma**, enter *1*.

4 Click **Options**. In **Significance level**, enter *0.01*. Click **OK** in each dialog box.

Session window output

Power and Sample Size

```
1-Sample t Test

Testing mean = null (versus not = null)
Calculating power for mean = null + difference
Alpha = 0.01  Sigma = 1

              Sample  Target  Actual
Difference     Size   Power   Power
         3        5   0.7000  0.8947
         3        5   0.8000  0.8947
         3        6   0.9000  0.9827
```

Interpreting the results

MINITAB displays the sample size required to obtain the requested power values. Because the target power values would result in non-integer sample sizes, MINITAB displays the power (Actual Power) that you would have to detect differences in volume greater than three ounces using the nearest integer value for sample size. If you take a sample of five cartons, power for your test is 0.895; for a sample of six cartons, power is 0.983.

Tests of Proportions

Proportion tests are used to perform hypothesis tests of a proportion (one-sample) or the difference in proportions (two-sample). For these tests, you can calculate the

- power
- sample size
- minimum difference (effect)

You need to determine what are acceptable values for any two of these parameters and MINITAB will solve for the third.

For example, to calculate the sample size, you need to determine the power and the minimum difference that you consider to be acceptable. Then, MINITAB solves for the sample size you need to be able to reject the null hypothesis when the true value differs from the hypothesized value by this minimum difference. See *Defining the minimum difference* on page 9-9.

▶ **To calculate power, sample size, or minimum difference**

1   Choose **Stat ➤ Power and Sample Size ➤ 1 Proportion** or **2 Proportions**.

1 Proportion   **2 Proportions**

Power and Sample Size for 1 Proportion	Power and Sample Size for 2 Proportions
Specify values for any two of the following:	Specify values for any two of the following:
Sample sizes:	Sample sizes:
Alternative values of p:	Proportion 1 values:
Power values:	Power values:
Hypothesized p: 0.5 Options...	Proportion 2: 0.5 Options...
Help OK Cancel	Help OK Cancel

   2 Do one of the following:

      ■ Solve for power

         1 In **Sample sizes**, enter one or more numbers. For two proportion test, the number you enter is considered the sample size for each group. For example, if you want to determine power for an analysis with 10 observations in each group for a total of 20, you would enter 10.

         2 In **Alternative values of p** or **Proportion 1 values**, enter one or more proportions.

      ■ Solve for sample size

         1 In **Alternative values of p** or **Proportion 1 values**, enter one or more proportions.

         2 In **Power values**, enter one or more numbers.

      ■ Solve for the minimum difference

         1 In **Sample sizes**, enter one or more numbers. For a two proportion test, the number you enter is considered the sample size for each group, not the total number for the experiment.

         2 In **Power values**, enter one or more numbers.

MINITAB will solve for all combinations of the specified values. For example, if you enter 3 values in **Sample sizes** and 2 values in **Alternative values of p**, MINITAB will compute the power for all 6 combinations of sample sizes and alternative proportions.

For a discussion of the values needed in **Alternative values of p** and **Proportion 1 values**, see *Defining the minimum difference* on page 9-9.

   3 Do one of the following:

      ■ For a one-sample test, enter the expected proportion under the null hypothesis in **Hypothesized p**. The default is 0.5.

      ■ For a two-sample test, enter the second proportion in **Proportion 2**. The default is 0.5.

For a discussion of the values needed in **Hypothesized p** and **Proportion 2**, see *Defining the minimum difference* on page 9-9.

   4 If you like, use one or more of the options listed below, then click **OK**.

Options

Options subdialog box

■ define the alternative hypothesis by choosing less than (lower-tailed), not equal (two-tailed), or greater than (upper-tailed). The default is a two-tailed test.

- specify the significance level of the test. The default is $\alpha = 0.05$.

- store the sample sizes, alternative values of p or proportion 1 values, and power values. When calculating sample size, MINITAB stores the power value that will generate the nearest integer sample size.

Defining the minimum difference

MINITAB uses two proportions to determine the minimum difference. The manner in which you express these proportions depends on whether you are performing a one- or two-sample proportion test.

- For a one-sample test of proportion, enter the expected proportion under the null hypothesis for **Hypothesized p** in the dialog box.

  Suppose you are testing whether the data are consistent with the following null hypothesis and would like to detect any differences where the true proportion is greater than .73.

  H_0: p = .7 H_1: p > .7   where p is the population proportion

  In MINITAB, enter .73 in **Alternative values of p**; enter .7 in **Hypothesized p**. (The alternative proportion is not the value of the alternative hypothesis, but the value at which you want to evaluate power.)

- For a two-sample test of proportion, enter the expected proportions under the null hypothesis for **Proportion 2** in the dialog box.

  Suppose a biologist wants to test whether or not there is a difference in the proportion of fish that have been affected by pollution in two lakes. Previous research suggests that approximately 25% of fish have been affected. The biologist would like to detect a difference in proportions of 0.03.

  H_0: $p_1 = p_2$ H_1: $p_1 \neq p_2$

  In MINITAB, enter 0.22 and 0.28 in **Proportion 1 values**; enter 0.25 in **Proportion 2**.

⮞ Example of calculating power for a two-sample test of proportion

As a political advisor, you want to determine whether there is a difference between the proportion of men and the proportion of women who support a tax reform bill. Results of a previous survey of registered voters indicate that 30% (p = .30) of the voters support the tax bill. If you mail 1000 surveys, what is the power to detect differences greater than .05 between the proportions of men and women who support the tax bill?

1 Choose **Stat ➤ Power and Sample Size ➤ 2 Proportions**.

2 In **Sample sizes**, enter *1000*.

3 In **Proportion 1 values**, enter *0.25* and *0.35*.

4 In **Proportion 2**, enter *0.30*. Click **OK**.

Power and Sample Size

Test for Two Proportions

Testing proportion 1 = proportion 2 (versus not =)
Calculating power for proportion 2 = 0.3
Alpha = 0.05

	Sample	
Proportion 1	Size	Power
0.250000	1000	0.7071
0.350000	1000	0.6656

Interpreting the results

If you mail 1000 surveys, you will have about a 71% chance of detecting a difference of −0.05 and a 67% chance of detecting a difference of + 0.05 in the proportions of males and females who support the tax bill.

One-Way Analysis Of Variance

A one-way ANOVA is used to test the equality of population means. For this test, you can calculate the

- power

- sample size

- minimum detectable difference between the smallest and largest factor means (maximum difference)

You need to determine what are acceptable values for any two of these parameters and MINITAB will solve for the third.

For example, to calculate sample size, you need to determine the power and the maximum difference between the factor level means that you consider to be meaningful. Then, MINITAB solves for the sample size you need to be able to reject the null hypothesis when the true value differs from the hypothesized value by the specified maximum difference. See *Defining the maximum difference* on page 9-12.

▶ **To calculate power, sample size, or maximum difference**

1   Choose **Stat ➤ Power and Sample Size ➤ One-way ANOVA**.

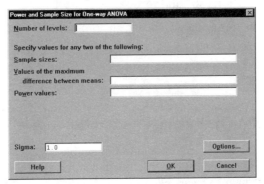

2   In **Number of levels**, enter the number of factor levels (treatment conditions).

3   Do one of the following:

   ■   Solve for power

      1   In **Sample sizes**, enter one or more numbers. Each number you enter is considered the number of observations in every factor level. For example, if you have 3 factor levels with 5 observations each, you would enter 5.

      2   In **Values of the maximum difference between means**, enter one or more numbers.

   ■   Solve for sample size

      1   In **Values of the maximum difference between means**, enter one or more numbers.

      2   In **Power values**, enter one or more numbers.

   ■   Solve for the maximum difference

      1   In **Sample sizes**, enter one or more numbers. Each number you enter is considered the number of observations in every factor level.

      2   In **Power values**, enter one or more numbers.

   MINITAB will solve for all combinations of the specified values. For example, if you enter 3 values in **Sample sizes** and 2 values in **Values of the maximum difference between means**, MINITAB will compute the power for all 6 combinations of sample sizes and maximum differences. See *Defining the maximum difference* on page 9-12.

3   In **Sigma**, enter an estimate of the population standard deviation (σ) for your data. See *Estimating* σ on page 9-6.

4   If you like, use one or more of the options listed below, then click **OK**.

Options

Options subdialog box

- specify the significance level of the test. The default is $\alpha = 0.05$.

- store the sample sizes, sums of squares, and power values. When calculating sample size, MINITAB stores the power value that will generate the nearest integer sample size.

Defining the maximum difference

In order to calculate power or sample size, you need to estimate the maximum difference between the smallest and largest actual factor level means. For example, suppose you are planning an experiment with four treatment conditions (four factor levels). You want to find a difference between a control group mean of 10 and a level mean that is 15. In this case, the maximum difference between the means is 5.

▷ Example of calculating power for a one-way ANOVA

Suppose you are about to undertake an investigation to determine whether or not 4 treatments affect the yield of a product using 5 observations per treatment. You know that the mean of the control group should be around 8, and you would like to find significant differences of +4. Thus, the maximum difference you are considering is 4 units. Previous research suggests the population σ is 1.64.

1 Choose **Stat ➤ Power and Sample Size ➤ One-way ANOVA**.

2 In **Number of levels**, enter 4.

3 In **Sample sizes**, enter 5.

4 In **Values of the maximum difference between means**, enter 4.

5 In **Sigma**, enter 1.64. Click **OK**.

Session window output

Power and Sample Size

One-way ANOVA

Sigma = 1.64 Alpha = 0.05 Number of Levels = 4

SS Means	Sample Size	Power	Maximum Difference
8	5	0.8269	4

Interpreting the results

If you assign five observations to each treatment level, you have power of 0.83 to detect differences of up to 4 units between the treatment means.

Two-Level Factorial and Plackett-Burman Designs

For two-level full and fractional factorial designs and Plackett-Burman designs, you can calculate

- number of replicates
- power
- minimum effect
- number of center points

You need to determine what are acceptable values for any three of these parameters and MINITAB will solve for the fourth.

For example, to calculate the number of replicates, you need to specify the minimum effect, power, and the number of center points that you consider to be acceptable. Then, MINITAB solves for the number of replicates you need to be able to reject the null hypothesis when the true value differs from the hypothesized value by the specified minimum effect. See *Defining the effect* on page 9-15.

▶ **To calculate power, replicates, minimum effect, or number of center points**

1 Choose Stat ➤ Power and Sample Size ➤ 2-Level Factorial Design or Plackett-Burman Design.

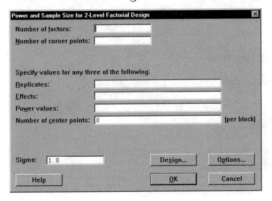

This dialog box is for a two-level factorial design. The dialog box for a Plackett-Burman design is identical.

2 In **Number of factors**, enter the number of factors (input variables).

3 In **Number of corner points**, enter a number. See *Determining the number of corner points* on page 9-14.

4 Do one of the following:

- Solve for power
  1 In **Replicates**, enter one or more numbers.
  2 In **Effects**, enter one or more numbers.
  3 In **Number of center points**, enter one or more numbers.

- Solve for the number of replicates
  1 In **Effects**, enter one or more numbers.
  2 In **Power values**, enter one or more numbers.
  3 In **Number of center points**, enter one or more numbers.

- Solve for the minimum effect
  1 In **Replicates**, enter one or more numbers.
  2 In **Power values**, enter one or more numbers.
  3 In **Number of center points**, enter one or more numbers.

- Solve the number of center points
  1 In **Replicates**, enter one or more numbers.
  1 In **Effects**, enter one or more numbers.
  2 In **Power values**, enter one or more numbers.

For information on the value needed in **Effects**, see *Defining the effect* on page 9-15.

5 In **Sigma**, enter an estimate of the population standard deviation (σ) for your data. See *Estimating* σ on page 9-6.

6 If you like, use one or more of the options listed below, then click **OK**.

Options

Designs subdialog box

- include blocks (two-level factorial designs only)
- omit terms from the model
- include the center points as a term in the model

Options subdialog box

- specify the significance level of the test. The default is $\alpha = 0.05$.
- store the number of replicates, effects, power values, and center points. When calculating the number of replicates, MINITAB stores the power value that will generate the nearest integer number of replicates.

Determining the number of corner points

For all designs, you need to specify the appropriate number of corner points given the number of factors. For example, for a 6 factor full factorial design you would have 64 corner points. However, for a 6 factor fractional factorial design, you can have either 8, 16, or 32 corner points. Use the information provided in *Summary of Two-Level*

Designs on page 19-28 to determine the correct number of corner points for your design.

Defining the effect

When calculating power or number of replicates, you need to specify the *minimum effect* you are interested in detecting. You express this effect as the difference between the low and high factor level means. For example, suppose you are trying to determine the effect of column temperature on the purity of your product. You are only interested in detecting a difference in purity that is greater than 0.007 between the low and high levels of temperature. In the dialog box, enter *0.007* in **Effects**.

Determining the number of replicates

Rather than using sample size to indicate the number of observations you need, factorial designs are expressed in terms of the number of replicates. A *replicate* is a repeat of each of the design points (experimental conditions) in the base design. For example, if you are doing a full factorial with three factors, one replicate would require eight runs. The set of experimental conditions would include all combinations of the low and high levels for all factors. Each time you replicate the design eight runs are added to the design; these runs are duplicates of the original eight runs.

For a discussion of replication, see *Replicating the design* on page 19-12. For a discussion of two-level factorial and Plackett-Burman designs, see Chapter 19, *Factorial Designs*.

▷ **Example of calculating power for a two-level fractional factorial design**

As a quality engineer, you need to determine the "best" settings for 4 input variables (factors) to improve the transparency of a plastic part. You have determined that a 4 factor, 8 run design (½ fraction) with 3 center points will allow you to estimate the effects you are interested in. Although you would like to perform as few replicates as possible, you must be able to detect effects of 5 or more. Previous experimentation suggests that 4.5 is a reasonable estimate of σ.

1 Choose **Stat ➤ Power and Sample Size ➤ 2-Level Factorial Design**.

2 In **Number of factors**, enter *4*.

3 In **Number of corner points**, enter *8*.

4 In **Replicates**, enter *1 2 3 4*.

5 In **Effects**, enter *5*.

6 In **Number of center points**, enter *3*.

7 In **Sigma**, enter *4.5*. Click **OK**.

*Session
window
output*

Power and Sample Size

2-Level Factorial Design

Sigma = 4.5   Alpha = 0.05

Factors: 4   Base Design: 4, 8
Blocks: none

Including a term for center points in model.

Center Points Per Block	Effect	Reps	Power
3	5	1	0.1577
3	5	2	0.5189
3	5	3	0.7305
3	5	4	0.8565

Interpreting the results

If you do not replicate your design (Reps = 1), you will only have a 16% chance of detecting effects that you have determined are important. However, if you use 4 replicates of your ½ fraction design for a total 35 runs (32 corner points and 3 center points), you will have an 86% chance of finding important effects.

part II

Quality Control

10
Quality Planning Tools

Quality Planning Tools Overview

MINITAB offers several graphical tools to help you explore and detect quality problems and improve your process:

- **Run charts** detect patterns in your process data, and perform two tests for non-random behavior. See *Run Chart* on page 10-2.

- **Pareto charts** help you identify which of your problems are most significant, so you can focus improvement efforts on areas where the largest gains can be made. See *Pareto Chart* on page 10-11.

- **Fishbone (cause-and-effect) diagrams** can help you organize brainstorming information about the potential causes of a problem. See *Cause-and-Effect Diagram* on page 10-14.

- **Multi-Vari charts** present analysis of variance data in graphical form to give you a "look" at your data. See *Multi-Vari Chart* on page 10-17.

- **Symmetry plots** can help you assess whether your data come from a symmetric distribution. See *Symmetry Plot* on page 10-19.

Run Chart

Use the Run Chart command to look for evidence of patterns in your process data, and perform two tests for non-random behavior. Run Chart plots all of the individual observations versus the subgroup number, and draws a horizontal reference line at the median. When the subgroup size is greater than 1, Run Chart also plots the subgroup means or medians and connects them with a line.

The two tests for non-random behavior detect trends, oscillation, mixtures, and clustering in your data. Such patterns suggest that the variation observed is due to "special causes"—causes arising from outside the system that can be corrected. Common cause variation, on the other hand, is variation that is inherent or a natural part of the process. A process is in control when only common causes—not special causes—affect the process output.

Data

You can use individual observations or subgroup data. Subgroup data can be structured in a single column or in rows across several columns. When you have subgroups of unequal size, enter the subgroups in a single column, then set up a second column of subgroup indicators. See *Data* on page 12-3 for examples.

▶ **To make a run chart**

1 Choose Stat ➤ Quality Tools ➤ Run Chart.

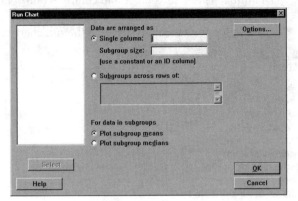

2 Do one of the following:

- When subgroups or individual observations are in one column, enter the data column in **Single column**. In **Subgroup size**, enter a subgroup size or column of subgroup indicators. For individual observations, enter a subgroup size of 1.

- When subgroups are in rows, enter a series of columns in **Subgroups across rows of**.

3 If you like, use any of the options described below, then click **OK**.

Options

Run Chart dialog box

- plot the subgroup medians rather than the subgroup means

Options subdialog box

- replace the default graph title with your own title

Interpreting the tests for randomness

A normal pattern for a process in control is one of randomness. If only common causes of variation exist in your process, the data will exhibit random behavior. A normal pattern for process data is shown in the run chart below:

Normal pattern

Characteristics of a normal pattern include a random distribution of points; the actual number of runs should be close to the expected number of runs.

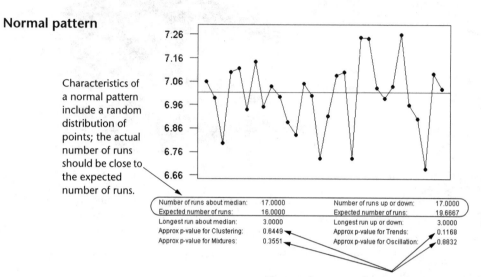

Number of runs about median:	17.0000		Number of runs up or down:	17.0000
Expected number of runs:	16.0000		Expected number of runs:	19.6667
Longest run about median:	3.0000		Longest run up or down:	3.0000
Approx p-value for Clustering:	0.6449		Approx p-value for Trends:	0.1168
Approx p-value for Mixtures:	0.3551		Approx p-value for Oscillation:	0.8832

The tests for non-random patterns are not significant at the .05 level. All p-values are greater than .05 which suggests the data come from a random distribution.

The first of Run Chart's two tests for randomness is based on the number of runs about the median. The second test is based on the number of runs up or down. The methods used to count the number of runs are described in *Interpreting the test for number of runs about the median* on page 10-6 and *Interpreting the test for number of runs up or down* on page 10-8. The following table illustrates what these two tests can tell you:

Test for randomness	Condition	Indicates
number of runs about the median	more runs observed than expected	mixed data from two population
	fewer runs observed than expected	clustering of data
number of runs up or down	more runs observed than expected	oscillation—data varies up and down rapidly
	fewer runs observed than expected	trending of data

Both tests are based on the individual observations when the subgroup size is equal to one. When the subgroup size is greater than one, the tests are based on either the subgroup means (the default) or the subgroup medians.

With both tests, the null hypothesis is that the data is a random sequence. Run Chart converts the observed number of runs into a test statistic that is approximately standard normal, then uses the normal distribution to obtain p-values. See [1] for details. The two p-values correspond to the one-sided probabilities associated with the test statistic. When either p-value is smaller than your α-value, also known as the significance level, you should reject the hypothesis of randomness. The α-value is the probability that you will incorrectly reject the hypothesis of randomness when the hypothesis is true. For illustrative purposes in the examples, assume the test for randomness is significant at an α-value of 0.05.

Interpreting the test for number of runs about the median

This first test is based on the total number of runs that occur both above and below the median. A run, in this case, is one or more consecutive points on the same side of the median. When the points are connected with a line, a run ends when the line crosses the median. A new run begins with the next plotted point.

The test for the number of runs about the median is sensitive to two types of non-random behavior—mixtures and clustering. An observed number of runs statistically greater than the expected number of runs supports the alternative of mixing (which corresponds to a right-tail rejection region); whereas, an observed number of runs that is statistically less than the expected number of runs supports the alternative of clustering (which corresponds to a left-tail rejection region).

Mixture pattern

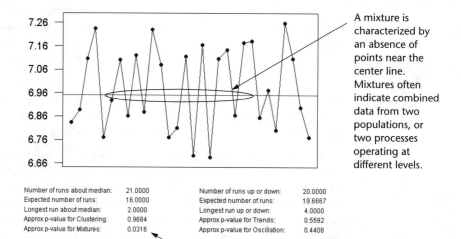

A mixture is characterized by an absence of points near the center line. Mixtures often indicate combined data from two populations, or two processes operating at different levels.

Number of runs about median:	21.0000	Number of runs up or down:	20.0000
Expected number of runs:	16.0000	Expected number of runs:	19.6667
Longest run about median:	2.0000	Longest run up or down:	4.0000
Approx p-value for Clustering:	0.9684	Approx p-value for Trends:	0.5592
Approx p-value for Mixtures:	0.0316	Approx p-value for Oscillation:	0.4408

The p-value for mixtures is less than 0.05, so you would reject the null hypothesis of randomness in favor of the alternative for mixtures—suggesting the data comes from different processes.

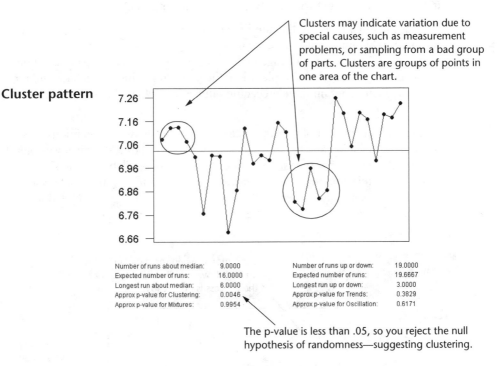

Cluster pattern

Clusters may indicate variation due to special causes, such as measurement problems, or sampling from a bad group of parts. Clusters are groups of points in one area of the chart.

Number of runs about median:	9.0000	Number of runs up or down:	19.0000
Expected number of runs:	16.0000	Expected number of runs:	19.6667
Longest run about median:	6.0000	Longest run up or down:	3.0000
Approx p-value for Clustering:	0.0046	Approx p-value for Trends:	0.3829
Approx p-value for Mixtures:	0.9954	Approx p-value for Oscillation:	0.6171

The p-value is less than .05, so you reject the null hypothesis of randomness—suggesting clustering.

Comparing run chart and runs test

MINITAB provides two commands which test for randomness: Runs Test (see *Runs Test* on page 5-22) and Run Chart. Runs Test is used with individual observations, and tests for randomness without looking for specific nonrandom patterns.

Runs Test (see *Runs Test* on page 5-22) bases its test for randomness on the number of runs above and below the mean by default, but you can specify the median. When the subgroup size is one, and you specify the median (instead of the default mean) for Runs Test, Runs Test and Run Chart perform the same test.

Run Chart displays the one-sided probabilities associated with the test statistic. In contrast, the Runs Test command uses a two-sided test. Thus, the p-value reported by Runs Test will be approximately twice as large as the smaller p-value reported by Run Chart.

Interpreting the test for number of runs up or down

The second test is based on the number of runs up or down—increasing or decreasing. A run, with this test, is one or more consecutive points in the same direction. A new run begins each time there is a change in the direction (either ascending or descending) in the sequence of data. For example, when the preceding value is smaller, a *run up* begins and continues until the preceding value is larger than the next point, then a *run down* begins.

The test for the number of runs up or down is sensitive to two types of non-random behavior—oscillation and trends. An observed number of runs statistically greater than the expected number of runs supports the alternative of oscillation (which corresponds to a right-tail rejection region); whereas, an observed number of runs that is statistically less than the expected number of runs supports the alternative of trends (which corresponds to a left-tail rejection region).

Oscillation is when the data fluctuates up and down rapidly, indicating that the process is not steady.

Oscillating pattern

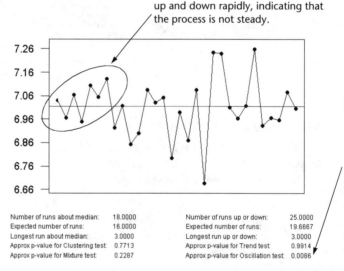

Since the p-value is less than .05, you would reject the null hypothesis of non-randomness in favor of the alternative for oscillation. Here, rapid oscillation—data that varies up and down quickly—is suggested.

Number of runs about median:	18.0000	Number of runs up or down:	25.0000
Expected number of runs:	16.0000	Expected number of runs:	19.6667
Longest run about median:	3.0000	Longest run up or down:	3.0000
Approx p-value for Clustering test:	0.7713	Approx p-value for Trend test:	0.9914
Approx p-value for Mixture test:	0.2287	Approx p-value for Oscillation test:	0.0086

Trends are sustained and systematic sources of variation characterized by a group of points that drift either up or down. Trends may warn that a process is about to go out of control, and may be due to such factors as worn tools, a machine that will not hold a setting, or periodic rotation of operators.

Trend pattern

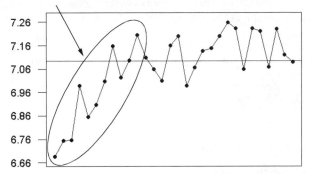

Number of runs about median:	13.0000		Number of runs up or down:	14.0000
Expected number of runs:	16.0000		Expected number of runs:	19.6667
Longest run about median:	7.0000		Longest run up or down:	5.0000
Approx p-value for Clustering:	0.1325		Approx p-value for Trends:	0.0057
Approx p-value for Mixtures:	0.8675		Approx p-value for Oscillation:	0.9943

The p-value is less than .05, suggesting a trend in the data. In this case, the upward trend is circled and easily visible.

☞ Example of a run chart

Suppose you work for a company that produces different kinds of devices to measure radiation. As the quality control engineer, you are concerned with a membrane type device's ability to consistently measure the amount of radiation. You want to analyze the data from tests of twenty devices (in groups of two) collected in an experimental chamber. After every test, you record the amount of radiation that each device measured.

As an exploratory measure, you decide to construct a run chart to evaluate the variation in your measurements.

1 Open the worksheet RADON.MTW.

2 Choose **Stat ➤ Quality Tools ➤ Run Chart**.

3 In **Single column**, enter *Membrane*.

4 In **Subgroup size**, enter 2. Click **OK**.

Graph window output

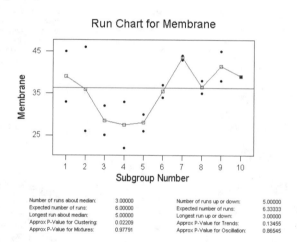

Number of runs about median:	3.00000	Number of runs up or down:	5.00000
Expected number of runs:	6.00000	Expected number of runs:	6.33333
Longest run about median:	5.00000	Longest run up or down:	3.00000
Approx P-Value for Clustering:	0.02209	Approx P-Value for Trends:	0.13455
Approx P-Value for Mixtures:	0.97791	Approx P-Value for Oscillation:	0.86545

Interpreting the results

The test for clustering is significant at the .05 level. Since the probability for the cluster test (p = 0.02) is less than .05, you would conclude that special causes are affecting your process, and you should investigate possible sources. Clusters may indicate sampling or measurement problems.

Note | The .05 level of significance was chosen for illustrative purposes, because it is conventional in many fields. You could evaluate the significance of the tests for non-random patterns at any level you choose. When the p-value displayed is less than the chosen level of significance, you reject the null hypothesis—a random sequence of data— in favor of one of the alternatives. See *Interpreting the tests for randomness* on page 10-4 for a complete discussion.

Pareto Chart

Pareto charts are a type of bar chart in which the horizontal axis represents categories of interest, rather than a continuous scale. The categories are often "defects." By ordering the bars from largest to smallest, a Pareto chart can help you determine which of the defects comprise the "vital few" and which are the "trivial many." A cumulative percentage line helps you judge the added contribution of each category. Pareto charts can help to focus improvement efforts on areas where the largest gains can be made.

Pareto chart can draw one chart for all your data (the default), or separate charts for groups within your data.

Data

You can structure your data in one of two ways:

■ as one column of raw data, where each observation is an occurrence of a type of defect

■ as two columns: one column of defect names and a corresponding column of counts

▶ To make a Pareto Chart

1 Choose **Stat ➤ Quality Tools ➤ Pareto Chart**.

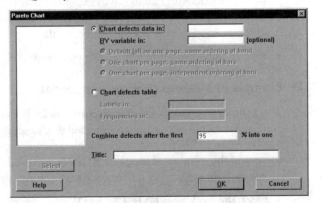

2 Do one of the following:

■ If you have a column of raw data, enter the column in **Chart defects data in**.

■ If you have a column of defect names and a column of counts:
 – Choose **Chart defects table**.
 – In **Labels in**, enter a column of defect names.
 – In **Frequencies in**, enter a column of counts.

3 If you like, use any of the options described below, then click **OK**.

Options

- draw separate Pareto charts for groups within your data. You can arrange the group charts one of three ways:
  - **All on one page, same ordering of bars.** All of the charts will be in the same Graph window, with the ordering of the bars determined by the first group. This means the bars in subsequent groups will usually not be in Pareto order (largest to smallest). But this can be useful for comparing importance of categories relative to a baseline, which is the first group.
  - **One chart per page, same ordering of bars.** Each chart is full-size in its own Graph window, with the ordering of the bars determined by the first group, as above. This means that the bars in subsequent groups will usually not be in Pareto order. But this can be useful for comparing importance of categories relative to a baseline, which is the first group.
  - **One chart per page, independent ordering of bars.** Each chart is full-size in its own Graph window, in Pareto order. In most cases, the order will be different between groups.

  Your worksheet must be structured as a column of raw data (not counts) and a "By" column to use this option. See *Example of a Pareto chart with a "by" column* on page 10-14 for an example.

- specify a cumulative percentage at which to stop generating bars for individual defects. By default, Pareto Chart generates bars until the cumulative percent of defects surpasses 95, then groups the remaining defects into a bar named "Others." You may want to stop at a different cumulative percentage, such as 90.

- replace the default graph title with your own title.

▷ Example of a Pareto chart using raw data

The company you work for manufactures metal bookcases. During final inspection, a certain number of bookcases are rejected due to scratches, chips, bends, or dents. You want to make a Pareto chart to see which defect is causing most of your problems. First you count the number of times each defect occurred, then you enter the name of the defect each time it occurs into a worksheet column called *Damage*.

1 Open the worksheet EXH_QC.MTW.

2 Choose **Stat ➤ Quality Tools ➤ Pareto Chart**.

3 Choose **Chart defects data in** and enter *Damage* in the text box. Click **OK**.

*Graph
window
output*

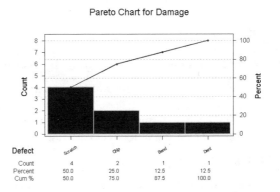

Pareto Chart for Damage

Interpreting the results

75% of the damage is due to scratches and chips, so you will focus improvement efforts
there.

⟩ Example of a Pareto chart using count data

Suppose you work for a company that manufactures motorcycles. You hope to reduce
quality costs arising from defective speedometers. During inspection, a certain number
of speedometers are rejected, and the types of defects recorded. You enter the name of
the defect into a worksheet column called *Defects*, and the corresponding counts into a
column called *Counts*. You know that you can save the most money by focusing on the
defects responsible for most of the rejections. A Pareto chart will help you identify
which defects are causing most of your problems.

1   Open the worksheet EXH_QC.MTW.

2   Choose **Stat ➤ Quality Tools ➤ Pareto Chart**.

3   Choose **Chart defects table**. Enter *Defects* in **Labels in** and *Counts* in **Frequencies
    in**. Click **OK**.

*Graph
window
output*

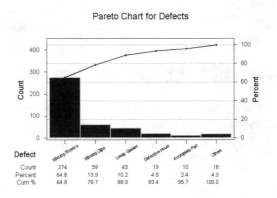

Pareto Chart for Defects

Interpreting the results

Over half of your speedometers are rejected due to missing screws, so you will focus improvement efforts there.

▷ Example of a Pareto chart with a "by" column

Imagine you work for a company which manufactures dolls. Lately, you have noticed that an increasing number of dolls are being rejected at final inspection due to scratches, peels, and smudges in their paint. You want to see if a relationship exists between the type and number of flaws, and the work shift producing the dolls.

1 Open the worksheet EXH_QC.MTW.

2 Choose **Stat ➤ Quality Tools ➤ Pareto Chart**.

3 Choose **Chart defects data in** and enter *Flaws* in the text box. In **BY variable in**, enter *Period*. Click **OK**.

Graph window output

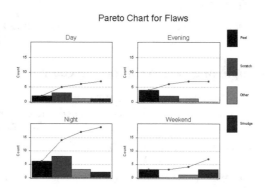

Interpreting the results

The night shift is producing more flaws overall. Most of the problems are due to scratches and peels. You may learn a lot about the problem if you examine that part of the process during the night shift.

Cause-and-Effect Diagram

Use a fishbone (cause-and-effect, or Ishikawa) diagram to organize brainstorming information about potential causes of a problem. Diagramming helps you to see relationships among potential causes. You can draw a blank diagram, or a diagram filled in as much as you like. Although there is no "correct" way to construct a fishbone diagram, some types lend themselves well to many different situations.

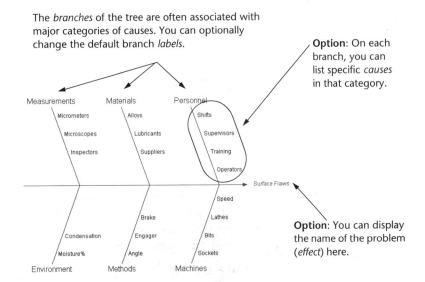

The *branches* of the tree are often associated with major categories of causes. You can optionally change the default branch *labels*.

Option: On each branch, you can list specific *causes* in that category.

Option: You can display the name of the problem (*effect*) here.

Data

If you want to enter causes on the branches of the diagram, create a column of causes for each branch.

▶ To make a cause-and-effect diagram

1 Choose Stat ➤ Quality Tools ➤ Cause-and-Effect.

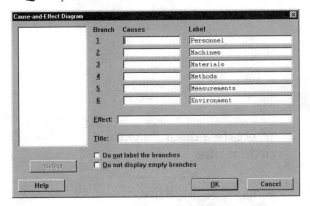

2 If you like, use any of the options described below, then click **OK**.

Options

- customize the diagram with your own labels, causes, and name of problem (or effect) you would like to solve

- draw a blank diagram—see *Example of drawing three common diagrams* on page 10-16 for an illustration

- suppress empty branches

- replace the default graph title with your own title

▷ Example of drawing three common diagrams

Using a Pareto chart (see page 10-11) you discovered that your parts were rejected most often due to surface flaws. This afternoon, you are meeting with members of various departments to brainstorm potential causes for these flaws. Beforehand, you decide to print a cause-and-effect diagram to help organize your notes during the meeting.

1 Choose **Stat ➤ Quality Tools ➤ Cause-and-Effect**.

2 Do one of the following:

To create a blank diagram

Check **Do not label the branches,** then click **OK**.

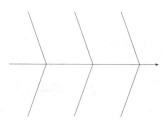
Cause-and-Effect Diagram

To create a diagram with custom title

In **Title**, enter *Sample FISHBONE Diagram*, then click **OK**.

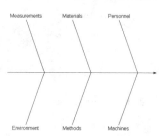
Sample FISHBONE Diagram

To create a diagram with causes and effect

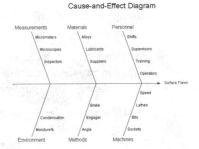

Cause-and-Effect Diagram

1 Open the worksheet EXH_QC.MTW.

2 Under **Causes**, enter *Personnel, Machines, Materials, Methods, Measurements,* and *Environment* in rows 1 through 6, respectively.

3 In **Effect**, enter *Surface Flaws,* then click **OK**.

Multi-Vari Chart

MINITAB draws Shainin multi-vari charts for up to four factors. Multi-vari charts are a way of presenting analysis of variance data in a graphical form providing a "visual" alternative to analysis of variance. These charts may also be used in the preliminary stages of data analysis to get a look at the data. The chart displays the means at each factor level for every factor. A chart for two factors (MetalType and SinterTime), each with three levels, is shown below:

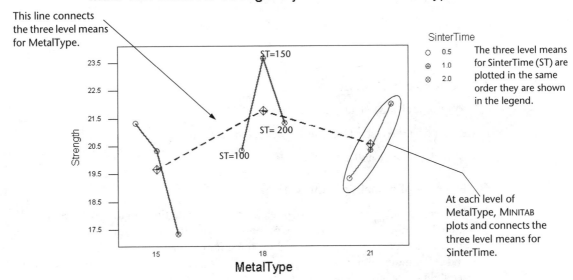

Multi-Vari Chart for Strength By SinterTime - MetalType

This line connects the three level means for MetalType.

SinterTime
- O   0.5
- ⊕   1.0
- ⊗   2.0

The three level means for SinterTime (ST) are plotted in the same order they are shown in the legend.

At each level of MetalType, MINITAB plots and connects the three level means for SinterTime.

Data

You need one numeric column for the response variable and up to four numeric, text, or date/time factor columns. Each row contains the data for a single observation.

Text categories (factor levels) are processed in alphabetical order by default. If you wish, you can define your own order—see *Ordering Text Categories* in the *Manipulating Data* chapter in MINITAB *User's Guide 1* for details.

MINITAB automatically omits missing data from the calculations.

▶ To draw a multi-vari chart

1 Choose Stat ➤ Quality Tools ➤ **Multi-Vari Chart**.

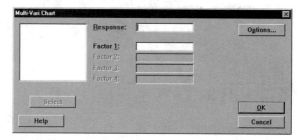

2 In **Response**, enter the column containing the response (measurement) data.

3 In **Factor 1**, enter a factor level column.

4 If you have more than one factor, enter columns in **Factor 2**, **Factor 3**, or **Factor 4** as needed.

5 If you like, use one or more of the options listed below, then click **OK**.

Options

Options subdialog box

- draw individual data points on the chart
- connect the factor level means for each factor with a line
- replace the default title with your own title

▷ Example of a Shainin multi-vari chart

You are responsible for evaluating the effects of sintering time on the compressive strength of three different metals. Compressive strength was measured for five specimens for each metal type at each of the sintering times: 100 minutes, 150 minutes, and 200 minutes. Before you engage in a full data analysis, you want to view the data to see if there are any visible trends or interactions by viewing a multi-vari chart.

1 Open the worksheet SINTER.MTW.

2 Choose **Stat ➤ Quality Tools ➤ Multi-Vari Chart**.

3 In **Response**, enter *Strength*.

4 In **Factor 1**, enter *SinterTime*. In **Factor 2**, enter *MetalType*.

5 Click **OK**.

*Graph
window
output*

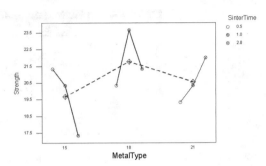

Multi-Vari Chart for Strength By SinterTime - MetalType

Interpreting the results

The multi-vari chart indicates that an interaction exists between the type of metal and the length of time it is sintered. The greatest compressive strength for Metal Type 1 is obtained by sintering for 100 minutes, for Metal Type 2 sintering for 150 minutes, and for Metal Type 3 sintering for 200 minutes.

To quantify this interaction, you could further analyze these data using techniques such as analysis of variance or general linear model.

Symmetry Plot

Symmetry plots can be used to assess whether sample data come from a symmetric distribution. Many statistical procedures assume that data come from a normal distribution. However, many procedures are robust to violations of normality, so having data from a symmetric distribution is often sufficient. Other procedures, such as nonparametric methods, assume symmetric distributions rather than normal distributions. Therefore, a symmetry plot is a useful tool in many circumstances.

Data

The data columns must be numeric. If you enter more than one data column, MINITAB draws a separate symmetry plot for each column.

MINITAB automatically omits missing data from the calculations.

▶ To draw a symmetry plot

1 Choose Stat ➤ Quality Tools ➤ Symmetry Plot.

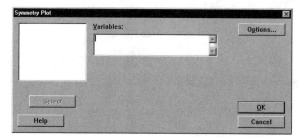

2 In **Variables**, enter the columns containing the numeric data you want to plot.

3 If you like, use the option listed below, then click **OK**.

Options

Options subdialog box

■ replace the default title with your own title

Method

MINITAB plots the distances from the median of ordered pairs of the data from the sample. The distances for each ordered pair make up the X and Y coordinates of a single point for each pair:

1 The first pair consists of the two values that are closest to the median, one above and one below.

2 The second pair consists of the two values that are second closest to the median, one above and one below.

3 This pattern continues to form pairs for the entire sample.

The distance from the median for the point in each pair that is less than the median becomes the Y coordinate for that point. The distance from the median for the point in each pair that is greater than the median becomes the X coordinate for that point.

MINITAB also displays a histogram to provide an alternative view of the distribution.

Interpreting the symmetry plot

When the sample data follow a symmetric distribution, the X and Y coordinates will be approximately equal for all points and the data will fall in a straight line. MINITAB draws a line on the plot to represent exact X-Y equality (a perfectly symmetric sample). By comparing the data points to the line, you can assess the degree of symmetry present in the data. The more symmetric the data, the closer the points will be to the line. Even with normally distributed data, you can expect to see runs of points above or below the line. The important thing to look for is whether the points remain close to or parallel to the line, versus the points diverging from the line. You can detect the following asymmetric conditions:

■ Data points diverging above the line indicate skewness to the left.

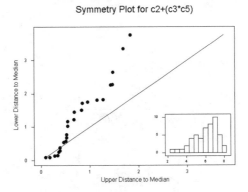

■ Data points diverging below the line indicate skewness to the right.

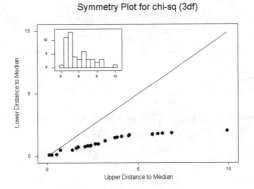

■ Points far away from the line in the upper right corner (where distances are large) indicate some degree of skewness in the tails of the distribution.

Caution As rule of thumb, you should have at least 25 to 30 data points. Interpreting a plot with too few data points may lead to incorrect conclusions.

> **Example of a symmetry plot**

Before doing further analysis, you would like to determine whether or not the sample data come from a symmetric distribution.

1 Open the worksheet EXH_QC.MTW.

2 Choose **Stat ➤ Quality Tools ➤ Symmetry Plot**.

3 In **Variables**, enter *Faults*. Click **OK**.

*Graph
window
output*

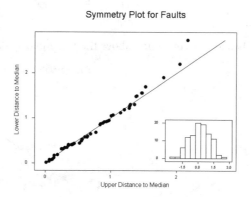

Interpreting the results

Here is a plot of data that are fairly symmetric. Notice the points above the line in the upper right corner. All this points out is a very slight extension in the left side of the histogram. The points in the plot do not diverge from the line, so we would not say there is much noticeable skewness.

References

[1] J.D. Gibbons (1986). "Randomness, Tests of" *Encyclopedia of Statistical Sciences*, 7, John Wiley & Sons, pp.555–562.

[2] T.P. Ryan (1989). *Statistical Methods for Quality Improvement*, John Wiley & Sons.

[3] W.A. Taylor (1991). *Optimization & Variation Reduction in Quality*, McGraw-Hill, Inc.

11 Measurement Systems Analysis

Measurement Systems Analysis Overview

MINITAB offers several commands to help you determine how much of your process variation arises from variation in your measurement system.

- **Gage R&R (Crossed)**, **Gage R&R (Nested)**, and **Gage Run Chart** examine measurement system precision.

- **Gage Linearity and Accuracy** examines gage linearity and accuracy.

Any time you measure the results of a process you will see some variation. This variation comes from two sources: one, there are always differences between parts made by any process, and two, any method of taking measurements is imperfect—thus, measuring the same part repeatedly does not result in identical measurements.

Statistical Process Control (SPC) is concerned with identifying sources of *part-to-part* variation, and reducing that variation as much as possible to get a more consistent product. But before you do any SPC analyses, you may want to check that the variation you observe is not overly due to errors in your measurement system.

Measurement system error

Measurement system errors can be classified into two categories: accuracy and precision.

- Accuracy describes the difference between the measurement and the part's actual value.

- Precision describes the variation you see when you measure the same part repeatedly with the same device.

Within any measurement system, you can have one or both of these problems. For example, you can have a device which measures parts precisely (little variation in the measurements) but not accurately. You can also have a device that is accurate (the average of the measurements is very close to the accurate value), but not precise, that is, the measurements have large variance. You can also have a device that is neither accurate nor precise.

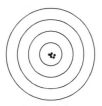   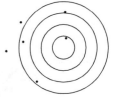

accurate and precise   precise but not accurate   accurate but not precise   not accurate or precise

Accuracy

The accuracy of a measurement system is usually broken into three components:

- linearity—a measure of how the size of the part affects the accuracy of the measurement system. It is the difference in the observed accuracy values through the *expected range* of measurements.

- accuracy—a measure of the bias in the measurement system. It is the difference between the observed average measurement and a *master value*.

- stability—a measure of how accurately the system performs over time. It is the total variation obtained with a particular device, on the same part, when measuring a single characteristic *over time*.

To examine your measurement system's accuracy, see *Gage Linearity and Accuracy Study* on page 11-27.

Precision

Precision, or measurement variation, can be broken down into two components:

- repeatability—the variation due to the measuring *device*. It is the variation observed when the same operator measures the same part repeatedly with the same device.

- reproducibility—the variation due to the measurement *system*. It is the variation observed when different operators measure the same parts using the same device.

To examine your measurement system's precision, see *Gage R&R Study* on page 11-4.

To look at a plot of all of the measurements by operator/part combination, and thus *visualize* the repeatability and reproducibility components of the measurement variation, see *Gage Run Chart* on page 11-23.

Data sets used in examples

The same two data sets are used in the Gage R&R (Crossed) Study and the Gage Run Chart examples:

- GAGE2.MTW, in which measurement system variation has a large effect on the overall observed variation

- GAGEAIAG.MTW, in which measurement system variation has a small effect on the overall observed variation

You can compare the output for the two data sets, as well as compare results from the various analyses.

The Gage Linearity and Accuracy Study example uses the GAGELIN.MTW data set.

GAGEAIAG.MTW and GAGELIN.MTW are reprinted with permission from the *Measurement Systems Analysis Reference Manual* (Chrysler, Ford, General Motors Supplier Quality Requirements Task Force).

Gage R&R Study

Gage repeatability and reproducibility studies determine how much of your observed process variation is due to measurement system variation. MINITAB allows you to perform either crossed or nested Gage R&R studies.

- Use Gage R&R Study (Crossed) when each part is measured multiple times by each operator.

- Use Gage R&R Study (Nested) when each part is measured by only one operator, such as in destructive testing. In destructive testing, the measured characteristic is different after the measurement process than it was at the beginning. Crash testing is an example of destructive testing.

MINITAB provides two methods for assessing repeatability and reproducibility: $\bar{X}$ and R, and ANOVA. The $\bar{X}$ and R method breaks down the overall variation into three categories: part-to-part, repeatability, and reproducibility. The ANOVA method goes one step further and breaks down reproducibility into its operator, and operator-by-part, components.

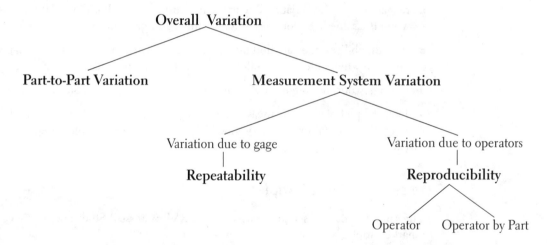

The ANOVA method is more accurate than the $\bar{X}$ and R method, in part, because it considers the operator by part interaction [3] and [4]. Gage R&R Study (Crossed) allows you to choose between the $\bar{X}$ and R method and the ANOVA method. Gage R&R Study (Nested) uses the ANOVA method only.

- If you need to use destructive testing, you must be able to assume that all parts within a single batch are identical enough to claim that they are the same part. If you are unable to make that assumption then part-to-part variation within a batch will mask the measurement system variation.

If you can make that assumption, then choosing between a crossed or nested Gage R&R Study for destructive testing depends on how your measurement process is set up.

If all operators measure parts from each batch, then use Gage R&R Study (Crossed). If each batch is only measured by a single operator, then you must use Gage R&R Study (Nested). In fact, whenever operators measure unique parts, you have a nested design.

Data

Gage R&R Study (Crossed)

Structure your data so that each row contains the part name or number, operator (optional), and the observed measurement. Parts and operators can be text or numbers.

PartNum	Operator	Measure
1	Daryl	1.48
1	Daryl	1.43
2	Daryl	1.83
2	Daryl	1.83
3	Daryl	1.53
3	Daryl	1.38
1	Beth	1.78
1	Beth	1.33
⋮	⋮	⋮

The Gage R&R studies require balanced designs (equal numbers of observations per cell) and replicates. You can estimate any missing observations with the methods described in [2].

Gage R&R Study (Nested)

Structure your data so that each row contains the part name or number, operator, and the observed measurement. Parts and operators can be text or numbers. Part is nested within operator, because each operator measures unique parts.

Note If you use destructive testing, you must be able to assume that all parts within a single batch are identical enough to claim that they are the same part.

In the example on the right, PartNum1 for Daryl is truly a different part from PartNum1 for Beth.

PartNum	Operator	Measure	PartNum	Operator	Measure
1	Daryl	1.48	1	Daryl	1.48
1	Daryl	1.43	1	Daryl	1.43
2	Daryl	1.83	2	Daryl	1.83
2	Daryl	1.83	2	Daryl	1.83
3	Daryl	1.53	3	Daryl	1.53
3	Daryl	1.52	3	Daryl	1.52
4	Beth	1.38	1	Beth	1.38
4	Beth	1.78	1	Beth	1.78
5	Beth	1.33	2	Beth	1.33
⋮	⋮	⋮	⋮	⋮	⋮

The Gage R&R studies require balanced designs (equal numbers of observations per cell) and replicates. You can estimate any missing observations with the methods described in [2].

▶ **To do a Gage R&R Study (Crossed)**

1 Choose Stat ➤ Quality Tools ➤ Gage R&R Study (Crossed).

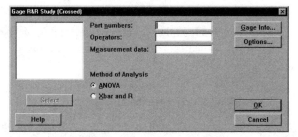

2 In **Part numbers**, enter the column of part names or numbers.

3 In **Measurement data,** enter the column of measurements.

4 If you like, use any of the options described below, then click **OK**.

▶ **To do a Gage R&R Study (Nested)**

   1 Choose Stat ➤ Quality Tools ➤ Gage R&R Study (Nested).

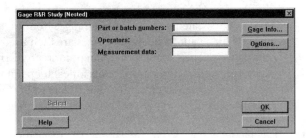

   2 In **Part or batch numbers**, enter the column of part or batch names or numbers.

   3 In **Operators**, enter the column of operator names or numbers.

   4 In **Measurement data**, enter the column of measurements.

   5 If you like, use any of the options described below, then click **OK**.

Options

Gage R&R Study dialog box

- (Gage R&R (Crossed) only) add operators as a factor in the model
- (Gage R&R (Crossed) only) use the ANOVA or $\bar{X}$ and R (default) method of analysis

Gage Info subdialog box

- fill in the blank lines on the graphical output label

Options subdialog box

- change the multiple in the Study Var (5.15∗SD) column by entering a study variation—see **StudyVar** in *Session window output* on page 11-9
- display a column showing the percentage of process tolerance taken up by each variance component (a measure of precision-to-tolerance for each component)
- display a column showing the percentage of process standard deviation taken up by each variance component
- choose not to display percent contribution or percent study variation
- draw plots on separate pages, one plot per page
- replace the default graph title with your own title

Method—Gage R&R Study (Crossed)

$\overline{X}$ and R method

MINITAB first calculates the sample ranges from each set of measurements taken by an operator on a part. The sample ranges are then used to calculate the average range for repeatability. The variance component for reproducibility is calculated from the range of the averages of all measurements for each operator. Reproducibility, in this case, is the same as the variance component for operator. The variance component for parts is calculated from the range of the averages of all measurements for each part.

Note | All ranges are divided by the appropriate d_2 factor.

ANOVA method

When both Parts and Operators are entered

When you enter Operators as well as Parts, your data are analyzed using a balanced two-factor factorial design. Both factors are considered to be random. The model includes the main effects of Parts and Operators, plus the Part by Operator interaction. (When operators are *not* entered, the model is a balanced one-way ANOVA with Part as a random factor, as described in the next section.)

MINITAB first calculates the ANOVA table for the appropriate model. That table is then used to calculate the variance components, which appear in the Gage R&R tables.

Note | Some of the variance components could be estimated as negative numbers when the Part by Operator term in the full model is not significant. MINITAB will first display an ANOVA table for the full model. If the p-value for the Part by Operator term is > 0.25, a reduced model is then fitted and used to calculate the variance components. This reduced model includes only the main effects of Part and Operator.

- **With the full model**, the variance component for Reproducibility is further broken down into variation due to Operator and variation due to the Part by Operator interaction:
  - The Operator component is the variation observed between different operators measuring the same part.
  - The Part by Operator interaction is the variation among the average part sizes measured by each operator. This interaction takes into account cases where, for instance, one operator gets more variation when measuring smaller parts, whereas another operator gets more variation when measuring larger parts.

  Use the table of variance components to interpret these effects.

- **With the reduced model**, the variance component for Reproducibility is simply the variance component for Operator.

When Operators are not entered

When you only enter the parts, the model is a balanced one-way ANOVA, and Part is considered a random factor. MINITAB calculates the ANOVA table and estimates the variance components for Part and Gage. The variance component for Gage is the same as Repeatability, and no Reproducibility component is estimated. Thus, the variance component for Gage is the error term from the ANOVA model.

Method—Gage R&R Study (Nested)

ANOVA Method

When you use Gage R&R Study (Nested), your data are analyzed using a nested design. The model includes the main effects for Operator and Part (Operator), in which part is nested in operator. Because each operator measures distinct parts, there is no Operator-by-Part interaction.

MINITAB first calculates the ANOVA table for the appropriate model. That table is then used to calculate the variance components—Repeatability, Reproducibility, and Part-to-Part.

Note | Some of the variance components could be estimated as negative numbers when the Part by Operator term in the full model is not significant. MINITAB will first display an ANOVA table for the full model. If the p-value for the Part by Operator term is > 0.25, a reduced model is then fitted and used to calculate the variance components. This reduced model includes only the main effects of Part and Operator.

Session window output

The Session window output consists of several tables:

- **ANOVA Table** (ANOVA method only)—displays the usual analysis of variance output for the fitted effects. See "Note" under *ANOVA method* on page 11-8 for more information.

- Gage R&R
  - **VarComp** (or **Variance**)—the variance component contributed by each source.
  - **%Contribution**—the percent contribution to the overall variation made by each variance component. (Each variance component divided by the total variation, then multiplied by 100.) The percentages in this column add to 100.
  - **StdDev**—the standard deviation for each variance component.
  - **StudyVar**—the standard deviations multiplied by 5.15. You can change the multiple from 5.15 to some other number. The default is 5.15*sigma, because 5.15 is the number of standard deviations needed to capture 99% of your process measurements. The last entry in the StudyVar column is 5.15*Total. This

number, usually referred to as the study variation, estimates the width of the interval you need to capture 99% of your process measurements.

- **%Study Var**—the percent of the study variation for each component (the standard deviation for each component divided by the total standard deviation). These percentages do not add to 100.

■ **Number of Distinct Categories**—the number of distinct categories within the process data that the measurement system can discern. For instance, imagine you measured ten different parts, and MINITAB reported that your measurement system could discern four distinct categories. This means that some of those ten parts are not different enough to be discerned as being different by your measurement system. If you want to distinguish a higher number of distinct categories, you need a more precise gage.

The number is calculated by dividing the standard deviation for Parts by the standard deviation for Gage, then multiplying by 1.41 and rounding down to the nearest integer. This number represents the number of non-overlapping confidence intervals that will span the range of product variation.

The Automobile Industry Action Group (AIAG) [1] suggests that when the number of categories is less than two, the measurement system is of no value for controlling the process, since one part cannot be distinguished from another. When the number of categories is two, the data can be divided into two groups, say high and low. When the number of categories is three, the data can be divided into three groups, say low, middle and high. A value of five or more denotes an acceptable measurement system.

Graph window output

■ **Components of Variation** is a visualization of the final table in the Session window output, showing bars for: Total Gage R&R, Repeatability, Reproducibility (but not Operator and Operator by Part), and Part-to-Part variation.

■ **R Chart by Operator** displays the variation in the measurements made by each operator, so you can compare operators to each other. This helps you determine if each operator has the variability of their measurements in control.

■ **$\bar{X}$ Chart by Operator** displays the measurements in relation to the overall mean for each operator, so you can compare operators to each other and to the mean. This helps you determine if each operator has the average of their measurements in control.

■ **By Part** displays the main effect for Part, so you can compare the mean measurement for each part. If you have many replicates, boxplots are displayed on the By Part graph.

- **By Operator** displays the main effect for Operator, so you can compare the mean measurement for each operator. If you have many replicates, boxplots are displayed on the By Operator graph.

- **Operator by Part Interaction** (Gage R&R Study (Crossed) only) displays the Operator by Part effect, so you can see how the relationship between Operator and Part changes depending on the operator.

▶ Example of a gage R&R study (crossed)—$\bar{X}$ and R method

In this example, we do a gage R&R study on two data sets: one in which measurement system variation contributes little to the overall observed variation (GAGEAIAG.MTW), and one in which measurement system variation contributes a lot to the overall observed variation (GAGE2.MTW). For comparison, we analyze the data using both the $\bar{X}$ and R method and the ANOVA method. You can also look at the same data plotted on a Gage Run Chart (page 11-24).

For the GAGEAIAG data set, ten parts were selected that represent the expected range of the process variation. Three operators measured the ten parts, two times per part, in a random order. For the GAGE2 data, three parts were selected that represent the expected range of the process variation. Three operators measured the three parts, three times per part, in a random order.

1 Open the file GAGEAIAG.MTW.

2 Choose **Stat ➤ Quality Tools ➤ Gage R&R Study (Crossed)**.

3 In **Part numbers**, enter *Part*. In **Operators**, enter *Operator*. In **Measurement data**, enter *Response*.

4 Under **Method of Analysis**, choose **Xbar and R**.

5 Click **OK**.

6 Now repeat steps 2 and 3 using the GAGE2.MTW data set.

▶ Example of a gage R&R study (crossed)—ANOVA method

1 Open the file GAGEAIAG.MTW.

2 Choose **Stat ➤ Quality Tools ➤ Gage R&R Study (Crossed)**.

3 In **Part numbers**, enter *Part*. In **Operators**, enter *Operator*. In **Measurement data**, enter *Response*.

4 Under **Method of Analysis**, choose **ANOVA**.

5 Click **OK**.

6 Now repeat steps 2 and 3 using the GAGE2.MTW data set.

X̄ and R method/Session window output/GAGEAIAG.MTW

Gage R&R Study - XBar/R Method

Gage R&R for Response

Source	Variance	%Contribution (of Variance)
Total Gage R&R	2.08E-03	6.33
Repeatability	1.15E-03	3.51
Reproducibility	9.29E-04	2.82
Part-to-Part	3.08E-02	93.67
Total Variation	3.29E-02	100.00

A

Source	StdDev (SD)	Study Var (5.15*SD)	%Study Var (%SV)
Total Gage R&R	0.045650	0.235099	25.16
Repeatability	0.033983	0.175015	18.73
Reproducibility	0.030481	0.156975	16.80
Part-to-Part	0.175577	0.904219	96.78
Total Variation	0.181414	0.934282	100.00

Number of distinct categories = 5

B

A The measurement system variation (Total Gage R&R) is much smaller than what was found for the same data with the ANOVA method. That is because the X̄ and R method does not account for the Operator by Part effect, which was very large for this data set. Here you get misleading estimates of the percentage of variation due to the measurement system.

B According to AIAG, 4 represents an adequate measuring system. However, as explained above, you would be better off using the ANOVA method for this data. (See *Session window output* on page 11-9.)

X̄ and R method/Session window output/GAGE2.MTW

Gage R&R Study - XBar/R Method

Gage R&R for Response

Source	Variance	%Contribution (of Variance)
Total Gage R&R	7229.94	78.11
Repeatability	7229.94	78.11
Reproducibility	0.00	0.00
Part-to-Part	2026.05	21.89
Total Variation	9255.99	100.00

A

Source	StdDev (SD)	Study Var (5.15*SD)	%Study Var (%SV)
Total Gage R&R	85.0291	437.900	88.38
Repeatability	85.0291	437.900	88.38
Reproducibility	0.0000	0.000	0.00
Part-to-Part	45.0116	231.810	46.79
Total Variation	96.2081	495.471	100.00

Number of distinct categories = 1

B

A A large percentage (78.111%) of the variation in the data is due to the measuring system (Gage R&R); little is due to differences between parts (21.889%).

B A 1 tells you the measurement system is poor; it cannot distinguish differences between parts. (See *Session window output* on page 11-9.)

X̄ and R method/Graph window output/GAGEAIAG.MTW

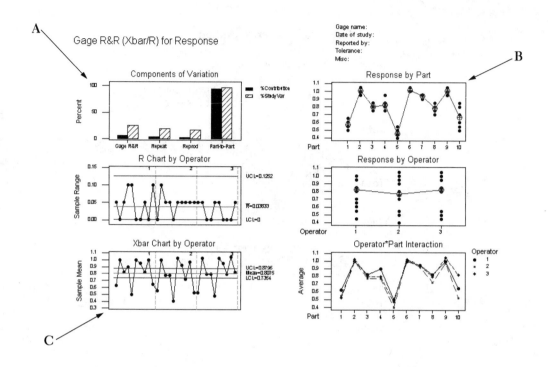

A A low percentage of variation (6%) is due to the measurement system (Gage R&R), and a high percentage (94%) is due to differences between parts.

B Although the X̄ and R method does not account for the Operator by Part interaction, this plot shows you that the interaction is significant. Here, the X̄ and R method grossly overestimates the capability of the gage. You may want to use the ANOVA method, which accounts for the Operator by Part interaction.

C Most of the points in the X̄ Chart are *outside* the control limits when the variation is mainly due to part-to-part differences.

$\bar{X}$ and R method/Graph window output/GAGE2.MTW

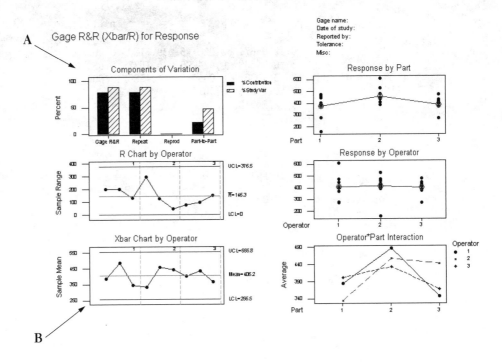

A A high percentage of variation (78%) is due to the measurement system (Gage R&R)—primarily repeatability, and the low percentage (22%) is due to differences between parts.

B Most of the points in the $\bar{X}$ chart will be *within* the control limits when the observed variation is mainly due to the measurement system.

ANOVA method/Session window output/GAGEAIAG.MTW

Two-Way ANOVA Table With Interaction

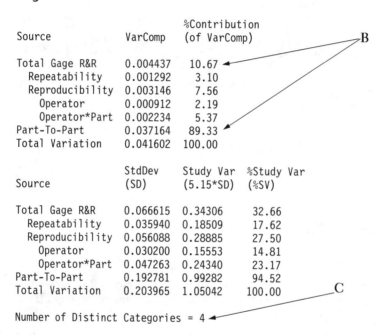

Source	DF	SS	MS	F	P
Part	9	2.05871	0.228745	39.7178	0.00000
Operator	2	0.04800	0.024000	4.1672	0.03256
Operator*Part	18	0.10367	0.005759	4.4588	0.00016
Repeatability	30	0.03875	0.001292		
Total	59	2.24912			

A

Gage R&R

Source	VarComp	%Contribution (of VarComp)
Total Gage R&R	0.004437	10.67
Repeatability	0.001292	3.10
Reproducibility	0.003146	7.56
Operator	0.000912	2.19
Operator*Part	0.002234	5.37
Part-To-Part	0.037164	89.33
Total Variation	0.041602	100.00

B

Source	StdDev (SD)	Study Var (5.15*SD)	%Study Var (%SV)
Total Gage R&R	0.066615	0.34306	32.66
Repeatability	0.035940	0.18509	17.62
Reproducibility	0.056088	0.28885	27.50
Operator	0.030200	0.15553	14.81
Operator*Part	0.047263	0.24340	23.17
Part-To-Part	0.192781	0.99282	94.52
Total Variation	0.203965	1.05042	100.00

C

Number of Distinct Categories = 4

A When the p-value for Operator by Part is < 0.25, MINITAB fits the full model. In this case, the ANOVA method will be more accurate than the $\bar{X}$ and R method, which does not account for this interaction.

B The percent contribution from Part-To-Part is larger than that of Total Gage R&R. This tells you that most of the variation is due to differences between parts; very little is due to measurement system error.

C According to AIAG, 4 represents an adequate measuring system. (See *Session window output* on page 11-9.)

ANOVA method/Session window output/GAGE2.MTW

Two-Way ANOVA Table With Interaction

Source	DF	SS	MS	F	P
Part	2	38990	19495.2	2.90650	0.16616
Operator	2	529	264.3	0.03940	0.96173
Operator*Part	4	26830	6707.4	0.90185	0.48352
Repeatability	18	133873	7437.4		
Total	26	200222			

Two-Way ANOVA Table Without Interaction

Source	DF	SS	MS	F	P
Part	2	38990	19495.2	2.66887	0.09168
Operator	2	529	264.3	0.03618	0.96452
Repeatability	22	160703	7304.7		
Total	26	200222			

Gage R&R

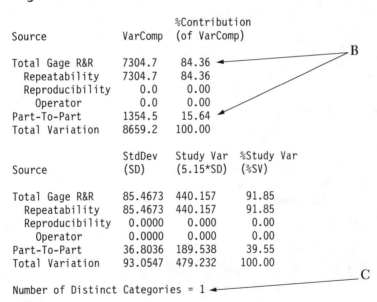

Source	VarComp	%Contribution (of VarComp)
Total Gage R&R	7304.7	84.36
Repeatability	7304.7	84.36
Reproducibility	0.0	0.00
Operator	0.0	0.00
Part-To-Part	1354.5	15.64
Total Variation	8659.2	100.00

Source	StdDev (SD)	Study Var (5.15*SD)	%Study Var (%SV)
Total Gage R&R	85.4673	440.157	91.85
Repeatability	85.4673	440.157	91.85
Reproducibility	0.0000	0.000	0.00
Operator	0.0000	0.000	0.00
Part-To-Part	36.8036	189.538	39.55
Total Variation	93.0547	479.232	100.00

A

B

Number of Distinct Categories = 1 ◄———— C

A When the p-value for Operator by Part is > 0.25, MINITAB fits the model without the interaction and uses the reduced model to define the Gage R&R statistics.

B The percent contribution from Total Gage R&R is larger than that of Part-To-Part. Thus, most of the variation arises from the measuring system; very little is due to differences between parts.

C A 1 tells you the measurement system is poor; it cannot distinguish differences between parts. (See *Session window output* on page 11-9.)

ANOVA method/Graph window output/GAGEAIAG.MTW

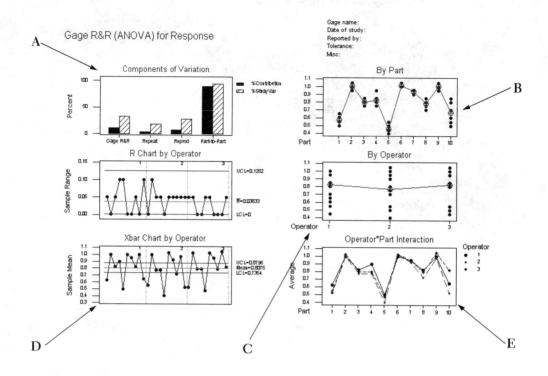

A   The percent contribution from Part-To-Part is larger than that of Total Gage R&R, telling you that most of the variation is due to differences between parts; little is due to the measurement system.

B   There are large differences between parts, as shown by the non-level line.

C   There are small differences between operators, as shown by the nearly level line.

D   Most of the points in the $\bar{X}$ Chart are *outside* the control limits, indicating the variation is mainly due to differences between parts.

E   This graph is a visualization of the p-value for Oper∗Part—0.00016 in this case— indicating a significant interaction between Part and Operator.

ANOVA method/Graph window output/GAGE2.MTW

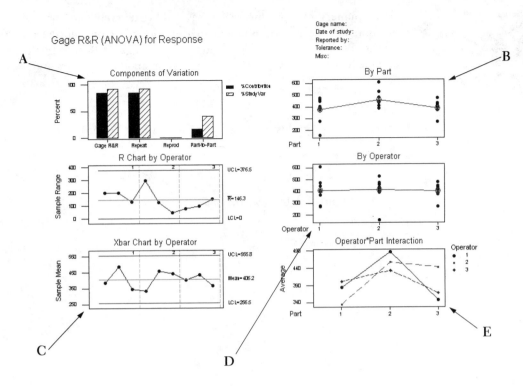

A The percent contribution from Total Gage R&R is larger than that of Part-to-Part, telling you that most of the variation is due to the measurement system—primarily repeatability; little is due to differences between parts.

B There is little difference between parts, as shown by the nearly level line.

C Most of the points in the $\bar{X}$ chart are *inside* the control limits, indicating the observed variation is mainly due to the measurement system.

D There are no differences between operators, as shown by the level line.

E This graph is a visualization of the p-value for Oper*Part—0.48352 in this case—indicating the differences between each operator/part combination are insignificant compared to the total amount of variation.

▷ **Example of a gage R&R study (nested)**

In this example, three operators each measured five different parts twice, for a total of 30 measurements. Each part is unique to operator; no two operators measured the same part. Because of this you decide to conduct a gage R&R study (nested) to determine how much of your observed process variation is due to measurement system variation.

1 Open the worksheet GAGENEST.MTW.

2 Choose **Stat ▶ Quality Tools ▶ Gage R&R Study (Nested)**.

3 In **Part or batch numbers**, enter *Part*.

4 In **Operators**, enter *Operator*.

5 In **Measurement data**, enter *Response*.

6 Click **OK**.

GAGE R&R Study (Nested)

Nested ANOVA Table

Source	DF	SS	MS	F	P
Operator	2	0.0142	0.00709	0.00386	0.99615
Part (Operator)	12	22.0548	1.83790	1.42545	0.25518
Repeatability	15	19.3403	1.28935		
Total	29	41.4093			

Gage R&R

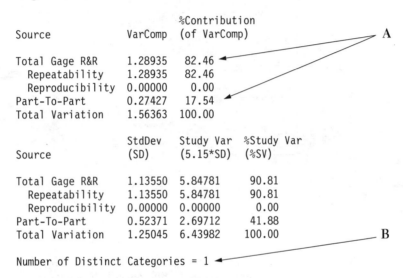

Source	VarComp	%Contribution (of VarComp)
Total Gage R&R	1.28935	82.46
Repeatability	1.28935	82.46
Reproducibility	0.00000	0.00
Part-To-Part	0.27427	17.54
Total Variation	1.56363	100.00

Source	StdDev (SD)	Study Var (5.15*SD)	%Study Var (%SV)
Total Gage R&R	1.13550	5.84781	90.81
Repeatability	1.13550	5.84781	90.81
Reproducibility	0.00000	0.00000	0.00
Part-To-Part	0.52371	2.69712	41.88
Total Variation	1.25045	6.43982	100.00

Number of Distinct Categories = 1 ◀ B

A The percent contribution for differences between parts (Part-To-Part) is much smaller than the percentage contribution for measurement system variation (Total Gage R&R). This indicates that most of the variation is due to measurement system error; very little is due to differences between part.

B A 1 in number of distinct categories tells you that the measurement system is not able to distinguish between parts.

Gage R&R Study (Nested)

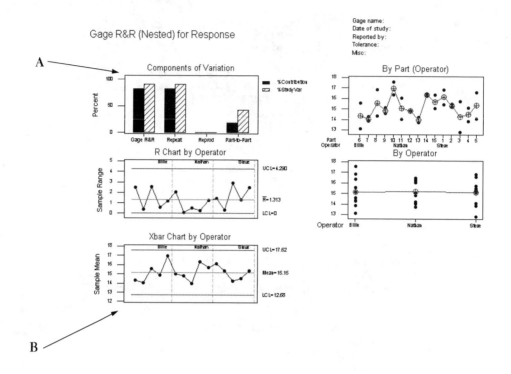

A Most of the variation is due to measurement system error (Gage R&R), while a low percentage of variation is due to differences between parts.

B Most of the points in the $\bar{X}$ chart are *inside* the control limits when the variation is mostly due to meaurement system error.

Gage Run Chart

A gage run chart is a plot of all of your observations by operator and part number. A horizontal reference line is drawn at the mean, which can be calculated from the data, or a value you enter from prior knowledge of the process. You can use this chart to quickly assess differences in measurements between different operators and parts. A stable process would give you a random horizontal scattering of points; an operator or part effect would give you some kind of pattern in the plot.

Data

Structure your data so each row contains the part name or number, operator (optional), and the observed measurement. Parts and operators can be text or numbers.

PartNum	Operator	Measure
1	Daryl	1.48
1	Daryl	1.43
2	Daryl	1.83
2	Daryl	1.83
3	Daryl	1.53
3	Daryl	1.38
1	Beth	1.78
1	Beth	1.33
⋮	⋮	⋮

▶ **To make a gage run chart**

1 Choose **Stat ➤ Quality Tools ➤ Gage Run Chart**.

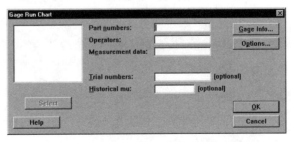

2 In **Part numbers,** enter the column of part names or numbers.

3 In **Operators,** enter the column of operator names or numbers.

4 In **Measurement data**, enter the column of measurements.

5 If you like, use any of the options described below, then click **OK**.

Options

Gage Run Chart dialog box

- enter trial numbers

- enter a location other than the mean for the horizontal reference line

Gage Info subdialog box

- fill in the blank lines on the graphical output label

Options subdialog box

- replace the default graph title with your own title

▶ Example of a gage run chart

In this example, you draw a gage run chart with two data sets: one in which measurement system variation contributes little to the overall observed variation (GAGEAIAG.MTW), and one in which measurement system variation contributes a lot to the overall observed variation (GAGE2.MTW). For comparison, see the same data sets analyzed by the gage R&R study using the ANOVA and $\bar{X}$ and R Methods (page 11-11).

For the GAGEAIAG data, ten parts were selected that represent the expected range of the process variation. Three operators measured the ten parts, two times per part, in a random order. For the GAGE2 data, three parts were selected that represent the expected range of the process variation. Three operators measured the three parts, three times per part, in a random order.

1 Open the worksheet GAGEAIAG.MTW.

2 Choose **Stat ➤ Quality Tools ➤ Gage Run Chart**.

3 In **Part numbers**, enter *C1*.

4 In **Operators**, enter *C2*.

5 In **Measurement data**, enter *C3*. Click **OK**.

6 Repeat these steps, using the GAGE2.MTW data set.

Gage run chart for GAGEAIAG.MTW

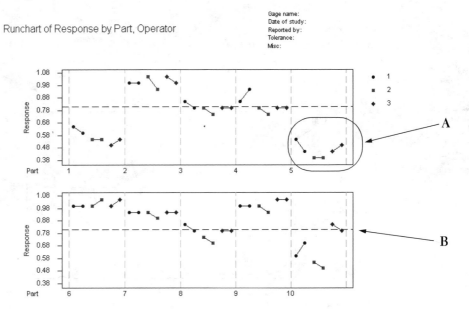

Runchart of Response by Part, Operator

Gage name:
Date of study:
Reported by:
Tolerance:
Misc:

A For each part, you can compare both the variation between measurements made by each operator, and differences in measurements between operators.

B You can also look at the measurements in relationship to the horizontal reference line. In this example, the reference line is the mean of all observations.

Most of the variation is due to differences between parts. Some smaller patterns also appear. For example, Operator 2's second measurement is consistently (seven times out of ten) smaller than the first measurement. Operator 2's measurements are consistently (eight times out of ten) smaller than Operator 1's measurements.

Gage run chart for GAGE2.MTW

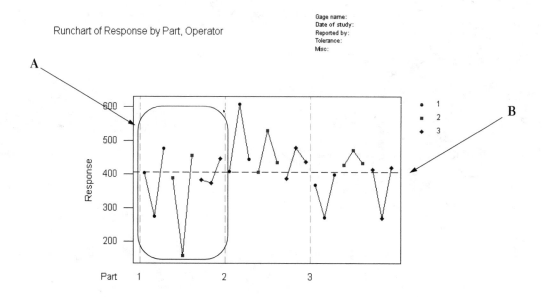

A For each part, you can compare both the variation between measurements made by each operator, and differences in measurements between operators.

B You can also look at the measurements in relationship to the horizontal reference line. In this example, the reference line is the mean of all observations.

The dominant factor here is repeatability—large differences in measurements when the same operator measures the same part. Oscillations might suggest the operators are "adjusting" *how* they measure between measurements.

Gage Linearity and Accuracy Study

A gage linearity study tells you how accurate your measurements are through the expected range of the measurements. It answers the question, "Does my gage have the same accuracy for all sizes of objects being measured?"

A gage accuracy study examines the difference between the observed average measurement and a reference or master value. It answers the question, "How accurate is my gage when compared to a master value?" Gage accuracy is also referred to as bias.

Data

Structure your data so each row contains a part, master measurement, and the observed measurement on that part (the response). Parts can be text or numbers.

PartNum	Master	Response
1	2	2.7
1	2	2.5
⋮	⋮	⋮
2	4	5.1
2	4	3.9
⋮	⋮	⋮

▶ **To do a gage linearity and accuracy study**

1 Choose **Stat ➤ Quality Tools ➤ Gage Linearity Study**.

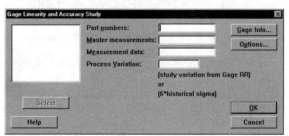

2 In **Part numbers**, enter the column of part names or numbers. In **Master Measurements**, enter the column of master measurements. In **Measurement data**, enter the column of observed measurements.

3 In **Process Variation**, enter a value. You can get this value from the Gage R&R Study—ANOVA method: it is the value in the Total row of the 5.15*Sigma column. This is the number that is usually associated with process variation. If you do not know the value for the process variation, you can enter the process tolerance instead.

4 If you like, use any of the options described below, then click **OK**.

Options

Gage Info subdialog box

■ fill in the blank lines on the graphical output label

Options subdialog box

■ replace the default graph title with your own title

Method

Both studies are done by selecting parts whose measurements cover the normal range of values for a particular process, measuring the parts with a master system, then having an operator make several measurements on each part using a common gage. MINITAB subtracts each measurement taken by the operator from the master measurement, then calculates, for each part, an average deviation from the master measurement.

To calculate the linearity of the gage, MINITAB finds the best-fit line relating the average deviations to the master measurements. Then,

Linearity = slope * process sigma

Generally, the closer the slope is to zero, the better the gage linearity. Linearity can also be expressed as a percentage of the process variation by multiplying the slope of the line by 100.

To calculate the accuracy of the gage, MINITAB combines the deviations from the master measurement for all parts. The mean of this combined sample is the gage accuracy. Accuracy can also be expressed as a percentage of the overall process variation by dividing the mean deviation by the process sigma, and multiplying by 100.

▷ **Example of a gage linearity and accuracy study**

A plant foreman chose five parts that represented the expected range of the measurements. Each part was measured by layout inspection to determine its reference value. Then, one operator randomly measured each part 12 times. A Gage R&R Study using the ANOVA method was done to get the process variation—the number in the Total row of the 5.15*Sigma column—in this case, 14.1941.

The data set used in this example has been reprinted with permission from the *Measurement Systems Analysis Reference Manual* (Chrysler, Ford, General Motors Supplier Quality Requirements Task Force).

1 Open the worksheet GAGELIN.MTW.

2 Choose **Stat ➤ Quality Tools ➤ Gage Linearity Study**.

3 In **Part numbers**, enter *C1*.

4 In **Master measurements**, enter *C2*. In **Measurement data**, enter *C3*.

5 In **Process Variation**, enter *14.1941*. Click **OK**.

Gage linearity and accuracy study

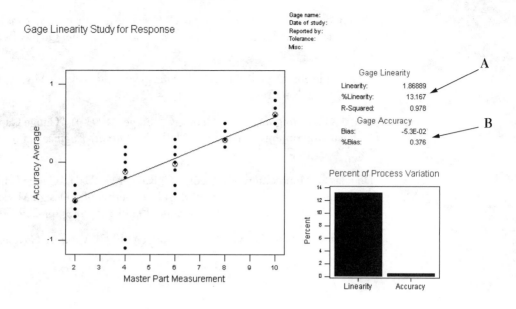

A %Linearity, which is the linearity expressed as a percent of the process variation. For a gage that measures consistently across parts, %linearity will be close to zero. Here, the %Linearity is 13.

B The variation due to accuracy for this gage is less than 1% of the overall process variation.

References

[1] Automotive Industry Task Force (AIAG) (1994). *Measurement Systems Analysis Reference Manual*. Chrysler, Ford, General Motors Supplier Quality Requirements Task Force.

[2] R.J.A. Little and D. B. Rubin (1987). *Statistical Analysis With Missing Data*, John Wiley & Sons, New York.

[3] Douglas C. Montgomery and George C. Runger (1993-4). "Gauge Capability and Designed Experiments. Part I: Basic Methods," *Quality Engineering* 6(1), pp.115–135.

[4] Douglas C. Montgomery and George C. Runger (1993-4). "Gauge Capability Analysis and Designed Experiments. Part II: Experimental Design Models and Variance Component Estimation," *Quality Engineering* 6(2), pp.289–305.

[5] S.R. Searle, G. Casella, and C. E. McCulloch (1992). *Variance Components*, John Wiley & Sons, New York.

12

Variables Control Charts

Variables Control Charts Overview

Control charts are useful for tracking process statistics over time and detecting the presence of special causes. A special cause results in variation that can be detected and controlled. Examples of special causes include supplier, shift, or day of the week differences. Common cause variation, on the other hand, is variation that is inherent in the process. A process is in control when only common causes—not special causes—affect the process output.

Variables control charts, described here, plot statistics from *measurement* data, such as length or pressure. Attributes control charts, described further on page 13-2, plot *count* data, such as the number of defects or defective units.

A process statistic, such as a subgroup mean, individual observation, or weighted statistic, is plotted versus sample number or time. A "center line" is drawn at the average of the statistic being plotted for the time being charted. Two other lines—the upper and lower control limits—are drawn, by default, 3σ above and below the center line. Control limits are calculated lines which indicate the range of expected variation.

Structure of a control chart

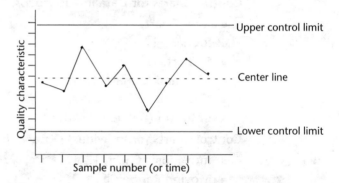

A process is in control when most of the points fall within the bounds of the control limits, and the points do not display any nonrandom patterns. The "tests for special causes" offered with MINITAB's control charts will detect nonrandom patterns in your data. You can change the threshold values for triggering a test failure—see *Defining Tests for Special Causes* on page 12-5.

Once a process is in control, control charts can be used to estimate process parameters needed to determine capability—see also Chapter 14, *Process Capability*.

Choosing a variables control chart

The variables control charts are grouped in this manner:

- control charts for data in subgroups
- control charts for individual observations
- control charts for subgroup combinations
- control charts for short runs

	To plot this...	Use this chart	On page
For data in subgroups:	subgroup means, $\bar{X}$	$\bar{X}$	12-11
	subgroup ranges, r	R	12-14
	subgroup standard deviations, s	S	12-17
	$\bar{X}$ and r on same screen	$\bar{X}$ and R	12-19
	$\bar{X}$ and s on same screen	$\bar{X}$ and S	12-22
For individual observations:	individual observations	Individuals	12-29
	moving ranges	Moving Range	12-32
	individual observations and moving ranges on same screen	I-MR	12-34
For subgroup combinations:	exponentially weighted moving averages	EWMA	12-37
	moving averages	Moving Average	12-41
	cumulative sums	CUSUM	12-44
	individual observations or subgroup means according to their distance from the center line	Zone	12-48
For short runs:	standardized individual observations and moving ranges from short run processes	Z-MR	12-54

Data

Structure individual observations down one column.

Structure subgroup data down a column or across rows. Here is the same data set, with subgroups of size 5, structured both ways. Note that the first 5 observations in the left-side data set (subgroup 1) are the first row of the right-side data set, the second 5 observations are the second row, and so on.

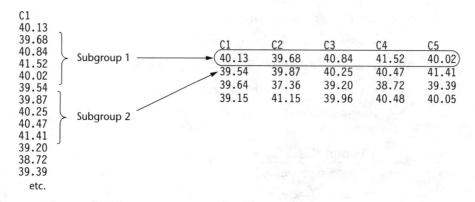

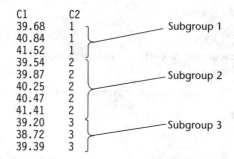

When subgroups are of unequal size, you must enter your data in one column, then create a second column of subscripts which serve as subgroup indicators. In the following example, C1 contains the process data and C2 contains subgroup indicators:

Each time a subscript changes in C2, a new subgroup begins in C1. In this example, subgroup 1 has three observations, subgroup 2 has six observations, and so on.

For information on data for specific charts, see the following sections:

- *Control Charts for Data in Subgroups* on page 12-10
- *Control Charts for Individual Observations* on page 12-28
- *Control Charts Using Subgroup Combinations* on page 12-36
- *Control Charts for Short Runs* on page 12-54

Non-normal data

To properly interpret MINITAB's quality control charts, you must enter data which approximate a normal distribution. If your data are highly skewed, you may want to use the Box-Cox transformation to induce normality.

You can access the Box-Cox transformation two ways: by using the Box-Cox transformation *option* provided with the control chart commands, or by using the *stand-alone* Box-Cox command. The stand-alone command can be used as an exploratory tool to help you determine the best lambda value for the transformation. Then, you can use the transformation option to transform the data at the same time you draw the control chart.

For information on the stand-alone Box-Cox transformation command, see *Box-Cox Transformation for Non-Normal Data* on page 12-6.

For information on the Box-Cox transformation option, see *Use the Box-Cox power transformation for non-normal data* on page 12-68.

Defining Tests for Special Causes

You can define the sensitivity of the tests for special causes used with quality control charts. The test definitions stay in effect until you restart MINITAB. The range of acceptable values you can enter depends on the test number, as shown below.

Test		K can be... (default in parentheses)
1	One point more than K sigmas from the center line	1–6 (3)
2	K points in a row on same side of center line	7–11 (9)
3	K points in a row, all increasing or all decreasing	5–8 (6)
4	K points in a row, alternating up and down	12–14 (14)
5	K out of K + 1 points in a row more than 2 sigmas from the center line (same side)	2–4 (2)
6	K out of K + 1 points in a row more than 1 sigma from the center line (same side)	3–6 (4)
7	K points in a row within 1 sigma of the center line (either side)	12–15 (15)
8	K points in a row more than 1 sigma from the center line (either side)	6–10 (8)

Note | R Chart, S Chart, Moving Range Chart, and the Attributes Control Charts (P, NP, C, and U) only support tests 1 through 4.

▶ **To define the tests for special causes**

1 Choose Stat ➤ Control Charts ➤ Define Tests.

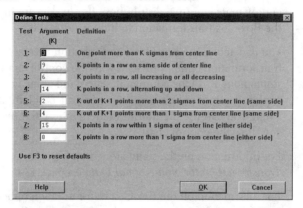

2 In one or more of the **Argument** boxes, enter a value for K. Click **OK**.

Box-Cox Transformation for Non-Normal Data

The Box-Cox transformation can be used to correct both non-normality in process data and subgroup process variation being related to the subgroup mean. Under most conditions, it is not necessary to correct for non-normality unless the data are highly skewed. Wheeler [27] and Wheeler and Chambers [26] suggest that it is not necessary to transform data that are used in control charts, because control charts work well in situations where data are not normally distributed. They give an excellent demonstration of the performance of control charts when data are collected from a variety of non-symmetric distributions.

MINITAB provides two Box-Cox transformations: a *stand-alone command*, described in this section, and a transformation *option* provided with each control chart, described on page 12-68. You can use these procedures in tandem. First, use the stand-alone command as an exploratory tool to help you determine the best lambda value for the transformation. Then, when you enter the control chart command, use the transformation option to transform the data at the same time you draw the chart.

Data

Use this command with subgroup data or individual observations. Structure individual observations down a single column.

Structure subgroup data in a single column or in rows across several columns—see *Data* on page 12-3 for examples.

Note | You can only use this procedure with positive data.

▶ **To do a Box-Cox transformation**

1 Choose Stat ➤ Control Charts ➤ Box-Cox Transformation.

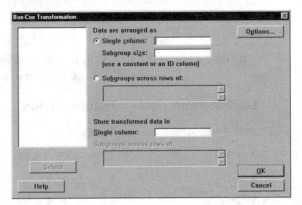

2 Do one of the following:

- For subgroups or individual observations in one column, enter the data column in **Single column**. In **Subgroup size**, enter a subgroup size or column of subgroup indicators. For individual observations, enter a subgroup size of 1.

- For subgroup in rows, enter a series of columns in **Subgroups across rows of**.

3 At this point, the command can be used several ways:

To...	Do this...
Estimate the best lambda value for the transformation	Click **OK**.
Estimate the best lambda value for the transformation, transform the data, and store the transformed data in the column(s) you specify	In **Store transformed data in**, enter a column(s) in which to store the transformed data, then click **OK**.
Transform the data with a lambda value you enter, and store the transformed data in a column(s) you specify	In **Store transformed data in**, enter a column(s) in which to store the transformed data. Click **Options**. In **Use lambda**, enter a value. Click **OK** in each dialog box.

Method

Box-Cox Transformation estimates a lambda value, as shown below, which minimizes the standard deviation of a standardized transformed variable. The resulting transformation is Y^λ when $\lambda \neq 0$ and $\text{Log}_e Y$ when $\lambda = 0$.

This method searches through many types of transformations. Here are some common transformations [20] where Y' is the transform of the data Y:

Lambda value	Transformation
$\lambda = 2$	$Y' = Y^2$
$\lambda = 0.5$	$Y' = \sqrt{Y}$
$\lambda = 0$	$Y' = \text{Log}_e Y$
$\lambda = -0.5$	$Y' = 1/(\sqrt{Y})$
$\lambda = -1$	$Y' = 1/Y$

See [18] for more details on this procedure. A Fibonacci search [2] is used to find the smallest standard deviation (and therefore the best transformation).

Graphical output

When you ask MINITAB to estimate a lambda value, you get a graph which displays:

- the best estimate of lambda for the transformation
- two closely competing values of lambda
- a 95% confidence interval for the true value of lambda

See *Example of a Box-Cox data transformation* on page 12-9 for an illustration.

The graph can be used to assess the appropriateness of the transformation. For example, you can use the 95% confidence interval for lambda to determine whether the optimal lambda value is "close" to 1, since a lambda of 1 indicates that a transformation should not be done. In the case that the optimal lambda is close to 1, you would gain very little by performing the transformation.

As another example, if the optimal lambda is "close" to 0.5, you could simply take the square root of the data, since this transformation is simple and understandable.

Note | In some cases, one of the closely competing values of lambda may end up having a slightly smaller standard deviation than the best estimate.

⮞ **Example of a Box-Cox data transformation**

The data used in the example are highly right skewed, and consist of 50 subgroups each of size 5. If you like, you can look at the spread of the data both before and after the transformation using **Graph ➤ Histogram**.

1 Open the worksheet BOXCOX.MTW.

2 Choose **Stat ➤ Control Charts ➤ Box-Cox Transformation**.

3 In **Single column**, enter *Skewed*. In **Subgroup size**, enter 5.

4 Under **Store transformed data in,** in **Single column**, enter C2. Click **OK**.

Graph window output

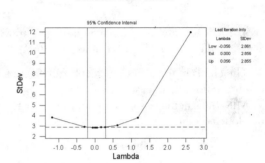

Interpreting the results

The Last Iteration Information table contains the best estimate of lambda (presented as "Est"), which is −0.000 (a very small negative number). Two other closely competing values (presented as "Low" and "Up") are −0.057 and 0.056. A 95% confidence interval for the "true" value of lambda is marked by vertical lines on the graph.

Although the best estimate of lambda is a very small negative number, in any practical situation you want a lambda value that corresponds to an understandable transformation, such as the square root (a lambda of 0.5) or the natural log (a lambda of 0). In this example, 0 is a reasonable choice because it falls within the 95% confidence interval. Therefore, the natural log transformation may be preferred to the transformation defined by the best estimate of lambda.

The 95% confidence interval includes all lambda values which have a standard deviation less than or equal to the horizontal dashed line. Therefore, any lambda value which has a standard deviation *close* to the dashed line is also a reasonable value to use for the transformation. In this example, this corresponds to an interval of −0.3 to 0.4.

Control Charts for Data in Subgroups

MINITAB offers these control charts for data in subgroups:

- $\bar{X}$ chart—a chart of the subgroup means. See *Xbar Chart* on page 12-11.

- R chart—a chart of the subgroup ranges. See *R Chart* on page 12-14.

- S chart—a chart of the subgroup standard deviations. See *S Chart* on page 12-17.

- $\bar{X}$ and R chart—an $\bar{X}$ chart and R chart in one window. See *Xbar and R Chart* on page 12-19.

- $\bar{X}$ and S chart—an $\bar{X}$ chart and S chart in one window. See *Xbar and S Chart* on page 12-22.

- I-MR-R/S chart—an individuals chart, moving range chart, and R chart in one window. See *I-MR-R/S (Between/Within) Chart* on page 12-24.

The charts in this section (except $\bar{X}$ chart) require that you have two or more observations in at least one subgroup. Subgroups do not need to be the same size. MINITAB calculates summary statistics for each subgroup. These summary statistics are plotted on the charts and used to estimate process parameters.

With $\bar{X}$ chart, you can also plot individual observations by entering a subgroup size of 1 in the dialog box.

An important consideration when constructing control charts for data in subgroups is in choosing subgroups that are free of special causes. The variation within a subgroup should be representative of the process variation if all special causes were removed.

Missing data

If a single observation is missing, it is omitted from the calculations of the summary statistics for the subgroup it was in. All formulas are adjusted accordingly. This may cause the control chart limits and the center line to have different values for that subgroup.

If an entire subgroup is missing, there is a gap in the chart where the summary statistic for that subgroup would have been plotted.

Unequal-size subgroups

All of the control chart commands in this section will handle unequal-size subgroups. Since the control limits are functions of the subgroup size, they are affected by unequal-size subgroups. If the sample sizes do not vary by very much, you may want to force the control limits to be constant. See *Force control limits and center line to be constant* on page 12-68 for details.

Xbar Chart

An $\bar{X}$ chart is a control chart of subgroup means. You can use $\bar{X}$ charts to track the process level and detect the presence of special causes.

By default, MINITAB's $\bar{X}$ chart estimates the process variation, σ, using a pooled standard deviation. You can also base the estimate on the average of the subgroup ranges or standard deviations, or enter an historical value for σ.

You can also plot individual observations with the $\bar{X}$ chart. When you plot individual observations, MINITAB estimates σ with $\overline{MR}$ / d2, the average of the moving range divided by an unbiasing constant. By default, the moving range is of length 2, since consecutive values have the greatest chance of being alike. You can also estimate σ using the median of the moving range, or change the length of the moving range.

For more information, see *Variables Control Charts Overview* on page 12-2 and *Control Charts for Data in Subgroups* on page 12-10.

Data

Use this command with subgroup data or individual observations. Subgroup data can be structured in a single column, or in rows across several columns. When you have subgroups of unequal size, structure the subgroups in a single column, then set up a second column of subgroup identifiers. See *Data* on page 12-3 for examples.

▶ **To make an $\bar{X}$ chart**

1 Choose **Stat ➤ Control Charts ➤ Xbar**.

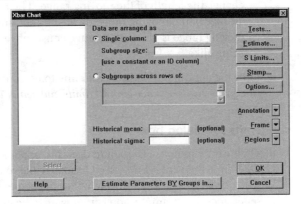

2 Do one of the following:

- When subgroups are in one column, enter the data column in **Single column**. In **Subgroup size**, enter a subgroup size or column of subgroup indicators.

- When subgroups are in rows, enter a series of columns in **Subgroups across rows of**.

3 If you like, use any of the options listed below, then click **OK**.

Options

Xbar Chart dialog box

- enter historical values for μ (the mean of the population distribution) and σ (the standard deviation of the population distribution) if you have a goal for μ or σ, or known parameters from prior data—see *Use historical values of μ and σ* on page 12-64. If you do not specify a value for μ or σ, they are estimated from the data.

- customize the chart annotation, frame, and region (placement of the chart within the Graph window)—see *Customize the data display, annotation, frame, and regions* on page 12-74.

Tests subdialog box

- do eight tests for special causes—see *Do tests for special causes* on page 12-64. To adjust the sensitivity of the tests, see *Defining Tests for Special Causes* on page 12-5.

Estimate subdialog box

- omit certain subgroups when estimating μ and σ—see *Omit subgroups from the estimate of μ or σ* on page 12-66.

- estimate σ various ways—see *Control how σ is estimated* on page 12-67.
  - with subgroup size > 1: base the estimate on the average of the subgroup ranges or standard deviations. The default estimate uses a pooled standard deviation.
  - with subgroup size = 1: base the estimate on the median of the moving range, or change the length of the moving range. The default method uses $\overline{MR}$ / d2, the average of the moving range divided by an unbiasing constant. By default, the moving range is of length 2, since consecutive values have the greatest chance of being alike.

- force the control limits and center line to be constant when subgroups are of unequal size—see *Force control limits and center line to be constant* on page 12-68.

S Limits subdialog box

- choose the positions at which to draw the upper and lower control (sigma) limits in relation to the center line—see *Customize the control (sigma) limits* on page 12-70. The default line is 3σ above and below the center line. You can draw more than one set of lines. For example, you can draw specification limits along with control limits on the chart.

- place bounds on the upper and lower control limits—see *Customize the control (sigma) limits* on page 12-70.

- choose the line type, color, and size for the control limits—see *Customize the control (sigma) limits* on page 12-70. The default line is solid red.

Stamp subdialog box

- add another row of tick labels below the default tick labels—see *Add additional rows of tick labels* on page 12-72. For example, you can place "time stamp" labels (or other descriptive labels) on your graph.

- choose the text font, color, and size for the axis and tick labels. The default labels are black Arial.

Options subdialog box

- use the Box-Cox transformation when you have very skewed data—see *Use the Box-Cox power transformation for non-normal data* on page 12-68.

- choose the symbol type, color, and size. The default symbol is a black cross.

- choose the connection line type, color, and size. The default line is solid black.

Estimate Parameters BY Groups subdialog box

- estimate control limits and center line independently for different groups (draws a "historical chart")—see page 12-61.

▷ Example of an Xbar chart with tests and customized control limits

Suppose you work at a car assembly plant in a department that assembles engines. In an operating engine, parts of the crankshaft move up and down a certain distance from an ideal baseline position. AtoBDist is the distance (in mm) from the actual (A) position of a point on the crankshaft to the baseline (B) position.

To ensure production quality, you took five measurements each working day, from September 28 through October 15, and then ten per day from the 18th through the 25th. You want to draw an $\bar{X}$ chart to track the process level through that time period and to test for the presence of special causes.

1 Open the worksheet CRANKSH.MTW.

2 Choose **Stat ➤ Control Charts ➤ Xbar**.

3 In **Single column**, enter *AtoBDist*. In **Subgroup size**, enter 5.

4 Click **Tests**. Check **Perform all eight tests**. Click **OK**.

5 Click **S Limits**. In **Sigma limit positions**, enter *1 2 3*. Click **OK** in each dialog box.

Session window output

```
TEST 6. 4 out of 5 points more than 1 sigma from center line
        (on one side of CL).
Test Failed at points: 5
```

Graph window output

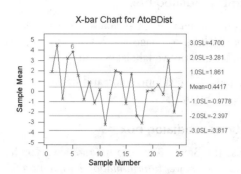

X-bar Chart for AtoBDist

Interpreting the output

Subgroup 5 failed Test 6, meaning it is the fourth point in a row in Zone B (1 to 2σ from the center line), which suggests the presence of special causes.

R Chart

An R chart is a control chart of subgroup ranges. You can use R charts to track process variation and detect the presence of special causes. R charts are typically used to track process variation for samples of size 5 or less, while S charts (page 12-17) are used for larger samples.

By default, MINITAB's R Chart command bases the estimate of the process variation, σ, on the average of the subgroup ranges. You can also use a pooled standard deviation, or enter an historical value for σ.

For more information, see *Variables Control Charts Overview* on page 12-2 and *Control Charts for Data in Subgroups* on page 12-10.

Data

Subgroup data can be structured in a single column, or in rows across several columns. When you have subgroups of unequal size, structure the subgroups in a single column, then set up a second column of subgroup identifiers. Subgroup size must be less than or equal to 100. See *Data* on page 12-3 for examples.

▶ **To make an R chart**

1 Choose Stat ➤ Control Charts ➤ R.

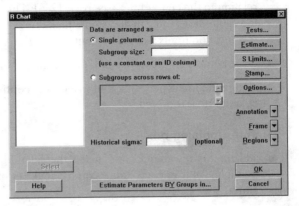

2 Do one of the following:

- When subgroups are in one column, enter the data column in **Single column**. In **Subgroup size**, enter a subgroup size or column of subgroup indicators.

- When subgroups are in rows, enter a series of columns in **Subgroups across rows of**.

3 If you like, use any of the options listed below, then click **OK**.

Options

R Chart dialog box

- enter an historical value for σ (the standard deviation of the population distribution) if you have a goal for σ, or a known σ from past data. If you do not specify a value for σ, it is estimated from the data.

- customize the chart annotation, frame, and region (placement of the chart within the Graph window)—see page 12-74.

Tests subdialog box

- do four tests for special causes—see page 12-64. To adjust the sensitivity of the tests, see *Defining Tests for Special Causes* on page 12-5.

Estimate subdialog box

- omit certain subgroups when estimating μ and σ—see page 12-66.

- base the estimate of σ on a pooled standard deviation—see page 12-67. By default, the estimate is based on the average of the subgroup ranges.

- force the control limits and center line to be constant when subgroups are of unequal size—see page 12-68.

S Limits subdialog box

- choose the positions at which to draw the upper and lower control (sigma) limits in relation to the center line—see page 12-70. The default line is 3σ above and below the center line. You can draw more than one set of lines. For example, you can draw specification limits along with control limits on the chart.

- place bounds on the upper and lower control limits—see page 12-70.

- choose the line type, color, and size for the control limits—see page 12-70. The default line is solid red.

Stamp subdialog box

- add another row of tick labels below the default tick labels—see page 12-72. For example, you can place "time stamp" labels (or other descriptive labels) on your graph.

- choose the text font, color, and size for the axis and tick labels—see page 12-72. The default labels are black Arial.

Options subdialog box

- use the Box-Cox transformation when you have very skewed data—see page 12-68.

- choose the connection line type, color, and size. The default line is solid black.

- choose the symbol type, color, and size. The default symbol is a black cross.

Estimate Parameters BY Groups subdialog box

- estimate control limits and center line independently for different groups (draws a "historical chart")—see page 12-61.

▷ Example of an R chart

Suppose you work at a car assembly plant in a department that assembles engines. In an operating engine, parts of the crankshaft move up and down a certain distance from an ideal baseline position. AtoBDist is the distance (in mm) from the actual (A) position of a point on the crankshaft to the baseline (B) position.

To ensure production quality, you took five measurements each working day, from September 28 through October 15, and then ten per day from the 18th through the 25th. You have already made an $\bar{X}$ chart with the data to track the process level and test for special causes. Now you want to draw an R chart to track the process variation using the same data.

1　Open the worksheet CRANKSH.MTW.

2　Choose **Stat ➤ Control Charts ➤ R**.

3　In **Single column**, enter *AtoBDist*. In **Subgroup size**, enter 5.

4　Click **Tests**. Check **Perform all four tests.** Click **OK** in each dialog box.

Graph window output

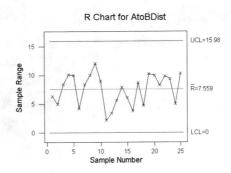

Interpreting the output

The points are randomly distributed between the control limits, implying a stable process. It is also important to compare points on the R chart with those on the $\bar{X}$ chart for the same data (see *Example of an Xbar chart with tests and customized control limits* on page 12-13) to see if the points follow each other. Yours do not—again, implying a stable process.

S Chart

An S Chart is a control chart of subgroup standard deviations. You can use S charts to track the process variation and detect the presence of special causes. S charts are typically used to track process variation for samples larger than size 5, while R charts (page 12-14) are used for smaller samples.

By default, MINITAB's S Chart command bases the estimate of the process variation, σ, on the average of the subgroup standard deviations. You can also use a pooled standard deviation, or enter an historical value for σ.

For more information, see *Variables Control Charts Overview* on page 12-2 and *Control Charts for Data in Subgroups* on page 12-10.

Data

Subgroup data can be structured in a single column, or in rows across several columns. When you have subgroups of unequal size, structure the subgroups in a single column, then set up a second column of subgroup identifiers. See *Data* on page 12-3 for examples.

▶ **To make an S chart**

1 Choose Stat ➤ Control Charts ➤ S.

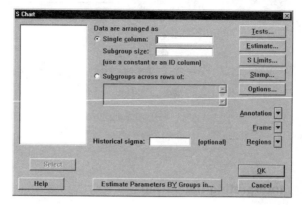

2 Do one of the following:

- When subgroups are in one column, enter the data column in **Single column**. In **Subgroup size**, enter a subgroup size or column of subgroup indicators.

- When subgroups are in rows, enter a series of columns in **Subgroups across rows of**.

3 If you like, use any of the options listed below, then click **OK**.

Options

S Chart dialog box

- enter an historical value for σ (the standard deviation of the population distribution) if you have a goal for σ, or a known σ from prior data—see page 12-64. If you do not specify a value for σ, it is estimated from the data.

- customize the chart annotation, frame, and region (placement of the chart within the Graph window)—see page 12-74.

Tests subdialog box

- do four tests for special causes—see page 12-64. To adjust the sensitivity of the tests, see *Defining Tests for Special Causes* on page 12-5.

Estimate subdialog box

- omit certain subgroups when estimating μ and σ—see page 12-66.

- base the estimate of σ on a pooled standard deviation—see page 12-67. By default, the estimate is based on the average of the subgroup standard deviations.

- force the control limits and center line to be constant when subgroups are of unequal size—see page 12-68.

S Limits subdialog box

- choose the positions at which to draw the upper and lower control (sigma) limits in relation to the center line—see page 12-70. The default line is 3σ above and below the center line. You can draw more than one set of lines. For example, you can draw specification limits along with control limits on the chart.

- place bounds on the upper and lower control limits—see page 12-70.

- choose the line type, color, and size for the control limits—see page 12-70. The default line is solid red.

Stamp subdialog box

- add another row of tick labels below the default tick labels—see page 12-72. For example, you can place "time stamp" labels (or other descriptive labels) on your graph.

- choose the text font, color, and size for the axis and tick labels—see page 12-72. The default labels are black Arial.

Options subdialog box

- use the Box-Cox transformation when you have very skewed data—see page 12-68.

- choose the connection line type, color, and size. The default line is solid black.

- choose the symbol type, color, and size. The default symbol is a black cross.

Estimate Parameters BY Groups subdialog box

- estimate control limits and center line independently for different groups (draws a "historical chart")—see page 12-61.

Xbar and R Chart

Use $\bar{X}$ and R Chart to draw a control chart for subgroup means (an $\bar{X}$ chart) and a control chart for subgroup ranges (an R chart) in the same graph window. The $\bar{X}$ chart is drawn in the upper half of the screen; the R chart in the lower half. Seeing both charts together allows you to track both the process level and process variation at the same time, as well as detect the presence of special causes. See [25] for a discussion of how to interpret joint patterns in the two charts.

$\bar{X}$ and R charts are typically used to track the process level and process variation for samples of size 5 or less, while $\bar{X}$ and S charts (page 12-17) are used for larger samples.

By default, MINITAB's $\bar{X}$ and R chart bases the estimate of the process variation, σ, on the average of the subgroup ranges. You can also use a pooled standard deviation, or enter an historical value for σ.

For more information, see *Variables Control Charts Overview* on page 12-2 and *Control Charts for Data in Subgroups* on page 12-10.

Data

Subgroup data can be structured in a single column, or in rows across several columns. When you have subgroups of unequal size, structure the subgroups in a single column, then set up a second column of subgroup identifiers. See *Data* on page 12-3 for examples.

To use an $\bar{X}$ and R chart your subgroup size must be less than or equal to 100. If your subgroup size is greater than 100, use an $\bar{X}$ and S chart.

▶ **To make an $\bar{X}$ and R chart**

1 Choose **Stat ➤ Control Charts ➤ Xbar-R**.

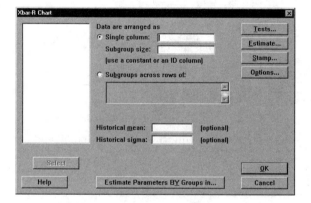

2 Do one of the following:

- When subgroups are in one column, enter the data column in **Single column**. In **Subgroup size**, enter a subgroup size or column of subgroup indicators.

- When subgroups are in rows, enter a series of columns in **Subgroups across rows of**.

3 If you like, use any of the options listed below, then click **OK**.

Options

Xbar/R Chart dialog box

- enter historical values for μ (the mean of the population distribution) and σ (the standard deviation of the population distribution) if you have a goal for μ or σ, or known parameters from prior data—see page 12-64. If you do not specify a value for μ or σ, they are estimated from the data.

Tests subdialog box

- do eight tests for special causes—see page 12-64. To adjust the sensitivity of the tests, see *Defining Tests for Special Causes* on page 12-5.

Estimate subdialog box

- omit certain subgroups when estimating μ and σ—see page 12-66.

- base the estimate of σ on a pooled standard deviation—see page 12-67. The default estimate of σ is based on the average of the subgroup ranges.

- force the control limits and center line to be constant when subgroups are of unequal size—see page 12-68.

Stamp subdialog box

- place an additional row of tick labels, such as dates or shifts, below the subgroup numbers on the x-axis—see page 12-72.

Options subdialog box

- use the Box-Cox transformation when you have very skewed data—see page 12-68.

- choose the positions at which to draw the upper and lower control (sigma) limits in relation to the center line—see page 12-70. The default line is 3σ above and below the center line. You can draw more than one set of lines. For example, you can draw specification limits along with control limits on the chart.

- replace the default graph title with your own title.

Estimate Parameters BY Groups subdialog box

- estimate control limits and center line independently for different groups (draws a "historical chart")—see page 12-61.

▷ Example of an $\bar{X}$ and R chart

Suppose you work at an automobile manufacturer in a department that assembles engines. One of the parts, a camshaft, must be 600 mm ±2 mm long to meet engineering specifications. There has been a chronic problem with camshaft length being out of specification—a problem which has caused poor-fitting assemblies down the production line and high scrap and rework rates. Your supervisor wants to run $\bar{X}$ and R charts to monitor this characteristic, so for a month, you collect a total of 100 observations (20 samples of 5 camshafts each) from all the camshafts used at the plant, and 100 observations from each of your suppliers. First you will look at camshafts produced by Supplier 2.

1 Open the worksheet CAMSHAFT.MTW.

2 Choose **Stat ➤ Control Charts ➤ Xbar-R**.

3 In **Single column**, enter *Supp2*. In **Subgroup size**, enter 5. Click **OK**.

*Graph
window
output*

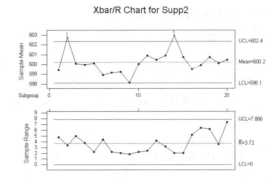

Interpreting the results

The center line on the $\bar{X}$ chart is at 600.2, implying that your process is falling within the specification limits, but two of the points fall outside the control limits, implying an unstable process. The center line on the R chart, 3.720 is also quite large considering the maximum allowable variation is ±2 mm. There may be excess variability in your process.

Xbar and S Chart

Use $\bar{X}$ and S Chart to draw a control chart for subgroup means (an $\bar{X}$ chart) and a control chart for subgroup standard deviations (an S chart) in the same graph window. The $\bar{X}$ chart is drawn in the upper half of the screen; the S chart in the lower half. Seeing both charts together allows you to track both the process level and process variation at the same time, as well as detect the presence of special causes. See [25] for a discussion of how to interpret joint patterns in the two charts.

$\bar{X}$ and S charts are typically used to track process variation for samples larger than size five, while $\bar{X}$ and R charts (page 12-14) are used for smaller samples.

By default, MINITAB's $\bar{X}$ and S Chart command bases the estimate of the process variation, σ, on the average of the subgroup standard deviations. You can also use a pooled standard deviation, or enter an historical value for σ.

For more information, see *Variables Control Charts Overview* on page 12-2 and *Control Charts for Data in Subgroups* on page 12-10.

Data

Subgroup data can be structured in a single column, or in rows across several columns. When you have subgroups of unequal size, structure the subgroups in a single column, then set up a second column of subgroup identifiers. See *Data* on page 12-3 for examples.

▶ To make an X̄ and S chart

1   Choose **Stat ➤ Control Charts ➤ Xbar-S**.

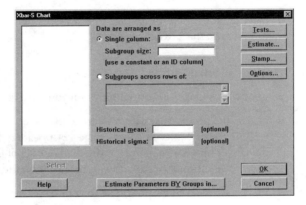

2   Do one of the following:

- When subgroups are in one column, enter the data column in **Single column**. In **Subgroup size**, enter a subgroup size or column of subgroup indicators.

- When subgroups are in rows, enter a series of columns in **Subgroups across rows of**.

3   If you like, use any of the options listed below, then click **OK**.

Options

Xbar/S Chart dialog box

- enter historical values for μ (the mean of the population distribution) and σ (the standard deviation of the population distribution) if you have goals for μ or σ, or known parameters from prior data—see page 12-64. If you do not specify a value for μ or σ, they are estimated from the data.

Tests subdialog box

- do eight tests for special causes—see page 12-64. To adjust the sensitivity of the tests, see *Defining Tests for Special Causes* on page 12-5.

Estimate subdialog box

■ omit certain subgroups when estimating μ and σ—see page 12-66.

■ base the estimate of σ on a pooled standard deviation—see page 12-67. The default estimate of σ is based on the average of the subgroup standard deviations.

■ force the control limits and center line to be constant when subgroups are of unequal size—see page 12-68.

Stamp subdialog box

■ place an additional row of tick labels, such as dates or shifts, below the subgroup numbers on the x-axis—see page 12-72.

Options subdialog box

■ use the Box-Cox transformation when you have very skewed data—see page 12-68.

■ choose the positions at which to draw the upper and lower control (sigma) limits in relation to the center line—see page 12-70. The default line is 3σ above and below the center line. You can draw more than one set of lines. For example, you can draw specification limits along with control limits on the chart.

■ replace the default graph title with your own title.

Estimate Parameters BY Groups subdialog box

■ estimate control limits and center line independently for different groups (draws a "historical chart")—see page 12-61.

I-MR-R/S (Between/Within) Chart

I-MR-R/S (Between/Within) Chart produces a three-way control chart using both between-subgroup and within-subgroup variations. An I-MR-R/S chart consists of

■ an individuals chart—see *Individuals Chart* on page 12-29

■ a moving range chart—see *Moving Range Chart* on page 12-32

■ an R chart or S chart—see *R Chart* on page 12-14 or *S Chart* on page 12-17

When collecting data in subgroups, random error may not be the only source of variation. For example, if you sample five parts in close succession every hour, the only differences should be due to random error. Over time, the process could shift or drift, so the next sample of five parts may be different from the previous sample. Under these conditions, the overall process variation is due to both between-sample variation and random error.

Variation within each sample also contributes to overall process variation. Suppose you sample one part every hour, and measure five locations across the part. While the parts can vary hour to hour, the measurements taken at the five locations can also be consistently different in all parts. Perhaps one location almost always produces the largest measurement, or is consistently smaller. This variation due to location is not accounted for, and the within-sample standard deviation no longer estimates random error, but actually estimates both random error and the location effect. This results in a standard deviation that is too large, causing control limits that are too wide, with most points on the control chart placed very close to the centerline. This process appears to be too good, and it probably is.

You can solve this problem by using I-MR-R/S (Between/Within) to create three separate evaluations of process variation:

Individuals chart: charts the **means from each sample** on an individuals control chart, rather than on an Xbar chart. This chart uses a moving range between consecutive means to determine the control limits. Since the distribution of the sample means is related to the random error, using a moving range to estimate the standard deviation of the distribution of sample means is similar to estimating just the random error component. This eliminates the within-sample component of variation in the control limits.

Moving range chart: charts the **subgroup means** using a moving range to remove the within-sample variation. Use this chart, along with the Individuals chart, to track both process location and process variation, using the between-sample component of variation.

R chart or S chart: charts process variation using the within-sample component of variation.

Whether MINITAB displays an R chart or an S chart depends on the chosen estimation method and the size of the subgroup. If you base estimates on the average of subgroup ranges, then an R chart will be displayed. If you base estimates on the average of subgroup standard deviations, then an S chart will be displayed. If you base estimates on the pooled standard deviation and your subgroup size is less than ten, an R chart will be displayed. If you base estimates on the pooled standard deviation and your subgroup size is ten or greater, an S chart will be displayed.

Thus, the combination of the three charts provides a method of assessing the stability of process location, the between-sample component of variation, and the within-sample component of variation.

Data

Subgroup data can be structured in a single column, or in rows across several columns. When you have subgroups of unequal size, structure the subgroups in a single column, then set up a second column of subgroup indicators. See *Data* on page 12-3 for examples.

▶ **To make an I-MR-R/S (Between/Within) Chart**

1 Choose Stat ➤ Control Charts ➤ I-MR-R/S (Between/Within).

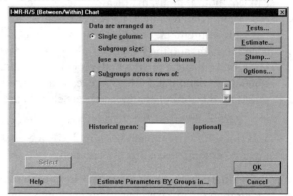

2 Do one of the following:

- When subgroups are in one column, enter the data columns in **Single column**. In **Subgroup size**, enter a subgroup size or column of subgroup indicators.

- When subgroups are in rows, enter a series of columns in **Subgroups across rows of**.

3 If you like use any of the dialog box options, then click **OK**.

Options

I-MR-R/S (Between/Within) Chart dialog box

- enter a historical value for μ (the mean of the population distribution) if you have a goal for μ, or know parameters from prior data—see *Use historical values of μ and σ* on page 12-64. If you do not specify a value for μ, it is estimated from the data.

Tests subdialog box

- do eight tests for special causes—see *Do tests for special causes* on page 12-64. To adjust the sensitivity of the test, see *Defining Tests for Special Causes* on page 12-5.

Estimate subdialog box

- omit certain subgroups when estimating μ and σ—see *Omit subgroups from the estimate of μ or σ* on page 12-66

- estimate σ various ways—see *Control how σ is estimated* on page 12-67
  - for I and MR chart only: base the estimate on the median of the moving range length the square root of the mean of squared successive differences, or change the length of the moving range. The default method uses $\overline{MR}/2$, the average of the moving range divided by an unbiasing constant. By default, the moving range is of length 2, since consecutive values have the greatest chance of being alike.

– for R chart or S chart only: base the estimate of σ on the average of subgroup standard deviations (displays S chart) or on a pooled standard deviation. With estimates based on pooled standard deviation, an R chart is displayed if subgroup size is less than ten, while an S chart is displayed if subgroup size is ten or greater. By default, the estimate is based on the average of the subgroup ranges (displays R chart).

Stamp subdialog box

■ place an additional row of tick labels, such as dates or shifts, below the subgroup numbers on the x-axis—see *Add additional rows of tick labels* on page 12-72.

Options subdialog box

■ use the Box-Cox transformation when you have very skewed data—see *Use the Box-Cox power transformation for non-normal data* on page 12-68.

■ choose the positions at which to draw the upper and lower control (sigma) limits in relation to the center line—see *Customize the control (sigma) limits* on page 12-70. The default line is three above and below the center line. You can draw more than one set of lines. For example, you can draw specification limits along with control limits on the chart.

■ replace the default graph title with your own title.

Estimate parameters BY groups in subdialog box

■ estimate control limits and center line independently for different groups (draws a "historical chart")—see *Estimate control limits and center line independently for different groups* on page 12-61.

➤ Example of I-MR-R/S chart

Suppose you are interested in determining whether or not a process that coats rolls of paper with a thin film is in control [27]. You are concerned that the paper is being coated with the correct thickness of film and that the coating is evenly distributed across the length of the roll. You take 3 samples from 15 consecutive rolls and measure coating weight.

Because you are interested in whether or not the coating is even throughout a roll and whether each roll is correctly coated, you use MINITAB to create an I-MR-R/S chart.

1 Open the worksheet COATING.MTW.

2 Choose **Stat ➤ Control Charts ➤ I-MR-R/S (Between/Within)**.

3 In **Single column**, enter *Coating*. In **Subgroup size**, enter *Roll*. Click **OK**.

Session
window
output

I-MR-R/S (Between/Within) Chart: Coating

```
Between standard deviation =    0.0000
 Within standard deviation =   13.5854
  Total standard deviation =   13.5854
```

BWChart for Coating

```
Test Results for I Chart of Subgroup Means
TEST 1. One point more than 3.00 sigmas from center line.
Test Failed at points: 7 8 9 14 15

Test Results for MR Chart of Subgroup Means
Test Results for R Chart
```

Graph
window
output

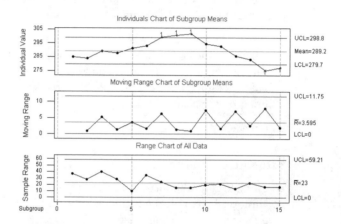

Interpreting the results

The individuals chart shows five points outside the control limits, suggesting that this process is out of control.

Control Charts for Individual Observations

Control charts for individual observations are typically used in situations where the data cannot easily be subgrouped. They are typically used when measurements are expensive (destructive testing), for continuous output that is homogenous, and for productions that have long cycle time. MINITAB offers these control charts for individual observations:

- **Individuals chart**—a chart of the individual observations. See *Individuals Chart* on page 12-29.

- **Moving Range chart**—a chart of the moving ranges. See *Moving Range Chart* on page 12-32.

- **I-MR chart**—an Individuals and Moving Range chart on one screen. See *I-MR Chart* on page 12-34.

Other charts that work with individual observations are $\bar{X}$, EWMA, Moving Average, CUSUM, and Zone chart.

You must have all of the process data in a single column when using these commands.

Missing data

If an observation is missing, there is a gap in the Individuals chart where that observation would have been plotted. When calculating moving ranges, each value is the range of K consecutive observations, where K is the length of the moving ranges. If any of the observations for a particular moving range are missing, it is not calculated. Hence, there is a gap in the Moving Range chart corresponding to each of the moving ranges that includes the missing observation.

Individuals Chart

An individuals chart is a control chart of individual observations. You can use individuals charts to track the process level and detect the presence of special causes when your sample size is 1.

By default, Individuals chart estimates the process variation, σ, with $\overline{MR}$ / d2, the average of the moving range divided by an unbiasing constant. Moving ranges are artificial subgroups created from the individual measurements. By default, the moving range is of length 2, since consecutive values have the greatest chance of being alike. You can also estimate σ using the median of the moving range, change the length of the moving range, or enter historical values of σ.

For more information, see *Variables Control Charts Overview* on page 12-2 and *Control Charts for Individual Observations* on page 12-28.

Data

Structure individual observations in one column.

▶ **To make an individuals chart**

1 Choose Stat ➤ Control Charts ➤ Individuals.

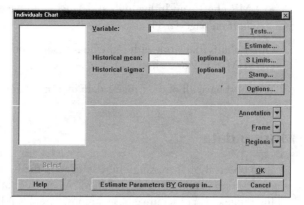

2 In **Variable**, enter a data column.

3 If you like, use any of the options listed below, then click **OK**.

Options

Individuals Chart dialog box

- enter historical values for μ (the mean of the population distribution) and σ (the standard deviation of the population distribution) if you have a goal for μ or σ, or known parameters from prior data—see page 12-64. If you do not specify a value for μ or σ, they are estimated from the data.

- customize the chart annotation, frame, and region (placement of the chart within the Graph window)—see page 12-74.

Tests subdialog box

- do eight tests for special causes—see page 12-64. To adjust the sensitivity of the tests, see *Defining Tests for Special Causes* on page 12-5.

Estimate subdialog box

- omit certain subgroups when estimating μ and σ—see page 12-66.

- base the estimate of σ on the median of the moving range—see page 12-67. The default estimate of σ is based on the average of the moving range of length 2. You can also change the length of the moving range.

S Limits subdialog box

■ choose the positions at which to draw the upper and lower control (sigma) limits in relation to the center line—see page 12-70. The default line is 3σ above and below the center line. You can draw more than one set of lines. For example, you can draw specification limits along with control limits on the chart.

■ place bounds on the upper and lower control limits—see page 12-70.

■ choose the line type, color, and size for the control limits—see page 12-70. The default line is solid red.

Stamp subdialog box

■ add another row of tick labels below the default tick labels—see page 12-72. For example, you can place "time stamp" labels (or other descriptive labels) on your graph.

■ choose the text font, color, and size for the axis and tick labels. The default labels are black Arial.

Options subdialog box

■ use the Box-Cox transformation when you have very skewed data—see page 12-68.

■ choose the connection line type, color, and size. The default line is solid black.

■ choose the symbol type, color, and size. The default symbol is a black cross.

Estimate Parameters BY Groups subdialog box

■ estimate control limits and center line independently for different groups (draws a "historical chart")—see page 12-61.

☞ Example of an individuals chart

In the following example, Weight contains the weight in pounds of each batch of raw material.

1 Open the worksheet EXH_QC.MTW.

2 Choose **Stat ➤ Control Charts ➤ Individuals**.

3 In **Variable**, enter *Weight*.

4 Click **Tests**. Check the first four tests. Click **OK** in each dialog box.

Session window output

```
TEST 1. One point more than 3.00 sigmas from center line.
Test Failed at points: 14 23 30 31 44 45

TEST 2. 9 points in a row on same side of center line.
Test Failed at points: 9 10 11 12 13 14 15 16 17 18 19 20 21 33 34 35 36
```

*Graph
window
output*

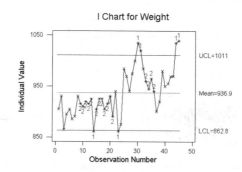

Interpreting the results

This chart shows 6 points outside the control limits and 17 points inside the control limits that failed one of the tests, which suggests the presence of special causes.

Moving Range Chart

A moving range chart is a chart of "moving ranges" — ranges calculated from artificial subgroups created from successive observations. You can use moving range charts to track the process variation and detect the presence of special causes when your sample size is 1.

By default, Moving Range chart estimates the process variation, σ, with $\overline{MR} / d2$, the average of the moving range divided by an unbiasing constant. The moving range is of length 2, since consecutive values have the greatest chance of being alike. You can also estimate σ using the median of the moving range, change the length of the moving range, or enter an historical value for σ.

For more information, see *Variables Control Charts Overview* on page 12-2 and *Control Charts for Individual Observations* on page 12-28.

Data

Structure individual observations in one column.

▶ **To make a moving range chart**

1 Choose Stat ➤ Control Charts ➤ Moving Range.

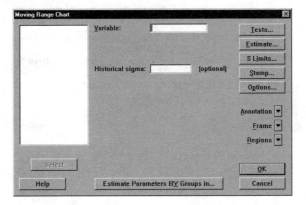

2 In **Variable**, enter a data column.

3 If you like, use any of the options listed below, then click **OK**.

Options

Moving Range Chart dialog box

■ enter an historical value for σ (the standard deviation of the population distribution) if you have a goal for σ, or a known σ from prior data—see page 12-64. If you do not specify a value for σ, it is estimated from the data.

■ customize the chart annotation, frame, and region (placement of the chart within the Graph window)—see page 12-74.

Tests subdialog box

■ do four tests for special causes—see page 12-64. To adjust the sensitivity of the tests, see *Defining Tests for Special Causes* on page 12-5.

Estimate subdialog box

■ omit certain subgroups when estimating μ and σ—see page 12-66.

■ base the estimate of σ on the median of the moving range, or change the length of the moving range—see page 12-67. The default estimate of σ is based on the average of the moving range of length 2.

S Limits subdialog box

- choose the positions at which to draw the upper and lower control (sigma) limits in relation to the center line—see page 12-70. The default line is 3σ above and below the center line. You can draw more than one set of lines. For example, you can draw specification limits along with control limits on the chart.

- place bounds on the upper and lower control limits—see page 12-70.

- choose the line type, color, and size for the control limits—see page 12-70. The default line is solid red.

Stamp subdialog box

- add another row of tick labels below the default tick labels—see page 12-72. For example, you can place "time stamp" labels (or other descriptive labels) on your graph.

- choose the text font, color, and size for the axis and tick labels—see page 12-72. The default labels are black Arial.

Options subdialog box

- use the Box-Cox transformation when you have very skewed data—see page 12-68.

- choose the connection line type, color, and size. The default line is solid black.

- choose the symbol type, color, and size. The default symbol is a black cross.

Estimate Parameters BY Groups subdialog box

- estimate control limits and center line independently for different groups (draws a "historical chart")—see page 12-61.

I-MR Chart

An I-MR chart is an Individuals chart and Moving Range chart in the same graph window. The Individuals chart is drawn in the upper half of the screen; the Moving Range chart in the lower half. Seeing both charts together allows you to track both the process level and process variation at the same time, as well as detect the presence of special causes. See [25] for a discussion of how to interpret joint patterns in the two charts.

By default, I-MR Chart estimates the process variation, σ, with $\overline{MR}$ / d2, the average of the moving range divided by an unbiasing constant. The moving range is of length 2, since consecutive values have the greatest chance of being alike. You can also estimate σ using the median of the moving range, change the length of the moving range, or enter an historical value for σ.

For more information, see *Variables Control Charts Overview* on page 12-2 and *Control Charts for Individual Observations* on page 12-28.

Data

Structure individual observations in one column.

▶ **To make an I-MR chart**

1 Choose Stat ➤ Control Charts ➤ I-MR.

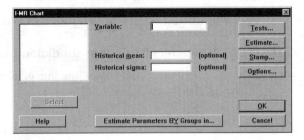

2 In **Variable**, enter a data column.

3 If you like, use any of the options listed below, then click **OK**.

Options

I/MR Chart dialog box

■ enter historical values for μ (the mean of the population distribution) and σ (the standard deviation of the population distribution) if you have a goal for μ or σ, or known parameters from prior data—see page 12-64. If you do not specify a value for μ or σ, they are estimated from the data.

Tests subdialog box

■ do eight tests for special causes—see page 12-64. To adjust the sensitivity of the tests, see *Defining Tests for Special Causes* on page 12-5.

Estimate subdialog box

■ omit certain subgroups when estimating μ and σ—see page 12-66.

■ base the estimate of σ on the median of the moving range, or change the length of the moving range—see page 12-67. The default estimate of σ is based on the average of the moving range of length 2.

Stamp subdialog box

■ place an additional row of tick labels, such as dates or shifts, below the subgroup numbers on the x-axis—see page 12-72.

Options subdialog box

- use the Box-Cox transformation when you have very skewed data—see page 12-68.

- choose the positions at which to draw the upper and lower control (sigma) limits in relation to the center line—see page 12-70. The default line is 3σ above and below the center line. You can draw more than one set of lines. For example, you can draw specification limits along with control limits on the chart.

- replace the default graph title with your own title.

Estimate Parameters BY Groups subdialog box

- estimate control limits and center line independently for different groups (draws a "historical chart")—see page 12-61.

Control Charts Using Subgroup Combinations

MINITAB offers these control charts that use subgroup combinations:

- **EWMA chart**—a chart of exponentially weighted moving averages. See page 12-37.

- **Moving Average chart**—a chart of unweighted moving averages. See page 12-41.

- **CUSUM chart**—a chart of cumulative sum of the deviations from a nominal specification. See page 12-44.

- **Zone chart**—a chart that assigns a weight to each point depending on its distance from the center line, and plots the cumulative scores. See page 12-48.

EWMA, Moving Average, CUSUM, and Zone Chart produce control charts for either data in subgroups or individual observations. They are typically used to evaluate the process level. However, both EWMA and CUSUM Chart may also be used to plot control charts for subgroup ranges or standard deviations to evaluate process variation. See [8] and [21] for a discussion.

EWMA, Moving Average, and Zone Chart work with equal or unequal-size subgroups, but CUSUM Chart requires all subgroups to be the same size. Zone Chart generates a standardized zone chart when subgroup sizes are unequal.

Missing data

If a single observation is missing and you have data in subgroups, it is omitted from the calculations of the summary statistics for the subgroup it was in. All formulas are adjusted accordingly. This may cause the EWMA and Moving Average Chart to produce control chart limits that are not straight lines.

Suppose an entire subgroup is missing:

- EWMA Chart plots an exponentially weighted moving average of all past subgroup means. Hence, once it finds a missing subgroup, it cannot calculate any more values. The chart will be blank starting with the missing subgroup.

- Moving Average Chart plots a moving average of K subgroup averages. If a subgroup is missing, there will be a gap in the chart corresponding to all of the moving averages that would have used that subgroup mean.

- CUSUM Chart plots a cumulative sum of deviations. Like EWMA Chart, when CUSUM Chart encounters a missing subgroup, the chart will be blank beginning with the missing subgroup.

- Zone Chart leaves a gap in the chart corresponding to the missing subgroup.

EWMA Chart

An EWMA chart is a chart of exponentially weighted moving averages. Each EWMA point incorporates information from all of the previous subgroups or observations. An EWMA chart can be custom tailored to detect any size shift in the process. Because of this, they are often used to monitor in-control processes for detecting small shifts away from the target.

The plot points can be based on either subgroup means or individual observations. When you have data in subgroups, the mean of all the observations in each subgroup is calculated. Exponentially weighted moving averages are then formed from these means. By default, the process standard deviation, σ, is estimated using a pooled standard deviation. You can also base the estimate on the average of subgroup ranges or subgroup standard deviations, or enter an historical value for σ.

When you have individual observations, exponentially weighted moving averages are formed from the individual observations. By default, σ is estimated with $\overline{MR}$ / d2, the average of the moving range divided by an unbiasing constant. Moving ranges are artificial subgroups created from the individual measurements. The moving range is of length 2, since consecutive values have the greatest chance of being alike. You can also estimate σ using the median of the moving range, change the length of the moving range, or enter an historical value for σ.

For more information, see *Variables Control Charts Overview* on page 12-2 and *Control Charts Using Subgroup Combinations* on page 12-36.

Data

You can use this command with subgroup data or individual observations. Subgroup data can be structured in a single column, or in rows across several columns. When you have subgroups of unequal size, structure the subgroups in a single column, then set up a second column of subgroup identifiers. See *Data* on page 12-3 for examples.

Individual observations should be structured in a single column.

▶ To make an EWMA chart

1 Choose **Stat ➤ Control Charts ➤ EWMA**.

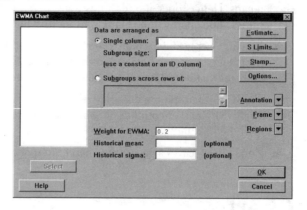

2 Do one of the following:

- When subgroups or individual observations are in one column, enter the data column in **Single column**. In **Subgroup size**, enter a subgroup size or column of subgroup indicators. For individual observations, enter a subgroup size of 1.

- When subgroups are in rows, enter a series of columns in **Subgroups across rows of**.

3 If you like, use any of the options listed below, then click **OK**.

Options

EWMA Chart dialog box

- specify the weight used in the exponentially weighted moving average—see page 12-39. Choose a value between 0 and 1. The default weight is 0.2.

- enter historical values for μ (the mean of the population distribution) and σ (the standard deviation of the population distribution) if you have goals for μ or σ, or known parameters from prior data—see page 12-64. If you do not specify a value for μ or σ, they are estimated from the data.

- customize the chart annotation, frame, and region (placement of the chart within the Graph window)—see page 12-74.

Estimate subdialog box

■ omit certain subgroups when estimating μ and σ—see page 12-66.

■ estimate σ various ways—see page 12-67.
  – with subgroup size > 1: estimate σ using the average of the subgroup ranges or standard deviations. The default estimate uses a pooled standard deviation.
  – with subgroup size = 1: estimate σ using the median of the moving range, or change the length of the moving range. The default estimate of σ is based on the average of the moving range of length 2.

■ force the control limits and center line to be constant when subgroups are of unequal size—see page 12-68.

S Limits subdialog box

■ choose the positions at which to draw the upper and lower control (sigma) limits in relation to the center line—see page 12-70. The default line is 3σ above and below the center line. You can draw more than one set of lines. For example, you can draw specification limits along with control limits on the chart.

■ place bounds on the upper and lower control limits—see page 12-70.

■ choose the line type, color, and size for the control limits—see page 12-70. The default line is solid red.

Stamp subdialog box

■ add another row of tick labels below the default tick labels—see page 12-72. For example, you can place "time stamp" labels (or other descriptive labels) on your graph.

■ choose the text font, color, and size for the axis and tick labels—see page 12-72. The default labels are black Arial.

Options subdialog box

■ use the Box-Cox transformation when you have very skewed data—see page 12-68.

■ choose the connection line type, color, and size. The default line is solid black.

■ choose the symbol type, color, and size. The default symbol is a black cross.

Calculating the EWMA

The table below contains eight subgroup means. It shows how the EWMA is calculated from these subgroup means, using a weight of 0.2.

subgroup	1	2	3	4	5	6	7	8
mean	14.000	9.000	7.000	9.000	13.000	4.000	9.000	11.000
EWMA	10.400	10.120	9.494	9.397	10.117	8.894	8.915	9.332

To get started, the EWMA for subgroup 0 is set to the mean of all data, 9.5. The EWMA for subgroup 1 is .2(14) + .8(9.5) = 10.4. The EWMA for subgroup 2 is .2(9) + .8(10.4) = 10.12. In general, the EWMA, z_i for subgroup i is

$$z_i = w\bar{x}_i + (1-w)z_{i-1} \quad \text{or}$$

$$z_i = w\bar{x}_i + w(1-w)\bar{x}_{i-1} + w(1-w)^2\bar{x}_{i-2} + \dots + w(1-w)^{i-1}\bar{x}_1 + (1-w)^i\bar{x}$$

where w is the weight, $\bar{x}_i$ is the mean of subgroup i, $\bar{x}$ is the mean of all data.

If you have individual observations, these are used in place of the subgroup means in the calculations.

The default weight used is 0.2. If you like, you can change the weight to a value between 0 and 1. By changing the weight used and the number of σ's for the control limits, you can construct a chart with very specific properties. Combinations of these two parameters are often chosen by using an ARL (Average Run Length) table. See [16] for a fairly extensive table.

▶ **To change the weight used in the EWMA**

1   In the EWMA chart main dialog box, enter a value between 0 and 1 in **Weight for EWMA**. The default weight is 0.2.

▷ **Example of an EWMA chart**

In the following example, Weight contains the weight in pounds of each batch of raw material.

1   Open the worksheet EXH_QC.MTW.

2   Choose **Stat ▸ Control Charts ▸ EWMA**.

3   In **Single column**, enter *Weight*. In **Subgroup size**, enter 5. Click **OK**.

*Graph
window
output*

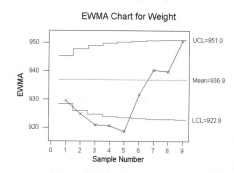

Interpreting the results

The EWMAs for sample numbers 2, 3, 4, and 5 fall slightly outside the control limits, suggesting small shifts away from the target.

Moving Average Chart

A Moving Average chart is a chart of "moving averages"—averages calculated from artificial subgroups created from consecutive observations. The observations in this case, however, can be either individual measurements or subgroup means. This chart is generally not preferred over an EWMA chart (page 12-37) because it does not weight the observations as the EWMA does.

When you have data in subgroups, the mean of all the observations in each subgroup is calculated. Moving averages are then formed from these means. By default, the process standard deviation, σ, is estimated using a pooled standard deviation. You can also base the estimate on the average of subgroup ranges or subgroup standard deviations, or enter an historical value for σ.

When you have individual observations, moving averages are formed from the individual observations. By default, σ is estimated with $\overline{MR}$ / d2, the average of the moving range divided by an unbiasing constant. Moving ranges are artificial subgroups created from consecutive measurements. The moving range is of length 2, since consecutive values have the greatest chance of being alike. You can also estimate σ using the median of the moving range, change the length of the moving range, or enter an historical value for σ.

For more information, see *Variables Control Charts Overview* on page 12-2 and *Control Charts Using Subgroup Combinations* on page 12-36.

Data

You can use this command with subgroup data or individual observations. Subgroup data can be structured in a single column, or in rows across several columns. When you have subgroups of unequal size, structure the subgroups in a single column, then set up a second column of subgroup identifiers. See *Data* on page 12-3 for examples.

Individual observations should be structured in a single column.

▶ **To make a moving average chart**

1 Choose **Stat ➤ Control Charts ➤ Moving Average**.

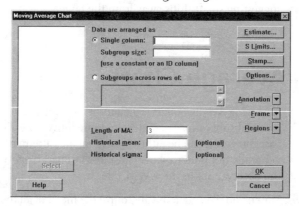

2 Do one of the following:

- When subgroups or individual observations are in one column, enter the data column in **Single column**. In **Subgroup size**, enter a subgroup size or column of subgroup indicators. For individual observations, enter a subgroup size of 1.

- When subgroups are in rows, enter a series of columns in **Subgroups across rows of**.

3 If you like, use any of the options listed below, then click **OK**.

Options

Moving Average Chart dialog box

- specify the length of the moving averages—see page 12-43. The default length is 3.

- enter historical values for μ (the mean of the population distribution) and σ (the standard deviation of the population distribution) if you have goals for μ or σ, or known parameters from prior data—see page 12-64. If you do not specify a value for μ or σ, they are estimated from the data.

- customize the chart annotation, frame, and region (placement of the chart within the Graph window)—see page 12-74.

Estimate subdialog box

- omit certain subgroups when estimating μ and σ—see page 12-66.

- estimate σ various ways—see page 12-67.
  - with subgroup size > 1: estimate σ using the average of the subgroup ranges or standard deviations. The default estimate of σ uses a pooled standard deviation.

– with subgroup size = 1: estimate σ using the median of the moving range, or change the length of the moving range. The default estimate of σ is based on the average of the moving range of length 2.

■ force the control limits and center line to be constant when subgroups are of unequal size—see page 12-68.

S Limits subdialog box

■ choose the positions at which to draw the upper and lower control (sigma) limits in relation to the center line—see page 12-70. The default line is 3σ above and below the center line. You can draw more than one set of lines. For example, you can draw specification limits along with control limits on the chart.

■ place bounds on the upper and lower control limits—see page 12-70.

■ choose the line type, color, and size for the control limits—see page 12-70. The default line is solid red.

Stamp subdialog box

■ add another row of tick labels below the default tick labels—see page 12-72. For example, you can place "time stamp" labels (or other descriptive labels) on your graph.

■ choose the text font, color, and size for the axis and tick labels—see page 12-72. The default labels are black Arial.

Options subdialog box

■ use the Box-Cox transformation when you have very skewed data—see page 12-68.

■ choose the connection line type, color, and size. The default line is solid black.

■ choose the symbol type, color, and size. The default symbol is a black cross.

Calculating the moving average

The table below contains 8 subgroup means. It shows how the moving averages of length 3 are calculated from these subgroup means.

subgroup	1	2	3	4	5	6	7	8
mean	14.000	9.000	7.000	9.000	13.000	4.000	9.000	11.000
MA	14.000	11.500	10.000	8.333	9.667	8.667	8.667	8.000

The MA for the first subgroup is 14.0, the first subgroup mean. The MA for the second subgroup is the average of the first two means, $(14 + 9) / 2 = 11.5$. These two are special because we do not have three subgroup means to average yet. Because of this, the UCL and LCL will be farther out than for the rest of the subgroups. The remaining values of the MA follow a general pattern. The MA for subgroup 3 is the average of the first 3 means, that is $(14 + 9 + 7) / 3 = 10.0$. The MA for subgroup 4 is the average of the means from subgroups 2 through 4, $(9 + 7 + 9) / 3 = 8.333$. In general, the MA for subgroup i is the average of the means from subgroups $i - 2$, $i - 1$, and i.

If you have individual observations, these are used in place of the subgroup means in all calculations.

You can specify the length of the moving average used, that is, the number of subgroup means to include in each average.

▶ **To change the length of the moving average**

In the Moving Average Chart main dialog box, enter the number of subgroup means to be included in each average in **Length of MA**. The default is 3. If you have individual observations (that is you specified a subgroup size of 1), these are used in place of the subgroup means in all calculations.

CUSUM Chart

A cumulative sum (CUSUM) chart plots the cumulative sums of the deviations of each sample value from the target value. You can plot a chart based on subgroup means or individual observations. With in-control processes, both the CUSUM chart and EWMA chart (page 12-37) are good at detecting small shifts away from the target.

You can plot two types of CUSUM chart. The default chart plots two one-sided CUSUMs. The upper CUSUM detects upward shifts in the level of the process, the lower CUSUM detects downward shifts. This chart uses control limits (UCL and LCL) to determine when an out-of-control situation has occurred. See [22] and [23] for a discussion of one-sided CUSUMs.

You can also plot one two-sided CUSUM. This chart uses a V-mask, rather than the usual 3σ control limits, to determine when an out-of-control situation has occurred. See [14] and [24] for a discussion of the V-mask chart.

When you have data in subgroups, the mean of all the observations in each subgroup is calculated. CUSUM statistics are then formed from these means. All subgroups must be the same size. By default, the process standard deviation, σ, is estimated using a pooled standard deviation. You can also base the estimate on the average of subgroup ranges or subgroup standard deviations, or enter an historical value for σ.

When you have individual observations, CUSUM statistics are formed from the individual observations. By default, σ is estimated with $\overline{MR} / d2$, the average of the moving range divided by an unbiasing constant. Moving ranges are artificial subgroups created from the individual measurements. The moving range is of length 2, since consecutive values have the greatest chance of being alike. You can also estimate σ using the median of the moving range, change the length of the moving range, or enter an historical value for σ.

For more information, see *Variables Control Charts Overview* on page 12-2 and *Control Charts Using Subgroup Combinations* on page 12-36.

Data

Subgroup data can be structured in a single column or in rows across several columns. Subgroups must be of equal size. See *Data* on page 12-3 for examples.

Individual observations should be structured in a single column.

▶ **To plot two one-sided CUSUMs**

1 Choose **Stat ➤ Control Charts ➤ CUSUM**.

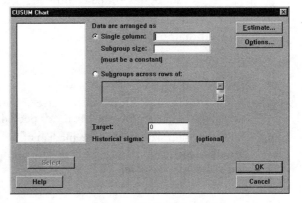

2 Do one of the following:

■ When subgroups or individual observations are in one column, enter the data column in **Single column**. In **Subgroup size**, enter a subgroup size. For individual observations, enter a subgroup size of 1.

■ When subgroups are in rows, enter a series of columns in **Subgroups across rows of**.

3 If you like, use any of the options listed below, then click **OK**.

▶ **To plot one two-sided (V-mask) CUSUM**

1 Choose **Stat ➤ Control Charts ➤ CUSUM**.

2 Do one of the following:

■ When subgroups or individual observations are in one column, enter the data column in **Single column**. In **Subgroup size**, enter a subgroup size. For individual observations, enter a subgroup size of 1.

■ When subgroups are in rows, enter a series of columns in **Subgroups across rows of**.

3 Click **Options**. Under **Type of CUSUM**, choose **Two-sided**.

4 In **Center on subgroup**, enter the subgroup number to center the V-mask on. Click **OK**.

5 If you like, use any of the options listed below, then click **OK**.

Options

CUSUM Chart dialog box

- specify a value other than 0 for the target. CUSUM statistics are cumulative deviations from this target, or nominal, specification.

- enter an historical value for σ (the standard deviation of the population distribution) if you have a goal for σ, or a known σ from prior data—see page 12-64. If you do not specify a value for σ, it is estimated from the data.

Estimate subdialog box

- omit certain subgroups when estimating μ and σ—see page 12-66.

- estimate σ various ways—see page 12-67.
  - with subgroup size > 1: use the average of the subgroup ranges or standard deviations. The default estimate uses a pooled standard deviation.
  - with subgroup size = 1: use the median of the moving range, or change the length of the moving range. The default estimate of σ is based on the average of the moving range of length 2.

Options subdialog box

- specify a "CUSUM plan," which is defined by the parameters h and k—see page 12-47.

- choose to conduct a one-sided or two-sided (V-mask) CUSUM.

For a one-sided CUSUM

- use the FIR (Fast Initial Response) method to initialize the one-sided CUSUMs. then specify the number of standard deviations above and below the center line. Normally, they are initialized at 0, but if the process is out f control at startup, the CUSUMs will not detect the situation for several subgroups. This has been shown by [15] to reduce the number of subgroups needed to detect problems at startup.

- reset the CUSUMs to their initial values whenever an out-of-control signal is generated (one-sided CUSUMS only). When a process goes out of control, an attempt should be made to find and eliminate the cause of the problem. If the problem has been corrected, the CUSUMs should be reset to their initial values.

For a two-sided (V-mask) CUSUM

- specify the subgroup number on which to center the V-mask.

For both one-sided and two-sided CUSUMs

- replace the default title with your own title.

Method

With in-control processes, CUSUM charts are good at detecting small shifts away from the target, because they incorporate information from the sequence of sample values. The plot points are the cumulative sums of the deviations of the sample values from the target. These points should fluctuate randomly around zero. If a trend develops upwards or downwards, it should be considered as evidence that the process mean has shifted, and you should look for special causes.

MINITAB generates two kinds of CUSUMs:

- **two one-sided CUSUMs** (the default). The upper CUSUM detects upward shifts in the level of the process and the lower CUSUM detects downward shifts. This chart uses control limits (UCL and LCL) to determine when an out-of-control situation has occurred. See [22] and [23] for a discussion of one-sided CUSUMs.

- **one two-sided CUSUM**. This chart uses a V-mask, rather than control limits, to determine when an out-of-control situation has occurred. See [14] and [24] for a discussion of the V-mask chart.

For the formulas used, see Help.

The CUSUM plan

CUSUM charts are defined by 2 parameters, h and k, which are often referred to as the "CUSUM plan." These values are often selected from ARL (Average Run Length) tables. See [14] and [15].

For this chart...	h is...	k is...
One-sided CUSUM	The number of standard deviations between the center line and the control limits; that is, the value at which an out of control signal occurs.	The allowable "slack" in the process. In the CUSUM point formula, k specifies the size of the shift you want to detect.
Two-sided CUSUM (V-mask)	Part of the equation used to calculate the half-width of the V-mask (H). The half-width of the V-mask (H) is calculated at the point of origination by $H = h * \sigma$.	The slope of the V-mask arms.

▶ To specify a different CUSUM plan (h and k)

1 In the CUSUM chart main dialog box, click **Options**.

2 Do one or both of the following, then click **OK**:

   - In **h**, enter a value greater than zero. The default value is 4.

   - In **k**, enter a value greater than zero. The default value is 0.5.

▷ Example of a two one-sided CUSUM charts

Suppose you work at a car assembly plant in a department that assembles engines. In an operating engine, parts of the crankshaft move up and down a certain distance from an ideal baseline position. AtoBDist is the distance (in mm) from the actual (A) position of a point on the crankshaft to the baseline (B) position.

To ensure production quality, you took five measurements each working day, from September 28 through October 15, and then ten per day from the 18th through the 25th. You already drew an $\bar{X}$ chart (page 12-13) and an R chart (page 12-16) of this data. On the $\bar{X}$ chart, subgroup 5 failed a test for special causes. Now, to look for small shifts away from the target, you want to plot the CUSUMS.

1 Open the worksheet CRANKSH.MTW.

2 Choose **Stat ➤ Control Charts ➤ CUSUM**.

3 In **Single column**, enter *AtoBDist*. In **Subgroup size**, enter 5. Click **OK**.

*Graph
window
output*

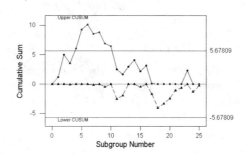

Interpreting the results

The CUSUMS for subgroups 4 through 10 fall outside the upper sigma limit, suggesting small shifts away from the target.

Zone Chart

A zone chart is a hybrid between an X (or Individuals) chart and a CUSUM chart. It plots a cumulative score, based on "zones" at 1, 2, and 3 sigmas from the center line. Zone charts are usually preferred over X or Individuals charts because of their utter simplicity: a point is out of control simply, by default, if its score is greater than or equal to 8. Thus, you do not need to recognize the patterns associated with non-random behavior as on a Shewhart chart. This method is equivalent to four of the standard tests for special causes in an X or Individuals chart. You can also modify the zone chart weighting scheme to provide the sensitivity needed for a specific process.

A zone chart is illustrated and further defined on page 12-51.

You can plot a chart based on subgroup means or individual observations. With data in subgroups, the mean of the observations in each subgroup is calculated, then plotted on the chart. When subgroup sizes are unequal, MINITAB generates a standardized zone chart. By default, the process standard deviation, σ, is estimated using a pooled standard deviation. You can also base the estimate on the average of subgroup ranges or subgroup standard deviations, or enter a historical value for σ.

With individual observations, a point is plotted for each observation. By default, σ is estimated σ, with $\overline{MR}$ / d2, the average of the moving range divided by an unbiasing constant. Moving ranges are artificial subgroups created from the individual measurements. The moving range is of length 2, since consecutive values have the greatest chance of being alike. You can also estimate σ using the median of the moving range, change the length of the moving range, or enter an historical value for σ.

For more information, see *Variables Control Charts Overview* on page 12-2 and *Control Charts Using Subgroup Combinations* on page 12-36.

Data

You can use this command with subgroup data or individual observations. Subgroup data can be structured in a single column, or in rows across several columns. When you have subgroups of unequal size, structure the subgroups in a single column, then set up a second column of subgroup identifiers. See *Data* on page 12-3 for examples.

Individual observations should be structured in a single column.

▶ To make a zone chart

1 Choose **Stat ➤ Control Charts ➤ Zone**.

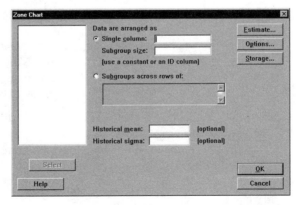

2   Do one of the following:

- When subgroups or individual observations are in one column, enter the data column in **Single column**. In **Subgroup size**, enter a subgroup size or column of subgroup indicators. For individual observations, enter a subgroup size of 1.

- When subgroups are in rows, enter a series of columns in **Subgroups across rows of**.

3   If you like, use any of the options listed below, then click **OK**.

Options

Zone Chart dialog box

- enter historical values for μ (the mean of the population distribution) and σ (the standard deviation of the population distribution) if you have goals for μ or σ, or known parameters from prior data—see page 12-64. If you do not specify values for μ or σ, they are estimated from the data.

Estimate subdialog box

- omit certain subgroups when estimating μ and σ—see page 12-66.

- estimate σ various ways—see page 12-67.
  - with subgroup size > 1: use the average of the subgroup ranges or standard deviations. The default estimate uses a pooled standard deviation.
  - with subgroup size = 1: use the median of the moving range, or change the length of the moving range. The default estimate of σ is based on the average of the moving range of length 2.

Options subdialog box

- change the weights or scores assigned to the points in each zone—see page 12-51. The weight assigned to Zone 4 is also used as the critical value for determining when a process is out of control. If you do not use this option, the default scores are 0, 2, 4, and 8. See [3] and [9] for a discussion of the various weighting schemes.

- reset the cumulative score to zero following each out of control signal—see page 12-51. When a process goes out of control, you should try to find and eliminate the cause of the problem. When the problem is corrected, the cumulative score should be reset to zero.

- display all subgroups on the zone chart, or the last n subgroups. By default, MINITAB plots the last 25 observations.

- replace the default graph title with your own title.

Storage subdialog box

- store the cumulative zone scores that appear in the circles at each point on the graph. Zone chart stores the exact cumulative score for each subgroup.

Method

The zone chart classifies observations or subgroup means according to their distance from the center line. For each observation or subgroup mean, the corresponding plot point is derived as follows.

1 Each observation is assigned a "zone score," as shown in this table:

If the observation or subgroup mean falls here...	it gets this zone score
Between the target and 1σ	0
Between 1 and 2σ	2
Between 2 and 3σ	4
Beyond 3σ	8

2 Each observation is assigned a "cumulative score," which is the value that is actually plotted:

- The first point is simply the zone score for the first observation or subgroup mean.

- For subsequent points, weights are summed sequentially. Each time a new point crosses the center line, the sum is reset to zero. If the sum totals 8 or more, the process is declared "out-of-control."

You can specify weights other than 0, 2, 4, and 8 for the zone scores in the Options subdialog box. You can also choose to reset the cumulative score after each signal.

A zone control chart is illustrated below:

Shows the weights assigned to each zone. By default, the weights are 0, 2, 4, and 8. You can change the scores assigned to each zone in the Options subdialog box.

Weights for points on the same side of the center line are added. A cumulative score ≥ the weight assigned to Zone 4 signals an out of control process. In this example using the default weights, the cumulative score of 8 indicates an out of control process.

Zones are defined by their distance are from the center line (mean).

Zone 1: within 1 standard deviation
Zone 2: between 1 and 2 standard deviations
Zone 3: between 2 and 3 standard deviations
Zone 4: 3 or more standard deviations

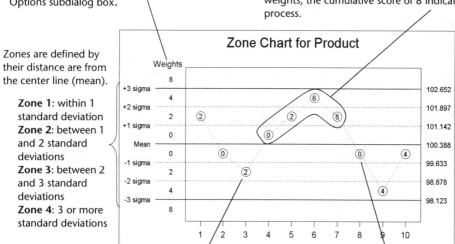

Each circle contains the cumulative score for each subgroup or observation.

The cumulative score is set to zero when the next plotted point crosses over the center line.

Comparing a zone chart with a Shewhart chart

The zone control chart procedure incorporates some statistical tests for detecting process shift used with conventional Shewhart control charts. The $\bar{X}$, S, R, and Individuals charts produce Shewhart control charts for process data. For example, using the default weights:

- a point in Zone 4 is given a score of 8. Keep in mind that a cumulative score equal to or greater than the weight assigned to Zone 4 signals an out of control situation. This is equivalent to a Shewhart chart Rule 1—a single value beyond three standard deviations from the center.

- a point in Zone 3 is given a score of 4. A second point in the same zone gives another score of 4. The cumulative sum of these two points is 8, which signals an out of control situation. This is equivalent to a Shewhart chart Rule 5—two out of three points in a row more than two standard deviations from the center line.

- a point in Zone 2 is given a score of 2. Three more points in the same zone gives a cumulative score of 8, which signals an out of control situation. This is equivalent to a Shewhart chart Rule 6—four out of five points in a row more than one standard deviation from the center line.

For further discussions of zone control chart properties, refer to [3], [9], [11], and [12].

☞ Example of a zone chart

Suppose you work in a manufacturing plant concerned about quality control. You decide to measure the length of ten sets of cylinders produced during each of five shifts for a total of 50 samples daily. Because a zone control chart is very easy to interpret, you decide to evaluate your data with it. You also decide to reset the cumulative score following each out-of-control signal.

1 Open the worksheet EXH_QC.MTW.

2 Choose **Stat ➤ Control Charts ➤ Zone**.

3 In **Single column**, enter *Length*. In **Subgroup size**, enter 5.

4 Click **Options**. Check **Reset cumulative score after each signal**. Click **OK** in each dialog box.

Graph window output

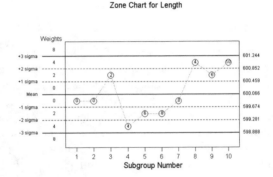

Interpreting the results

The cumulative score at subgroup 6 equals eight which indicates the process is out of control. You find that the operator reset the machine following subgroup 6, as he believed the machine was slipping. However, the zone chart detects the process is out of control again at subgroup 10. After seeing the subsequent rise in subgroups 7 to 10 on the zone chart, you decide the operator may have overcompensated for the problem identified at subgroup 6.

Control Charts for Short Runs

Standard control charting techniques rely upon a sufficiently large amount of data to reliably estimate process parameters, such as the process means (μ) and process standard deviations (σ). With short run processes, there is often not enough data in each run to produce good estimates of the process parameters. A single machine or process may be used to produce many different parts, or different products. For example, you may produce only 20 units of a part, then reset the machine to produce a different part in the next run. Even if the runs are large enough that estimates can be obtained, you would need a separate control chart for each part made by the process, since it is likely that all parts would not have the same mean and the same standard deviation.

Short run charts provide a solution to these problems by pooling and standardizing the data in various ways. MINITAB provides Z-MR Chart to produce variables control charts for short run processes. Z-MR Chart generates standardized control charts for individual observations (Z) and moving ranges (MR).

Several methods are commonly used for short runs. See [4] and [7] for details. The most general method assumes that each part or batch produced by a process has its own unique average and standard deviation. If the average and the standard deviation can be obtained, then the process data can be standardized by subtracting the mean and dividing the result by the standard deviation. The standardized data all come from a population with $\mu = 0$ and $\sigma = 1$. Now you can use a single plot for the standardized data from different parts or products. The resulting control chart has a center line at 0, and upper and lower limits at +3 and −3, respectively.

Z-MR Chart

A Z-MR chart is a chart of standardized individual observations (Z) and moving ranges (MR) from a short run process. The chart for individual observations (Z) displays above the chart for moving ranges (MR). Seeing both charts together lets you track both the process level and process variation at the same time. See [25] for a discussion of how to interpret joint patterns in the two charts.

Use Z-MR Chart with short run processes when there is not enough data in each run to produce good estimates of process parameters. Z-MR Chart standardizes the measurement data by subtracting the mean to center the data, then dividing by the standard deviation. Standardizing allows data collected from different runs to be evaluated by interpreting a single control chart.

You can estimate the mean and process variation from the data various ways, or supply historical values.

See page 12-2 for a control charts overview, or page 12-54 for information specific to control charts for short run processes.

Data

Your worksheet should consist of a pair of columns: a data column and column containing the corresponding part/product name or number. The part/product data defines the groupings for estimating process parameters. In addition, each time MINITAB encounters a change in the part/product name column, a new run is defined. You may find **Calc ➤ Make Patterned Data ➤ Simple Set of Numbers** useful for entering the part/product number.

➤ To make a Z-MR chart

1 Choose Stat ➤ Control Charts ➤ Z-MR.

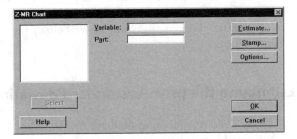

2 In **Variable**, enter a data column. In **Part**, enter a column containing the part/product name or number for each measurement.

3 If you like, use any of the options listed below, then click **OK**.

Options

Estimate subdialog box

- standardize the data with historical means, or target values, for each part/product, rather than the means estimated from the data. See *Estimating the process means* on page 12-56 for more information. When you use historical means to center the data, you can compare your process with past performance. When you use target values to center the data, you can compare your process to the desired performance.

- estimate σ various ways, or enter historical values for each part/product. See *Estimating the process standard deviations* on page 12-56 for more information.

Stamp subdialog box

- place an additional row of tick labels, such as dates or shifts, below the subgroup numbers on the x-axis—see page 12-72

Options subdialog box

- display *all* observations on the chart, or the last n observations. By default, the last 25 observations are displayed.

- replace the default graph title with your own title.

Estimating the process means

Z-MR Chart estimates the mean for each different part or product separately. Z-MR Chart pools all the data for a common part, and obtains the average of the pooled data. The result is the estimate of μ for that part. The part name data define the groupings for estimating the process means. When you use the **Relative to size (pool all data, use log (data))** option for estimating σ (see below), the means are also taken on the natural log of the data.

Estimating the process standard deviations

Z-MR Chart provides four methods for estimating σ, the process standard deviation. You should choose an estimation method based on the properties of your particular process/product. You can also choose to enter a historical value. You need to make assumptions about the process variation.

Use this table to help you choose a method:

Use this method...	When...	Which does this...
Constant (pool all data)	All the output from your process has the same variance—regardless of the size of the measurement.	Pools all the data across runs and parts to obtain a common estimate of σ.
Relative to size (pool all data, use log (data))	The variance increases in a fairly constant manner as the size of the measurement increases.	Takes the natural log of the data, pools the transformed data across all runs and all parts, and obtains a common estimate of σ for the transformed data. The natural log transformation stabilizes the variation in cases where variation increases as the size of the measurement increases.

Use this method...	When...	Which does this...
By Parts (pool all runs of same part/ batch)	All runs of a particular part or product have the same variance.	Combines all runs of the same part or product to estimate σ.
By Runs (no pooling)	You cannot assume all runs of a particular part or product have the same variance.	Estimates σ for each run independently.

By Parts is a good choice when you have very short runs and want to combine runs of the same part or product to obtain a more reliable estimate of σ. If the runs are sufficiently long, **By Runs** can provide reliable estimates of σ.

Regardless of the method used to estimate σ, Z-MR Chart uses a moving range of length 2 to estimate σ for each group of pooled data.

The methods that can be used to estimate σ, the process standard deviation, result in different standardized values that are plotted on the control charts. The assumptions you are willing to make about your process variation will determine the estimation method you choose. See the table above for guidance in choosing a method.

Suppose you are measuring the thickness, in centimeters, of fibers from a spinning process. There are 3 different fibers being made (#134, #221, #077) as seen in the Fiber # column in the table below. The table shows the estimated σ for each measurement, using the various methods:

Run #	Fiber #	Thickness	Mean	Constant	Relative to size	By Parts	By Runs
1	134	1.435	1.5015	.0716	.0463	.0696	.0988
1	134	1.572	1.5015	.0716	.0463	.0696	.0988
1	134	1.486	1.5015	.0716	.0463	.0696	.0988
2	221	1.883	1.7847	.0716	.0461	.0821	.1117
2	221	1.715	1.7847	.0716	.0461	.0821	.1117
2	221	1.799	1.7847	.0716	.0461	.0821	.1117
3	134	1.511	1.5015	.0716	.0461	.0696	.0643
3	134	1.457	1.5015	.0716	.0463	.0696	.0643
3	134	1.548	1.5015	.0716	.0463	.0696	.0643
4	221	1.768	1.7847	.0716	.0461	.0821	.0789
4	221	1.711	1.7847	.0716	.0461	.0821	.0789
4	221	1.832	1.7847	.0716	.0461	.0821	.0789
5	077	1.427	1.3883	.0716	.0459	.0634	.0634
5	077	1.344	1.3883	.0716	.0459	.0634	.0634
5	077	1.404	1.3883	.0716	.0459	.0634	.0634

Z-MR Chart estimates the mean for each different part or product separately. To calculate the mean, Z-MR Chart pools all the data for a common part, and obtains the average of the pooled data. This average is the estimate of μ for that part. The part name data are used to define the groupings for estimating the process means.

Notice the mean for each fiber is the same for all runs of that fiber. You can see in the table that the mean for run 1 and run 3 are the same, since they were both the same fiber—fiber #134. Also, the mean for run 2 and run 4 are the same, since they are both runs for fiber #221.

When the **Relative to size** option is used, the means are taken on the natural log of the data.

In this example, the data comes from a process where the variance increases as the size of the measurement increases. For example,

Fiber#	Mean	σ
221	1.7847	.0821
134	1.5015	.0696
077	1.3883	.0634

You probably want to use the **Relative to size** method for estimating σ for this process.

When you use the **Constant** option, Z-MR Chart subtracts the mean for each part from the raw data of that part. This process is required to center the data before estimating σ. The deviations from the mean are then pooled into one sample, and the average moving range of the deviations is used to estimate σ.

Standardizing the data

In all cases, the standardized values (Z) are obtained by:

$$Z = (X - \mu)/\sigma$$

where μ is the overall mean for a particular part, and σ is the estimate of the process standard deviation for each X. The estimate of σ depends on the method chosen.

When you choose the **Relative to size** option for estimating σ, X is the natural log of the data.

The following table shows how the Z values vary depending on the method chosen to estimate σ:

Run #	Fiber #	Thickness	Mean	Constant Z	Relative to size Z	By Parts Z	By Runs Z
1	134	1.435	1.5015	−0.9288	−0.9674	−0.9554	−0.6731
1	134	1.572	1.5015	0.9846	1.0022	1.0129	0.7136
1	134	1.486	1.5015	−0.2165	−0.2131	−0.2227	−0.1569
2	221	1.883	1.7847	1.3729	1.1774	1.1973	0.8800
2	221	1.715	1.7847	−0.9735	−0.8518	−0.8490	−0.6240

Run #	Fiber #	Thickness	Mean	Constant Z	Relative to size Z	By Parts Z	By Runs Z
2	221	1.799	1.7847	0.1997	0.1865	0.1742	0.1280
3	134	1.511	1.5015	0.1327	0.1473	0.1365	0.1477
3	134	1.457	1.5015	−0.6215	−0.6388	−0.6394	−0.6921
3	134	1.548	1.5015	0.6494	0.6698	0.6681	0.7232
4	221	1.768	1.7847	−0.2332	−0.1909	−0.2034	−0.2117
4	221	1.711	1.7847	−1.0293	−0.9024	−0.8977	−0.9341
4	221	1.832	1.7847	0.6606	0.5812	0.5761	0.5995
5	077	1.427	1.3883	0.5405	0.5529	0.6104	0.6104
5	077	1.344	1.3883	−0.6187	−0.7520	−0.6987	−0.6987
5	077	1.404	1.3883	0.2193	0.1991	0.2476	0.2476

▶ Example of a Z-MR chart

Suppose you work in a paper manufacturing plant and are concerned about quality control. Because your process makes paper in short runs, you need to employ standardized control charting techniques to assess quality control. You know that the variation in your process is proportional to the thickness of the paper being produced, so you plan to use the **Relative to size** option to estimate σ.

You collect data from 5 runs including 3 different grades of paper. You then use MINITAB's Z-MR chart command to produce a standardized control chart for the individual observations (Z) and the moving ranges (MR) from your short run paper-making process.

1 Open the worksheet EXH_QC.MTW.

2 Choose **Stat ➤ Control Charts ➤ Z-MR**.

3 In **Variable**, enter *Thicknes*. In **Part**, enter *Grade*.

4 Click **Estimate**. Choose **Relative to size**. Click **OK** in each dialog box.

Graph window output

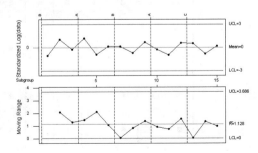

Options Shared by Quality Control Charts

This table lists the options shared by the quality control charts. A • means the option is available; a + means a scaled-down version of the option is available.

Option	Page	data in subgroups						individual observations			subgroup combinations				short runs
		Xbar	R	S	Xbar-R	Xbar-S	I-MR-R/S	Individuals	Moving Range	I-MR	EWMA	Moving Average	CUSUM	Zone	Z-MR
Use historical values of μ	12-64	•			•	•	•	•		•	•	•		•	•
Use historical values of σ	12-64	•	•	•	•	•	•	•	•	•	•	•	•	•	•
Do tests for special causes	12-64	•	•	•	•	•	•	•	•	•					
Omit subgroups from parameter estimates	12-66	•	•	•	•	•	•	•	•	•	•	•	•	•	
Control how σ is estimated	12-67														page 12-52
Use average of subgroup ranges		•	•		•		•				•	•	•	•	
Use average of subgroup standard deviations		•		•		•					•	•	•	•	
Use median of moving range		•						•	•	•	•	•	•	•	
Specify length of moving range		•					•	•	•	•	•	•	•	•	
Force control limits/center line to be constant	12-68	•	•	•	•	•					•	•			
Use Box-Cox transformation on data	12-68	•	•	•	•	•	•	•	•	•	•	•			
Estimate control limits and center line independently for different groups	12-61	•	•	•	•	•	•	•	•	•					
Customize control (sigma) limits	12-70	•	•	•	+	+	+	•	•	+	•	•			
Add additional rows of tick labels	12-72	•	•	•	+	+	+	•	•	+	•	•	+	+	+
Customize the data display, annotation, frame, and regions	12-74	•	•	•	+	+	+	•	•	+	•	•	+	+	

Estimate control limits and center line independently for different groups

Commands | Xbar, R, S, Xbar-R, Xbar-S, Individuals, I-MR, I-MR-R/S, Moving Range, all attributes control charts (P, NP, C, and U)

You can display stages in your process by drawing a "historical chart"—a control chart in which the control limits and center line are estimated independently for different groups in your data. Historical charts are particularly useful for comparing data before and after a process improvement.

Suppose you work for a company which manufactures light bulbs. As the light bulbs move along a conveyer belt, they are stamped with the company logo. Sometimes the stamp lands off center. To improve the process, you first tighten the conveyer belt. To improve the process further, you adjust the stamping device.

This chart groups the data collected before and after each adjustment:

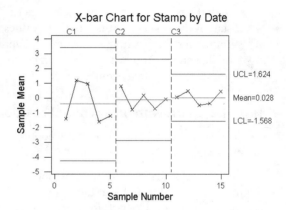

Note | With the following charts, you must have at least one subgroup with two or more observations: R chart, S chart, I-MR-R/S chart, or $\bar{X}$ chart with the Rbar or Sbar estimation method.

▶ To make a historical chart

To define stages in your process, you must set up a column of grouping indicators. The indicators can be numbers, dates, or text. When executing the command, you can tell MINITAB to start a new stage in one of two ways:

- each time the value in the column changes
- at the first occurrence of one or more values

The column must be the same length as the data column (or columns, when subgroups are across rows).

1 In the control chart main dialog box, click **Estimate Parameters BY Groups in**.

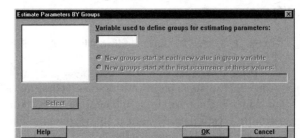

2 In **Variable used to define groups for estimating parameters**, enter the column which contains the stage indicators.

3 Do one of the following, and then click **OK**:

- to start a new stage each time the value in the column changes, choose **New groups start at each new value in group variable** (the default).

- to start a new stage at the first occurrence of a certain value, choose **New groups start at the first occurrence of these values** and enter the values, or a column containing those values, in the box. Date/time or text entries must be enclosed in double quotes. You can enter the same value more than once; each repeat will be treated as a separate occurrence.

Historical charts with other control chart options

In a sense you are creating two or more control charts in one: so how do the control chart options work with these "separate charts?"

Most of the time what goes for one goes for all. If you specify that you want three control limit lines drawn, for instance, three lines are drawn for each stage. There are exceptions, however. The tests for special causes, for instance, are performed independently for each stage. Each time a new stage begins, the tests restart.

Some options offer choices:

With this option...	You can...
Historical mean, Historical sigma, and **Historical p**	Enter one value to be used for all stages, or enter a column containing different values for each stage.
Box-Cox power transformation	Enter one value to be used for all stages, or enter a column containing different values for each stage.

▷ Example of a historical chart

As manager of a hospital's intensive care unit, you are concerned about the length of time it takes to admit patients to your unit. To gain an understanding of the process, you begin monitoring admission times. You find that the process is in control, but the variability is large. So before making any changes in the process, your team decides to first standardize the admission procedure for all shifts. This standardization takes place in July.

While studying the admissions process, you discover that you can cut down on switchover time by using the same type of IV line used in the operating room. You implement this change in August.

To share your findings with the staff, you draw an historical chart.

1 Open the worksheet ICU.MTW.

2 Choose **Stat ➤ Control Charts ➤ Individuals**.

3 In **Variable**, enter *ICUadmit*.

4 Click **Estimate Parameters BY Groups In**. In **Variable used to define groups for estimating parameters**, enter *Month*. Click **OK** in each dialog box.

Graph window output

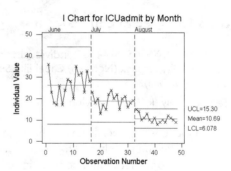

Interpreting the results

The data in the first part of the Individuals chart are the admission times (in minutes) before any improvements were made. As you can see, the initial standardization in July reduced both the mean admission time and the variation in admission time. In August, improvements to standardized procedure further reduced mean admission time, as well as the variation.

Use historical values of μ and σ

Commands | Historical μ: Xbar, Xbar-R, Xbar-S, I-MR-R/S, Individuals, I-MR, EWMA, Moving Average, Zone, C, U

Historical σ: All control charts *except* Z-MR and I-MR-R/S

For variables control charts, the process is assumed to produce data from a stable population that often follows a normal distribution. The mean and standard deviation of a population distribution are denoted by mu (μ) and sigma (σ), respectively. If μ and σ are not specified, they are estimated from the data. Alternatively, you can enter known process parameters, estimates obtained from past data, or your goals.

When you choose to enter historical values for μ and σ it overrides any options relating to estimating μ or σ from the data—specifically: **Omit the following samples when estimating parameters**, and any of the **Methods for estimating sigma**.

▶ **To use historical values of μ and σ**

In the chart's main dialog box, enter a value in **Historical mean** and/or **Historical sigma**.

Do tests for special causes

Commands | Xbar, Xbar-R, Xbar-S, I-MR-R/S, Individuals, and I-MR, all attributes charts (P, NP, C, and U), Capability Sixpack (Normal), Capability Sixpack (Between/Within), and Capability Sixpack (Weibull)

Tests 1-4 only: R, S, and Moving Range

Each of the tests for special causes, shown in Exhibit 12.1, detects a specific pattern in the data plotted on the chart. The occurrence of a pattern suggests a special cause for the variation, one that should be investigated. See [5] and [25] for guidance on using these tests.

When a point fails a test, it is marked with the test number on the chart. If a point fails more than one test, the number of the first test in your list is the number printed on the chart. In addition, a summary table is printed in the Session window with complete information.

You can change the threshold values for triggering a test failure—see *Defining Tests for Special Causes* on page 12-5 for details.

Subgroup sizes must be equal to perform these tests.

Exhibit 12.1 Eight Tests for Special Causes

Test 1
One point more than
3 sigmas from center
line

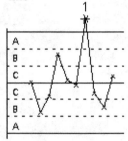

Test 2
Nine points in a row
on same side of center
line

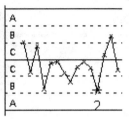

Test 3
Six points in a row, all
increasing or all
decreasing

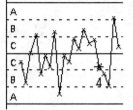

Test 4
Fourteen points in a
row, alternating up
and down

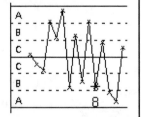

Test 5
Two out of three
points in a row more
than 2 sigmas from
center line (same
side)

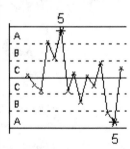

Test 6
Four out of five points
in a row more than 1
sigma from center
line (same side)

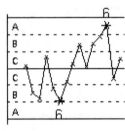

Test 7
Fifteen points in a
row within 1 sigma of
center line (either
side)

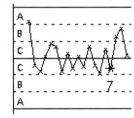

Test 8
Eight points in a row
more than 1 sigma
from center line
(either side)

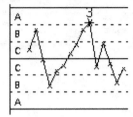

▶ **To do the tests for special causes**

1 In the control chart's main dialog box, click **Tests**.

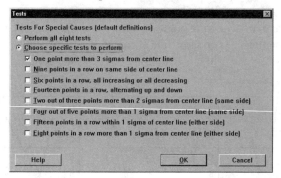

2 Do one of the following, then click **OK**:

■ To select certain tests, choose **Choose specific tests to perform** (the default). Check the tests you would like to perform.

■ To do all of the tests, choose **Perform all eight tests** or **Perform all four tests**, depending on the command.

Omit subgroups from the estimate of μ or σ

Commands │ All variables control charts except Z-MR and all attributes control charts

By default, MINITAB estimates the process parameters from all the data. But you may want to omit certain data if it shows abnormal behavior.

▶ **To omit subgroups from the estimates of μ and σ**

1 In the chart's main dialog box, click **Estimate**.

2 In **Omit the following samples when estimating parameters**, enter the subgroups or observation (sample) numbers that you want to omit from the calculations. With some charts ($\bar{X}$, R, S, Individuals, Moving Range, EWMA and Moving Average), you can also enter a column which contains those values.

Note │ MINITAB assumes the values you enter are subgroup numbers, except with the I-MR-R/S, Individuals, Moving Range, and I-MR charts. With these charts, the values are interpreted as observation (sample) numbers.

3 Click **OK**.

Control how σ is estimated

Commands

Pooled standard deviation: All control charts *except* I-MR, Individuals, Moving Range, and capability charts not based on normal distributions

Average of subgroup ranges: Xbar, R, Xbar-R, I-MR-R/S, EWMA, Moving Average, CUSUM, Zone, Capability Analysis (Normal), Capability Sixpack (Normal)

Average of subgroup standard deviations: Xbar, S, Xbar-S, I-MR-R/S, EWMA, Moving Average, CUSUM, Zone, Capability Analysis (Normal), Capability Sixpack (Normal)

Median of moving range/Specify length of moving range: Xbar, I-MR-R/S, Individuals, Moving Range, I-MR, EWMA, Moving Average, CUSUM, Zone, Capability Analysis (Normal), Capability Sixpack (Normal)

Square root of mean of squared successive differences: I-MR-R/S

MINITAB has several methods of estimating σ, depending on whether your data is in subgroups or individual observations.

Data in subgroups

All commands, except for R chart, S chart, and I-MR-R/S chart, estimate σ with a pooled standard deviation. The pooled standard deviation is the most efficient method of estimating sigma when you can assume constant variation across subgroups. Choose **Rbar** to base the estimate on the average of the subgroup ranges. Choose **Sbar** to base your estimate on the average of the subgroup standard deviations. See [1] for a discussion of the relative merits of each estimator.

Individual observations

The estimate of σ is based on $\overline{MR}$ / d2, the average of the moving range divided by an unbiasing constant. By default, the moving range is of length 2, since consecutive values have the greatest chance of being alike. **Use moving range of length** to change the length of the moving range. Alternatively, use **Median moving range** to estimate σ using the median of the moving range.

▶ **To choose how σ is estimated**

1 In the chart's main dialog box, click **Estimate**.

2 Under **Methods of estimating sigma**, click the method of choice, then click **OK**.

Note

When **Omit the following samples when estimating parameters** is used with **Use moving range of length**, any moving ranges which include omitted data are excluded from the calculations.

Force control limits and center line to be constant

Commands | Xbar, R, S, Xbar-R, Xbar-S, EWMA, Moving Average

When subgroup sizes are not equal, the control limits will not be straight lines, but will vary with the subgroup size. The center line of charts for ranges and standard deviations also varies with the subgroup size. If the sizes do not vary much, you may want to force these lines to be constant. For instance, you could enter the average sample size as the subgroup size. When you use this option, the plot points themselves are not changed; only the control limits and center line.

▶ **To force control limits and center line to be constant**

1 In the chart's main dialog box, click **Estimate**.

2 Under **Calculate control limits using**, enter a value in **Subgroup size**. For example, entering a value of 6 says to calculate the control limits and center line as if all subgroups were of size 6. Click **OK**.

Note | It is usually recommended that you force the control limits and center line to be constant only when the difference in size between the largest and smallest subgroup is no more than 25%.

Use the Box-Cox power transformation for non-normal data

Commands | Xbar, R, S, Xbar-R, Xbar-S, I-MR-R/S, Individuals, Moving Range, I-MR, EWMA, Moving Average, Z-MR, Capability Analysis (Normal), Capability Sixpack (Normal), Capability Analysis (Between/Within), Capability Sixpack (Between/Within)

You can use the Box-Cox power transformation when your data are very skewed or where the within-subgroup variation is unstable to make the data "more normal." The transformation takes the original data to the power λ, unless $\lambda = 0$, in which case the natural log is taken. (λ is pronounced "lambda.")

To use this option, the data must be positive.

The Options subdialog box lists the common transformations natural log ($\lambda = 0$) and square root ($\lambda = 0.5$). You can also choose any value between −5 and 5 for λ. In most cases, you should not choose a λ outside the range of -2 and 2. You may want to first run the command described under *Box-Cox Transformation for Non-Normal Data* on page 12-6 to help you find the optimal transformation value.

Caution | If you use **Stat ➤ Control Charts ➤ Box-Cox Transformation** to find the optimal lambda value *and* choose to store the transformed data with that command, take care not to select the Box-Cox option if making the control chart with that data; you will double transform the data.

When you use this transformation, MINITAB does not accept any values you enter in **Historical mean** or **Historical sigma**.

Box-Cox transformation with control charts

When you use the Box-Cox power transformation, the control chart will be based on the transformed data. The process parameters (mean and standard deviation) are also calculated using the transformed data.

Box-Cox transformation with process capability commands

When you use the Box-Cox power transformation, MINITAB displays a capability histogram for the transformed data. (A small histogram of the original data displays in the upper left side of the plot.) The normal curve included in the capability histogram helps you determine whether the transformation was successful in making the data "more normal."

This method also transforms the specification limits and target automatically, so that all the data are on the same scale. Process parameters (mean, short-term standard deviation, and long-term standard deviation) and capability statistics (both long-term and short-term) are calculated using the transformed data and specification limits. The transformed statistics display with an * next to their names in the table "Process Data."

With Capability Sixpack (Normal) and Capability Sixpack (Between/Within), when you enter a $\lambda \geq 0$, the capability plot is in the original scale; when $\lambda < 0$, the plot is in the transformed scale.

▶ To do the Box-Cox power transformation

1 From the main control chart or capability dialog box, click **Options**. We use the **Xbar** dialog box for an illustration.

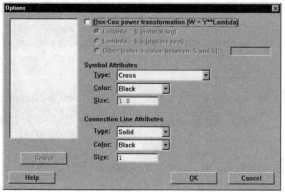

2 Check **Box-Cox power transformation (W = Y**Lambda)**, then do one of the following:

- use the natural log of the data—choose **Lambda = 0 (natural log)**

- use the square root of the data—choose **Lambda = 0.5 (square root)**

- transform the data using some other lambda value—choose **Other** and enter a value between −5 and 5 in the box

For help choosing a lambda value, see the independent Box-Cox transformation command described in *Box-Cox Transformation for Non-Normal Data* on page 12-6.

3 Click **OK**.

Customize the control (sigma) limits

Commands | Full options: Xbar, R, S, Individuals, Moving Range, EWMA, and Moving Average
Partial option: Xbar-R, Xbar-S, I-MR-R/S, and I-MR

With the full and partial options, you can draw control limits above and below the mean at the multiples of any standard deviation.

To specify the positions of control limits, you enter positive numbers, or a column containing the values. Each value you give draws two horizontal lines, one above and one below the mean. For example, entering a 2 draws control limits at two standard deviations above and below the center line. Entering 1 2 3 gives three lines above and three lines below the center line at 1σ, 2σ, and 3σ. Entering C1 also gives three lines above and below the center line at 1σ, 2σ, and 3σ when C1 contains the values 1 2 3.

With the full option (S Limits subdialog box), you can also:

- set bounds on the upper and lower control limits. When the calculated upper control limit is greater than the upper bound, a horizontal line labeled UB will be drawn at the upper bound instead. Similarly, if the calculated lower control limit is less than the lower bound, a horizontal line labeled LB will be drawn at the lower bound instead.

- specify the line type, color, and size. By default, the line is solid red.

For an example, see *Example of an Xbar chart with tests and customized control limits* on page 12-13.

Tip | You can also modify the control limits using the graph editing features explained in *MINITAB User's Guide 1*.

▶ **To customize the control limits (full option)**

1 In the chart's main dialog box, click **S Limits**.

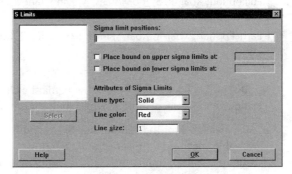

2 Do any of the following:

– To specify where control limits are drawn: in **Sigma limit positions**, enter one or more values, or a column of values. Each value is the number of standard deviations the lines should be drawn at, above and below the mean.

– To set bounds on the control limits: check **Place bound on upper sigma limits at** (and/or **Place bound on lower sigma limits at**) and enter a value. Each value represents the number of standard deviations above and below the mean.

– To change line attributes: under **Line type** or **Line color**, click a choice. In **Line size**, enter a positive real number. Larger numbers correspond to wider lines. The number you enter is in relation to the base unit of 1 pixel.

3 Click **OK** in each dialog box.

▶ **To customize the control limits (partial option)**

1 In the chart's main dialog box, click **Options**.

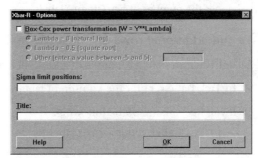

2 In **Sigma limit positions**, specify where control limits are drawn by entering one or more values, or a column of values. Each value is the number of standard deviations the lines should be drawn at, above and below the mean.

3 Click **OK**.

Add additional rows of tick labels

Commands

Full option: Xbar, R, S, Individuals, Moving Range, EWMA, Moving Average, all attributes charts

Partial option: Xbar-R, Xbar-S, I-MR-R/S, I-MR, CUSUM, Zone

With the *full option*, you can:

- add row(s) of tick labels below the regular tick labels on the horizontal (x-) axis. This allows you to place "time stamp" labels (or other descriptive labels) on your chart.

- specify a label for the added line. The default label is the name of the column variable specified in the control chart command. If the column has a name (for example, Sales), that name is the default label. If not, the column number (for example, C20) is the default label.

- specify the font, color, and size of the tick labels. By default, the labels are black Arial.

With the *partial option*, you can add rows of tick labels below the regular labels, but you cannot label the line.

The column used for tick labels can contain date/time, text, or numeric data, but must contain the same number of entries as the column of data you use to generate the control chart.

To control the number of tick marks and whether the tick marks appear on the top or bottom of a chart, see *Tick* in on-line Help. Changing the number of tick marks also changes the number of tick (stamp) labels.

Tip

You can modify stamp text using the graph editing features explained in *MINITAB User's Guide 1*. For example, you can control the number of tick marks and whether the tick marks appear on the top or bottom of a chart. Changing the number of tick marks also changes the number of tick (stamp) labels.

▶ **To add additional rows of tick labels (full option)**

1 In the control chart's main dialog box, click **Stamp**.

2 In **Tick Labels**, enter the column of labels.

3 If you like, do one of the following:
   – In **Axis Label**, enter an axis label for the added line. The default is the name of the column of labels.
   – In **Text Font**, specify a font. The default is Arial.
   – In **Text Color**, specify a color. The default is black.

4 Click **OK**.

▶ **To add additional rows of tick labels (partial option)**

1 In the control chart's main dialog box, click **Stamp**.

2 In **Stamp**, enter the column of labels.

3 Click **OK**.

▷ **Example of adding a time stamp**

In this example, we add two rows of tick labels below the original tick labels (the subgroup number)—Month and Day.

1 Open the worksheet CRANKSHD.MTW (a variation of CRANKSH.MTW).

2 Choose **Stat ➤ Control Charts ➤ R**.

3 In **Single column**, enter *AtoBDist*. In **Subgroup size**, enter 5.

4 Click **Stamp**. Under **Tick Labels**, enter *Month* in row 1 and *Day* in row 2, then click **OK** in each dialog box.

Graph window output

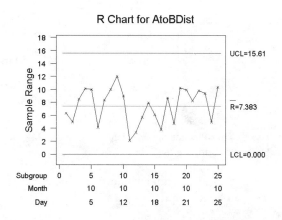

Customize the data display, annotation, frame, and regions

Commands | Full option: Xbar, R, S, Individuals, Moving Range, EWMA, Moving Average, all attributes charts
Partial option: Xbar-R, Xbar-S, I-MR-R/S, I-MR, CUSUM, Zone

The control charts share basic options with other MINITAB graphs. These options can be accessed in the main dialog box through the Annotation, Frame, and Regions drop-down lists, and in the Options subdialog box. For more information, refer to the indicated chapters in MINITAB *User's Guide 1*.

Core Graphs: Displaying Data	Core Graphs: Annotating	Core Graphs: Customizing the Frame	Core Graphs: Controlling Regions
Symbols	Titles	Axes	Figure
Connection lines	Footnotes	Ticks	Data
	Text	Grids	Aspect ratio of a page
	Lines	Reference lines	
	Polygons	Min and max values	
	Markers	Suppressing frame elements	

Note | With Xbar-R, Xbar-S, I-MR-R/S, I-MR, and Z-MR, you can enter your own graph title; no other options are available.

To save an active graph window, use **File ➤ Save Window As**. To view it later, use **File ➤ Open Graph**.

References

[1] I.W. Burr (1976). *Statistical Quality Control Methods*, Marcel Dekker, Inc.

[2] Ward Cheney and David Kincaid. (1985). *Numerical Mathematics and Computing*, Second Edition, Brook/Cole Publishing Company.

[3] J. Fang and K.E. Case (1990). *Improving the Zone Control Chart*, ASQC Quality Congress Transactions, San Francisco.

[4] N.R. Farnum (1994). *Modern Statistical Quality Control and Improvement*, Wadsworth Publishing.

[5] Ford Motor Company (1983). *Continuing Process Control and Process Capability Improvement*, Ford Motor Company, Dearborn, Michigan.

[6] E.L. Grant and R.S. Leavenworth (1988). *Statistical Quality Control*, 6th Edition, McGraw-Hill.

[7] G.K. Griffith (1989). *Statistical Process Control Methods for Long and Short Runs*, ASQC Quality Press, Milwaukee.

[8] D.M. Hawkins (1981). "A Cusum for a Scale Parameter," *Journal of Quality Technology*, 13, pp.228–231.

[9] C.D. Hendrix and J.L. Hansen (1990). *Zone Charts: an SPC Tool for the 1990's*, Union Carbide Chemicals & Plastics, South Charleston.

[10] K. Ishikawa (1967). *Guide to Quality Control*, Asian Productivity Organization.

[11] A. Jaehn (1987). "Zone Control Charts: A New Tool for Quality Control," *Tappi*, pp.159–161.

[12] A. Jaehn (1987). "Zone Control Charts—SPC Made Easy," *Quality*, pp.51–52.

[13] V.E. Kane (1989). *Defect Prevention*, Marcel Dekker, Inc.

[14] J.M. Lucas (1976). "The Design and Use of V-Mask Control Schemes," *Journal of Quality Technology*, 8, pp.1–12.

[15] J.M. Lucas and R.B. Crosier (1982). "Fast Initial Response for CUSUM Quality-Control Schemes: Give Your CUSUM a Head Start," *Technometrics*, 24, pp.199–205.

[16] J.M. Lucas and M.S. Saccucci (1990). "Exponentially Weighted Moving Average Control Schemes: Properties and Enhancements," *Technometrics*, 32, pp.1–12.

[17] D.C. Montgomery (1985). *Introduction to Statistical Quality Control*, John Wiley & Sons.

[18] Raymond H. Myers. (1990). *Classical and Modern Regression with Applications*, Second Edition, PWS-KENT Publishing Company.

[19] L.S. Nelson (1984). "The Shewhart Control Chart—Tests for Special Causes," *Journal of Quality Technology*, 16, pp.237–239.

[20] John Neter, William Wasserman, and Michael Kutner. (1990). *Applied Linear Statistical Models: Regression, Analysis of Variance, and Experimental Designs*, Third Edition, Richard D. Irwin, Inc.

[21] C.H. Ng and K.E. Case (1989). "Development and Evaluation of Control Charts Using Exponentially Weighted Moving Averages," *Journal of Quality Technology*, 21, pp.242–250.

[22] E.S. Page (1961). "Cumulative Sum Charts," *Technometrics*, 3, pp.1–9.

[23] T.P. Ryan (1989). *Statistical Methods for Quality Improvement*, John Wiley & Sons.

[24] H.M. Wadsworth, K.S. Stephens, and A.B. Godfrey (1986). *Modern Methods for Quality Control and Improvement*, John Wiley & Sons.

[25] Western Electric (1956). *Statistical Quality Control Handbook*, Western Electric Corporation, Indianapolis, Indiana.

[26] Donald J. Wheeler and David S. Chambers. (1992). *Understanding Statistical Process Control*, Second Edition, SPC Press, Inc.

[27] Donald J. Wheeler. (1995). *Advanced Topics in Statistical Process Control: The Power of Shewhart Charts*, SPC Press, Inc.

13

Attributes
Control Charts

Attributes Control Charts Overview

Attributes control charts are similar in structure to variables control charts, except that they plot statistics from *count* data rather than *measurement* data. For instance, products may be compared against a standard and classified as either being defective or not. Products may also be classified by their number of defects.

As with variables control charts, a process statistic, such as the number of defects, is plotted versus sample number or time. A *center line* is drawn at the average of the statistic being plotted for the time being charted. Two other lines—the *upper and lower control limits*—are drawn, by default, 3σ above and below the center line.

 Structure of a control chart

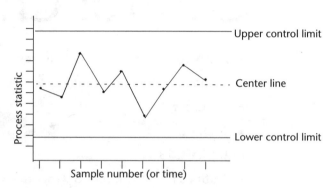

A process is in control when most of the points fall within the bounds of the control limits and the points do not display any nonrandom patterns. The "tests for special causes" will detect nonrandom patterns. If you like, you can change the threshold values for triggering a test failure.

Special causes are causes arising from outside the system that can be corrected. Examples of special causes include supplier, shift, or day of the week differences. Common cause variation, on the other hand, is variation that is inherent or a natural part of the process. A process is in control when only common causes—not special causes—affect the process output.

Control charts for defectives

You can compare a product to a standard and classify it as being defective or not. For example, a length of wire either meets the strength requirements or not. The control charts for defectives are:

■ **P Chart**, which charts the *proportion* of defectives in each subgroup

■ **NP Chart**, which charts the *number* of defectives in each subgroup

See [2], [3], [6], [8], [9], and [10] for a discussion of these charts.

Control charts for defects

When a product is complex, a defect doesn't always result in a defective product. Here it is sometimes more convenient to classify a product by the number of defects it contains. For example, you might count the number of scratches on the surface of an appliance. The control charts for defects are:

- **C Chart**, which charts the number of defects in each subgroup. Use C Chart when the subgroup size is constant.

- **U Chart**, which charts the number of defects *per unit sampled* in each subgroup. Use U Chart when the subgroup size varies.

For example, if you were counting the number of flaws on the inner surface of a television screen, C Chart would chart the actual number of flaws while U Chart would chart the number of flaws per square inch sampled.

See [2], [3], [6], [8], [9], and [10] for a discussion of these charts.

Data

Each entry in the worksheet column should contain the number of defectives or defects for a subgroup. When subgroup sizes are unequal, you must also enter a corresponding column of subgroup sizes.

Suppose you have collected daily data on the number of parts that have been inspected and the number of parts that failed to pass inspection. On any given day both numbers may vary. You enter the number that failed to pass inspection in one column. In this case, the total number inspected varies from day to day, so you enter the subgroup size in another column:

```
Failed  Inspect
     8      968
    13     1216
    13     1004
    16     1101
    14     1076
    15      995
    13     1202
    10     1028
    24     1184
    12      992
```

P Chart (and U Chart) divide the number of defectives or defects by the subgroup size to get the proportion of defectives, or defects per unit. NP Chart and C Chart plot raw data.

P Chart, NP Chart, and U Chart handle unequal-size subgroups. With P Chart and U Chart, the control limits are a function of the subgroup size, while the center line is always constant. With NP Chart, both the control limits and the center line are affected by differing subgroup sizes. In general, the control limits are further from the center line for smaller subgroups than they are for larger ones. You can force the control limits and center line to be constant, as described on page 13-16.

When an observation is missing, a gap exists in the chart where the summary statistic for that subgroup would have been plotted.

P Chart

Use P chart to draw a chart of the proportion of defectives—the number of defectives divided by the subgroup size. P charts track the proportion defective and detect the presence of special causes. Each entry in the worksheet column is the number of defectives for one subgroup, assumed to have come from a binomial distribution with parameters n and p.

By default, the *process proportion defective*, p, is estimated by the overall sample proportion. This is the value of the center line on the chart. The control limits are also calculated using this value.

Data

Arrange the data in your worksheet as illustrated in *Data* on page 13-3.

▶ **To make a P chart**

1 Choose **Stat ➤ Control Charts ➤ P**.

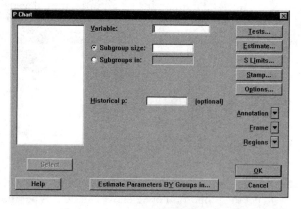

2 In **Variable**, enter the column containing the number of defectives.

3 Do one of the following:

- When subgroups are of equal size, enter their size in **Subgroup size**.

- When subgroups are of unequal size, choose **Subgroups in**, and enter the column of subgroup sizes.

4 If you like, use any of the options described below, then click **OK**.

Options

P Chart dialog box

- enter an historical value for p that will be used for calculating the center line and control limits—see *Use historical values of p* on page 13-14. Use this option if you have a goal for p, or a known p from prior data.

- customize the chart annotation, frame, and region (placement of the chart within the Graph window)—see *Customize the data display, annotation, frame, and regions* on page 13-17.

Tests subdialog box

- do four tests for special causes—see *Do tests for special causes* on page 13-15. To adjust the sensitivity of the tests, see *Defining Tests for Special Causes* on page 12-5.

Estimate subdialog box

- omit certain subgroups when estimating p, for calculating the center line and control limits—see *Omit subgroups from the estimate of μ or p* on page 13-15.

- force the control limits to be constant when subgroups are of unequal size—see *Force control limits and center line to be constant* on page 13-16.

S Limits subdialog box

- choose the positions at which to draw the upper and lower control (sigma) limits in relation to the center line—see *Customize the control (sigma) limits* on page 13-16. The default line is 3σ above and below the center line. You can draw more than one set of lines. For example, you can draw specification limits along with control limits on the chart.

- place bounds on the upper and/or lower control limits—see *Customize the control (sigma) limits* on page 13-16.

- choose the line type, color, and size for the control limits—see *Customize the control (sigma) limits* on page 13-16. The default line is solid red.

Stamp subdialog box

- add another row of tick labels below the default tick labels—see *Add additional rows of tick labels* on page 12-72. For example, you can place "time stamp" labels, or other descriptive labels, on your graph.

- choose the text font, color, and size for the axis and tick labels—see *Customize the data display, annotation, frame, and regions* on page 13-17. The default labels are black Arial.

Options subdialog box

- choose the symbol type, color, and size—see page 13-17. The default symbol is a black cross.

- choose the connection line type, color, and size—see page 13-17. The default line is solid black.

Estimate Parameters BY Groups subdialog box

- estimate control limits and center line independently for different groups (draws a "historical chart")—see page 12-61.

▷ Example of a P chart with unequal subgroup sizes

Suppose you work in a plant that manufactures picture tubes for televisions. For each lot, you pull some of the tubes and do a visual inspection. If a tube has scratches on the inside, it is rejected. If a lot has too many rejects, you will do a 100% inspection on that lot. A P chart can define when you need to inspect the whole lot.

1 Open the worksheet EXH_QC.MTW.

2 Choose **Stat ➤ Control Charts ➤ P**.

3 In **Variable**, enter *Rejects*.

4 Choose **Subgroups in** and enter *Sampled* in the text box. Click **OK**.

Graph window output

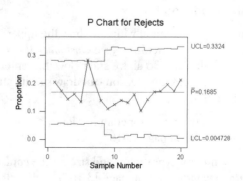

Interpreting the results

Sample 6 is outside the upper control limit, therefore you decide to do a 100% inspection on that lot.

NP Chart

Use NP chart to draw a chart of the number of defectives. NP charts track the number of defectives and detect the presence of special causes. Each entry in the worksheet column is the number of defectives for one subgroup, assumed to have come from a binomial distribution with parameters n and p.

By default, the *process proportion defective*, p, is estimated by the overall sample proportion. The center line and control limits are then calculated using this value.

Data

Arrange the data in your worksheet as illustrated in *Data* on page 13-3.

▶ **To make an NP chart**

1 Choose **Stat ➤ Control Charts ➤ NP**.

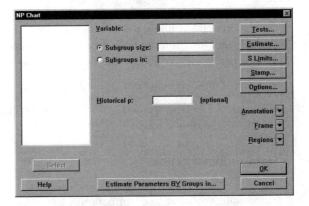

2 In **Variable**, enter the column containing the number of defectives.

3 Do one of the following:

■ When subgroups are of equal size, enter their size in Subgroup size.

■ When subgroups are of unequal size, choose Subgroups in and enter the column of subgroup sizes.

4 If you like, use any of the options described below, then click **OK**.

Options

NP Chart dialog box

- enter an historical value for p that will be used for calculating the center line and control limits—see page 13-14. Use this option if you have a goal for p, or a known p from prior data.

- customize the chart annotation, frame, and region (placement of the chart within the Graph window)—see page 13-17.

Tests subdialog box

- do four tests for special causes—see page 13-15. To adjust the sensitivity of the tests, see *Defining Tests for Special Causes* on page 12-5.

Estimate subdialog box

- omit certain subgroups when estimating p, for calculating the center line and control limits—see page 13-15.

- force the control limits and center line to be constant when subgroups are of unequal size—see page 13-16.

S Limits subdialog box

- choose the positions at which to draw the upper and lower control (sigma) limits in relation to the center line—see page 13-16. The default line is 3σ above and below the center line. You can draw more than one set of lines. For example, you can draw specification limits along with control limits on the chart.

- place bounds on the upper and/or lower control limits—see page 13-16.

- choose the line type, color, and size for the control limits—see page 13-16. The default line is solid red.

Stamp subdialog box

- add another row of tick labels below the default tick labels—see page 12-72. For example, you can place "time stamp" labels, or other descriptive labels, on your graph.

- choose the text font, color, and size for the axis and tick labels—see page 13-17. The default labels are black Arial.

Options subdialog box

- choose the symbol type, color, and size—see page 13-17. The default symbol is a black cross.

- choose the connection line type, color, and size—see page 13-17. The default line is solid black.

Estimate Parameters BY Groups subdialog box

- estimate control limits and center line independently for different groups (draws a "historical chart")—see page 12-61.

C Chart

Use C chart to draw a chart of the number of defects. C charts track the number of defects and detect the presence of special causes. Each entry in the specified column contains the number of defects for one subgroup, assumed to have come from a Poisson distribution with parameter μ. This is both the mean and the variance.

By default, the *process average number of defects*, μ, is estimated from the data. This value is the center line on the C Chart. The control limits are also calculated using this value.

Data

Each entry in the worksheet column should contain the number of defects for one subgroup. Each subgroup must be the same size.

▶ **To make a C chart**

1 Choose **Stat ➤ Control Charts ➤ C**.

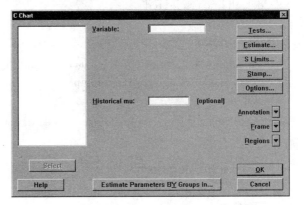

2 In **Variable**, enter the column containing the number of defects.

3 If you like, use any of the options described below, then click **OK**.

Options

C Chart dialog box

- enter an historical value for μ that will be used for calculating the center line and control limits—see page 13-14. Use this option if you have a goal for μ, or a known μ from prior data.

- customize the chart annotation, frame, and region (placement of the chart within the Graph window)—see page 13-17.

Tests subdialog box

- do four tests for special causes—see page 13-15. To adjust the sensitivity of the tests, see *Defining Tests for Special Causes* on page 12-5.

Estimate subdialog box

- omit certain subgroups when estimating μ, for calculating the center line and control limits—see page 13-15.

S Limits subdialog box

- choose the positions at which to draw the upper and lower control (sigma) limits in relation to the center line—see page 13-16. The default line is 3σ above and below the center line. You can draw more than one set of lines. For example, you can draw specification limits along with control limits on the chart.

- place bounds on the upper and/or lower control limits—see page 13-16.

- choose the line type, color, and size for the control limits—see page 13-16. The default line is solid red.

Stamp subdialog box

- add another row of tick labels below the default tick labels—see page 12-72. For example, you can place "time stamp" labels, or other descriptive labels, on your graph.

- choose the text font, color, and size for the axis and tick labels—see page 13-17. The default labels are black Arial.

Options subdialog box

- choose the symbol type, color, and size—see page 13-17. The default symbol is a black cross.

- choose the connection line type, color, and size—see page 13-17. The default line is solid black.

Estimate Parameters BY Groups subdialog box

■ estimate control limits and center line independently for different groups (draws a "historical chart")—see page 12-61.

➤ Example of a C chart with a customized control limits

Suppose you work for a linen manufacturer. Each 100 square yards of fabric is allowed to contain a certain number of blemishes before it is rejected. For quality control, you want to track the number of blemishes per 100 square yards over a period of several days, to see if your process is behaving predictably. You would like the control chart to show control limits at 1σ, 2σ, as well as 3σ above and below the center line.

1 Open the worksheet EXH_QC.MTW.

2 Choose **Stat ➤ Control Charts ➤ C**.

3 In **Variable**, enter *Blemish*.

4 Click **S Limits**. In **Sigma limit positions**, enter *1 2 3*.

5 Check **Place bound on lower sigma limits at** and enter *0* in the box. Click **OK** in each dialog box.

Graph window output

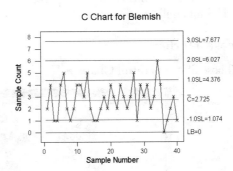

Interpreting the results

Because the points fall in a random pattern, within the bounds of the 3σ control limits, you conclude the process is behaving predictably and is in control.

U Chart

Use U Chart to draw a chart of the number of defects per unit sampled, X / n. U charts track the number of defects per unit sampled and detect the presence of special causes. Each entry in the worksheet column is the number of defects in a sample (or subgroup), assumed to come from a Poisson distribution with the parameter μ, which is both the mean and the variance.

By default, the *process average number of defects*, μ, is estimated from the data. This value is the center line on a U Chart. The control limits are also calculated using this value.

For general information on attributes control charts, see *Attributes Control Charts Overview* on page 13-2.

Data

Each entry in the worksheet column should contain the number of defects in a sample (or subgroup). Subgroups need not be of equal size. When they are unequal, a second column should contain, in the corresponding row, the subgroup size. See *Data* on page 13-3 for an illustration.

▶ **To make a U chart**

1 Choose **Stat ➤ Control Charts ➤ U**.

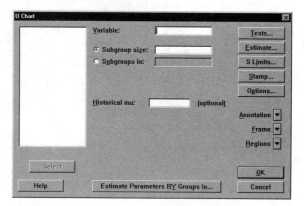

2 In **Variable**, enter the column containing the number of defects per unit.

3 Do one of the following:

- When subgroups are of equal size, enter their size in **Subgroup size**.

- When subgroups are of unequal size, choose **Subgroups in** and enter the column of unit sizes.

4 If you like, use any of the options described below, then click **OK**.

Options

U Chart dialog box

■ enter an historical value for μ that will be used for calculating the center line and control limits—see page 13-14. Use this option if you have a goal for μ, or a known μ from prior data.

■ customize the chart annotation, frame, and region (placement of the chart within the Graph window)—see page 13-17.

Tests subdialog box

■ do four tests for special causes—see page 13-15. To adjust the sensitivity of the tests, see *Defining Tests for Special Causes* on page 12-5.

Estimate subdialog box

■ omit certain subgroups when estimating μ, for calculating the center line and control limits—see page 13-15.

■ force the control limits to be constant when subgroups are of unequal size—see page 13-16.

S Limits subdialog box

■ choose the positions at which to draw the upper and lower control (sigma) limits in relation to the center line—see page 13-16. The default line is 3σ above and below the center line. You can draw more than one set of lines. For example, you can draw specification limits along with control limits on the chart.

■ place bounds on the upper and/or lower control limits—see page 13-16.

■ choose the line type, color, and size for the control limits—see page 13-16. The default line is solid red.

Stamp subdialog box

■ add another row of tick labels below the default tick labels—see page 12-72. For example, you can place "time stamp" labels, or other descriptive labels, on your graph.

■ choose the text font, color, and size for the axis and tick labels—see page 13-17. The default labels are black Arial.

Options subdialog box

■ choose the connection line type, color, and size—see page 13-17. The default line is solid black.

■ choose the symbol type, color, and size—see page 13-17. The default symbol is a black cross.

Options for Attributes Control Charts

Here are the attributes control chart options and a page number for instructions.

Option	Page	Applies to chart type			
		P	NP	C	U
Use historical values of μ	13-14			•	•
Use historical values of p	13-14	•	•		
Do four tests for special causes	13-15	•	•	•	•
Omit subgroups from estimate of μ or p	13-15	•	•	•	•
Force control limits/center line to be constant	13-16	•	•		•
Customize control (sigma) limits	13-16	•	•	•	•
Add additional rows of tick labels	12-72	•	•	•	•
Customize the data display, annotation, frame, and regions	13-17	•	•	•	•

Use historical values of μ

With C chart and U chart, the process is assumed to produce data from a population that follows a Poisson distribution. The mean and variance of this distribution are both denoted by μ. If μ is not specified, it is estimated from the data. Alternatively, you can enter a known process mean, an estimate obtained from past data, or a goal.

▶ **To use historical values of μ**

In the chart's main dialog box, enter a value in **Historical mu**.

Use historical values of p

With P chart and NP chart, the process is assumed to produce data from a population that follows a binomial distribution. The parameters of the binomial distribution are the sample size, n, and the proportion of defectives, p. If p is not specified, it is estimated from the data. Alternatively, you can enter an actual known process proportion, an estimate obtained from past data, or a goal.

▶ **To use historical values of p**

In the attributes control chart's main dialog box, enter a value in **Historical p**.

Do tests for special causes

With any of the attributes control charts, you can perform the four tests for special causes. Each test, as shown in Exhibit 13.1, detects a specific pattern in the plotted data. The occurrence of a pattern suggests a special cause for the variation, one that should be investigated. See [2] and [10] for guidance on using these tests.

When a point fails a test, it is marked with the test number on the plot. If a point fails more than one test, the number of the first test you request is the number printed on the plot. MINITAB prints a summary table in the Session window with the complete information.

If you like, you can change the threshold values for triggering a test failure—see *Defining Tests for Special Causes* on page 12-5.

Subgroup sizes must be equal in order to perform these tests.

▶ **To do tests for special causes**

1 In the chart's main dialog box, click **Tests**.

2 Check any of the tests you would like to perform, then click **OK**.

Exhibit 13.1 Four Tests for Special Causes

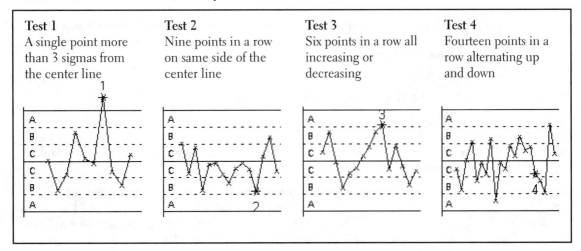

Test 1	Test 2	Test 3	Test 4
A single point more than 3 sigmas from the center line	Nine points in a row on same side of the center line	Six points in a row all increasing or decreasing	Fourteen points in a row alternating up and down

Omit subgroups from the estimate of μ or p

With any of the attributes control charts, you can omit subgroups from the parameter estimates (μ or p, depending on the chart). By default, MINITAB estimates the parameters from all the data. But you may want to omit data from certain subgroups if these samples show abnormal behavior.

▶ **To omit subgroups from estimate of μ or p**

1 In the attributes control chart's main dialog box, click **Estimate**.

2 In **Omit the following samples when estimating parameters**, enter the subgroup numbers you would like to omit, then click **OK**.

Force control limits and center line to be constant

With P, NP, and U Chart, you can force the control limits and center line to be constant. This option is relevant when you have subgroups of unequal size. When subgroups are of unequal size, the control limits will not be straight lines, but will vary with the subgroup size. The center line of an NP chart also varies with the subgroup size. When the sizes do not vary much, you may want to force these lines to be constant by entering a constant subgroup size. For instance, you could use the average sample size as the subgroup size. When you use this option, the plot points themselves are not changed, only the control limits and center line.

▶ **To force the control limits and/or center line to be constant**

1 In the attributes control chart's main dialog box, click **Estimate**.

2 Under **Calculate control limits using**, enter a value in **Subgroup size**, then click **OK**.

Note | It is usually recommended that you force the control limits and/or center line to be constant only when the difference in size between the largest and smallest subgroup is no more than 25%.

Customize the control (sigma) limits

With any of the attributes control charts, you can:

- draw control limits above and below the mean at the multiples of any standard deviation.

- set bounds on the upper and/or lower control limits. When the calculated upper control limit is greater than the upper bound, a horizontal line labeled UB will be drawn at the upper bound instead. Similarly, if the calculated lower control limit is less than the lower bound, a horizontal line labeled LB will be drawn at the lower bound instead.

- specify the line type, color, and size. By default, the line is solid red.

For an example, see *Example of an Xbar chart with tests and customized control limits* on page 12-13.

Tip | You can also modify the control limits using the graph editing features explained in *MINITAB User's Guide 1*.

▶ **To customize the control limits**

1   In the attributes control chart's main dialog box, click **S Limits**.

2   Do any of the following, then click **OK**:

- To specify where control limits are drawn: In **Sigma limit positions**, enter one or more values, or a column of values. Each value you enter draws two horizontal lines, one above and one below the mean. For example, entering a 2 draws control limits at two standard deviations above and below the center line. Entering 1 2 3 gives three lines above and three lines below the center line at 1σ, 2σ, and 3σ. When C1 contains the values 1 2 3, entering C1 also draws three lines above and below the center line at 1σ, 2σ, and 3σ.

- To set bounds on the control limits: Check **Place bound on upper sigma limits at** (and/or **Place bound on lower sigma limits at**) and enter a value. Each value represents the number of standard deviations above and below the mean.

- To change line attributes: Under **Line type** or **Line color**, click a choice. In **Line size**, enter a positive real number. Larger numbers correspond to wider lines. The number you enter is in relation to the base unit of 1 pixel.

Customize the data display, annotation, frame, and regions

The attributes control charts share basic options with other MINITAB graphs. These options can be accessed in the main dialog box through the Annotation, Frame, and Regions drop-down lists, and in the Options subdialog box. For more information, refer to the indicated chapters in MINITAB *User's Guide 1*.

Core Graphs: Displaying Data	Core Graphs: Annotating	Core Graphs: Customizing the Frame	Core Graphs: Controlling Regions
Symbols	Titles	Axes	Figure
Connection lines	Footnotes	Ticks	Data
	Text	Grids	Aspect ratio of a page
	Lines	Reference lines	
	Polygons	Min and max values	
	Markers	Suppressing frame elements	

To save an active graph window, use **File ▶ Save Window As**. To view it later, use **File ▶ Open Graph**.

References

[1] I.W. Burr (1976). *Statistical Quality Control Methods*, Marcel Dekker, Inc.

[2] Ford Motor Company (1983). *Continuing Process Control and Process Capability Improvement*, Ford Motor Company, Dearborn, Michigan.

[3] E.L. Grant and R.S. Leavenworth (1988). *Statistical Quality Control*, 6th Edition, McGraw-Hill.

[4] K. Ishikawa (1967). *Guide to Quality Control*, Asian Productivity Organization.

[5] V.E. Kane (1989). *Defect Prevention*, Marcel Dekker, Inc.

[6] D.C. Montgomery (1985). *Introduction to Statistical Quality Control*, John Wiley & Sons.

[7] L.S. Nelson (1984). "The Shewhart Control Chart—Tests for Special Causes," *Journal of Quality Technology*, 16, pp. 237–239.

[8] T.P. Ryan (1989). *Statistical Methods for Quality Improvement*, John Wiley & Sons.

[9] H.M. Wadsworth, K.S. Stephens, and A.B. Godfrey, (1986). *Modern Methods for Quality Control and Improvement*, John Wiley & Sons.

[10] Western Electric (1956). *Statistical Quality Control Handbook*, Western Electric Corporation, Indianapolis, Indiana.

14

Process Capability

Process Capability Overview

Once a process is in statistical control, that is producing consistently, you probably then want to determine if it is capable, that is meeting specification limits and producing "good" parts. You determine capability by comparing the width of the process variation with the width of the specification limits. The process needs to be in control before you assess its capability; if it is not, then you will get incorrect estimates of process capability.

You can assess process capability graphically by drawing capability histograms and capability plots. These graphics help you assess the distribution of your data and verify that the process is in control. You can also calculate capability indices, which are ratios of the specification tolerance to the natural process variation. Capability indices, or statistics, are a simple way of assessing process capability. Because they are unitless, you can use capability statistics to compare the capability of one process to another.

Choosing a capability command

MINITAB provides a number of different capability analysis commands from which you can choose depending on the the nature of data and its distribution. You can perform capability analyses for:

- normal or Weibull probability models (for measurement data)

- normal data that might have a strong source of between-subgroup variation

- binomial or Poisson probability models (for attributes or count data)

Note | If your data are badly skewed, you can use the Box-Cox transformation or use a Weibull probability model—see *Non-normal data* on page 14-6.

It is essential to choose the correct distribution when conducting a capability analysis. For example, MINITAB provides capability analyses based on both normal and Weibull probability models. The commands that use a normal probability model provide a more complete set of statistics, but your data must approximate the normal distribution for the statistics to be appropriate for the data.

For example, Capability Analysis (Normal) estimates expected parts per million out-of-spec using the normal probability model. Interpretation of these statistics rests on two assumptions: that the data are from a stable process, and that they follow an approximately normal distribution. Similarly, Capability Analysis (Weibull) calculates parts per million out-of-spec using a Weibull distribution. In both cases, the validity of the statistics depends on the validity of the assumed distribution.

If the data are badly skewed, probabilities based on a normal distribution could give rather poor estimates of the actual out-of-spec probabilities. In that case, it is better to either transfom the data to make the normal distribution a more appropriate model, or choose a different probability model for the data. With MINITAB, you can use the

Box-Cox power transformation or a Weibull probability model. *Non-normal data* on page 14-6 compares these two methods.

If you suspect that there may be a strong between-subgroup source of variation in your process, use Capability Analysis (Between/Within) or Capability Sixpack (Between/Within). Subgroup data may have, in addition to random error within subgroups, random variation between subgroups. Understanding both sources of subgroup variation may provide you with a more realistic estimate of the potential capability of a process. Capability Analysis (Between/Within) and Capability Sixpack (Between/Within) computes both within and between standard deviations and then pools them to calculate the total standard deviation.

MINITAB also provides capability analyses for attributes (count) data, based on the binomial and Poisson probability models. For example, products may be compared against a standard and classified as defective or not (use Capability Analysis (Binomial)). You can also classify products based on the number of defects (use Capability Analysis (Poisson)).

MINITAB's capability commands

- **Capability Analysis (Normal)** draws a capability histogram of the individual measurements overlaid with normal curves based on the process mean and standard deviation. This graph helps you make a visual assessment of the assumption of normality. The report also includes a table of process capability statistics, including both within and overall statistics.

- **Capability Analysis (Between/Within)** draws a capability histogram of the individual measurements overlaid with normal curves, which helps you make a visual assessment of the assumption of normality. Use this analysis for subgroup data in which there is a strong between-subgroup source of variation, in addition to the within-subgroup variation. The report also includes a table of between/within and overall process capability statistics.

- **Capability Analysis (Weibull)** draws a capability histogram of the individual measurements overlaid with a Weibull curve based on the process shape and scale. This graph helps you make a visual assessment of the assumption that your data follow a Weibull distribution. The report also includes a table of overall process capability statistics.

- **Capability Sixpack (Normal)** combines the following charts into a single display, along with a subset of the capability statistics:
  - an $\bar{X}$ (or Individuals), R or S (or Moving Range), and run chart, which can be used to verify that the process is in a state of control
  - a capability histogram and normal probability plot, which can be used to verify that the data are normally distributed
  - a capability plot, which displays the process variability compared to the specifications

■ **Capability Sixpack (Between/Within)** is appropriate for subgroup data in which there is a strong between-subgroup source of variation. Capability Sixpack (Between/Within) combines the following charts into a single display, along with a subset of the capability statistics:

– an Individuals Chart, Moving Range Chart, and R Chart or S Chart, which can be used to verify that the process is in a state of control

– a capability histogram and normal probability plot, which can be used to verify that the data are normally distributed

– a capability plot, which displays the process variability compared to specifications

■ **Capability Sixpack (Weibull)** combines the following charts into a single display, along with a subset of the capability statistics:

– an $\bar{X}$ (or Individuals), R (or Moving Range), and run chart, which can be used to verify that the process is in a state of control

– a capability histogram and Weibull probability plot, which can be used to verify that the data come from a Weibull distribution

– a capability plot, which displays the process variability compared to the specifications

Although the Capability Sixpack commands give you fewer statistics than the Capability Analysis commands, the array of charts can be used to verify that the process is in control and that the data follow the chosen distribution.

Note | Capability statistics are simple to use, but they have distributional properties that are not fully understood. In general, it is not good practice to rely on a single capability statistic to characterize a process. See [2], [4], [5], [6], [9], [10], and [11] for a discussion.

■ **Capability Analysis (Binomial)** is appropriate when your data consists of the number of defectives out of the total number of parts sampled. The report draws a P chart, which helps you verify that the process is in a state of control. The report also includes a chart of cumulative %defectives, histogram of %defectives, and defective rate plot.

■ **Capability Analysis (Poisson)** is appropriate when your data take the form of the number of defects per item. The report draws a U chart, which helps you to verify that the process is in a state of control. The report also includes a chart of the cumulative mean DPU (defects per unit), histogram of DPU, and a defect rate plot.

Capability statistics

Process capability statistics are numerical measures of process capability—that is, they measure how capable a process is of meeting specifications. These statistics are simple and unitless, so you can use them to compare the capability of different processes. Capability statistics are basically a ratio between the allowable process spread (the width of the specification limits) and the actual process spread (6σ). Some of the statistics take into account the process mean or target.

Process capability command	Capability statistics
Capability Analysis (Normal) and Capability Sixpack (Normal)	■ Cp, Cpk, CPU, CPL, and Cpm (if you specify a target)—associated with within variation ■ Pp, Ppk, PPU, PPL—associated with overall variation
Capability Analysis (Between/Within) and Capability Sixpack (Between/Within)	■ Cp, Cpk, CPU, CPL, and Cpm (if you specify a target)—associated with within and between variation ■ Pp, Ppk, PPU, PPL—associated with overall variation
Capability Analysis (Weibull) and Capability Sixpack (Weibull)	■ Pp, Ppk, PPU, PPL—associated with overall variation

For more information, see *Capability statistics* on page 14-9, *Capability statistics* on page 14-21, and *Capability statistics* on page 14-26.

Many practitioners consider 1.33 to be a minimum acceptable value for the process capability statistics, and few believe that a value less than 1 is acceptable. A value less than 1 indicates that your process variation is wider than the specification tolerance.

Here are some guidelines for how the statistics are used:

This statistic...	is used when...	Definition
Cp or Pp	the process is centered between the specification limits	ratio of the tolerance (the width of the specification limits) to the actual spread (the process tolerance): $(USL - LSL) / 6\sigma$
Cpk or Ppk	the process is *not* centered between the specification limits, but falls on or between them	ratio of the tolerance (the width of the specification limits) to the actual spread, taking into account the process mean relative to the midpoint between specifications: minimum $[(USL - \mu) / 3\sigma, (\mu - LSL) / 3\sigma]$
CPU or PPU	the process only has an upper specification limit	$USL - \mu / 3\sigma$
CPL or PPL	the process only has a lower specification limit	$\mu - LSL / 3\sigma$

Note | If the process target is not the midpoint between specifications, you may prefer to use **Cpm** in place of Cpk, since Cpm measures process mean relative to the *target* rather than the midpoint between specifications. See [9] for a discussion. You can calculate Cpm by entering a target in the Options subdialog box.

Non-normal data

When you have non-normal data, you can either transfom the data in such a way that the normal distribution is a more appropriate model, or choose a Weibull probability model for the data.

■ To transform the data, use Capability Analysis (Normal), Capability Sixpack (Normal), Capability Analysis (Between/Within), or Capability Sixpack (Between/ Within) with the optional Box-Cox power transformation. See *Box-Cox Transformation for Non-Normal Data* on page 12-6.

■ To use a Weibull probability model, use Capability Analysis (Weibull) and Capability Sixpack (Weibull).

This table summarizes the differences between the methods.

Normal model with Box-Cox transformation	Weibull model
Uses *transformed data* for the histogram, specification limits, target, process parameters (mean, within and overall standard deviations), and capability statistics	Uses *actual data units* for the histogram, process parameters (shape and scale), and capability statistics
Calculates both *within* and *overall* process parameters and capability statistics	Calculates only *overall* process parameters and capability statistics
Draws a *normal curve* over the histogram to help you determine whether the transformation made the data "more normal"	Draws a *Weibull curve* over the histogram to help you determine whether the data fit the Weibull distribution

Which method is better? The only way to answer that question is to see which model fits the data better. If both models fit the data about the same, it is probably better to choose the normal model, since it provides estimates of both overall and within process capability.

Capability Analysis (Normal Distribution)

Use Capability Analysis (Normal) to produce a process capability report when your data are from a normal distribution or when you have Box-Cox transformed data. The report includes a capability histogram overlaid with two normal curves, and a complete table of overall and within capability statistics. The two normal curves are generated using the process mean and within standard deviation and the process mean and overall standard deviation.

The report also includes statistics of the process data, such as the process mean, the target (if you enter one), the within and overall standard deviation, and the process specifications; the observed performance; and the expected within and overall performance. The report can be used to visually assess whether the data are normally distributed, whether the process is centered on the target, and whether it is capable of consistently meeting the process specifications.

A model which assumes the data are from a normal distribution suits most process data. If your data are very skewed, see the discussion under *Non-normal data* on page 14-6.

Data

You can use individual observations or data in subgroups. Individual observations should be structured in one column. Subgroup data can be structured in one column, or in rows across several columns. When you have subgroups of unequal size, enter the data in a single column, then set up a second column of subgroup indicators. For examples, see *Data* on page 12-3.

If you have data in subgroups, you must have two or more observations in at least one subgroup in order to estimate the process standard deviation.

To use the Box-Cox transformation, data must be positive.

If an observation is missing, MINITAB omits it from the calculations.

▶ **To perform a capability analysis (normal probability model)**

1 Choose **Stat ➤ Quality Tools ➤ Capability Analysis (Normal)**.

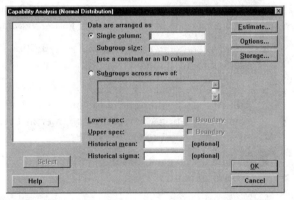

2 Do one of the following:

- When subgroups or individual observations are in one column, enter the data column in **Single column**. In **Subgroup size**, enter a subgroup size or column of subgroup indicators. For individual observations, enter a subgroup size of 1.

- When subgroups are in rows, choose **Subgroups across rows of**, and enter the columns containing the rows in the box.

3 In **Lower spec** or **Upper spec**, enter a lower and/or upper specification limit, respectively. You must enter at least one of them.

4 If you like, use any of the options listed below, then click **OK**.

Options

Capability Analysis (Normal) dialog box

- define the upper and lower specification limits as "boundaries," meaning measurements cannot fall outside those limits. As a result, the expected % out of spec is set to 0 for "boundaries." If you choose boundaries, then USL (upper specification limits) and LSL (lower specification limit) will be replaced by UB (upper boundary) and LB (lower boundary) on the analysis.

Note | When you define the upper and lower specification limits as boundaries, MINITAB still calculates the observed % out-of-spec. If the observed % out-of-spec comes up nonzero, this is an obvious indicator of incorrect data.

- enter historical values for μ (the process mean) and σ (the process potential standard deviation) if you have known process parameters or estimates from past data. If you do not specify a value for μ or σ, MINITAB estimates them from the data.

Estimate subdialog box

- estimate the process standard deviation (σ) various ways — see *Estimating the process variation* on page 14-10.

Options subdialog box

- use the Box-Cox power transformation when you have very skewed data — see *Use the Box-Cox power transformation for non-normal data* on page 12-68.

- enter a process target, or nominal specification. MINITAB calculates Cpm in addition to the standard capability statistics.

- calculate the capability statistics using an interval other than six standard deviations wide (three on either side of the process mean) by entering a sigma tolerance. For example, entering 12 says to use an interval 12 standard deviations wide, six on either side of the process mean.

- perform only the within-subgroup analysis or only the overall analysis. The default is to perform both.

- display observed performance, expected "within" performance, and expected "overall" performance in percents or parts per million. The default is parts per million.

- enter a minimum and/or maximum scale to appear on the capability histogram.

- display benchmark Z scores instead of capability statistics. The default is to display capability statistics.

- display the capability analysis graph or not. The default is to display the graph.

- replace the default graph title with your own title.

Storage subdialog box

■ store your choice of statistics in worksheet columns. The statistics available for storage depend on the options you have chosen in the Capability Analysis (Normal) dialog box and subdialog boxes.

Capability statistics

When you use the normal distribution model for the capability analysis, MINITAB calculates the capability statistics associated with within variation (Cp, Cpk, CPU, and CPL) and with overall variation (Pp, Ppk PPU, PPL). To interpret these statistics, see *Capability statistics* on page 14-4.

Cp, Cpk, CPU, and CPL represents the potential capability of your process—what your process would be capable of if the process did not have shifts and drifts in the subgroup means. To calculate these, Minitab estimates σ_{within} considering the variation within subgroups, but not the shift and drift between subgroups.

Note | When your subgroup size is one, the within variation estimate is based on a moving range, so that adjacent observations are effectively treated as subgroups.

Pp, Ppk, PPU, and PPL represent the *overall* capability of the process. When calculating these statistics, MINITAB estimates $\sigma_{overall}$ considering the variation for the whole study.

Each small curve represents within (or potential) variation, or variation for one subgroup (one moment in time).

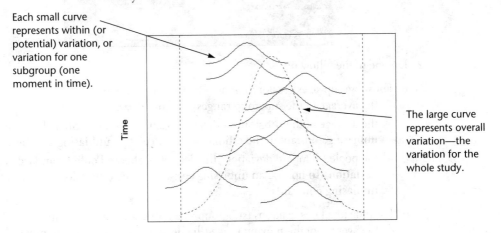

The large curve represents overall variation—the variation for the whole study.

Overall capability depicts how the process is *actually* performing relative to the specification limits. Within capability depicts how the process *could* perform relative to the specification limits, if shifts and drifts could be eliminated. A substantial difference between overall and within variation may indicate that the process is out of control, or it may indicate sources of variation not estimated by within capability.

Estimating the process variation

An important step in a capability analysis with normal data is estimating the process variation using the standard deviation, sigma (σ). Both Capability Analysis (Normal) and Capability Sixpack (Normal) calculate within (within-subgroup) and overall variation. The capability statistics associated with the within variation are Cp, Cpk, CPU, and CPL. The statistics associated with the overall variation are Pp, Ppk, PPU, and PPL.

To calculate $\sigma_{overall}$, MINITAB uses the standard deviation of all of the data.

To calculate σ_{within}, MINITAB provides several options, which are listed below. For a discussion of the relative merits of these methods, see [1].

▶ **To specify a method for estimating σ_{within}**

1 In the Capability Analysis (Normal) or Capability Sixpack (Normal) main dialog box, click **Estimate**.

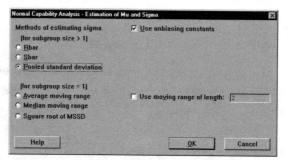

2 Do one of the following:

- For subgroup sizes greater than one, to base the estimate on:
  – the average of the subgroup ranges—choose **Rbar**.
  – the average of the subgroup standard deviations—choose **Sbar**. To not use an unbiasing constant in the estimation, uncheck **Use unbiasing constants**.
  – the pooled standard deviation (the default)—choose **Pooled standard deviation**. To not use an unbiasing constant in the estimation, uncheck **Use unbiasing constants**.

- For individual observations (subgroup size is one), to base the estimate on:
  – the average of the moving range (the default)—choose **Average moving range**. To change the length of the moving range from 2, check **Use moving range of length** and enter a number in the box.
  – the median of the moving range—choose **Median moving range**. To change the length of the moving range from 2, check **Use moving range of length** and enter a number in the box.

   – the square root of MSSD (mean of the squared successive differences)—
    choose **Square root of MSSD**. To not use an unbiasing constant in the
    estimation, uncheck **Use unbiasing constants**.

3 Click **OK**.

▷ Example of a capability analysis (normal probability model)

Suppose you work at an automobile manufacturer in a department that assembles
engines. One of the parts, a camshaft, must be 600 mm ±2 mm long to meet
engineering specifications. There has been a chronic problem with camshaft lengths
being out of specification—a problem which has caused poor-fitting assemblies down
the production line and high scrap and rework rates.

Upon examination of the inventory records, you discovered that there were two
suppliers for the camshafts. An $\overline{X}$ and R chart showed you that Supplier 2's camshaft
production was out of control, so you decided to stop accepting production runs from
them until they get their production under control.

After dropping Supplier 2, the number of poor quality assemblies has dropped
significantly, but the problems have not completely disappeared. You decide to run a
capability study to see whether Supplier 1 alone is capable of meeting your engineering
specifications.

1 Open the worksheet CAMSHAFT.MTW.

2 Choose **Stat ➤ Quality Tools ➤ Capability Analysis (Normal)**.

3 In **Single column**, enter *Supp1*. In **Subgroup size**, enter *5*.

4 In **Lower spec**, enter *598*. In **Upper spec**, enter *602*.

5 Click **Options**. In **Target (adds Cpm to table)**, enter *600*. Click **OK** in each dialog
  box.

*Graph
window
output*

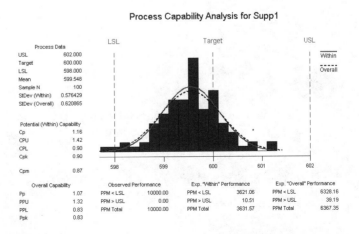

Interpreting the results

If you want to interpret the process capability statistics, your data should approximately follow a normal distribution. This requirement appears to have been fulfilled, as shown by the histogram overlaid with a normal curve.

But you can see that the process mean (599.55) falls short of the target (600). And the left tail of the distribution falls outside the lower specification limits. This means you will sometimes see camshafts that do not meet the lower specification of 598 mm.

The Cpk index indicates whether the process will produce units within the tolerance limits. The Cpk index for Supplier 1 is only 0.90, indicating that they need to improve their process by reducing variability and centering the process around the target.

Likewise, the PPM < LSL—the number of parts per million whose characteristic of interest is less than the lower spec—is 3621.06. This means that approximately 3621 out of a million camshafts do not meet the lower specification of 598 mm.

Since Supplier 1 is currently your best supplier, you will work with them to improve their process, and therefore, your own.

▶ Example of a capability analysis with a Box-Cox transformation

Suppose you work for a company that manufactures floor tiles and are concerned about warping in the tiles. To ensure production quality, you measure warping in ten tiles each working day for ten days.

A histogram shows that your data do not follow a normal distribution, so you decide to use the Box-Cox power transformation to try to make the data "more normal."

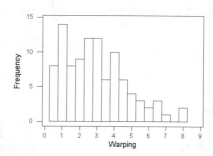

First you need to find the optimal lambda (λ) value for the transformation. Then you will do the capability analysis, performing the Box-Cox transformation with that value.

1 Open the worksheet TILES.MTW.

2 Choose **Stat ▶ Control Charts ▶ Box-Cox Transformation**.

3 In **Single column**, enter *Warping*. In **Subgroup size**, type *10*. Click **OK**.

*Graph
window
output*

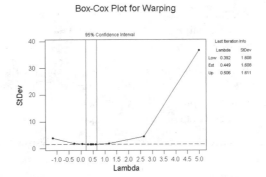

Box-Cox Plot for Warping

The best estimate of lambda is 0.449, but practically speaking, you may want a lambda value that corresponds to an intuitive transformation, such as the square root (a lambda of 0.5). In our example, 0.5 is a reasonable choice because it falls within the 95% confidence interval, as marked by vertical lines on the graph. So you will run the Capability Analysis with a Box-Cox transformation, using $\lambda = 0.5$.

1 Choose **Stat ➤ Quality Tools ➤ Capability Analysis (Normal)**.

2 In **Single column**, enter *Warping*. In **Subgroup size**, enter *10*.

3 In **Upper spec**, enter *8*.

4 Click **Options**.

5 Check **Box-Cox power transformation (W = Y**Lambda)**. Choose **Lambda = 0.5 (square root)**. Click **OK** in each dialog box.

*Graph
window
output*

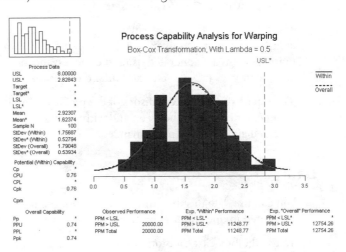

Process Capability Analysis for Warping

Interpreting the results

As you can see from the normal curve overlaying the histogram, the Box-Cox transformation "normalized" the data. Now the process capability statistics are appropriate for this data.

Because you only entered an upper specification limit, the capability statistics printed are CPU and Cpk. Both statistics are 0.76, below the guideline of 1.33, so your process does not appear to be capable. You can also see on the histogram that some of the process data fall beyond the upper spec limit.

You decide to perform a capability analysis with this data using a Weibull model, to see how the fit compares—see *Example of a capability analysis (Weibull probability model)* on page 14-22.

Capability Analysis (Between/Within)

Use Capability Analysis (Between/Within) to produce a process capability report using both between-subgroup and within-subgroup variation. When you collect data in subgroups, random error within subgroups may not be the only source of variation to consider. There may also be random error between subgroups. Under these conditions, the overall process variation is due to both the between-subgroup variation and the within-subgroup variation.

Capability Analysis (Between/Within) computes standard deviations within subgroups and between subgroups, or you may specify historical standard deviations. These will be combined (pooled) to compute the total standard deviation. The total standard deviation will be used to calculate the capability statistics, such as Cp and Cpk.

The report includes a capability histogram overlaid with two normal curves, and a complete table of overall and total (between and within) capability statistics. The normal curves are generated using the process mean and overall standard deviation and the process mean and total standard deviation.

The report also includes statistics of the process data, such as the process mean, target, if you enter one, total (between and within) and overall standard deviation, and observed and expected performance.

Data

You can use data in subgroups, with two or more observations. Subgroup data can be structured in one column, or in rows across several columns.

To use the Box-Cox transformation, data must be positive.

Ideally, all subgroups should be the same size. If your subgroups are not all the same size, due to missing data or unequal subgroup sizes, only subgroups of the majority size are used for estimating the between-subgroup variation.

▶ **To perform a capability analysis (between/within)**

1 Choose Stat ➤ Quality Tools ➤ Capability Analysis (Between/Within).

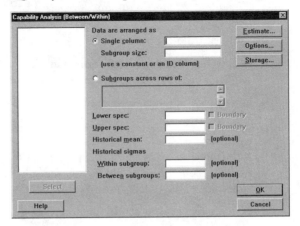

2 Do one of the following:

■ When subgroups are in one column, enter the data column in **Single column**. In **Subgroup size**, enter a subgroup size or column of subgroup indicators.

■ When subgroups are in rows, choose **Subgroups across rows of**, and enter the columns containing the rows in the box.

3 In **Lower spec** or **Upper spec**, enter a lower and/or upper specification limit, respectively. You must enter at least one of them.

4 If you like, use any of the options listed below, then click **OK**.

Options

Capability Analysis (Between/Within) dialog box

■ define the upper and lower specification limits as "boundaries," meaning measurements cannot fall outside those limits. As a result, the expected % out of spec is set to 0 for a boundary. If you choose a boundary, MINITAB does not calculate capability statistics for that side.

Note | When you define the upper and lower specification limits as boundaries, MINITAB still calculates the observed % out-of-spec. If the observed % out-of-spec comes up nonzero, this is an obvious indicator of incorrect data.

■ enter historical values for μ (the process mean) and σ within subgroups and/or σ between subgroups if you have known process parameters or estimates from past data. If you do not specify a value for μ or σ, MINITAB estimates them from the data.

Estimate subdialog box

- estimate the within and between standard deviations (σ) various ways—see *Estimating the process variation* on page 14-17.

Options subdialog box

- use the Box-Cox power transformation when you have very skewed data—see *Use the Box-Cox power transformation for non-normal data* on page 12-68.

- enter a process target, or nominal specifications. MINITAB calculates Cpm in addition to the standard capability statistics.

- calculate the capability statistics using an interval other than six standard deviations wide (three on either side of the process mean) by entering a sigma tolerance. For example, entering 12 says to use an interval 12 standard deviations wide, six on either side of the process mean.

- perform the between/within subgroup analysis only, or the overall analysis only. The default is to perform both.

- display observed performance, expected "between/within" performance, and expected "overall" performance in percents or parts per million. The default is parts per million.

- display the capability analysis graph or not. The default is to display the graph.

- enter a minimum and/or maximum scale to appear on the capability histogram.

- replace the default graph title with your own title.

Storage subdialog box

- store your choice of statistics in worksheet columns. The statistics available for storage depend on the options you have chosen in the Capability Analysis (Between/Within) dialog box and subdialog boxes.

Capability statistics

When you use Capability Analysis (Between/Within), MINITAB calculates both overall capability statistics (Pp, Ppk, PPU, and PPL) and between/within capability statistics (Cp, Cpk, CPU, and CPL). To interpret these statistics, see *Capability statistics* on page 14-4.

Cp, Cpk, CPU, and CPL represents the potential capability of your process—what your process would be capable of if the process did not have shifts and drifts in the subgroup means. To calculate these, Minitab estimates σ_{within} and $\sigma_{between}$ and pools them to estimate σ_{total}. Then, σ_{total} is used to calculate the capability statistics.

Pp, Ppk, PPU, and PPL represent the *overall* capability of the process. When calculating these statistics, MINITAB estimates $\sigma_{overall}$ considering the variation for the whole study.

Estimating the process variation

An important step in a capability analysis with normal data is estimating the process variation using the standard deviation, sigma (σ). Both Capability Analysis (Between/Within) and Capability Sixpack (Between/Within) calculate within, between, total (between/within), and overall variation. The capability statistics associated with total variation are Cp, Cpk, CPU, and CPL. The statistics associated with overall variation are Pp, Ppk, PPU, and PPL.

To calculate $\sigma_{overall}$, MINITAB uses the standard deviation of all of the data.

To calculate σ_{within} and $\sigma_{between}$, MINITAB provides several options, which are listed below. For a discussion of the relative merits of these methods, see [1].

To calculate σ_{total}, MINITAB pools σ_{within} and $\sigma_{between}$.

For the formulas used to estimate the process standard deviations (σ), see Help.

▶ **To specify methods for estimating σ_{within} and $\sigma_{between}$**

1   In the Capability Analysis (Between/Within) or Capability Sixpack (Between/Within) main dialog box, click **Estimate**.

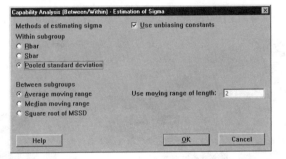

2   To change the method for estimating σ_{within}, choose one of the following:

- the average of the subgroup ranges—choose **Rbar**.

- the average of the subgroup standard deviations—choose **Sbar**. To not use an unbiasing constant in the estimation, uncheck **Use unbiasing constants**.

- the pooled standard deviation (the default)—choose **Pooled standard deviation**. To not use an unbiasing constant in the estimation, uncheck **Use unbiasing constants**.

3   To change the method for estimating $\sigma_{between}$, choose one of the following:

- the average of the moving range (the default)—choose **Average moving range**. To change the length of the moving range from 2, check **Use moving range of length** and enter a number in the box.

■ the median of the moving range—choose **Median moving range**. To change the length of the moving range from 2, check **Use moving range of length** and enter a number in the box.

■ the square root of MSSD (mean of the squared successive differences)—choose **Square root of MSSD**. To not use an unbiasing constant in the estimation, uncheck **Use unbiasing constants**.

4 Click **OK**.

▷ Example of a capability analysis (between/within)

Suppose you are interested in the capability of a process that coats rolls of paper with a thin film. You are concerned that the paper is being coated with the correct thickness of film and that the coating is applied evenly throughout the roll. You take three samples from 25 consecutive rolls and measure coating thickness. The thickness must be 50 ±3 to meet engineering specifications.

1 Open the worksheet BWCAPA.MTW.

2 Choose **Stat ➤ Quality Tools ➤ Capability Analysis (Between/Within)**.

3 In **Single column**, enter *Coating*. In **Subgroup size**, enter *Roll*.

4 In **Lower spec**, enter *47*. In **Upper spec**, enter *53*. Click **OK**.

Graph window output

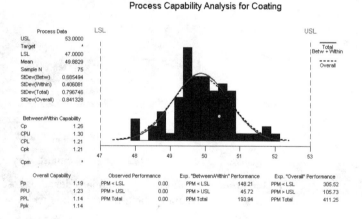

Process Capability Analysis for Coating

Process Data	
USL	53.0000
Target	*
LSL	47.0000
Mean	49.8829
Sample N	75
StDev(Betw)	0.685494
StDev(Within)	0.406081
StDev(Total)	0.796746
StDev(Overall)	0.841328

Between/Within Capability	
Cp	1.26
CPU	1.30
CPL	1.21
Cpk	1.21
Cpm	*

Overall Capability	
Pp	1.19
PPU	1.23
PPL	1.14
Ppk	1.14

Observed Performance	
PPM < LSL	0.00
PPM > USL	0.00
PPM Total	0.00

Exp. "Between/Within" Performance	
PPM < LSL	148.21
PPM > USL	45.72
PPM Total	193.94

Exp. "Overall" Performance	
PPM < LSL	305.52
PPM > USL	105.73
PPM Total	411.25

Interpreting results

You can see that the process mean (49.8829) falls close to the target of 50. The Cpk index indicates whether the process will produce units within the tolerance limits. The Cpk index is only 1.21, indicating that the process is fairly capable, but could be improved.

The PPM Total for Expected "Between/Within" Performance is 193.94. This means that approximately 194 out of a million coatings will not meet the specification limits. This analysis tells you that your process is fairly capable.

Capability Analysis (Weibull Distribution)

Use the Capability Analysis (Weibull) command to produce a process capability report when your data are from a Weibull distribution. The report includes a capability histogram overlaid with a Weibull curve and a table of overall capability statistics. The Weibull curve is generated from the process shape and scale.

The report also includes statistics of the process data, such as the mean, shape, scale, target (if you enter one), and process specifications; the actual overall capability; and the observed and expected overall performance. The report can be used to visually assess the distribution of the process relative to the target, whether the data follow a Weibull distribution, and whether the process is capable of meeting the specifications consistently.

When using the Weibull model, MINITAB calculates the overall capability statistics, Pp, Ppk, PPU, and PPL. The calculations are based on maximum likelihood estimates of the shape and scale parameters for the Weibull distribution, rather than mean and variance estimates as in the normal case. If you have data that do not follow a normal distribution, and you want to calculate the within capability statistics, Cp and Cpk, use *Capability Analysis (Normal Distribution)* on page 14-6 with the optional Box-Cox power transformation. For a comparison of the methods used for non-normal data, see *Non-normal data* on page 14-6.

Data

You can enter your data in a single column or in multiple columns if you have arranged subgroups across rows. Because the Weibull capability analysis does not calculate within capability statistics, MINITAB does not used subgroups in calculations. For examples, see *Data* on page 12-3.

Data must be positive.

If an observation is missing, MINITAB omits it from the calculations.

▶ **To perform a capability analysis (Weibull probability model)**

1 Choose **Stat ➤ Quality Tools ➤ Capability Analysis (Weibull)**.

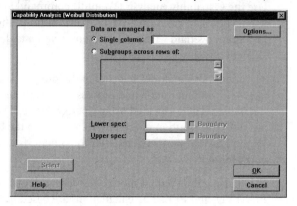

2 Do one of the following:

- When subgroups or individual observations are in one column, choose **Single column** and enter the column containing the data.

- When subgroups are in rows, choose **Subgroups across rows of**, and enter the columns containing the rows in the box.

3 In **Lower spec** or **Upper spec**, enter a lower and/or upper specification limit, respectively. You must enter at least one of them. These limits must be positive numbers, though the lower spec can be 0.

4 If you like, use any of the options listed below, then click **OK**.

Options

Capability Analysis (Weibull) dialog box

- define the upper and lower specification limits as "boundaries," meaning that it is impossible for a measurement to fall outside that limit. As a result, when calculating the expected % out-of-spec, MINITAB sets this value to 0 for a boundary.

Note │ When you define the upper or lower specification limits as boundaries, MINITAB still
        │ calculates the observed % out-of-spec. If the observed % out-of-spec comes up nonzero,
        │ this is an obvious indicator of incorrect data.

Options subdialog box

- enter historical values for the Weibull shape and scale parameters—see *Weibull family of distributions* on page 14-21.

- enter a process target or nominal specification. MINITAB calculates Cpm in addition to the standard capability statistics.

- calculate the capability statistics using an interval other than six standard deviations wide (three on either side of the process mean) by entering a sigma tolerance. For example, entering 12 says to use an interval 12 standard deviations wide, six on either side of the process mean.

- replace the default graph title with your own title.

Capability statistics

When you use the Weibull model for the capability analysis, MINITAB only calculates the overall capability statistics, Pp, Ppk, PPU, and PPL. The calculations are based on maximum likelihood estimates of the shape and scale parameters for the Weibull distribution, rather than mean and variance estimates as in the normal case.

To interpret these statistics, see *Capability statistics* on page 14-4.

Pp, Ppk, PPU, and PPL represent the *overall* capability of the process. When calculating these statistics, MINITAB estimates $\sigma_{overall}$ considering the variation for the whole study.

Weibull family of distributions

The Weibull distribution is actually a family of distributions, including such distributions as the exponential and Rayleigh. Its defining parameters are the shape (β) and scale (δ). The appearance of the distribution varies widely, depending on the size of β. A $\beta = 1$, for instance, gives an exponential distribution; a $\beta = 2$ gives a Rayleigh distribution.

If you like, you can enter historical values for the shape and scale. If you do not enter historical values, MINITAB obtains maximum likelihood estimates from the data.

Caution | Because the shape and scale parameters define the properties of the Weibull distribution, they also define the probabilities used to calculate the capability statistics. If you enter "known" values for the parameters, keep in mind that small changes in the parameters, especially the shape, can have large effects on the associated probabilities.

▶ **To enter historical values for the shape and scale parameters**

1 In the Capability Analysis (Weibull) or Capability Sixpack (Weibull) main dialog box, click **Options**.

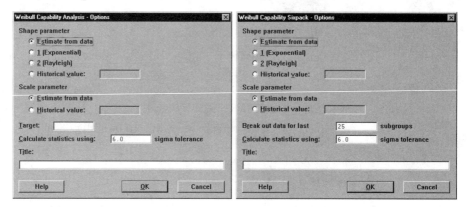

2 Under **Shape parameter**, choose one of the following:

- 1 (Exponential)

- 2 (Rayleigh)

- **Historical value,** and enter a positive value in the box

3 In **Scale parameter**, choose **Historical value**, and enter a positive value for the scale. Click **OK**.

▷ **Example of a capability analysis (Weibull probability model)**

Suppose you work for a company that manufactures floor tiles, and are concerned about warping in the tiles. To ensure production quality, you measured warping in ten tiles each working day for ten days.

A histogram of the data showed that it did not come from a normal distribution — see *Example of a capability analysis with a Box-Cox transformation* on page 14-12. So you decide to perform a capability analysis based on a Weibull probability model.

1 Open the worksheet TILES.MTW.

2 Choose **Stat ➤ Quality Tools ➤ Capability Analysis (Weibull)**.

3 In **Single column**, enter *Warping*.

4 In **Upper spec**, type 8. Click **OK**.

*Graph
window
output*

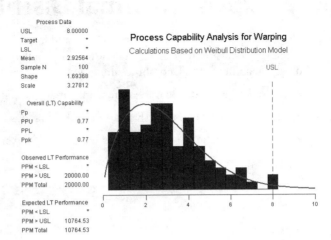

Process Data	
USL	8.00000
Target	*
LSL	*
Mean	2.92564
Sample N	100
Shape	1.69368
Scale	3.27812

Overall (LT) Capability

Pp	*
PPU	0.77
PPL	*
Ppk	0.77

Observed LT Performance

PPM < LSL	*
PPM > USL	20000.00
PPM Total	20000.00

Expected LT Performance

PPM < LSL	*
PPM > USL	10764.53
PPM Total	10764.53

Process Capability Analysis for Warping
Calculations Based on Weibull Distribution Model

Interpreting the results

The capability histogram does not show evidence of any serious discrepancies between the assumed model and the data.

But you can see that the right tail of the distribution falls over the upper specification limit. This means you will sometimes see warping higher than the upper specification of 8 mm.

The Ppk and PPU indices tell you whether the process will produce tiles within the tolerance limits. Both indices are 0.77, below the guideline of 1.33. Thus, your process does not appear to be capable.

Likewise, the PPM > USL—the number of parts per million above the upper spec—is 20000.00. This means that 20,000 out of a million tiles will warp more than the upper specification of 8 mm.

To see the same data analyzed with Capability Analysis (Normal), see *Example of a capability analysis with a Box-Cox transformation* on page 14-12.

Capability Sixpack (Normal Distribution)

Use the Capability Sixpack (Normal) command to assess process capability in a glance when your data are from the normal distribution or you have Box-Cox transformed data. Capability Sixpack combines the following information into a single display:

- an $\bar{X}$ chart (or Individuals chart for individual observations)
- an R chart or S chart (or MR chart for individual observations)
- a run chart of the last 25 subgroups (or last 25 observations)
- a histogram of the process data
- a normal probability plot
- a process capability plot
- within and overall capability statistics: Cp, Cpk, Cpm (if you enter a target), and σ_{within}; Pp, Ppk, and $\sigma_{overall}$

The $\bar{X}$, R, and run charts can be used to verify that the process is in a state of control. The histogram and normal probability plot can be used to verify that the data are normally distributed. Lastly, the capability plot gives a graphical view of the process variability compared to the specifications. Combined with the capability statistics, this information can help you assess whether your process is in control and the product meets specifications.

A model that assumes the data are from a normal distribution suits most process data. If your data are either very skewed or the within-subgroup variation is not constant (for example, when this variation is proportional to the mean), see the discussion under *Non-normal data* on page 14-6.

Data

You can enter individual observations or data in subgroups. Individual observations should be structured in one column. Subgroup data can be structured in one column, or in rows across several columns. When you have subgroups of unequal size, enter the subgroups in a single column, then set up a second column of subgroup indicators. For examples, see *Data* on page 12-3.

To use the Box-Cox transformation, data must be positive.

If you have data in subgroups, you must have two or more observations in at least one subgroup in order to estimate the process standard deviation. Subgroups need not be the same size.

If a single observation in the subgroup is missing, MINITAB omits it from the calculations of the statistics for that subgroup. Such an omission may cause the control chart limits and the center line to have different values for that subgroup. If an entire subgroup is missing, there is a gap in the chart where the statistic for that subgroup would have been plotted.

▶ **To make a capability sixpack (normal probability model)**

1 Choose Stat ➤ Quality Tools ➤ Capability Sixpack (Normal).

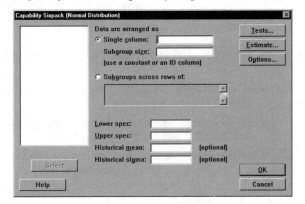

2 Do one of the following:

- When subgroups or individual observations are in one column, enter the data column in **Single column**. In **Subgroup size**, enter a subgroup size or column of subgroup indicators. For individual observations, enter a subgroup size of 1.

- When subgroups are in rows, choose **Subgroups across rows of**, and enter the columns containing the rows in the box.

3 In **Lower spec** or **Upper spec**, enter a lower and/or upper specification limit, respectively. You must enter at least one of them.

4 If you like, use any of the options listed below, then click **OK**.

Options

Capability Sixpack (Normal) dialog box

- enter your own value for μ (the process mean) and σ (the process potential standard deviation) if you have known process parameters or estimates from past data. If you do not specify a value for μ or σ, MINITAB estimates them from the data.

Tests subdialog box

- do your choice of eight tests for special causes—see *Do tests for special causes* on page 12-64. To adjust the sensitivity of the tests, use *Defining Tests for Special Causes* on page 12-5.

Estimate subdialog box

- estimate the process standard deviation (σ) various ways — see *Estimating the process variation* on page 14-10. The default estimate of σ is based on a pooled standard deviation.

Note

- When you estimate σ using the average of subgroup ranges (Rbar), MINITAB displays an R chart.
- When you estimate σ using the average of subgroup standard deviations (Sbar), MINITAB displays an S chart.
- When you estimate σ using the pooled standard deviation and your subgroup size is less than ten, MINITAB displays an R chart.
- When you estimate σ using the pooled standard deviation and your subgroup size is ten or greater, MINITAB displays an S chart.

Options subdialog box

- use the Box-Cox power transformation when you have very skewed data — see *Use the Box-Cox power transformation for non-normal data* on page 12-68.

- change the number of subgroups or observations to display in the run chart. The default is 25.

- enter the process target or nominal specification. MINITAB calculates Cpm in addition to the standard capability statistics.

- calculate the capability statistics using an interval other than six standard deviations wide (three on either side of the process mean) by entering a sigma tolerance. For example, entering 12 says to use an interval 12 standard deviations wide, six on either side of the process mean.

- replace the default graph title with your own title.

Capability statistics

Capability Sixpack (Normal) displays both the within and overall capability statistics, Cp, Cpk, Cpm (if you specify a target), and σ_{within}, and Pp, Ppk, and $\sigma_{overall}$. To interpret these statistics, see *Capability statistics* on page 14-4.

Cp, Cpk, CPU, and CPL represents the potential capability of your process — what your process would be capable of if the process did not have shifts and drifts in the subgroup means. To calculate these, Minitab estimates σ_{within} considering the variation within subgroups, but not the shift and drift between subgroups.

Pp, Ppk, PPU, and PPL represent the *overall* capability of the process. When calculating these statistics, MINITAB estimates $\sigma_{overall}$ considering the variation for the whole study.

► **Example of a capability sixpack (normal probability model)**

Suppose you work at an automobile manufacturer in a department that assembles engines. One of the parts, a camshaft, must be 600 mm ±2 mm long to meet engineering specifications. There has been a chronic problem with camshaft lengths being out of specification—a problem which has caused poor-fitting assemblies down the production line and high scrap and rework rates.

Upon examination of the inventory records, you discovered that there were two suppliers for the camshafts. An X̄ and R chart showed you that Supplier 2's camshaft production was out of control, so you decided to stop accepting production runs from them until they get their production under control.

After dropping Supplier 2, the number of poor quality assemblies have dropped significantly, but the problems have not completely disappeared. You decide to run a capability sixpack to see whether Supplier 1 alone is capable of meeting your engineering specifications.

1   Open the worksheet CAMSHAFT.MTW.

2   Choose **Stat ➤ Quality Tools ➤ Capability Sixpack (Normal)**.

3   In **Single column**, enter *Supp1*. In **Subgroup size**, enter 5.

4   In **Lower spec**, enter 598. In **Upper spec**, enter 602. Click **OK**.

Graph window output

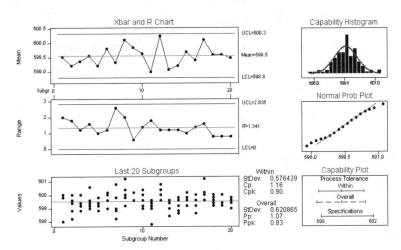

Process Capability Sixpack for Supp1

Interpreting the results

On both the X̄ chart and the R chart, the points are randomly distributed between the control limits, implying a stable process. It is also important to compare points on the R chart with those on the X̄ chart to see if the points follow each other. Yours do not, again, implying a stable process.

The points on the run chart make a random horizontal scatter, with no trends or shifts—also indicating process stability.

If you want to interpret the process capability statistics, your data should approximately follow a normal distribution. On the capability histogram, the data approximately follow the normal curve. On the normal probability plot, the points approximately follow a straight line. These patterns indicate that the data are normally distributed.

But from the capability plot, you can see that the process tolerance falls below the lower specification limit. This means you will sometimes see camshafts that do not meet the lower specification of 598 mm. Also, the values of Cp (1.16) and Cpk (0.90) are below the guideline of 1.33, indicating that Supplier 1 needs to improve their process.

Example of a capability sixpack with a Box-Cox tranformation

Suppose you work for a company that manufactures floor tiles, and are concerned about warping in the tiles. To ensure production quality, you measure warping in ten tiles each working day for ten days.

From previous analyses, you found that the tile data do not come from a normal distribution, and that a Box-Cox transformation using a lambda value of 0.5 makes the data "more normal." For details, see *Example of a capability analysis with a Box-Cox transformation* on page 14-12.

So you will run the capability sixpack using a Box-Cox transformation on the data.

1 Open the worksheet TILES.MTW.

2 Choose **Stat ➤ Quality Tools ➤ Capability Sixpack (Normal)**.

3 In **Single column**, enter *Warping*. In **Subgroup size**, type *10*.

4 In **Upper spec**, type *8*.

5 Click **Options**.

6 Check **Box-Cox power transformation (W = Y**Lambda)**. Choose **Lambda = 0.5 (square root)**. Click **OK** in each dialog box.

*Graph
window
output*

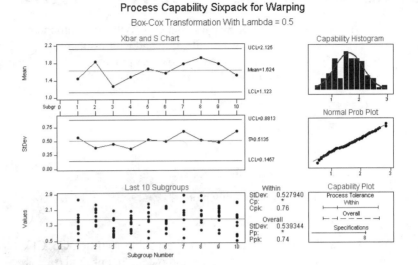

Interpreting the results

On both the X̄ chart and the R chart, the points are randomly distributed between the control limits, implying a stable process. It is also important to compare points on the R chart with those on the X̄ chart for the same data to see if the points follow each other. Yours do not—again, implying a stable process.

The points on the run chart make a random horizontal scatter, with no trends or shifts—also indicating process stability.

As you can see from the capability histogram, the data follow the normal curve. Also, on the normal probability plot, the points approximately follow a straight line. These patterns indicate that the Box-Cox transformation "normalized" the data. Now the process capability statistics are appropriate for this data.

The capability plot, however, shows that the process is not meeting specifications. And the values of Cpk (0.76) and Ppk (0.75) fall below the guideline of 1.33, so your process does not appear to be capable.

Capability Sixpack (Between/Within)

Use the Capability Sixpack (Between/Within) command when you suspect that you may have both between-subgroup and within-subgroup variation. Capability Sixpack (Between/Within) allows you to assess process capability at a glance and combines the following information into a single display:

- an Individuals chart
- a Moving Range chart
- an R chart or S chart
- a histogram of the process data
- a normal probability plot
- a process capability plot
- between/within and overall capability statistics; Cp, Cpk, Cpm (if you specify a target), σ_{within}, $\sigma_{between}$, and σ_{total}; Pp, Ppk, and $\sigma_{overall}$.

The Individuals, Moving Range, and R or S charts can verify whether or not the process is in control. The histogram and normal probability plot can verify whether or not the data are normally distributed. Lastly, the capability plot gives a graphical view of the process variability compared to specifications. Combined with the capability statistics, this information can help you assess whether your process is in control and the product meets specifications.

A model that assumes that the data are from a normal distribution suits most process data. If your data are either very skewed or the within subgroup variation is not constant (for example, when the variation is proportional to the mean), see the discussion under *Non-normal data* on page 14-6.

Data

You can enter data in subgroups, with two or more observations per subgroup. Subgroup data can be structured in one column or in rows across several columns.

To use the Box-Cox transformation, data must be positive.

Ideally, all subgroups should be the same size. If your subgroups are not all the same size, due to missing data or unequal sample sizes, only subgroups of the majority size are used for estimating the between-subgroup variation. Control limits for the Individuals and Moving Range charts are based on the majority subgroup size.

▶ **To make a capability sixpack (between/within)**

1 Choose Stat ➤ Quality Tools ➤ Capability Sixpack (Between/Within).

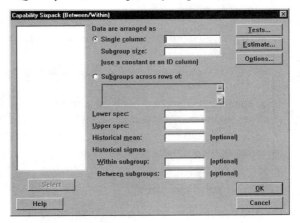

2 Do one of the following:

■ When subgroups are in one column, enter the data column in **Single column**. In **Subgroup size**, enter a subgroup size or column of subgroup indicators.

■ When subgroups are in rows, choose **Subgroups across rows of**, and enter the columns containing the rows in the box.

3 In **Lower spec** or **Upper spec**, enter a lower and/or upper specification limit, respectively. You must enter at least one of them.

4 If you like, use any of the options listed below, then click **OK**.

Options

Capability Sixpack (Between/Within) dialog box

■ enter a historical value for μ (the process mean) and/or σ (within-subgroup and/or between-subgroup standard deviations) if you have known process parameters or estimates from past data. If you do not specify a value for μ or σ, MINITAB estimates them from the data.

Tests subdialog box

■ do your choice of the eight tests for special causes—see *Do tests for special causes* on page 12-64. To adjust the sensitivity of the tests, use *Defining Tests for Special Causes* on page 12-5.

Estimate subdialog box

- estimate the process standard deviation (σ) various ways—see *Estimating the process variation* on page 14-17.

Note

- When you estimate σ using the average of subgroup ranges (Rbar), MINITAB displays an R chart.
- When you estimate σ using the average of subgroup standard deviations (Sbar), MINITAB displays an S chart.
- When you estimate σ using the pooled standard deviation and your subgroup size is less than ten, MINITAB displays an R chart.
- When you estimate σ using the pooled standard deviation and your subgroup size is ten or greater, MINITAB displays an S chart.

Options subdialog box

- use the Box-Cox power transformation when you have very skewed data—see *Non-normal data* on page 14-6.

- enter the process target or nominal specification. MINITAB calculates Cpm in addition to the standard capability statistics.

- calculate the capability statistics using an interval other than six standard deviations wide (three on either side of the process mean) by entering a sigma tolerance. For example, entering 12 says to use an interval 12 standard deviations wide, six on either side of the process mean.

- replace the default graph title with your own title.

Capability statistics

When you use Capability Analysis (Between/Within), MINITAB calculates both overall capability statistics (Pp, Ppk, PPU, and PPL) and between/within capability statistics (Cp, Cpk, CPU, and CPL). To interpret these statistics, see *Capability statistics* on page 14-4.

▷ Example of a capability sixpack (between/within)

Suppose you are interested in the capability of a process that coats rolls of paper with a thin film. You are concerned that the paper is being coated with the correct thickness of film and that the coating is applied evenly throughout the roll. You take three samples from 25 consecutive rolls and measure coating thickness. The thickness must be 50 ±3 to meet engineering specifications.

Because you are interested in determining whether or not the coating is even throughout a roll, you use MINITAB to conduct a Capability Sixpack (Between/Within).

1 Open the worksheet BWCAPA.MTW.

2 Select **Stat ➤ Quality Tools ➤ Capability Sixpack (Between/Within)**.

3 In **Single column**, enter *Coating*. In **Subgroup size**, enter *Roll*.

4 In **Lower spec**, enter 47. In **Upper spec**, enter 53.

5 Click **Tests**. Choose **Perform all eight tests**. Click **OK** in each dialog box.

Graph window output

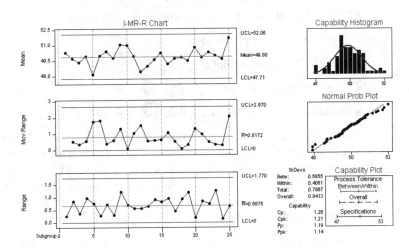

Process Capability Sixpack for Coating

Interpreting results

If you want to interpret the process capability statistics, your data need to come from a normal distribution. This criteria appears to have been met. In the capability histogram, the data approximately follow the normal curve. Also, on the normal probability plot, the points approximately follow a straight line.

No points failed the eight tests for special causes, thereby implying that your process is in control. The points on the Individuals and Moving Range chart do not appear to follow each other, again indicating a stable process.

The capability plot shows that the process is meeting specifications. The values of Cpk (1.21) and Ppk (1.14) fall just below the guideline of 1.33, so your process could use some improvement.

Capability Sixpack (Weibull Distribution)

When a Weibull distribution is a good approximation of the distribution of your process data, you can use the Capability Sixpack (Weibull) command to assess process capability in a glance. Capability Sixpack (Weibull) combines the following information into a single display:

- an $\bar{X}$ chart (or I chart for individual observations)

- an R chart (or MR chart for individual observations)

- a run chart of the last 25 subgroups (or last 25 observations)

- a histogram of the process data

- a Weibull probability plot

- a process capability plot

- overall capability statistics Pp, Ppk, shape (β), and scale (δ)

The $\bar{X}$, R, and run charts can be used to verify that the process is in a state of control. The histogram and Weibull probability plot can be used to verify that the data approximate a Weibull distribution. Lastly, the capability plot gives a graphical view of the process variability compared to the specifications. Combined with the capability statistics, this information can help you assess whether your process is in control and can produce output that consistently meets the specifications.

When using the Weibull model, MINITAB only calculates the overall capability statistics, Pp and Ppk. The calculations are based on maximum likelihood estimates of the shape and scale parameters for the Weibull distribution, rather than mean and variance estimates as in the normal case. If you have data that do not follow a normal distribution, and you want to calculate the within statistics (Cp, Cpk, σ_{within}), see *Capability Analysis (Normal Distribution)* on page 14-6 with the optional Box-Cox power transformation. For a comparison of the methods used for non-normal data, see *Non-normal data* on page 14-6.

Tip | To make a control chart that you can interpret properly, your data must follow a normal distribution. If the Weibull distribution fits your data well, a lognormal distribution would probably also provide a good fit. To transform your data, use the control chart command with the optional Box-Cox transformation, entering Lambda = 0(natural log). For more details, see *Use the Box-Cox power transformation for non-normal data* on page 12-68.

Data

You can enter individual observations or data in subgroups. Individual observations should be structured in one column. Subgroup data can be structured in one column or in rows across several columns. When you have subgroups of unequal size, enter the subgroups in a single column, then set up a second column of subgroup indicators. For examples, see *Data* on page 12-3.

Data must be positive.

If a single observation in the subgroup is missing, MINITAB omits it from the calculations of the statistics for that subgroup. This may cause the control chart limits and the center line to have different values for that subgroup. If an entire subgroup is missing, there is a gap in the chart where the statistic for that subgroup would have been plotted.

▶ To make a capability sixpack (Weibull probability model)

1 Choose Stat ➤ Quality Tools ➤ Capability Sixpack (Weibull).

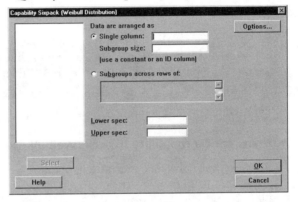

2 Do one of the following:

- When subgroups or individual observations are in one column, enter the data column in **Single column**. In **Subgroup size**, enter a subgroup size or column of subgroup indicators. For individual observations, enter a subgroup size of 1.

- When subgroups are in rows, choose **Subgroups across rows of**, and enter the columns containing the rows in the box.

3 In **Lower spec** or **Upper spec**, enter a lower and/or upper specification limit. You must enter at least one of them. These limits must be positive numbers, though the lower spec can be 0.

4 If you like, use any of the options listed below, then click **OK**.

Options

Options subdialog box

- enter your own value for the Weibull shape and scale parameters—see *Weibull family of distributions* on page 14-21. If you do not enter values, MINITAB obtains maximum likelihood estimates from the data.

Caution | When you enter "known" values for the parameters, keep in mind that small changes in the parameters, especially the shape, can have large effects on the associated probabilities.

- change the number of subgroups or observations to display in the run chart. The default is 25.

- calculate the capability statistics using an interval other than six standard deviations wide (three on either side of the process mean) by entering a sigma tolerance. For example, entering 12 says to use an interval 12 standard deviations wide, six on either side of the process mean.

- replace the default graph title with your own title.

Capability statistics

Capability Sixpack (Weibull) displays the overall capability statistics, Pp and Ppk. These calculations are based on maximum likelihood estimates of the shape and scale parameters for the Weibull distribution, rather than mean and variance estimates as in the normal case.

For information on interpreting these statistics, see *Capability statistics* on page 14-4.

▷ Example of a capability sixpack (Weibull probability model)

Suppose you work for a company that manufactures floor tiles, and are concerned about warping in the tiles. To ensure production quality, you measured warping in ten tiles each working day for ten days.

A histogram of the data revealed that it did not come from a normal distribution—see *Example of a capability analysis with a Box-Cox transformation* on page 14-12. So you decide to make a capability sixpack based on a Weibull probability model.

1 Open the worksheet TILES.MTW.

2 Choose **Stat ➤ Quality Tools ➤ Capability Sixpack (Weibull)**.

3 In **Single column**, enter *Warping*. In **Subgroup size**, type *10*.

4 In **Upper spec**, type 8. Click **OK**.

Graph window output

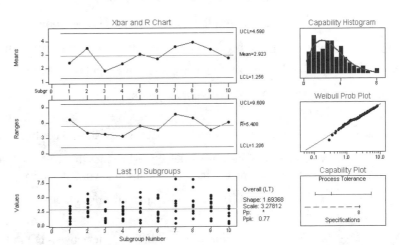

Process Capability Sixpack for Warping

Interpreting the results

The capability histogram does not show evidence of any serious discrepancies between the assumed model and the data. Also, on the Weibull probability plot, the points approximately follow a straight line.

The capability plot, however, shows that the process is not meeting specifications. And the value of Ppk (0.77) falls below the guideline of 1.33, so your process does not appear to be capable.

To see the same data analyzed with Capability Sixpack (Normal), see *Example of a capability sixpack with a Box-Cox tranformation* on page 14-28.

Capability Analysis (Binomial)

Use Capability Analysis (Binomial) to produce a process capability report when your data are from a binomial distribution. Binomial distributions are usually associated with recording the number of defective items out of the total number sampled.

For example, you might have a pass/fail gage that determines whether an item is defective or not. You could then record the total number of parts inspected and the number failed by the gage. Or, you could record the number of people who call in sick on a particular day and the number of people scheduled to work each day.

Use Capability Analysis (Binomial) if your data meet the following conditions:

- each item is the result of identical conditions
- each item can result in one or two possible outcomes (success/failure, go/no-go)
- the probability of a success (or failure) is constant for each item
- the outcomes of the items are independent of each other

Capability Analysis (Binomial) produces a process capability report that includes the following:

- **P chart**—verifies that the process is in a state of control
- **Chart of cumulative %defective**—verifies that you have collected data from enough samples to have a stable estimate of %defective
- **Histogram of %defective**—displays the overall distribution of the %defectives from the samples collected
- **Defective rate plot**—verifies that the %defective is not influenced by the number of items sampled

Data

Use data from a binomial distribution. Each entry in the worksheet column should contain the number of defectives for a subgroup. When subgroup sizes are unequal, you must also enter a corresponding column of subgroup sizes.

Suppose you have collected data on the number of parts inspected and the number of parts that failed inspection. On any given data, both numbers may vary. Enter the number that failed inspection in one column. If the total number inspected varies, enter subgroup size in another column:

Failed	Inspected
11	1003
12	968
9	897
13	1293
9	989
15	1423

Missing data

If an observation is missing, there is a gap in the P chart where that subgroup would have been plotted. The other plots and charts simply exclude the missing observations.

Unequal subgroup sizes

In the P chart, the control limits are a function of the subgroup size. In general, the control limits are further from the center line for smaller subgroups than they are for larger ones. When you do have unequal subgroup sizes, the plot of %defective versus sample size will permit you to verify that there is no relationship between the two. For example, if you tend to have a smaller %defective when more items are sampled, this could be caused by fatigued inspectors, a common problem. The subgroup size has no bearing on the other charts because they only display the %defective.

▶ **To perform a capability analysis (binomial probability model)**

1 Choose **Stat ➤ Quality Tools ➤ Capability Analysis (Binomial)**.

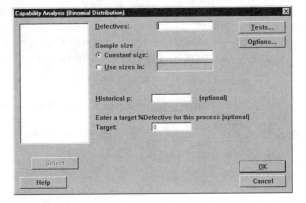

2 In **Defectives**, enter the column containing the number of defectives.

3 Do one of the following:

   ▪ When your sample size is constant, enter the sample size value in **Constant size**.

   ▪ When your sample sizes vary, enter the column containing sample sizes in **Use sizes in**.

4 If you like, use any of the options listed below, then click **OK**.

Options

Capability Analysis (binomial) dialog box

▪ enter a historical value for the proportion of defectives. This value must be between 0 and 1.

▪ enter a value for the % defective target.

Tests subdialog box

- perform your choice of the four tests for special causes—see *Do tests for special causes* on page 13-15. To adjust the sensitivity of the tests, use *Defining Tests for Special Causes* on page 12-5.

Options subdialog box

- choose a color scheme for printing.

- replace the default graph title with your own title.

▷ Example of capability analysis (binomial probability model)

Suppose you are responsible for evaluating the responsiveness of your telephone sales department, that is, how capable it is of answering incoming calls. You record the number of calls that were not answered (a defective) by sales representatives due to unavailability each day for 20 days. You also record the total number of incoming calls.

1 Open the worksheet BPCAPA.MTW.

2 Choose **Stat ➤ Quality Tools ➤ Capability Analysis (Binomial)**.

3 In **Defectives**, enter *Unavailable*.

4 In **Use sizes in**, enter *Calls*. Click **OK**.

Graph window output

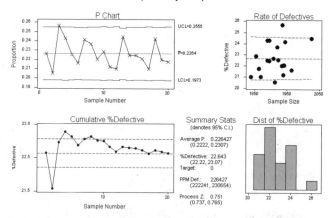

Interpreting results

The P chart indicates that there is one point out of control. The chart of cumulative %defect shows that the estimate of the overall defective rate appears to be settling down around 22%, but more data may need to be collected to verify this. The rate of defectives does not appear to be affected by sample size. The process Z is around 0.75, which is very poor. This process could use a lot of improvement.

Capability Analysis (Poisson)

Use Capability Analysis (Poisson) to produce a process capability report when your data are from a Poisson distribution. Poisson data is usually associated with the number of defects observed in an item, where the item occupies a specified amount of time or specified space. The size of the item may vary, so you may also keep track of the size.

For example, if you manufacture electrical wiring, you may want to record the number of breaks in a piece of wire. If the lengths of the wire vary, you will have to record the size of each piece sampled. Or, if you manufacture appliances, you may want to record the number of scratches on the surface of the appliance. Since the sizes of the surface may be different, you may also record the size of each surface sampled, say in square inches.

Use Capability Analysis (Poisson) when your data meet the following conditions:

- the rate of defects per unit of space or time is the same for each item

- the number of defects observed in the items are independent of each other

Capability Analysis (Poisson) produces a process capability report for data from a Poisson distribution. The report includes the following:

- **U chart**—verifies that the process was in a state of control at the time the report was generated

- **Chart of cumulative mean DPU (defects per unit)**—verifies that you have collected data from enough samples to have a stable estimate of the mean

- **Histogram of DPU**—displays the overall distribution of the defects per unit from the samples collected

- **Defect plot rate**—verifies that DPU is not influenced by the size of the items sampled

Data

Each entry in the worksheet column should contain the number of or defects for a subgroup. When subgroup sizes are unequal, you must also enter a corresponding column of subgroup sizes.

Suppose you have collected data on the number of defects per unit and the size of the unit. For any given unit, both numbers may vary. Enter the number of defects in one column. If the unit size varies, enter unit size in another column:

Failed	Inspected
3	89
4	94
7	121
2	43
11	142
6	103

Missing data

If an observation is missing, there is a gap in the U chart where the subgroup would have been plotted. The other plots and charts simply exclude the missing observation(s).

Unequal subgroup sizes

In the U chart, the control limits are a function of the subgroup size. In general, the control limits are further from the centerline for smaller subgroups than they are for larger ones. When you do have unequal subgroup sizes, the plot of defects per unit (DPU) versus sample size will permit you to verify that there is no relationship between the two. For example, if you tend to have a **smaller** DPU when more items are sampled, this could be caused by fatigued inspectors, a common problem. The subgroup size has no bearing on the other charts, because they only display the DPU.

▶ **To perform a capability analysis (Poisson distribution model)**

1 Choose **Stat ➤ Quality Tools ➤ Capability Analysis (Poisson)**.

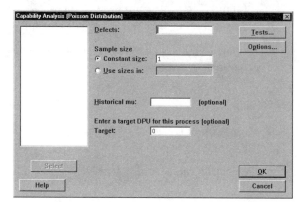

2 In **Defects**, enter the column containing the number of defects.

3 Do one of the following:

   ■ When your unit size is constant, enter the unit size value in **Constant size**.

   ■ When your unit sizes vary, enter the column containing unit sizes in **Use sizes in**.

4 If you like, use any of the options listed below, then click **OK**.

Options

Capability Analysis (Poisson) dialog box

- enter historical values for μ (the process mean) if you have known process parameters or estimates from past data. If you do not specify a value for μ, MINITAB estimates it from the data.

- enter a target DPU (defects per unit) for the process.

Tests subdialog box

- perform the four tests for special causes—see *Do tests for special causes* on page 13-15. To adjust the sensitivity of the tests, use *Defining Tests for Special Causes* on page 12-5.

Options subdialog box

- choose to use a full color, partial color, or black and white color scheme for printing.

- replace the default graph title with your own title.

▷ Example of capability analysis (Poisson probability distribution)

Suppose you work for a wire manufacturer and are concerned about the effectiveness of the wire insulation process. You take random lengths of electrical wiring and test them for weak spots in their insulation by subjecting them to a test voltage. You record the number of weak spots and the length of each piece of wire (in feet).

1 Open the worksheet BPCAPA.MTW.

2 Choose **Stat ➤ Quality Tools ➤ Capability Analysis (Poisson)**.

3 In **Defects**, enter *Weak Spots*.

4 In **Uses sizes in**, enter *Length*. Click **OK**.

Graph window output

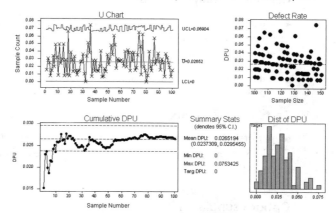

Poisson Process Capability Report for Weak Spots

Interpreting results

The U Chart indicates that there are three points out of control. The chart of cumulative mean DPU (defects per unit) has settled down around the value 0.0265, signifying that enough samples were collected to have a good estimate of the mean DPU. The rate of DPU does not appear to be affected by the lengths of the wire.

References

[1] L.K. Chan, S.W. Cheng, and F.A. Spiring (1988). "A New Measure of Process Capability: C_{pm}," *Journal of Quality Technology*, 20, July, pp.162–175.

[2] Y. Chou, D. Owen, S. Borrego (1990). "Lower Confidence Limits on Process Capability Indices," *Journal of Quality Technology*, 22, July, pp.223–229.

[3] Ford Motor Company (1983). *Continuing Process Control and Process Capability Improvement*, Ford Motor Company, Dearborn, Michigan.

[4] L.A. Franklin and G.S. Wasserman (1992). "Bootstrap Lower Confidence Limits for Capability Indices," *Journal of Quality Technology*, 24, October, pp.196–210.

[5] B. Gunter (1989). "The Use and Abuse of Cpk, Part 2," *Quality Progress*, 22, March, pp.108, 109.

[6] B. Gunter (1989). "The Use and Abuse of Cpk, Part 3," *Quality Progress*, 22, May, pp.79, 80.

[7] A.H. Jaehn (1989). "How to Estimate Percentage of Product Failing Specifications," *Tappi*,72, pp.227–228.

[8] V.E. Kane (1986). "Process Capability Indices," *Journal of Quality Technology*, 18, pp. 41–52.

[9] R.H. Kushler and P. Hurley (1992). "Confidence Bounds for Capability Indices," *Journal of Quality Technology*, 24, October, pp.188–195.

[10] W.L. Pearn, S. Kotz, and N.L. Johnson (1992). "Distributional and Inferential Properties of Process Capability Indices," *Journal of Quality Technology*, 24, October, pp. 216–231.

[11] R.N. Rodriguez (1992). "Recent Developments in Process Capability Analysis," *Journal of Quality Technology*, 24, October, pp.176–187.

[12] T.P. Ryan (1989). *Statistical Methods for Quality Improvement*, John Wiley & Sons.

[13] L.P. Sullivan (1984). "Reducing Variability: A New Approach to Quality," *Quality Progress*, July, 1984, pp.15– 21.

[14] H.M. Wadsworth, K.S. Stephens, and A.B. Godfrey (1986). *Modern Methods for Quality Control and Improvement*, John Wiley & Sons.

[15] Western Electric (1956). *Statistical Quality Control Handbook*, Western Electric Corporation, Indianapolis, Indiana.

part III

Reliability and Survival Analysis

15

Distribution Analysis

Distribution Analysis Overview

Use MINITAB's distribution analysis commands to understand the lifetime characteristics of a product, part, person, or organism. For instance, you might want to estimate how long a part is likely to last under different conditions, or how long a patient will survive after a certain type of surgery.

Your goal is to estimate the failure-time distribution of a product. You do this by estimating percentiles, survival probabilities, and distribution parameters and by drawing survival or hazard plots. You can use either parametric or nonparametric estimates. Parametric estimates are based on an assumed parametric distribution, while nonparametric estimates assume no parametric distribution.

Life data can be described using a variety of distributions. Once you have collected your data, you can use the commands in this chapter to select the best distribution to use for modeling your data, and then estimate the variety of functions that describe that distribution. These methods are called *parametric* because you assume the data follow a parametric distribution. If you cannot find a distribution that fits your data, MINITAB provides *nonparametric* estimates of the same functions.

Life data are often censored or incomplete in some way. Suppose you're testing how long a certain part lasts before wearing out and plan to cut off the study at a certain time. Any parts that did not fail before the study ended are censored, meaning their exact failure time is unknown. In this case, the failure is known only to be "on the right," or *after* the present time. This type of censoring is called right-censoring. Similarly, all you may know is that a part failed *before* a certain time (left-censoring), or *within* a certain interval of time (interval-censoring). When you know exactly when the part failed it is not censored, but is an exact failure.

Choosing a distribution analysis command

How do you know which distribution analysis command to use? You need to consider two things: 1) whether or not you can assume a parametric distribution for your data, and 2) the type of censoring you have.

- Use the **parametric distribution analysis** commands when you can assume your data follow a parametric distribution.

- Use the **nonparametric distribution analysis** commands when you cannot assume a parametric distribution.

Then, once you have decided which type of analysis to use, you need to choose whether you will use the right censoring or arbitrary censoring commands, which perform similar analyses.

- Use the **right-censoring** commands when you have exact failures and right-censored data.

■ Use the **arbitrary-censoring** commands when your data include both exact failures and a varied censoring scheme, including right-censoring, left-censoring, and interval-censoring.

For details on creating worksheets for censored data, see *Distribution Analysis Data* on page 15-5.

Parametric distribution analysis commands

All parametric distribution analysis commands in this chapter can be used for both right censored and arbitrarily censored data. The parametric distribution analysis commands include Parametric Distribution Analysis, which performs the full analysis, and the specialty graphs, Distribution ID Plot and Distribution Overview Plot. The specialty graphs are often used before the full analysis to help choose a distribution or view summary information.

■ **Distribution ID Plot—Right Censoring** and **Distribution ID Plot—Arbitrary Censoring** draw a layout of up to four probability plots, from your choice of eight common distributions: Weibull, extreme value, exponential, normal, lognormal base$_e$, lognormal base$_{10}$, logistic, and loglogistic. The layout helps you determine which, if any, of the parametric distributions best fits your data. See *Distribution ID Plot* on page 15-9.

■ **Distribution Overview Plot—Right Censoring** and **Distribution Overview Plot—Arbitrary Censoring** draw a probability plot, probability density function, survival plot, and hazard plot on one page. The layout helps you assess the fit of the chosen distribution and view summary graphs of your data. See *Distribution Overview Plot* on page 15-19.

■ **Parametric Distribution Analysis—Right Censoring** and **Parametric Distribution Analysis—Arbitrary Censoring** fit one of eight common parametric distributions to your data, then use that distribution to estimate percentiles and survival probabilities, and draw survival, hazard, and probability plots. See *Parametric Distribution Analysis* on page 15-27.

Nonparametric distribution analysis commands

The nonparametric distribution analysis commands include Nonparametric Distribution Analysis—Right Censoring and Nonparametric Distribution Analysis—Arbitrary Censoring, which perform the full analysis, and the specialty graph—Distribution Overview Plot—Right Censoring and Distribution Overview Plot—Arbitrary Censoring. Distribution Overview Plot is often used before the full analysis to view summary information.

■ **Distribution Overview Plot** (uncensored/right censored data only) draws a Kaplan-Meier survival plot and hazard plot, or an Actuarial survival plot and hazard plot, on one page. See *Distribution Overview Plot* on page 15-19.

- **Distribution Overview Plot** (uncensored/arbitrarily censored data only) draws a Turnbull survival plot or an Actuarial survival plot and hazard plot. See *Distribution Overview Plot* on page 15-19.

- **Nonparametric Distribution Analysis — Right Censoring** and **Nonparametric Distribution Analysis — Arbitrary Censoring** give you nonparametric estimates of the survival probabilities, hazard estimates, and other estimates depending on the nonparametric technique chosen, and draw survival and hazard plots. When you have multiple samples, Nonparametric Distribution Analysis — Right Censoring also tests the equality of their survival curves. See *Nonparametric Distribution Analysis* on page 15-52.

Estimation methods

As described above, MINITAB provides both parametric and nonparametric methods to estimate functions. If a parametric distribution fits your data, then use the parametric estimates. If no parametric distribution adequately fits your data, then use the nonparametric estimates.

For the parametric estimates in this chapter, you can choose either the maximum likelihood method or least squares approach. Nonparametric methods differ, depending on the type of censoring. For the formulas used, see Help.

Estimation methods

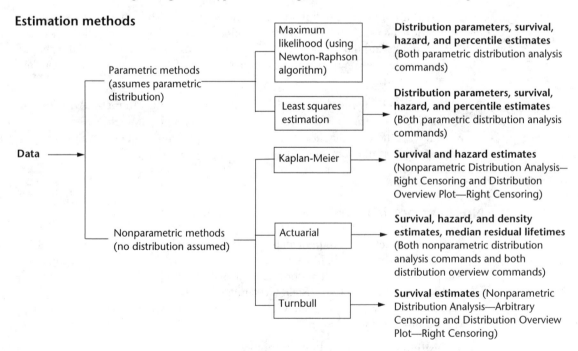

Distribution Analysis Data

The data you gather for the commands in this chapter are individual failure times. For example, you might collect failure times for units running at a given temperature. You might also collect samples of failure times under different temperatures, or under different combinations of stress variables.

Life data are often censored or incomplete in some way. Suppose you are monitoring air conditioner fans to find out the percentage of fans that fail within a three-year warranty period. This table describes the types of observations you can have:

Type of observation	Description	Example
Exact failure time	You know *exactly* when the failure occurred.	The fan failed at exactly 500 days.
Right censored	You only know that the failure occurred *after* a particular time.	The fan had not yet failed at 500 days.
Left censored	You only know that the failure occurred *before* a particular time.	The fan failed sometime before 500 days.
Interval censored	You only know that the failure occurred *between* two particular times.	The fan failed sometime between 475 and 500 days.

How you set up your worksheet depends, in part, on the type of censoring you have:

- when your data consist of exact failures and right-censored observations, see *Distribution analysis—right censored data* on page 15-5.

- when your data have exact failures and a varied censoring scheme, including right-censoring, left-censoring, and interval-censoring, see *Distribution analysis— arbitrarily censored data* on page 15-8.

Distribution analysis—right censored data

Right-censored data can be **singly** or **multiply censored**. Singly censored means that the censored items all ran for the same amount of time, and all of the exact failures occurred earlier than that censoring time. Multiply censored means that items were censored at different times, with failure times intermixed with those censoring times.

Multiply censored data are more common in the field, where units go into service at different times. Singly censored data are more common in controlled studies.

In these two examples, the Months column contains failure times, and the Censor column contains indicators that say whether that failure was censored (C) or an exact failure time (F):

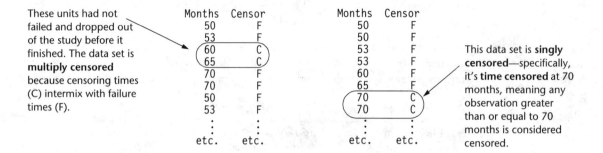

These units had not failed and dropped out of the study before it finished. The data set is **multiply censored** because censoring times (C) intermix with failure times (F).

This data set is **singly censored**—specifically, it's **time censored** at 70 months, meaning any observation greater than or equal to 70 months is considered censored.

Singly censored data can be either:

- **time censored**, meaning that you run the study for a specified period of *time*. All units still running at the end time are time censored. This is known as Type I censoring on the right.

- **failure censored**, meaning that you run the study until you observe a specified *number of failures*. All units running from the last specified failure onward are failure censored. This is known as Type II censoring on the right.

Worksheet structure

Do one of the following, depending on the type of censoring you have:

Singly censored data

- to use a constant *failure time* to define censoring, enter a column of failure times for each sample. Later, when executing the command, you will specify the failure time at which to begin censoring.

- to use a specified *number of failures* to define censoring, enter a column of failure times for each sample. Later, when executing the command, you will specify the number of failures at which to begin censoring.

Singly or multiply censored data

- to use censoring columns to define censoring, enter two columns for each sample — one column of failure times and a corresponding column of censoring indicators. You must use this method for multiply censored data.

  Censoring indicators can be numbers or text. If you don't specify which value indicates censoring in the Censor subdialog box, MINITAB assumes the lower of the two values indicates censoring, and the higher of the two values indicates an exact failure.

The data column and associated censoring column must be the same length, although pairs of data and censor columns (from different samples) can have different lengths.

This data set uses censoring columns:

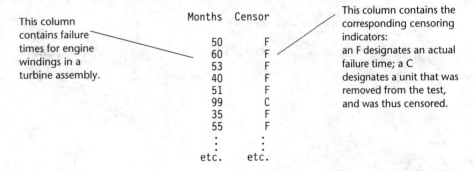

This column contains failure times for engine windings in a turbine assembly.

Months	Censor
50	F
60	F
53	F
40	F
51	F
99	C
35	F
55	F
⋮	⋮
etc.	etc.

This column contains the corresponding censoring indicators:
an F designates an actual failure time; a C designates a unit that was removed from the test, and was thus censored.

Using frequency columns

You can structure each column so that it contains individual observations (one row = one observation), as shown above, or unique observations with a corresponding column of frequencies (counts).

Here are the same data structured both ways:

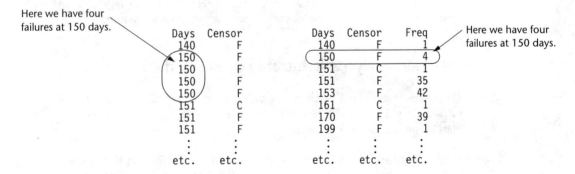

Here we have four failures at 150 days.

Days	Censor
140	F
150	F
150	F
150	F
150	F
151	C
151	F
151	F
⋮	⋮
etc.	etc.

Days	Censor	Freq
140	F	1
150	F	4
151	C	1
151	F	35
153	F	42
161	C	1
170	F	39
199	F	1
⋮	⋮	⋮
etc.	etc.	etc.

Here we have four failures at 150 days.

Frequency columns are useful for data where you have large numbers of observations with common failure and censoring times. For example, warranty data usually includes large numbers of observations with common censoring times.

Stacked vs. unstacked data

In the discussion so far, we have shown illustrations of unstacked data: that is, data from different samples are in separate columns. You can optionally stack all of the data in one column, then set up a column of grouping indicators. The grouping indicators define each sample. Grouping indicators, like censoring indicators, can be numbers or text.

Here is the same data set structured both ways:

Unstacked data			Stacked data	
Drug A	Drug B		Drug	Group
20	2		20	A
30	3		30	A
43	6		43	A
51	14		51	A
57	24		57	A
82	26		82	A
85	27		85	A
89	31		89	A
			2	B
			3	B
			6	B
			14	B
			24	B
			26	B
			27	B
			31	B

Note | You cannot analyze more than one column of stacked data per analysis. So when you use grouping indicators, the data for each sample must be in one column.

Distribution analysis—arbitrarily censored data

Arbitrarily-censored data includes exact failure times and a varied censoring scheme, including right, left, and interval censored data. Enter your data in table form, using a Start column and End column:

For this observation...	Enter in the Start column...	Enter in the End column...
Exact failure time	failure time	failure time
Right censored	time that the failure occurred after	the missing value symbol '*'
Left censored	the missing value symbol '*'	time that the failure occurred before
Interval censored	time at start of interval during which the failure occurred	time at end of interval during which the failure occurred

This data set illustrates tabled data, as well as the use of a frequency column. Frequency columns are described in *Using frequency columns* on page 15-7.

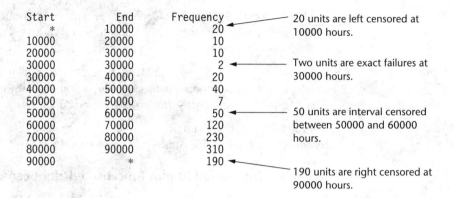

Start	End	Frequency
*	10000	20
10000	20000	10
20000	30000	10
30000	30000	2
30000	40000	20
40000	50000	40
50000	50000	7
50000	60000	50
60000	70000	120
70000	80000	230
80000	90000	310
90000	*	190

20 units are left censored at 10000 hours.

Two units are exact failures at 30000 hours.

50 units are interval censored between 50000 and 60000 hours.

190 units are right censored at 90000 hours.

When you have more than one sample, you can use separate columns for each sample. Alternatively, you can stack all of the samples in one column, then set up a column of grouping indicators. Grouping indicators can be numbers or text. For an illustration, see *Stacked vs. unstacked data* on page 15-8.

Distribution ID Plot

Use Distribution ID Plot to plot up to four different probability plots (with distributions chosen from Weibull, extreme value, exponential, normal, lognormal base$_e$, lognormal base$_{10}$, logistic, and loglogistic) to help you determine which of these distributions best fits your data. Usually this is done by comparing how closely the plot points lie to the best-fit lines—in particular those points in the tails of the distribution.

MINITAB also provides two goodness-of-fit tests—Anderson-Darling for the maximum likelihood and least squares estimation methods and Pearson correlation coefficient for the least squares estimation method—to help you assess how the distribution fits your data. See *Goodness-of-fit statistics* on page 15-13.

The data you gather are the individual failure times, which may be censored. For example, you might collect failure times for units running at a given temperature. You might also collect samples of failure times under different temperatures, or under varying conditions of any combination of stress variables.

You can display up to ten samples on each plot. All of the samples display on a single plot, in different colors and symbols.

For a discussion of probability plots, see *Probability plots* on page 15-37.

Data

Distribution ID Plot accepts different kinds of data:

- Distribution ID Plot—Right Censoring accepts exact failure times and right censored data. For information on how to set up your worksheet see *Distribution analysis—right censored data* on page 15-5.

- Distribution ID Plot—Arbitrary Censoring accepts exact failure times and right-, left-, and interval-censored data. For information on how to set up your worksheet see *Distribution analysis—arbitrarily censored data* on page 15-8.

You can enter up to ten samples per analysis. For general information on life data and censoring, see *Distribution Analysis Data* on page 15-5.

▶ To make a distribution ID plot (uncensored/right censored data)

1 Choose **Stat ➤ Reliability/Survival ➤ Distribution ID Plot–Right Cens**.

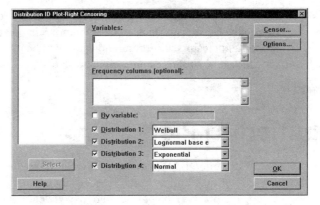

2 In **Variables**, enter the columns of failure times. You can enter up to ten columns (ten different samples).

3 If you have frequency columns, enter the columns in **Frequency columns**.

4 If all of the samples are stacked in one column, check **By variable**, and enter a column of grouping indicators in the box.

Note | If you have no censored values, you can skip steps 5 & 6.

5 Click **Censor**.

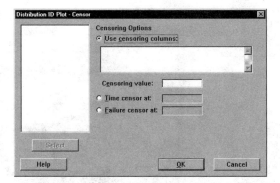

6 Do one of the following, then click **OK**.

- For data with censoring columns: Choose **Use censoring columns**, then enter
  the censoring columns in the box. The first censoring column is paired with the
  first data column, the second censoring column is paired with the second data
  column, and so on.

  If you like, enter the value you use to indicate censoring in **Censoring value**. If
  you do not enter a value, MINITAB uses the lowest value in the censoring
  column.

- For time censored data: Choose **Time censor at**, then enter a failure time at
  which to begin censoring. For example, entering *500* says that any observation
  from 500 time units onward is considered censored.

- For failure censored data: Choose **Failure censor at**, then enter a number of
  failures at which to begin censoring. For example, entering *150* says to censor all
  (ordered) observations from the 150th observed failure on, and leave all other
  observations uncensored.

7 If you like, use any of the options listed below, then click **OK**.

▶ **To make a distribution ID plot (arbitrarily censored data)**

    1 Choose **Stat ▶ Reliability/Survival ▶ Distribution ID Plot–Arbitrary Cens.**

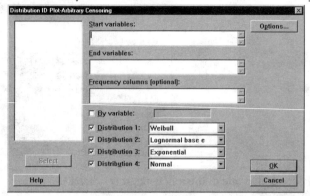

    2 In **Start variables**, enter the column of start times. You can enter up to ten columns (ten different samples).

    3 In **End variables**, enter the column of end times. You can enter up to ten columns (ten different samples). The first start column is paired with the first end column, the second start column is paired with the second end column, and so on.

    4 If you have frequency columns, enter the columns in **Frequency columns**.

    5 If all of the samples are stacked in one column, check **By variable**, and enter a column of grouping indicators in the box.

    6 If you like, use any of the options described below, then click **OK**.

Options

Distribution ID Plot dialog box

■ choose to create up to four probability plots. The default is to create four plots.

■ choose to fit up to four common lifetime distributions for the parametric analysis, including the Weibull, extreme value, exponential, normal, lognormal base$_e$, lognormal base$_{10}$, logistic, and loglogistic distributions. The four default distributions are Weibull, lognormal base$_e$, exponential, and normal.

More | MINITAB's extreme value distribution is the smallest extreme value (Type 1).

Options subdialog box

■ estimate parameters using the maximum likelihood (default) or least squares methods.

■ estimate percentiles for additional percents. The default is 1, 5, 10, and 50.

- obtain the plot points for the probability plot using various nonparametric methods—see *Probability plots* on page 15-37.
  - With Distribution ID Plot—Right Censoring, you can choose the Default method, Modified Kaplan-Meier method, Herd-Johnson method, or Kaplan-Meier method. The Default method is the normal score for uncensored data; the modified Kaplan-Meier method for censored data.
  - With Distribution ID Plot—Arbitrary Censoring, you can choose the Turnbull or Actuarial method. The Turnbull method is the default.
- (Distribution ID Plot—Right Censoring only) handle ties by plotting all of the points (default), the maximum of the tied points, or the average (median) of the tied points.
- enter minimum and/or maximum values for the x-axis scale.
- replace the default graph title with your own title.

Output

The default output consists of:

- goodness-of-fit statistics for the chosen distributions—see *Goodness-of-fit statistics* on page 15-13
- table of percents and their percentiles, standard errors, and 95% confidence intervals
- table of MTTFs (mean time to failures) and their standard errors and 95% confidence intervals
- four probability plots for the Weibull, lognormal base$_e$, exponential, and normal distributions

Goodness-of-fit statistics

MINITAB provides two goodness-of-fit statistics—Anderson-Darling for the maximum likelihood and least squares estimation methods and Pearson correlation coefficient for the least squares estimation method—to help you compare the fit of competing distributions.

The Anderson-Darling statistic is a measure of how far the plot points fall from the fitted line in a probability plot. The statistic is a weighted squared distance from the plot points to the fitted line with larger weights in the tails of the distribution. Minitab uses an adjusted Anderson-Darling statistic, because the statistic changes when a different plot point method is used. A smaller Anderson-Darling statistic indicates that the distribution fits the data better.

For least squares estimation, Minitab calculates a Pearson correlation coefficient. If the distribution fits the data well, then the plot points on a probability plot will fall on a straight line. The correlation measures the strength of the linear relationship between the X and Y variables on a probability plot. The correlation will range between 0 and 1, and higher values indicate a better fitting distribution.

Use the Anderson-Darling statistic and Pearson correlation coefficient to compare the fit of different distributions.

▷ **Example of a distribution ID plot for right-censored data**

Suppose you work for a company that manufactures engine windings for turbine assemblies. Engine windings may decompose at an unacceptable rate at high temperatures. You want to know—at given high temperatures—the time at which 1% of the engine windings fail. You plan to get this information by using the Parametric Distribution Analysis—Right Censoring command, which requires you to specify the distribution for your data. Distribution ID Plot—Right Censoring can help you choose that distribution.

First you collect failure times for the engine windings at two temperatures. In the first sample, you test 50 windings at 80° C; in the second sample, you test 40 windings at 100° C. Some of the units drop out of the test for unrelated reasons. In the MINITAB worksheet, you use a column of censoring indicators to designate which times are actual failures (1) and which are censored units removed from the test before failure (0).

1 Open the worksheet RELIABLE.MTW.

2 Choose **Stat ➤ Reliability/Survival ➤ Distribution ID Plot—Right Cens.**

3 In **Variables**, enter *Temp80 Temp100*.

4 Click **Censor**. Choose **Use censoring columns** and enter *Cens80 Cens100* in the box. Click **OK** in each dialog box.

Session window output

Distribution ID Plot

```
Variable:  Temp80

Goodness of Fit

Distribution         Anderson-Darling
Weibull              67.64
Lognormal base e     67.22
Exponential          70.33
Normal               67.73
```

Table of Percentiles

Distribution	Percent	Percentile	Standard Error	95.0% Normal CI Lower	CI Upper
Weibull	1	10.0765	2.78453	5.8626	17.3193
Lognormal base e	1	19.3281	2.83750	14.4953	25.7722
Exponential	1	0.8097	0.13312	0.5867	1.1176
Normal	1	-0.5493	8.37183	-16.9578	15.8592
Weibull	5	20.3592	3.79130	14.1335	29.3273
Lognormal base e	5	26.9212	3.02621	21.5978	33.5566
Exponential	5	4.1326	0.67939	2.9942	5.7037
Normal	5	18.2289	6.40367	5.6779	30.7798

------the rest of this table omitted for space-----

Table of MTTF

Distribution	Mean	Standard Error	95% Normal CI Lower	CI Upper
Weibull	64.9829	4.6102	56.5472	74.677
Lognormal base e	67.4153	5.5525	57.3656	79.225
Exponential	80.5676	13.2452	58.3746	111.198
Normal	63.5518	4.0694	55.5759	71.528

Variable: Temp100

Goodness of Fit

Distribution	Anderson-Darling
Weibull	16.60
Lognormal base e	16.50
Exponential	18.19
Normal	17.03

Table of Percentiles

Distribution	Percent	Percentile	Standard Error	95.0% Normal CI Lower	CI Upper
Weibull	1	2.9819	1.26067	1.3020	6.8290
Lognormal base e	1	6.8776	1.61698	4.3383	10.9034
Exponential	1	0.5025	0.08618	0.3591	0.7033
Normal	1	-18.8392	8.80960	-36.1057	-1.5727
Weibull	5	8.1711	2.36772	4.6306	14.4189
Lognormal base e	5	11.3181	2.07658	7.8995	16.2162
Exponential	5	2.5647	0.43984	1.8325	3.5893
Normal	5	-0.2984	6.86755	-13.7585	13.1618

-----the rest of this table omitted for space-----

Table of MTTF

Distribution	Mean	Standard Error	95% Normal CI Lower	Upper
Weibull	45.9448	4.87525	37.3177	56.5663
Lognormal base e	49.1969	6.91761	37.3465	64.8076
Exponential	50.0000	8.57493	35.7265	69.9761
Normal	44.4516	4.37371	35.8793	53.0240

Graph window output

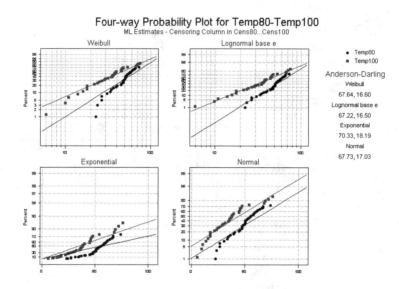

Interpreting the results

The points fall approximately on the straight line on the lognormal probability plot, so the lognormal base$_e$ distribution would be a good choice when running the parametric distribution analysis. You can also compare the Anderson-Darling goodness-of-fit values to determine which distribution best fits the data. A smaller Anderson-Darling statistic means that the distribution provides a better fit. Here, the Anderson-Darling values for the lognormal base$_e$ distribution are lower than the Anderson-Darling values for other distributions, thus supporting your conclusion that the lognormal base$_e$ distribution provides the best fit.

The table of percentiles and MTTFs allow you to see how your conclusions may change with different distributions.

► Example of a distribution ID plot for arbitrarily-censored data

Suppose you work for a company that manufactures tires. You are interested in finding out how many miles it takes for various proportions of the tires to "fail," or wear down to 2/32 of an inch of tread. You are especially interested in knowing how many of the tires last past 45,000 miles. You plan to get this information by using the Parametric

Distribution Analysis—Arbitrary Censoring command, which requires you to specify the distribution for your data. Distribution ID Plot—Arbitrary Censoring can help you choose that distribution.

You inspect each good tire at regular intervals (every 10,000 miles) to see if the tire has failed, then enter the data into the MINITAB worksheet.

1   Open the worksheet TIREWEAR.MTW.

2   Choose **Stat ➤ Reliability/Survival ➤ Distribution ID Plot–Arbitrary Cens**.

3   In **Start variables**, enter *Start*. In **End variables**, enter *End*.

4   In **Frequency columns**, enter *Freq*.

5   Under **Distribution 4**, choose **Extreme value**. Click **OK**.

Session window output

Distribution ID Plot

```
Variable
Start: Start    End: End
Frequency: Freq

Goodness of Fit

Distribution        Anderson-Darling
Weibull             2.534
Lognormal base e    2.685
Exponential         3.903
Extreme value       2.426

Table of Percentiles
```

			Standard	95.0% Normal	CI
Distribution	Percent	Percentile	Error	Lower	Upper
Weibull	1	27623.0	998.00	25734.6	29650.0
Lognormal base e	1	27580.2	781.26	26090.7	29154.8
Exponential	1	762.4	28.80	708.0	821.0
Extreme value	1	13264.5	2216.24	8920.8	17608.3
Weibull	5	39569.8	975.59	37703.1	41528.9
Lognormal base e	5	35793.9	795.52	34268.2	37387.6
Exponential	5	3891.0	146.96	3613.4	4190.0
Extreme value	5	36038.3	1522.71	33053.9	39022.8

```
-----the rest of this table omitted for space-----

Table of MTTF
```

		Standard	95% Normal	CI
Distribution	Mean	Error	Lower	Upper
Weibull	69545.4	629.34	68322.8	70789.9
Lognormal base e	72248.6	1066.42	70188.4	74369.3
Exponential	75858.8	2865.18	70446.0	81687.6
Extreme value	69473.3	646.64	68205.9	70740.7

*Graph
window
output*

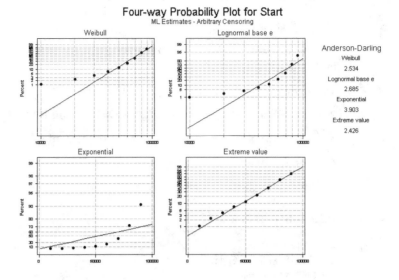

Interpreting results

The points fall approximately on the straight line on the extreme value probability plot, so the extreme value distribution would be a good choice when running the parametric distribution analysis.

You can also compare the Anderson-Darling goodness-of-fit values to determine which distribution best fits the data. A smaller Anderson-Darling statistic means that the distribution provides a better fit. Here, the Anderson-darling values for the extreme value distribution are lower than the Anderson-Darling values for other distributions, thus supporting your conclusion that the extreme value distribution provides the best fit.

The table of percentiles and MTTFs allow you to see how your conclusions may change with different distributions.

Distribution Overview Plot

Use Distribution Overview Plot to generate a layout of plots that allow you to view your life data in different ways on one page. You can draw a *parametric* overview plot by selecting a distribution for your data, or a *nonparametric* overview plot.

The parametric display includes a probability plot (for a selected distribution), a survival (or reliability) plot, a probability density function, and a hazard plot. The nonparametric display depends on the type of data: if you have right-censored data MINITAB displays a Kaplan-Meier survival plot and a hazard plot or an Actuarial survival plot and hazard plot, and if you have arbitrarily-censored data, MINITAB displays a Turnbull survival plot or an Actuarial survival plot and hazard plot. These functions are all typical ways of describing the distribution of failure time data.

The data you gather are the individual failure times, some of which may be censored. For example, you might collect failure times for units running at a given temperature. You might also collect samples of failure times under different temperatures, or under various combination of stress variables.

You can enter up to ten samples per analysis. MINITAB estimates the functions independently for each sample. All of the samples display on a single plot, in different colors and symbols, which helps you compare their various functions.

To draw these plots with more information, see *Parametric Distribution Analysis* on page 15-27 or *Nonparametric Distribution Analysis* on page 15-52.

Data

Distribution Overview Plot accepts different kinds of data:

- Distribution Overview Plot—Right Censoring accepts exact failure times and right censored data. For information on how to set up your worksheet, see *Distribution analysis—right censored data* on page 15-5.

- Distribution Overview Plot—Arbitrary Censoring accepts exact failure times and right-, left-, and interval-censored data. The data must be in tabled form. For information on how to set up your worksheet, see *Distribution analysis—arbitrarily censored data* on page 15-8.

You can enter up to ten samples per analysis. For general information on life data and censoring, see *Distribution Analysis Data* on page 15-5.

▶ **To make a distribution overview plot (uncensored/right-censored data)**

1   Choose **Stat ➤ Reliability/Survival ➤ Distribution Overview Plot—Right Censoring**.

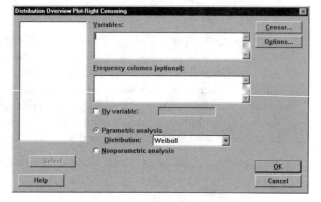

2   In **Variables**, enter the columns of failure times. You can enter up to ten columns (ten different samples).

3   If you have frequency columns, enter the columns in **Frequency columns**.

4   If all of the samples are stacked in one column, check **By variable**, and enter a column of grouping indicators in the box.

5   Choose to draw a parametric or nonparametric plot:

   ■ *Parametric plot*—Choose **Parametric analysis**. From **Distribution**, choose to plot one of the eight available distributions.

   ■ *Nonparametric plot*—Choose **Nonparametric analysis**.

Note | If you have no censored values, you can skip steps 5 & 6.

6   Click **Censor**.

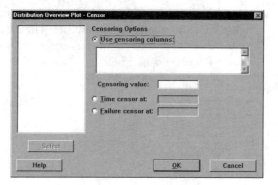

7   Do one of the following, then click **OK**.

  ■   For data with censoring columns: Choose **Use censoring columns**, then enter
      the censoring columns in the box. The first censoring column is paired with the
      first data column, the second censoring column is paired with the second data
      column, and so on.

      If you like, enter the value you use to indicate censoring in **Censoring value**. If
      you don't enter a value, by default MINITAB uses the lowest value in the
      censoring column.

  ■   For time censored data: Choose **Time censor at**, then enter a failure time at
      which to begin censoring. For example, entering *500* says that any observation
      from 500 time units onward is considered censored.

  ■   For failure censored data: Choose **Failure censor at**, then enter a number of
      failures at which to begin censoring. For example, entering *150* says to censor all
      (ordered) observations from the 150th observed failure on, and to leave all other
      observations uncensored.

8   If you like, use any of the options listed below, then click **OK**.

▶ **To make a distribution overview plot (arbitrarily censored data)**

1   Choose **Stat ➤ Reliability/Survival ➤ Distribution Overview Plot–Arbitrarily
    Censored**.

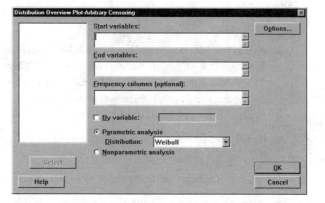

2   In **Start variables**, enter the columns of start times. You can enter up to ten columns
    (ten different samples).

3   In **End variables**, enter the columns of end times. You can enter up to ten columns
    (ten different samples).

4   If you have frequency columns, enter the columns in **Frequency columns**.

5   If all of the samples are stacked in one column, check **By variable**, and enter a
    column of grouping indicators in the box.

6 Choose to draw a parametric or nonparametric plot:

- *Parametric plot*—Choose **Parametric analysis**. From **Distribution**, choose to plot one of eight distributions.

- *Nonparametric plot*—Choose **Nonparametric analysis**.

7 If you like, use any of the options described below, then click **OK**.

Options

Distribution Overview Plot dialog box

- for the parametric display of plots, choose one of eight common lifetime distributions for the data—Weibull (default), extreme value, exponential, normal, lognormal base$_e$, lognormal base$_{10}$, logistic, or loglogistic.

More | MINITAB's extreme value distribution is the smallest extreme value (Type 1).

- draw a nonparametric display of plots.

Options subdialog box (right censoring)

When you have chosen to conduct a parametric analysis

- estimate parameters using the maximum likelihood (default) or least squares methods

- obtain the plot points for the probability plot using various nonparametric methods—see *Probability plots* on page 15-37. You can choose the Default method, Modified Kaplan-Meier, Herd-Johnson, or Kaplan-Meier method. The Default method is the normal score for uncensored data; the modified Kaplan-Meier method is for censored data.

- handle ties by plotting all of the points (default), the maximum of the tied points, or the average (median) of the tied points.

When you have chosen to conduct a nonparametric analysis:

- estimate parameters using the Kaplan-Meier method (default) or Actuarial method.

For both parametric and nonparametric analyses:

- enter minimum and/or maximum values for the x-axis scale.

- replace the default graph title with your own title.

Options subdialog box (arbitrary censoring)

When you have chosen to conduct a parametric analysis:

- estimate parameters using the maximum likelihood (default) or least squares methods

- obtain the plot points for the probability plot using various nonparametric methods—see *Probability plots* on page 15-37. You can choose from the Turnbull method (default) or Actuarial method.

When you have chosen to conduct a nonparametric analysis:

- estimate parameters using the Turnbull method (default) or Actuarial method (default).

For both parametric and nonparametric analyses:

- enter minimum and/or maximum values for the x-axis scale.

- replace the default graph title with your own title.

Output

The distribution overview plot display differs depending on whether you select the parametric or nonparametric display.

When you select a parametric display, you get:

- goodness-of-fit statistics for the chosen distribution.

- a probability plot, which displays estimates of the cumulative distribution function $F(y)$ vs. failure time—see *Probability plots* on page 15-37.

- a parametric survival (or reliability) plot, which displays the survival (or reliability) function $1-F(y)$ vs. failure time—see *Survival plots* on page 15-40.

- a probability density function, which displays the curve that describes the distribution of your data, or $f(y)$.

- a parametric hazard plot, which displays the hazard function or instantaneous failure rate, $f(y)/(1-F(y))$ vs. failure time—see *Hazard plots* on page 15-41.

When you select a nonparametric display, you get:

- For right-censored data with Kaplan-Meier method
  - a Kaplan-Meier survival plot
  - a nonparametric hazard plot based on the empirical hazard function

- For right-censored data with Actuarial method
  - an Actuarial survival plot
  - a nonparametric hazard plot based on the empirical hazard function

- For arbitrarily-censored data with Turnbull method
  - a Turnbull survival plot

- For arbitrarily-censored data with Actuarial method
  - an Actuarial survival plot
  - a nonparametric hazard plot based on the empirical hazard function

The Kaplan-Meier survival estimates, Turnbull survival estimates, and empirical hazard function change values only at exact failure times, so the nonparametric survival and hazard curves are step functions. Parametric survival and hazard estimates are based on a fitted distribution and the curve will therefore be smooth.

▷ **Example of a distribution overview plot with right-censored data**

Suppose you work for a company that manufactures engine windings for turbine assemblies. Engine windings may decompose at an unacceptable rate at high temperatures. You want to know, at given high temperatures, at what time do 1% of the engine windings fail. You plan to get this information by using the Parametric Distribution Analysis—Right Censoring command, but you first want to have a quick look at your data from different perspectives.

First you collect data for times to failure for the engine windings at two temperatures. In the first sample, you test 50 windings at 80° C; in the second sample, you test 40 windings at 100° C. Some of the units drop out of the test due to failures from other causes. These units are considered to be right censored because their failures were not due to the cause of interest. In the MINITAB worksheet, you use a column of censoring indicators to designate which times are actual failures (1) and which are censored units removed from the test before failure (0).

1 Open the worksheet RELIABLE.MTW.

2 Choose **Stat ➤ Reliability/Survival ➤ Distribution Overview Plot—Right Cens**.

3 In **Variables**, enter *Temp80 Temp100*.

4 From **Distribution**, choose **Lognormal base e**.

5 Click **Censor**. Choose **Use censoring columns** and enter *Cens80 Cens100* in the box. Click **OK** in each dialog box.

Session window output

Distribution Overview Plot
```
Distribution:    Lognormal base e
Variable  Anderson-Darling
Temp80    67.22
Temp100   16.50
```

*Graph
window
output*

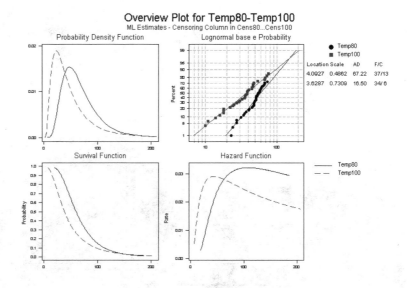

Interpreting the results

These four plots describe the failure rate of engine windings at two different temperatures. With these plots, you can determine how much more likely it is that the engine windings will fail when running at 100° C as opposed to 80° C.

▷ Example of a distribution overview plot with arbitrarily-censored data

Suppose you work for a company that manufactures tires. You are interested in finding out how many miles it takes for various proportions of the tires to "fail," or wear down to 2/32 of an inch of tread. You are especially interested in knowing how many of the tires last past 45,000 miles. You plan to get this information by using the Parametric Distribution Analysis—Arbitrary Censoring command, but first you want to have a quick look at your data from different perspectives.

You inspect each good tire at regular intervals (every 10,000 miles) to see if the tire has failed, then enter the data into the MINITAB worksheet.

1 Open the worksheet TIREWEAR.MTW.

2 Choose **Stat ➤ Reliability/Survival ➤ Distribution Overview Plot–Arbitrary Cens**.

3 In **Start variables**, enter *Start*. In **End variables**, enter *End*.

4 In **Frequency columns**, enter *Freq*.

5 From **Distribution**, choose **Extreme value**. Click **OK**.

*Session
window
output*

Distribution Overview Plot

```
Variable
Start: Start    End: End
Frequency: Freq


Anderson-Darling
2.426
```

*Graph
window
output*

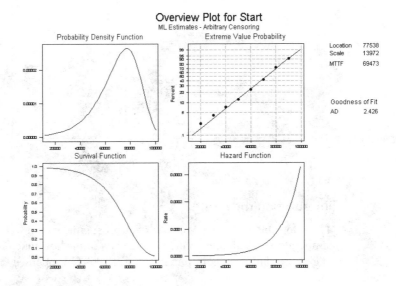

Interpreting the results

These four plots describe the failure rate for tires over time. With these plots, you can approximately determine how many tires last past 45,000 miles.

Parametric Distribution Analysis

Use the parametric distribution analysis commands to fit one of eight common distributions to your data, estimate percentiles and survival probabilities, evaluate the appropriateness of the distribution, and draw survival, hazard, and probability plots. The command you choose, Parametric Distribution Analysis—Right Censoring or Parametric Distribution Analysis—Arbitrary Censoring, depends on the type of data you have, as described in *Data* on page 15-27.

Use the probability plot to see if the distribution fits your data. To compare the fits of four different distributions, see *Distribution ID Plot* on page 15-9, which draws four probability plots on one page. If no parametric distribution fits your data, use *Nonparametric Distribution Analysis* on page 15-52.

The data you gather are the individual failure times, some of which may be censored. For example, you might collect failure times for units running at a given temperature. You might also collect failure times under different temperatures, or under various combinations of stress variables.

You can enter up to ten samples per analysis. MINITAB estimates the functions independently for each sample, unless you assume a common shape (Weibull) or scale (other distributions). All of the samples display on a single plot, in different colors and symbols, which helps you compare the various functions between samples.

To view your data in different ways on one page, see *Distribution Overview Plot* on page 15-19.

Data

The parametric distribution analysis commands accept different kinds of data:

- Parametric Distribution Analysis—Right Censoring accepts exact failure times and right-censored data. For information on how to set up your worksheet, see *Distribution analysis—right censored data* on page 15-5.

- Parametric Distribution Analysis—Arbitrary Censoring accepts exact failure times, right-, left-, and interval-censored data. The data must be in table form. For information on how to set up your worksheet, see *Distribution analysis—arbitrarily censored data* on page 15-8.

You can enter up to ten samples per analysis. For general information on life data and censoring, see *Distribution Analysis Data* on page 15-5.

Occasionally, you may have life data with no failures. Under certain conditions, MINITAB allows you to draw conclusions based on that data. See *Drawing conclusions when you have few or no failures* on page 15-33.

▶ **To do a parametric distribution analysis (uncensored/right censored data)**

  1 Choose Stat ➤ Reliability/Survival ➤ Parametric Dist Analysis—Right Cens.

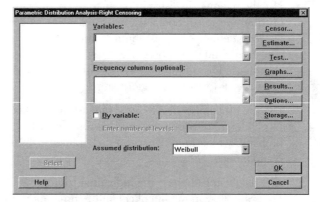

  2 In **Variables**, enter the columns of failure times. You can enter up to ten columns
     (ten different samples).

  3 If you have frequency columns, enter the columns in **Frequency columns**.

  4 If all of the samples are stacked in one column, check **By variable**, and enter a
     column of grouping indicators in the box. In **Enter number of levels**, enter the
     number of levels the indicator column contains.

Note │ If you have no censored values, you can skip steps 5 & 6.

  5 Click **Censor**.

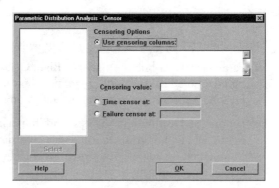

  6 Do one of the following, then click **OK**.

     ■ For data with censoring columns: Choose **Use censoring columns**, then enter
        the censoring columns in the box. The first censoring column is paired with the
        first data column, the second censoring column is paired with the second data
        column, and so on.

If you like, enter the value you use to indicate censoring in **Censoring value**. If you don't enter a value, by default MINITAB uses the lowest value in the censoring column.

- For time censored data: Choose **Time censor at**, then enter a failure time at which to begin censoring. For example, entering *500* says that any observation from 500 time units onward is considered censored.

- For failure censored data: Choose **Failure censor at**, then enter a number of failures at which to begin censoring. For example, entering *150* says to censor all (ordered) observations from the 150th observed failure on, and leave all other observations uncensored.

7 If you like, use any of the options listed below, then click **OK**.

▶ **To do a parametric distribution analysis (arbitrarily censored data)**

1 Choose **Stat ➤ Reliability/Survival ➤ Parametric Dist Analysis–Arbitrary Cens**.

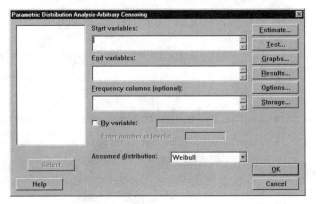

2 In **Start variables**, enter the columns of start times. You can enter up to ten columns (ten different samples).

3 In **End variables**, enter the columns of end times. You can enter up to ten columns (ten different samples).

4 If you have frequency columns, enter the columns in **Frequency columns**.

5 If all of the samples are stacked in one column, check **By variable**, and enter a column of grouping indicators in the box. In **Enter number of levels**, enter the number of levels the indicator column contains.

6 If you like, use any of the options described below, then click **OK**.

Options

Parametric Distribution Analysis dialog box

- fit one of eight common lifetime distributions for the parametric analysis, including Weibull (default), extreme value, exponential, normal, lognormal base$_e$, lognormal base$_{10}$, logistic, and loglogistic

More | MINITAB's extreme value distribution is the the smallest extreme value (Type 1).

Estimate subdialog box

- estimate parameters using the maximum likelihood (default) or least squares methods—see *Estimating the distribution parameters* on page 15-42.

- estimate parameters assuming a common shape (Weibull distribution) or scale (other distributions).

- estimate the scale parameter while holding the shape fixed (Weibull distribution), or estimate the location parameter while keeping the scale fixed (all other distributions)—see *Estimating the distribution parameters* on page 15-42.

- draw conclusions when you have few or no failures—*Drawing conclusions when you have few or no failures* on page 15-33.

- estimate percentiles for additional percents—see *Percentiles* on page 15-36.

- estimate survival probabilities for times (values) you specify—see *Survival probabilities* on page 15-39.

- specify a confidence level for all of the confidence intervals. The default is 95.0%.

- choose to calculate two-sided confidence intervals, or lower or upper bounds. The default is two-sided.

Test subdialog box

- test whether the distribution parameters (scale, shape, or location) are consistent with specified values—see *Comparing parameters* on page 15-34.

- test whether two or more samples come from the same population—see *Comparing parameters* on page 15-34.

- test whether the shape, scale, or location parameters from K distributions are the same—see *Comparing parameters* on page 15-34.

Graphs subdialog box

- obtain the plot points for the probability plot using various nonparametric methods—see *Probability plots* on page 15-37.

With Parametric Distribution Analysis—Right Censoring, you can choose the Default method, Modified Kaplan-Meier method, Herd-Johnson method, or Kaplan-Meier method. The Default method is the normal score for uncensored data; the modified Kaplan-Meier method for censored data.

With Parametric Distribution Analysis—Arbitrary Censoring, choose the Turnbull or Actuarial method. Turnbull is the default method.

- (Parametric Distribution Analysis—Right Censoring only) handle tied failure times in the probability plot by plotting all of the points (default), the average (median) of the tied points, or the maximum of the tied points.

- draw a survival plot—see *Survival plots* on page 15-40.

- suppress confidence intervals on the probability and survival plots.

- draw a hazard plot—see *Hazard plots* on page 15-41.

- enter minimum and/or maximum values for the x-axis scale.

- enter a label for the x-axis.

Results subdialog box

- display the following Session window output:
  - no output
  - the basic output, which includes variable information, censoring information, estimated parameters, the log-likelihood, goodness-of-fit statistics, and tests of parameters
  - the above output, plus characteristics of the distribution, and tables of percentiles and survival probabilities

- show the log-likelihood for each iteration of the algorithm

Options subdialog box

- enter starting values for model parameters—see *Estimating the distribution parameters* on page 15-42.

- change the maximum number of iterations for reaching convergence (the default is 20). MINITAB obtains maximum likelihood estimates through an iterative process. If the maximum number of iterations is reached before convergence, the command terminates—see *Estimating the distribution parameters* on page 15-42.

- use historical estimates for the parameters rather than estimate them from the data. In this case, no estimation is done; all results—such as the percentiles and survival probabilities—are based on these historical estimates. See *Estimating the distribution parameters* on page 15-42.

Storage subdialog box

- store characteristics of the fitted distribution:
  - percentiles and their percents, standard errors, and confidence limits
  - survival probabilities and their times and confidence limits

- store information on parameters:
  - estimates of the parameters and their standard errors and confidence limits
  - the variance/covariance matrix
  - the log-likelihood for the last iteration

Output

The default output for Parametric Distribution Analysis—Right Censoring and Parametric Distribution Analysis—Arbitrary Censoring consists of:

- the censoring information

- parameter estimates and their
  - standard errors
  - 95% confidence intervals

- log-likelihood and Anderson-Darling goodness-of-fit statistic—see *Goodness-of-fit statistics* on page 15-13

- characteristics of distribution and their
  - standard errors
  - 95% confidence intervals

- table of percentiles and their
  - standard errors
  - 95% confidence intervals

- probability plot

Fitting a distribution

You can fit one of eight common lifetime distributions to your data, including the Weibull (default), extreme value, exponential, normal, lognormal base$_e$, lognormal base$_{10}$, logistic, and loglogistic distributions.

More | MINITAB's extreme value distribution is the the smallest extreme value (Type 1).

The Session window output includes two tables that describe the distribution. Here is some sample output from a default Weibull distribution:

```
Estimation Method:  Maximum Likelihood
Distribution:  Weibull

Parameter Estimates
                          Standard      95.0% Normal CI
Parameter    Estimate       Error     Lower      Upper
Shape         2.3175       0.3127    1.7790     3.0191
Scale         73.344        5.203    63.824     84.286


Log-Likelihood = -186.128


Goodness-of-Fit
Anderson-Darling = 67.6366

Characteristics of Distribution
                              Standard        95.0% Normal CI
                   Estimate      Error     Lower      Upper
Mean(MTTF)          64.9829     4.6102    56.5472    74.6771
Standard Deviation  29.7597     4.1463    22.6481    39.1043
Median              62.6158     4.6251    54.1763    72.3700
First Quartile(Q1)  42.8439     4.3240    35.1546    52.2151
Third Quartile(Q3)  84.4457     6.2186    73.0962    97.5575
Interquartile Range(IQR)  41.6018  5.5878  31.9730   54.1305
```

■ **Parameter Estimates** displays the maximum likelihood or the least squares estimates of the distribution parameters, their standard errors and approximate 95.0% confidence intervals, and the log-likelihood and Anderson-Darling goodness-of-fit statistic for the fitted distribution.

■ **Characteristics of Distribution** displays common measures of the center and spread of the distribution with 95.0% lower and upper confidence intervals. The mean and standard deviation are not resistant to large lifetimes, while the median, Q1 (25th percentile), Q3 (75th percentile), and the IQR (interquartile range) are resistant.

The Newton-Raphson algorithm is used to calculate maximum likelihood estimates of the parameters. These parameters define the distribution. All resulting functions, such as the percentiles and survival probabilities, are calculated from that distribution. For computations, see [6].

Drawing conclusions when you have few or no failures

MINITAB allows you to use historical values for distribution parameters to improve the current analysis. Providing the shape (Weibull) or scale (other distributions) parameter makes the resulting analysis more precise, if your shape/scale is an appropriate choice. An added benefit of providing historical values, is that, when your data are from a Weibull or exponential distribution, you can do a Bayes analysis and draw conclusions when your data has few or no failures.

Sometimes you may collect life data and have no failures. MINITAB offers the ability to draw conclusions based on that data under certain conditions:

- The data come from a Weibull or exponential distribution.

- The data are right-censored.

- The maximum likelihood method will be used to estimate parameters.

- You provide a historical value for the shape parameter (Weibull or exponential).

MINITAB provides lower confidence bounds for the scale parameter (Weibull or exponential), percentiles, and survival probabilities. The lower confidence bound helps you to draw some conclusions; if the value of the lower confidence bound is better than the specifications, then you may be able to terminate the test.

For example, your reliability specifications require that the 5th percentile is at least 12 months. You run a Bayes analysis on data with no failures, and then examine the lower confidence bound to substantiate that the product is at least as good as specifications. If the lower confidence bound for the 5th percentile is 13.1 months, then you can conclude that your product meets specifications and terminate the test.

▶ **To draw conclusions when you have no failures**

1 In the main dialog box, click **Estimate**.

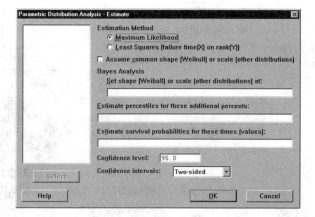

2 In **Set shape (Weibull) or scale (other distributions) at** enter the shape or scale value. Click **OK**.

Comparing parameters

Are the distribution parameters for a sample equal to specified values; for example, does the scale equal 1.1? Does the sample come from the historical distribution? Do two or more samples come from the same population? Do two or more samples share the same shape, scale, or location parameters? To answer these questions you need to perform hypothesis tests on the distribution parameters.

MINITAB performs Wald Tests [7] and provides Bonferroni 95.0% confidence intervals for the following hypothesis tests:

- Test whether the distribution parameters (scale, shape, or location) are consistent with specified values

- Test whether the sample comes from the historical distribution

- Test whether two or more samples come from the same population

- Test whether two or more samples share the same shape, scale or location parameters

▶ **To compare distribution parameters to a specified value**

1 In the main dialog box, click **Test**.

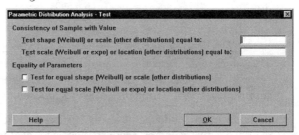

2 In **Test shape (Weibull) or scale (other distributions) equal to** or **Test scale (Weibull or expo) or location (other distributions) equal to** enter the value to be tested. Click **OK**.

▶ **To test whether a sample comes from a historical distribution**

1 In the main dialog box, click **Test**.

2 In **Test shape (Weibull) or scale (other distributions) equal to** and **Test scale (Weibull or expo) or location (other distributions) equal to** enter the parameters of the historical distribution. Click **OK**.

▶ **To determine whether two or more samples come from the same population**

1 In the main dialog box, click **Test**.

2 Check **Test for equal shape (Weibull) or scale (other distributions)** and **Test for equal scale (Weibull or expo) or location (other distributions)**. Click **OK**.

▶ **To compare the shape, scale, or location parameters from two or more samples**

1 In the main dialog box, click **Test**.

2 Check **Test for equal shape (Weibull) or scale (other distributions)** or **Test for equal scale (Weibull or expo) or location (other distributions)**. Click **OK**.

Percentiles

By what time do half of the engine windings fail? How long until 10% of the blenders stop working? You are looking for *percentiles*. The parametric distribution analysis commands automatically display a table of percentiles in the Session window. By default, MINITAB displays the percentiles 1–10, 20, 30, 40, 50, 60, 70, 80, and 90–99.

In this example, we entered failure times (in months) for engine windings.

Table of Percentiles

		Standard	95.0% Normal CI	
Percent	Percentile	Error	Lower	Upper
1	10.0765	2.7845	5.8626	17.3193
2	13.6193	3.2316	8.5543	21.6834
3	16.2590	3.4890	10.6767	24.7601
4	18.4489	3.6635	12.5009	27.2270

At about 10 months, 1% of the windings failed.

The values in the Percentile column are estimates of the times at which the corresponding percent of the units failed. The table also includes standard errors and approximate 95.0% confidence intervals for each percentile.

In the Estimate subdialog box, you can specify a different confidence level for all confidence intervals. You can also request percentiles to be added the default table.

▶ **To request additional percentiles**

1 In the main dialog box, click **Estimate**.

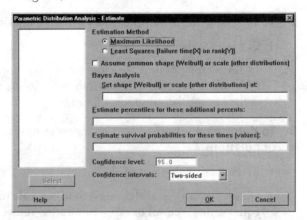

2 In **Estimate percentiles for these additional percents**, enter the additional percents for which you want to estimate percentiles. You can enter individual percents (0 < P < 100) or a column of percents. Click **OK**.

Probability plots

Use the probability plot to assess whether a particular distribution fits your data. The plot consists of:

- *plot points*, which represent the proportion of failures up to a certain time. The plot points are calculated using a nonparametric method, which assumes no parametric distribution—for formulas, see Calculations in Help. The proportions are transformed and used as the y variable, while their corresponding times may be transformed and used as the x variable.

- the *fitted line*, which is a graphical representation of the percentiles. To make the fitted line, MINITAB first calculates the percentiles for the various percents, based on the chosen distribution. The associated probabilities are then transformed and used as the y variables. The percentiles may be transformed, depending on the distribution, and are used as the x variables. The transformed scales, chosen to linearize the fitted line, differ depending on the distribution used.

- a set of approximate 95.0% *confidence intervals* for the fitted line.

Because the plot points do not depend on any distribution, they would be the same (before being transformed) for any probability plot made. The fitted line, however, differs depending on the parametric distribution chosen. So you can use the probability plot to assess whether a particular distribution fits your data. In general, the closer the points fall to the fitted line, the better the fit.

Tip | To quickly compare the fit of up to four different distributions at once see *Distribution ID Plot* on page 15-9.

MINITAB provides two goodness of fit measures to help assess how the distribution fits your data: the Anderson-Darling statistic for both the maximum likelihood and the least squares methods and the Pearson correlation coefficient for the least squares method. A smaller Anderson-Darling statistic indicates that the distribution provides a better fit. A larger Pearson correlation coefficient indicates that the distribution provides a better fit. See *Goodness-of-fit statistics* on page 15-13.

Here is a Weibull probability plot for failure times associated with running engine windings at a temperature of 80° C:

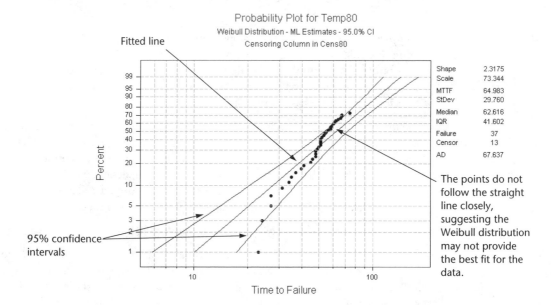

With the commands in this chapter, you can choose from various methods to estimate the plot points. You can also choose the method used to obtain the fitted line. The task below describes all the ways you can modify the probability plot.

▶ To modify the default probability plot

1 In the main dialog box, click **Graphs**.

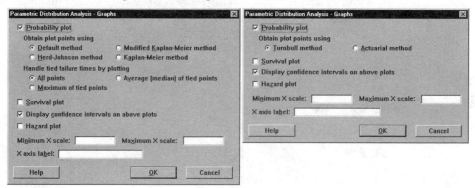

2   Do any or all of the following:

- specify the method used to obtain the plot points—under **Obtain plot points using**, choose one of the following:
  - with Parametric Distribution Analysis—Right Censoring: **Default method, Modified Kaplan-Meier method, Herd-Johnson method**, or **Kaplan-Meier method**. The Default method is the normal score for uncensored data; the modified Kaplan-Meier method for censored data.
  - with Parametric Distribution Analysis—Arbitrary Censoring: **Turnbull method** or **Actuarial method**.

- Parametric Distribution Analysis—Right Censoring only: Choose what to plot when you have tied failure times—under **Handle tied failure times by plotting**, choose **All points** (default), **Maximum of the tied points**, or **Average (median) of tied points**.

- turn off the 95.0% confidence interval—uncheck **Display confidence intervals on above plots**.

- specify a minimum and/or maximum value for the x-axis scale.

- enter a label for the x axis.

3   Click **OK**.

4   If you want to change the confidence level for the 95.0% confidence interval to some other level, click **Estimate**. In **Confidence level**, enter a value. Click **OK**.

5   If you want to change the method used to obtain the fitted line, click Estimate. In **Estimation Method**, choose **Maximum Likelihood** (default) or **Least Squares**. Click **OK**.

Survival probabilities

What is the probability of an engine winding running past a given time? How likely is it that a cancer patient will live five years after receiving a certain drug? You are looking for *survival probabilities*, which are estimates of the proportion of units that survive past a given time.

When you request survival probabilities in the Estimate subdialog box, the parametric distribution analysis commands display them in the Session window. Here, for example, we requested a survival probability for engine windings running at 70 months:

```
                        Table of Survival Probabilities
40.76% of the                                        95.0% Normal CI
engine windings last       Time   Probability     Lower      Upper
past 70 months.         70.0000        0.4076     0.2894     0.5222
```

▶ **To request parametric survival probabilities**

 1 In the main dialog box, click **Estimate**.

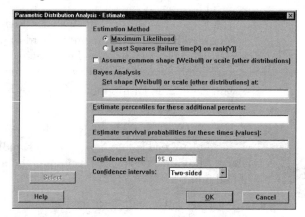

 2 In **Estimate survival probabilities for these times (values)**, enter one or more times
   or a column of times for which you want to calculate survival probabilities. Click **OK**.

Survival plots

Survival (or reliability) plots display the survival probabilities versus time. Each plot
point represents the proportion of units surviving at time t. The survival curve is
surrounded by two outer lines—the approximate 95.0% confidence interval for the
curve, which provide reasonable values for the "true" survival function.

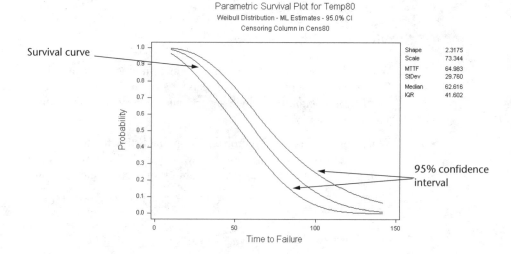

▶ **To draw a parametric survival plot**

1 In the main dialog box, click **Graphs**.

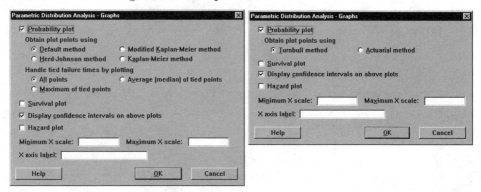

2 Check **Survival plot**.

3 If you like, do any of the following:

- turn off the 95.0% confidence interval—uncheck **Display confidence intervals on above plots**. Click **OK**.

- change the confidence level for the 95.0% confidence interval. First, click **OK** in the Graphs subdialog box. Click **Estimate**. In **Confidence level for confidence intervals**, enter a value. Click **OK**.

- specify minimum and/or maximum values for the x-axis scale.

- enter a label for the x-axis.

Hazard plots

The hazard plot displays the instantaneous failure rate for each time t. Often, the hazard rate is high at the beginning of the plot, low in the middle of the plot, then high again at the end of the plot. Thus, the curve often resembles the shape of a bathtub. The early period with high failure rate is often called the infant mortality stage. The middle section of the curve, where the failure rate is low, is the normal life stage. The end of the curve, where failure rate increases again, is the wearout stage.

Note | MINITAB's distributions will not resemble a bathtub curve. The failures at different parts of the bathtub curve are likely caused by different failure modes. MINITAB estimates the distribution of the failure time caused by one failure mode.

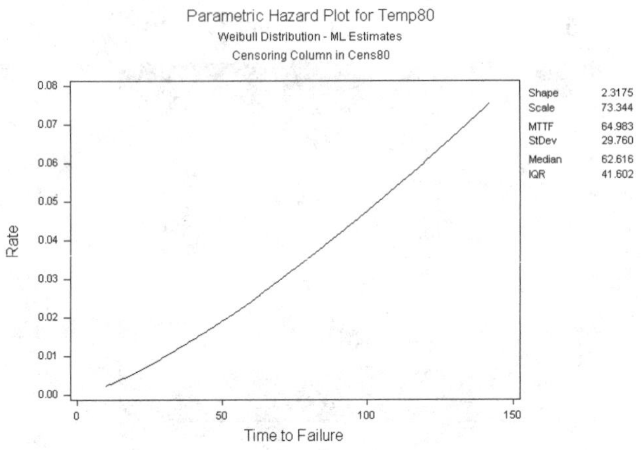
Parametric Hazard Plot for Temp80
Weibull Distribution - ML Estimates
Censoring Column in Cens80
Rate
0.00
0.01
0.02
0.03
0.04
0.05
0.06
0.07
0.08
0
50
100
150
Time to Failure
Shape 2.3175
Scale 73.344
MTTF 64.983
StDev 29.760
Median 62.616
IQR 41.602

▶ To draw a parametric hazard plot

1 In the main dialog box, click **Graphs**.

2 Check **Hazard plot**.

3 If you like, do any of the following, then click **OK**.

- specify minimum and/or maximum values for the x-axis scale
- enter a label for the x-axis

Estimating the distribution parameters

MINITAB uses a the maximum likelihood estimations method (modified Newton-Raphson algorithm) or least squares (XY) method to estimate the parameters of the distribution. Or, if you like, you can use your own parameters. In this case, no estimation is done; all results—such as the percentiles—are based on the parameters you enter.

You can choose to estimate the parameters using either the maximum likelihood method or the least squares method—see *Maximum likelihood estimates versus least squares estimates* on page 15-44.

When you let MINITAB estimate the parameters from the data using the maximum likelihood method, you can optionally:

- enter starting values for the algorithm.
- change the maximum number of iterations for reaching convergence (the default is 20). MINITAB obtains maximum likelihood estimates through an iterative process. If the maximum number of iterations is reached before convergence, the command terminates.

Why enter starting values for the algorithm? The maximum likelihood solution may not converge if the starting estimates are not in the neighborhood of the true solution, so you may want to specify what you think are good starting values for parameter estimates. In these cases, enter the distribution parameters. For the Weibull distribution, enter the shape and scale. For the exponential distribution, enter the scale. For all other distributions, enter the location and scale.

You can also choose to

- estimate the scale parameter while keeping the shape fixed (Weibull and exponential distributions)

- estimate the location parameter while keeping the scale fixed (other distributions)

▶ To control estimation of the parameters

1 In the main dialog box, click **Options**.

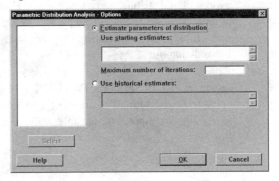

2 Do one of the following:

- To estimate the distribution parameters from the data (the default), choose **Estimate parameters of distribution**.

  If you like, do any of the following:
  - Enter starting estimates for the parameters: In **Use starting estimates,** enter one column of values to be used for all samples, or several columns of values that match the order in which the corresponding variables appear in the **Variables** box in the main dialog box.
  - Specify the maximum number of iterations: In **Maximum number of iterations**, enter a positive integer.

- To enter your own estimates for the distribution parameters, choose **Use historical estimates** and enter one column of values to be used for all samples, or several columns of values that match the order in which the corresponding variables appear in the **Variables** box in the main dialog box.

3 Click **OK**.

▶ **To choose the method for estimating parameters**

1 In the main dialog box, choose **Estimate**.

2 Under **Estimation Method**, choose **Maximum Likelihood** (the default) or **Least Squares**. Click **OK**.

▶ **To estimate one parameter while keeping the other parameter fixed**

You can estimate the scale parameter while keeping the shape parameter fixed (Weibull and exponential) or estimate the location parameter while keeping the scale fixed (other distributions).

1 In the main dialog box, click **Estimate**.

2 Do one of the following:
  – Estimate the scale parameter while keeping the shape fixed (Weibull and exponential distributions): In **Set shape (Weibull) or scale (other distributions) at**, enter one value to be used for all samples, or a series of values that match the order in which the corresponding variables appear in the **Variables** box in the main dialog box.
  – Estimate the location parameter while keeping the scale fixed (other distributions): In **Set shape (Weibull) or scale (other distributions) at**, enter one value to be used for all samples, or a series of values that match the order in which the corresponding variables appear in the **Variables** box in the main dialog box.

3 Click **OK**.

Maximum likelihood estimates versus least squares estimates

Maximum likelihood estimates are calculated by maximizing the likelihood function. The likelihood function describes, for each set of distribution parameters, the chance that the true distribution has the parameters based on the sample.

Least squares estimates are calculated by fitting a regression line to the points in a probability plot. The line is formed by regressing time (X) to failure (Y) or log (time to failure) on the transformed percent.

Here are the major advantages of each method:

Maximum likelihood (MLE)

■ Distribution parameter estimates are more precise than least squares (XY).

■ MLE allows you to perform an analysis when there are no failures. When there is only one failure and some right-censored observations, the maximum likelihood parameter estimates may exist for a Weibull distribution.

■ The maximum likelihood estimation method has attractive mathematical qualities.

Least squares (LSXY)

- Better graphical display to the probability plot because the line is fitted to the points on a probability plot.

- For small or heavily censored sample, LSXY is more accurate than MLE. MLE tends to overestimate the shape parameter for a Weibull distribution and underestimate the scale parameter in other distributions. Therefore, MLE will tend to overestimate the low percentiles.

When possible, both methods should be tried; if the results are consistent, then there is more support for your conclusions. Otherwise, you may want to use the more conservative estimates or consider the advantages of both approaches and make a choice for your problem.

▷ Example of a parametric distribution analysis with exact failure/ right-censored data

Suppose you work for a company that manufactures engine windings for turbine assemblies. Engine windings may decompose at an unacceptable rate at high temperatures. You decide to look at failure times for engine windings at two temperatures, 80 and 100°C. You want to find out the following information for each temperature:

- the times at which various percentages of the windings fail. You are particularly interested in the 0.1st percentile.

- the proportion of windings that survive past 70 months.

You also want to draw two plots: a probability plot to see if the lognormal$_e$ distribution provides a good fit for your data, and a survival plot.

In the first sample, you collect failure times (in months) for 50 windings at 80°C; in the second sample, you collect failure times for 40 windings at 100°C. Some of the windings drop out of the test for unrelated reasons. In the MINITAB worksheet, you use a column of censoring indicators to designate which times are actual failures (1) and which are censored units removed from the test before failure (0).

1 Open the worksheet RELIABLE.MTW.

2 Choose **Stat ➤ Reliability/Survival ➤ Parametric Dist Analysis–Right Cens.**

3 In **Variables**, enter *Temp80 Temp100*.

4 From **Assumed distribution**, choose **Lognormal base e**.

5 Click **Censor**. Choose **Use censoring columns** and enter *Cens80 Cens100* in the box. Click **OK**.

6 Click **Estimate**. In **Estimate percentiles for these additional percents**, enter *.1*.

7 In **Estimate survival probabilities for these times (values)**, enter *70*. Click **OK**.

8 Click **Graphs**. Check **Survival plot**. Click **OK** in each dialog box.

Session
window
output

Distribution Analysis: Temp80

Variable: Temp80

Censoring Information	Count
Uncensored value	37
Right censored value	13
Censoring value: Cens80 = 0	

Estimation Method: Maximum Likelihood
Distribution: Lognormal base e

Parameter Estimates

Parameter	Estimate	Standard Error	95.0% Normal CI Lower	95.0% Normal CI Upper
Location	4.09267	0.07197	3.95161	4.23372
Scale	0.48622	0.06062	0.38080	0.62082

Log-Likelihood = -181.625

Goodness-of-Fit
Anderson-Darling = 67.2208

Characteristics of Distribution

	Estimate	Standard Error	95.0% Normal CI Lower	95.0% Normal CI Upper
Mean(MTTF)	67.4153	5.5525	57.3656	79.2255
Standard Deviation	34.8145	6.7983	23.7435	51.0476
Median	59.8995	4.3109	52.0192	68.9735
First Quartile(Q1)	43.1516	3.2953	37.1531	50.1186
Third Quartile(Q3)	83.1475	7.3769	69.8763	98.9392
Interquartile Range(IQR)	39.9959	6.3332	29.3245	54.5505

Table of Percentiles

Percent	Percentile	Standard Error	95.0% Normal CI Lower	95.0% Normal CI Upper
0.1	13.3317	2.5156	9.2103	19.2975
1.0	19.3281	2.8375	14.4953	25.7722
2.0	22.0674	2.9256	17.0178	28.6154
3.0	24.0034	2.9726	18.8304	30.5975
4.0	25.5709	3.0036	20.3126	32.1906
5.0	26.9212	3.0262	21.5978	33.5566
6.0	28.1265	3.0440	22.7506	34.7727
7.0	29.2276	3.0588	23.8074	35.8819
8.0	30.2501	3.0717	24.7910	36.9113
9.0	31.2110	3.0833	25.7170	37.8788
10.0	32.1225	3.0941	26.5962	38.7970
20.0	39.7837	3.2100	33.9646	46.5999
30.0	46.4184	3.4101	40.1936	53.6073
40.0	52.9573	3.7567	46.0833	60.8568
50.0	59.8995	4.3109	52.0192	68.9735

-----the rest of this table omitted for space-----

Table of Survival Probabilities

		95.0% Normal CI	
Time	Probability	Lower	Upper
70.0000	0.3743	0.2631	0.4971

Distribution Analysis: Temp100

Variable: Temp100

Censoring Information	Count
Uncensored value	34
Right censored value	6

Censoring value: Cens100 = 0

Estimation Method: Maximum Likelihood
Distribution: Lognormal base e

Parameter Estimates

		Standard	95.0% Normal CI	
Parameter	Estimate	Error	Lower	Upper
Location	3.6287	0.1178	3.3978	3.8595
Scale	0.73094	0.09198	0.57117	0.93540

Log-Likelihood = -160.688

Goodness-of-Fit
Anderson-Darling = 16.4987

Characteristics of Distribution

		Standard	95.0% Normal CI	
	Estimate	Error	Lower	Upper
Mean(MTTF)	49.1969	6.9176	37.3465	64.8076
Standard Deviation	41.3431	11.0416	24.4947	69.7806
Median	37.6636	4.4362	29.8995	47.4439
First Quartile(Q1)	23.0044	2.9505	17.8910	29.5791
Third Quartile(Q3)	61.6643	8.4984	47.0677	80.7876
Interquartile Range(IQR)	38.6600	7.2450	26.7759	55.8185

Table of Percentiles

		Standard	95.0% Normal CI	
Percent	Percentile	Error	Lower	Upper
0.1	3.9350	1.1729	2.1940	7.0577
1.0	6.8776	1.6170	4.3383	10.9034
2.0	8.3941	1.7942	5.5212	12.7619
3.0	9.5253	1.9111	6.4283	14.1144
4.0	10.4756	2.0015	7.2036	15.2338
5.0	11.3181	2.0766	7.8995	16.2162
6.0	12.0884	2.1419	8.5418	17.1076
7.0	12.8069	2.2003	9.1453	17.9343
8.0	13.4863	2.2538	9.7195	18.7129
9.0	14.1354	2.3034	10.2707	19.4544

10.0	14.7606	2.3502	10.8036	20.1667
20.0	20.3589	2.7526	15.6197	26.5362
30.0	25.6717	3.1662	20.1592	32.6916
40.0	31.2967	3.6950	24.8316	39.4451
50.0	37.6636	4.4362	29.8995	47.4439

-----the rest of this table omitted for space-----

Table of Survival Probabilities

		95.0% Normal CI	
Time	Probability	Lower	Upper
70.0000	0.1982	0.1072	0.3248

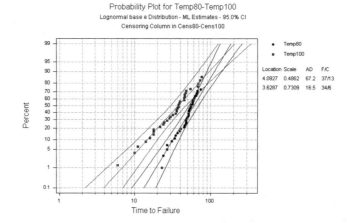

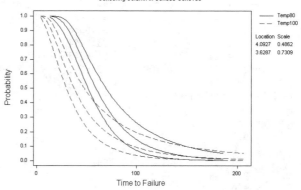

Interpreting the results

To see the times at which various percentages of the windings fail, look at the Table of Percentiles. At 80° C, for example, it takes 19.3281 months for 1% of the windings fail.

You can find the .1st percentile, which you requested, within the Table of Percentiles. At 80° C, .1% of the windings fail by 13.3317 months; at 100° C, .1% of the windings fail by 3.9350 months. So the increase in temperature decreased the percentile by about 9.5 months.

What proportion of windings would you expect to still be running past 70 months? In the Table of Survival Probabilities you find your answer. At 80° C, 37.43% survive past 70 months; at 100° C, 19.82% survive.

☞ Example of parametric distribution analysis with arbitrarily censored data

Suppose you work for a company that manufactures tires. You are interested in finding out how many miles it takes for various proportions of the tires to "fail," or wear down to 2/32 of an inch of tread. You are especially interested in knowing how many of the tires last past 45,000 miles.

You inspect each good tire at regular intervals (every 10,000 miles) to see if the tire has failed, then enter the data into the MINITAB worksheet.

1 Open the worksheet TIREWEAR.MTW.

2 Choose **Stat ➤ Reliability/Survival ➤ Parametric Dist Analysis–Arbitrary Cens**.

3 In **Start variables**, enter *Start*. In **End variables**, enter *End*.

4 In **Frequency columns**, enter *Freq*.

5 From **Assumed distribution**, choose **Extreme value**.

6 Click **Graphs**. Check **Survival plot**, then click **OK**.

7 Click **Estimate**. In **Estimate survival probabilities for these times (values)**, enter 45000. Click **OK** in each dialog box.

Session window output

Distribution Analysis, Start = Start and End = End

```
Variable
Start:  Start    End:  End
Frequency:  Freq


Censoring Information             Count
Right censored value               71
Interval censored value           694
Left censored value                 8


Estimation Method:  Maximum Likelihood
Distribution:  Extreme value


Parameter Estimates
                       Standard      95.0% Normal CI
Parameter   Estimate    Error     Lower      Upper
Location     77538.0    547.0    76465.8    78610.2
Scale        13972.0    445.0    13126.5    14872.1
```

```
Log-Likelihood = -1465.913

Goodness-of-Fit
Anderson-Darling = 2.4259

Characteristics of Distribution
```

	Estimate	Standard Error	95.0% Normal CI Lower	95.0% Normal CI Upper
Mean(MTTF)	69473.32	646.6352	68205.94	70740.70
Standard Deviation	17919.83	570.7594	16835.36	19074.15
Median	72417.04	599.5413	71241.97	73592.12
First Quartile(Q1)	60130.23	849.0361	58466.15	61794.31
Third Quartile(Q3)	82101.72	538.9283	81045.44	83158.00
Interquartile Range(IQR)	21971.49	699.8078	20641.82	23386.80

Table of Percentiles

Percent	Percentile	Standard Error	95.0% Normal CI Lower	95.0% Normal CI Upper
1	13264.55	2216.243	8920.791	17608.30
2	23019.97	1916.275	19264.14	26775.80
3	28756.49	1741.644	25342.93	32170.05
4	32847.96	1618.183	29676.38	36019.54
5	36038.31	1522.706	33053.87	39022.76
6	38658.95	1444.905	35826.99	41490.91
7	40886.63	1379.291	38183.26	43589.99
8	42826.87	1322.593	40234.64	45419.11
9	44547.76	1272.702	42053.31	47042.21
10	46095.77	1228.182	43688.58	48502.97
20	56580.77	939.3041	54739.76	58421.77
30	63133.78	777.3208	61610.26	64657.30
40	68152.58	670.9556	66837.54	69467.63
50	72417.04	599.5413	71241.97	73592.12

```
-----the rest of this table omitted for space-----

Table of Survival Probabilities
```

Time	Probability	95.0% Normal CI Lower	95.0% Normal CI Upper
45000.00	0.9072	0.8903	0.9216

*Graph
window
output*

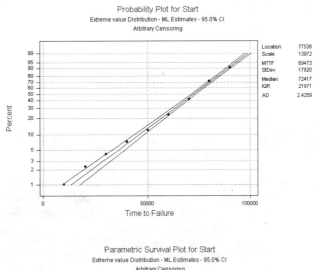

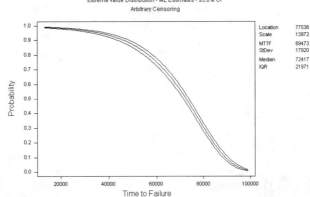

Interpreting the results

As shown in the Characteristics of Distribution table, the mean and median miles until the tires fail are 69,473.32 and 72,417.04 miles, respectively.

To see the times at which various percentages or proportions of the tires fail, look at the Table of Percentiles. For example, 5% of the tires fail by 36,038.31 miles and 50% fail by 72,417.04 miles.

In the Table of Survival Probabilities, you can see that 90.72% of the tires last past 45,000 miles.

Nonparametric Distribution Analysis

When no distribution fits your data, use the nonparametric distribution analysis commands to estimate survival probabilities, hazard estimates, and other functions, and draw survival and hazard plots.

When you have exact failure/right-censored data, you can request Kaplan-Meier or Actuarial estimates. When you have tabled data with a varied censoring scheme, you can request Turnbull or Actuarial estimates.

When you have exact failure/right-censored data and multiple samples, MINITAB tests the equality of survival curves.

The data you gather are the individual failure times, some of which may be censored. For example, you might collect failure times for units running at a given temperature. You might also collect failure times under different temperatures, or under various combination of stress variables.

You can enter up to ten samples per analysis. When you enter more than one sample, MINITAB estimates the functions independently. All of the samples display on a single plot, in different colors and symbols, which helps you compare the various functions between samples.

To make a quick Kaplan-Meier survival plot and empirical hazard plot, see *Distribution Overview Plot* on page 15-19.

If a distribution fits your data, use *Parametric Distribution Analysis* on page 15-27.

Data

The nonparametric distribution analysis commands accept different kinds of data:

- Nonparametric Distribution Analysis—Right Censoring accepts exact failure times and right-censored data—for information on how to set up your worksheet, see *Distribution analysis—right censored data* on page 15-5.

- Nonparametric Distribution Analysis—Arbitrary Censoring accepts exact failure times, right-, left-, and interval-censored data. The data must be in table form. For information on how to set up your worksheet, see *Distribution analysis—arbitrarily censored data* on page 15-8.

You can enter up to ten samples per analysis. For general information on life data and censoring, see *Distribution Analysis Data* on page 15-5.

▶ **To do a nonparametric distribution analysis (uncensored/right censored data)**

1 Choose Stat ➤ Reliability/Survival ➤ Nonparametric Distribution Analysis–Right Cens.

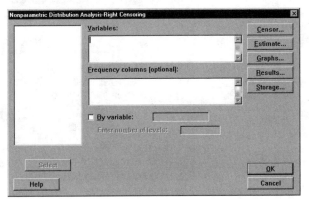

2 In **Variables**, enter the columns of failure times. You can enter up to ten columns (ten different samples).

3 If you have frequency columns, enter the columns in **Frequency columns**.

4 If all of the samples are stacked in one column, enter a column of grouping indicators in **By variable**. In **Enter number of levels**, enter the number of levels the indicator column contains.

Note | If you have no censored values, you can skip steps 5 & 6.

5 Click **Censor**.

6 Do one of the following, then click **OK**.

   ■ For data with censoring columns: Choose **Use censoring columns**, then enter the censoring columns in the box. The first censoring column is paired with the first data column, the second censoring column is paired with the second data column, and so on.

   If you like, enter the value you use to indicate a censored value in **Censoring value**. If you do not enter a censoring value, MINITAB uses the lowest value in the censoring column by default.

   ■ For time censored data: Choose **Time censor at**, then enter a failure time at which to begin censoring. For example, entering *500* says that any observation from 500 time units onward is considered censored.

   ■ For failure censored data: Choose **Failure censor at**, then enter a number of failures at which to begin censoring. For example, entering *150* says to censor all (ordered) observations starting with the 150th observed failures, and leave all other observations uncensored.

7 If you like, use any of the options listed below, then click **OK**.

▶ **To do a nonparametric distribution analysis (arbitrarily censored data)**

1   Choose Stat ➤ Reliability/Survival ➤ Nonparametric Dist Analysis–Arbitrary
    Cens.

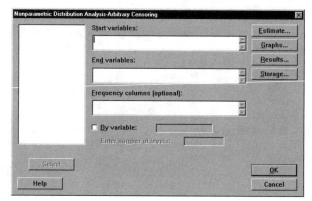

2   In **Start variables**, enter the columns of start times. You can enter up to ten columns
    (ten different samples).

3   In **End variables**, enter the columns of end times. You can enter up to ten columns
    (ten different samples).

4   When you have frequency columns, enter the columns in **Frequency columns**.

5   If all of the samples are stacked in one column, enter a column of grouping
    indicators in **By variable**. In **Enter number of levels**, enter the number of levels the
    indicator column contains.

6   If you like, use any of the options described below, then click **OK**.

Options

Estimate subdialog box

■   estimate survival probabilities using the Kaplan-Meier or Actuarial method
    (Nonparametric Distribution Analysis—Right Censoring), or the Turnbull or
    Actuarial method (Nonparametric Distribution Analysis—Arbitrary Censoring)—
    see *Survival probabilities* on page 15-56.

■   specify a confidence level for all confidence intervals. The default is 95.0%.

■   choose to calculate two-sided confidence intervals, or lower or upper bounds. The
    default is two-sided.

Graphs subdialog box

■   draw a survival plot, with or without confidence intervals—see *Nonparametric
    survival plots* on page 15-61.

- draw a hazard plot—see *Hazard plots* on page 15-62.

- specify minimum and/or maximum values for the x-axis scale.

- enter a label for the x axis.

Results subdialog box

- display the following Session window output:

  Nonparametric Distribution Analysis—Right Censoring
  - no output.
  - the basic output, which includes variable information, censoring information, characteristics of variable, and test statistics for comparing survival curves.
  - the basic output, plus the Kaplan-Meier survival probabilities or actuarial table.
  - the above output, plus hazard, density (actuarial method) estimates, and log-rank and Wilcoxon statistics. The log-rank and Wilcoxon statistics are used to compare survival curves when you have more than one sample—*Comparing survival curves (nonparametric distribution analysis—right censoring only)* on page 15-62.

  Nonparametric Distribution Analysis—Arbitrary Censoring
  - no output
  - the basic output, which includes variable information, censoring information, and characteristics of the variable (actuarial method)
  - the basic output, plus the Turnbull survival probabilities or actuarial table
  - the above output, plus hazard and density estimates (actuarial method)

Storage subdialog box

- store any of these nonparametric estimates:
  - survival probabilities and their times, standard errors, and confidence limits
  - hazard rates and their times

Output

The nonparametric distribution analysis output differs depending on whether your data are uncensored/right censored or arbitrarily censored.

When your data are uncensored/right censored you get

- the censoring information

- characteristics of the variable, which includes the mean, its standard error and 95% confidence intervals, median, interquartile range, Q1, and Q3

- Kaplan-Meier estimates of survival probabilities and their
  - standard error
  - 95% confidence intervals

When your data are arbitrarily censored you get

- the censoring information

- Turnbull estimates of the probability of failure and their standard errors

- Turnbull estimates of the survival probabilities and their standard errors and 95% confidence intervals

Survival probabilities

What is the probability of an engine winding running past a given time? How likely is it that a cancer patient will live five years after receiving a certain drug? You are looking for *survival probabilities*. Survival probabilities estimate the proportion of units surviving at time t.

You can choose various estimation methods, depending on the command.

- **Nonparametric Distribution Analysis—Right Censoring** automatically displays a table of Kaplan-Meier survival estimates. Alternatively, you can request Actuarial survival estimates. The two methods are very similar, but where the Kaplan-Meier method displays information for individual failure times, the Actuarial method displays information for *groupings* of failure times. The Actuarial method is generally used for large samples where you have natural groupings, such as human mortality data, which are commonly grouped into one-year intervals, or warranty data. The intervals may be equal or unequal in size.

- **Nonparametric Distribution Analysis—Arbitrary Censoring** automatically displays a table of Turnbull survival estimates. Alternatively, you can request Actuarial survival estimates.

To plot the survival probabilities versus time, see *Nonparametric survival plots* on page 15-61.

Kaplan-Meier survival estimates (Nonparametric Distribution Analysis—Right Censoring only)

With Nonparametric Distribution Analysis—Right Censoring, the default output includes the characteristics of the variable, and a table of Kaplan-Meier survival estimates. You can also request hazard estimates (empirical hazard function) in the Results subdialog box.

Here we entered failure times for engine windings:

```
Characteristics of Variable

Standard          95.0% Normal CI
Mean(MTTF)        Error        Lower        Upper
   55.7000        2.2069      51.3746      60.0254
Median =      55.0000
IQR =                 *   Q1 =    48.0000   Q3 =              *

Kaplan-Meier Estimates
Number     Number    Survival    Standard     95.0% Normal CI
     Time  at Risk   Failed   Probability     Error      Lower      Upper
   23.0000      50       1       0.9800      0.0198     0.9412     1.0000
   24.0000      49       1       0.9600      0.0277     0.9057     1.0000
   27.0000      48       2       0.9200      0.0384     0.8448     0.9952
   31.0000      46       1       0.9000      0.0424     0.8168     0.9832
   34.0000      45       1       0.8800      0.0460     0.7899     0.9701
   35.0000      44       1       0.8600      0.0491     0.7638     0.9562
   etc.
```

At 35 months, 86% of the units are still running.

- **Characteristics of Variable** displays common measures of the center and spread of the distribution. The mean is not resistant to large lifetimes, while the median, Q1 (25th percentile), Q3 (75th percentile) and the IQR (interquartile range) are resistant.

- **Kaplan-Meier Estimates** contains the *Survival Probability* column—estimates of the proportion of units still surviving at time t.

For each failure time t, MINITAB also displays the number of units at risk, the number failed, and the standard error and 95.0% confidence interval for the survival probabilities.

Additional output

You can request this additional output in the Results subdialog box:

```
Empirical Hazard Function

                    Hazard
         Time    Estimates
       23.0000      0.02000
       24.0000      0.02041
       27.0000      0.02128
       31.0000      0.02174
       34.0000      0.02222
       etc.
```

- *Hazard Estimates* are measures of the instantaneous failure rate for each time t.

Turnbull survival estimates (Nonparametric Distribution Analysis—Arbitrary Censoring only)

With Nonparametric Distribution Analysis—Arbitrary Censoring, the default output includes a table of Turnbull survival estimates.

Here we entered failure times (in miles) for tires.

Turnbull Estimates

Interval lower	upper	Probability of Failure	Standard Error
*	10000.00	0.0103	0.0036
10000.00	20000.00	0.0129	0.0041
20000.00	30000.00	0.0181	0.0048
30000.00	40000.00	0.0323	0.0064
40000.00	50000.00	0.0479	0.0077
50000.00	60000.00	0.1125	0.0114
60000.00	70000.00	0.1876	0.0140
70000.00	80000.00	0.2988	0.0165
80000.00	90000.00	0.1876	0.0140
90000.00	*	0.0918	*

At 40,000 miles, 92.63% of the tires have survived.

Time	Survival Probability	Standard Error	95.0% Normal CI lower	upper
10000.00	0.9897	0.0036	0.9825	0.9968
20000.00	0.9767	0.0054	0.9661	0.9873
30000.00	0.9586	0.0072	0.9446	0.9726
40000.00	0.9263	0.0094	0.9078	0.9447
50000.00	0.8784	0.0118	0.8554	0.9014
60000.00	0.7658	0.0152	0.7360	0.7957
70000.00	0.5783	0.0178	0.5435	0.6131
80000.00	0.2794	0.0161	0.2478	0.3111
90000.00	0.0918	0.0104	0.0715	0.1122

The *Probability of Failure* column contains estimates of the probability of failing during the interval.

The *Survival Probability* column contains estimates of the proportion of units still surviving at time t—in our case, the number of miles.

For each time t, the table also displays the standard errors for both the probability of failures and survival probabilities, and 95.0% approximate confidence intervals for the survival probabilities.

Actuarial survival estimates

Instead of the default Kaplan-Meier or Turnbull survival estimates, you can request Actuarial estimates in the Estimate subdialog box. Actuarial output includes median residual lifetimes, conditional probabilities of failure, and survival probabilities. When using the actuarial method, you can also request hazard estimates and density estimates in the Results subdialog box.

With Nonparametric Distribution Analysis—Right Censoring, you can request specific time intervals. In this example, we requested equally spaced time intervals from 0–110, in increments of 20:

Characteristics of Variable

	Standard	95.0% Normal CI	
Median	Error	lower	upper
56.1905	3.3672	49.5909	62.7900

Additional Time from Time T until 50% of Running Units Fail

	Proportion of	Additional	Standard	95.0% Normal CI	
Time T	Running Units	Time	Error	lower	upper
20.0000	1.0000	36.1905	3.3672	29.5909	42.7900
40.0000	0.8400	20.0000	3.0861	13.9514	26.0486

Actuarial Table

Interval		Number	Number	Number	Conditional Probability	Standard
lower	upper	Entering	Failed	Censored	of Failure	Error
0.000000	20.0000	50	0	0	0.0000	0.0000
20.0000	40.0000	50	8	0	0.1600	0.0518
40.0000	60.0000	42	21	0	0.5000	0.0772
60.0000	80.0000	21	8	4	0.4211	0.1133
80.0000	100.0000	9	0	6	0.0000	0.0000
100.0000	120.0000	3	0	3	0.0000	0.0000

	Survival	Standard	95.0% Normal CI	
Time	Probability	Error	lower	upper
20.0000	1.0000	0.0000	1.0000	1.0000
40.0000	0.8400	0.0518	0.7384	0.9416
60.0000	0.4200	0.0698	0.2832	0.5568
80.0000	0.2432	0.0624	0.1208	0.3655
100.0000	0.2432	0.0624	0.1208	0.3655

Characteristics of Variable displays the median, its standard error, and 95% confidence interval.

Additional Time from Time T Until 50% of Running Units Fail

- *Additional Time* contains the median residual lifetimes, which estimate the additional time from Time t until half of the running units fail. For example, at 40 months, it will take an estimated additional 20 months until 42% (1/2 of 84%) of the running units fail.

Actuarial Table

- *Conditional Probability of Failure* displays conditional probabilities, which estimate the chance that a unit fails in the interval, given that it had not failed up to this point. For example, between 40 and 60 months, 0.5000 of the units failed, given the unit was running at 40 months.

■ *Survival Probability* displays the survival probabilities, which estimate the probability that a unit is running at a given time. For example, 0.8400 of the units are running at 40 months.

For each estimate, MINITAB displays the associated standard errors and, for the survival probabilities, 95.0% approximate confidence intervals.

Additional output

You can request this additional output in the Results subdialog box:

Time	Hazard Estimates	Standard Error	Density Estimates	Standard Error
10.0000	0.000000	*	0.000000	*
30.0000	0.008696	0.003063	0.008000	0.002592
50.0000	0.03333	0.006858	0.02100	0.003490
70.0000	0.02667	0.009087	0.008842	0.002796
90.0000	0.000000	*	0.000000	*
110.0000	0.000000	*	0.000000	*

■ *Hazard Estimates* estimate the hazard function at the midpoint of the interval. The hazard function is a measure of the instantaneous failure rate for each time t.

■ *Density Estimates* estimate the density function at the midpoint of the interval. The density function describes the distribution of failure times.

For each estimate, MINITAB also displays the standard errors.

▶ To request actuarial estimates

1 In the main dialog box, click **Estimate**.

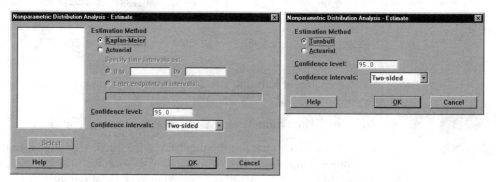

2 Under **Estimation Method**, check **Actuarial**.

    3 With Nonparametric Distribution Analysis—Right Censoring, do one of the following:

- use equally spaced time intervals—choose **0 to_by_** and enter numbers in the boxes. For example, **0 to** 100 **by** 20 gives you these time intervals: 0–20, 20–40, and so on up to 80–100.

- use unequally spaced time intervals—choose **Enter endpoints of intervals**, and enter a series of numbers, or a column of numbers, in the box. For example, entering 0 4 6 8 10 20 30, gives you these time intervals: 0–4, 4–6, 6–8, 8–10, 10–20, and 20–30.

    4 Click **OK**.

More | To display hazard and density estimates in the Actuarial table, from the main dialog box, click **Results**. Do one of the following, then click **OK**:

- With Nonparametric Distribution Analysis—Right Censoring, choose **In addition, hazard, density (actuarial method) estimates, and log-rank and Wilcoxon statistics**.

- With Nonparametric Distribution Analysis—Arbitrary Censoring, choose **In addition, hazard and density estimates (actuarial method)**.

Nonparametric survival plots

Survival (or reliability) plots display the survival probabilities versus time. Each plot point represents the proportion of units surviving at time t. The survival curve is surrounded by two outer lines—the 95% confidence interval for the curve, which provide reasonable values for the "true" survival function.

You can choose from various estimation methods, depending on the command you use:

- With Nonparametric Distribution Analysis—Right Censoring, the survival plot uses Kaplan-Meier survival estimates by default, but you can choose to plot Actuarial estimates.

- With Nonparametric Distribution Analysis—Arbitrary Censoring, the survival plot uses Turnbull survival estimates by default, but you can choose to plot Actuarial estimates.

You can interpret the nonparametric survival curve in a similar manner as you would the parametric survival curve on page 15-40. The major difference is that the nonparametric survival curve is a step function while the parametric survival curve is a smoothed function.

To draw a nonparametric survival plot, check Survival plot in the Graphs subdialog box. By default, the survival plot uses Kaplan-Meier (Nonparametric Distribution Analysis—Right Censoring) or Turnbull (Nonparametric Distribution Analysis—Arbitrary Censoring) estimates of the survival function. If you want to plot Actuarial estimates, choose Actuarial method in the Estimate subdialog box. See *To request actuarial estimates* on page 15-60.

For computations, see Help.

Comparing survival curves (nonparametric distribution analysis—right censoring only)

When you enter more than one sample, Nonparametric Distribution Analysis—Right Censoring automatically compares their survival curves, and displays this table in the Session window:

```
Comparison of Survival Curves

Test Statistics
Method      Chi-Square   DF   P-Value
Log-Rank       7.7152    1    0.0055
Wilcoxon      13.1326    1    0.0003
```

This table contains measures that tell you if the survival curves for various samples are significantly different. A p-value $< \alpha$ indicates that the survival curves are significantly different.

To get more detailed log-rank and Wilcoxon statistics, choose **In addition, hazard, density (actuarial method) estimates and log-rank and Wilcoxon statistics** in the Results subdialog box.

Hazard plots

Nonparametric hazard estimates are calculated various ways:

- Nonparametric Distribution Analysis—Right Censoring automatically plots the empirical hazard function. You can optionally plot Actuarial estimates.

- Nonparametric Distribution Analysis—Arbitrary Censoring only plots Actuarial estimates. Since the Actuarial method is not the default estimation method, be sure to choose Actuarial method in the Estimate subdialog box when you want to draw a hazard plot.

For a general description, see *Hazard plots* on page 15-41. For computations, see Help.

▶ **To draw a hazard plot (nonparametric distribution analysis—right censoring command)**

1 In the Nonparametric Distribution Analysis—Right Censoring dialog box, click **Graphs**.

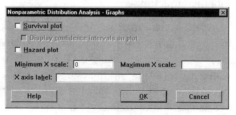

2   Check **Hazard plot**, then click **OK**.

More | By default, Nonparametric Distribution Analysis—Right Censoring's hazard plot uses the empirical hazard function. If you want to plot Actuarial estimates, choose **Actuarial method** in the Estimate subdialog box. See *To request actuarial estimates* on page 15-60.

▶ **To draw a hazard plot (nonparametric distribution analysis—arbitrary censoring command)**

1   In the Nonparametric Distribution Analysis—Arbitrary Censoring dialog box, click **Estimate**. Choose **Actuarial**. Click **OK**.

2   Click **Graphs**.

3   Check **Hazard plot**, then click **OK**.

▷ **Example of a nonparametric distribution analysis with exact failure/right censored data**

Suppose you work for a company that manufactures engine windings for turbine assemblies. Engine windings may decompose at an unacceptable rate at high temperatures. You decide to look at failure times for engine windings at two temperatures, 80 and 100°C. You want to find out the following information for each temperature:

■ the times at which half of the windings fail

■ the proportion of windings that survive past various times

You also want to know whether or not the survival curves at the two temperatures are significantly different.

In the first sample, you collect times to failure for 50 windings at 80°C; in the second sample, you collect times to failure for 40 windings at 100°C. Some of the windings drop out of the test for unrelated reasons. In the MINITAB worksheet, you use a column of censoring indicators to designate which times are actual failures (1) and which are censored units removed from the test before failure (0).

1   Open the worksheet RELIABLE.MTW.

2   Choose **Stat ➤ Reliability/Survival ➤ Nonparametric Dist Analysis–Right Cens**.

3   In **Variables**, enter *Temp80 Temp100*.

4 Click **Censor**. Choose **Use censoring columns** and enter *Cens80 Cens100* in the box. Click **OK**.

5 Click **Graphs**. Check **Survival plot** and **Display confidence intervals on plot**. Click **OK** in each dialog box.

The output for the 100°C sample follows that of the 80°C sample. The comparison of survival curves shows up last.

Session window output

Distribution Analysis: Temp80

Variable: Temp80

Censoring Information	Count
Uncensored value	37
Right censored value	13

Censoring value: Cens80 = 0

Nonparametric Estimates

Characteristics of Variable

Mean (MTTF)	Standard Error	95.0% Normal CI Lower	Upper
55.7000	2.2069	51.3746	60.0254

Median =   55.0000
IQR =   * Q1 =   48.0000   Q3 =   *

Kaplan-Meier Estimates

Time	Number at Risk	Number Failed	Survival Probability	Standard Error	95.0% Normal CI Lower	Upper
23.0000	50	1	0.9800	0.0198	0.9412	1.0000
24.0000	49	1	0.9600	0.0277	0.9057	1.0000
27.0000	48	2	0.9200	0.0384	0.8448	0.9952
31.0000	46	1	0.9000	0.0424	0.8168	0.9832
34.0000	45	1	0.8800	0.0460	0.7899	0.9701
35.0000	44	1	0.8600	0.0491	0.7638	0.9562
37.0000	43	1	0.8400	0.0518	0.7384	0.9416
40.0000	42	1	0.8200	0.0543	0.7135	0.9265
41.0000	41	1	0.8000	0.0566	0.6891	0.9109
45.0000	40	1	0.7800	0.0586	0.6652	0.8948

Distribution Analysis: Temp100

Variable: Temp100

Censoring Information	Count
Uncensored value	34
Right censored value	6

Censoring value: Cens100 = 0

Nonparametric Estimates

Characteristics of Variable

	Standard	95.0% Normal CI	
Mean(MTTF)	Error	Lower	Upper
41.6563	3.4695	34.8561	48.4564

Median =   38.0000
IQR =   30.0000 Q1 =   24.0000 Q3 =   54.0000

Kaplan-Meier Estimates

Time	Number at Risk	Number Failed	Survival Probability	Standard Error	95.0% Normal CI Lower	Upper
6.0000	40	1	0.9750	0.0247	0.9266	1.0000
10.0000	39	1	0.9500	0.0345	0.8825	1.0000
11.0000	38	1	0.9250	0.0416	0.8434	1.0000
14.0000	37	1	0.9000	0.0474	0.8070	0.9930
16.0000	36	1	0.8750	0.0523	0.7725	0.9775
18.0000	35	3	0.8000	0.0632	0.6760	0.9240
22.0000	32	1	0.7750	0.0660	0.6456	0.9044
24.0000	31	1	0.7500	0.0685	0.6158	0.8842
25.0000	30	1	0.7250	0.0706	0.5866	0.8634
27.0000	29	1	0.7000	0.0725	0.5580	0.8420
29.0000	28	1	0.6750	0.0741	0.5299	0.8201
30.0000	27	1	0.6500	0.0754	0.5022	0.7978
32.0000	26	1	0.6250	0.0765	0.4750	0.7750
35.0000	25	1	0.6000	0.0775	0.4482	0.7518

Distribution Analysis: Temp80, Temp100

Comparison of Survival Curves

Test Statistics

Method	Chi-Square	DF	P-Value
Log-Rank	7.7152	1	0.0055
Wilcoxon	13.1326	1	0.0003

Graph window output

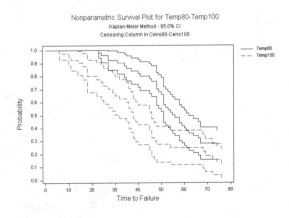

Nonparametric Survival Plot for Temp80-Temp100
Kaplan-Meier Method - 95.0% CI
Censoring Column in Cens80-Cens100

Interpreting the results

The estimated median failure time for Temp80 is 55 months and 38 months for Temp100. So the increase in temperature decreased the median failure time by approximately 17 months.

The survival estimates are displayed in the Kaplan-Meier Estimates table. For example, at 80° C, 0.9000 of the windings survive past 31 months, while at 100° C, 0.9000 of the windings survive past 14 months.

Are the survival curves for Temp80 and Temp100 significantly different? In the Test Statistics table, a p-value $< \alpha$ indicates that the survival curves are significantly different. In this case, the small p-values (0.0055 and 0.003) suggest that a change of 20° C plays a significant role in the breakdown of engine windings.

▷ Example of a nonparametric distribution analysis with arbitrarily censored data

Suppose you work for a company that manufactures tires. You are interested in finding out how likely it is that a tire will "fail," or wear down to 2/32 of an inch of tread, within given mileage intervals. You are especially interested in knowing how many of the tires last past 45,000 miles.

You inspect each good tire at regular intervals (every 10,000 miles) to see if the tire fails, then enter the data into the MINITAB worksheet.

1 Open the worksheet TIREWEAR.MTW.

2 Choose **Stat ➤ Reliability/Survival ➤ Nonparametric Dist Analysis–Arbitrary Cens**.

3 In **Start variables**, enter *Start*. In **End variables**, enter *End*.

4 In **Frequency columns**, enter *Freq*, then click **OK**.

Session window output

Distribution Analysis, Start = Start and End = End

```
Variable
Start:  Start     End:  End
Frequency:  Freq

Censoring Information              Count
Right censored value               71
Interval censored value           694
Left censored value                 8

Turnbull Estimates

            Interval      Probability    Standard
     Lower      Upper      of Failure      Error
         *   10000.00         0.0103      0.0036
  10000.00   20000.00         0.0129      0.0041
  20000.00   30000.00         0.0181      0.0048
  30000.00   40000.00         0.0323      0.0064
  40000.00   50000.00         0.0479      0.0077
  50000.00   60000.00         0.1125      0.0114
  60000.00   70000.00         0.1876      0.0140
  70000.00   80000.00         0.2988      0.0165
  80000.00   90000.00         0.1876      0.0140
  90000.00          *         0.0918         *

              Survival    Standard     95.0% Normal CI
     Time   Probability     Error     Lower      Upper
  10000.00     0.9897      0.0036     0.9825     0.9968
  20000.00     0.9767      0.0054     0.9661     0.9873
  30000.00     0.9586      0.0072     0.9446     0.9726
  40000.00     0.9263      0.0094     0.9078     0.9447
  50000.00     0.8784      0.0118     0.8554     0.9014
  60000.00     0.7658      0.0152     0.7360     0.7957
  70000.00     0.5783      0.0178     0.5435     0.6131
  80000.00     0.2794      0.0161     0.2478     0.3111
  90000.00     0.0918      0.0104     0.0715     0.1122
```

Interpreting the results

The Turnbull Estimates table displays the probabilities of failure. For example, between 60,000 and 70,000 miles, 18.76% of the tires fail.

You can see in the column of survival probabilities that 92.63% of the tires last past 40,000 miles.

References

[1] R.B. D'Agostino and M.A. Stephens (1986). *Goodness-of-Fit Techniques*, Marcel Dekker.

[2] J.D. Kalbfleisch and R.L. Prentice (1980). *The Statistical Analysis of Failure Time Data*, John Wiley & Sons.

[3] D. Kececioglu (1991). *Reliability Engineering Handbook*, Vols 1 and 2, Prentice Hall.

[4] J.F. Lawless (1982). *Statistical Models and Methods for Lifetime Data*, John Wiley & Sons, Inc.

[5] W.Q. Meeker and L.A. Escobar (1998). *Statistical Methods for Reliability Data*, John Wiley & Sons, Inc.

[6] W. Murray, Ed. (1972). *Numerical Methods for Unconstrained Optimization*, Academic Press.

[7] W. Nelson (1982). *Applied Life Data Analysis*, John Wiley & Sons.

[8] R. Peto (1973). "Experimental Survival Curves for Interval-censored Data," *Applied Statistics* 22, pp. 86-91.

[9] B.W. Turnbull (1976). "The Empirical Distribution Function with Arbitrarily Grouped, Censored and Truncated Data," *Journal of the Royal Statistical Society* 38, pp. 290-295.

[10] B.W. Turnbull (1974). "Nonparametric Estimation of a Survivorship Function with Doubly Censored Data," *Journal of the American Statistical Association* 69, 345, pp. 169-173.

16

Regression with Life Data

Regression with Life Data Overview

Use MINITAB's regression with life data commands to investigate the relationship between failure time and one or more predictors. For example, you might want to examine how a predictor affects the lifetime of a person, part, product, or organism. The goal is to come up with a model that predicts failure time. Based on these predictions you can estimate the reliability of the system.

- **Accelerated Life Testing** performs a simple regression with one predictor that is used to model failure times for highly reliable products. The predictor is an accelerating variable; its levels exceed those normally found in the field. The data obtained under the high stress conditions can then be used to extrapolate back to normal use conditions. In order to do this, you must have a good model of the relationship between failure time and the accelerating variable.

- **Regression with Life Data** performs a regression with one or more predictors. The model can include factors, covariates, interactions, and nested terms. This model will help you understand how different factors and covariates affect the lifetime of your part or product.

Both regression with life data commands differ from other regression commands in MINITAB in that they use different distributions and accept censored data. You can choose to model your data on one of the following eight distributions: Weibull, extreme value, exponential, normal, lognormal base$_e$, lognormal base$_{10}$, logistic, and loglogistic.

Life data is often incomplete or censored in some way. Censored observations are those for which an exact failure time is unknown. Suppose you are testing how long a product lasts and you plan to end the study after a certain amount of time. Any products that have not failed *before* the study ends are right-censored, meaning that the part failed sometime after the present time. Similarly, you may only know that a product failed before a certain time, which is left-censored. Failure times that occur within a certain interval of time are interval-censored.

MINITAB uses a modified Newton-Raphson algorithm to calculate maximum likelihood estimates of the model parameters.

Worksheet Structure for Regression with Life Data

The basic worksheet structure for regression with life data is three columns, although you may have more than three. The three columns are:

- the *response variable* (failure times) — see *Failure times* on page 16-4

- *censoring indicators* (for the failure times, if needed) — see *Uncensored/right censored data* on page 16-4

- *predictor variables*
    - For Accelerated Life Testing, enter one predictor column containing various levels of an accelerating variable. For example, an accelerating variable may be stresses or catalysts whose levels exceed normal operating conditions.
    - For Regression with Life Data, enter one or more predictor columns. These predictor variables may be treated as factors or covariates in the model. For more information, see *How to specify the model terms* on page 16-24.

Structure each column so that it contains individual observations (one row = one observation), or unique observations with a corresponding column of frequencies. Frequency columns are useful when you have large numbers of data with common failure or censoring times, and identical predictor values. Here is the same worksheet structured both ways:

Raw Data: one row for each observation

Frequency Data: one row for each combination of response, censoring indicator, factor, and covariate.

C1	C2	C3	C4
Response	Censor	Factor	Covar
29	F	1	12 ——1
31	F	1	12
31	F	1	12
.	.	.	. ⎬ 19
.	.	.	.
37	F	1	12 ——1
37	C	2	12 ——1
41	F	2	12
.	.	.	. ⎬ 19
.	.	.	.

C1	C2	C3	C4	C5
Response	Censor	Covar	Factor	Count
29	F	12	1	1
31	F	12	1	19
37	F	12	1	1
37	C	12	2	1
41	F	12	2	19

Text categories (factor levels) are processed in alphabetical order by default. If you wish, you can define your own order — see *Ordering Text Categories* in the *Manipulating Data* chapter of MINITAB *User's Guide 1* for details.

The way you set up the worksheet depends on the type of censoring you have, as described in *Failure times* below.

Failure times

The response data you gather for the commands in this chapter are the individual failure times. For example, you might collect failure times for units running at a given temperature. You might also collect samples under different temperatures, or under varying conditions of any combination of accelerating variables. Individual failure times are the same type of data used for *Distribution Analysis* on page 15-1.

Life data is often censored or incomplete in some way. Suppose you are monitoring air conditioner fans to find out the percentage of fans which fail within a three-year warranty period. The table below describes the types of observations you can have:

Type of observation	Description	Example
Exact failure time	You know *exactly* when the failure occurred.	The fan failed at exactly 500 days.
Right censored	You only know that the failure occurred *after* a particular time.	The fan failed sometime after 500 days.
Left censored	You only know that the failure occurred *before* a particular time.	The fan failed sometime before 500 days.
Interval censored	You only know that the failure occurred *between* two particular times.	The fan failed sometime between 475 and 500 days.

How you set up your worksheet depends, in part, on the type of censoring you have:

- When your data consist of exact failures and right-censored observations, see *Uncensored/right censored data* on page 16-4.

- When your data have a varied censoring scheme, see *Uncensored/arbitrarily censored data* on page 16-5.

Uncensored/right censored data

Enter two columns for each sample—one column of failure (or censoring) times and a corresponding column of censoring indicators.

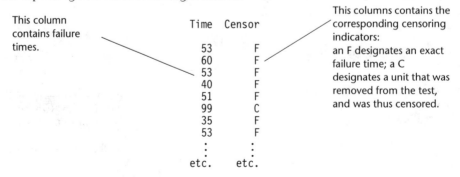

This column contains failure times.

Time	Censor
53	F
60	F
53	F
40	F
51	F
99	C
35	F
53	F
⋮	⋮
etc.	etc.

This columns contains the corresponding censoring indicators: an F designates an exact failure time; a C designates a unit that was removed from the test, and was thus censored.

Censoring indicators can be numbers, text, or date/time values. If you do not specify which value indicates censoring in the Censor subdialog box, MINITAB assumes the lower of the two values indicates censoring, and the higher of the two values indicates an exact failure.

The data column and associated censoring column must be the same length, although pairs of data/censor columns (each pair corresponds to a sample) can have different lengths.

Uncensored/arbitrarily censored data

When you have any combination of exact failure times, right-, left- and interval-censored data, enter your data using a Start column and End column:

For this observation...	Enter in the Start column...	Enter in the End column...
Exact failure time	failure time	failure time
Right censored	time after which the failure occurred	the missing value symbol '*'
Left censored	the missing value symbol '*'	time before which the failure occurred
Interval censored	time at start of interval during which the failure occurred	time at end of interval during which the failure occurred

This example uses a frequency column as well.

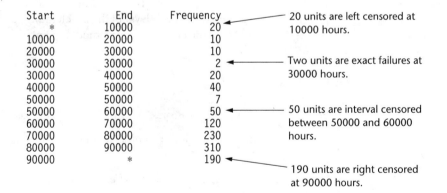

Start	End	Frequency	
*	10000	20	← 20 units are left censored at 10000 hours.
10000	20000	10	
20000	30000	10	
30000	30000	2	← Two units are exact failures at 30000 hours.
30000	40000	20	
40000	50000	40	
50000	50000	7	
50000	60000	50	← 50 units are interval censored between 50000 and 60000 hours.
60000	70000	120	
70000	80000	230	
80000	90000	310	
90000	*	190	← 190 units are right censored at 90000 hours.

Accelerated Life Testing

Use Accelerated Life Testing to investigate the relationship between failure time and one predictor. The most common application of accelerated life testing is for studies in which you impose a series of variable levels far exceeding normal field conditions to accelerate the failure process. The variable is thus called the *accelerating variable*. Accelerated tests are performed to save time and money, since, under normal field conditions, it can take a very long time for a unit to fail. Accelerated life testing requires knowledge of the relationship between the accelerating variable and failure time.

Here are the steps:

1   Impose levels of the accelerating variable on the units.

2   Record the failure (or censoring) times.

3   Run the Accelerated Life Testing analysis, asking MINITAB to extrapolate to the *design value*, or common field condition. This way, you can find out how the units behave under normal field conditions.

You can request an Arrhenius, inverse temperature, $\log_e$, $\log_{10}$ transformation, or no transformation for the accelerating variable. By default, MINITAB assumes the relationship is linear (no transformation).

The simplest output includes a regression table, relation plot, and probability plot for each level of the accelerating variable based on the fitted model. The relation plot displays the relationship between the accelerating variable and failure time by plotting percentiles for each level of the accelerating variable. By default, lines are drawn at the 10th, 50th, and 90th percentiles. The 50th percentile is a good estimate for the time a part will last when exposed to various levels of the accelerating variable. The probability plot is created for each level of the accelerating variable based on the fitted model (line) and based on a nonparametric model (points).

Data

See *Worksheet Structure for Regression with Life Data* on page 16-3.

MINITAB automatically excludes all observations with missing values from all calculations.

How you run the analysis depends on whether your data is uncensored/right censored or uncensored/arbitrarily censored.

▶ To perform accelerated life testing with uncensored/right censored data

1   Choose Stat ➤ Reliability/Survival ➤ Accelerated Life Testing.

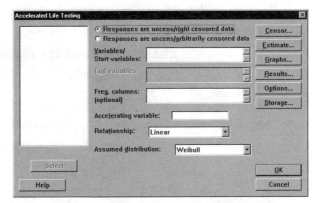

2   In **Variables/Start variables**, enter the columns of failure times. You can enter up to ten columns (ten different samples).

3   If you have frequency columns, enter them in **Freq. columns**.

4   In **Accelerating variable**, enter the column of predictors.

Note | If you have no censored values, you can skip steps 5 & 6.

5   Click **Censor**.

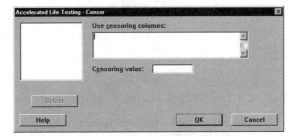

6   In **Use censoring columns**, enter the censoring columns. The first censoring column is paired with the first data column, the second censoring column is paired with the second data column, and so on.

By default, MINITAB uses the lowest value in the censoring column to indicate a censored observation. To use some other value, enter that value in **Censoring value**.

Note | If your censoring indicators are date/time values, store the value as a constant and then enter the constant.

7   If you like, use any of the options listed below, then click **OK**.

▶ **To perform accelerated life testing with uncensored/arbitrarily censored data**

1 Choose Stat ➤ Reliability/Survival ➤ Accelerated Life Testing.

2 Choose **Responses are uncens/arbitrarily censored data.**

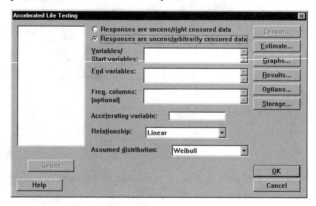

3 In **Variables/Start variables**, enter the columns of start times. You can enter up to ten columns (ten different samples).

4 In **End variables**, enter the columns of end times. You can enter up to ten columns (ten different samples).

5 If you have frequency columns, enter them in **Freq. columns**.

6 In **Accelerating variable**, enter the column of predictor values.

7 If you like, use any of the options described below, then click **OK**.

Options

Accelerated Life Testing dialog box

- transform the accelerating variable one of four common ways: Arrhenius, inverse temperature, $\log_e$, or $\log_{10}$. By default, MINITAB uses no transformation (linear). See *Transforming the accelerating variable* on page 16-12.

- choose one of eight common lifetime distributions for the error distribution, including the Weibull (default), extreme value, exponential, normal, lognormal $base_e$, lognormal $base_{10}$, logistic, and loglogistic distributions.

More | MINITAB's extreme value distribution is the smallest extreme value (Type 1).

Estimate subdialog box

- enter predictor values (levels of accelerating variable) for which to estimate percentiles and/or survival probabilities. Most often, you would enter the design value. You can also use the predictor values (levels of accelerating variable) from the data.

- estimate percentiles for the percents you specify—see *Percentiles and survival probabilities* on page 16-16. By default, MINITAB estimates the 50th percentile.

- store the percentiles, their standard errors, and confidence intervals.

- estimate survival probabilities for the times you specify—see *Percentiles and survival probabilities* on page 16-16. For example, if you enter 10 hours, MINITAB estimates (for each predictor value) the proportion of units that survive at least 10 hours.

- store the survival probabilities and confidence intervals.

- specify a confidence level for all of the confidence intervals. The default is 95.0%.

Graphs subdialog box

- enter a design value to include on the plots based on the fitted model (relation plot and probability plot for each accelerating level).

- draw a relation plot to display the relationship between an accelerating variable and failure time—see *Relation plot* on page 16-11. You can:
  - plot percentiles for the percents you specify. By default, MINITAB plots the 10th, 50th, and 90th percentiles.
  - display confidence intervals for all of the percentiles or the middle percentiles only. You can also suppress their display.
  - display points for failure times (exact failure time or midpoint of interval for interval censored observation) on the plot.

- draw a probability plot for each level of the accelerating variable based on the fitted model—see *Probability plots* on page 16-14. You can:
  - display confidence intervals for the design value or for all levels of the accelerating variable. You can also suppress their display.

- draw a probability plot for each level of the accelerating variable based on the individual fits—see *Probability plots* on page 16-14.

- draw a probability plot for the standardized residuals and an exponential probability plot for the Cox-Snell residuals—see *Probability plots* on page 16-14.

- include confidence intervals on the diagnostic plots.

Results subdialog box

- display the following Session window output:
  - no output
  - the basic output, which includes the response information, censoring information, regression table, the log-likelihood, and goodness-of-fit measures
  - the basic output, plus the table of percentiles and/or survival probabilities (the default)
- show the log-likelihood for each iteration of the algorithm

Options subdialog box

- enter starting values for model parameters for the Newton-Raphson algorithm—see *Estimating the model parameters* on page 16-28.

- change the maximum number of iterations for reaching convergence (the default is 20). MINITAB obtains maximum likelihood estimates through an iterative process. If the maximum number of iterations is reached before convergence, the command terminates—see *Estimating the model parameters* on page 16-28.

- estimate other model coefficients while holding the shape parameter (Weibull) or the scale parameter (other distributions) fixed at a specific value—see *Estimating the model parameters* on page 16-28.

- use historical estimates for the parameters rather than estimate them from the data—see *Estimating the model parameters* on page 16-28. In this case, no estimation is done; all results—such as the percentiles—are based on these parameters.

Storage subdialog box

- store the ordinary, standardized, and Cox-Snell residuals.

- store information on the estimated equation, including the estimated coefficients, their standard errors and confidence intervals, the variance/covariance matrix, and the log-likelihood for the last iteration.

Output

The default output consists of the regression table, a relation plot, a probability plot for each level of the accelerating variable based on the fitted model, and Anderson-Darling goodness-of-fit statistics for the probability plot.

Regression table

The regression table displays:

- the estimated *coefficients* for the regression model and their
  - standard errors.
  - Z-values and p-values. The Z-test tests that the coefficient is significantly different than zero; in other words, is it a significant predictor?
  - 95% confidence interval.

- the *Shape parameter* (Weibull or exponential) or *Scale parameter* (other distributions), a measure of the overall variability, and its
  - standard error.
  - 95% confidence interval.

- the log-likelihood.

- Anderson-Darling goodness-of-fit statistics for each level of the accelerating variable based on the fitted model.

Relation plot

The relation plot displays failure time versus an accelerating variable. By default, lines are drawn at the 10th, 50th, and 90th percentiles. The 50th percentile is a good estimate for the time a part will last for the given conditions. For an illustration, see *Example of accelerated life testing* on page 16-17.

You can optionally specify up to ten percentiles to plot and display the failure times (exact failure time or midpoint of interval for interval censored observation) on the plot. You can enter a design value to include on the plot.

▶ **To modify the relation plot**

  1 In the Accelerated Life Testing dialog box, click **Graphs**.

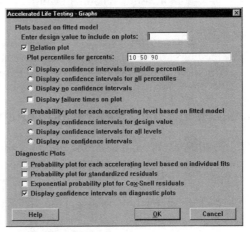

2 Do any of the following:

- To include a design value on the plot, specify a value in **Enter design value to include on plots**.

- To plot percentiles for the percents you specify, enter the percents or a column of percents in **Plot percentiles for percents**. For example, to plot the 30th percentile (how long it takes 30% of the units to fail), enter 30. By default, MINITAB plots the 10th, 50th, and 90th percentiles.

- Choose one:
  - **Display confidence intervals for middle percentile**
  - **Display confidence intervals for all percentiles**
  - **Display no confidence intervals**

- To include failure times (exact failure time or midpoint of interval for interval censored observation) on the plot, check **Display failure times on plot**.

3 Click **OK**.

4 If you like, change the confidence level for the intervals (default = 95%): Click **Estimate**. In **Confidence level**, enter a value, then click **OK**.

Probability plot for each accelerating level based on fitted model

The probability plot displays the percents for each level of the accelerating variable based on the fitted model (line) and a nonparametric model (points). By default, the probability plot includes the shape and scale parameters (Weibull and exponential distributions) or the location and scale parameters (other distributions). These parameters are based on the fitted model. This plot assumes that the observations for each accelerating variable level share a common shape (Weibull and exponential distributions) or scale (other distributions).

The probability plot also includes the Anderson-Darling statistic, which is a goodness-of-fit measure. A count of failures and right-censored data appears when your data are exact failures/right-censored.

You can choose to display confidence intervals for the design value, for all levels of the accelerating variable, or no confidence intervals. For more information on creating and interpreting probability plots see *Probability plots* on page 16-14.

Transforming the accelerating variable

If you assume a linear relationship then no transformation is needed. Any change in failure time or log failure time is directly proportional to the change in the accelerating variable.

A log relationship is used to model the life of products running under constant stress. The log relationship is most often used in combination with a log-based failure time distribution. When it is used in combination with a log-based failure time distribution, an **inverse power** relationship results. Common applications of the log transformations include electrical insulations, metal fatigue, and ball bearings.

Based on the Arrhenius Rate Law, the rate of a simple chemical reaction depends on the temperature. This relationship is often used to describe failures due to degradation caused by a chemical reaction. Common applications of the Arrhenius transformation include electrical insulations, semiconductor devices, solid state devices, and plastics.

$$\text{Arrhenius transformation} = \frac{11604.83}{C° + 273.16}$$

The inverse temperature transformation is a simple relationship that assumes that failure time is inversely proportional to Kelvin temperature. The inverse and Arrhenius transformations have similar results, but the coefficients have different interpretations.

$$\text{Inverse temperature transformation} = \frac{1}{C° + 273.16}$$

Interpreting the regression equation

The regression model estimates the percentiles of the failure time distribution:

$$Y_p = \beta_0 + \beta_1 X + \sigma\varepsilon_p$$

where:

Y_p = pth percentile of the failure time distribution, either failure time or log (failure time)

β_0 = y-intercept (constant)

β_1 = regression coefficient

X = predictor values (may be transformed)

σ = scale parameter

ε_p = pth percentile of the error distribution

Depending on the distribution, Y_p = failure time or log (failure time):

- For the Weibull, exponential, lognormal base$_e$, lognormal base$_{10}$ and loglogistic distributions, Y_p = log (failure time)

- For the normal, extreme value, and logistic distributions, Y_p = failure time

When Y_p = log (failure time), MINITAB takes the antilog to display the percentiles on the original scale.

You can find the values for the y-intercept, the regression coefficient(s), and the shape or scale parameter in the regression table. When you enter predictor values in the Estimate subdialog box, the percentiles are displayed in the table of percentiles.

Note   You will often have more than one regression coefficient and predictor (X) with *Regression with Life Data* on page 16-19.

The value of the error distribution ε_p also depends on the distribution chosen.

- For the normal distribution, the error distribution is the standard normal distribution—normal $(0,1)$. For the lognormal base$_{10}$ and lognormal base$_e$ distributions, MINITAB takes the log base$_{10}$ or log base$_e$ of the data, respectively, and uses a normal distribution.

- For the logistic distribution, the error distribution is the standard logistic distribution—logistic $(0, 1)$. For the loglogistic distribution, MINITAB takes the log of the data and uses a logistic distribution.

- For the extreme value distribution, the error distribution is the standard extreme value distribution—extreme value $(0, 1)$. For the Weibull distribution and the exponential distribution (a type of Weibull distribution), MINITAB takes the log of the data and uses the extreme value distribution.

Probability plots

The Accelerated Life Testing command draws several probability plots to help you assess the fit of the chosen distribution. You can draw probability plots for the standardized and Cox-Snell residuals. You can use these plots to assess whether a particular distribution fits your data. In general, the closer the points fall to the fitted line, the better the fit.

You can also choose to draw probability plots for each level of the accelerating variable based on individual fits or on the fitted model. You can use these plots to assess whether the distribution, transformation, and assumption of equal shape (Weibull or exponential) or scale (other distributions) are appropriate. The probability plot based on the fitted model includes fitted lines that are based on the chosen distribution and transformation. If the points do not fit the lines adequately, then consider a different transformation or distribution.

The probability plot based on the individual fits includes fitted lines that are calculated by individually fitting the distribution to each level of the accelerating variable. If the distributions have equal shape (Weibull or exponential) or scale (other distributions) parameters, then the fitted lines should be approximately parallel. The points should fit the line adequately if the chosen distribution is appropriate.

MINITAB provides one goodness-of-fit measure: the Anderson-Darling statistic. A smaller Anderson-Darling statistic indicates that the distribution provides a better fit. You can use the Anderson-darling statistic to compare the fit of competing models.

For a discussion of probability plots, see *Probability plots* on page 15-37.

▶ **To draw a probability plot for each level of the accelerating variable**

1   In the Accelerated Life Testing dialog box, click **Graphs**.

2   Do any of the following, then click **OK**.

   ■   To plot based on the fitted model, check **Probability plot for each accelerating level based on fitted model**. Choose one of the following:
      –   **Display confidence intervals for design value**
      –   **Display confidence intervals for all levels**
      –   **Display no confidence intervals**

      To include a design value on the fitted model plot, enter a value in **Enter a design value to include on plots**.

   ■   To plot based on the individual fits, check **Probability plot for each accelerating level based on individual fits**.

▶ **To draw a probability plot of the residuals**

1   In the Accelerated Life Testing dialog box, click **Graphs**.

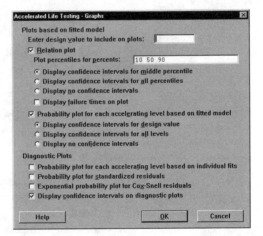

2   Do any of the following, then click **OK**:

   ■   To plot the standardized residuals, check **Probability plot for standardized residuals**

   ■   To plot the Cox-Snell residuals, check **Exponential probability plot for Cox-Snell residuals**

Tip | To draw a probability plot with more options, store the residuals in the Storage subdialog box, then use the probability plot included with *Parametric Distribution Analysis* on page 15-27.

Percentiles and survival probabilities

When doing accelerated life testing, you subject units to levels of an accelerating variable far exceeding normal field conditions to accelerate the failure process. But most likely, the information you ultimately want is, How do the units behave under normal field conditions?

In the Estimate subdialog box, you can ask MINITAB to extrapolate information gained from the accelerated situation to the *design value*, or common field condition.

▶ **To estimate percentiles and survival probabilities**

1 In the **Accelerated Life Testing** dialog box, click **Estimate**.

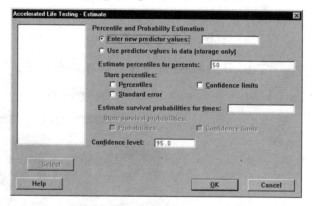

2 In **Enter new predictor values**, enter one new value or column of new values. Often you will enter the design value, or common running condition, for the units.

3 Do any of the following, then click **OK**:

■ To estimate percentiles, enter the percents in **Estimate percentiles for percents.** By default, MINITAB estimates the 50th percentile. If you want to look at the beginning, middle, and end of the product's lifetime for a given predictor value, enter 10 50 90 (the 10th, 50th, 90th percentiles). MINITAB then estimates how long it takes for 10% of the units to fail, 50% of the units to fail, and 90% of the units to fail.

■ To estimate survival probabilities, enter the times in **Estimate survival probabilities for times**. For example, when you enter 70 (units in hours), MINITAB estimates the probability, for each predictor value, that the unit will survive past 70 hours.

More | Sometimes you may want to estimate percentiles or survival probabilities for the accelerating variable levels used in the study:

In the Estimate subdialog box, choose **Use predictor values in data (storage only)**. Because of the potentially large amount of output, MINITAB stores the results in the worksheet rather then printing them in the Session window.

▷ **Example of accelerated life testing**

Suppose you want to investigate the deterioration of an insulation used for electric motors. The motors normally run between 80 and 100° C. To save time and money, you decide to use accelerated life testing.

First you gather failure times for the insulation at abnormally high temperatures—110, 130, 150, and 170° C—to speed up the deterioration. With failure time information at these temperatures, you can then extrapolate to 80 and 100° C. It is known that an Arrhenius relationship exists between temperature and failure time.

To see how well the model fits, you will draw a probability plot based on the standardized residuals.

1 Open the worksheet INSULATE.MTW.

2 Choose **Stat ➤ Reliability/Survival ➤ Accelerated Life Testing**.

3 In **Variables/Start variables**, enter *FailureT*. In **Accelerating variable**, enter *Temp*.

4 From **Relationship**, choose **Arrhenius**.

5 Click **Censor**. In **Use censoring columns**, enter *Censor*, then click **OK**.

6 Click **Graphs**. In **Enter design value to include on plot**, enter *80*. Click **OK**.

7 Click **Estimate**. In **Enter new predictor values**, enter *Design*, then click **OK** in each dialog box.

Session window output

Regression with Life Data: FailureT versus Temp

```
Response Variable:  FailureT

Censoring Information              Count
Uncensored value                    66
Right censored value                14
Censoring value:  Censor = C

Estimation Method:  Maximum Likelihood
Distribution:  Weibull
Transformation on accelerating variable:  Arrhenius

Regression Table
                      Standard                    95.0% Normal CI
Predictor    Coef      Error      Z      P      Lower      Upper
Intercept  -15.1874   0.9862  -15.40  0.000   -17.1203   -13.2546
Temp         0.83072  0.03504   23.71  0.000     0.76204    0.89940
Shape        2.8246   0.2570                     2.3633     3.3760

Log-Likelihood = -564.693
```

Anderson-Darling (adjusted) Goodness-of-Fit

At each accelerating level
Level	Fitted Model
110	22.30
130	0.6750
150	4.996
170	2.435

Table of Percentiles

Percent	Temp	Percentile	Standard Error	95.0% Normal CI Lower	Upper
50	80.0000	159584.5	27446.85	113918.2	223557.0
50	100.0000	36948.57	4216.511	29543.36	46209.94

*Graph
window
output*

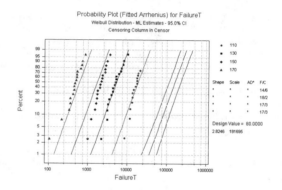

Probability Plot (Fitted Arrhenius) for FailureT
Weibull Distribution - ML Estimates - 95.0% CI
Censoring Column in Censor

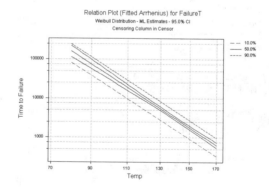

Relation Plot (Fitted Arrhenius) for FailureT
Weibull Distribution - ML Estimates - 95.0% CI
Censoring Column in Censor

Interpreting the results

From the Regression Table, you get the coefficients for the regression model. For a Weibull distribution, this model describes the relationship between temperature and failure time for the insulation:

$$\text{Log}_e \text{ (failure time)} = -15.1874 + 0.83072 \text{ (ArrTemp)} + 2.8246 \; \varepsilon_p$$

where ε_p = the pth percentile of the standard extreme value distribution

$$\text{ArrTemp} = \left(\frac{11604.83}{\text{Temp} + 273.16} \right)$$

The Table of Percentiles displays the 50th percentiles for the temperatures that you entered. The 50th percentile is a good estimate of how long the insulation will last in the field. At 80° C, the insulation lasts about 159,584.5 hours, or 18.20 years; at 100° C, the insulation lasts about 36,948.57 hours, or 4.21 years.

With the relation plot, you can look at the distribution of failure times for each temperature—in this case, the 10th, 50th, and 90th percentiles.

The probability plot based on the fitted model can help you determine whether the distribution, transformation, and assumption of equal shape (Weibull) at each level of the accelerating variable are appropriate. In this case, the points fit the lines adequately, thereby verifying that the assumptions of the model are appropriate for the accelerating variable levels.

Regression with Life Data

Use Regression with Life Data to see whether one or more predictors affect the failure time of a product. The goal is to come up with a model which predicts failure time. This model uses explanatory variables to explain changes in the response variable, for example why some products fail quickly and some survive for a long time. The model can include factors, covariates, interactions, and nested terms.

Regression with Life Data differs from MINITAB's regression commands in that it accepts censored data and uses different distributions.

To do regression with life data, you must enter the following information:

- the *response variable* (failure times).
- *model terms*, which consist of any number of predictor variables and when appropriate, various interactions between predictors. See *How to specify the model terms* on page 16-24. Some of these terms may be *factors*.

Data

Enter three types of columns in the worksheet:

- the *response variable* (failure times)—see *Failure times* on page 16-4.
- *censoring indicators* for the response variables, if needed.
- *predictor variables*, which may be factors (categorical variables) or covariates (continuous variables). For factors, MINITAB estimates the coefficients for k − 1 design variables (where k is the number of levels), to compare the effect of different levels on the response variable. For covariates, MINITAB estimate the coefficient associated with the covariate to describe its effect on the response variable.

Unless you specify a predictor as a factor, the predictor is assumed to be a covariate. In the model, terms may be created from these predictor variables and treated as factors, covariates, interactions, or nested terms. The model can include up to 9 factors and 50 covariates. Factors may be crossed or nested. Covariates may be crossed with each other or with factors, or nested within factors. See *How to specify the model terms* on page 16-24.

You can enter up to ten samples per analysis.

Depending on the type of censoring you have, you will set up your worksheet in column or table form. You can also structure the worksheet as raw data, or as frequency data. For details, see *Worksheet Structure for Regression with Life Data* on page 16-3.

Factor columns can be numeric or text. MINITAB by default designates the lowest numeric or text value as the *reference level*. To change the reference level, see *Factor variables and reference levels* on page 16-25.

MINITAB automatically excludes all observations with missing values from all calculations.

How you run the analysis depend on whether your data are uncensored/right censored or uncensored/arbitrarily censored.

▶ **To perform regression with uncensored/right censored data**

   1 Choose Stat ➤ Reliability/Survival ➤ Regression with Life Data.

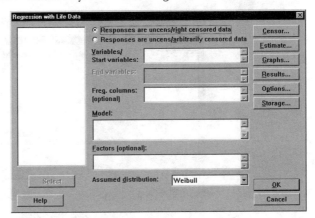

   2 In **Variables/Start variables**, enter up to ten columns of failure times (10 different samples).

   3 If you have frequency columns, enter them in **Freq. columns**.

   4 In **Model**, enter the model terms—see *How to specify the model terms* on page 16-24. If any of those predictors are factors, enter them again in **Factors**.

Note | If you have no censored values, you can skip steps 5 & 6.

   5 Click **Censor**.

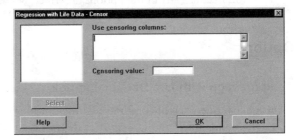

   6 In **Use censoring columns**, enter the censoring columns. The first censoring column is paired with the first data column, the second censoring column is paired with the second data column, and so on.

      By default, MINITAB uses the lowest value in the censoring column to indicate a censored value. To use some other value, enter that value in **Censoring value**.

Note | If your censoring indicators are date/time values, store the values as constants and then enter them as constants.

   7 If you like, use any of the options listed below, then click **OK**.

▶ **To perform regression with uncensored/arbitrarily censored data**

1 Choose Stat ➤ Reliability/Survival ➤ Regression with Life Data.

2 Choose **Responses are uncens/arbitrarily censored data**.

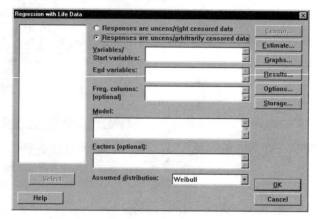

3 In **Variables/Start variables**, enter up to ten columns of start times (ten different samples).

4 In **End variables**, enter up to ten columns of end times (ten different samples).

5 If you have frequency columns, enter them in **Freq. columns**.

6 In **Model**, enter the model terms—see *How to specify the model terms* on page 16-24. If any of those predictors are factors, enter them again in **Factors**.

7 If you like, use any of the options described below, then click **OK**.

Options

Regression with Life Data dialog box

■ choose one of eight common lifetime distributions for the error distribution, including the Weibull (default), extreme value, exponential, normal, lognormal base$_e$, lognormal base$_{10}$, logistic, and loglogistic distributions.

More | MINITAB's extreme value distribution is the smallest extreme value (Type 1).

Estimate subdialog box

■ enter new predictor values for which to estimate percentiles and/or survival probabilities—see *Percentiles and survival probabilities* on page 16-27. You can also use the predictor values from the data.

■ estimate percentiles for the percents you specify—see *Percentiles and survival probabilities* on page 16-27. By default, MINITAB estimates the 50th percentile.

- store the percentiles, their standard errors, and confidence intervals.

- estimate survival probabilities for the times you specify—see *Percentiles and survival probabilities* on page 16-27. For example, if you enter ten hours, MINITAB estimates (for each predictor value) the proportion of units that survive past ten hours.

- store the survival probabilities and confidence intervals.

- specify a confidence level for all of the confidence intervals. The default is 95.0%.

Graphs subdialog box

- draw a probability plot for the standardized residuals or an exponential probability plot for the Cox-Snell residuals—*Probability plots* on page 16-26.

- choose not to include confidence intervals on the plots.

Results subdialog box

- display the following Session window output:
  - no output.
  - the basic output, which includes the response information, censoring information, regression table, the log-likelihood, and goodness-of-fit measures.
  - the basic output, plus the table of percentiles and/or survival probabilities (the default).
  - the previous levels of output, plus the list of factor level values, and the tests for terms with more than one degree of freedom—see *Multiple degrees of freedom test* on page 16-28.

- show the log-likelihood for each iteration of the algorithm.

Options subdialog box

- enter starting values for model parameters for the Newton-Raphson algorithm—see *Estimating the model parameters* on page 16-28.

- change the maximum number of iterations for reaching convergence (the default is 20). MINITAB obtains maximum likelihood estimates through an iterative process. If the maximum number of iterations is reached before convergence, the command terminates—see *Estimating the model parameters* on page 16-28.

- estimate other model coefficients while holding the shape parameter (Weibull) or the scale parameter (other distributions) fixed at a specific value—see *Estimating the model parameters* on page 16-28.

- use historical estimates for the parameters rather than estimate them from the data—see *Estimating the model parameters* on page 16-28. In this case, no estimation is done; all results—such as the percentiles—are based on these parameters.

- change the reference levels for the factors—see *Factor variables and reference levels* on page 16-25.

Storage subdialog box

- store the ordinary, standardized, and Cox-Snell residuals.

- store the information on the estimated equation, including the coefficients, their standard errors and confidence intervals, the variance/covariance matrix, and the log-likelihood for the last iteration.

Default output

The default output consists of the regression table which displays:

- the estimated *coefficients* for the regression model and their
  - standard errors.
  - Z-values and p-values. The Z-test tests that the coefficient is significantly different than zero; in other words, is it a significant predictor?
  - 95% confidence interval.

- the *Shape parameter* (Weibull or exponential) or *Scale parameter* (other distributions), a measure of the overall variability, and its
  - standard error.
  - 95% confidence interval.

- the log-likelihood.

How to specify the model terms

You can fit models with:

- up to 9 factors and up to 50 covariates

- crossed or nested factors—see *Crossed vs. nested factors* on page 3-19

- covariates that are crossed with each other or with factors, or nested within factors

Here are some examples. A is a factor and X is a covariate.

Model terms

A X A∗X	fits a full model with a covariate crossed with a factor
A | X	an alternative way to specify the previous model
A X X∗X	fits a model with a covariate crossed with itself making a squared term
A X(A)	fits a model with a covariate nested within a factor

This model is a generalization of the model used in MINITAB's general linear model (GLM) procedure. Any model fit by GLM can also be fit by the life data procedures. For a general discussion of specifying models, see *Specifying the model terms* on page 3-21 and *Specifying reduced models* on page 3-22. In the regression with life data commands, MINITAB assumes any variable in the model is a covariate unless the variable is specified as a factor. In contrast, GLM assumes any variable in the model is a factor unless the variable is specified as a covariate.

Model restrictions

Life data models in MINITAB have the same restrictions as general linear models:

- The model must be *full rank*, meaning there must be enough data to estimate all the terms in your model. Suppose you have a two-factor crossed model with one empty cell. You can then fit the model with terms A B, but not A B A∗B. Do not worry about figuring out whether or not your model is of full rank. MINITAB will tell you if it is not. In most cases, eliminating some of the high order interactions in your model (assuming, of course, they are not important) will solve your problem.

- The model must be hierarchical. In a hierarchical model, if an interaction term is included, all lower order interactions and main effects that comprise the interaction term must appear in the model.

Factor variables and reference levels

You can enter numeric, text, or date/time factor levels. MINITAB assigns one factor level to be the *reference level*, meaning that the estimated coefficients are interpreted relative to this level.

Regression with Life Data creates a set of design variables for each factor in the model. If there are k levels, there will be k − 1 design variables and the reference level will be coded as 0. Here are two examples of the default coding scheme:

Factor A with 4 levels (1 2 3 4)	A1	A2	A3
reference level → 1	0	0	0
2	1	0	0
3	0	1	0
4	0	0	1

Factor B with 3 levels (High Low Medium)	B1	B2
reference level → High	0	0
Low	1	0
Medium	0	1

By default, MINITAB designates the lowest numeric, date/time, or text value as the reference factor level. If you like, you can change this reference value in the Options subdialog box.

▶ **To change the reference factor level**

1   In the Regression with Life Data dialog box, click **Options**.

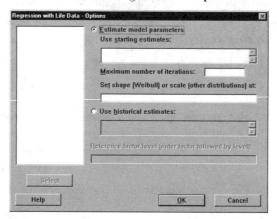

2   In **Reference factor level**, for each factor you want to set the reference level for, enter a factor column followed by a value specifying the reference level. For text values, the value must be in double quotes. For date/time values, store the value as a constant and then enter the constant. Click **OK**.

Probability plots

The Regression with Life Data command draws probability plots for the standardized and Cox-Snell residuals. You can use these plots to assess whether a particular distribution fits your data. In general, the closer the points fall to the fitted line, the better the fit.

MINITAB provides one goodness-of-fit measure: the Anderson-Darling statistic. The Anderson-darling statistic is useful in comparing the fit of different distributions. It measures the distances from the plot points to the fitted line; therefore, a smaller Anderson-Darling statistic indicates that the distribution provides a better fit.

For a discussion of probability plots, see *Probability plots* on page 15-37.

▶ **To draw a probability plot of the residuals**

1   In the Regression with Life Data dialog box, click **Graphs**.

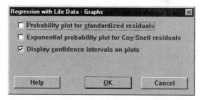

2 Do any of the following, then click **OK**:

- To plot the standardized residuals, check **Probability plot for standardized residuals**

- To plot the Cox-Snell residuals, check **Exponential probability plot for Cox-Snell residuals**

Tip | To draw a probability plot with more options, store the residuals in the Storage subdialog box, then use the probability plot included with *Parametric Distribution Analysis* on page 15-27.

Percentiles and survival probabilities

You can estimate percentiles and survival probabilities for new predictor values, or the values in your data.

▶ To estimate percentiles and survival probabilities

1 In the Regression with Life Data dialog box, click **Estimate**.

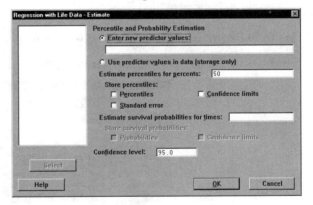

2 Do one of the following:

- To enter new predictor values: In **Enter new predictor values**, enter a set of predictor values (or columns containing sets of predictor values) for which you want to estimate percentiles or survival probabilities. The predictor values must be in the same order as the main effects in the model. For an illustration, see *Example of regression with life data* on page 16-30.

- To use the predictor values in the data, choose **Use predictor values in data (storage only)**. Because of the potentially large amount of output, MINITAB stores the results in the worksheet rather then printing them in the Session window.

3 Do any of the following, then click **OK**:

- To estimate percentiles, enter the percents or a column of percents in **Estimate percentiles for percents**. By default, MINITAB estimates the 50th percentile. If you want to look at the beginning, middle, and end of the product's lifetime for a given predictor value, enter 10 50 90 (the 10th, 50th, 90th percentiles). MINITAB then estimates how long it takes for 10% of the units to fail, 50% of the units to fail, and 90% of the units to fail.

- To estimate survival probabilities, enter the times or a column of times in **Estimate survival probabilities for times**. For example, when you enter 70 (units in hours in this example), MINITAB estimates the probability, for each predictor value, that the unit will survive past 70 hours.

Multiple degrees of freedom test

When you have a term with more than one degree of freedom, you can request a multiple degrees of freedom test. This procedure tests whether or not the term is significant. In other words: Is at least one of the coefficients associated with this term significantly different than zero?

▶ To perform multiple degrees of freedom tests

1 In the Regression with Life Data dialog box, click **Results**.

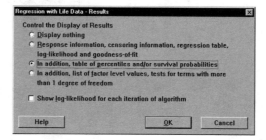

2 Choose **In addition, list of factor level values, tests for terms with more than 1 degree of freedom**, then click **OK**.

Estimating the model parameters

MINITAB uses a modified Newton-Raphson algorithm to estimate the model parameters. If you like, you can enter your own parameters. In this case, no estimation is done; all results—such as the percentiles—are based on these parameters.

When you let MINITAB estimate the parameters from the data, you can optionally:

- enter starting values for the algorithm.

- change the maximum number of iterations for reaching convergence (the default is 20). MINITAB obtains maximum likelihood estimates through an iterative process. If the maximum number of iterations is reached before convergence, the command terminates.

- estimate other model coefficients while holding the shape parameter (Weibull) or the scale parameter (other distributions) fixed at a specific value.

Why enter starting values for the algorithm? The maximum likelihood solution may not converge if the starting estimates are not in the neighborhood of the true solution, so you may want to specify what you think are good starting values for parameter estimates.

In all cases, enter a column with entries which correspond to the model terms in the order you entered them in the Model box. With complicated models, find out the order of entries for the starting estimates column by looking at the regression table in the output.

▶ To control estimation of the parameters

1 In the Regression with Life Data dialog box, click **Options**.

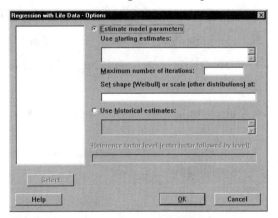

2 Do one of the following:

- To estimate the model parameters from the data (the default), choose **Estimate model parameters**.
  - To enter starting estimates for the parameters: In **Use starting estimates,** enter one column to be used for all of the response variables, or a number of columns equal to the number of response variables.
  - To specify the **Maximum number of iterations**, enter a positive integer.
  - To estimate other model coefficients while holding the shape (Weibull) or the scale (other distributions) parameter fixed: In **Set shape (Weibull) or scale**

parameter (other distributions) at, enter one value to be used for all of the response variables, or a number of values equal to the number of response variables.

- To enter your own estimates for the model parameters, choose **Use historical estimates** and enter one column to be used for all of the response variables, or a number of columns equal to the number of response variables.

3 Click **OK**.

▷ Example of regression with life data

Suppose you want to investigate the deterioration of an insulation used for electric motors. You want to know if you can predict failure times for the insulation based on the plant in which it was manufactured, and the temperature at which the motor runs. It is known that an Arrhenius relationship exists between temperature and failure time.

You gather failure times at plant 1 and plant 2 for the insulation at four temperatures—110, 130, 150, and 170°C. Because the motors generally run at between 80 and 100°C, you want to predict the insulation's behavior at those temperatures.

To see how well the model fits, you will draw a probability plot based on the standardized residuals.

1 Open the worksheet INSULATE.MTW.

2 Choose **Stat ▸ Reliability/Survival ▸ Regression with Life Data**.

3 In **Variables/Start variables**, enter *FailureT*.

4 In **Model**, enter *ArrTemp Plant*. In **Factors (optional)**, enter *Plant*.

5 Click **Censor**. In **Use censoring columns**, enter *Censor*, then click **OK**.

6 Click **Estimate**. In **Enter new predictor values**, enter *ArrNewT NewPlant*, then click **OK**.

7 Click **Graphs**. Check **Probability plot for standardized residuals**, then click **OK** in each dialog box.

*Session
window
output*

Regression with Life Data: FailureT versus ArrTemp, Plant

Response Variable: FailureT

Censoring Information   Count
Uncensored value   66
Right censored value   14
Censoring value: Censor = C

Estimation Method: Maximum Likelihood
Distribution: Weibull

Regression Table

Predictor	Coef	Standard Error	Z	P	95.0% Normal CI Lower	Upper
Intercept	-15.3411	0.9508	-16.13	0.000	-17.2047	-13.4775
ArrTemp	0.83925	0.03397	24.71	0.000	0.77267	0.90584
Plant						
2	-0.18077	0.08457	-2.14	0.033	-0.34652	-0.01501
Shape	2.9431	0.2707			2.4577	3.5244

Log-Likelihood = -562.525

Anderson-Darling (adjusted) Goodness-of-Fit

Standardized Residuals = 0.5078

Table of Percentiles

Percent	Predictor Row Number	Percentile	Standard Error	95.0% Normal CI Lower	Upper
50	1	182093.6	32466.16	128389.8	258260.9
50	2	151980.8	25286.65	109689.6	210577.6
50	3	41530.38	5163.756	32548.44	52990.94
50	4	34662.51	3913.866	27781.00	43248.61

*Graph
window
output*

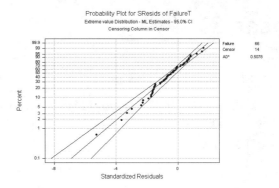

Interpreting the results

From the Regression Table, you get the coefficients for the regression model. For the Weibull distribution, here is the equation that describes the relationship between temperature and failure time for the insulation for plant 1 and 2, respectively:

$$\text{Log}_e \text{ (failure time)} = -15.3411 + 0.83925 \text{ (ArrTemp)} + 2.9431 \, \varepsilon_p$$

$$\text{Log}_e \text{ (failure time)} = -15.52187 + 0.83925 \text{ (ArrTemp)} + 2.9431 \, \varepsilon_p$$

where ε_p = the pth percentile of the error distribution

$$\text{ArrTemp} = \left(\frac{11604.83}{\text{Temp} + 273.16} \right)$$

The Table of Percentiles displays the 50th percentiles for the combinations of temperatures and plants that you entered. The 50th percentile is a good estimate of how long the insulation will last in the field:

- For motors running at 80° C, insulation from plant 1 lasts about 182093.6 hours or 20.77 years; insulation from plant 2 lasts about 151980.8 hours or 17.34 years.

- For motors running at 100° C, insulation from plant 1 lasts about 41530.38 hours or 4.74 years; insulation from plant 2 lasts about 34662.51 hours or 3.95 years.

As you can see from the low p-values, the plants are significantly different at the $\alpha = .05$ level, and temperature is a significant predictor.

The probability plot for standardized residuals will help you determine whether the distribution, transformation, and equal shape (Weibull or exponential) or scale parameter (other distributions) assumption is appropriate. Here, the plot points fit the fitted line adequately; therefore you can assume the model is appropriate.

References

[1] J.D. Kalbfleisch and R.L. Prentice (1980). *The Statistical Analysis of Failure Time Data*, John Wiley & Sons, Inc.

[2] J.F. Lawless (1982). *Statistical Models and Methods for Lifetime Data*, John Wiley & Sons, Inc.

[3] W.Q. Meeker and L.A. Escobar (1998). *Statistical Methods for Reliability Data*, John Wiley & Sons, Inc.

[4] W. Murray (Ed.) (1972). *Numerical Methods for Unconstrained Optimization*, Academic Press.

[5] W. Nelson (1990). *Accelerated Testing*, John Wiley & Sons, Inc.

17

Probit Analysis

Probit Analysis Overview

A probit study consists of imposing a stress (or stimulus) on a number of units, then recording whether the unit failed or not. Probit analysis differs from accelerated life testing (page 16-6) in that the response data is binary (success or failure), rather than an actual failure time.

In the engineering sciences, a common experiment would be destructive inspecting. Suppose you are testing how well submarine hull materials hold up when exposed to underwater explosions. You subject the materials to various magnitudes of explosions, then record whether or not the hull cracked. In the life sciences, a common experiment would be the bioassay, where you subject organisms to various levels of a stress and record whether or not they survive.

Probit analysis can answer these kinds of questions: For each hull material, what shock level cracks 10% of the hulls? What concentration of a pollutant kills 50% of the fish? Or, at a given pesticide application, what is the probability that an insect dies?

Probit Analysis

Use probit analysis when you want to estimate percentiles, survival probabilities, and cumulative probabilities for the distribution of a stress, and draw probability plots. When you enter a factor and choose a Weibull, lognormal, or loglogistic distribution, you can also compare the potency of the stress under different conditions.

MINITAB calculates the model coefficients using a modified Newton-Raphson algorithm.

Data

Enter the following columns in the worksheet:

- two columns containing the *response variable*, set up in success/trial or response/frequency format

- one column containing a *stress variable* (treated as a covariate in MINITAB)

- (optional) one column containing a *factor*

Response variable

The response data is binomial, so you have two possible outcomes, success or failure. You can enter the data in either success/trial or response/frequency format. Here is the same data arranged both ways:

Success/trial format

Temp	Success	Trials
80	2	10
120	4	10
140	7	10
160	9	10

The Success column contains the number of successes; the Trials column contains the number of trials.

Response/frequency format

Response	Frequency	Temp
1	2	80
0	8	80
1	4	120
0	6	120
1	7	140
0	3	140
1	9	160
0	1	160

The Response column contains values which indicate whether the unit succeeded or failed. The higher value corresponds to a success. The Frequency column indicates how many times that observation occurred.

Factors

Text categories (factor levels) are processed in alphabetical order by default. If you wish, you can define your own order—see *Ordering Text Categories* in the *Manipulating Data* chapter of MINITAB *User's Guide 1* for details.

▶ To perform a probit analysis

How you run the analysis depend on whether your worksheet is in "success/trial" or "response/frequency" format.

1 Choose **Stat ➤ Reliability/Survival ➤ Probit Analysis**.

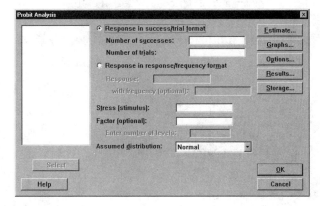

2 Do one of the following:

- Choose **Responses in success/trial format**.

    1 In **Number of successes**, enter one column of successes.

    2 In **Number of trials**, enter one column of trials.

- Choose **Responses in response/frequency format**.

    1 In **Response**, enter one column of response values.

    2 If you have a frequency column, enter the column in **with frequency**.

3 In **Stress (stimulus)**, enter one column of stress or stimulus levels.

4 If you like, use any of the options described below, then click **OK**.

Options

Probit Analysis dialog box

- include a factor in the model—see *Probit Analysis* on page 17-2.

- choose one of seven common lifetime distributions, including the normal (default), lognormal base$_e$, lognormal base$_{10}$, logistic, loglogistic, Weibull, and extreme value distributions.

Estimate subdialog box

- estimate percentiles for the percents you specify—see *Percentiles* on page 17-8. These percentiles are added to the default table of percentiles.

- estimate survival probabilities for the stress values you specify—see *Survival and cumulative probabilities* on page 17-9.

- specify fiducial (default) or normal approximation confidence intervals.

- specify a confidence level for all of the confidence intervals. The default is 95%.

Graphs subdialog box

- suppress the display of the probability plot.

- draw a survival plot—see *Survival plots* on page 17-10.

- do not include confidence intervals on the above plots.

- plot the Pearson or deviance residuals versus the event probability. Use these plots to identify poorly fit observations.

Options subdialog box

- enter starting values for model parameters—see *Estimating the model parameters* on page 17-11.

- change the maximum number of iterations for reaching convergence (the default is 20). MINITAB obtains maximum likelihood estimates through an iterative process. If the maximum number of iterations is reached before convergence, the command terminates—see *Estimating the model parameters* on page 17-11.

- use historical estimates for the model parameters. In this case, no estimation is done; all results—such as the percentiles—are based on these historical estimates. See *Estimating the model parameters* on page 17-11.

- estimate the natural response rate from the data or specify a value—see *Natural response rate* on page 17-12.

- if you have response/frequency data, you can define the value used to signify the occurrence of a success. Otherwise, the highest value in the column is used.

- enter a reference level for the factor—see *Factor variables and reference levels* on page 17-11. Otherwise, the lowest value in the column is used.

- perform a Hosmer-Lemeshow test to assess how well your model fits the data. This test bins the data into 10 groups by default; if you like, you can specify a different number.

Results subdialog box

- display the following in the Session window:
  - no output
  - the basic output, which includes the response information, regression table, test for equal slopes, the log-likelihood, multiple degrees of freedom test, and two goodness-of-fit tests
  - the basic output, plus distribution parameter estimates and the table of percentiles and/or survival probabilities (default)
  - the above output, plus characteristics of the distribution and the Hosmer-Lemeshow goodness-of-fit test

Note | When you select fiducial confidence intervals, MINITAB will display fiducial confidence intervals for the median, Q1, and Q2 and normal confidence intervals for mean, standard deviation, and IQR in the characteristics of distribution table.

- show the log-likelihood for each iteration of the algorithm.

Storage subdialog box

- store the Pearson and deviance residuals
- store the characteristics of the fitted distribution, including
  - percentiles and their percents, standard errors, and confidence limits
  - survival probabilities and their stress level and confidence limits
- store information on the estimated equation, including
  - event probability
  - estimated coefficients and standard error of the estimates
  - variance/covariance matrix
  - natural response rate and standard error of the natural response
  - log-likelihood for the last iteration

Output

The default output consists of:

- the *response information*
- the *factor information*
- the *regression table*, which includes the estimated coefficients and their
  - standard errors.
  - Z-values and p-values. The Z-test tests that the coefficient is significantly different than 0; in other words, is it a significant predictor?
  - natural response rate—the probability that a unit fails without being exposed to any of the stress.
- the *test for equal slopes*, which tests that the slopes associated with the factor levels are significantly different.
- the *log-likelihood* from the last iteration of the algorithm.
- two *goodness-of-fit tests*, which evaluate how well the model fits the data. The null hypothesis is that the model fits the data adequately. Therefore, the higher the p-value the better the model fits the data.
- the *parameter estimates* for the distribution and their standard errors and 95% confidence intervals. The parameter estimates are transformations of the estimated coefficients in the regression table.
- the *table of percentiles*, which includes the estimated percentiles, standard errors, and 95% fiducial confidence intervals.
- the *probability plot*, which helps you to assess whether the chosen distribution fits your data—see *Probability plots* on page 17-10.

- the *relative potency*—compares the potency of a stress for two levels of a factor. To get this output, you must have a factor, and choose a Weibull, lognormal, or loglogistic distribution.

  Suppose you want to compare how the amount of voltage affects two types of light bulbs, and the relative potency is .98. This means that light bulb 1 running at 117 volts would fail at approximately the same time as light bulb 2 running at 114.66 volts (117 × .98).

Probit model and distribution function

MINITAB provides three main distributions—normal, logistic, and extreme value— allowing you to fit a broad class of binary response models. You can take the log of the stress to get the lognormal, loglogistic, and Weibull distributions, respectively. This class of models (for the situation with no factor) is defined by:

$$\pi_j = c + (1 - c)g(\beta_0 + x_j\beta)$$

where

π_j	=	the probability of a response for the jth stress level
$g(y_j)$	=	the distribution function (described below)
β_0	=	the constant term
x_j	=	the jth level of the stress variable
β	=	unknown coefficient associated with the stress variable
c	=	natural response rate

The distribution functions are outlined below:

Distribution	Distribution function	Mean	Variance
logistic	$g(y_j) = 1/(1 + e^{-y_j})$	0	$pi^2 / 3$
normal	$g(y_j) = \Phi(y_j)$	0	1
extreme value	$g(y_j) = 1 - e^{-e^{y_j}}$	$-\gamma$ (Euler constant)	$pi^2 / 6$

Here, pi in the Variance column of the table is 3.14159.

The distribution function you choose should depend on your data. You want to choose a distribution function that results in a good fit to your data. Goodness-of-fit statistics can be used to compare fits using different distributions. Certain distributions may be used for historical reasons or because they have a special meaning in a discipline.

Percentiles

At what stress level do half of the units fail? How much pesticide do you need to apply to kill 90% of the insects? You are looking for *percentiles*.

Common percentiles used are the 10th, 50th, and 90th percentiles, also known in the life sciences as the ED 10, ED 50 and ED 90 (ED = effective dose).

The probit analysis automatically displays a table of percentiles in the Session window, along with 95% fiducial confidence intervals. You can also request:

- additional percentiles to be added to the table

- normal approximation rather than fiducial confidence intervals

- a confidence level other than 95%

The Percentile column contains the stress level required for the corresponding percent of the events to occur.

In this example, you exposed light bulbs to various voltages and recorded whether or not the bulb burned out before 800 hours.

```
                           Table of Percentiles
                                          Standard      95.0% Fiducial CI
At 104.9931 volts,    Percent  Percentile    Error      Lower      Upper
1% of the bulbs burn      1     104.9931     1.3715    101.9273   107.3982
out before 800 hours.     2     106.9313     1.2661    104.1104   109.1598
                          3     108.1795     1.1997    105.5144   110.2980
                          4     109.1281     1.1504    106.5795   111.1656
                        etc.
```

▶ To modify the table of percentiles

1 In the Probit Analysis main dialog box, click **Estimate**.

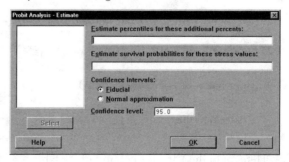

2 Do any of the following:

- In **Estimate percentiles for these additional percents**, enter the percents or a column of percents.

- Choose **Normal approximation** to request normal approximation rather than fiducial confidence intervals.

- Change the confidence level for the percentiles (default is 95%): In **Confidence level**, enter a value. This changes the confidence level for *all* confidence intervals.

Survival and cumulative probabilities

What is the probability that a submarine hull will survive a given strength of shock? At a given pesticide application, what is the probability that an insect survives? You are looking for *survival probabilities*—estimates of the proportion of units that survive at a certain stress level.

When you request survival probabilities, they are displayed in a table in the Session window. In this example, we exposed light bulbs to various voltages and recorded whether or not the bulb burned out before 800 hours. Then we requested a survival probability for light bulbs subjected to 117 volts:

The probability of a bulb lasting past 800 hours is 0.7692 at 117 volts.

Table of Survival Probabilities

		95.0% Fiducial CI	
Stress	Probability	Lower	Upper
117.0000	0.7692	0.6224	0.8825

To calculate *cumulative probabilities* (the likelihood of failing rather than surviving), subtract the survival probability from 1. In this case, the probability of failing before 800 hours at 117 volts is 0.2308.

▶ **To request survival probabilities**

1   In the Probit Analysis main dialog box, click **Estimate**.

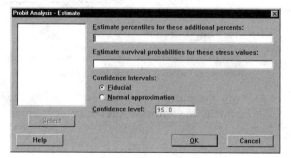

2   In **Estimate survival probabilities for these stress values**, enter one or more stress values or columns of stress values.

Probability plots

A probability plot displays the percentiles. You can use the probability plot to assess whether a particular distribution fits your data. In general, the closer the points fall to the fitted line, the better the fit.

For a discussion of probability plots, see *Probability plots* on page 15-37.

When you have more than one factor level, lines and confidence intervals are drawn for each level. If the plot looks cluttered, you can turn off the confidence intervals in the Graphs subdialog box. You can also change the confidence level for the 95% confidence by entering a new value in the Estimate subdialog box.

Survival plots

Survival plots display the survival probabilities versus stress. Each point on the plot represents the proportion of units surviving at a stress level. The survival curve is surrounded by two outer lines—the 95% confidence interval for the curve, which provide reasonable values for the "true" survival function.

For an illustration of a survival plot, see *Survival plots* on page 15-40.

▶ To draw a survival plot

1 In the Probit Analysis dialog box, click **Graphs**.

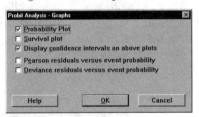

2 Check **Survival plot**.

3 If you like, turn off the 95% confidence interval—uncheck **Display confidence intervals on above plots**. Click **OK**.

4 If you like, change the confidence level for the 95% confidence interval—click **Estimate**. In **Confidence level**, enter a value. Click **OK**.

Factor variables and reference levels

You can enter numeric, text, or date/time factor levels. MINITAB needs to assign one factor level to be the *reference level*, meaning that the estimated coefficients are interpreted relative to this level.

Probit analysis creates a set of design variables for the factor in the model. If there are k levels, there will be k-1 design variables and the reference level will be coded with all 0's. Here are two examples of the default coding scheme:

	Factor A with 4 levels (1 2 3 4)				Factor B with 3 levels (High Low Medium)	
	A1	A2	A3		B1	B2
reference level → 1	0	0	0	reference level → High	0	0
2	1	0	0	Low	1	0
3	0	1	0	Medium	0	1
4	0	0	1			

By default, MINITAB designates the lowest numeric, date/time, or text value as the reference factor level. If you like, you can change this reference value in the Options subdialog box.

Estimating the model parameters

MINITAB uses a modified Newton-Raphson algorithm to estimate the model parameters. If you like, you can enter historical estimates for these parameters. In this case, no estimation is done; all results—such as the percentiles—are based on these historical estimates.

When you let MINITAB estimate the parameters from the data, you can optionally:

- enter starting values for the algorithm.
- change the maximum number of iterations for reaching convergence (the default is 20). MINITAB obtains maximum likelihood estimates through an iterative process. If the maximum number of iterations is reached before convergence, the command terminates.

Why enter starting values for the algorithm? The maximum likelihood solution may not converge if the starting estimates are not in the neighborhood of the true solution, so you may want to specify what you think are good starting values for parameter estimates.

▶ **To control estimation of the parameters**

1 In the Probit Analysis main dialog box, click **Options**.

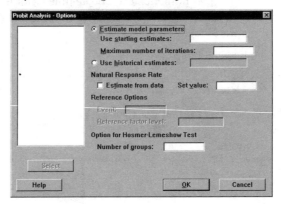

2 Do one of the following:

■ To estimate the model parameters from the data (the default), choose **Estimate model parameters**.
   – To enter starting estimates for the parameters: In **Use starting estimates,** enter one starting value for each coefficient in the regression table. Enter the values in the order that they appear in the regression table.

Note | Do not enter a starting value for the natural response rate here.

   – To specify the maximum number of iterations, enter a positive integer.

■ To enter your own estimates for the model parameters, choose **Use historical estimates** and enter one starting value for each coefficient in the regression table. Enter the values in the order that they appear in the regression table.

Natural response rate

The regression table includes the natural response rate—the probability that a unit fails without being exposed to any of the stress. This statistic is used in situations with high mortality or high failure rates. For example, you might want to know the probability that a young fish dies without being exposed to a certain pollutant. If the natural response rate is greater than 0, you may want to consider the fact that the stress does not cause all of the deaths in the analysis.

You can choose to estimate the natural response rate from the data, or set the value. You would set the value when you have a historical estimate, or to use as a starting value for the algorithm.

▶ Example of a probit analysis

Suppose you work for a lightbulb manufacturer and have been asked to determine bulb life for two types of bulbs at typical household voltages. The typical line voltage entering a house is 117 volts ± 10% (or 105 to 129 volts).

You subject the two bulbs to five stress levels within that range—108, 114, 120, 126, and 132 volts, and define a success as: The bulb fails before 800 hours.

1 Open the worksheet LIGHTBUL.MTW.

2 Choose **Stat ➤ Reliability/Survival ➤ Probit Analysis**.

3 Choose **Response in success/trial format**.

4 In **Number of successes**, enter *Blows*. In **Number of trials**, enter *Trials*.

5 In **Stress (stimulus)**, enter *Volts*.

6 In **Factor (optional)**, enter *Type*. In **Enter number of levels**, enter 2.

7 From **Assumed distribution**, choose **Weibull**.

8 Click **Estimate**. In **Estimate survival probabilities for these stress values**, enter *117*. Click **OK**.

9 Click **Graphs**. Uncheck **Display confidence intervals on above plots**. Click **OK** in each dialog box.

Session window output

Probit Analysis: Blows, Trials versus Volts, Type

```
Distribution:  Weibull

Response  Information

Variable  Value       Count
Blows     Success       192
          Failure       308
Trials    Total         500

Factor Information

Factor    Levels Values
Type        2 A B

Estimation Method:  Maximum Likelihood
```

Regression Table

Variable	Coef	Standard Error	Z	P
Constant	-97.019	7.673	-12.64	0.000
Volts	20.019	1.587	12.61	0.000
Type				
B	0.1794	0.1598	1.12	0.262
Natural				
Response	0.000			

Test for equal slopes: Chi-Square = 0.2585, DF = 1, P-Value = 0.611
Log-Likelihood = -214.213

Goodness-of-Fit Tests

Method	Chi-Square	DF	P
Pearson	2.516	7	0.926
Deviance	2.492	7	0.928

Type = A

Tolerance Distribution

Parameter Estimates

Parameter	Estimate	Standard Error	95.0% Normal CI Lower	Upper
Shape	20.019	1.587	17.138	23.384
Scale	127.269	0.737	125.832	128.722

Table of Percentiles

Percent	Percentile	Standard Error	95.0% Fiducial CI Lower	Upper
1	101.1409	1.8424	96.9868	104.3407
2	104.7307	1.6355	101.0429	107.5731
3	106.9008	1.5090	103.5009	109.5267
4	108.4760	1.4171	105.2866	110.9457
5	109.7203	1.3449	106.6975	112.0680
6	110.7531	1.2854	107.8683	113.0007
7	111.6387	1.2348	108.8717	113.8017
8	112.4158	1.1909	109.7516	114.5057
9	113.1096	1.1523	110.5364	115.1354
10	113.7373	1.1177	111.2458	115.7062
20	118.0817	0.8986	116.1208	119.7003
30	120.8808	0.7901	119.2012	122.3424
40	123.0693	0.7358	121.5505	124.4720
50	124.9600	0.7179	123.5231	126.3718

-----the rest of this table omitted for space-----

Table of Survival Probabilities

		95.0% Fiducial CI	
Stress	Probability	Lower	Upper
117.0000	0.8306	0.7807	0.8785

Type = B

Tolerance Distribution

Parameter Estimates

Parameter	Estimate	Standard Error	95.0% Normal CI	
			Lower	Upper
Shape	20.019	1.587	17.138	23.384
Scale	126.134	0.704	124.761	127.522

Table of Percentiles

Percent	Percentile	Standard Error	95.0% Fiducial CI	
			Lower	Upper
1	100.2388	1.8617	96.0399	103.4706
2	103.7965	1.6562	100.0595	106.6728
3	105.9472	1.5303	102.4960	108.6073
4	107.5084	1.4386	104.2667	110.0121
5	108.7416	1.3663	105.6661	111.1226
6	109.7652	1.3065	106.8277	112.0453
7	110.6429	1.2556	107.8234	112.8374
8	111.4131	1.2113	108.6967	113.5335
9	112.1007	1.1722	109.4760	114.1558
10	112.7228	1.1371	110.1805	114.7197
20	117.0285	0.9108	115.0289	118.6590
30	119.8026	0.7929	118.1018	121.2561
40	121.9716	0.7280	120.4520	123.3436
50	123.8454	0.6989	122.4294	125.2031

-----the rest of this table omitted for space-----

Table of Survival Probabilities

		95.0% Fiducial CI	
Stress	Probability	Lower	Upper
117.0000	0.8009	0.7460	0.8546

Table of Relative Potency

Factor: Type

Comparison	Relative Potency	95.0% Fiducial CI	
		Lower	Upper
A VS B	0.9911	0.9754	1.0068

Graph
window
output

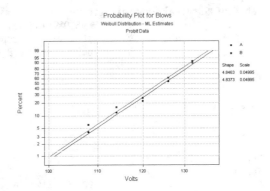

Interpreting the results

The goodness-of-fit tests (p-values = 0.926, 0.928) and the probability plot suggest that the Weibull distribution fits the data adequately. Since the test for equal slopes is not significant (p-value = .611), the comparison of lightbulbs will be similar regardless of the voltage level. In this case, the lightbulbs A and B are not significantly different because the coefficient associated with type B is not significantly different than 0 (p-value = .262).

At 117 volts, what percentage of the bulbs last beyond 800 hours? Eight-three percent of the bulb A's and 80% of the bulb B's last beyond 800 hours.

At what voltage do 50% of the bulbs fail before 800 hours? The table of percentiles shows you that 50% of bulb A's fail before 800 hours at 124.96 volts; 50% of bulb B's fail before 800 hours at 123.85 volts.

References

[1] D.J. Finney (1971). *Probit Analysis*, Cambridge University Press.

[2] D.W. Hosmer and S. Lemeshow (1989). *Applied Logistic Regression*, John Wiley & Sons, Inc.

[3] P. McCullagh and J.A. Nelder (1992). *Generalized Linear Models*, Chapman & Hall.

[4] W. Murray, Ed. (1972). *Numerical Methods for Unconstrained Optimization*, Academic Press.

[5] W. Nelson (1982). *Applied Life Data Analysis*, John Wiley & Sons.

part IV

Design of Experiments

18

Design of Experiments Overview

- **Design of Experiments (DOE) Overview**, 18-2
- **Modifying and Using Worksheet Data**, 18-4

See also,

- *Session Five: Designing an Experiment* in *Meet MINITAB*

Design of Experiments (DOE) Overview

In industry, designed experiments can be used to systematically investigate the process or product variables that influence product quality. After you identify the process conditions and product components that influence product quality, you can direct improvement efforts to enhance a product's manufacturability, reliability, quality, and field performance.

For example, you may want to investigate the influence of coating type and furnace temperature on the corrosion resistance of steel bars. You could design an experiment that allows you to collect data at combinations of coatings/temperature, measure corrosion resistance, and then use the findings to adjust manufacturing conditions.

Because resources are limited, it is very important to get the most information from each experiment you perform. Well-designed experiments can produce significantly more information and often require fewer runs than haphazard or unplanned experiments. In addition, a well-designed experiment will ensure that you can evaluate the effects that you have identified as important. For example, if you believe that there is an interaction between two input variables, be sure to include both variables in your design rather than doing a "one factor at a time" experiment. An interaction occurs when the effect of one input variable is influenced by the level of another input variable.

Designed experiments are often carried out in four phases: planning, screening (also called process characterization), optimization, and verification.

Planning

Careful planning can help you avoid problems that can occur during the execution of the experimental plan. For example, personnel, equipment availability, funding, and the mechanical aspects of your system may affect your ability to complete the experiment. If your project has low priority, you may want to carry out small sequential experiments. That way, if you lose resources to a higher priority project, you will not have to discard the data you have already collected. When resources become available again, you can resume experimentation.

The preparation required before beginning experimentation depends on your problem. Here are some steps you may need to go through:

- *Define the problem*. Developing a good problem statement helps make sure you are studying the right variables. At this step, you identify the questions that you want to answer.

- *Define the objective*. A well-defined objective will ensure that the experiment answers the right questions and yields practical, usable information. At this step, you define the goals of the experiment.

- *Develop an experimental plan that will provide meaningful information.* Be sure to review relevant background information, such as theoretical principles, and knowledge gained through observation or previous experimentation. For example, you may need to identify which factors or process conditions affect process performance and contribute to process variability. Or, if the process is already established and the influential factors have been identified, you may want determine optimal process conditions.

- *Make sure the process and measurement systems are in control.* Ideally, both the process and the measurements should be in statistical control as measured by a functioning statistical process control (SPC) system. Even if you do not have the process completely in control, you *must* be able to reproduce process settings. You also need to determine the variability in the measurement system. If the variability in your system is greater than the difference/effect that you consider important, experimentation will not yield useful results.

MINITAB provides numerous tools to evaluate process control and analyze your measurement system. See Part II *Quality Control* in this book.

Screening

In many process development and manufacturing applications, potentially influential variables are numerous. Screening reduces the number of variables by identifying the key variables that affect product quality. This reduction allows you to focus process improvement efforts on the really important variables, or the "vital few." Screening may also suggest the "best" or optimal settings for these factors, and indicate whether or not curvature exists in the responses. Then, you can use optimization methods to determine the best settings and define the nature of the curvature.

Chapter 19, *Factorial Designs*, describes methods that are often used for screening:

- two-level full and fractional factorial designs are used extensively in industry

- Plackett-Burman designs have low resolution, but their usefulness in some screening experimentation and robustness testing is widely recognized

- general full factorial designs (designs with more than two-levels) may also be useful for small screening experiments

Optimization

After you have identified the "vital few" by screening, you need to determine the "best" or optimal values for these experimental factors. Optimal factor values depend on the process objective. For example, you may want to maximize process yield or reduce product variability.

The optimization methods available in MINITAB include general full factorial designs (designs with more than two-levels), response surface designs, mixture designs, and Taguchi designs.

- Chapter 19, *Factorial Designs*, describes methods for designing and analyzing general full factorial designs.

- Chapter 20, *Response Surface Designs*, describes methods for designing and analyzing central composite and Box-Behnken designs.

- Chapter 21, *Mixture Designs*, describes methods for designing and analyzing simplex centroid, simplex lattice, and extreme vertices designs. Mixture designs are special class of response surface designs where the proportions of the components (factors), rather than their magnitude, are important.

- Chapter 23, *Response Optimization*, describes methods for optimizing multiple responses. MINITAB provides numerical optimization, an interactive graph, and an overlaid contour plot to help you determine the "best" settings to simultaneously optimize multiple responses.

- Chapter 24, *Taguchi Designs*, describes methods for analyzing Taguchi designs. Taguchi designs may also be called orthogonal array designs, robust designs, or inner-outer array designs. These designs are used for creating products that are robust to conditions in their expected operating environment.

Verification

Verification involves performing a follow-up experiment at the predicted "best" processing conditions to confirm the optimization results. For example, you may perform a few verification runs at the optimal settings, then obtain a confidence interval for the mean response.

More | Our intent is to provide only a brief introduction to the design of experiments. There are many resources that provide a thorough treatment of these methods. For a list of resources, see *References* on pages 19-65, 20-38, 21-54, and 24-39.

Modifying and Using Worksheet Data

When you create a design using one of the Create Design procedures, MINITAB creates a design object that stores the appropriate design information in the worksheet. MINITAB needs this stored information to analyze and plot data properly.

The following columns contain your design:

- StdOrder

- RunOrder

- CenterPt (two-level factorial and Plackett-Burman designs only)

- PtType (mixture designs only)

- Blocks

- factor or component columns

If you want to analyze your design with the Analyze Design procedures, you must follow certain rules when modifying worksheet data. If you make changes that corrupt your design, you may still be able to analyze it with the Analyze Design procedures after you use one of the Define Custom Design procedures.

- You **cannot** delete or move the columns that contain the design.

- You can enter, edit, and analyze data in all the other columns of the worksheet, that is, all columns beyond the last design column. You can place the response and covariate data here, or any other data you want to enter into the worksheet.

- You can delete runs from your design. If you delete runs, you may not be able to fit all terms in your model. In that case, MINITAB will automatically remove any terms that cannot be fit and do the analysis using the remaining terms.

- You can add runs to your design. For example, you may want to add center points or a replicate of a particular run of interest. Make sure the levels are appropriate for each factor or component and that you enter appropriate values in StdOrder, RunOrder, CenterPt, PtType and Blocks. These columns and the factor or component columns must all be the same length. You can use any numbers that seem reasonable for StdOrder and RunOrder. MINITAB uses these two columns to order data in the worksheet.

- You can change the level of a factor for a botched run in the Data window—see *Analyzing designs with botched runs* on page 19-44.

- You can change factor level settings using Modify Design. However, you cannot change a factor type from numeric to text or text to numeric.

- You can change the name of factors and components using Modify Design.

- You can use any procedures to analyze the data in your design, not just the procedures in the DOE menu.

- You can add factors to your design by entering them in the worksheet. Then, use one of the Define Custom Design procedures.

Note | If you make changes that corrupt your design, you may still be able to analyze it. You can redefine the design using one of the Define Custom Design procedures.

19

Factorial Designs

Factorial Designs Overview

Factorial designs allow for the simultaneous study of the effects that several factors may have on a process. When performing an experiment, varying the levels of the factors simultaneously rather than one at a time is efficient in terms of time and cost, and also allows for the study of interactions between the factors. Interactions are the driving force in many processes. Without the use of factorial experiments, important interactions may remain undetected.

Screening designs

In many process development and manufacturing applications, the number of potential input variables (factors) is large. Screening (process characterization) is used to reduce the number of input variables by identifying the key input variables or process conditions that affect product quality. This reduction allows you to focus process improvement efforts on the few really important variables, or the "vital few." Screening may also suggest the "best" or optimal settings for these factors, and indicate whether or not curvature exists in the responses. Optimization experiments can then be done to determine the best settings and define the nature of the curvature.

In industry, two-level full and fractional factorial designs, and Plackett-Burman designs are often used to "screen" for the really important factors that influence process output measures or product quality. These designs are useful for fitting first-order models (which detect linear effects), and can provide information on the existence of second-order effects (curvature) when the design includes center points.

In addition, general full factorial designs (designs with more than two-levels) may be used with small screening experiments.

Full factorial designs

In a full factorial experiment, responses are measured at *all* combinations of the experimental factor levels. The combinations of factor levels represent the conditions at which responses will be measured. Each experimental condition is a called a "run" and the response measurement an observation. The entire set of runs is the "design."

The following diagrams show two and three factor designs. The points represent a unique combination of factor levels. For example, in the two-factor design, the point on the lower left corner represents the experimental run when Factor A is set at its low level and Factor B is also set at its low level.

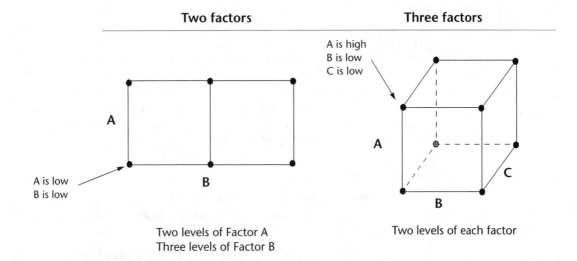

Two factors — Two levels of Factor A, Three levels of Factor B

Three factors — Two levels of each factor

Two-level full factorial designs

In a two-level full factorial design, each experimental factor has only two levels. The experimental runs include *all* combinations of these factor levels. Although two-level factorial designs are unable to explore fully a wide region in the factor space, they provide useful information for relatively few runs per factor. Because two-level factorials can indicate major trends, you can use them to provide direction for further experimentation. For example, when you need to further explore a region where you believe optimal settings may exist, you can augment a factorial design to form a central composite design (see page *Central composite designs* on page 20-4).

General full factorial designs

In a general full factorial design, the experimental factors can have any number of levels. For example, Factor A may have two levels, Factor B may have three levels, and Factor C may have five levels. The experimental runs include *all* combinations of these factor levels. General full factorial designs may be used with small screening experiments, or in optimization experiments.

Fractional factorial designs

In a full factorial experiment, responses are measured at all combinations of the factor levels, which may result in a prohibitive number of runs. For example, a two-level full factorial design with 6 factors requires 64 runs; a design with 9 factors requires 512 runs. To minimize time and cost, you can use designs that exclude some of the factor level combinations. Factorial designs in which one or more level combinations are excluded are called *fractional factorial designs*. MINITAB generates two-level fractional factorial designs for up to 15 factors.

Fractional factorial designs are useful in factor screening because they reduce the number of runs to a manageable size. The runs that are performed are a selected subset or *fraction* of the full factorial design. When you do not run all factor level combinations, some of the effects will be confounded. Confounded effects cannot be estimated separately and are said to be *aliased*. MINITAB displays an alias table which specifies the confounding patterns. Because some effects are confounded and cannot be separated from other effects, the fraction must be carefully chosen to achieve meaningful results. Choosing the "best fraction" often requires specialized knowledge of the product or process under investigation.

Plackett-Burman designs

Plackett-Burman designs are a class of resolution III, two-level fractional factorial designs that are often used to study main effects. In a resolution III design, main effects are aliased with two-way interactions.

MINITAB generates designs for up to 47 factors. Each design is based on the number of runs, from 8 to 48 and always a multiple of 4. The number of factors must be less than the number of runs.

More | Our intent is to provide only a brief introduction to factorial designs. There are many resources that provide a thorough treatment of these designs. For a list of resources, see *References* on page 19-65.

Factorial experiments in MINITAB

Performing a factorial experiment may consist of the following steps:

1 Before you begin using MINITAB, you need to complete all pre-experimental planning. For example, you must determine what the influencing factors are, that is, what processing conditions influence the values of the response variable. See *Planning* on page 18-2.

2 In MINITAB, create a new design or use data that is already in your worksheet.

- Use **Create Factorial Design** to generate a full or fractional factorial design—see *Creating Two-Level Factorial Designs* on page 19-6, *Creating Plackett-Burman Designs* on page 19-24, and *Creating General Full Factorial Designs* on page 19-33.

- Use **Define Custom Factorial Design** to create a design from data you already have in the worksheet. **Define Custom Factorial Design** allows you to specify which columns are your factors and other design characteristics. You can then easily fit a model to the design and generate plots. See *Defining Custom Designs* on page 19-35.

3 Use **Modify Design** to rename the factors, change the factor levels, replicate the design, and randomize the design. For two-level designs, you can also fold the

design, add axial points, and add center points to the axial block. See *Modifying Designs* on page 19-38.

4 Use **Display Design** to change the display order of the runs and the units (coded or uncoded) in which MINITAB expresses the factors in the worksheet. See *Displaying Designs* on page 19-42.

5 Perform the experiment and collect the response data. Then, enter the data in your MINITAB worksheet. See *Collecting and Entering Data* on page 19-43.

6 Use **Analyze Factorial Design** to fit a model to the experimental data—see page 19-44.

7 Display plots to look at the design and the effects. Use **Factorial Plots** to display main effects, interactions, and cube plots—see page 19-53. For two-level designs, use **Contour/Surface (Wireframe) Plots** to display contour and surface plots—see page 19-60.

8 If you are trying to optimize responses, use **Response Optimizer** (page 23-2) or **Overlaid Contour Plot** (page 23-19) to obtain a numerical and graphical analysis.

Depending on your experiment, you may do some of the steps in a different order, perform a given step more than once, or eliminate a step.

Choosing a Design

The design, or layout, provides the specifications for each experimental run. It includes the blocking scheme, randomization, replication, and factor level combinations. This information defines the experimental conditions for each run. When performing the experiment, you measure the response (observation) at the predetermined settings of the experimental conditions. Each experimental condition that is employed to obtain a response measurement is a *run*.

MINITAB provides two-level full and fractional factorial designs, Plackett-Burman designs, and full factorials for designs with more than two levels. When choosing a design you need to

- identify the number of factors that are of interest.

- determine the number of runs you can perform.

- determine the impact that other considerations (such as cost, time, or the availability of facilities) have on your choice of a design.

Depending on your problem, there are other considerations that make a design desirable. You may want to choose a design that allows you to

- increase the order of the design sequentially. That is, you may want to "build up" the initial design for subsequent experimentation.

- perform the experiment in orthogonal blocks. Orthogonally blocked designs allow for model terms and block effects to be estimated independently and minimize the variation in the estimated coefficients.

- detect model lack of fit.

- estimate the effects that you believe are important by choosing a design with adequate resolution. The resolution of a design describes how the effects are confounded. Some common design resolutions are summarized below:
  - Resolution III designs—no main effect is aliased with any other main effect. However, main effects are aliased with two-factor interactions and two-factor interactions are aliased with each other.
  - Resolution IV designs—no main effect is aliased with any other main effect or two-factor interaction. Two-factor interactions are aliased with each other.
  - Resolution V designs—no main effect or two-factor interaction is aliased with any other main effect or two-factor interaction. Two-factor interactions are aliased with three-factor interactions.

More | For more information on design considerations, explanations of desirable design properties, and definitions, see *References* on page 19-65.

Creating Two-Level Factorial Designs

Use MINITAB's two-level factorial options to generate settings for two-level

- full factorial designs with up to seven factors
- fractional factorial designs with up to 15 factors

You can use default designs from MINITAB's catalog (these designs are shown in the Display Available Designs subdialog box) or create your own design by specifying the design generators (see *Specifying generators to add factors to the base design* on page 19-9).

The default designs cover many industrial product design and development applications. They are fully described in the *Summary of Two-Level Designs* on page 19-28.

To create full factorial designs when any factor has more than two levels or you have more than seven factors, see *Creating General Full Factorial Designs* on page 19-33.

Note | To create a design from data that you already have in the worksheet, see *Defining Custom Designs* on page 19-35.

► **To create a two-level factorial design**

1   Choose **Stat ➤ DOE ➤ Factorial ➤ Create Factorial Design**.

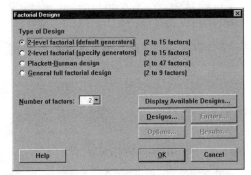

2   If you want to see a summary of the factorial designs, click **Display Available Designs**. Use this table to compare design features. Click **OK**.

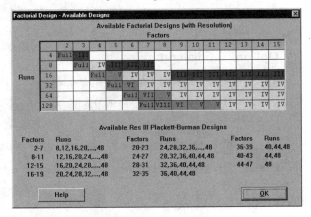

3   Under **Type of Design**, choose **2-level factorial (default generators)**.

4   From **Number of factors**, choose a number from 2 to 15.

5   Click **Designs**.

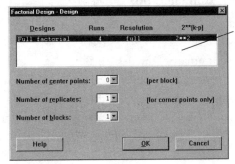

The designs that display depend on the number of factors in your design.

6 In the box at the top, highlight the design you want to create. If you like, use any of the options listed under *Designs subdialog box* below.

7 Click **OK** even if you do not change any of the options. This selects the design and brings you back to the main dialog box.

8 If you like, click **Options**, **Factors**, and/or **Results** to use any of the options listed below. Then, click **OK** in each dialog box to create your design.

Options

Designs subdialog box

■ add center points—see *Adding center points* on page 19-11

■ replicate the *corner points* of the design—see *Replicating the design* on page 19-12

■ block a design that was created using the default generators—see *Blocking the design* on page 19-13

Options subdialog box

■ fold the design—see *Folding the design* on page 19-14

■ for fractional factorials, specify the fraction to use—see *Choosing a fraction* on page 19-16

■ randomize the design—see *Randomizing the design* on page 19-16

■ store the design—see *Storing the design* on page 19-17

Factors subdialog box

■ name factors—see *Naming factors* on page 19-18

■ set factor levels—see *Setting factor levels* on page 19-18

Results subdialog box

■ display the following in the Session window:
  – no results.
  – a summary of the design.
  – the default results, which includes the summary and alias tables.
  – the default results, plus the data table.
  – all the results described above, plus the defining relation. When the design is a full factorial, there is no defining relation.

- if you choose to display the alias table, you can specify the highest order interaction to print in the alias table. The default alias table for designs with
  - up to 7 factors, shows all terms.
  - 8 to 10 factors, shows up to four-way interactions.
  - 11 or more factors, shows up to three-way interactions.

Caution | Be careful! High-order interactions with a large number of factors could take a very long time to compute.

Specifying generators to add factors to the base design

You can add factors to the base design to create your own design rather than using a design from MINITAB's catalog. You can add up to 15 factors to the base design by specifying the appropriate generators. You can use a minus interaction for a generator, for example D = −AB.

If you want to block the design, you also need to specify block generators—see *Blocking the design* on page 19-13.

▶ To add factors to the base design by specifying generators

1 Choose **Stat ➤ DOE ➤ Factorial ➤ Create Factorial Design**.

2 Under **Type of Design**, choose **2-level factorial (specify generators)**.

3 From **Number of factors**, choose a number from 2 to 15.

4 Click **Designs**.

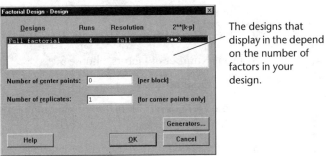

The designs that display in the depend on the number of factors in your design.

5 In the box at the top, highlight the design you want to create. The selected design will serve as the base design. If you like, use any of the options listed under *Designs subdialog box* on page 19-8.

6 Click **Generators**.

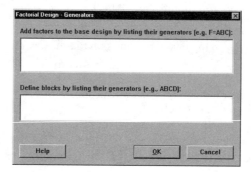

7 In **Add factors to the base design by listing their generators**, enter the generators for up to 15 additional factors in alphabetical order. Click **OK** in the Generators and Design subdialog boxes.

8 If you want to block the design, in **Define blocks by listing their generators**, enter the block generators. Click **OK** in the Generators and Design subdialog boxes. For more information, see *Blocking the design* on page 19-13.

9 If you like, click **Options**, **Factors**, and/or **Results** to use any of the options listed on page 19-8, then click **OK** in each dialog box to create your design.

More | For a thorough explanation of design generators, see [1] and [3].

▷ **Example of specifying generators**

Suppose you want to add two factors to a base design with three factors and eight runs.

1 Choose **Stat ➤ DOE ➤ Factorial ➤ Create Factorial Design**.

2 Choose **2-level factorial (specify generators)**.

3 From **Number of factors**, choose 3.

4 Click **Designs**.

5 In the **Designs** box at the top, highlight the row for a **full factorial**. This design will serve as the base design.

6 Click **Generators**. In **Add factors to the base design by listing their generators**, enter $D = AB$ $E = AC$. Click **OK** in each dialog box.

*Session
window
output*

Factorial Design

Fractional Factorial Design

```
Factors:      5   Base Design:        3, 8   Resolution: III
Runs:         8   Replicates:            1   Fraction:  1/4
Blocks:    none   Center pts (total):    0
```

*** NOTE *** Some main effects are confounded with two-way interactions

Design Generators: D = AB E = AC

Alias Structure (up to order 3)

```
I + ABD + ACE

A + BD + CE + ABCDE
B + AD + CDE + ABCE
C + AE + BDE + ABCD
D + AB + BCE + ACDE
E + AC + BCD + ABDE
BC + DE + ABE + ACD
BE + CD + ABC + ADE
BCDE
```

Interpreting the results

The base design has three factors labeled A, B, and C. Then MINITAB adds factors D and E. Because of the generators selected, D is confounded with the AB interaction and E is confounded with the AC interaction. This gives a $2^{(5-2)}$ or resolution III design. Look at the alias structure to see how the other effects are confounded.

Adding center points

Adding center points to a factorial design may allow you to detect curvature in the fitted data. If there is curvature that involves the center of the design, the response at the center point will be either higher or lower than the fitted value of the factorial (corner) points.

The way MINITAB adds center points to the design depends on whether you have text, numeric, or a combination of text and numeric factors. Here is how MINITAB adds center points:

- When all factors are numeric and the design is
  - not blocked, MINITAB adds the specified number of center points to the design.
  - blocked, MINITAB adds the specified number of center points to each block.
- When all of the factors in a design are text, you cannot add center points.

- When you have a combination of numeric and text factors, there is no true center to the design. In this case, center points are called pseudo-center points. When the design is
  - not blocked, MINITAB adds the specified number of center points for each combination of the levels of the text factors.
  - blocked, MINITAB adds the specified number of center points for each combination of the levels of the text factors to each block.

For example, consider an unblocked 2^3 design. Factors A and C are numeric with levels 0, 10 and .2, .3, respectively. Factor B is text indicating whether a catalyst is present or absent. If you specify three center points in the Designs subdialog box, MINITAB adds a total of $2 \times 3 = 6$ pseudo-center points, three points for the low level of factor B and three for the high level. These six points are

```
5   present   .25
5   present   .25
5   present   .25
5    absent   .25
5    absent   .25
5    absent   .25
```

Next, consider a blocked 2^5 design where three factors are text, and there are two blocks. There are $2 \times 2 \times 2 = 8$ combinations of text levels. If you specify two center points per block, MINITAB will add $8 \times 2 = 16$ pseudo-center points to each of the two blocks.

▶ **To add center points to the design**

1 In the Create Factorial Design dialog box, click **Designs**.

2 From **Number of center points**, choose a number up to 25. Click **OK**.

Replicating the design

You can have up to ten replicates of your design. When you replicate a design, you duplicate the complete set of "corner point" runs from the initial design. MINITAB does not replicate center points.

For example, suppose you are creating a full factorial design with 4 factors and 16 runs, and you specify 2 replicates. Each of the 16 runs will be repeated for a total of 32 runs in the experiment.

The runs that would be added to a two-factor full factorial design are as follows:

Initial design (one replicate)		One replicate added (total of two replicates)		Two replicates added (total of three replicates)	
A	B	A	B	A	B
-	-	-	-	-	-
+	+	+	+	+	+
+	-	+	-	+	-
-	+	-	+	-	+
		-	-	-	-
		+	+	+	+
		+	-	+	-
		-	+	-	+
				-	-
				+	+
				+	-
				-	+

True replication provides an estimate of the error or noise in your process and may allow for more precise estimates of effects.

▶ **To replicate the design**

1 In the Create Factorial Design dialog box, click **Designs**.

2 From **Number of replicates**, choose a number up to 10. Click **OK**.

More | You can also replicate a design after it has been created using **Modify Design** (page 19-38).

Blocking the design

Although every observation should be taken under identical experimental conditions (other than those that are being varied as part of the experiment), this is not always possible. Nuisance factors that can be classified can be eliminated using a blocked design. For example, an experiment carried out over several days may have large variations in temperature and humidity, or data may be collected in different plants, or by different technicians. Observations collected under the same experimental conditions are said to be in the same *block*.

The way you block a design depends on whether you are creating a design using the default generators or specifying your own generators.

Note | When you have more than one block, MINITAB randomizes each block independently.

▶ **To block a design created with the default generators**

1 In the Create Factorial Design dialog box, click **Designs**.

2 From **Number of blocks**, choose a number. Click **OK**.

The list shows all the possible blocking combinations for the selected design with the number of specified replicates. If you change the design or the number of replicates, the list will reflect a new set of possibilities.

If your design has replicates, MINITAB attempts to put the replicates in different blocks. For details, see *Rule for blocks with replicates for default designs* on page 19-28.

▶ **To block a design created by specifying your own generators**

You need to specify your own block generators because MINITAB cannot automatically determine "good" generators when you are adding factors.

Suppose you generate a 64 run design with 8 factors (labeled alphabetically) and specify the block generators to be ABC CDE. This gives four blocks which are shown in "standard" (Yates) order below:

Block	ABC	CDE
1	–	–
2	+	–
3	–	+
4	+	+

Note | Blocking a design can reduce its resolution. Let r_1 = the resolution before blocking. Let r_2 = the length of the shortest term that is confounded with blocks. Then the resolution after blocking is the smaller of r_1 and $(r_2 + 1)$.

1 In the Designs subdialog box, click **Generators**.

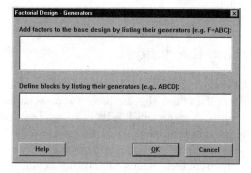

2 In **Define blocks by listing their generators**, type the block generators. Click **OK**.

Folding the design

Folding is a way to reduce *confounding*. Confounding occurs when you have a fractional factorial design and one or more effects cannot be estimated separately. The effects that cannot be separated are said to be *aliased*.

Resolution IV designs may be obtained from resolution III designs by folding. For example, if you fold on one factor, say A, then A and all its two-factor interactions will be free from other main effects and two-factor interactions. If you fold on all factors, then all main effects will be free from each other and from all two-factor interactions.

▶ **To fold the design**

1   In the Create Factorial Design dialog box, click **Options**.

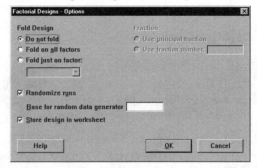

2   Do one of the following, then click **OK**.

■ Choose **Fold on all factors** to make all main effects free from each other and all two-factor interactions.

■ Choose **Fold just on factor** and then choose a factor from the list to make the specified factor and all its two-factor interactions free from other main effects and two-factor interactions.

Method

For example, suppose you are creating a three-factor design in four runs.

■ When you fold on all factors, MINITAB adds to the original four runs, four runs with all the signs reversed thereby doubling the number of runs.

■ When you fold on one factor, MINITAB reverses the signs on the specified factor while the signs on the remaining factors are left alone. These rows are then appended to the end of the data matrix, doubling the number of runs.

Original fraction	Folded on all factors	Folded on factor A
A B C	A B C	A B C
– – +	– – +	– – +
+ – –	+ – –	+ – –
– + –	– + –	– + –
+ + +	+ + +	+ + +
	+ + –	+ – +
	– + +	– – –
	+ – +	+ + –
	– – –	– + +

When you fold a design, the defining relation is usually shortened. Specifically, any word in the defining relation that has an odd number of the letters on which you folded the design is omitted. If you fold a design and the defining relation is not shortened, then the folding just adds replicates. It does not reduce confounding. In this case, MINITAB gives you an error message.

If you fold a design that is blocked, the same block generators are used for the folded design as for the unfolded design.

Choosing a fraction

When you create a fractional factorial design, MINITAB uses the principal fraction by default. The principal fraction is the fraction where all signs are positive. However, there may be situations when a design contains points that are impractical to run and choosing an appropriate fraction can avoid these points.

A full factorial design with 5 factors requires 32 runs. If you want just 8 runs, you need to use a one-fourth fraction. You can use any of the four possible fractions of the design. MINITAB numbers the runs in "standard" (Yates) order using the design generators as follows:

```
1  D = -AB   E = -AC
2  D =  AB   E = -AC
3  D = -AB   E =  AC
4  D =  AB   E =  AC
```

The default fraction is called the principal fraction. This is the fraction where all signs are positive (D = AB   E = AC). In the blocking example, shown on page 19-22, we asked for the third fraction. This is the one with design generators D = −AB and E = AC.

Choosing an appropriate fraction can avoid points that are impractical or impossible to run. For example, suppose you could not run the design in the previous example with all five factors set at their high level. The principal fraction contains this point, but the third fraction does not.

Note | If you choose to use a fraction other than the principal fraction, you cannot use minus signs for the design generators in the Generators subdialog box. Using minus signs in this case is not useful anyway.

Randomizing the design

By default, MINITAB randomizes the run order of the design. The ordered sequence of the factor combinations (experimental conditions) is called the *run order*. It is usually a good idea to randomize the run order to lessen the effects of factors that are not included in the study, particularly effects that are time-dependent.

However, there may be situations when randomization leads to an undesirable run order. For instance, in industrial applications, it may be difficult or expensive to change factor levels. Or, after factor levels have been changed, it may take a long time for the system to return to a steady state. Under these conditions, you may not want to randomize the design in order to minimize the level changes.

Every time you create a design, MINITAB reserves and names C1 (StdOrder) and C2 (RunOrder) to store the standard order and run order, respectively.

- StdOrder shows what the order of the runs in the experiment would be if the experiment was done in standard order—also called Yates' order.

- RunOrder shows what the order of the runs in the experiment would be if the experiment was run in random order.

If you do not randomize, the run order and standard order are the same.

If you want to re-create a design with the same ordering of the runs (that is, the same design order), you can choose a base for the random data generator. Then, when you want to re-create the design, you just use the same base.

Note | When you have more than one block, MINITAB randomizes each block independently.

More | You can use **Stat ➤ DOE ➤ Display Design** (page 19-42) to switch back and forth between a random and standard order display in the worksheet.

Storing the design

If you want to analyze a design, you *must* store it in the worksheet. By default, MINITAB stores the design. If you want to see the properties of various designs, such as alias structures before selecting the design you want to store, uncheck **Store design in worksheet** in the Options subdialog box.

Every time you create a design, MINITAB reserves and names the following columns:

- C1 (StdOrder) stores the standard order.

- C2 (RunOrder) stores run order.

- C3 (CenterPt) (two-level factorials and Plackett-Burman designs only) contains a 0 if the row is a center point run. Otherwise, it contains a 1.

- C4 (Blocks) stores the blocking variable. When the design is not blocked, MINITAB sets all column values to 1.

- C5– C*n* stores the factors. MINITAB stores each factor in your design in a separate column.

If you name the factors, these names display in the worksheet. If you did not provide names, MINITAB names the factors alphabetically. After you create the design, you can change the factor names directly in the Data window or with Modify Design (page 19-42).

If you did not assign factor levels in the Factors subdialog box, MINITAB stores factor levels in coded form (all factor levels are −1 or +1). If you assigned factor levels, the uncoded levels display in the worksheet. After you create the design, you can change the factor levels with Modify Design (page 19-42).

More | You can use **Stat ➤ DOE ➤ Display Design** (page 19-42) to switch back and forth between a coded and uncoded display in the worksheet.

Caution | When you create a design using Create Factorial Design, MINITAB stores the appropriate design information in the worksheet. MINITAB needs this stored information to analyze and plot data. If you want to use Analyze Factorial Design, you must follow certain rules when modifying the worksheet data. If you do not, you may corrupt your design. See *Modifying and Using Worksheet Data* on page 18-4.

| If you make changes that corrupt your design, you may still be able to analyze it with Analyze Factorial Design after you use **Define Custom Factorial Design** (page 19-35).

Naming factors

By default, MINITAB names the factors alphabetically, skipping the letter I.

▶ To name factors

1 In the Create Factorial Design dialog box, click **Factors**.

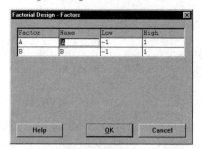

2 Under **Name**, click in the first row and type the name of the first factor. Then, use the ⬇ key to move down the column and enter the remaining factor names. Click **OK**.

More | After you have created the design, you can change the factor names by typing new names in the Data window or with Modify Design (page 19-38).

Setting factor levels

You can enter factor levels as numeric or text. If your factors could be *continuous*, use numeric levels; if your factors are *categorical*, use text levels. Continuous variables can take on any value on the measurement scale being used (for example, length of reaction time). In contrast, categorical variables can only assume a limited number of possible values (for example, type of catalyst).

By default, MINITAB sets the low level of all factors to −1 and the high level to +1.

▶ **To assign factor levels**

1 In the Create Factorial Design dialog box, click **Factors**.

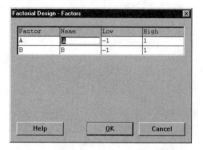

2 Under **Low**, click in the factor row you would like to assign values and enter any numeric or text value. Use the ⟶ key to move to **High** and enter a value. For numeric levels, the **High** value must be larger than **Low** value.

3 Repeat step 2 to assign levels for other factors. Click **OK**.

More | To change the factor levels after you have created the design, use **Stat ➤ DOE ➤ Modify Design**. Unless some runs result in botched runs, do not change levels by typing them in the worksheet.

▶ **Example of creating a fractional factorial design**

Suppose you want to study the influence six input variables (factors) have on shrinkage of a plastic fastener of a toy. The goal of your pilot study is to screen these six factors to determine which ones have the greatest influence. Because you assume that three-way and four-way interactions are negligible, a resolution IV factorial design is appropriate. You decide to generate a 16-run fractional factorial design from MINITAB's catalog.

1 Choose **Stat ➤ DOE ➤ Factorial ➤ Create Factorial Design**.

2 From **Number of factors**, choose 6.

3 Click **Designs**.

4 In the box at the top, highlight the line for **1/4 fraction**. Click **OK**.

5 Click **Results**. Choose **Summary table, alias table, data table, defining relation**.

6 Click **OK** in each dialog box.

Session
window
output

Factorial Design

Fractional Factorial Design

Factors:	6	Base Design:	6, 16	Resolution: IV
Runs:	16	Replicates:	1	Fraction: 1/4
Blocks: none		Center pts (total):	0	

Design Generators: E = ABC   F = BCD

Defining Relation: I = ABCE = BCDF = ADEF

Alias Structure

I + ABCE + ADEF + BCDF

A + BCE + DEF + ABCDF
B + ACE + CDF + ABDEF
C + ABE + BDF + ACDEF
D + AEF + BCF + ABCDE
E + ABC + ADF + BCDEF
F + ADE + BCD + ABCEF
AB + CE + ACDF + BDEF
AC + BE + ABDF + CDEF
AD + EF + ABCF + BCDE
AE + BC + DF + ABCDEF
AF + DE + ABCD + BCEF
BD + CF + ABEF + ACDE
BF + CD + ABDE + ACEF
ABD + ACF + BEF + CDE
ABF + ACD + BDE + CEF

Data Matrix (randomized)

Run	A	B	C	D	E	F
1	+	+	+	-	+	-
2	-	-	-	+	-	+
3	+	-	+	+	-	-
4	+	-	+	-	-	+
5	-	+	-	-	+	+
6	-	+	+	+	-	+
7	-	-	+	-	+	+
8	-	+	-	+	+	-
9	+	+	-	-	-	+
10	+	+	-	+	-	-
11	-	+	+	-	-	-
12	-	-	-	-	-	-
13	+	-	-	+	+	+
14	+	+	+	+	+	+
15	+	-	-	-	+	-
16	-	-	+	+	+	-

Interpreting the results

The first table gives a summary of the design: the total number of factors, runs, blocks, replicates, and center points.

With 6 factors, a full factorial design would have 2^6 or 64 runs. Because resources are limited, you chose a 1/4 fraction with 16 runs.

The resolution of a design that has not been blocked is the length of the shortest word in the defining relation. In this example, all words in the defining relation have four letters so the resolution is IV. In a resolution IV design, some main effects are confounded with three-way interactions, but not with any two-way interactions or other main effects. Because two-way interactions are confounded with each other, any significant interactions will need to be evaluated further to define their nature.

Because you chose to display the summary and data tables, MINITAB shows the experimental conditions or settings for each of the factors for the design points. When you perform the experiment, use the order that is shown to determine the conditions for each run. For example, in the first run of your experiment, you would set Factor A high, Factor B high, Factor C high, Factor D low, Factor E high, and Factor F low, and measure the shrinkage of the plastic fastener.

Note | MINITAB randomizes the design by default, so if you try to replicate this example, your runs may not match the order shown.

Studying specific interactions

When you are interested in studying specific interactions, you do not want these interactions confounded with each other or with main effects. Look at the alias structure to see how the interactions are confounded, then assign factors to appropriate letters in MINITAB's design.

For example, suppose you wanted to use a 16-run design to study 6 factors: pressure, speed, cooling, thread, hardness, and time. The alias structure for this design is shown on page 19-20. Suppose you were interested in the two-factor interactions among pressure, speed, and cooling. You could assign pressure to A, speed to B, and cooling to C. The following lines of the alias table demonstrate that AB, AC, and BC are not confounded with each other or with main effects

```
AB + CE + ACDF + BDEF
AC + BE + ABDF + CDEF
...
AE + BC + DF + ABCDEF
```

You can assign the remaining three factors to D, E, and F in any way.

If you also wanted to study the three-way interaction among pressure, speed, and cooling, this assignment would not work because ABC is confounded with E. However, you could assign pressure to A, speed to B, and cooling to D.

➤ **Example of creating a blocked design**

You would like to study the effects of five input variables on the impurity of a vaccine. Each batch only contains enough raw material to manufacture four tubes of the vaccine. To remove the effects due to differences in the four batches of raw material, you decide to perform the experiment in four blocks. To determine the experimental conditions that will be used for each run, you create a 5-factor, 16-run design, in 4 blocks.

1 Choose **Stat ➤ DOE ➤ Factorial ➤ Create Factorial Design**.

2 From **Number of factors**, choose 5.

3 Click **Designs**.

4 In the box at the top, highlight the line for **1/2 fraction**.

5 From **Number of blocks**, choose **4**.

6 Click **Results**. Choose **Summary table, alias table, data table, defining relation**. Click **OK** in each dialog box.

Session window output

Factorial Design

Fractional Factorial Design

Factors:	5	Base Design:	5, 16	Resolution with blocks: III
Runs:	16	Replicates:	1	Fraction: 1/2
Blocks:	4	Center pts (total):	0	

*** NOTE *** Blocks are confounded with two-way interactions

Design Generators: E = ABCD

Block Generators: AB AC

Defining Relation: I = ABCDE

Alias Structure

I + ABCDE

Blk1 = AB + CDE
Blk2 = AC + BDE
Blk3 = BC + ADE

```
A + BCDE
B + ACDE
C + ABDE
D + ABCE
E + ABCD
AD + BCE
AE + BCD
BD + ACE
BE + ACD
CD + ABE
CE + ABD
DE + ABC
```

Data Matrix (randomized)

```
Run Block  A  B  C  D  E
 1    1    +  +  -  -  +
 2    1    +  +  -  +  -
 3    1    -  -  +  +  +
 4    1    -  -  +  -  -
 5    2    -  +  -  -  -
 6    2    +  -  +  -  +
 7    2    +  -  +  +  -
 8    2    -  +  -  +  +
 9    3    +  +  +  +  +
10    3    -  -  -  +  -
11    3    -  -  -  -  +
12    3    +  +  +  -  -
13    4    +  -  -  +  +
14    4    -  +  +  +  -
15    4    +  -  -  -  -
16    4    -  +  +  -  +
```

Interpreting the results

The first table gives a summary of the design: the total number of factors, runs, blocks, replicates, center points, and resolution. After blocking, this is a resolution III design because blocks are confounded with two-way interactions.

Because you chose to display the summary and data tables, MINITAB shows the experimental conditions or settings for each of the factors for the design points. When you perform the experiment, use the order that is shown to determine the conditions for each run.

The first four runs of your experiment would all be performed using raw material from the same batch (Block 1). For the first run in block one, you would set Factor A high, Factor B high, Factor C low, Factor D low, and Factor E high, and measure the impurity of the vaccine.

Note | MINITAB randomizes the design by default, so if you try to replicate this example, your runs may not match the order shown.

Creating Plackett-Burman Designs

Plackett-Burman designs are a class of resolution III, two-level fractional factorial designs that are often used to study main effects. In a resolution III design, main effects are aliased with two-way interactions. Therefore, you should only use these designs when you are willing to assume that two-way interactions are negligible.

MINITAB generates designs for up to 47 factors. Each design is based on the number of runs, from 8 to 48, and is always a multiple of 4. The number of factors must be less than the number of runs. For example, a design with 20 runs allows you to estimate the main effects for up to 19 factors. The Plackett-Burman designs that MINITAB generates are shown on page 19-32.

MINITAB displays alias tables only for saturated 8- and 16-run designs. For 12-, 20-, and 24-run designs, each main effect gets partially confounded with more than one two-way interaction thereby making the alias structure difficult to determine.

After you create the design, perform the experiment to obtain the response data, and enter the data in the worksheet, you can use Analyze Factorial Design (page 19-44).

▶ **To create a Plackett-Burman design**

1   Choose **Stat ➤ DOE ➤ Factorial ➤ Create Factorial Design**.

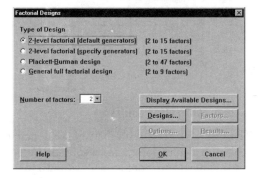

2 If you want to see a summary of the Plackett-Burman designs, click **Display Available Designs**. Use this table to compare design features. Click **OK**.

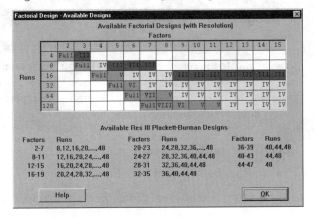

3 Choose **Plackett-Burman design**.

4 From **Number of factors**, choose a number from 2 to 47.

5 Click **Designs**.

6 From **Number of runs**, choose the number of runs for your design. This list contains only acceptable numbers of runs based on the number of factors you choose in step 4. (Each design is based on the number of runs, from 8 to 48, and is always a multiple of 4. The number of factors must be less than the number of runs.)

7 If you like, use any of the options listed under *Design subdialog box* below.

Even if you do not use any of these options, click **OK**. This selects the design and brings you back to the main dialog box.

8 If you like, click **Options** or **Factors** to use any of the options listed below, then click **OK** to create your design.

Options

Design subdialog box

- add center points—see *Adding center points* on page 19-26.

- replicate the *corner points* of the design. For example, suppose you are creating a design with 3 factors and 12 runs, and you specify 2 replicates. Each of the 12 runs will be repeated for a total of 24 runs in the experiment. MINITAB does not replicate center points. See *Replicating the design* on page 19-12.

Options subdialog box

- randomize the design—see *Randomizing the design* on page 19-16

- store the design—see *Storing the design* on page 19-17

Factors subdialog box

- name factors—see *Naming factors* on page 19-18

- set factor levels—see *Setting factor levels* on page 19-18

Adding center points

The way MINITAB adds center points to the design depends on whether you have text, numeric, or a combination of text and numeric factors. Here is how MINITAB adds center points:

- When all factors are numeric, MINITAB adds the specified number of center points to the design.

- When all of the factors in a design are text, you cannot add center points.

- When you have a combination of numeric and text factors, there is no true center to the design. In this case, center points are called pseudo-center points. MINITAB adds the specified number center points for each combination of the levels of the text factors.

For an example, see *Adding center points* on page 19-11.

▷ Example of creating a Plackett-Burman design with center points

Suppose you want to study the effects of 9 factors using only 12 runs, with 3 center points. In this 12-run design, each main effect is partially confounded with more than one two-way interaction.

1 Choose **Stat ➤ DOE ➤ Factorial ➤ Create Factorial Design**.

2 Choose **Plackett-Burman design**.

3 From **Number of factors**, choose 9.

4 Click **Designs**.

5 From **Number of runs**, choose 12.

6 In **Number of center points**, enter 3. Click **OK** in each dialog box.

Session window output

Factorial Design

Plackett-Burman Design

Factors:	9	Replicates:	1	Design:	12
Runs:	15	Center pts (total):	3		

Data Matrix (randomized)

Run	A	B	C	D	E	F	G	H	J
1	-	+	+	+	-	+	+	-	+
2	-	+	-	-	-	+	+	+	-
3	+	-	-	-	+	+	+	-	+
4	0	0	0	0	0	0	0	0	0
5	0	0	0	0	0	0	0	0	0
6	-	-	+	+	+	-	+	+	-
7	+	+	-	+	-	-	-	+	+
8	+	-	+	+	-	+	-	-	-
9	+	+	+	-	+	+	-	+	-
10	+	+	-	+	+	-	+	-	-
11	+	-	+	-	-	-	+	+	+
12	-	+	+	-	+	-	-	-	+
13	-	-	-	+	+	+	-	+	+
14	0	0	0	0	0	0	0	0	0
15	-	-	-	-	-	-	-	-	-

Interpreting the results

In the first table, Runs shows the total number of runs including any runs created by replicates and center points. For this example, you specified 12 runs and added 3 runs for center points, for a total of 15.

MINITAB does not display an alias tables for this 12 run design because each main effect is partially confounded with more than one two-way interaction.

MINITAB shows the experimental conditions or settings for each of the factors for the design points. When you perform the experiment, use the order that is shown to determine the conditions for each run. For example, in the first run of your experiment, you would set Factor A low, Factor B high, Factor C high, Factor D high, Factor E low, Factor F high, Factor G high, Factor H low, and Factor J high.

Note | MINITAB randomizes the design by default, so if you try to replicate this example, your runs may not match the order shown.

Summary of Two-Level Designs

Two-level designs

The table below summarizes the two-level default designs and the base designs for designs in which you specify generators for additional factors. Table cells with entries show available run/factor combinations. The first number in a cell is the resolution of the unblocked design. The lower number in a cell is the maximum number of blocks you can use.

Number of runs	Number of factors													
	2	3	4	5	6	7	8	9	10	11	12	13	14	15
4	full 2	III 1												
8		full 4	IV 4	III 2	III 2	III 1								
16			full 8	V 8	IV 8	IV 8	IV 8	III 4	III 4	III 4	III 4	III 2	III 2	III 1
32				full 16	VI 16	IV 8	IV 8	IV 8	IV 8	IV 8	IV 8	IV 8	IV 8	IV 8
64					full 32	VII 16	V 16	IV 16	IV 16	IV 16	IV 16	IV 16	IV 16	IV 16
128						full 64	VIII 32	VI 16	V 16	V 16	IV 16	IV 16	IV 16	IV 16

Rule for blocks with replicates for default designs

For a blocked default design with replicates, MINITAB puts replicates in different blocks to the extent that it can.

The following rule is used to assign runs to blocks: Let k = the number of factors, b = the number of blocks, r = the number of replicates, and n = the number of runs (corner points).

Let D = the greatest common divisor of b and r. Then b = B*D and r = R*D, for some B and R. Start with the standard design for k factors, n runs, and B blocks. (If there is no such design, you will get an error message.) Replicate this entire design r times. This gives a total of B*r blocks, numbered 1, 2, ..., B, 1, 2, ... , B, ..., 1, 2, ..., B. Renumber these blocks as 1, 2, ..., b, 1, 2, ..., b, ..., 1, 2, ..., b. This will give b blocks, each replicated R times, which is what you want.

For example, suppose you have a factorial design with 3 factors and 8 runs, run in 6 blocks, and you want to add 15 replicates.

Then k = 3, b = 6, r = 15, and n = 8. The greatest common divisor of b and r is 3. Then B = 2 and R = 5. Start with the design for 3 factors, 8 runs, and 2 blocks. Replicate this design 15 times. This gives a total of 2*15 = 30 blocks, numbered 1, 2, 1, 2, 1, 2, ..., 1, 2. Renumber these blocks as 1, 2, 3, 4, 5, 6, 1, 2, 3, 4, 5, 6, ..., 1, 2, 3, 4, 5, 6. This gives 6 blocks, each replicated 5 times.

Generators for two-level designs

The first line for each design gives the number of factors, the number of runs, the resolution (R) of the design without blocking, and the design generators. On the following lines, there is one entry for each number of blocks. The number before the parentheses is the number of blocks, in the parentheses are the block generators, and the number after the parentheses is the resolution of the blocked design.

factor	runs	R	design generators
2	4	–	full
			2(AB)3
3	4	3	C=AB
			no blocking
3	8	–	full
			2(ABC)4 4(AB,AC)3
4	8	4	D=ABC
			2(AB)3 4(AB,AC)3
4	16	–	full
			2(ABCD)5 4(BC,ABD)3 8(AB,BC,CD)3
5	8	3	D=AB E=AC
			2(BC)3
5	16	5	E=ABCD
			2(AB)3 4(AB,AC)3
5	32	–	full
			2(ABCDE)6 4(ABC,CDE)4 8(AC,BD,ADE)3 16(AB,AC,CD,DE)3
6	8	3	D=AB E=AC F=BC
			2(BE)3
6	16	4	E=ABC F=BCD
			2(ACD)4 4(AE,ACD)3 8(AB,BC,BF)3
6	32	6	F=ABCDE
			2(ABF)4 4(BC,ABF)3 8(AD,BC,ABF)3 16(AB,BC,CD,DE)3
6	64	–	full
			2(ABCDEF)7 4(ABCF,ABDE)5 8(ACE,ADF,BCF)4
			16(AD,BE,CE,ABF)3 32(AB,BC,CD,DE,EF)

factor	runs	R	design generators
7	8	3	D=AB E=AC F=BC G=ABC
			no blocking
7	16	4	E=ABC F=BCD G=ACD
			2(ABD)4 4(AB,AC)3 8(AB,AC,AD)3
7	32	4	F=ABCD G=ABDE
			2(CDE)4 4(CF,CDE)3 8(AB,AD,CG)3
7	64	7	G=ABCDEF
			2(CDE)4 4(ACF,CDE)4 8(ACF,ADG,CDE)4 16(AB,AC,EF,EG)3
7	128	–	full
			2(ABCDEFG)8 4(ABDE,ABCFG)5 8(ABC,AFG,DEF)4 16(ABE,ADG,CDE,EFG)4
			32(AC,BD,CE,DF,ABG)3 64(AB,BC,CD,DE,EF,FG)3
8	16	4	E=BCD F=ACD G=ABC H=ABD
			2(AB)3 4(AB,AC)3 8(AB,AC,AD)3
8	32	4	F=ABC G=ABD H=BCDE
			2(ABE)4 4(EH,ABE)3 8(AB,AC,BD)3
8	64	5	G=ABCD H=ABEF
			2(ACE)4 4(ACE,BDF)4 8(BC,FH,BDF)3 16(BC,DE,FH,BDF)3
8	128	8	H=ABCDEFG
			2(ABCD)5 4(ABCD,ABEF)5 8(ABCD,ABEF,BCEG)5
			16(BF,DE,ABG,AEH)3 32(AC,BD,BF,DE,AEH)3
9	16	3	E=ABC F=BCD G=ACD H=ABD J=ABCD
			2(AB)3 4(AB,AC)3
9	32	4	F=BCDE G=ACDE H=ABDE J=ABCE
			2(AEF)4 4(AB,CD)3 8(AB,AC,CD)3
9	64	4	G=ABCD H=ACEF J=CDEF
			2(BCE)4 4(ABF,ACJ)4 8(AD,AH,BDE)3 16(AC,AD,AJ,BF)3
9	128	6	H=ACDFG J=BCEFG
			2(CDEJ)5 4(ABFJ,CDEJ)5 8(ACF,AHJ,BCJ)4 16(AE,CG,BCJ,BDE)3
10	16	3	E=ABC F=BCD G=ACD H=ABD J=ABCD K=AB
			2(AC)3 4(AD,AG)3
10	32	4	F=ABCD G=ABCE H=ABDE J=ACDE K=BCDE
			2(AB)3 4(AB,BC)3 8(AB,AC,AH)3
10	64	4	G=BCDF H=ACDF J=ABDE K=ABCE
			2(AGJ)4 4(CD,AGJ)3 8(AG,CJ,CK)3 16(AC,AG,CJ,CK)3
10	128	5	H=ABCG J=BCDE K=ACDF
			2(ADG)4 4(ADG,BDF)4 8(AEH,AGK,CDH)4 16(BH,EG,JK,ADG)3
11	16	3	E=ABC F=BCD G=ACD H=ABD J=ABCD K=AB L=AC
			2(AD)3 4(AE,AH)3
11	32	4	F=ABC G=BCD H=CDE J=ACD K=ADE L=BDE
			2(ABD)4 4(AK,ABD)3 8(AB,AC,AD)3

factor	runs	R	design generators
11	64	4	G=CDE H=ABCD J=ABF K=BDEF L=ADEF
			2(AHJ)4 4(FL,AHJ)3 8(CD,CE,DL)3 16(AB,AC,AE,AF)3
11	128	5	H=ABCG J=BCDE K=ACDF L=ABCDEFG
			2(ADJ)4 4(ADJ,BFH)4 8(ADJ,AHL,BFH)4 16(BC,DF,GL,BFH)3
12	16	3	E=ABC F=ABD G=ACD H=BCD J=ABCD K=AB L=AC M=AD
			2(AG)3 4(AF,AG)3
12	32	4	F=ACE G=ACD H=ABD J=ABE K=CDE L=ABCDE M=ADE
			2(ABC)4 4(DG,DH)3 8(AB,AC,AD)3
12	64	4	G=DEF H=ABC J=BCDE K=BCDF L=ABEF M=ACEF
			2(ABM)4 4(AB,AC)3 8(AB,AC,BM)3 16(AB,AD,BE,BM)3
12	128	4	H=ACDG J=ABCD K=BCFG L=ABDEFG M=CDEF
			2(ACF)4 4(BG,BJ)3 8(BG,BJ,AGM)3 16(BG,BJ,FM,AGM)3
13	16	3	E=ABC F=ABD G=ACD H=BCD J=ABCD K=AB L=AC M=AD N=BC
			2(AG)3
13	32	4	F=ACE G=BCE H=ABC J=CDE K=ABCDE L=ABE M=ACD N=ADE
			2(ABD)4 4(CG,GH)3 8(AB,AC,AD)3
13	64	4	G=ABC H=DEF J=BCDF K=BCDE L=ABEF M=ACEF N=BCEF
			2(AB)3 4(AB,AC)3 8(AB,AC,AN)3 16(AB,AD,BE,BM)3
13	128	4	H=DEFG J=BCEG K=BCDFG L=ABDEF M=ACEF N=ABC
			2(ADE)4 4(AB,AC)3 8(AB,AC,AGK)3 16(AB,AC,ABM,AGK)3
14	16	3	E=ABC F=ABD G=ACD H=BCD J=ABCD K=AB L=AC M=AD N=BC O=BD
			2(AG)3
14	32	4	F=ABC G=ABD H=ABE J=ACD K=ACE L=ADE M=BCD N=BCE O=BDE
			2(ACL)4 4(AB,ACL)3 8(AC,AL,AO)3
14	64	4	G=BEF H=BCF J=DEF K=CEF L=BCE M=CDF N=ACDE O=BCDEF
			2(ABC)4 4(BC,BE)3 8(BC,BE,BG)3 16(AB,BC,BE,BG)3
14	128	4	H=EFG J=BCFG K=BCEG L=ABEF M=ACEF N=BCDEF O=ABC
			2(ADE)4 4(AB,AC)3 8(AB,AC,BM)3 16(AB,AC,BM,DG)3
15	16	3	E=ABC F=ABD G=ACD H=BCD J=ABCD K=AB L=AC M=AD N=BC O=BD P=CD
			no blocking
15	32	4	F=ABC G=ABD H=ABE J=ACD K=ACE L=ADE M=BCD N=BCE O=BDE P=CDE
			2(ABP)4 4(AB,BP)3 8(AB,AD,AK)3
15	64	4	G=ABC H=ABD J=ABE K=ABF L=ACD M=ACE N=ACF O=ADE P=ADF
			2(ABL)4 4(AM,ABL)3 8(AB,AC,AD)3 16(AB,AC,AD,AE)3
15	128	4	H=ABFG J=ACDEF K=BEF L=ABCEG M=CDFG N=ACDEG O=EFG P=ABDEFG
			2(ADE)4 4(EG,GP)3 8(EG,GP,OP)3 16(BO,EG,GP,OP)3

Plackett-Burman designs

These are the designs given in [4], up through n = 48, where n is the number of runs. In all cases except n = 28, the design can be specified by giving just the first column of the design matrix. In the table below, we give this first column (written as a row to save space). This column is permuted cyclically to get an (n − 1) × (n − 1) matrix. Then a last row of all minus signs is added. For n = 28, we start with the first 9 rows. These are then divided into 3 blocks of 9 columns each. Then the 3 blocks are permuted (rowwise) cyclically and a last column of all minus signs is added to get the full design.

Each design can have up to k = (n − 1) factors. If you specify a k that is less than (n − 1), just the first k columns are used.

8 Runs
+ + + - + - -

12 Runs
+ + - + + + - - - + -

16 Runs
+ + + + - + - + + - - + - - -

20 Runs
+ + - - + + + + - + - + - - - - + + -

24 Runs
+ + + + + - + - + + - - + + - - + - + - - - -

28 Runs
+ - + + + + - - - - + - - - + - - + + + - + - + + - - +
+ + - + + + - - - - - + + - - + - - - + + + + - + + -
- + + + + + - - - + - - - + - + - + - + - + + - + + +
- - - + - + + + + + - - + - + - - - + + - + + + - + - +
- - - + + - + + + + - - - - + + - - + + - - + + + + + -
- - - - + + + + + - + - + - - - + - - + + + - + - + +
+ + + - - - + - + - - + - + - + - + - + - + + - + + + -
+ + + - - - + + - + - + - - - + + + - + + - + + - - + +
+ + + - - - - + + - + - + - - + - + - - - + + - + + + - +

32 Runs
- - - - + - + - + + + - + + - - - + + + + + + - - + + - + - - - +

36 Runs
- + - + + + - - - + + + + + - + + + - - + - - - - + - + - + + - - + -

40 Runs (derived by duplicating the 20 run design)
+ + - - + + + + - + - + - - - - + + - + + - - + + + + - + - + - - - - + + - + -

44 Runs
+ + - - + - + - - + + + - + + + + + - - - + - + + + - - - - - + - - - + + - + - + + + -

48 Runs
+ + + + + - + + + + + - - + - + - + + + - - + - + + - + + - + - - - + - + - + + - - - - + - - - -

Creating General Full Factorial Designs

Use MINITAB's general full factorial design option when any factor has more than two levels. You can create designs with up to nine factors. Each factor can have from two to ten levels.

▶ **To create a general full factorial design**

1 Choose **Stat ➤ DOE ➤ Factorial ➤ Create Factorial Design**.

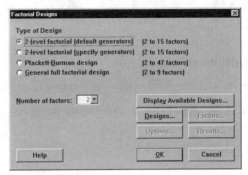

2 Choose **General full factorial design**.

3 From **Number of factors**, choose a number from 2 to 9.

4 Click **Designs**.

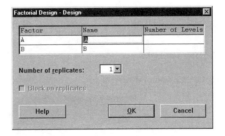

5 Click in **Number of Levels** in the row for Factor A and enter a number from 2 to 10. Use the ⊥ key to move down the column and specify the number of levels for each factor.

6 If you like, use any of the options listed under *Designs subdialog box* on page 19-8.

7 Click **OK**. This selects the design and brings you back to the main dialog box.

8 If you like, click **Options** or **Factors** and use any of the options listed on page 19-34, then click **OK** to create your design.

Options

Design subdialog box

- name factors.

- replicate the design up to 10 times. For example, suppose you are creating a design with 3 factors and 12 runs, and you specify 2 replicates. Each of the 12 runs will be repeated for a total of 24 runs in the experiment.

- block the design on replicates. Each set of replicate points will be placed in a separate block.

Options subdialog box

- randomize the design—see *Randomizing the design* on page 19-16

- store the design—see *Storing the design* on page 19-17

Factors subdialog box

- name factors—see *Naming factors* below

- set factor levels—see *Setting factor levels* on page 19-35

Naming factors

By default, MINITAB names the factors alphabetically, skipping the letter I.

▶ To name factors

1   In the Create Factorial Design dialog box, click **Factors**.

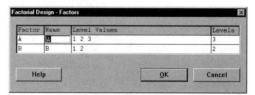

2   Under **Name**, click in the first row and type the name of the first factor. Then, use the ⬇ arrow key to move down the column and enter the remaining factor names. Click **OK**.

More | After you have created the design, you can change the factor names by typing new names in the Data window, or with Modify Design (page 19-38).

Setting factor levels

You can enter factor levels as numeric or text. If your factors could be *continuous*, use numeric levels; if your factors are *categorical*, use text levels. Continuous variables can take on any value on the measurement scale being used (for example, length of reaction time). In contrast, categorical variables can only assume a limited number of possible values (for example, type of catalyst).

You can have up to ten levels for each factor. By default, MINITAB sets the level values in numerical order. For example if you have a factor with four levels, MINITAB assigns the values 1 2 3 4.

▶ To assign factor levels

1 In the Create Factorial Design dialog box, click **Factors**

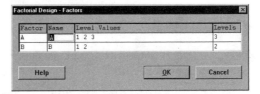

2 Under **Level Values**, click in the factor row to which you would like to assign values and enter any numeric or text value. Enter numeric levels from lowest to highest.

3 Use the ⬇ key to move down the column and assign levels for the remaining factors. Click **OK**.

More | To change the factor levels after you have created the design, use **Stat ➤ DOE ➤ Modify Design**. Unless some runs result in botched runs, do not change levels by typing them in the worksheet.

Defining Custom Designs

Use **Define Custom Factorial Design** to create a design from data you already have in the worksheet. For example, you may have a design that you created using MINITAB session commands, entered directly into the Data window, imported from a data file, or created with earlier releases of MINITAB. You can also use **Define Custom Factorial Design** to redefine a design that you created with Create Factorial Design and then modified directly in the worksheet.

Define Custom Factorial Design allows you to specify which columns contain your factors and other design characteristics. After you define your design, you can use Modify Design (page 19-38), Display Design (page 19-42), and Analyze Factorial Design (page 19-44).

▶ **To define a custom factorial design**

1 Choose Stat ➤ DOE ➤ Factorial ➤ Define Custom Factorial Design.

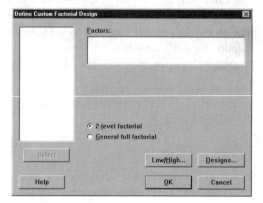

2 In **Factors**, enter the columns that contain the factor levels.

3 Depending on the type of design you have in the worksheet, choose **2-level factorial** or **General full factorial**.

4 By default, for each factor, MINITAB designates the smallest value in a factor column as the low level; the highest value in a factor column as the high level.

■ If you do not need to change this designation, go to step 5.

■ If you need to change this designation, click **Low/High**.

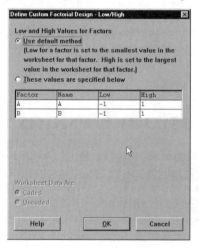

1 Under **Low and High Values for Factors**, choose **These values are specified below**.

2 Under **Low**, click in the factor row you would like to assign values and enter the appropriate numeric or text value. Use the ➡ key to move to **High** and enter a value. For numeric levels, the **High** value must be larger than **Low** value.

3 Repeat step 2 to assign levels for other factors.

4 Under **Worksheet Data Are**, choose **Coded** or **Uncoded**.

5 Click **OK**.

6 Do one of the following:

- If you do not have any worksheet columns containing the standard order, run order, center point indicators, or blocks, click **OK** in each dialog box.

- If you have worksheet columns that contain data for the blocks, center point identification (two-level designs only), run order, or standard order, click **Designs**.

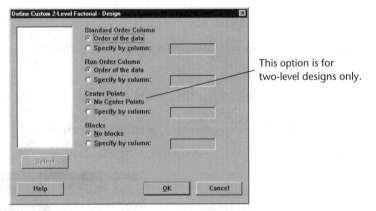

This option is for two-level designs only.

1 If you have a column that contains the standard order of the experiment, under **Standard Order Column**, choose **Specify by column** and enter the column containing the standard order.

2 If you have a column that contains the run order of the experiment, under **Run Order Column**, choose **Specify by column** and enter the column containing the run order.

3 For two-level designs, if you have a column that contains the center point identification values, under **Center points**, choose **Specify by column** and enter the column containing these values. The column must contain only 0's and 1's. MINITAB considers 0 a center point; 1 not a center point.

4 If your design is blocked, under **Blocks**, choose **Specify by column** and enter the column containing the blocks.

5 Click **OK** in each dialog box.

Modifying Designs

After creating a factorial design and storing it in the worksheet, you can use Modify Design to make the following modifications:

- rename the factors and change the factor levels
- replicate the design
- randomize the design

For two-level factorial designs, you can also

- fold the design.
- add axial points to the design. You can also add center points to the axial block.

By default, MINITAB will replace the current design with the modified design.

Renaming factors and changing factor levels

▶ To rename factors or change factor levels

1 Choose **Stat ➤ DOE ➤ Modify Design**.

These two options are available for two-level designs only.

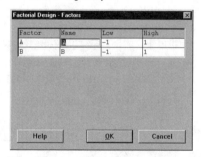

2 Choose **Modify factors** and click **Specify**.

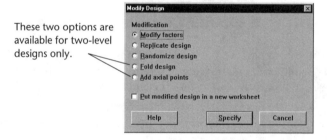

3 Enter new factor names or factor levels as shown in *Naming factors* on page 19-18 and *Setting factor levels* on page 19-18. Click **OK**.

Tip | You can also type new factor names directly into the Data window.

Replicating the design

You can add up to ten replicates of your design. When you replicate a design, you duplicate the complete set of runs from the initial design. The runs that would be added to a two factor full factorial design are as follows:

Initial design	One replicate added (total of two replicates)	Two replicates added (total of three replicates)
A B	A B	A B
- -	- -	- -
+ +	+ +	+ +
+ -	+ -	+ -
- +	- +	- +
	- -	- -
	+ +	+ +
	+ -	+ -
	- +	- +
		- -
		+ +
		+ -
		- +

True replication provides an estimate of the error or noise in your process and may allow for more precise estimates of effects.

▶ **To replicate the design**

1 Choose **Stat ➤ DOE ➤ Modify Design**.

2 Choose **Replicate design** and click **Specify**.

3 From **Number of replicates to add**, choose a number up to 10. Click **OK**.

Randomizing the design

You can randomize the entire design or just randomize one of the blocks. For a general discussion of randomization, see page 19-16.

▶ **To randomize the design**

1 Choose **Stat ➤ DOE ➤ Modify Design**.

2 Choose **Randomize design** and click **Specify**.

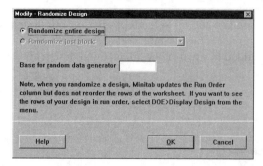

3 Do one of the following:

- Choose **Randomize entire design**.

- Choose **Randomize just block**, and choose a block number from the list.

4 If you like, in **Base for random data generator**, enter a number. Click **OK**.

More | You can use **Stat ➤ DOE ➤ Display Design** (page 19-42) to switch back and forth
between a random and standard order display in the worksheet.

Folding the design (two-level designs only)

Folding is a way to reduce *confounding*. Confounding occurs when you have a
fractional factorial design and one or more effects cannot be estimated separately. For a
discussion of folding, see *Folding the design* on page 19-14.

▶ **To fold the design**

1 Choose **Stat ➤ DOE ➤ Modify Design**.

2 Choose **Fold design** and click **Specify**.

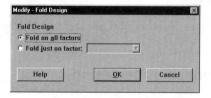

3 Do one of the following, then click **OK**.

- Choose **Fold on all factors** to make all main effects free from each other and all
  two-factor interactions.

- Choose **Fold just on factors** and then choose a factor from the list to make the
  specified factor and all its two-factor interactions free from other main effects and
  two-factor interactions.

Adding axial points (two-level designs only)

You can add axial points to a two-level factorial design to "build" it up to a central composite design. The position of the axial points in a central composite design is denoted by α. The value of α, along with the number of center points, determines whether a design can be orthogonally blocked and is rotatable. For a discussion of axial points and the value of α, see *Changing the value of α for a central composite design* on page 20-10.

Note | Orthogonally blocked designs allow for model terms and block effects to be estimated independently and minimize the variation in the estimated coefficients. Rotatable designs provide the desirable property of constant prediction variance at all points that are equidistant from the design center, thus improving the quality of the prediction.

▶ To add axial points

1   Choose **Stat ➤ DOE ➤ Modify Design**.

2   Choose **Add axial points** and click **Specify**.

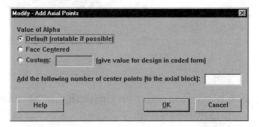

3   Do one of the following:

   ■ To have MINITAB assign a value to α, choose **Default**.

   ■ To set α equal to 1, choose **Face Centered**. When $\alpha = 1$, the axial points are placed on the "cube" portion of the design. This is an appropriate choice when the "cube" points of the design are at the operational limits.

   ■ Choose **Custom** and enter a positive number in the box. A value less than 1 places the axial points inside the "cube" portion of the design; a value greater than 1 places the axial points outside the "cube."

4   If you want to add center points to the axial block, enter a number in **Add the following number of center points (in the axial block)**. Click **OK**.

Note | If you are building up a factorial design into a central composite design and would like to consider the properties of orthogonal blocking and rotatability, use the table on page 20-18 for guidance on choosing α and the number of center points to add.

Displaying Designs

After you create the design, you can use Display Design to change the way the design points display in the worksheet. You can change the design points in two ways:

- display the points in either random or standard order. Standard order is the order of the runs if the experiment was done in Yates' order. Run order is the order of the runs if the experiment was done in random order.

- express the factor levels in coded or uncoded form.

▶ **To change the display order of points in the worksheet**

1 Choose **Stat ➤ DOE ➤ Display Design**.

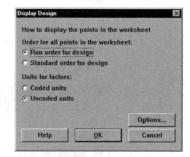

2 Choose **Run order for the design** or **Standard order for the design**. If you do not randomize a design, the columns that contain the standard order and run order are the same.

3 Do one of the following:

- If you want to reorder all worksheet columns that are the same length as the design columns, click **OK**.

- If you have worksheet columns that you do not want to reorder:
  1 Click **Options**.
  2 In **Exclude the following columns when sorting**, enter the columns. These columns *cannot* be part of the design. Click **OK** in each dialog box.

Displaying the design in coded or uncoded units

If you assigned factor levels in the Factors subdialog box, the uncoded or actual levels initially display in the worksheet. For example, if you entered 2 for the low level of pressure and 4 for the high level of pressure in the Factors subdialog box, these uncoded levels display in the worksheet. The coded levels are −1 and +1.

If you do not assign factor levels, displaying the design in coded and uncoded units is the same.

▶ **To change the display units for the factors**

1 Choose **Stat ➤ DOE ➤ Display Design**.

2 Choose **Coded units** or **Uncoded units**. Click **OK**.

Collecting and Entering Data

After you create your design, you need to perform the experiment and collect the response (measurement) data. To print a data collection form, follow the instructions below. After you collect the response data, enter the data in any worksheet column not used for the design. For a discussion of the worksheet structure, see *Storing the design* on page 19-17.

Printing a data collection form

You can generate a data collection form in two ways. You can simply print the Data window contents, or you can use a macro. A macro can generate a "nicer" data collection form—see Help for more information. Although printing the Data window will not produce the prettiest form, it is the easiest method. Just follow these steps:

1 When you create your experimental design, MINITAB stores the run order, block assignment, and factor settings in the worksheet. These columns constitute the basis of your data collection form. If you did not name factors or specify factor levels when you created the design, and you want names or levels to appear on the form, use Modify Design (page 19-38).

2 In the worksheet, name the columns in which you will record the measurement data obtained when you perform your experiment.

3 Choose **File ➤ Print Worksheet**. Make sure **Print Grid Lines** is checked, then click **OK**.

More | You can also copy the worksheet cells to the Clipboard by choosing **Edit ➤ Copy Cells**. Then paste the Clipboard contents into a word-processing application, such as Microsoft WordPad or Microsoft Word, where you can create your own form.

Analyzing Factorial Designs

To use Analyze Factorial Design to fit a model, you must

■ create and store the design using Create Factorial Design, or

■ create a design from data that you already have in the worksheet with **Define Custom Factorial Design**

You can fit models with up to 127 terms.

When you have center points in your data set, MINITAB automatically does a test for curvature. When you have pseudo-center points, MINITAB calculates pure error but does not do a test for curvature. For a description of pseudo-center points, see *Adding center points* on page 19-11.

You can also generate effects plots—normal and Pareto—to help you determine which factors are important (page 19-49) and diagnostic plots to help assess model adequacy.

Data

Enter up to 25 numeric response data columns that are equal in length to the design variables in the worksheet. Each row will contain data corresponding to one run of your experiment. You may enter the response data in any column(s) not occupied by the design data. The number of columns reserved for the design data is dependent on the number of factors in your design.

If there is more than one response variable, MINITAB fits separate models for each response.

MINITAB omits missing data from all calculations.

Note | When all the response variables do not have the same missing value pattern, MINITAB displays a message. Since you would get different results, you may want to repeat the analysis separately for each response variable.

Analyzing designs with botched runs

A *botched run* occurs when the actual value of a factor setting differs from the planned factor setting. When a botched run occurs, you need to change the factor levels for that run in the worksheet. You can only have botched runs with two-level designs; general factorial designs cannot have botched runs. MINITAB can automatically detect botched runs and analyze the data accordingly.

Note	When you have a botched run, you need to determine the extent to which the actual factor settings deviate from the planned settings. When the executed settings fall within the normal range of their set points, you may not wish to alter the factor levels in the worksheet. The variability in the actual factor levels will simply contribute to the overall experimental error. However, if the executed levels differ notably from the planned levels, you should change them in the worksheet.

▶ To fit a factorial model

1 Choose **Stat ➤ DOE ➤ Factorial ➤ Analyze Factorial Design**.

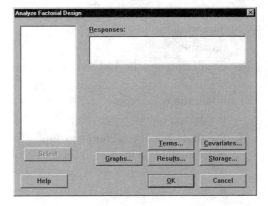

2 In **Responses**, enter up to 25 columns that contain the response data.

3 If you like, use any of the options listed below, then click **OK**.

Options

Graphs subdialog box

- for two-level factorial and Plackett-Burman designs, draw two effects plots—a normal plot and a Pareto chart—see *Effects plots* on page 19-49.

- draw five different residual plots for regular, standardized, or deleted residuals—see *Choosing a residual type* on page 2-5. Available residual plots include a

   - histogram.

   - normal probability plot.

   - plot of residuals versus the fitted values ($\hat{Y}$).

   - plot of residuals versus data order. The row number for each data point is shown on the x-axis—for example, 1 2 3 4... *n*.

   - separate plot for the residuals versus each specified column.

   For a discussion, see *Residual plots* on page 2-6.

Terms subdialog box

- fit a model by specifying the maximum order of the terms, or choose which terms to include from a list of all estimable terms—see *Specifying the model* on page 19-47.

- include blocks in the model.

- for two-level factorial and Plackett-Burman designs, include center points in the model.

Results subdialog box

- for two-level factorial and Plackett-Burman designs, display the following in the Session window:
  - no results.
  - coefficients and the ANOVA table.
  - the default results, which includes the coefficients, ANOVA table, and unusual observations.
  - the default output plus a table of fits and residuals.
  - the alias table. If you choose to display the alias table, you can specify the highest order interaction to print in the alias table. The default alias table for designs with
    - up to 6 factors, shows all terms.
    - 7 to 10 factors, shows up to two-way interactions.
    - 11 or more factors, shows up to three-way interactions.

Caution   Be careful! High-order interactions with a large number of factors could take a very long time to compute.

  - display the adjusted (also called fitted or least squares) means for factors and interactions that are in the model. If the design is orthogonal and there are no covariates, each adjusted mean is just the average of all the observations in the corresponding cell.

- for general full factorial designs, display the following in the Session window:
  - no results.
  - the ANOVA table.
  - the default results, which includes the ANOVA table, covariate coefficients, and unusual observations.
  - the ANOVA table, all coefficients, and unusual observations.
  - display the adjusted (also called fitted or least squares) means for factors and interactions that are in the model. If the design is orthogonal and there are no covariates, each adjusted mean is just the average of all the observations in the corresponding cell.

Covariates subdialog box

- include up to 50 covariates in your model. Covariates are fit first, then the blocks, then all other terms.

Storage subdialog box

- store the fits and regular, standardized, and deleted residuals separately for each response—see *Choosing a residual type* on page 2-5.

- for two-level factorial and Plackett-Burman designs, store the effects for each response in a separate column. The effects for the constant, covariates, center points or blocks are not stored.

- store the coefficients, and design matrix for the model, separately for each response. The design matrix multiplied by the coefficients will yield the fitted values.

- for two-level factorial and Plackett-Burman designs, store information about the fitted model in a column by checking **Factorial**—see Help for the structure of this column.

- store the leverages, Cook's distances, and DFITS for identifying outliers—see *Identifying outliers* on page 2-9.

Specifying the model

The model you choose determines what terms are fit and whether or not you can model linear or curvilinear aspects of the responses. By default, the terms MINITAB fits depend on the number of factors and whether or not you have a full or fractional factorial design.

- For a *full factorial design*, by default MINITAB fits all terms up to the maximum order. For example, MINITAB will fit all terms up to the four-way interaction for a four-factor design. If you do not want the default model, you select terms by specifying the maximum order, or you can fit a model that is a subset of these terms. The table below shows the terms that would be fit for a four-factor design.

If you choose	Minitab fits these terms	
1	linear	A B C D
2	linear	A B C D
	two-way interactions	AB AC AD BC BD CD
3	linear	A B C D
	two-way interactions	AB AC AD BC BD CD
	three-way interactions	ABC ABD ACD BCD
4	linear	A B C D
	two-way interactions	AB AC AD BC BD CD
	three-way interactions	ABC ABD BCD
	four-way interaction	ABCD

- For a *fractional factorial design*, the default terms selected are based on the alias structure. For example, suppose a five-factor design has the following alias structure:

```
A  + BD + CE + ABCDE
B  + AD + CDE + ABCE
C  + AE + BDE + ABCD
D  + AB + BCE + ACDE
E  + AC + BCD + ABDE
BC + DE + ABE + ACD
BE + CD + ABC + ADE
```

By default, MINITAB fits the highlighted terms. If you do not want the default model, select terms by specifying the maximum order, or fit a model that is a subset of these terms.

▶ **To specify the model**

1 In the Analyze Factorial Design dialog box, click **Terms**.

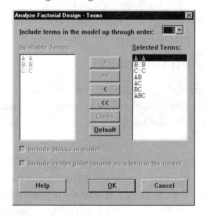

2 Do one of the following:

- from **Include terms in the model up through order**, choose a number. The available choices depend on the number of factors in your design.

3 Move the terms you want to fit from the **Available** box to the **Selected** box using the arrow buttons. Click **OK**.

- to move the terms one at a time, highlight a term then click ![<] or ![>]
- to move all of the terms, click ![<<] or ![>>]

You can also move a term by double-clicking it.

4 If you have blocks in your design and you would like to include a block term in the model, check **Include blocks in model**.

5 If you have center points in your design and you would like to include a center point term in the model, check **Include center point column as a term in the model**. Click **OK**.

Effects plots

The primary goal of screening designs is to identify the "vital" few factors or key variables that influence the response. MINITAB provides two graphs that help you identify these influential factors: a normal plot and a Pareto chart. These graphs allow you to compare the relative magnitude of the effects and evaluate their statistical significance.

Normal plot of the effects

In the normal plot of the effects, points that do not fall near the line usually signal important effects. Important effects are larger and further from the fitted line than unimportant effects. Unimportant effects tend to be smaller and centered around zero.

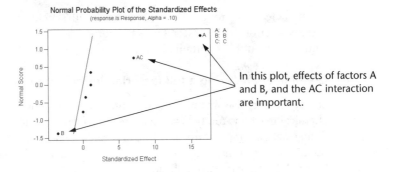

The normal probability plot labels important effects using $\alpha = 0.10$, by default. You can change the α-level in the Graphs subdialog box.

When there is no error term, MINITAB uses Lenth's method [2] to identify important effects. When there is an error term, MINITAB uses the corresponding p-values shown in the Session window to identify important effects.

Pareto chart of the effects

You can also draw a Pareto chart of the effects. MINITAB displays the

- absolute value of the unstandardized effects when there is not an error term

- absolute value of the standardized effects when there is an error term

The Pareto chart allows you to look at both the magnitude and the importance of an effect. This chart displays the absolute value of the effects, and draws a reference line on the chart. Any effect that extends past this reference line is potentially important.

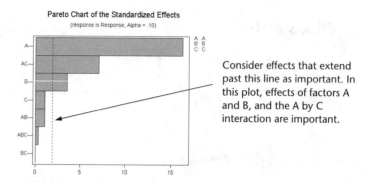

Consider effects that extend past this line as important. In this plot, effects of factors A and B, and the A by C interaction are important.

The reference line corresponds to $\alpha = 0.10$, by default. You can change the α-level in the Graphs subdialog box.

When there is no error term, MINITAB uses Lenth's method [2] to draw the line. When there is an error term, MINITAB uses the corresponding t-value shown in the Session window to identify important effects.

▷ Example of analyzing a full factorial design with replicates and blocks

You are an engineer investigating how processing conditions affect the yield of a chemical reaction. You believe that three processing conditions (factors)—reaction time, reaction temperature, and type of catalyst—affect the yield. You have enough resources for 16 runs, but you can only perform 8 in a day. Therefore, you create a full factorial design, with two replicates, and two blocks.

1 Open the worksheet YIELD.MTW. (The design and response data have been saved for you.)

2 Choose **Stat ➤ DOE ➤ Factorial ➤ Analyze Factorial Design**.

3 In **Responses**, enter *Yield*.

4 Click **Graphs**. Under **Effects Plots**, check **Normal** and **Pareto**. In **Alpha**, enter *0.05*. Click **OK** in each dialog box.

*Session
window
output*

Fractional Factorial Fit: Yield versus Time, Temp, Catalyst

Estimated Effects and Coefficients for Yield (coded units)

Term	Effect	Coef	SE Coef	T	P
Constant		45.5592	0.09546	477.25	0.000
Block		-0.0484	0.09546	-0.51	0.628
Time	2.9594	1.4797	0.09546	15.50	0.000
Temp	2.7632	1.3816	0.09546	14.47	0.000
Catalyst	0.1618	0.0809	0.09546	0.85	0.425
Time*Temp	0.8624	0.4312	0.09546	4.52	0.003
Time*Catalyst	0.0744	0.0372	0.09546	0.39	0.708
Temp*Catalyst	-0.0867	-0.0434	0.09546	-0.45	0.663
Time*Temp*Catalyst	0.0230	0.0115	0.09546	0.12	0.907

Analysis of Variance for Yield (coded units)

Source	DF	Seq SS	Adj SS	Adj MS	F	P
Blocks	1	0.0374	0.0374	0.0374	0.26	0.628
Main Effects	3	65.6780	65.6780	21.8927	150.15	0.000
2-Way Interactions	3	3.0273	3.0273	1.0091	6.92	0.017
3-Way Interactions	1	0.0021	0.0021	0.0021	0.01	0.907
Residual Error	7	1.0206	1.0206	0.1458		
Total	15	69.7656				

Estimated Coefficients for Yield using data in uncoded units

Term	Coef
Constant	39.4786
Block	-0.0483750
Time	-0.102585
Temp	0.0150170
Catalyst	0.48563
Time*Temp	0.00114990
Time*Catalyst	-0.0028917
Temp*Catalyst	-0.00280900
Time*Temp*Catalyst	0.000030700

Alias Structure

I
Blocks =
Time
Temp
Catalyst
Time*Temp
Time*Catalyst
Temp*Catalyst
Time*Temp*Catalyst

*Graph
window
output*

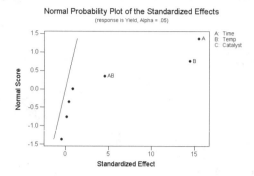

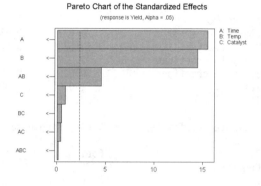

Interpreting the results

The analysis of variance table gives a summary of the main effects and interactions.
MINITAB prints both the sequential sums of squares (Seq SS) and adjusted sums of
squares (Adj SS). If the model is orthogonal and does not contain covariates, these will
be the same. Look at the p-values to determine whether or not you have any significant
effects. The effects are summarized below:

Effect	P-Value	Significant[a]
Blocks	0.628	no
Main	0.000	yes
Two-way interactions	0.017	yes
Three-way interactions	0.907	no

[a] significant at $\alpha = .05$

The nonsignificant block effect indicates that the results are not affected by the fact that you had to collect your data on two different days.

After identifying the significant effects (main and two-way interactions) in the analysis of variance table, look at the estimated effects and coefficients table. This table shows the p-values associated with each individual model term. The p-values indicate that just one two-way interaction Time * Temp (p = 0.003), and two main effects Time (p = 0.000) and Temp (p = 0.000) are significant. However, because both of these main effects are involved in an interaction, you need to understand the nature of the interaction before you can consider these main effects. See *Example of factorial plots* on page 19-58 for a discussion of this interaction.

The residual error that is shown in the ANOVA table can be made up of three parts: (1) curvature, if there are center points in the data, (2) lack of fit, if a reduced model was fit, and (3) pure error, if there are any replicates. If the residual error is just due to lack of fit, MINITAB does not print this breakdown. In all other cases, it does.

The normal and Pareto plots of the effects allow you to visually identify the important effects and compare the relative magnitude of the various effects.

You should also plot the residuals versus the run order to check for any time trends or other nonrandom patterns. Residual plots are found in the Graphs subdialog box. For a discussion, see *Residual plots* on page 2-6.

Displaying Factorial Plots

You can produce two types of plots to help you visualize the effects:

- factorial plots—main effects, interactions, and cube plots. These plots can be used to show how a response variable relates to one or more factors.

- response surface plots—contour and surface (wireframe) plots. These plots show how a response variable relates to two factors based on a model equation. See *Displaying Response Surface Plots* on page 19-60.

You must have a design in the worksheet created by Create Factorial Design or Define Custom Factorial Design before using Factorial Plots.

Main effects plots

A main effects plot is a plot of the means at each level of a factor. You can draw a main effects plot for either the

- raw response data—the means of the response variable for each level of a factor

- fitted values after you have analyzed the design—predicted values for each level of a factor

For a balanced design, the main effects plot using the two types of responses are identical. However, with an unbalanced design, the plots are sometimes quite different. While you can use raw data with unbalanced designs to obtain a general idea of which main effects may be important, it is generally good practice to use the predicted values to obtain more precise results.

MINITAB plots the means at each level of the factor and connects them with a line. Center points and factorial points are represented by different symbols. A reference line at the grand mean of the response data is drawn.

MINITAB draws a single main effects plot if you enter one factor, or a series of plots if you enter more than one factor. You can use these plots to compare the magnitudes of the various main effects. MINITAB also draws a separate plot for each factor-response combination.

A main effect occurs when the mean response changes across the levels of a factor. You can use main effects plots to compare the relative strength of the effects across factors. Notice on the plots below that the main effect for pressure (on the left) is much smaller than the main effect for temperature (on the right).

Main Effect for Pressure	**Main Effect for Temperature**
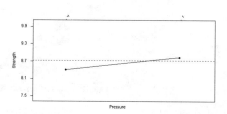	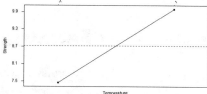
The tensile strength remains virtually the same when you move from the low level to the high level of pressure.	The tensile strength increases when you move from the low level to the high level of temperature.

Note | Although you can use these plots to compare factor effects, be sure to evaluate significance by looking at the effects in the analysis of variable table.

Interactions plots

You can plot two-factor interactions for each pair of factors in your design. An interactions plot is a plot of means for each level of a factor with the level of a second factor held constant. You can draw an interactions plot for either the

- raw response data—the means of the response variable for each level of a factor

- fitted values after you have analyzed the design—predicted values for each level of a factor

For a balanced design, the interactions plot using the two types of responses are identical. However, with an unbalanced design, the plots are sometimes quite different. While you can use raw data with unbalanced designs to obtain a general idea of which interactions may important, it is generally good practice to use the predicted values to obtain more precise results.

MINITAB draws a single interactions plot if you enter two factors, or a matrix of interactions plots if you enter more than two factors.

An interaction between factors occurs when the change in response from the low level to the high level of one factor is not the same as the change in response at the same two levels of a second factor. That is, the effect of one factor is dependent upon a second factor. You can use interactions plots to compare the relative strength of the effects across factors. Notice on the plots below that the interaction between pressure and rate (on the left) is much smaller than the interaction between temperature and rate (on the right).

Pressure by Rate Interaction

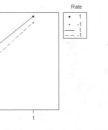

Temperature by Rate Interaction

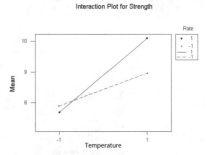

The change in tensile strength when you move from the low level to the high level of pressure is about the same at both levels of stirring rate.

The change in tensile strength when you move from the low level to the high level temperature is different depending on the level of stirring rate.

Note Although you can use these plots to compare interaction effects, be sure to evaluate significance by looking at the effects in the analysis of variable table.

Cube plots

Cube plots can be used to show the relationship between up to eight factors—with or without a response measure. Viewing the factors without the response allows you to see what a design "looks like." If there are only two factors, MINITAB displays a square plot. You can draw a cube plot for either the

- data means—the means of the raw response variable data for each factor level

- fitted means after analyzing the design—predicted values for each factor level

The plots below illustrate a three-factor cube plot with and without a response variable.

No response	**Response**
Factorial Design	Cube Plot - Means for Strength

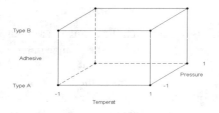 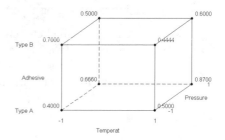

Points are drawn on the cube for each of the factor levels that are in your model.	This cube plot shows the response means at each point on the cube where observations were measured.

Data

You must create a factorial design, and enter the response data in your worksheet for both main effects and interactions plots.

For cube plots, you do not need to have a response variable, but you must create a factorial design first. If you enter a response column, MINITAB displays the means for the raw response data or fitted values at each point in the cube where observations were measured. If you do not enter a response column, MINITAB draws points on the cube for the effects that are in your model.

If you are plotting the means of the raw response data, you can generate the plots before you fit a model to the data. If you are using the fitted values (least-squares means), you need to use Analyze Factorial Design before you can display a factorial plot.

▶ **To display factorial plots**

1 Choose Stat ➤ DOE ➤ Factorial ➤ Factorial Plots.

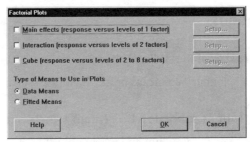

2 Do one or more of the following:

- To generate a main effects plot, check **Main effects (response versus levels of 1 factor)**, then click **Setup**

- To generate a interactions plot, check **Interaction (response versus levels of 2 factors)**, then click **Setup**

- To generate a cube plot, check **Cube (response versus levels of 2 to 8 factors, then click Setup)**

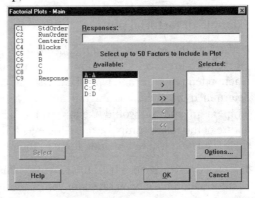

The setup subdialog box shown above is for a main effects plot. The setup dialog box for the other factorial plots will differ slightly.

3 In **Responses**, enter the numeric columns that contain the response (measurement) data. MINITAB draws a separate plot for each column. (You can create a cube plot without entering any response columns.)

4 Move the factors you want to plot from the **Available** box to the **Selected** box using the arrow buttons. Click **OK**.

You can plot up to 50 factors with main effects, up to 15 factors with interactions plots, and up to 8 factors with cube plots.

- to move the factors one at a time, highlight a factor then click < or >
- to move all of the factors, click << or >>

You can also move a factor by double-clicking it.

5 If you like, use any of the options listed below, then click **OK**.

Options

Factorial Plots dialog box

- plot the data means or the fitted (least-squares) means as the response

Options subdialog box (main effects and interactions plots only)

- set the minimum and maximum values on the y-axis. Each plot will then be on the same scale, which can be useful when you are comparing several plots of related data.
- replace the default title with your own title.
- for interactions plots, display the full interaction matrix when you have more than two factors—by default, MINITAB only displays the upper right portion of the matrix. In the full matrix, the transpose of each plot in the upper right displays in the lower left portion of the matrix.

▷ Example of factorial plots

In the *Example of analyzing a full factorial design with replicates and blocks* on page 19-50, you were investigating how processing conditions (factors)—reaction time, reaction temperature, and type of catalyst—affect the yield of a chemical reaction. You determined that there was a significant interaction between reaction time and reaction temperature and you would like to view the factorial plots to help you understand the nature of the relationship. Because the effects due to block and catalyst are not significant, you will not include them in the plots.

1 Open the worksheet YIELDPLT.MTW. (The design, response data, and model information have been saved for you.)

2 Choose **Stat ➤ DOE ➤ Factorial ➤ Factorial Plots**.

3 Check **Main effects (response versus levels of 1 factor)** and click **Setup**.

4 In **Responses**, enter *Yield*.

5 Click ▶ to move **Time** to the **Selected** box.

6 Click ▶ to move **Temp** to the **Selected** box. Click **OK**.

7 Repeat steps 3-6 to set up the interaction plot. Click **OK**.

*Graph
window
output*

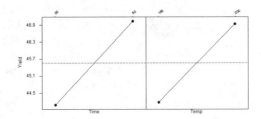

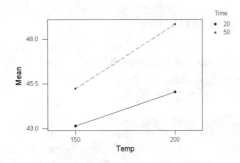

Interpreting the results

The Main Effects Plot indicates that both reaction time and reaction temperature have similar effects on yield. For both factors, yield increases as you move from the low level to the high level of the factor.

However, the interaction plot shows that the increase in yield is greater when reaction time is high (50) than when reaction time is low (20). Therefore, you should be sure to understand this interaction before making any judgments about the main effects.

Although you can use factorial plots to compare the magnitudes of effects, be sure to evaluate significance by looking at the effects in an analysis of variance table (page 19-51) or the normal or Pareto effects plots (page 19-59).

Displaying Response Surface Plots

You can produce two types of plots to help you visualize the response surface—contour plots and surface plots (also called wireframe). These plots show how a response variable relates to two factors based on a model equation.

More | You can also produce three factorial plots—main effects, interactions, and cube plots. These plots can be used to show how a response variable relates to one or more factors. See *Displaying Factorial Plots* on page 19-53.

Generating contour and surface (wireframe) plots

In a contour plot, the response surface is viewed as a two-dimensional plane where all points that have the same response are connected to produce contour lines of constant responses. Contour plots are useful for establishing desirable response values and operating conditions.

A surface plot displays a three-dimensional view of the surface. Although useful for establishing desirable response values and operating conditions, surface plots may provide a clearer picture of the response surface. The illustrations below compare these two types of response surface plots.

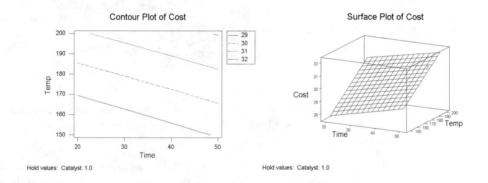

Note | When the model has more than two factors, the factor(s) that are not in the plot are held constant. Any covariates in the model are also held constant. You can specify the constant values at which to hold the remaining factors and covariates. See *Settings for covariates and extra factors* on page 19-62.

Data

Contour plots and surface plots are model dependent. Thus, you *must* fit a model using Analyze Factorial Design before you can generate response surface plots. MINITAB looks in the worksheet for the necessary model information to generate these plots.

▶ **To plot the response surface**

1 Choose **Stat ➤ DOE ➤ Factorial ➤ Contour/Surface (Wireframe) Plots**.

2 Do one or both of the following, then click **OK**:

   ■ to generate a contour plot, check **Contour plot** and click **Setup**. If you have
      analyzed more than one response, from **Response**, choose the desired response.

   ■ to generate a surface (wireframe) plot, check **Surface (wireframe) plot** and click
      Setup. If you have analyzed more than one response, from **Response**, choose the
      desired response.

3 If you like, use any of the options listed below, then click **OK** in each dialog box.

Options

Setup subdialog box

■ display a single graph for a selected factor pair

■ display separate graphs for every combination of numeric factors in the model

■ display the data in coded or uncoded units

Contours subdialog box

■ for contour plots, specify the number or location of the contour levels, and the
   contour line color and style—see *Controlling the number, type, and color of the
   contour lines* on page 19-63

Wireframe subdialog box

■ for surface (wireframe) plots, specify the color of the wireframe (mesh) and the
   surface

Settings subdialog box

■ specify values for covariates and factors that are not included in the response surface
   plot. By default, MINITAB holds factors at their low levels and covariates at their
   middle (calculated median) levels. See *Settings for covariates and extra factors* on
   page 19-62.

Options subdialog box

- define minimum and maximum values for the x-axis and y-axis.
- replace the default title with your own title.

Settings for covariates and extra factors

You can set the holding level for factors that are not in the plot at their highest, lowest (default), or middle (calculated median) settings, or you can set specific levels to hold each factor.

If you have covariates in your model, you can also set their holding levels. By default, MINITAB holds covariates at their middle (calculated median) levels.

▶ **To set the holding level for factors not in the plot**

1 In the Contour/Surface (Wireframe) Plots dialog box, click **Setup**.

2 Click **Settings**.

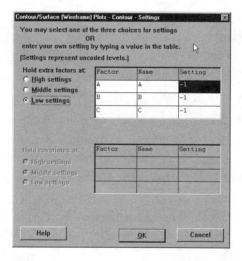

3 Do one of the following:

- To use the preset values, choose **High settings**, **Middle settings**, or **Low settings** under **Hold extra factors at** and/or **Hold covariates at**. When you use a preset value, *all* factors or covariates not in the plot will be held at their specified settings.

- To specify the value at which to hold a factor or covariate, enter a number in **Setting** for each one you want control. This option allows you to set a different holding value for each factor or covariate.

4 Click **OK**.

Controlling the number, type, and color of the contour lines

MINITAB displays from 4 to 7 contour levels—depending on the data—by default. However, you can specify from 2 to 15 contour lines.

You can also change the line type and color of the lines.

▶ To control plotting of contour lines

1 In the Contour/Surface (Wireframe) Plots dialog box, check **Contour plot** and click **Setup**.

2 Click **Contours**.

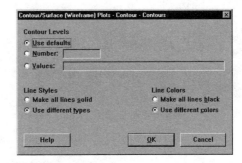

3 To change the number of contour lines, do one of the following:

- Choose **Number** and enter a number from 2 to 15.

- Choose **Values** and enter from 2 to 15 contour level values in the units of your data. You must enter the values in increasing order.

4 To define the line style, choose **Make all lines solid** or **Use different types** under **Line Styles**.

5 To define the line color, choose **Make all lines black** or **Use different colors** under **Line Colors**. Click **OK** in each dialog box.

▷ Example of a contour plot and a surface plot

In the *Example of analyzing a full factorial design with replicates and blocks* on page 19-50, you were investigating how processing conditions (factors)—reaction time, reaction temperature, and type of catalyst—affect the yield of a chemical reaction. You determined that there was a significant interaction between reaction time and reaction temperature and you would like to view the response surface plots to help you understand the nature of the relationship. Because the effects due to block and catalyst are not significant, you did not include them in the plots.

To view the main effects and interactions plots, see page 19-59.

1 Open the worksheet YIELDPLT.MTW. (The design, response data, and model information have been saved for you.)

2 Choose **Stat ➤ DOE ➤ Factorial ➤ Contour/Surface (Wireframe) Plots**.

3 Choose **Contour plot** and click **Setup**. Click **OK**.

4 Choose **Surface (wireframe) plot** and click **Setup**. Click **OK** in each dialog box.

*Graph
window
output*

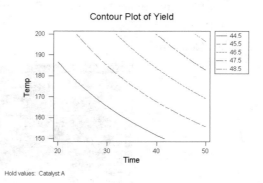

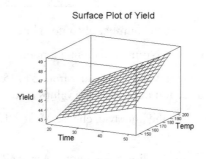

Interpreting the results

Both the contour plot and the surface plot show that Yield increases as both reaction time and reaction temperature increase. The surface plot also illustrates that the increase in yield from the low to the high level of time is greater at the high level of temperature.

References

[1] G.E.P. Box, W.G. Hunter, and J.S. Hunter (1978). *Statistics for Experimenters. An Introduction to Design, Data Analysis, and Model Building.* New York: John Wiley & Sons.

[2] R.V. Lenth (1989). "Quick and Easy Analysis of Unreplicated Factorials," *Technometrics,* 31, pp.469-473.

[3] D.C. Montgomery (1991). *Design and Analysis of Experiments,* Third Edition, John Wiley & Sons.

[4] R.L. Plackett and J.P. Burman (1946). "The Design of Optimum Multifactorial Experiments," *Biometrika,* 34, pp.255–272.

Acknowledgment

The two-level factorial and Plackett-Burman design and analysis procedures were developed under the guidance of James L. Rosenberger, Statistics Department, The Pennsylvania State University.

20

Response Surface Designs

Response Surface Designs Overview

Response surface methods are used to examine the relationship between one or more response variables and a set of quantitative experimental variables or factors. These methods are often employed after you have identified a "vital few" controllable factors and you want to find the factor settings that optimize the response. Designs of this type are usually chosen when you suspect curvature in the response surface.

Response surface methods may be employed to

- find factor settings (operating conditions) that produce the "best" response
- find factor settings that satisfy operating or process specifications
- identify new operating conditions that produce demonstrated improvement in product quality over the quality achieved by current conditions
- model a relationship between the quantitative factors and the response

Many response surface applications are sequential in nature in that they require more than one stage of experimentation and analysis. The steps shown below are typical of a response surface experiment. Depending on your experiment, you may carry out some of the steps in a different order, perform a given step more than once, or eliminate a step.

1 Choose a response surface design for the experiment. Before you begin using MINITAB, you must determine what the influencing factors are, that is, what the process conditions are that influence the values of the response variable. See *Choosing a Design* on page 20-3.

2 Use **Create Response Surface Design** to generate a central composite or Box-Behnken design—see *Creating Response Surface Designs* on page 20-4.

  Use **Define Custom Response Surface Design** to create a design from data you already have in the worksheet. Custom designs allows you to specify which columns are your factors and other design characteristics. You can then easily fit a model to the design and generate plots. See *Defining Custom Designs* on page 20-19.

3 Use **Modify Design** to rename the factors, change the factor levels, replicate the design, and randomize the design. See *Modifying Designs* on page 20-20.

4 Use **Display Design** to change the order of the runs and the units in which MINITAB expresses the factors in the worksheet. See *Displaying Designs* on page 20-24.

5 Perform the experiment and collect the response data. Then, enter the data in your MINITAB worksheet. See *Collecting and Entering Data* on page 20-25.

6 Use **Analyze Response Surface Design** to fit a model to the experimental data. See *Analyzing Response Surface Designs* on page 20-26.

7 Use **Contour/Surface (Wireframe) Plots** to visualize response surface patterns. You can display contour and surface (wireframe) plots—see page 20-34.

8 If you are trying to optimize responses, use **Response Optimizer** (page 23-2) or **Overlaid Contour Plot** (page 23-19) to obtain a numerical and graphical analysis.

Choosing a Design

Before you use MINITAB, you need to determine what design is most appropriate for your experiment. Choosing your design correctly will ensure that the response surface is fit in the most efficient manner. MINITAB provides central composite and Box-Behnken designs. When choosing a design you need to

- identify the number of factors that are of interest.

- determine the number of runs you can perform.

- ensure adequate coverage of the region of interest on the response surface. You should choose a design that will adequately predict values in the region of interest.

- determine the impact that other considerations (such as cost, time, or the availability of facilities) have on your choice of a design.

Depending on your problem, there are other considerations that make a design desirable. You need to choose a design that shows consistent performance in the criteria that you consider important, such as the ability to

- increase the order of the design sequentially.

- perform the experiment in orthogonal blocks. Orthogonally blocked designs allow for model terms and block effects to be estimated independently and minimize the variation in the estimated coefficients.

- rotate the design. Rotatable designs provide the desirable property of constant prediction variance at all points that are equidistant from the design center, thus improving the quality of the prediction.

- detect model lack of fit.

More | Our intent is to provide only a brief introduction to response surface methods. There are many resources that provide a thorough treatment of these designs. For a list of resources, see *References* on page 20-38.

Creating Response Surface Designs

MINITAB provides two response surface designs: central composite designs (page 20-4) and Box-Behnken designs (page 20-5).

Central composite designs

You can create blocked or unblocked central composite designs. Central composite designs consist of

- 2^k factorial or "cube" points, where K is the number of factors
- axial points (also called star points)
- center points

A central composite design with two factors is shown below. Points on the diagrams represent the experimental runs that are performed:

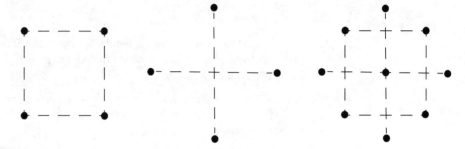

The points in the "cube" portion of the design are coded to be –1 and +1.

The points in the axial or star portion of the design are at
$(+\alpha, 0)\ (-\alpha, 0)$
$(0, +\alpha)\ (0, -\alpha)$

Here, the "cube" and axial portions along with the center point is shown. The design center is at (0,0).

Central composite designs are often recommended when the design plan calls for sequential experimentation because these designs can incorporate information from a properly planned factorial experiment. The factorial or "cube" portion and center points may serve as a preliminary stage where you can fit a first-order (linear) model, but still provide evidence regarding the importance of a second-order contribution or curvature.

You can then build the "cube" portion of the design up into a central composite design to fit a second-degree model by adding axial and center points. Central composite designs allow for efficient estimation of the quadratic terms in the second-order model, and it is also easy to obtain the desirable design properties of orthogonal blocking and rotatability.

More Orthogonally blocked designs allow for model terms and block effects to be estimated independently and minimize the variation in the regression coefficients. Rotatable designs provide the desirable property of constant prediction variance at all points that are equidistant from the design center, thus improving the quality of the prediction.

Box-Behnken designs

You can create blocked or unblocked Box-Behnken designs. The illustration below shows a three-factor Box-Behnken design. Points on the diagram represent the experimental runs that are performed:

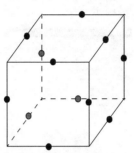

You may want to use Box-Behnken designs when performing non-sequential experiments. That is, you are only planning to perform the experiment once. These designs allow efficient estimation of the first- and second-order coefficients. Because Box-Behnken designs have fewer design points, they are less expensive to run than central composite designs with the same number of factors.

Box-Behnken designs can also prove useful if you know the safe operating zone for your process. Central composite designs usually have axial points outside the "cube" (unless you specify an α that is less than or equal to one). These points may not be in the region of interest, or may be impossible to run because they are beyond safe operating limits. Box-Behnken designs do not have axial points, thus, you can be sure that all design points fall within your safe operating zone. Box-Behnken designs also ensure that all factors are never set at their high levels simultaneously.

▶ **To create a response surface design**

  1 Choose Stat ➤ DOE ➤ Response Surface ➤ Create Response Surface Design

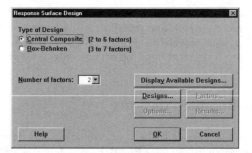

  2 If you want to see a summary of the response surface designs, click **Display Available Designs**. Use this table to compare design features. Click **OK**.

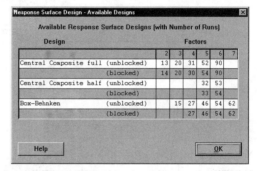

  3 Under **Type of Design**, choose **Central composite** or **Box-Behnken**.

  4 From **Number of factors**, choose a number:

   ■ for a central composite design, choose a number from 2 to 6

   ■ for a Box-Behnken design, choose a number from 3 to 7

  5 Click **Designs**.

The subdialog box that displays depends whether you choose **Central composite** or **Box-Behnken** in step 3.

Central Composite Design   **Box-Behnken Design**

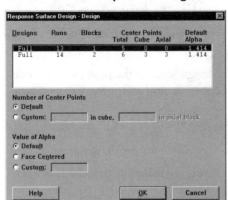

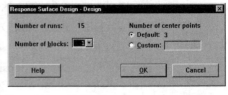

6 Do one of the following:

■ for a central composite design, choose the design you want to create from the list shown at the top of the subdialog box

■ for a Box-Behnken design, you do not have to choose a design because the number of factors determines the number of runs

7 If you like, use any of the options listed under *Design subdialog box* below.

8 Click **OK** even if you do not change any of the options. This selects the design and brings you back to the main dialog box.

9 If you like, click **Options**, **Factors**, or **Results** to use any of the options listed below, then click **OK** to create your design.

Note | *Central composite designs* on page 20-18 shows the central composite designs you can generate with **Create Response Surface Design**. The default values of α provide orthogonal blocking and, whenever possible, rotatability. The "cube" portions of central composite designs are identical to those generated by **Create Factorial Design** with the same number of center points and blocks. Thus, a design generated by **Create Factorial Design** with the same number of runs, center points, and blocks can be built up into an orthogonally-blocked central composite design.

Any factorial design with the right number of runs and blocks can be built up into a blocked central composite design. However, to make the blocks orthogonal, **Create Factorial Design** must use the number of center points shown in *Central composite designs* on page 20-18.

Options

Design subdialog box

- block the design—see *Blocking the design* on page 20-8

- change the number of center points—see *Changing the number of center points* on page 20-9

- for a central composite design, change the position of the axial settings (α)—see *Changing the value of α for a central composite design* on page 20-10

Options subdialog box

- randomize the design—see *Randomizing the design* on page 20-10

- store the design—see *Storing the design* on page 20-11

Factors subdialog box

- name factors—see *Naming factors* on page 20-12

- set factor levels—see *Setting factor levels* on page 20-12

- for a central composite design, define the low and high values of the experiment in terms of the axial points rather than the "cube" points—see *Setting factor levels* on page 20-12

Results subdialog box

- display the summary and data tables or suppress all Session window results

Blocking the design

When the number of runs is too large to be completed under steady state conditions, you need to be concerned with the error that may be introduced into the experiment. Running an experiment in blocks allows you to separately and independently estimate the block effects (or different experimental conditions) from the factor effects. For example, blocks might be days, suppliers, batches of raw material, machine operators, or manufacturing shift.

Central composite designs

For a central composite design, the number of orthogonal blocks depends on the number of factors, the number of runs, and the design fraction you choose. A central composite design can always be separated into a factorial block and an axial point block. With three or more factors, the factorial block can also be divided into two or more blocks. When you are creating a design, MINITAB displays the appropriate choices.

More   The value of α, in combination with the number of center points, determines whether a design exhibits the properties of rotatability and orthogonal blocking. MINITAB provides default designs that achieve rotatability and orthogonal blocking, when both properties can be achieved simultaneously. When the design is blocked and you cannot achieve both properties simultaneously, the default designs provide for orthogonal blocking.

Box-Behnken designs

For a Box-Behnken design, the number of ways to block a design depends on the number of factors. All of the blocked designs have orthogonal blocks. A design with

- three factors cannot be blocked
- four factors can be run in three blocks
- five, six, or seven factors can be run in two blocks

When you are creating a design, MINITAB displays the appropriate choices.

Changing the number of center points

The number of center points, along with α (for a central composite design), determines whether or not a design can be orthogonally blocked. By default, MINITAB chooses the number of center points to achieve orthogonal blocking.

The inclusion of center points provides an estimate of experimental error and allows you to check the adequacy of the model (lack of fit). Checking the adequacy of the fitted model is important as an incorrect or under-specified model can result in misleading conclusions.

The default number of center points is shown in the Designs subdialog box. For a table showing the default number of center points for all designs, see *Central composite designs* on page 20-18 and *Box-Behnken designs* on page 20-18.

▶ **To change the default number of center points**

1 In the Create Response Surface Design dialog box, click **Designs**.

2 Do one of the following, then click **OK**.

- For a central composite design, under **Number of center points** choose **Custom** and enter a number in **in cube**. When you have more than one block in your design, you also need to enter a number to indicate the number of center points in **in axial block**.

- For a Box-Behnken design, under **Number of center points** choose **Custom** and enter a number in the box.

Note   When a Box-Behnken design is blocked, the center points are divided equally (as much as possible) among the blocks.

Changing the value of α for a central composite design

The position of the axial points in a central composite design is denoted by α. The value of α, along with the number of center points, determines whether a design can be orthogonally blocked and is rotatable. Orthogonally blocked designs allow for model terms and block effects to be estimated independently and minimize the variation in the regression coefficients. Rotatable designs provide the desirable property of constant prediction variance at all points that are equidistant from the design center, thus improving the quality of the prediction.

MINITAB's default designs achieve rotatability and orthogonal blocking when both properties can be achieved simultaneously. When the design is blocked and you cannot achieve both properties simultaneously, the default designs use α such that the design is orthogonally blocked. When there are no blocks, the default designs use α such that the design is rotatable.

The default value for α for each central composite design is shown on page 20-18.

▶ **To change the default value of α**

1 In the Create Response Surface Design dialog box, click **Designs**.

2 Do one of the following, then click **OK**.

   ■ To set α equal to 1, choose **Face Centered**. When $\alpha = 1$, the axial points are placed on the "cube" portion of the design. This is an appropriate choice when the "cube" points of the design are at the operational limits.

   ■ Choose **Custom** and enter a positive number in the box. A value less than one places the axial points inside the "cube" portion of the design; a value greater than one places the axial points outside the "cube."

Note | A value of $\alpha = (F)^{1/4}$, where F is the number of factorial points in the design, guarantees rotatability.

Randomizing the design

By default, MINITAB randomizes the run order of the design. The ordered sequence of the factor combinations (experimental conditions) is called the *run order*. It is usually a good idea to randomize the run order to lessen the effects of factors that are not included in the study, particularly effects that are time-dependent.

However, there may be situations when randomization leads to an undesirable run order. For instance, in industrial applications, it may be difficult or expensive to change factor levels. Or, after factor levels have been changed, it may take a long time for the system to return to steady state. Under these conditions, you may not want to randomize the design in order to minimize the level changes.

Every time you create a design, MINITAB reserves and names C1 (StdOrder) and C2 (RunOrder) to store the standard order and run order, respectively.

- StdOrder shows what the order of the runs in the experiment would be if the experiment was done in standard order—also called Yates' order.

- RunOrder shows what the order of the runs in the experiment would be if the experiment was run in random order.

If you do not randomize, the run order and standard order are the same.

If you want to re-create a design with the same ordering of the runs (that is, the same design order), you can choose a base for the random data generator. Then, when you want to re-create the design, you just use the same base.

More | You can use **Stat ➤ DOE ➤ Display Design** (page 20-24) to switch back and forth between a random and standard order display in the worksheet.

Storing the design

If you want to analyze a design, you *must* store it in the worksheet. By default, MINITAB stores the design. If you want to see the properties of various designs before selecting the design you want to store, uncheck **Store design in worksheet** in the Options subdialog box.

Every time you create a design, MINITAB reserves and names the following columns:

- C1 (StdOrder) stores the standard order.
- C2 (RunOrder) stores run order.
- C3 (Blocks) stores the blocking variable. When the design is not blocked, MINITAB sets all column values to one.
- C4 – Cn stores the factors. MINITAB stores each factor in your design in a separate column.

If you named the factors, these names display in the worksheet. If you did not provide names, MINITAB names the factors alphabetically. After you create the design, you can change the factor names directly in the Data window or with **Stat ➤ DOE ➤ Modify Design** (page 20-20).

If you did not assign factor levels in the Factors subdialog box, MINITAB stores factor levels in coded form (all factor levels are −1 or +1). If you assigned factor levels, the uncoded levels display in the worksheet. To switch back and forth between a coded and an uncoded display, use **Stat ➤ DOE ➤ Display Design** (page 20-24).

Caution | When you create a design using Create Response Surface Design, MINITAB stores the appropriate design information in the worksheet. MINITAB needs this stored information to analyze and plot data. If you want to use Analyze Response Surface Design, you must follow certain rules when modifying the worksheet data. See *Modifying and Using Worksheet Data* on page 18-4.

If you make changes that corrupt your design, you may still be able to analyze it with Analyze Response Surface Design after you use Define Custom Response Surface Design (page 20-19).

Naming factors

By default, MINITAB names the factors alphabetically.

▶ To name factors

1 In the Create Response Surface Design dialog box, click **Factors**.

2 Under **Name**, click in the first row and type the name of the first factor. Then, use the ⬇ key to move down the column and enter the remaining factor names. Click **OK**.

More | After you have created the design, you can change the factor names by typing new names in the Data window or with Modify Design (page 20-20).

Setting factor levels

In a response surface design, you designate a low level and a high level for each factor. These factor levels define the proportions of the "cube" around which the design is built. The "cube" is often centered around the current operating conditions for the process. For a central composite design, you may have design points inside the "cube," on the "cube," or outside the "cube." For a Box-Behnken design, the factor levels are the lowest and highest points in the design. See the illustrations on pages 20-4 and 20-6.

By default, MINITAB sets the low level of all factors to −1 and high level to +1.

▶ **To assign factor levels**

1 In the Create Response Surface Design dialog box, click **Factors**.

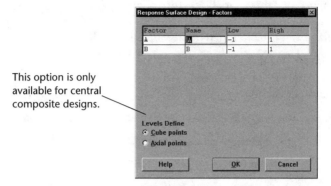

This option is only available for central composite designs.

2 Under **Low**, click in the row for the factor you would like to assign values and enter any numeric value. Use the → key to move to **High** and enter a numeric value that is greater than the value you entered in **Low**.

3 Repeat step 2 to assign levels for other factors.

4 For a central composite design, under **Levels Define**, choose **Cube points** or **Axial points** to specify which values you entered in **Low** and **High**. Click **OK**.

Note In a central composite design, the values you enter for the factor levels are usually not the minimum and maximum values in the design. They are the low and high settings for the "cube" portion of the design. The axial points are usually outside the "cube" (unless you specify an α that is less than or equal to 1). If you are not careful, this could lead to axial points that are not in the region of interest or may be impossible to run.

Choosing **Axial points** in the Factors subdialog box guarantees all of the design points will fall between the defined minimum and maximum value for the factor(s). MINITAB will then determine the appropriate low and high settings for the "cube" as follows:

$$\text{Low Level Setting} = \frac{(\alpha - 1)\ \text{max} + (\alpha + 1)\ \text{min}}{2\alpha}$$

$$\text{High Level Setting} = \frac{(\alpha - 1)\ \text{min} + (\alpha + 1)\ \text{max}}{2\alpha}$$

More To change the factor levels after you have created the design, use **Stat ▶ DOE ▶ Modify Design**.

► Example of a central composite design

Suppose you want to conduct an experiment to maximize crystal growth. You have determined that three variables—time the crystals are exposed to a catalyst, temperature in the exposure chamber, and percentage of the catalyst in the air inside the chamber—explain much of the variability in the rate of crystal growth.

You generate the default central composite design for three factors and two blocks (to represent the two days you conduct the experiment). You assign the factor levels and randomize the design.

1 Choose **Stat ► DOE ► Response Surface ► Create Response Surface Design**.

2 Under **Type of Design**, choose **Central Composite**.

3 From **Number of factors**, choose 3.

4 Click **Designs**. To create the design with 2 blocks, highlight the second row in the **Design** box at the top. Click **OK**.

5 Click **Factors**. Complete the **Name**, **Low**, and **High** columns of the table as shown below:

Factor	Name	Low	High
A	Time	6	9
B	Temperature	40	60
C	Catalyst	3.5	7.5

6 Click **OK**.

7 Click **Results**. Choose **Summary table and data table**. Click **OK** in each dialog box. .

*Session
window
output*

Central Composite Design

Central Composite Design

Factors:	3	Blocks:	2	Center points in cube:	4
Runs:	20	Alpha:	1.633	Center points in star:	2

Data Matrix (randomized)

Run	Block	A	B	C
1	1	1.000	-1.000	-1.000
2	1	1.000	1.000	-1.000
3	1	-1.000	1.000	1.000
4	1	0.000	0.000	0.000
5	1	0.000	0.000	0.000
6	1	-1.000	1.000	-1.000
7	1	-1.000	-1.000	-1.000
8	1	-1.000	-1.000	1.000
9	1	0.000	0.000	0.000
10	1	0.000	0.000	0.000
11	1	1.000	1.000	1.000
12	1	1.000	-1.000	1.000
13	2	0.000	-1.633	0.000
14	2	0.000	0.000	0.000
15	2	-1.633	0.000	0.000
16	2	0.000	0.000	1.633
17	2	0.000	0.000	0.000
18	2	0.000	1.633	0.000
19	2	0.000	0.000	-1.633
20	2	1.633	0.000	0.000

Interpreting the results

You have created a central composite design with three factors which will be run in two blocks. This design is both rotatable and orthogonally blocked—see *Central composite designs* on page 20-18.

Because you chose to display the summary and data tables, MINITAB shows the experimental conditions or settings for each of the factors for the design points. When you perform the experiment, use the order that is shown to determine the conditions for each run. For example, in the first run of your experiment, you would set the time (A) at 9 minutes (1 = high), the temperature (B) at $40°$ (−1 = low), and use 3.5 grams of the catalyst (C) (−1 = low).

Note | MINITAB randomizes the design by default, so if you try to replicate this example, your runs may not match the order shown.

⯈ Example of a Box-Behnken design

Suppose you have a process for pressure treating utility poles with creosote. In the treating step of the process, you place air-dried poles inside a treatment chamber. The pressure in the chamber is increased and the chamber is flooded with hot creosote. The poles are left in the chamber until they have absorbed 12 pounds of creosote per cubic foot. You would like to experiment with different settings for the air pressure, temperature of the creosote, and time in the chamber. Your goal is to get the creosote absorption as close to 12 pounds per cubic foot as possible, with minimal variation. Previous investigation suggests that the response surface for absorption exhibits curvature.

The chamber will withstand internal pressures up to 220 psi, although the strain on equipment is pronounced at over 200 psi. The current operating value is at 175 psi, so you feel comfortable with a range of values between 150 and 200. Current operating values for temperature and time are 210° F and 5 hours, respectively. You feel that temperature cannot vary by more than 10° from the current value. Time can be varied from 4 to 6 hours.

A Box-Behnken design is a practical choice when you cannot run all of the factors at their high (or low) levels at the same time. Here, the high level for pressure is already at the limit of what the chamber can handle. If temperature were also at its high level, this increases the effective pressure, and running at these settings for a long period of time is not recommended. The Box-Behnken design will assure that no runs require all factors to be at their high settings simultaneously.

1 Choose **Stat ➤ DOE ➤ Response Surface ➤ Create Response Surface Design**.

2 Under **Type of Design**, choose **Box-Behnken**.

3 From **Number of factors**, choose 3.

4 Click **Designs**. Click **OK**.

5 Click **Factors**. Complete the **Name**, **Low**, and **High** columns of the table as shown below:

Factor	Name	Low	High
A	Pressure	150	200
B	Temperature	200	220
C	Time	4	6

6 Click **OK**.

7 Click **Results**. Choose **Summary table and data table**. Click **OK** in each dialog box.

*Session
window
output*

Box-Behnken Design

Box-Behnken Design

```
Factors:    3      Blocks:          none
Runs:      15      Center points:    3


Data Matrix (randomized)

    Run   A   B   C
      1   0   +   -
      2   +   -   0
      3   -   0   -
      4   0   -   -
      5   +   0   -
      6   +   +   0
      7   0   0   0
      8   0   +   +
      9   -   0   +
     10   0   0   0
     11   0   0   0
     12   -   +   0
     13   0   -   +
     14   +   0   +
     15   -   -   0
```

Interpreting the results

Because you chose to display the summary and data tables, MINITAB shows the experimental conditions or settings for each of the factors for the design points. When you perform the experiment, use the order that is shown to determine the conditions for each run. For example, in the first run of your experiment, you would set the pressure at 175 psi (0 = center), the temperature at 220°F (+ = high), and treat the utility poles for 4 hours (− = low).

Note | MINITAB randomizes the design by default, so if you try to replicate this example, your runs may not match the order shown.

Summary of Available Designs

Central composite designs

factors	total runs	total blocks	cube blocks	cube runs	total center points	cube center points	axial center points	default alpha	orthogonal blocks	rotatable
2	13	—	—	4	5	—	—	1.414	—	y
	14	2	1	4	6	3	3	1.414	y	y
3	20	—	—	8	6	—	—	1.682	—	y
	20	2	1	8	6	4	2	1.633	y	n
	20	3	2	8	6	4	2	1.633	y	n
4	31	—	—	16	7	—	—	2.000	—	y
	30	2	1	16	6	4	2	2.000	y	y
	30	3	2	16	6	4	2	2.000	y	y
5 half	32	—	—	16	6	—	—	2.000	—	y
	33	2	1	16	7	6	1	2.000	y	y
5	52	—	—	32	10	—	—	2.378	—	y
	54	2	1	32	12	8	4	2.366	y	n
	54	3	2	32	12	8	4	2.366	y	n
6 half	53	—	—	32	9	—	—	2.378	—	y
	54	2	1	32	10	8	2	2.366	y	n
	54	3	2	32	10	8	2	2.366	y	n
6	90	—	—	64	14	—	—	2.828	—	y
	90	2	1	64	14	8	6	2.828	y	y
	90	3	2	64	14	8	6	2.828	y	y
	90	5	4	64	14	8	6	2.828	y	y

Box-Behnken designs

factors	runs	blocks	center points
3	15	1	3
4	27	3	3
5	46	2	6
6	54	2	6
7	62	2	6

Defining Custom Designs

Use **Define Custom Response Surface Design** to create a design from data you already have in the worksheet. For example, you may have a design that you created using MINITAB session commands, entered directly into the Data window, imported from a data file, or created with earlier releases of MINITAB. You can also use **Define Custom Response Surface Design** to redefine a design that you created with Create Response Surface Design and then modified directly in the worksheet.

Define Custom Response Surface Design allows you to specify which columns contain your factors and other design characteristics. After you define your design, you can use Modify Design (page 20-20), Display Design (page 20-24), and Analyze Response Surface Design (page 20-26).

▶ **To define a custom response surface design**

1 Choose **Stat ➤ DOE ➤ Response Surface ➤ Define Custom Response Surface Design**.

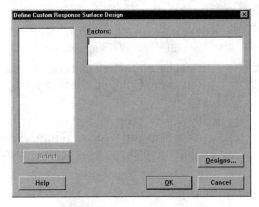

2 In **Factors**, enter the columns that contain the factor levels.

3 Do one of the following:

- If you do not have any columns containing the blocks, run order, or standard order, click **OK**.

- If you have additional columns that contain data for the blocks, run order, or standard order, click **Designs**.

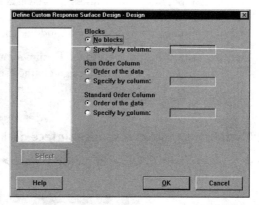

1 If your design is blocked, under **Blocks**, choose **Specify by column** and enter the column containing the blocks.

2 If you have a column that contains the run order of the experiment, under **Run Order Column**, choose **Specify by column** and enter the column containing the run order.

3 If you have a column that contains the standard order of the experiment, under **Standard Order Column**, choose **Specify by column** and enter the column containing the standard order. Click **OK** in each dialog box.

Modifying Designs

After creating a design and storing it in the worksheet, you can use Modify Design to make the following modifications:

- rename the factors and change the factor levels—see *Renaming factors and changing factor levels* below

- replicate the design—see *Replicating the design* on page 20-22

- randomize the design—see *Randomizing the design* on page 20-23

By default, MINITAB will replace the current design with the modified design.

Renaming factors and changing factor levels

If you did not name the factors, MINITAB assigns letter names alphabetically. You can use Modify Design to change the default names or names that you assigned when you created the design. You can also change factor levels from the default values of −1 and +1 or change previously assigned values.

▶ To rename factors or change factor levels

1 Choose **Stat ➤ DOE ➤ Modify Design**.

2 Choose **Modify factors** and click **Specify**.

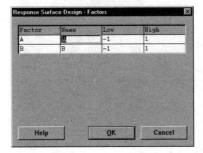

3 Enter new factor names or factor levels as shown in *Naming factors* on page 20-12 and *Setting factor levels* on page 20-12. Click **OK**.

Tip │ You can also type new factor names directly into the Data window.

Replicating the design

You can add up to ten replicates of your design. When you replicate a design, you duplicate the complete set of runs from the initial design. The runs that would be added to a two-factor central composite design are as follows:

Initial design		One replicate added (total of two replicates)		Two replicates added (total of three replicates)	
A	B	A	B	A	B
-1.414	0.000	-1.414	0.000	-1.414	0.000
1.000	-1.000	1.000	-1.000	1.000	-1.000
0.000	1.414	0.000	1.414	0.000	1.414
0.000	0.000	0.000	0.000	0.000	0.000
0.000	0.000	0.000	0.000	0.000	0.000
1.414	0.000	1.414	0.000	1.414	0.000
0.000	0.000	0.000	0.000	0.000	0.000
0.000	0.000	0.000	0.000	0.000	0.000
0.000	0.000	0.000	0.000	0.000	0.000
0.000	-1.414	0.000	-1.414	0.000	-1.414
1.000	1.000	1.000	1.000	1.000	1.000
-1.000	-1.000	-1.000	-1.000	-1.000	-1.000
-1.000	1.000	-1.000	1.000	-1.000	1.000
		-1.414	0.000	-1.414	0.000
		1.000	-1.000	1.000	-1.000
		0.000	1.414	0.000	1.414
		0.000	0.000	0.000	0.000
		0.000	0.000	0.000	0.000
		1.414	0.000	1.414	0.000
		0.000	0.000	0.000	0.000
		0.000	0.000	0.000	0.000
		0.000	0.000	0.000	0.000
		0.000	-1.414	0.000	-1.414
		1.000	1.000	1.000	1.000
		-1.000	-1.000	-1.000	-1.000
		-1.000	1.000	-1.000	1.000
				-1.414	0.000
				1.000	-1.000
				0.000	1.414
				0.000	0.000
				0.000	0.000
				1.414	0.000
				0.000	0.000
				0.000	0.000
				0.000	0.000
				0.000	-1.414
				1.000	1.000
				-1.000	-1.000
				-1.000	1.000

True replication provides an estimate of the error or noise in your process and may allow for more precise estimates of effects.

▶ **To replicate the design**

1 Choose **Stat ▶ DOE ▶ Modify Design**.

2 Choose **Replicate design** and click **Specify**.

3 From **Number of replicates to add**, choose a number up to ten. Click **OK**.

Randomizing the design

You can randomize the entire design or just randomize one of the blocks. For a general discussion of randomization, see page 20-10.

▶ **To randomize the design**

1 Choose **Stat ▶ DOE ▶ Modify Design**.

2 Choose **Randomize design** and click **Specify**.

3 Do one of the following:

  ■ Choose **Randomize entire design**.

  ■ Choose **Randomize just block**, and choose a block number from the list.

4 If you like, in **Base for random data generator**, enter a number. You can recreate a design by using the same base each time. Click **OK**.

More | You can use **Stat ▶ DOE ▶ Display Design** (page 20-24) to switch back and forth between a random and standard order display in the worksheet.

Displaying Designs

After you create the design, you can use Display Design to change the way the design points are stored in the worksheet. You can change the design points in two ways:

- display the points in either run or standard order. Standard order is the order of the runs if the experiment was done in Yates' order. Run order is the order of the runs if the experiment was done in random order.

- express the factor levels in coded or uncoded form.

▶ **To change the display order of points in the worksheet**

1 Choose **Stat ▶ DOE ▶ Display Design**.

2 Choose **Run order for the design** or **Standard order for the design**. If you do not randomize a design, the columns that contain the standard order and run order are the same.

3 Do one of the following:

- If you want to reorder all worksheet columns that are the same length as the design columns, click **OK**.

- If you have worksheet columns that you do not want to reorder:
  1 Click **Options**.
  2 In **Exclude the following columns when sorting**, enter the columns. These columns *cannot* be part of the design. Click **OK** in each dialog box.

Displaying the design in coded or uncoded units

If you assigned factor levels in the Factors subdialog box, the uncoded or actual levels initially display in the worksheet. For example, if you entered 50 for the low level of temperature and 80 for the high level of temperature in the Factors subdialog box, these uncoded levels display in the worksheet. The coded levels are −1 and +1.

If you do not assign factor levels, displaying the design in coded and uncoded units is the same.

▶ **To change the display units for the factors**

   1 Choose **Stat ➤ DOE ➤ Display Design**.

   2 Choose **Coded units** or **Uncoded units**. Click **OK**.

Collecting and Entering Data

After you create your design, you need to perform the experiment and collect the response (measurement) data. To print a data collection form, follow the instructions below. After you collect the response data, enter the data in any worksheet column not used for the design. For a discussion of the worksheet structure, see *Storing the design* on page 20-11.

Printing a data collection form

You can generate a data collection form in two ways. You can simply print the Data window contents, or you can use a macro. A macro can generate a "nicer" data collection form—see Help for more information. Although printing the Data window will not produce the prettiest form, it is the easiest method. Just follow these steps:

1 When you create your experimental design, MINITAB stores the run order, block assignment, and factor settings in the worksheet. These columns constitute the basis of your data collection form. If you did not name factors or specify factor levels when you created the design, and you want names or levels to appear on the form, use Modify Design (page 20-20).

2 In the worksheet, name the columns in which you will enter the measurement data obtained when you perform your experiment.

3 Choose **File ➤ Print Worksheet**. Make sure **Print Grid Lines** is checked, then click **OK**.

More | You can also copy the worksheet cells to the Clipboard by choosing **Edit ➤ Copy Cells**. Then paste the Clipboard contents into a word-processing application, such as Microsoft Wordpad or Microsoft Word, where you can create your own form.

Analyzing Response Surface Designs

To use Analyze Response Surface Design to fit a model, you must create and store the design using Create Response Surface Design, or create a design from data that you already have in the worksheet with **Define Custom Response Surface Design**.

You can choose to fit models with the following terms:

- all linear terms

- all linear terms and all squared terms

- all linear terms and all two-way interactions

- all linear terms, all squared terms, and all two-way interactions (the default)

- a subset of linear terms, squared terms, and two-way interactions

The model you fit will determine the nature of the effect, linear or curvilinear, that you can detect—see *Selecting model terms* on page 20-29.

Data

Enter up to 25 numeric response data columns that are equal in length to the design variables in the worksheet. Each row will contain data corresponding to one run of your experiment. You may enter the response data in any column(s) not occupied by the design data. The number of columns reserved for the design data is dependent on the number of factors in your design.

If there is more than one response variable, MINITAB fits separate models for each response.

MINITAB omits missing data from all calculations.

Note   When all the response variables do not have the same missing value pattern, MINITAB displays a message. Since you would get different results, you may want to repeat the analysis separately for each response variable.

▶ To fit a response surface model

1 Choose **Stat ➤ DOE ➤ Response Surface ➤ Analyze Response Surface Design**.

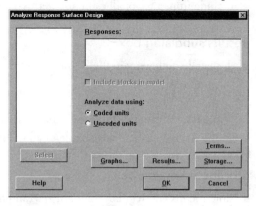

2 In **Responses**, enter up to 25 columns that contain the response data.

3 If you like, use any of the options listed below, then click **OK**.

Options

Analyze Response Surface Design dialog box

- include blocks in the model. This option is available when the blocks column contains more than one distinct value.

- fit the model with coded or uncoded factor levels. See *Choosing data units* on page 20-28.

Graphs subdialog box

- draw five different residual plots for regular, standardized, or deleted residuals—see *Choosing a residual type* on page 2-5. Available residual plots include a
  - histogram.
  - normal probability plot.
  - plot of residuals versus the fitted values ($\hat{Y}$).
  - plot of residuals versus data order. The row number for each data point is shown on the x-axis—for example, 1 2 3 4... *n*.
  - separate plot for the residuals versus each specified column.

For a discussion, see *Residual plots* on page 2-6.

Terms subdialog box

■ fit a model by specifying the maximum order of the terms, or choose which terms to include from a list of all estimable terms—see *Selecting model terms* on page 20-29.

Results subdialog box

■ display the following in the Session window:
  - no results
  - the default results, which includes a table of coefficients, s, R^2, adjusted R^2, the analysis of variance table, and the unusual values in the table of fits and residuals
  - the default results, plus a table of all the fits and residuals

Storage subdialog box

■ store the fits and regular, standardized, and deleted residuals separately for each response—see *Choosing a residual type* on page 2-5.

■ store the coefficients for the model and the design matrix, separately for each response. The design matrix multiplied by the coefficients will yield the fitted values.

■ store information about the fitted model in a column by checking **Quadratic** in the Storage subdialog box—see Help for the structure of this column.

■ store leverages, Cook's distances, and DFITS for identifying outliers—see *Identifying outliers* on page 2-9.

Choosing data units

The following results differ depending on whether you analyze the data in coded or uncoded units (the actual factor levels):

■ coefficients and their standard deviations

■ t-value for the constant term

■ p-value for the constant term

Additional results would be the same, including which terms in the model are significant.

▶ To specify the data units for analysis

1 In the Create Response Surface Design dialog box, under **Analyze data using,** choose **coded units** or **uncoded units**.

More | Analyze Response Surface Design uses the same method of coding as General Linear Model—see *Design matrix used by General Linear Model* on page 3-43.

Selecting model terms

The model you choose determines what terms are fit and whether or not you can model linear or curvilinear aspects of the response surface. If you include any second-order terms (squares or interactions), you can model curvilinearity.

You can fit a linear, linear and squares, linear and two-way interactions, or full quadratic (default) model. Or, you can fit a model that is a subset of these terms. The table below shows what terms would be fit for a model with four factors.

This model type	fits these terms
linear	A B C D
linear and squares	A B C D A*A B*B C*C D*D
linear and two-way interactions	A B C D A*B A*C A*D B*C B*D C*D
full quadratic (default)	A B C D A*A B*B C*C D*D A*B A*C A*D B*C B*D C*D

▶ To specify the model

1 In the Analyze Response Surface Design dialog box, click **Terms**.

2 Do one of the following:

■ from **Include the following terms,** choose **linear, linear + squares, linear + interactions,** or **full quadratic**

- move the terms you do not want to include in the model from **Selected Terms** to **Available Terms** using the arrow buttons
    - to move one or more factors, highlight the desired terms then click [<] or [>]
    - to move all of the terms, click [<<] or [>>]

    You can also move a term by double-clicking it.

Example of fitting a response surface model

The following examples use data from [3]. The experiment uses three factors—nitrogen, phosphoric acid, and potash—all ingredients in fertilizer. The effect of the fertilizer on snap bean yield was studied in a central composite design using the default (coded) factor levels.

The actual (uncoded) units for the −1 and +1 levels are 2.03 and 5.21 for nitrogen, 1.07 and 2.49 for phosphoric acid, 1.35 and 3.49 for potash. If we were to analyze the design in uncoded units, a few things would change: the coefficients and their standard deviations, and the t-value and p-value for the constant term. Additional results would be the same, including which terms in the model are significant.

Step 1: Generating the central composite design

1 Choose **Stat ➤ DOE ➤ Response Surface ➤ Create Response Surface Design**.

2 Under **Type of Design**, choose **Central composite**.

3 From **Number of factors**, choose 3.

4 Click **Designs**. Click **OK**.

5 Click **Factors**. In the **Name** column, enter *Nitrogen PhosAcid Potash* in rows one through three, respectively. Click **OK** in each dialog box.

Step 2: Fitting a linear model

1 Open the worksheet CCD_EX1.MTW. (The design from the previous step and the response data have been saved for you.)

2 Choose **Stat ➤ DOE ➤ Response Surface ➤ Analyze Response Surface Design**.

3 In **Variables**, enter *BeanYield*.

4 Click **Terms**.

5 From **Include the following terms**, choose **Linear**. Click **OK** in each dialog box.

Response Surface Regression

The analysis was done using coded units.

Estimated Regression Coefficients for BeanYiel

Term	Coef	StDev	T	P
Constant	10.1980	0.3473	29.364	0.000
Nitrogen	-0.5738	0.4203	-1.365	0.191
PhosAcid	0.1834	0.4203	0.436	0.668
Potash	0.4555	0.4203	1.084	0.295

s = 1.553   R-Sq = 16.8%   R-Sq(adj) = 1.2%
Analysis of Variance for BeanYiel

Source	DF	Seq SS	Adj SS	Adj MS	F	P
Regression	3	7.789	7.789	2.5962	1.08	0.387
Linear	3	7.789	7.789	2.5962	1.08	0.387
Residual Error	16	38.597	38.597	2.4123		
Lack-of-Fit	11	36.057	36.057	3.2779	6.45	0.026
Pure Error	5	2.540	2.540	0.5079		
Total	19	46.385				

Unusual Observations for BeanYiel

Observation	BeanYiel	Fit	StDev Fit	Residual	St Resid
15	8.260	11.163	0.788	-2.903	-2.17R
18	13.190	10.500	0.807	2.690	2.03R

R denotes an observation with a large standardized residual

Interpreting the results

It is important to check the adequacy of the fitted model, because an incorrect or under-specified model can result in misleading conclusions. By checking the fit of the linear (first-order) model you can tell if the model is under specified. The small p-value (p = 0.026) for the lack of fit test indicates the linear model does not adequately fit the response surface. The F-statistic for this test is (Adj MS for Lack of Fit) / (Adj MS for Pure Error).

Because the linear model does not adequately fit the response surface, you need to fit a quadratic (second-order) model.

▷ **Example of fitting a quadratic model**

In the previous example, you determined that the linear model did not adequately represent the response surface. The next step is to fit the quadratic model. The quadratic model allows detection of curvature in the response surface.

1 Open the worksheet CCD_EX1.MTW. (The design and response data have been saved for you.)

2 Choose **Stat ➤ DOE ➤ Response Surface ➤ Analyze Response Surface Design**.

3 In **Responses**, enter *BeanYield*.

4 Click **Terms**.

5 From **Include the following terms**, choose **Full quadratic**. Click **OK**.

6 Click **Graphs**.

7 Under **Residual Plots**, check **Histogram, Normal plot, Residuals versus fits**, and **Residuals versus order**. Click **OK** in each dialog box

Session window output

Response Surface Regression

The analysis was done using coded units.

Estimated Regression Coefficients for BeanYiel

Term	Coef	StDev	T	P
Constant	10.4623	0.4062	25.756	0.000
Nitrogen	-0.5738	0.2695	-2.129	0.059
Phospori	0.1834	0.2695	0.680	0.512
Potash	0.4555	0.2695	1.690	0.122
Nitrogen*Nitrogen	-0.6764	0.2624	-2.578	0.027
Phospori*Phospori	0.5628	0.2624	2.145	0.058
Potash*Potash	-0.2734	0.2624	-1.042	0.322
Nitrogen*Phospori	-0.6775	0.3521	-1.924	0.083
Nitrogen*Potash	1.1825	0.3521	3.358	0.007
Phospori*Potash	0.2325	0.3521	0.660	0.524

s = 0.9960   R-Sq = 78.6%   R-Sq(adj) = 59.4%

Analysis of Variance for BeanYiel

Source	DF	Seq SS	Adj SS	Adj MS	F	P
Regression	9	36.465	36.465	4.0517	4.08	0.019
Linear	3	7.789	7.789	2.5962	2.62	0.109
Square	3	13.386	13.386	4.4619	4.50	0.030
Interaction	3	15.291	15.291	5.0970	5.14	0.021
Residual Error	10	9.920	9.920	0.9920		
Lack-of-Fit	5	7.380	7.380	1.4760	2.91	0.133
Pure Error	5	2.540	2.540	0.5079		
Total	19	46.385				

```
Unusual Observations for BeanYiel

Observation    BeanYiel          Fit    StDev Fit    Residual    St Resid
        14      11.060       12.362        0.776      -1.302       -2.09R
        15       8.260        9.514        0.776      -1.254       -2.01R
        18      13.190       12.004        0.815       1.186        2.07R

R denotes an observation with a large standardized residual
```

Graph window output

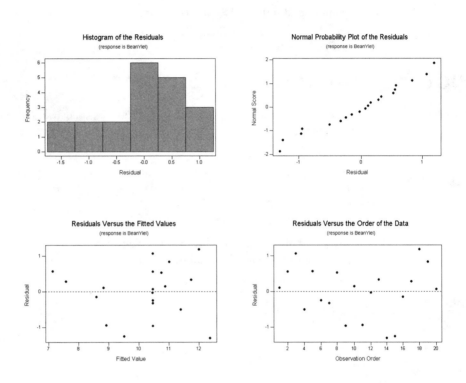

Interpreting the results

Since the linear model suggested that a higher model is needed to adequately model the response surface, you fit the full quadratic model. For the full quadratic model, the p-value for lack of fit is 0.133 suggesting that this model adequately fits the data.

The first table on the results gives the coefficients for all the terms in the model. Because you used an orthogonal design, each effect is estimated independently. Therefore, the coefficients for the linear terms are the same as when you fit just the linear model (page 20-30). The error term, s = 0.996, is smaller because you reduced the variability accounted for by error.

The Analysis of Variance table summarizes the linear terms, the squared terms, and the interactions. The small p-values for the interactions (p = 0.021) and the squared terms (p = 0.030) suggest there is curvature in the response surface. In the table of Estimated Regression Coefficients, you will see small p-values for the Nitrogen by Potash interaction (p = 0.007), Nitrogen squared (p = 0.027), and Phosphoric acid squared (p = 0.058) suggesting these effects may be important.

In addition, MINITAB draws four residual plots. The residual plots do not indicate any problems with the model. For assistance in interpreting the residual plots, see *Residual plots* on page 2-6.

For contour and surface plots of this response surface, see page 20-37.

Plotting the Response Surface

You can use Contour/Surface (Wireframe) Plots to display two types of response surface plots: contour plots and surface plots (also called wireframe). These plots show how a response variable relates to two factors based on a model equation.

Contour and surface plots are useful for establishing desirable response values and operating conditions. In a contour plot, the response surface is viewed as a two-dimensional plane where all points that have the same response are connected to produce contour lines of constant responses.

A surface plot displays a three-dimensional view that may provide a clearer picture of the response surface. The illustrations below compare these two types of plots.

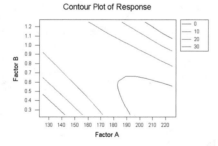
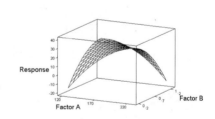

Note When the model has more than two factors, the factor(s) that are not in the plot are held constant. You can specify the constant values at which to hold the remaining factors. See *Settings for extra factors* on page 20-36.

Data

Contour plots and surface plots are model dependent. Thus, you *must* fit a model using Analyze Response Surface Design before you can generate response surface plots with Contour/Surface (Wireframe) Plots. MINITAB looks in the worksheet for the necessary model information to generate these plots.

▶ **To plot the response surface**

   1 Choose Stat ➤ DOE ➤ Response Surface ➤ Contour/Surface (Wireframe) Plots.

   2 Do one or both of the following:

- to generate a contour plot, check **Contour plot** and click **Setup**

- to generate a surface (wireframe) plot, check **Surface (wireframe) plot** and click **Setup**

   3 If you like, use any of the options listed below, then click **OK** in each dialog box.

Options

Setup subdialog box

- display a single graph for a selected factor pair
- display separate graphs for every combination of factors in the model
- display the data in coded or uncoded units

Settings subdialog box

- specify values for factors that are not included in the response surface plot, instead of using the default of median (middle) values—see *Settings for extra factors* on page 20-36

Contours subdialog box

- for contour plots, specify the number or location of the contour levels, and the contour line color and style—see *Controlling the number, type, and color of the contour lines* on page 20-36

Wireframe subdialog box

- for surface (wireframe) plots, specify the color of the wireframe (mesh) and the surface

Options subdialog box

- define minimum and maximum values for the x-axis and y-axis
- replace the default title with your own title

Settings for extra factors

You can set the holding level for factors that are not in the plot at their highest, lowest, or middle (calculated median) settings, or you can set specific levels at which to hold each factor.

▶ **To set the holding level for factors not in the plot**

1 In the Contour/Surface (Wireframe) dialog box, click **Setup**.

2 Click **Settings**.

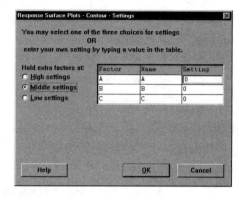

3 Do one of the following:

- To use the preset values, choose **High settings**, **Middle settings**, or **Low settings** under **Hold extra factors at**. When you use a preset value, *all* factors not in the plot will be held at their high, middle (calculated median), or low settings. (Not available for custom designs.)

- To specify the value(s) at which to hold the factor(s), enter a number in **Setting** for each factor you want control. This option allows you to set different hold settings for different factors.

4 Click **OK**.

Controlling the number, type, and color of the contour lines

MINITAB displays from four to seven contour levels—depending on the data—by default. However, you can specify from 2 to 15 contour lines.

You can also change the line type and color of the lines.

▶ **To control plotting of contour lines**

1 In the Contour/Surface (Wireframe) dialog box, check **Contour plot** and click **Setup**.

2 Click **Contours**.

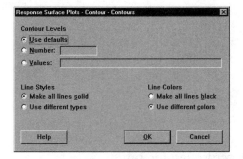

3 To change the number of contour lines, do one of the following:

■ Choose **Number** and enter a number from 2 to 15.

■ Choose **Values** and enter from 2 to 15 contour level values in the units of your data. You must enter the values in increasing order.

4 To define the line style, choose **Make all lines solid** or **Use different types** under **Line Styles**.

5 To define the line color, choose **Make all lines black** or **Use different colors** under **Line Colors**. Click **OK**.

▷ **Example of a contour plot and a surface plot**

In the fertilizer example on page 20-30, you generated a design, supplied the response data, and fit a linear model. Since this linear model suggested that a higher model is needed to adequately model the response surface, you fit the full quadratic model. The full quadratic provides a better fit, with the squared terms for nitrogen and phosphoric acid and the nitrogen by potash interaction being important. The example below is a continuation of this analysis. Now you want to try an understand these effects by looking at a contour plot and a surface plot of snap bean yield versus the significant factors—nitrogen and phosphoric acid. By default, MINITAB selects the first factor, in this case nitrogen, for the vertical axis, and the second factor, phosphoric acid, for the horizontal axis.

1 Open the worksheet CCD_EX1.MTW. (The design, response data, and model information have been saved for you.)

2 Choose **Stat ▶ DOE ▶ Response Surface ▶ Contour/Surface (Wireframe) Plot**s.

3 Choose **Contour plot** and click **Setup**. Click **OK**.

4 Choose **Surface (wireframe) plot** and click **Setup**. Click **OK** in each dialog box.

*Graph
window
output*

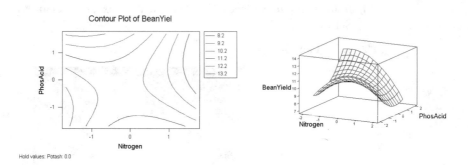

Interpreting the results

The contour plots indicates that the highest yield is obtained when nitrogen levels are low and phosphoric acid levels are high. This area appears at the upper left corner of the plot.

The surface plot also shows that the highest yield is obtained when nitrogen levels are low and phosphoric acid levels are high. In addition, you can see the shape of the response surface and get a general idea of yield at various settings of nitrogen and phosphoric acid.

Keep in mind that these plots are based on a model equation. You should be sure that your model is adequate before interpreting the plots.

References

[1] G.E.P. Box and D.W. Behnken (1960). "Some New Three Level Designs for the Study of Quantitative Variables," *Technometrics* 2, pp.455–475.

[2] G.E.P. Box and N.R. Draper (1987). *Empirical Model-Building and Response Surfaces*, John Wiley & Sons. p.249.

[3] A.I. Khuri and J.A. Cornell (1987). *Response Surfaces: Designs and Analyses*, Marcel Dekker, Inc.

[4] D.C. Montgomery (1991). *Design and Analysis of Experiments*, Third Edition, John Wiley & Sons.

21

Mixture Designs

Mixture Designs Overview

Mixture experiments are a special class of response surface experiments in which the product under investigation is made up of several components or ingredients. Designs for these experiments are useful because many product design and development activities in industrial situations involve formulations or mixtures. In these situations, the response is a function of the proportions of the different ingredients in the mixture. For example, you may be developing a pancake mix that is made of flour, baking powder, milk, eggs, and oil. Or, you may be developing an insecticide that blends four chemical ingredients.

In the simplest mixture experiment, the response (the quality or performance of the product based on some criterion) depends on the *relative proportions* of the components (ingredients). The quantities of components, measured in weights, volumes, or some other units, add up to a common total. In contrast, in a factorial design, the response varies depending on the *amount* of each factor (input variable).

MINITAB can create designs and analyze data from three types of experiments:

- mixture experiments
- mixture-amounts (MA) experiments (page 21-11)
- mixture-process variable (MPV) experiments (21-15)

The difference in these experiments is summarized below:

Type	Response depends on...	Example
mixture	the relative proportions of the components *only*.	the taste of lemonade depends *only* on the proportions of lemon juice, sugar, and water
mixture-amounts	the relative proportions of the components *and* the total amount of the mixture.	the yield of a crop depends on the amount of an insecticide applied *and* the proportions of the insecticide ingredients
mixture-process variable	the relative proportions of the components *and* process variables. Process variables are factors that are not part of the mixture but may affect the blending properties of the mixture.	the taste of a cake depends on the cooking time and cooking temperature, *and* the proportions of cake mix ingredients

Mixture experiments in MINITAB

The design and subsequent analysis of a mixture experiment might consist of the following steps:

1 Choose a mixture design for the experiment. Before you begin using MINITAB, you need to determine what design is appropriate for your problem. See *Choosing a Design* on page 21-3.

2 Use **Create Mixture Design** to generate a simplex centroid, simplex lattice, or extreme vertices mixture design (page 21-5). In addition, you can include amounts or process variables in your design to create mixture-amounts designs (page 21-11) and mixture-process variable designs (page 21-15).

   Use **Define Custom Mixture Design** to create a design from data you already have in the worksheet. Define Custom Mixture Design allows you to specify which columns contain your components and other design characteristics. You can then easily fit a model to the design. See *Defining Custom Designs* on page 21-28.

3 Use **Modify Design** to rename the components, replicate the design, randomize the design, and renumber the design. See *Modifying Designs* on page 21-31.

4 Use **Display Design** to change the display order of the runs and to change the units in which MINITAB expresses the components or process variables in the worksheet. See *Displaying Designs* on page 21-35.

5 Perform the mixture experiment and collect the response data. Then, enter the data in your MINITAB worksheet. See *Collecting and Entering Data* on page 21-37.

6 Use **Analyze Mixture Design** to fit a model to the experimental data. See *Analyzing Mixture Designs* on page 21-38.

7 Use plots to visualize the design space or response surface patterns. Use **Simplex Design Plot** (page 21-24) to view the design space, or **Response Trace Plot** (page 21-45) and **Contour/Surface (Wireframe) Plots** to visualize response surface patterns (21-49).

8 If you are trying to optimize responses, use **Response Optimizer** (page 23-2) or **Overlaid Contour Plot** (page 23-19) to obtain a numerical and graphical analysis.

Depending on your experiment, you may do some of the steps in a different order, perform a given step more than once, or eliminate a step.

Choosing a Design

Before you use MINITAB, you need to determine what design is most appropriate for your experiment. MINITAB provides simplex centroid, simplex lattice, and extreme vertices designs.

When you are choosing a design you need to

- identify the components, process variables, and mixture amounts that are of interest
- determine the model you want to fit—see *Selecting model terms* on page 21-41
- ensure adequate coverage of the region of interest on the response surface
- determine the impact that other considerations (such as cost, time, availability of facilities, or lower and upper bound constraints) have on your choice of a design

For a complete discussion of choosing a design, see [1].

To help you visualize a mixture design, the following illustrations show design points using triangular coordinates. Each point on the triangle represents a particular blend of components that you would use in your experiment. For simplicity, the illustrations show three component designs. The diagrams below only show a few of the mixture designs you can create. MINITAB can also create simplex lattice designs up to degree 10 and extreme vertices designs. For an explanation of triangular coordinates, see page 21-55.

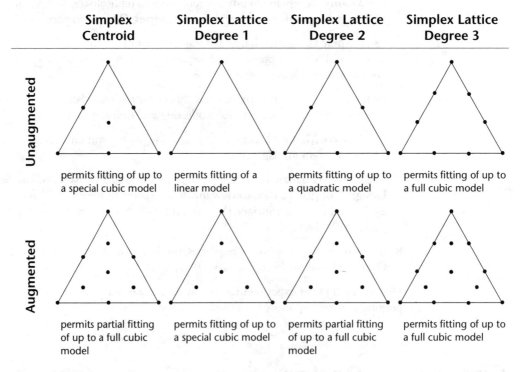

Simplex Centroid	Simplex Lattice Degree 1	Simplex Lattice Degree 2	Simplex Lattice Degree 3
Unaugmented			
permits fitting of up to a special cubic model	permits fitting of a linear model	permits fitting of up to a quadratic model	permits fitting of up to a full cubic model
Augmented			
permits partial fitting of up to a full cubic model	permits fitting of up to a special cubic model	permits partial fitting of up to a full cubic model	permits fitting of up to a full cubic model

Note | When selecting a design, it is important to consider the maximum order of the fitted model required to adequately model the response surface. Mixture experiments frequently require a higher-order model than is initially planned. Therefore, it is usually a good idea, whenever possible, to perform additional runs beyond the minimum required to fit the model. For guidelines, see [1].

Creating Mixture Designs

You can create simplex centroid, simplex lattice, or extreme vertices designs.

Simplex centroid and simplex lattice designs

In the simplex designs, the points are arranged in a uniform manner (or lattice) over an L-simplex. An L-simplex is similar to and has sides parallel to the 0–1 triangle shown on page 21-4.

For both simplex centroid and simplex lattice designs, you can add points to the interior of the design space. These points provide information on the interior of the response surface thereby improving coverage of the design space. See *Augmenting the design* on page 21-8.

Extreme vertices designs

In extreme vertices designs, MINITAB employs an algorithm that generates extreme vertices and their blends up to the specified degree. These designs must be used when your chosen design space is not an L-simplex. The presence of both lower and upper bound constraints on the components often create this condition. The goal of an extreme vertices design is to choose design points that adequately cover the design space. The illustration below shows the extreme vertices for two three-component designs with both upper and lower constraints:

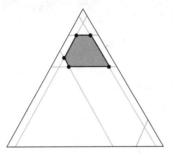 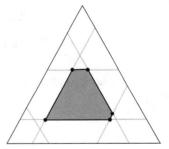

The light gray lines represent the lower and upper bound constraints on the components. The dark gray area represents the design space. The points are placed at the extreme vertices of design space.

More | For a discussion of upper and lower bound constraints, see *Setting lower and upper bounds* on page 21-13.

Note | To create a design from data that you already have in the worksheet, see *Defining Custom Designs* on page 21-28.

▶ **To create a mixture design**

1 Choose Stat ➤ DOE ➤ Mixture ➤ Create Mixture Design.

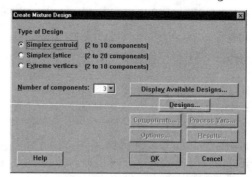

2 If you want to see a summary of the simplex designs, click **Display Available Designs**. Use this table to compare design features. Click **OK**.

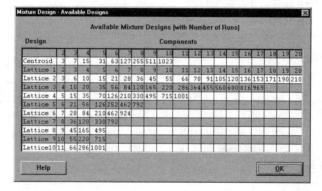

3 Under **Type of Design**, choose **Simplex centroid**, **Simplex lattice**, or **Extreme vertices**.

4 From **Number of components**, choose a number.

5 Click **Designs**.

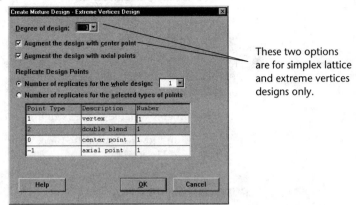

These two options are for simplex lattice and extreme vertices designs only.

6 If you like, use any of the options listed under *Design subdialog box* on page 21-7.

7 Click **OK** even if you do not change any of the options. This selects the design and brings you back to the main dialog box.

8 If you like, click **Components**, **Process Vars**, **Options**, or **Results** to use any of the options listed below, then click **OK** to create your design.

Options

Design subdialog box

- choose the degree of a simplex lattice or extreme vertices design—see *Choosing a Design* on page 21-3 and *Calculation of design points* on page 21-57

- add a center point (simplex lattice and extreme vertices designs only) or add axial points to the interior of the design (by default, MINITAB adds these points to the design)—see *Augmenting the design* on page 21-8

- replicate the design—see *Replicating the design* on page 21-9

Components subdialog box

- generate the design in units of the actual measurements rather than the proportions of the components—see *Generating the design in actual measurements* on page 21-11

- perform a mixture amounts experiment with up to five amount totals—see *Mixture-amounts designs* on page 21-11

- name components—see *Naming components* on page 21-12

- set lower and upper bounds for constrained designs—see *Setting lower and upper bounds* on page 21-13

- for extreme vertices designs, set linear constraints for the set of components—see *Setting linear constraints for extreme vertices designs* on page 21-14

Process variables subdialog box

- include up to seven process variables (factors) in your design—see *Mixture-process variable designs* on page 21-15

- specify the type of design (full or fractional factorial designs) and the fraction number to use for fractional factorial designs—see *Fractionating a mixture-process variable design* on page 21-15

- name the process variables—see *Naming process variables* on page 21-17

- set the high and low levels for the process variables—see *Setting process variable levels* on page 21-18

Options subdialog box

- randomize the design—see *Randomizing the design* on page 21-19

- store the design—see *Storing the design* on page 21-19

- store the design parameters (amounts, upper and lower bounds of the components, and linear constraints) in separate columns in the worksheet—see *Storing the design* on page 21-19

Results subdialog box

- display the following in the Session window:
  - no results
  - a summary of the design
  - the default results, which includes a detailed description of the design
  - the default results, plus the data table

Augmenting the design

In order to adequately cover the response surface, you want to use a design that has interior points. By default, MINITAB augments a design by adding interior points to the design. MINITAB adds axial points and a center point if it is not already in the base design. Each of these additional points is a complete mixture—that is, a mixture in which all components are simultaneously present. A design with these interior points would provide information on the inner portion of the response surface and allow you to model more complicated curvature.

These points are primarily used to examine the lack-of-fit of a model. In addition, a design with these interior points would provide information on the inner portion of the response surface and allow you to model more complicated curvature.

Each axial point is added halfway between a vertex and the center of the design. See *Appendix for Mixture Designs* on page 21-55 and Help for details.

The illustrations below show the points that are added when you augment a second-degree three-component simplex lattice design with both axial points and a center point.

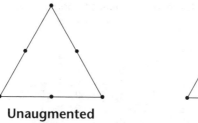
Unaugmented

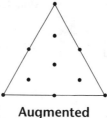
Augmented

To compare some other three-component designs, see the table under *Choosing a Design* on page 21-3. To view any design in MINITAB, use Simplex Design Plot.

Note | If you do not want to augment your design, uncheck **Augment the design with a center point** and/or **Augment the design with axial points** in the Designs subdialog box.

Replicating the design

You can replicate your design in one of two ways. You can replicate

- the whole design up to 50 times

- only certain types of points as many times as you want

When you replicate the whole design, you duplicate the complete set of design points from the base design. The design points that would be added to a first-degree three-component simplex lattice design are as follows:

Base design	One replicate added (total of two replicates)	Two replicates added (total of three replicates)
A B C	A B C	A B C
1 0 0	1 0 0	1 0 0
0 1 0	0 1 0	0 1 0
0 0 1	0 0 1	0 0 1
	1 0 0	1 0 0
	0 1 0	0 1 0
	0 0 1	0 0 1
		1 0 0
		0 1 0
		0 0 1

When you choose which types of points to replicate, you duplicate only the design points of the specified types of points from the base design. For example, the design points for a replicated second-degree three-component simplex lattice design are as follows:

Base design			One replicate of each vertex and two replicates of each double blend			Two replicates of each vertex and two replicates of each double blend		
A	B	C	A	B	C	A	B	C
1	0	0	1	0	0	1	0	0
.5	.5	0	.5	.5	0	.5	.5	0
.5	0	.5	.5	0	.5	.5	0	.5
0	1	0	0	1	0	0	1	0
0	.5	.5	0	.5	.5	0	.5	.5
0	0	1	0	0	1	0	0	1
			.5	.5	0	1	0	0
			.5	0	.5	0	1	0
			0	.5	.5	0	0	1
						.5	.5	0
						.5	0	.5
						0	.5	.5

True replication provides an estimate of the error or noise in your process and may allow for more precise estimates of effects.

▶ **To replicate the design**

1 In the Create Mixture Design dialog box, click **Designs**.

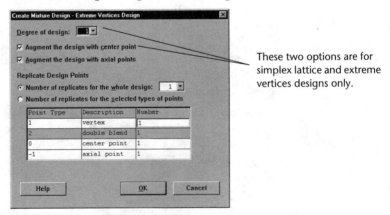

These two options are for simplex lattice and extreme vertices designs only.

1 Under **Replicate design points**, do one of the following:

- To replicate the entire base design, choose **Number of replicates for the whole design** and choose a number up to 50.

- To replicate only certain types of points, choose **Number of replicates for the selected types of points** and enter the number of replicates for each point type in the **Number** column of the table.

2 Click **OK**.

Generating the design in actual measurements

By default, MINITAB expresses the design points in terms of the proportions of all components, where the sum of the proportions is one. This is equivalent to an amount total equal to one.

▶ **To express a design in actual measurements**

1 In the Create Mixture Design dialog box, click **Components**.

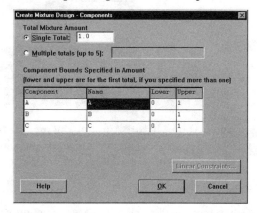

2 Under **Total Mixture Amount**, choose **Single total** and enter the sum of all the component measurements. Suppose you measure all the components of your mixture in liters. If the measurements add up to a total of 5.2 liters, you would enter 5.2.

3 Click **OK**.

Mixture-amounts designs

In the simplest mixture experiment, the response is assumed to only depend on the proportions of the components in the mixture. In the mixture-amounts experiment, the response is assumed to depend on the proportions of the components *and* the amount of the mixture. For example, the amount applied *and* the proportions of the ingredients of a plant food may affect the growth of a house plant. When a mixture experiment is performed at two or more levels of the total mixture amount, it is called a *mixture-amounts experiment*.

▶ **To create a mixture-amounts design**

1 In the Create Mixture Design dialog box, click **Components**.

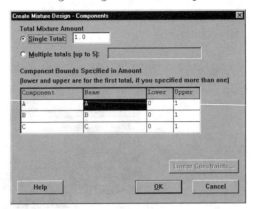

2 Under **Total Mixture Amount**, choose **Multiple totals** and enter up to five mixture totals. Suppose you are testing plant food and would like evaluate plant growth when one gram versus two grams of food are applied. You would enter *1 2*.

3 Click **OK**.

More │ For a complete discussion of mixture-amounts experiments, see [1] and [2].

Naming components

By default, MINITAB names the components alphabetically, skipping the letter T.

▶ **To name components**

1 In the Create Mixture Design dialog box, click **Components**.

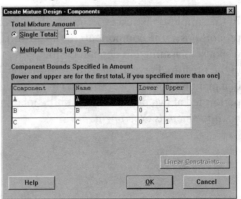

2 Under **Name**, click in the first row and type the name of the first component. Then, use the ⬇ key to move down the column and enter the remaining names.

More | After you have created the design, you can change the component names by typing new names in the Data window, or with Modify Design (page 21-31).

Setting lower and upper bounds

By default, MINITAB generates settings for an unconstrained design, that is, the lower bound is zero and the upper bound is one for all the components. However, in some mixture experimentation, it is necessary to set a lower bound and/or an upper bound on some or all of the components.

- Lower bounds are necessary when any of the components must be present in the mixture. For example, lemonade must contain lemon juice.

- Upper bounds are necessary when the mixture cannot contain more than a given proportion of an ingredient. For example, a cake mix cannot contain more than 5% baking powder.

Constrained designs (those in which you specify lower or upper bounds) produce coefficients that are highly correlated. Generally, you can reduce the correlations among the coefficients by transforming the components to pseudocomponents. For information on displaying or analyzing the design in pseudocomponents, see *Specifying the units for components* on page 21-36 and *Analyzing Mixture Designs* on page 21-38. For a complete discussion, see [1] and [3].

▶ To set lower and upper bounds

1 In the Create Mixture Design dialog box, click **Components**.

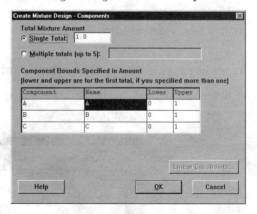

2 Under **Lower**, click in the component row for which you want set a lower bound, and type a positive number.

Each lower bound must be less than the corresponding upper bound. The sum of the lower bounds for all the components must be less than the value of **Single total** or the first value in **Multiple totals**.

3 Use the ▣ key to move to **Upper** and enter a positive number.

Each upper bound must be greater than the corresponding lower bound. Each upper bound must be less than the value of **Single total** or the first value in **Multiple totals**. The sum of the upper bounds for all the components must be greater than the value of **Single total** or the first value in **Multiple totals**.

4 Repeat steps 2 and 3 to assign bounds for other components.

5 Click **OK**.

When you change the default lower or upper bounds of a component, the achievable bounds on the other components may need to be adjusted. See Help for calculations.

Setting linear constraints for extreme vertices designs

In addition to the individual bounds on the components, you may have up to ten linear constraints on the set of components. Suppose the wet ingredients (eggs, milk, oil) of a cake mix cannot be less 40% or greater than 60% of the total mixture. If you are willing to allow equal amounts of these three ingredients, the lower value is 0.4, the upper value is 0.6, and the component coefficients are all 1. Examples for a four-component blend are shown in the table below:

Condition	Lower Value	Coefficients				Upper Value
		A	B	C	D	
$A + B \geq 10$ and $A + B \leq 20$	10	1	1			20
$5A + 3B + 8D \leq 0.1$		5	3		8	0.1
$0.5B + 0.8D \geq 0.9$	0.9		0.5	0.8		

▶ **To set linear constraints for a set of components**

1 In the Create Mixture Design dialog box, click **Components**.

2 Click **Linear Constraints**.

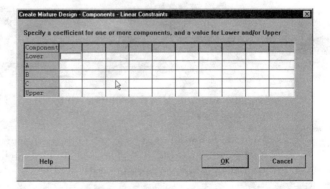

3 In the first column of the table, enter a coefficient for one or more of the components and a lower and/or upper value. Use the ⬇ key to move down the column and enter desired values. The lower and upper values that you enter must be consistent with value of **Single total** or the first value in **Multiple totals**.

You must enter at least one coefficient and an upper or lower value. If you do not enter a coefficient for a component, MINITAB assumes it to be zero.

4 Repeat step 3 to enter up to ten different linear constraints on the set of components.

5 Click **OK**.

Mixture-process variable designs

Process variables are factors in an experiment that are not part of the mixture but may affect the blending properties of the mixture. For example, the adhesive properties of a paint may depend on the temperature at which it is applied.

You can include up to seven two-level process variables in the mixture design. The process variables may be included as full or fractional factorial designs. The mixture design will be generated at each combination of levels of the process variables or at a fraction of the level combinations.

Fractionating a mixture-process variable design

When you generate a "complete" mixture-process variable design, the mixture design is generated at each combination of levels of the process variables. This may result in a prohibitive number of runs because the number of design points in the complete design increases quickly as the number of process variables increase. For example, a complete simplex centroid design with 3 mixture components and 2 process variables has 28 runs. The same 3-component design with three process variables has 56 runs; this design with 4 process variables has 112 runs.

Tip | You can also use an optimal design to reduce the number of runs—see Chapter 22, *Optimal Designs*.

The illustrations below show a 3-component mixture with 3 process variables:

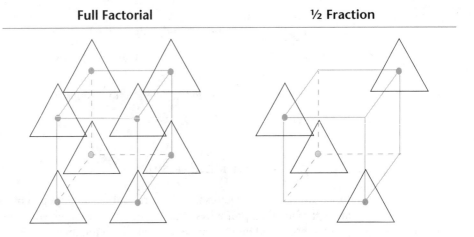

Full Factorial   **½ Fraction**

Notice that the full factorial design contains twice as many design points as the ½ fraction design. The response is only measured at four of the possible eight corner points of the factorial portion of the design.

The types of factorial designs that are available depend on the number of process variables. Factorial design availability is summarized in the table below:

Number of process variables	full	Type of factorial design			
		1/2 **fraction**	1/4 **fraction**	1/8 **fraction**	1/16 **fraction**
one	✗				
two	✗				
three	✗	✗			
four	✗	✗			
five	✗	✗	✗		
six	✗	✗	✗	✗	
seven	✗	✗	✗	✗	✗

▶ **To add process variables to a design**

1 In the Create Mixture Design dialog box, click **Process Vars**.

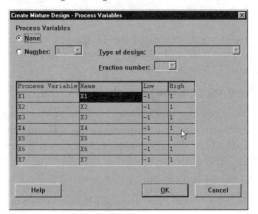

2 Under **Process Variables**, choose **Number**, then choose a value from 1 to 7.

3 From **Type of design**, choose a full or fractional factorial design. The available designs depend on the number of process variables chosen.

4 If you like, you can select the fraction number you want to use. By default, MINITAB uses the principal fraction. See *Choosing a fraction* on page 19-16.

5 If you like, you can name the process variables (described below) and set the process variable levels (described on page 21-18).

6 Click **OK**.

Naming process variables

By default, MINITAB names the process variables as X1,…,Xn, where n is the number of process variables.

▶ **To name process variables**

1 In the Create Mixture Design dialog box, click **Process Vars**.

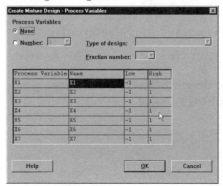

2 Under **Name**, click in the first row and type the name of the first process variable. Then, use the ↓ key to move down the column and enter the remaining names.

3 Click **OK**.

More After you have created the design, you can change the process variable names by typing new names in the Data window or with Modify Design (page 21-31).

Setting process variable levels

You can enter process variable levels as numeric or text. If your process variables could be *continuous*, use numeric levels; if your process variables are *categorical*, use text levels. Continuous variables can take on any value on the measurement scale being used (for example, length of reaction time). In contrast, categorical variables can only assume a limited number of possible values (for example, type of catalyst).

By default, MINITAB sets the low level of all factors to −1 and the high level to +1.

▶ To assign process variable levels

1 In the Create Mixture Design dialog box, click **Process Vars**.

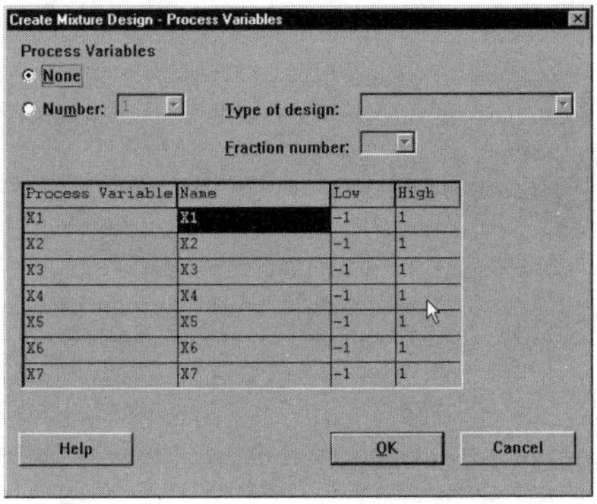

2 Under **Low**, click in the process variable row to which you would like to assign values and enter any value. Use the → key to move to **High** and enter a value. If you use numeric levels, the value you enter in **High** must be larger than the value you enter in **Low**.

3 Repeat step 2 to assign levels for other process variables.

4 Click **OK**.

More To change the process variable levels after you have created the design, use **Stat ➤ DOE ➤ Modify Design**.

Randomizing the design

By default, MINITAB randomizes the run order of the design. The ordered sequence of the design points is called the *run order*. It is usually a good idea to randomize the run order to lessen the effects of factors that are not included in the study, particularly effects that are time-dependent.

However, there may be situations when randomization leads to an undesirable run order. For instance, in industrial applications, it may be difficult or expensive to change component levels. Or, after component levels have been changed, it may take a long time for the system to return to steady state. Under these conditions, you may not want to randomize the design in order to minimize the level changes.

Every time you create a design, MINITAB reserves and names C1 (StdOrder) and C2 (RunOrder) to store the standard order and run order, respectively.

- StdOrder shows what the order of the runs in the experiment would be if the experiment was done in standard order.

- RunOrder shows what the order of the runs in the experiment would be if the experiment was run in random order.

If you did not randomize, the run order and standard order are the same.

If you want to re-create a design with the same ordering of the runs (that is, the same design order), you can choose a base for the random data generator. Then, when you want to re-create the design, you just use the same base.

More | You can use **Stat ➤ DOE ➤ Display Design** (page 21-35) to switch back and forth between a random and standard order display in the worksheet.

Storing the design

If you want to analyze a design, you *must* store it in the worksheet. By default, MINITAB stores the design. If you want to see the properties of various designs before selecting the design you want to store, uncheck **Store design in worksheet** in the Options subdialog box.

Every time you create a design, MINITAB reserves and names the following columns:

- C1 (StdOrder) stores the standard order.

- C2 (RunOrder) stores run order.

- C3 (PtType) stores a numerical representation of the type of design point.

- C4 (Blocks) stores the blocking variable. When a design is not blocked, as with mixture designs, MINITAB sets all column values to one.

- $C5,\ldots,C_{number\ of\ components\ +\ 4}$ stores the components. MINITAB stores each component in your design in a separate column.

■ In addition, depending on your design and storage options, MINITAB may store the following:

– each process variable in a separate column (named X1,...,Xn)

– an amount variable (named Amount)

– the design parameters (named Totals, Lower, Upper, Linear)

If you named the components or process variables, these names display in the worksheet. After you create the design, you can change the component names directly in the Data window or with **Stat ► DOE ► Modify Design** (page 21-31).

If you did not change the total for the mixture from the default value of one, MINITAB uses proportions to store your data. If you did change the total for the mixture, MINITAB uses amounts—what you actually measure—to express your data. After you create the design, you can specify one of three scales (described on page 21-36) to represent the data: amounts, proportions, or pseudocomponents. To change which of the three scales is displayed in the worksheet, use **Stat ► DOE ► Display Design** (page 21-35).

Caution | When you create a design using Create Mixture Design, MINITAB stores the appropriate design information in the worksheet. MINITAB needs this stored information to analyze the data properly. If you want to use Analyze Mixture Design, you must follow certain rules when modifying the worksheet data. See *Modifying and Using Worksheet Data* on page 18-4.

If you make changes that corrupt your design, you may still be able to analyze it with Analyze Mixture Design after you use Define Custom Mixture Design (page 21-28).

► Example of a simplex centroid design

Suppose you want to study how the proportions of three ingredients in an herbal blend household deodorizer affect the acceptance of the product based on scent. The three components are neroli oil, rose oil, and tangerine oil.

1 Choose **Stat ► DOE ► Mixture ► Create Mixture Design**.

2 Under **Type of Design**, choose **Simplex centroid**.

3 From **Number of components**, choose 3.

4 Click **Designs**. Make sure **Augment the design with axial points** is checked. Click **OK**.

5 Click **Components**. In **Name**, enter *Neroli, Rose,* and *Tangerine* in rows 1 to 3, respectively. Click **OK**.

6 Click **Results**. Choose **Detailed description and data table**.

7 Click **OK** in each dialog box.

*Session
window
output*

Simplex Centroid Design

```
Components:          3      Design points:   10
Process variables: 0        Design degree:    3

Mixture total: 1

Number of Boundaries for Each Dimension

Point Type      1    2    0
Dimension       0    1    2
Number          3    3    1

Number of Design Points for Each Type

Point Type      1    2    3    0    -1
Distinct        3    3    0    1     3
Replicates      1    1    0    1     1
Total Number    3    3    0    1     3
```

Bounds of Mixture Components

Comp	Amount Lower	Amount Upper	Proportion Lower	Proportion Upper	Pseudocomponent Lower	Pseudocomponent Upper
A	0.0000	1.0000	0.0000	1.0000	0.0000	1.0000
B	0.0000	1.0000	0.0000	1.0000	0.0000	1.0000
C	0.0000	1.0000	0.0000	1.0000	0.0000	1.0000

Data Matrix (randomized)

Run	Type	A	B	C
1	-1	0.1667	0.1667	0.6667
2	-1	0.6667	0.1667	0.1667
3	2	0.5000	0.5000	0.0000
4	2	0.5000	0.0000	0.5000
5	-1	0.1667	0.6667	0.1667
6	2	0.0000	0.5000	0.5000
7	1	0.0000	0.0000	1.0000
8	1	0.0000	1.0000	0.0000
9	0	0.3333	0.3333	0.3333
10	1	1.0000	0.0000	0.0000

Interpreting the results

MINITAB creates an augmented three-component simplex centroid design. The base design provides seven runs; augmentation adds three runs for a total of ten runs.

Because you chose to display the detailed description and data tables, MINITAB shows the component proportions you will use to create ten blends of your mixture. When you perform the experiment, use the blends in the run order that is shown. (Because you did not change the mixture total from the default of one, MINITAB expresses each component in proportions.) For example, the first blend you will test will be made up of equal amounts of neroli (0.1667) and rose oils (0.1667), and tangerine oil will make up the remaining 0.6667.

Note | MINITAB randomizes the design by default, so if you try to replicate this example, your runs may not match the order shown.

▶ Example of an extreme vertices design

Suppose you need to determine the proportions of flour, milk, baking powder, eggs, and oil in a pancake mix that would produce an optimal product based on taste. Because previous experimentation suggests that a mix that does not contain all of the ingredients or has too much baking powder will not meet the taste requirements, you decide to constrain the design by setting lower bounds and upper bounds.

You decide that quadratic model will sufficiently model the response surface, so you decide to create a second-degree design.

1 Choose **Stat ➤ DOE ➤ Mixture ➤ Create Mixture Design**.

2 Under **Type of Design**, choose **Extreme vertices**.

3 From **Number of components**, choose 5.

4 Click **Designs**. From **Degree of design**, choose 2.

5 Make sure **Augment the design with center point** and **Augment the design with axial points** are checked. Click **OK**.

6 Click **Components**. Complete the **Name**, **Lower**, and **Upper** columns of the table as shown below, then click **OK**.

Component	Name	Lower	Upper
A	Flour	.425	1
B	Milk	.30	1
C	Baking powder	.025	.05
D	Eggs	.10	1
E	Oil	.10	1

7 Click **Results**. Choose **Detailed description and data table**. Click **OK** in each dialog box.

Session window output

Extreme Vertices Design

Components: 5   Design points: 33
Process variables: 0   Design degree: 2

Mixture total: 1

Number of Boundaries for Each Dimension

Point Type	1	2	3	4	0
Dimension	0	1	2	3	4
Number	8	16	14	6	1

Number of Design Points for Each Type

Point Type	1	2	3	4	5	0	-1
Distinct	8	16	0	0	0	1	8
Replicates	1	1	0	0	0	1	1
Total Number	8	16	0	0	0	1	8

Bounds of Mixture Components

	Amount		Proportion		Pseudocomponent	
Comp	Lower	Upper	Lower	Upper	Lower	Upper
A	0.425000	0.475000	0.425000	0.475000	0.000000	1.000000
B	0.300000	0.350000	0.300000	0.350000	0.000000	1.000000
C	0.025000	0.050000	0.025000	0.050000	0.000000	0.500000
D	0.100000	0.150000	0.100000	0.150000	0.000000	1.000000
E	0.100000	0.150000	0.100000	0.150000	0.000000	1.000000

* NOTE * Bounds were adjusted to accommodate specified constraints.

Data Matrix (randomized)

Run	Type	A	B	C	D	E
1	2	0.462500	0.300000	0.037500	0.100000	0.100000
2	-1	0.429687	0.304688	0.043750	0.104688	0.117188
3	2	0.425000	0.300000	0.037500	0.100000	0.137500
4	-1	0.454687	0.304688	0.031250	0.104688	0.104688
5	2	0.425000	0.300000	0.037500	0.137500	0.100000
6	1	0.475000	0.300000	0.025000	0.100000	0.100000
7	2	0.425000	0.312500	0.050000	0.112500	0.100000
8	-1	0.429687	0.304688	0.031250	0.129688	0.104688
9	2	0.437500	0.312500	0.050000	0.100000	0.100000
10	2	0.450000	0.300000	0.025000	0.100000	0.125000
11	2	0.437500	0.300000	0.050000	0.112500	0.100000
12	2	0.425000	0.325000	0.025000	0.125000	0.100000
13	-1	0.429687	0.304688	0.043750	0.117188	0.104688
14	1	0.425000	0.300000	0.025000	0.150000	0.100000
15	2	0.450000	0.325000	0.025000	0.100000	0.100000
16	-1	0.429687	0.304688	0.031250	0.104688	0.129688
17	-1	0.429687	0.317188	0.043750	0.104688	0.104688
18	1	0.425000	0.300000	0.025000	0.100000	0.150000
19	1	0.425000	0.350000	0.025000	0.100000	0.100000
20	-1	0.442187	0.304688	0.043750	0.104688	0.104688

21	-1	0.429687	0.329687	0.031250	0.104688	0.104688
22	0	0.434375	0.309375	0.037500	0.109375	0.109375
23	2	0.425000	0.337500	0.037500	0.100000	0.100000
24	2	0.437500	0.300000	0.050000	0.100000	0.112500
25	2	0.425000	0.325000	0.025000	0.100000	0.125000
26	2	0.425000	0.312500	0.050000	0.100000	0.112500
27	2	0.425000	0.300000	0.025000	0.125000	0.125000
28	1	0.425000	0.300000	0.050000	0.100000	0.125000
29	1	0.425000	0.325000	0.050000	0.100000	0.100000
30	2	0.450000	0.300000	0.025000	0.125000	0.100000
31	1	0.450000	0.300000	0.050000	0.100000	0.100000
32	2	0.425000	0.300000	0.050000	0.112500	0.112500
33	1	0.425000	0.300000	0.050000	0.125000	0.100000

Interpreting the results

MINITAB creates an augmented five-component extreme vertices design. The base design provides 24 design points; augmentation adds 9 design points for a total of 33 runs. Augmenting this design adds 8 axial points and 1 center point to the design.

Because you chose to display the summary and data tables, MINITAB shows the component proportions you will use to create 33 blends of your mixture. When you perform the experiment, use the blends in the run order that is shown. (Because you did not change the mixture total from the default of one, MINITAB expresses each component in proportions.)

Note | MINITAB randomizes the design by default, so if you try to replicate this example, your runs may not match the order shown.

Displaying Simplex Design Plots

You can use a simplex design plot to visualize the mixture design space (or a slice of the design space if you have more than three components). MINITAB plots the design points on triangular axes. You can plot the following:

- components only

- components and process variables

- components and an amount variable

Data

You must create and store a design using Create Mixture Design.

▶ **To display a simplex design plot**

1 Choose Stat ➤ DOE ➤ Mixture ➤ Simplex Design Plot.

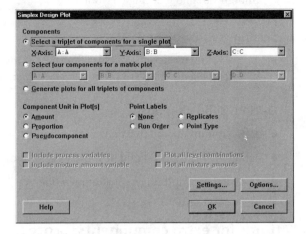

2 Do one of the following to select the number of plots to display:

- To display a single simplex design plot for any three components, choose **Select a triplet of components for a single plot**. Then, choose any three components that are in your design.

- To display a layout with four simplex design plots (each plot displays three components), choose **Select four components for a matrix plot**. Then, choose any four components that are in your design.

- To display a simplex design plot for all combinations of components, each in a separate window, choose **Generate plots for all triplets of components**.

3 If you like, use any of the options listed below, then click **OK**.

Options

Simplex Design Plot dialog box

- display four simplex design plots in a single page layout

- generate plots for all triplets of components

- display the plot in amounts, proportions, or pseudocomponents

- use the run order, number of replicates, or point type for design point labels on the plot

- include process variables, and for a single simplex design plot include all the levels of the process variables in a single layout

- include an amount variable (by default, MINITAB will plot the amount variable at its first defined value), and for a single simplex design plot include all the levels of the amount variable in a single layout

Settings subdialog box

- specify values for design variables that are not included in the plot—see *Settings for extra components, process variables, and an amount variable* below

Options subdialog box

- define minimum and maximum values for the x-axis, y-axis, and z-axis
- define the background grid or suppress grid lines
- replace the default title with your own title

Settings for extra components, process variables, and an amount variable

You can set the holding level for components and process variables that are not in the plot at their highest or lowest settings, or you can set specific levels to hold each. For an amount variable, you can set the hold value at any of the totals. The hold values must be expressed in the following units:

- components in the *units displayed in the worksheet*
- process variables in *coded units*

Note If you have text process variables in your design, you can only set their holding values at one of the text levels.

▶ To set the holding level for design variables not in the plot

1 In the Simplex Design Plot dialog box, click **Settings**.

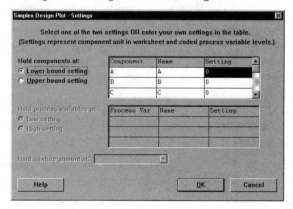

2 Do one or more of the following to set the holding values:

- For components (only available for design with more than three components):
  - To use the preset values for components, choose **Lower bound setting** or **Upper bound setting** under **Hold components at**. When you use a preset value, *all* components not in the plot will be held at their lower bound or upper bound.
  - To specify the value at which to hold the components, enter a number in **Setting** for each component that you want to control. This option allows you to set a different holding value for each component.

- For process variables:
  - To use the preset values for process variables, choose **High setting** or **Low setting** under **Hold process variables at**. When you use a preset value, *all* variables not in the plot will be held at their high or low settings.
  - To specify the value at which to hold the process variables, enter a number in **Setting** for each of the process variables you want to control. This option allows you to set a different holding value for each process variable.

- For an amount variable:
  - In **Hold mixture amount at**, choose one of the mixture totals. MINITAB displays the multiple totals that you entered in the Components subdialog box when you were creating the design.

3 Click **OK**.

▷ Example of simplex design plot

In the *Example of a simplex centroid design* on page 21-20, you created a design to study how the proportions of three ingredients in an herbal blend household deodorizer affect the acceptance of the product based on scent. The three components are neroli oil, rose oil, and tangerine oil. To help you visualize the design space, you want to display a simplex design plot.

1 Open the worksheet DEODORIZ.MTW.

2 Choose **Stat ➤ DOE ➤ Mixture ➤ Simplex Design Plot**.

3 Click **OK**.

*Graph
window
output*

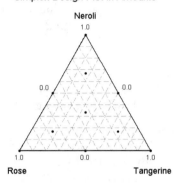

Interpreting the results

The simplex design plot shows that there are ten points in the design space. The points are as follows:

- three pure mixtures, one for each component (Neroli, Rose, and Tangerine). These points are found at the vertices of the triangle.

- three binary blends, one for each possible two-component blend (Neroli-Rose, Rose-Tangerine, and Tangerine-Neroli). These design points are found at the midpoint of each edge of the triangle.

- three complete blends. All three components are included in these blends, but not in equal proportions.

- one center point (or centroid). Equal proportions of all three components are included in this blend.

Defining Custom Designs

Use Define Custom Mixture Design to create a design from data you already have in the worksheet. For example, you may have a design that you created using MINITAB session commands, entered directly into the Data window, imported from a data file, or created with earlier releases of MINITAB. You can also use Define Custom Mixture Design to redefine a design that you created with Create Mixture Design and then modified directly in the worksheet.

Custom designs allow you to specify which columns contain your components and other design characteristics. After you define your design, you can use Modify Design (page 21-31), Display Design (page 21-35), and Analyze Mixture Design (page 21-38).

▶ **To define a custom mixture design**

1 Choose Stat ➤ DOE ➤ Mixture ➤ Define Custom Mixture Design.

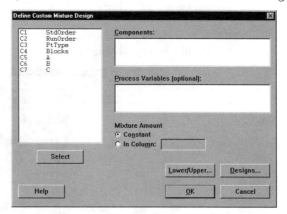

2 In **Components**, enter the columns that contain the component data. Data must be in the form of amounts. (When the mixture total is one, amounts and proportions are equivalent.) For information the data units, see *Mixture-amounts designs* on page 21-11 and *Specifying the units for components* on page 21-36.

3 If you have process variables in your design, enter the columns in **Process variables**.

4 If you have an amount variable, under **Mixture Amount**, choose **In column**, and enter the column that contains the amount data.

5 Click **Lower/Upper**.

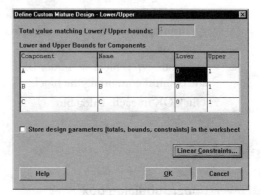

6 If you have an mixture-amounts experiment, MINITAB will enter the smallest value in your amount column in **Total value matching Lower/Upper bounds**. If this is not the value you want, change it to any other total in your amount column.

7 MINITAB will fill in the lower and upper bound table from the worksheet. Make any necessary corrections, then click **OK**.

8 Do one of the following:

- If you do not have any columns containing the standard order, run order, point type, or blocks, click **OK**.

- If you have columns that contain data for the standard order, run order, point type, or blocks, click **Designs**.

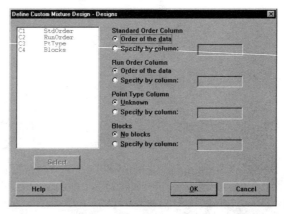

1 If you have a column that contains the standard order of the experiment, under **Standard Order Column**, choose **Specify by column** and enter the column containing the standard order.

2 If you have a column that contains the run order of the experiment, under **Run Order Column,** choose **Specify by column** and enter the column containing the run order.

3 If you have a column that contains the design point type, under **Point Type Column**, choose **Specify by column** and enter the column containing the point types.

4 If your design is blocked, under **Blocks**, choose **Specify by column** and enter the column containing the blocks.

5 Click **OK** in each dialog box.

Options

Lower/Upper subdialog box

- store the design parameters (amounts, upper and lower bounds of the components, and linear constraints) in separate columns in the worksheet—see *Storing the design* on page 21-19

- set one or more linear constraints for the set of components—see *Setting linear constraints for extreme vertices designs* on page 21-14

Modifying Designs

After creating a design and storing it in the worksheet, you can use Modify Design to make the following modifications:

- rename the components (below)
- rename process variables and change levels (page 21-32)
- replicate the design (page 21-33)
- randomize the design (page 21-34)
- renumber the design (page 21-34)

By default, MINITAB will replace the current design with the modified design in the worksheet. To store the modified design in a new worksheet, check **Put modified design in a new worksheet**.

Renaming components

▶ To rename components

1 Choose Stat ➤ DOE ➤ Modify Design.

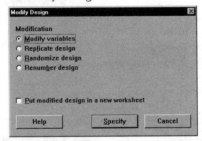

2 Choose **Modify variables** and click **Specify**.

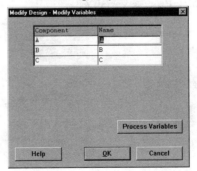

3 Under **Name**, click in the first row and type the name of the first component. Then, use the ⬇ key to move down the column and enter the remaining names.

4 Click **OK**.

Tip	You can also type new component or process variable names directly into the Data window.

Renaming process variables or changing levels

▶ **To rename process variables or change levels**

1 Choose Stat ➤ DOE ➤ Modify Design.

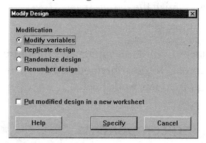

2 Choose **Modify variables** and click **Specify**.

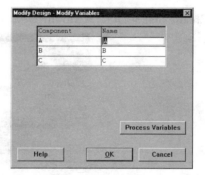

3 Click **Process Variables**.

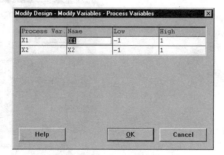

4 Do one or both of the following:

- Under **Name**, click in the first row and type the name of the first process variable. Then, use the ⊥ key to move down the column and name the remaining process variables.

- Under **Low**, click in the process variable row you would like to assign values and enter any numeric or text value. Use the → key to move to **High** and enter a value. For numeric levels, the **High** value must be larger than **Low** value.

  Repeat to assign levels for other factors.

5 Click **OK**.

Tip | You can also type new component or process variable names directly into the Data window.

Replicating the design

You can add up to ten replicates of your design. When you replicate a design, you duplicate the complete set of runs from the initial design. The runs that would be added to a three-component simplex lattice design are as follows:

Initial design	One replicate added (total of two replicates)	Two replicates added (total of three replicates)
A B C	A B C	A B C
1 0 0	1 0 0	1 0 0
0 1 0	0 1 0	0 1 0
0 0 1	0 0 1	0 0 1
	1 0 0	**1 0 0**
	0 1 0	**0 1 0**
	0 0 1	**0 0 1**
		1 0 0
		0 1 0
		0 0 1

True replication provides an estimate of the error or noise in your process and may allow for more precise estimates of effects.

▶ **To replicate the design**

1 Choose Stat ➤ DOE ➤ Modify Design.

2 Choose **Replicate design** and click **Specify**.

3 From **Number of replicates to add**, choose a number up to ten. Click **OK**.

Randomizing the design

You can randomize the entire design or just randomize one of the blocks. For a general discussion of randomization, see page 21-19.

▶ **To randomize the design**

1 Choose **Stat ➤ DOE ➤ Modify Design**.

2 Choose **Randomize design** and click **Specify**.

3 Do one of the following:

- Choose **Randomize entire design**.

- Choose **Randomize just block**, and choose a block number from the list. (Mixture designs are not usually blocked.)

4 If you like, in **Base for random data generator**, enter a number. Click **OK**.

More | You can use **Stat ➤ DOE ➤ Display Design** (page 21-35) to switch back and forth between a random and standard order display in the worksheet.

Renumbering the design

You can renumber the design. MINITAB will renumber the RunOrder column based on the order of design points in the worksheet. This is especially useful if you have selected an optimal design (see Chapter 22, *Optimal Designs*) and you would like to renumber the design to determine an order in which to perform the experiment.

▶ **To renumber the design**

1 Choose **Stat ➤ DOE ➤ Modify Design**.

2   Choose **Renumber design** and click **OK**.

Displaying Designs

After you create a design, you can use Display Design to change the way the design points are stored in the worksheet. You can change the design points in two ways:

- display the points in either random and standard order. Run order is the order of the runs if the experiment was done in random order.

- express the components in amounts, proportions, or pseudocomponents.

- express process variables in coded or uncoded units.

▶ **To change the display order of points in the worksheet**

1   Choose Stat ➤ DOE ➤ Display Design.

2   Choose **Run order for the design** or **Standard order for the design**. If you do not randomize a design, the columns that contain the standard order and run order are the same.

3   Do one of the following:

- If you want to reorder all worksheet columns that are the same length as the design columns, click **OK**.

- If you have worksheet columns that you do not want to reorder:
    1 Click **Options**.
    2 In **Exclude the following columns when sorting**, enter the columns. These columns *cannot* be part of the design. Click **OK** in each dialog box.

Specifying the units for components

If you did not change the total for the mixture from the default value of one, MINITAB uses proportions to store your data. (This is equivalent to an amount total equal to one.) If you did change the total for the mixture, MINITAB uses amounts—what you actually measure—to express your data. Depending on the mixture total and the presence of constraints, you may want to represent the design in another scale.

You can choose one of three scales to represent the design: amounts, proportions, or pseudocomponents. With certain combinations of the mixture total and lower bound constraints, the various scalings are equivalent as shown in the following table:

Total mixture	Lower bounds	Equivalent scales
equal to 1	0	amounts proportions pseudocomponents
equal to 1	greater than 0	amounts proportions
not equal to 1	0	proportions pseudocomponents
not equal to 1	greater than 0	none

▶ **To change the units for the components**

1 Choose **Stat ➤ DOE ➤ Display Design**.

2 Choose **Amount**, **Proportions**, or **Pseudocomponents**. Click **OK**.

Pseudocomponents

Constrained designs (those in which you specify lower or upper bounds) produce coefficients which are highly correlated.

- Lower bounds are necessary when any of the components must be present in the mixture. For example, lemonade must contain lemon juice.

- Upper bounds are necessary when the mixture cannot contain more than a given proportion of an ingredient. For example, a cake mix cannot contain more than 5% baking powder.

Generally, you can reduce the correlations among the coefficients by transforming the components to pseudocomponents. For a complete discussion, see [1] and [3].

Pseudocomponents, in effect, rescale the constrained data area so the minimum allowable amount (the lower bound) of each component is zero. This makes a constrained design in pseudocomponents the same as an unconstrained design in proportions.

The table below shows two components expressed in amounts, proportions, and pseudocomponents. Suppose the total mixture is 50 ml. Let X1 and X2 be the amount scale. Thus X1 + X2 = 50. Suppose X1 has a lower bound of 20 (this means that the upper bound of X2 is 50 minus 20, or 30). Here are some points on the three scales:

Amounts		Proportions		Pseudocomponents	
X1	X2	X1	X2	X1	X2
50	0	1.0	0.0	1.0	0.0
20	30	0.4	0.6	0.0	1.0
35	15	0.7	0.3	0.5	0.5

Collecting and Entering Data

After you create your design, you need to perform the experiment and collect the response (measurement) data. To print a data collection form, follow the instructions below. After you collect the response data, enter the data in any worksheet column not used for the design. For a discussion of worksheet structure, see *Storing the design* on page 21-19.

Printing a data collection form

You can generate a data collection form in two ways. You can simply print the Data window contents, or you can use a macro. A macro can generate a "nicer" data collection form—see Help for more information. Although printing the Data window will not produce the prettiest form, it is the easiest method. Just follow these steps:

1 When you create your experimental design, MINITAB stores the run order, components, process variables, and amount variable in the worksheet. These columns constitute the basis of your data collection form. If you did not name components or process variables when you created the design, and you want names on the form, use Modify Design (page 21-31).

2 In the worksheet, name the columns in which you will record the measurement data obtained when you perform your experiment.

3 Choose **File ➤ Print Worksheet**. Make sure **Print Grid Lines** is checked. Click **OK**.

More | You can also copy the worksheet cells to the Clipboard by choosing **Edit ➤ Copy Cells**. Then paste the Clipboard contents into a word-processing application, such as Microsoft WordPad or Microsoft Word, where you can create your own form.

Analyzing Mixture Designs

To use Analyze Mixture Design, you must first create and store the design using Create Mixture Design, or create a design from data that you already have in the worksheet with Define Custom Mixture Design.

You can choose from six standard models (linear, quadratic, special cubic, full cubic, special quartic, or full quartic) or choose specific terms from a list of all estimable terms. See *Selecting model terms* on page 21-41 for details.

You can also select from four model fitting methods:

- mixture regression
- stepwise regression
- forward selection
- backward elimination

Data

Enter numeric response data column(s) that are equal in length to the design variables in the worksheet. Each row in the worksheet will contain the data for one run of your experiment. You may enter the response data in any columns not occupied by the design data. The number of columns reserved for the design data is dependent on the number of components in your design and whether or not you chose to store the design parameters (see *Storing the design* on page 21-19).

If there is more than one response variable, MINITAB fits separate models for each response.

MINITAB omits the rows containing missing data from all calculations.

Note | When all the response variables do not have the same missing value pattern, MINITAB displays a message. When the responses do not have the same missing value pattern, you may want to perform the analysis separately for each response because you would get different results than if you included them all in a single analysis.

▶ **To fit a mixture model**

1 Choose **Stat ➤ DOE ➤ Mixture ➤ Analyze Mixture Design**.

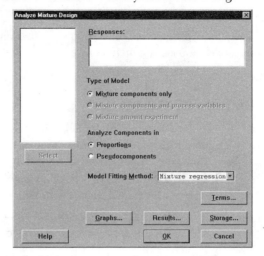

2 In **Responses**, enter up to 25 columns that contain the measurement data.

3 If you like, use any of the options listed below, then click **OK**.

Options

Analyze Mixture Design dialog box

- fit a model for mixture components only (default), or include process variables or amounts in the model. See *Mixture-amounts designs* on page 21-11 and *Mixture-process variable designs* on page 21-15 for more information.

- fit the model with the components expressed as proportions or pseudocomponents.

- choose from four model fitting methods: mixture regression (default), stepwise regression, forward selection, backward elimination.

Graphs subdialog box

- draw five different residual plots for regular, standardized, or deleted residuals — see *Choosing a residual type* on page 2-5. Available residual plots include a:
  - histogram.
  - normal probability plot.
  - plot of residuals versus the fitted values ($\hat{Y}$).
  - plot of residuals versus data order. The row number for each data point is shown on the x-axis (for example, 1 2 3 4... *n*).
  - separate plot for the residuals versus each specified column.

  For a discussion, see *Residual plots* on page 2-6.

Terms subdialog box

- fit a model by specifying the maximum order of the terms, or choose which terms to include from a list of all estimable terms—see *Selecting model terms* on page 21-41.

- include inverse component terms, process variable terms, or an amount term in the model. You cannot include inverse terms if the lower bound for any component is zero or if you choose to analyze the design in pseudocomponents.

Options subdialog box

- If you choose the stepwise model fitting method, you can
    - designate a set of predictor variables that *cannot* be removed from the model, even when their p-values are less than α to enter.
    - specify a starting set of predictor variables. These variables *are* removed if their p-values are greater than α to enter.
    - set the α-value for entering a new variable in the model.
    - set the α-value for removing a variable from the model.

- If you choose the forward selection model fitting method, you can
    - designate a set of predictor variables that *cannot* be removed from the model, even when their p-values are less than α to enter.
    - set the α-value for entering a new variable in the model.

- If you choose the backward elimination model fitting method, you can
    - designate a set of predictor variables that *cannot* be removed from the model, even when their p-values are less than α to enter.
    - set the α-value for removing a variable from the model.

- display the next best alternate predictors up to the number requested. If a new predictor is entered into the model, MINITAB displays the predictor which was the second best choice, the third best choice, and so on, up to the requested number.

Results subdialog box

- display the following in the Session window:
    - no results
    - model selection information, a table of coefficients, and the analysis of variance table
    - the default results, which includes model selection information, a table of coefficients, the analysis of variance table, and the unusual values in the table of fits and residuals
    - the default results, plus a table of all fits and residuals

Storage subdialog box

- store the fits, and regular, standardized, and deleted residuals separately for each response—see *Choosing a residual type* on page 2-5.

- store the coefficients for the model, the design matrix, and model terms separately for each response. The design matrix multiplied by the coefficients will yield the fitted values. Since Analyze Mixture Design does not allow a constant in the model, the design matrix does not contain a column of ones.

- store the leverages, Cook's distances, and DFITS, for identifying outliers—see *Identifying outliers* on page 2-9.

Selecting model terms

The model terms that are available depend on the type of mixture design. You can fit a model to a simple mixture design (components only), a mixture-process variable design (components and process variables), or a mixture-amounts design (components and amounts).

The order of the model you choose determines which terms are fit and whether or not you can model linear or curvilinear aspects of the response surface.

In the Terms subdialog box, you can choose a linear, quadratic, special cubic, full cubic model, special quartic, or full quartic model. Or, you can fit a model that is a subset of these terms. The following table summarizes these models. For a discussion of the various blending effects you can model, see [1].

This model type	fits these terms	and models this type of blending
linear (first-order)	linear	additive
quadratic (second-order)	linear and quadratic	additive nonlinear synergistic binary *or* additive nonlinear antagonistic binary
special cubic (third-order)	linear, quadratic, and special cubic	additive nonlinear synergistic ternary nonlinear antagonistic ternary
full cubic (third-order)	linear, quadratic, special cubic, and full cubic	additive nonlinear synergistic binary nonlinear antagonistic binary nonlinear synergistic ternary nonlinear antagonistic ternary

This model type	fits these terms	and models this type of blending
special quartic (fourth-order)	linear, quadratic, special cubic, full cubic, and special quartic	additive nonlinear synergistic binary nonlinear antagonistic binary nonlinear synergistic ternary nonlinear antagonistic ternary nonlinear synergistic quaternary nonlinear antagonistic quaternary
full quartic (fourth-order)	linear, quadratic, special cubic, full cubic, special quartic, and full quartic	additive nonlinear synergistic binary nonlinear antagonistic binary nonlinear synergistic ternary nonlinear antagonistic ternary nonlinear synergistic quaternary nonlinear antagonistic quaternary

You can fit inverse terms with any of the above models as long as the lower bound for any component is not zero and you choose to analyze the design in proportions. Inverse terms allow you to model extreme changes in the response as the proportion of one or more components nears its boundary. Suppose you are formulating lemonade and you are interested in the acceptance rating for taste. An extreme change in the acceptance of lemonade occurs when the proportion of sweetener goes to zero. That is, the taste becomes unacceptably sour.

Analyze Mixture Design fits a model without a constant term. For example, a quadratic in three components is as follows:

$$Y = b_1A + b_2B + b_3C + b_{12}AB + b_{13}AC + b_{23}BC$$

▶ **To specify the model**

1 In the Analyze Mixture Design dialog box, click **Terms**.

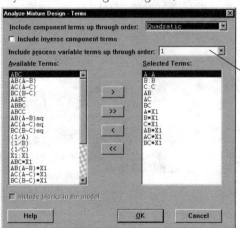

This option only displays when the mixture design contains process variables or amounts. The label changes depending on the variable type.

2 Do one of the following:

- from **Include the component terms up through order**, choose one of the following:

  linear, **quadratic**, **special cubic**, **full cubic**, **special quartic**, or **full quartic**

- move the terms you want to include in the model to **Selected Terms** using the arrow buttons
  - to move one or more terms, highlight the desired terms, then click ⬛◄ or ⬛►
  - to move all of the terms, click ⬛◄◄ or ⬛►►

  You can also move a term by double-clicking it.

Note | MINITAB represents components with the letters A, B, C, …, skipping the letter T, process variables with X1…Xn, and amounts with the letter T.

3 If you want to include inverse component terms, do one of the following:

- to include all the inverse component terms, check **Include inverse component terms**

- to include a subset of the inverse component terms, highlight the desired terms, then click ⬛►

4 If you want to include process variable or amount terms, do one of the following:

- from **Include process variables/mixture amount terms up through order**, and choose an order

- move terms you want to include in the model to **Selected Terms** using the arrow buttons
  - to move one or more terms, highlight the desired terms, then click ⬛◄ or ⬛►
  - to move all of the terms, click ⬛◄◄ or ⬛►►

  You can also move a term by double-clicking it.

☛ **Example of analyzing a simplex centroid design**

This example fits a model for the design created in *Example of a simplex centroid design* on page 21-20. Recall that you are trying determine how the proportions of the components in an herbal blend household deodorizer affect the acceptance of the product based on scent. The three components are neroli oil, rose oil, and tangerine oil. Based on the design points, you mixed ten blends. The response measure (Acceptance) is the mean of five acceptance scores for each of the blends.

1 Open the worksheet DEODORIZ.MTW.

2 Choose **Stat ➤ DOE ➤ Mixture ➤ Analyze Mixture Design**.

3 In **Responses**, enter *Acceptance*. Click **OK**.

Session window output

Regression for Mixtures: Acceptance versus Neroli, Rose, Tangerine

Estimated Regression Coefficients for Acceptance (component proportions)

Term	Coef	SE Coef	T	P	VIF
Neroli	5.856	0.4728	*	*	1.964
Rose	7.141	0.4728	*	*	1.964
Tangerin	7.448	0.4728	*	*	1.964
Neroli*Rose	1.795	2.1791	0.82	0.456	1.982
Neroli*Tangerin	5.090	2.1791	2.34	0.080	1.982
Rose*Tangerin	-1.941	2.1791	-0.89	0.423	1.982

S = 0.49023   PRESS = 11.440
R-Sq = 73.84%   R-Sq(pred) = 0.00%   R-Sq(adj) = 41.14%

Analysis of Variance for Acceptance (component proportions)

Source	DF	Seq SS	Adj SS	Adj MS	F	P
Regression	5	2.71329	2.71329	0.542659	2.26	0.225
Linear	2	1.04563	1.56873	0.784366	3.26	0.144
Quadratic	3	1.66766	1.66766	0.555887	2.31	0.218
Residual Error	4	0.96132	0.96132	0.240329		
Total	9	3.67461				

Interpreting the results

The magnitude of the coefficients for the three pure mixtures indicate that tangerine oil (7.448) and rose oil (7.141) produce deodorizers with higher acceptance levels than neroli oil (5.856).

Positive coefficients for two-blend mixtures indicate that the two components act synergistically or are complementary. That is, the mean acceptance score for the blend is greater than you would obtain by calculating the simple mean of the two acceptance scores for each pure mixture.

Negative coefficients indicate that the two components are antagonistic towards one another. That is, the mean acceptance score is lower than you would obtain by calculating the simple mean of the two acceptance scores.

The neroli oil by tangerine mixture is the only two-blend mixture that might be judged as significant (t = 2.34; p = 0.08).

For a general discussion of analysis results, see [1].

Displaying Factorial Plots

Factorial plots are available for process variables in a mixture design. You can produce three types of factorial plots to help you visualize process variable effects: main effects plots, interaction plots, and cube plots. These plots can be used to show how a response variable relates to one or more process variable.

These plots are described in Chapter 19, *Factorial Designs*. See *Displaying Factorial Plots* on page 19-53 for details.

Displaying Mixture Plots

You can produce three types of mixture plots to help you visualize effects:

- response trace plot—see *Response trace plots* on page 21-45
- contour plot—see *Contour and surface (wireframe) plots* on page 21-49
- surface (wireframe) plot—see *Contour and surface (wireframe) plots* on page 21-49

These plots show how a response variable relates to the design variables based on a model equation.

More | You can use a simplex design plot to visualize the mixture design space (or a slice of the design space if you have more than three components). MINITAB plots the design points on triangular axes. See *Displaying Simplex Design Plots* on page 21-24.

Data

Trace plots, contour plots, and surface plots are model dependent. Thus, you *must* fit a model using Analyze Mixture Design before you can display these plots. MINITAB looks in the worksheet for the necessary model information to generate these plots.

Response trace plots

A response trace plot (also called a component effects plot) shows the effect of each component on the response. Several response traces, which are a series of predictions from the fitted model, are plotted along a component direction. The trace curves show the effect of changing the corresponding component along an imaginary line (direction) connecting the reference blend to the vertex.

Each component in the mixture has a corresponding trace direction. The points along a trace direction of a component are connected thereby producing as many curves as there are components in the mixture.

Response trace plots are especially useful when there are more than three components in the mixture and the complete response surface cannot be visualized on a contour or surface plot. You can use the response trace plot to identify the most influential components and then use them for a contour or surface plot.

▶ **To display a response trace plot.**

1 Choose Stat ➤ DOE ➤ Mixture ➤ Response Trace Plot.

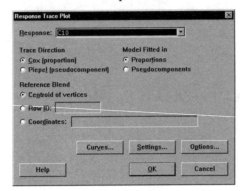

2 From **Response**, choose a response to plot. If an expected response is not in the list, fit a model to it with Analyze Mixture Design.

3 Click **OK**.

Options

Response Trace Plot dialog box

- specify the trace direction: Cox (proportion) or Piepel (pseudocomponent)—see *Component direction* on page 21-47

- specify the model units: proportions or pseudocomponents

- define the reference blend (the default is the centroid of the experimental region)

Curves subdialog box

- specify the line style and line color for the trace curves

Settings subdialog box

- specify hold values for process variables (the default is the low setting) and the amount variable (the default is the average amount)

Options subdialog box

- define minimum and maximum values for the x-axis and y-axis

- replace the default title with your own title

Component direction

When changing the proportion of a component in a mixture to determine its effect on a response, you must make offsetting changes in the other mixture components because the sum of the proportions must always be one. The changes in the component whose effect you are evaluating along with the offsetting changes in the other components can be thought of as a *direction* through the experimental region.

There are two commonly used trace directions along which the estimated responses are calculated: Cox's direction and Piepel's direction.

■ When the design is not constrained and the reference point lies at the centroid of the unconstrained experimental region, both Cox's directions and Piepel's directions are the axes of the simplex.

■ When the design is constrained, the default reference mixture point lies at the centroid of the constrained experimental region that is different than the centroid of the unconstrained experimental region. In this case, Cox's direction is defined in the original design space, whereas, Piepel's direction is defined in the L-pseudocomponent space.

▶ **Example of a response trace plot**

In the *Example of a simplex centroid design* on page 21-20, you created a design to study how the proportions of three ingredients (neroli oil, rose oil, and tangerine oil) in an herbal blend household deodorizer affect the acceptance of the product based on scent. Next, you analyzed the response (Acceptance) in the *Example of analyzing a simplex centroid design* on page 21-43. Now, to help you visualize the component effects, you display a response trace plot.

1 Open the worksheet DEODORIZ2.MTW.

2 Choose **Stat ➤ DOE ➤ Mixture ➤ Response Trace Plot**.

3 Click **Curves**.

4 Under **Line Styles**, choose **Use different types**. Click **OK** in each dialog box.

*Graph
window
output*

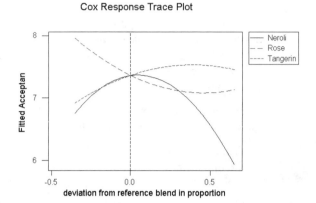

Interpreting the results

The trace plot shows how each component effects the response relative to the reference blend. In this example, the reference blend is the centroid of the design vertices. This trace plot provides the following information about the component effects. Starting at the location corresponding to the reference blend:

- As the proportion of neroli oil (solid curve) in the mixture
  - increases (and the other mixture components decrease), the acceptance rating of the deodorizer decreases
  - decreases (and the other mixture components increase), the acceptance rating of the deodorizer decreases

  The proportion of neroli oil in the reference blend is near optimal.

- As the proportion of rose oil (long-dashed curve) in the mixture
  - increases (and the other mixture components decrease), the acceptance rating of the deodorizer decreases slightly
  - decreases (and the other mixture components increase), the acceptance rating of the deodorizer increases

  A decrease in the proportion of rose oil relative to the reference blend may improve the acceptance rating.

- As the proportion of tangerine oil (short-dashed curve) in the mixture
  - increases (and the other mixture components decrease), the acceptance rating of the deodorizer increases slightly
  - decreases (and the other mixture components decrease), the acceptance rating of the deodorizer decreases

  An increase in the proportion of tangerine oil relative to the reference blend may improve the acceptance rating.

Keep the following in mind when you are interpreting a response trace plot:

- All components are interpreted relative to the reference blend.

- Components with the greatest effect on the response will have the steepest response traces.

- Components with larger ranges (upper bound – lower bound) will have longer response traces; components with smaller ranges will have shorter response traces.

- The total effect of a component depends on both the range of the component and the steepness of its response trace. The total effect is defined as the difference in the response between the effect direction point at which the component is at its upper bound and the effect direction point at which the component is at its lower bound.

- Components with approximately horizontal response traces, with respect to the reference blend, have virtually no effect on the response.

- Components with similar response traces will have similar effects on the response.

Contour and surface (wireframe) plots

In a contour plot, the response surface is viewed as a two-dimensional plane where all points that have the same response are connected to produce contour lines of constant responses. Contour plots are useful for establishing desirable response values and mixture blends.

A surface plot displays a three-dimensional view of the surface. Like contour plots, they are useful for establishing desirable response values and mixture blends. Surface plots may provide a clearer picture of the response surface. The illustrations below compare these two types of response surface plots.

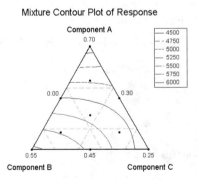

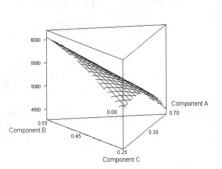

▶ **To plot the response surface**

1 Choose Stat ➤ DOE ➤ Mixture ➤ Contour/Surface (Wireframe) Plots.

2 Do one or both of the following:

- to generate a contour plot, check **Contour plot** and click **Setup**
- to generate a surface (wireframe) plot, check **Surface (wireframe) plot** and click **Setup**

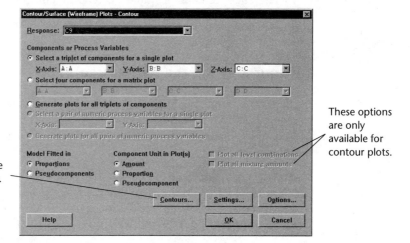

This button is labeled Wireframe for the Surface (wireframe) Plot.

These options are only available for contour plots.

3 From **Response**, choose a response to plot. If an expected response is not in the list, fit a model to it with Analyze Mixture Design.

4 If you like, use any of the options listed below, then click **OK**.

Options

Setup subdialog box

- select a triplet of components for a single plot
- display four contour plots in a single page layout
- generate plots for all triplets of components
- display plots for numeric process variables
- display the plot in amounts, proportions, or pseudocomponents

- for a single contour plot, include all the levels of the process variables in a single layout

- include an amount variable (by default, MINITAB will hold the amount variable at its first defined value)

Contours subdialog box

- for contour plots, specify the number or location of the contour levels, and the contour line color and style—see *Controlling the number, type, and color of the contour lines* on page 21-53

Wireframe subdialog box

- for surface (wireframe) plots, specify the color of the wireframe (mesh) and the surface

Settings subdialog box

- specify values for design variables that are not included in the plot—see *Settings for extra components, process variables, and an amount variable* below

Options subdialog box

- define minimum and maximum values for the x-axis, y-axis, and z-axis

- for contour plots, define the background grid or suppress grid lines

- for contour plots, suppress or display design points on the plot

- replace the default title with your own title

Settings for extra components, process variables, and an amount variable

You can set the holding level for components, and process variables that are not in the plot at their highest or lowest settings, or you can set specific levels to hold each. The hold values must be expressed in the following units:

- components in the *units displayed in the worksheet*

- process variables in *coded units*

Note | If you have text process variables in your design, you can only set their holding values at one of the text levels.

▶ **To set the holding level for design variables not in the plot**

1 In the Setup subdialog box, click **Settings**.

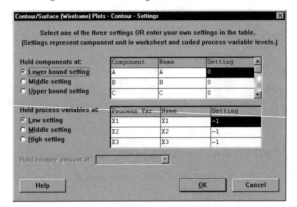

2 Do one or more of the following to set the holding values:

- For components (only available for design with more than three components):
   - To use the preset values for components, choose **Lower bound setting**, **Middle setting**, or **Upper bound setting** under **Hold components at**. When you use a preset value, *all* components not in the plot will be held at their lower bound, middle, or upper bound.
   - To specify the value at which to hold the components, enter a number in **Setting** for each component that you want to control. This option allows you to set a different holding value for each component.

- For process variables:
   - To use the preset values for process variables, choose **High setting** or **Low setting** under **Hold process variables at**. When you use a preset value, *all* variables not in the plot will be held at their high or low settings.
   - To specify the value at which to hold the process variables, enter a number in **Setting** for each of the process variables you want to control. This option allows you to set a different holding value for each process variable.

- For an amount variable:
   - In **Hold mixture amount at**, choose one of the mixture totals. MINITAB displays the multiple totals that you entered in the Components subdialog box when you were creating the design. The default hold value is the average of the multiple totals.

3 Click **OK**.

Controlling the number, type, and color of the contour lines

MINITAB displays from four to seven contour levels—depending on the data—by default. However, you can specify from 2 to 15 contour lines.

You can also change the line type and color of the lines.

▶ To control plotting of contour lines

1   In the **Contour/Surface (Wireframe) Plots** dialog box, check **Contour plot** and click **Setup**.

2   Click **Contours**.

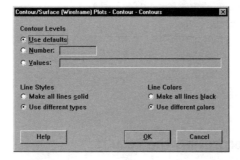

3   To change the number of contour lines, do one of the following:

  ■ Choose **Number** and enter a number from 2 to 15.

  ■ Choose **Values** and enter from 2 to 15 contour level values in the units of your data. You must enter the values in increasing order.

4   To define the line style, choose **Make all lines solid** or **Use different types** under **Line Styles**.

5   To define the line color, choose **Make all lines black** or **Use different colors** under **Line Colors**.

6   Click **OK**.

▷ Example of a contour plot and a surface plot

In the deodorizer example on page 21-43, you fit a model to try and determine how the proportions of the components in an herbal blend household deodorizer affect the acceptance of the product based on scent. The three components are neroli oil, rose oil, and tangerine oil. Based on the design points, you mixed ten blends. The response measure (Acceptance) is the mean of five acceptance scores for each of the blends.

Now you generate a contour and a surface plot to help identify the component proportions that yield the highest acceptance score for the herbal blend.

1   Open the worksheet DEODORIZ2.MTW.

2   Choose **Stat ➤ DOE ➤ Mixture ➤ Contour/Surface (Wireframe) Plots**.

3 Choose **Contour plot** and click **Setup**. Click **OK**.

4 Choose **Surface (wireframe) plot** and click **Setup**. Click **OK** in each dialog box.

*Graph
window
output*

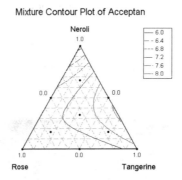

Mixture Contour Plot of Acceptan

Mixture Surface Plot of Acceptan

Interpreting the results

The area of the highest acceptance is located on the right edge of the plots. Both the contour and the surface plot show that the acceptance of the herbal deodorizer is highest when the mixture contains little or no rose oil and slightly more tangerine oil than neroli oil.

References

[1] J.A. Cornell (1990). Experiments With Mixtures: Designs, Models, and the Analysis of Mixture Data, John Wiley & Sons.

[2] D.C. Montgomery and S.R. Voth (1994). "Multicollinearity and Leverage in Mixture Experiments," Journal of Quality Technology 26, pp. 96–108.

[3] R.H Meyers and D.C. Montgomery (1995). Response Surface Methodology: Process and Product Optimization Using Designed Experiments, John Wiley & Sons.

[4] R. D. Snee and D. W. Marquardt (1974). "Extreme Vertices Designs for Linear Mixture Models," Technometrics 16 (3), pp. 399–408.

[5] R.C. St. John (1984). "Experiments With Mixtures in Conditioning and Ridge Regression," Journal of Quality Technology 16, pp.81–96.

Appendix for Mixture Designs

Triangular coordinate systems

Triangular coordinate systems allow you to visualize the relationships between the components in a three-component mixture. In a mixture, the components are restricted by one another in that the components must add up to the total amount or whole. Triangular coordinate systems in this section show the minimum of the x_1, x_2, and x_3 components as 0, with the maximums at 1.

The following illustration shows the general layout of a triangular coordinate system. The components in mixture models are referred to in terms of their proportion to the whole, with the whole as 1. The vertices of the triangle represent *pure* mixtures (also called single-component blends). In pure mixtures, the proportion of one component is 1 and the rest are 0.

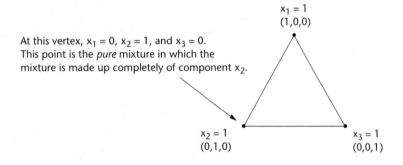

At this vertex, $x_1 = 0$, $x_2 = 1$, and $x_3 = 0$.
This point is the *pure* mixture in which the
mixture is made up completely of component x_2.

$x_1 = 1$
$(1,0,0)$

$x_2 = 1$
$(0,1,0)$

$x_3 = 1$
$(0,0,1)$

Any points along the edges of the triangle represent blends where one of the components is absent. The illustrations below show the location of different blends.

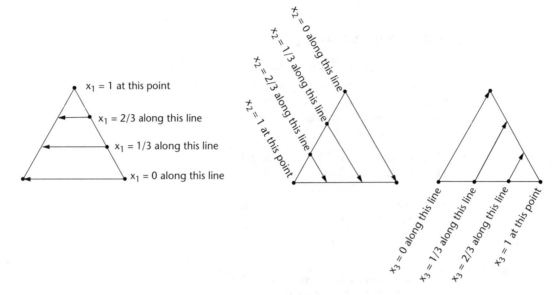

Now let's look at some points on the coordinate system.

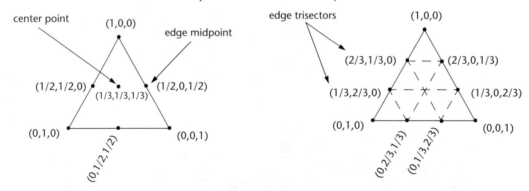

Each location on the triangles in the above illustrations represents a different blend of the mixture. For example,

- edge midpoints are two-blend mixtures in which one component makes up 1/2 and a second component makes up 1/2 of the mixture.

- edge trisectors are two-blend mixtures in which one component makes up 1/3 and another component makes up 2/3 of the mixture. These points divide the triangle edge into 3 equal parts.

- the center point (or centroid) is the complete mixture in which all components are present in equal proportions (1/3,1/3,1/3). Complete mixtures are on the interior of the design space and are mixtures in which all of the components are simultaneously present.

Calculation of design points

Simplex centroid designs

A *simplex centroid design* for a mixture with q components consists of $2^q - 1$ points. Design points are as follows:

- all points $(x_1, x_2, ..., x_q)$ where one component, $x_i = 1$, and the rest are 0. These are called vertex points.

- all points where one component, $x_i = 1/2$, another component, $x_j = 1/2$, and the rest are 0.

- all points where one component, $x_i = 1/3$, another component, $x_j = 1/3$, another component, $x_k = 1/3$, and the rest are 0.

- this pattern continues until all components are $1/q$. This last point (where all components are equal) is called the center or centroid of the design.

Simplex lattice designs

A *simplex lattice design* has q components (variables) of degree m. The degree m can be 1 to 10. MINITAB supports the following designs:

Degree of design (m)	Number of components (q)
1	2 to 20
2	2 to 20
3	2 to 17
4	2 to 11
5	2 to 8
6	2 to 7
7	2 to 6
8	2 to 5
9	2 to 5
10	2 to 5

Extreme vertices designs

MINITAB generates the extreme vertices of the constrained design space using the XVERT algorithm, and then calculates the centroid points up to the specified degree using Piepel's CONAEV algorithm. See [1] and [4] for details.

22

Optimal Designs

Optimal Designs Overview

The purpose of an optimal design is to select design points according to some criteria. MINITAB's optimal design capabilities can be used with response surface designs and mixture designs. You can use Select Optimal Design to

- select an "optimal" set of design points (described below)

- augment (add points to) an existing design—see *Augmenting or Improving a Design* on page 22-9

- improve the D-optimality of an existing design—see *Augmenting or Improving a Design* on page 22-9

- evaluate and compare designs—see *Evaluating a Design* on page 22-18

MINITAB provides two optimality criteria for the selection of design points:

- D-optimality—A design selected using this criterion minimizes the variance in the regression coefficients of the fitted model. You specify the model, then MINITAB selects design points that satisfy the D-optimal criterion from a set of candidate design points.

- distance-based optimality—A design selected using this criterion spreads the design points uniformly over the design space. The distance-based method can be used when it is not possible or desirable to select a model in advance.

Selecting an Optimal Design

Use the Select optimal design task to select design points from a candidate set to achieve an optimal design. This selection process is usually used to reduce the number of experimental runs. Often, a design as originally proposed contains more points than are feasible due to time or financial constraints. In the presence of such constraints, you may want to select a subset of design points in an "optimal" manner.

You can also use the Select optimal design task to obtain a D-optimal design where the number of design points in the final design is greater than the number of design points in the candidate set. For a distance-based design, the number of points in the final design must be less than or equal to the number of *distinct* points in the candidate set.

Data

The worksheet *must* contain a design generated by Create Response Surface Design, Define Custom Response Surface Design, Create Mixture Design, or Define Custom Mixture Design. For information on creating these designs, see Chapters 20 and 21.

The design columns in the worksheet comprise the candidate set of design points. For descriptions of a DOE worksheet, see *Storing the design* on page 20-11 and page 21-19.

▶ **To select an optimal design using D-optimality**

1 Choose Stat ➤ DOE ➤ Response Surface or Mixture ➤ Select Optimal Design.

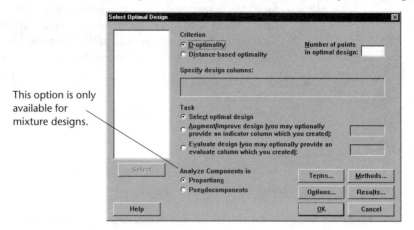

This option is only available for mixture designs.

2 Under **Criterion**, choose **D-optimality**. See *Method* on page 22-6 for a discussion.

3 In **Number of points in optimal design**, enter the number of points to be selected for the optimal design. You must select at least as many design points as there are terms in the model.

More | The feasible number of design points is dictated by various constraints (for example, time, budget, or ease of data collection). It is strongly recommended that you select more than the minimum number so you obtain estimates of pure error and lack-of-fit of the fitted model.

4 Under **Task**, choose **Select optimal design**.

5 Click **Terms**.

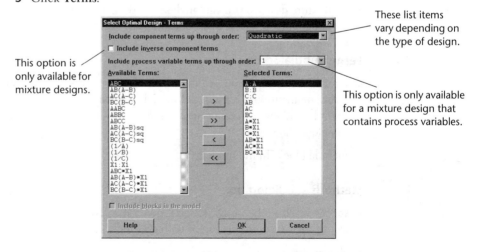

These list items vary depending on the type of design.

This option is only available for mixture designs.

This option is only available for a mixture design that contains process variables.

6 Do one of the following:

- from **Include the following terms**, choose the order of the model you want to fit:
  - for response surface designs, choose one of the following:
    linear, linear + squares, linear + interactions, or **full quadratic**
  - for mixture designs, choose one of the following:
    linear, quadratic, special cubic, full cubic, special quartic, or **full quartic**

- move the terms you want to include in the model to **Selected Terms** using the arrow buttons
  - to move one or more terms, highlight the desired terms, then click [<] or [>]
  - to move all of the terms, click [«] or [»]

  You can also move a term by double-clicking it.

7 Click **OK.**

Note | MINITAB represents factors and components with the letters A, B, C, ..., skipping the letter I for factors and the letter T for components. For mixture designs, process variables are represented by X1,...,Xn , and the amount variable by the letter T.

More | For more on specifying a response surface model, see *Selecting model terms* on page 20-29. For more information on specifying a mixture model, see *Selecting model terms* on page 21-41.

8 If you like, use one or more of the options listed below, then click **OK**.

Options

Select Optimal Design dialog box

- for mixture designs, you can analyze the design in proportions or pseudocomponents—see *Pseudocomponents* on page 21-36.

Terms subdialog box

- for mixture designs, you can include inverse component terms, process variable terms, or an amount term in the model. You cannot include inverse terms if the lower bound for any component is zero or if you choose to analyze the design in pseudocomponents.

- include blocks in the model.

Methods subdialog box

- specify whether the initial design is generated using a sequential or random algorithm, or a combination of both methods—see *Method* on page 22-6.

- choose the search procedure for improving the initial design—see *Method* on page 22-6.

Options subdialog box

- store a column (named OptPoint) in the original worksheet that indicates how many times a design point has been selected by the optimal procedure.

- store the design points that have been selected by the optimal procedure in a new worksheet.

- in addition to the design columns, store the rows of any non-design columns for the design points that were selected in a new worksheet.

Results subdialog box

- display the following Session window results:
  - no results
  - a summary table for the final design only
  - the default output, which includes summary tables for intermediate and final designs
  - the default output, plus the final design matrix

▶ **To select an optimal design using distance-based optimality**

1 Choose **Stat ➤ DOE ➤ Response Surface** or **Mixture ➤ Select Optimal Design**.

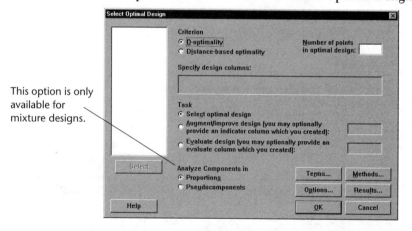

This option is only available for mixture designs.

2 Under **Criterion**, choose **Distance-based optimality**. See *Method* on page 22-6 for a discussion.

3 In **Number of points in optimal design**, enter the number of points to be included in the design. The number of points you enter must be less than or equal to the number of *distinct* design points in the candidate set.

4 In **Specify design columns**, delete the design columns that you do not want to include in the optimal design.

- For a response surface design, you can include all the factors or a subset of the factors.

- For a mixture design, you *must* include all components. You can also include all the process variables or a subset of the process variables, and an amount variable.

By default, MINITAB will include all input variables in the candidate design.

5 Under **Task**, choose **Select optimal design**.

6 If you like, use one or more of the options listed below, then click **OK**.

Options

Select Optimal Design dialog box

- for mixture designs, you can analyze the design in proportions or pseudocomponents — see *Pseudocomponents* on page 21-36

Options subdialog box

- store a column (named OptPoint) in the original worksheet that indicates how many times a design point has been selected by the optimal procedure

- store the design points that have been selected by the optimal procedure in a new worksheet

- in addition to the design columns, store the rows of any non-design columns for the design points that were selected in a new worksheet

Results subdialog box

- display the following Session window results:
  - no results
  - a summary table for the final design only
  - the default output, which includes summary tables for intermediate and final designs
  - the default output, plus the final design matrix

Method

There are two optimality criteria for MINITAB's select optimal design capability: D-optimality and distance-based optimality.

D-optimality

The D-optimality criterion minimizes the variance of the regression coefficients in the model. You specify the model, then MINITAB selects design points that satisfy the D-optimal criterion from a set of candidate points. The selection process consists of two steps:

- generating an *initial design*

- improving the initial design to obtain the *final design*

The design columns in the worksheet comprise the candidate set of design points. The two-step optimization process is summarized below.

1 MINITAB selects design points from the candidate set to obtain the *initial design*. You can choose which algorithm will be used to select these points in the Methods subdialog box. Choices include: sequential selection, random selection, or a combination of sequential and random selection.

By default, MINITAB selects all points sequentially.

2 MINITAB then tries to improve the initial design by adding and removing points to obtain the *final design* (referred to simply as the optimal design). You can choose the improvement method in the Methods subdialog box. Choices include:

- exchange method. MINITAB will first add the best points from the candidate set, and then drop the worst points until the D-optimality of the design cannot be improved further. You can specify the number of points to be exchanged in the Methods subdialog box.

- Fedorov's method. MINITAB will simultaneously switch pairs of points. This is accomplished by adding one point from the candidate set and dropping another point so that the switch results in maximum improvement in D-optimality. This process continues until the design cannot be improved further.

- suppress improvement of the initial design. In this case, the final design will be the same as the initial design.

By default, MINITAB improves the design by exchanging one point.

Candidate design points may be added with replacement to the final design during the optimization procedure. Therefore, the final design may contain duplicate design points.

Distance-based optimality

If you do not want to select a model in advance, a good strategy is to spread the design points uniformly over the design space. In this case, the distance-based method provides one solution for selecting the design points.

The distance-based optimality algorithm selects design points from the candidate set, such that the points are spread evenly over the design space. MINITAB selects the candidate point with the largest Euclidean distance from the origin (response surface design) or the point that is closest to a pure component (mixture design) as the starting point. Then, MINITAB adds additional design points in a stepwise manner such that each new point is as far as possible from the points already selected for the design.

There is no replacement and no replicates in distance-based designs.

▷ Example of selecting a D-optimal response surface design

Suppose you want to conduct an experiment to maximize crystal growth. You have determined that four variables—time the crystals are exposed to a catalyst, temperature in the exposure chamber, pressure within the chamber, and percentage of the catalyst in the air inside the chamber—explain much of the variability in the rate of crystal growth.

You generate the default central composite design for four factors and two blocks (the blocks represent the two days you conduct the experiment). This design, which contains 30 design points, serves as the candidate set for the D-optimal design.

Available resources restrict the number of design points that you can include in your experiment to 20. You want to obtain a D-optimal design which reduces the number of design points.

1 Open the worksheet OPTDES.MTW.

2 Choose **Stat ➤ DOE ➤ Response Surface ➤ Select Optimal Design**.

3 In **Number of points in optimal design**, type *20*.

4 Click **Terms**. Click **OK** in each dialog box.

Session window output

Optimal Design

Response surface design selected according to D-optimality

Number of candidate design points: 30   ⟵――――― A
Number of design points in optimal design: 20

Model terms

Block A B C D AA BB CC DD AB AC AD BC BD CD ⟵
                                                              ⟍ B

Initial design generated by Sequential method
                                                  ⎱
                                                   ├― C
Initial design improved by Exchange method   ⎰
Number of design points exchanged is 1

Optimal Design   D

Row number of selected design points:
    24   14   27   25   22   30   26   28   4   10   3   8   17   16   9
    21   1   5   6   19

      Condition number: 1.5138E+04 ⎫
      D-optimality   (determinant of XTX):   1.2622E+18 ⎪
      A-optimality   (trace of inv(XTX)):   5.9014E+03   ├ E
      G-optimality(ave leverage/max leverage):   0.8000   ⎪
      Maximum leverage: 1.0000   ⎪
      Average leverage: 0.8000   ⎭

Interpreting the results

The Session window output contains the following five parts:

A A summary of the D-optimal design that was obtained by selecting a subset of 20 points from a candidate set of 30 points.

B The model terms that you chose. D-optimal designs are dependent on the specified model. In this example, the terms include:
Block A B C D AA BB CC DD AB AC AD BC BD CD

These are the full quadratic model terms that were the default in the Terms subdialog box. Remember, a design that is D-optimal for one model will most likely not be D-optimal for another model.

C This section summarizes the method by which the initial design was generated and whether or not an improvement of the initial design was requested. In this example, the initial design was generated sequentially and the exchange method (using one design point) was used to improve the initial design.

D The selected design points in the order they were chosen. The numbers shown identify the row of the design points in the original worksheet.

Note | The design points that are selected depend on the row order of the points in the candidate set. Therefore, MINITAB may select a different optimal design from the same set of candidate points if they are in a different order. This can occur because there may be more than one D-optimal design for a given candidate set of points.

E MINITAB displays some *variance-minimizing* optimality measures. You can use this information to compare designs.

Augmenting or Improving a Design

If you have a response surface or a mixture design in your worksheet, you can augment the design by adding points to it or try to improve the D-optimality of the design. You can augment both D-optimal and distance-based designs, but you can only improve D-optimal designs.

Data

The worksheet *must* contain a design generated by Create Response Surface Design, Define Custom Response Surface Design, Create Mixture Design, or Define Custom Mixture Design. For information on creating these designs, see Chapters 20 and 21.

The design columns in the worksheet comprise the candidate set of design points. For descriptions of a DOE worksheet, see *Storing the design* on page 20-11 and page 21-19.

In addition to the design columns, you may also have a column that indicates how many times a design point is to be included in the initial design, and whether a point must be kept in (protected) or may be omitted from the final design. See below for more information.

Design indicator column

There are two ways that you can define the initial design. You can use all of the rows of the design columns in the worksheet or you can create an indicator column to specify certain rows to include in the initial design. In addition, you can use this column to "protect" design points during the optimization process. If you protect a point, MINITAB will not drop this design point from the final design. The indicator column can contain any positive or negative integers.

MINITAB interprets the indicators as follows:

- the magnitude of the indicator determines the number of replicates of the corresponding design point in the initial design

- the sign of the indicator determines whether or not the design point will be protected during the optimization process
    - a positive sign indicates that the design point *may be excluded* from the final design
    - a negative sign indicates that the design point *may not be excluded* from the final design

▶ To augment or improve a D-optimal design

1 Choose Stat ➤ DOE ➤ Response Surface or Mixture ➤ Select Optimal Design.

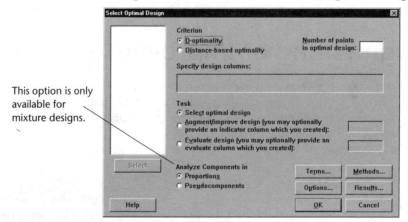

This option is only available for mixture designs.

2 Under **Criterion**, choose **D-optimality**. See *Method* on page 22-6 for a discussion.

3 Under **Task**, choose **Augment/improve design**. If you have a design point indicator column, enter this column in the box. See *Design indicator column* on page 22-10.

4 Do one of the following:

- To augment (add points) a design, in **Number of points in optimal design**, enter the number of points to be included in the final design. The number of points you enter must be greater than the number of points in the design you are augmenting.

- To improve a design's D-optimality but not add any additional points, in **Number of points in optimal design**, enter 0. In this case, the final design will have the same number of design points as the initial design.

5 Click **Terms**.

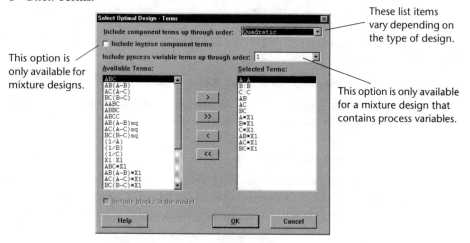

These list items vary depending on the type of design.

This option is only available for mixture designs.

This option is only available for a mixture design that contains process variables.

6 Do one of the following:

- from **Include the following terms**, choose the order of the model you want to fit:
  - for response surface designs, choose one of the following:
    linear, linear + squares, linear + interactions, or **full quadratic**
  - for mixture designs, choose one of the following:
    linear, quadratic, special cubic, full cubic, special quartic, or **full quartic**

- move the terms you want to include in the model to **Selected Terms** using the arrow buttons
  - to move one or more terms, highlight the desired terms, then click [<] or [>]
  - to move all of the terms, click [<<] or [>>]

  You can also move a term by double-clicking it.

7 Click **OK**.

Note | MINITAB represents factors and components with the letters A, B, C, ..., skipping the letter I for factors and the letter T for components. For mixture designs, process variables are represented by X1,...,Xn , and the amount variable by the letter T.

More | For more on specifying a response surface model, see *Selecting model terms* on page 20-29. For more information on specifying a mixture model, see *Selecting model terms* on page 21-41.

8 If you like, use one or more of the options listed below, then click **OK**.

Options

Select Optimal Design dialog box

- for mixture designs, you can analyze the design in proportions or pseudocomponents—see *Pseudocomponents* on page 21-36

Terms subdialog box

- for mixture designs, you can include inverse component terms, process variable terms, or an amount term in the model. You cannot include inverse terms if the lower bound for any component is zero or if you choose to analyze the design in pseudocomponents.

- include blocks in the model

Methods subdialog box

- choose the search procedure for improving the initial design—see *Method* on page 22-14

Options subdialog box

- store a column (named OptPoint) in the original worksheet that indicates how many times a design point has been selected by the optimal procedure

- store the design points that have been selected by the optimal procedure in a new worksheet

- in addition to the design columns, store the rows of any non-design columns for the design points that were selected in a new worksheet

Results subdialog box

- display the following Session window results:
  - no results

– a summary table for the final design only
– the default output, which includes summary tables for intermediate and final designs
– the default output, plus the final design matrix

▶ To augment a distance-based optimal design

1 Choose **Stat ➤ DOE ➤ Response Surface** or **Mixture ➤ Select Optimal Design**.

This option is only available for mixture designs.

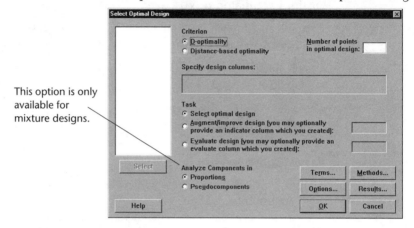

2 Under **Criterion**, choose **Distance-based optimality**. See *Method* on page 22-6 for a discussion.

3 In **Number of points in optimal design**, enter the number of points to be in the final design. The number of points you enter must be greater than the number of points in the initial design but not greater then the number of "distinct" points in the candidate set.

4 In **Specify design columns**, delete the design columns that you do not want to include in the optimal design.

- For a response surface design, you can include all the factors or a subset of the factors.

- For a mixture design, you *must* include all components. You can also include all the process variables or a subset of the process variables, and an amount variable.

By default, MINITAB will include all design variables in the candidate design.

5 Under **Task**, choose **Augment/improve design**. If you have a design point indicator column, enter this column in the box. See *Design indicator column* on page 22-10.

6 If you like, use one or more of the options listed below, then click **OK**.

Options

Select Optimal Design dialog box

- for mixture designs, you can analyze the design in proportions or pseudocomponents—see *Pseudocomponents* on page 21-36

Options subdialog box

- store a column (named OptPoint) in the original worksheet that indicates how many times a design point has been selected by the optimal procedure
- store the design points that have been selected by the optimal procedure in a new worksheet
- in addition to the design columns, store the rows of any non-design columns for the design points that were selected in a new worksheet

Results subdialog box

- display the following Session window results:
  - no results
  - a summary table for the final design only
  - the default output, which includes summary tables for intermediate and final designs
  - the default output, plus the final design matrix

Method

There are two optimality criteria for MINITAB's augment/improve optimal design capability: D-optimality and distance-based optimality.

D-optimality

The D-optimality criterion minimizes the variance of the regression coefficients in the model. You specify the model, then MINITAB selects design points that satisfy the D-optimal criterion from a set of candidate points. The selection process consists of two steps:

- generating an *initial design*
- improving the initial design to obtain the *final design*

The design columns in the worksheet make up the candidate set of design points. The two-step optimization process is summarized below.

1 The initial design can be obtained in one of two ways:

■ You can use all the design points in the worksheet for the *initial design*.

■ You can use an indicator column to specify which design points and how many replicates of each point comprise the *initial design*. For information on the structure of this indicator column, see *Design indicator column* on page 22-10.

If you are augmenting the design, MINITAB adds the "best" points in the candidate set sequentially.

2 MINITAB then tries to improve the initial design by adding and removing points to obtain the *final design* (referred to simply as the optimal design). You can choose the improvement method in the Methods subdialog box. Choices include:

■ exchange method. MINITAB will first add the best points from the candidate set, and then drop the worst points until the D-optimality of the design cannot be improved further. You can specify the number of points to be exchanged in the Methods subdialog box.

■ Fedorov's method. MINITAB will simultaneously switch pairs of points. This is accomplished by adding one point from the candidate set and dropping another point so that the switch results in maximum improvement in D-optimality. This process continues until the design cannot be improved further.

■ suppress improvement of the initial design. In this case, the final design will be the same as the initial design.

By default, MINITAB improves the design by exchanging one point.

Candidate design points may be added with replacement to the final design during the optimization procedure. Therefore, the final design may contain duplicate design points.

Tip | In numerical optimization, there is always a danger of finding a local optimum instead of the global optimum. To avoid finding a local optimum, you could perform multiple trials of the optimization procedure starting from different initial designs. MINITAB will identify the design with the highest D-optimality, and for this design

■ create an indicator column (OptPoint) in the original worksheet that shows whether or not a point was selected and the number of replicates of that design point

■ copy the selected design points to a new worksheet

There is only one trial possible if you generate the initial design by purely sequential selection or if you specify the initial design with an indicator column.

Distance-based optimality

If you do not want to select a model in advance, a good strategy is to spread the design points uniformly over the design space. In this case, the distance-based method provides one solution for selecting the design points.

The distance-based optimality algorithm selects design points from a candidate set, such that the points are spread evenly over the design space. You may choose to begin the optimization from all the design points in the candidate set or just points that you specify with an indicator column. If you begin with the entire candidate set, MINITAB selects the candidate point with the largest Euclidean distance from the origin (response surface design) or the point that is closest to a pure component (mixture design) as the starting point. Then, MINITAB adds additional design points in a stepwise manner such that each new point is as far as possible from the points already selected for the design.

There is no replacement and no replicates in distance-based designs.

▶ Example of augmenting a D-optimal design

In the *Example of selecting a D-optimal response surface design* on page 22-8, you selected a subset of 20 design points from a candidate set of 30 points. After you collected the data for the 20 selected design points, you found out that you could run five additional design points. Because you already collected the data for the original design, you need to protect these points in the augmented design so they can not be excluded during the augmentation/optimization procedure. To protect these points, you need to have negative indicators for the design points that were already selected for the first optimal design.

1 Open the worksheet OPTDES2.MTW. (The design and indicator column have been saved for you.)

2 Choose **Stat ➤ DOE ➤ Response Surface ➤ Select Optimal Design**.

3 Choose **Augment/improve design** and type *OptPoint* in the box.

4 In **Number of points in optimal design**, type *25*.

5 Click **Terms**. Click **OK** in each dialog box.

Session window output

Optimal Design

Response surface design augmented according to D-optimality

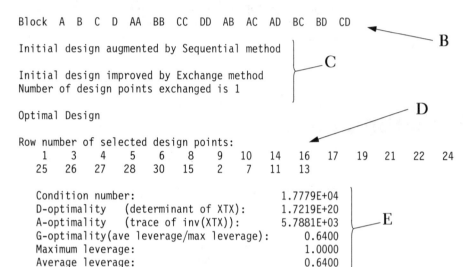

Number of candidate design points: 30
Number of design points to augment/improve: 20 ← A
Number of design points in optimal design: 25

Model terms

Block A B C D AA BB CC DD AB AC AD BC BD CD ← B

Initial design augmented by Sequential method
                                                    C
Initial design improved by Exchange method
Number of design points exchanged is 1

Optimal Design
                                                    D
Row number of selected design points:
   1   3   4   5   6   8   9   10   14   16   17   19   21   22   24
  25   26   27   28   30   15   2   7   11   13

      Condition number: 1.7779E+04
      D-optimality   (determinant of XTX):   1.7219E+20
      A-optimality   (trace of inv(XTX)):   5.7881E+03 E
      G-optimality(ave leverage/max leverage):   0.6400
      Maximum leverage: 1.0000
      Average leverage: 0.6400

Interpreting the results

The Session window output contains the following five parts:

A A summary of the D-optimal design that was obtained by augmenting a design with containing 20 points by adding 5 more design points. The candidate set contains 30 design points.

B The model terms that you chose. D-optimal designs depend on the specified model. In this example, the terms include:
Block A B C D AA BB CC DD AB AC AD BC BD CD

These full quadratic model terms are the default in the Terms subdialog box. Remember, a design that is D-optimal for one model will most likely not be D-optimal for another model.

C This section summarizes the method by which the initial design was augmented and whether or not an improvement of the initial design was requested. In this example, two design points were added sequentially and the exchange method (using one design point) was used to improve the initial design.

D The selected design points in the order they were chosen. The numbers shown identify the row of the design points in the worksheet.

Note The design points that are selected depend on the row order of the points in the candidate set. Therefore, MINITAB may select a different optimal design from the same candidate points if they are in a different order. This can occur because there may be more than one D-optimal design for a given candidate set of points.

E MINITAB displays some *variance-minimizing* optimality measures. You can use this information to compare designs. You can use this information to compare designs. For example, if you compare the optimality of the original 20 point design shown on page 22-8 with this 25 point design, you will notice that the D-optimality increased from 1.2622E+18 to 1.7219E+20.

Evaluating a Design

If you have a response surface or a mixture design in your worksheet, you can evaluate this design. MINITAB will display a number of optimality statistics. You can use this information to compare designs or to evaluate changes in the optimality of a design if you change the model.

For example, recall that a design that is D-optimal for a specific model only. Suppose you generated a D-optimal design for a certain model, but then decided to fit a model with different terms. You can determine the change in optimality using the Evaluate design task.

Data

The worksheet *must* contain a design generated by Create Response Surface Design, Define Custom Response Surface Design, Create Mixture Design, or Define Custom Mixture Design. For information on creating these designs, see Chapters 20 and 21.

In addition to the design columns, you may also have a column that indicates how many times a design point is to be included in the evaluation. This column must contain only positive integers. See below for more information.

Design indicator column

There are two ways that you can define the design you want to evaluate. You can use all of the rows of the design columns in the worksheet or you can create an indicator column to specify certain rows to include in the design. The magnitude of the indicator determines the number of replicates of the corresponding design point.

▶ **To evaluate a design**

1 Choose Stat ➤ DOE ➤ Response Surface or Mixture ➤ Select Optimal Design.

This option is only
available for
mixture designs.

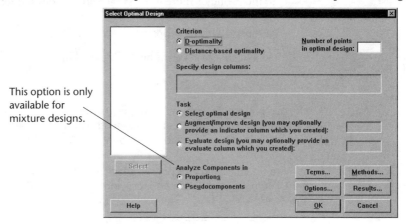

2 Under **Task**, choose **Evaluate design**. If you have an indicator column that defines
the design, enter the column in the box. See *Design indicator column* above.

3 Click **Terms**.

These list items
vary depending on
the type of design.

This option is
only available for
mixture designs.

This option is only available
for a mixture design that
contains process variables.

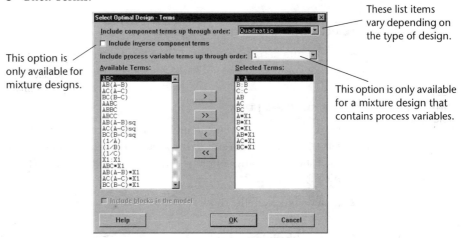

4 Do one of the following:

■ from **Include the component terms up through order**, choose the order of the
model you want to fit:
  – for response surface designs, choose one of the following:
    linear, linear + squares, linear + interactions, or **full quadratic**
  – for mixture designs, choose one of the following:
    linear, quadratic, special cubic, full cubic, special quartic, or **full quartic**

- move the terms you want to include in the model to **Selected Terms** using the arrow buttons
    - to move one or more terms, highlight the desired terms, then click ![<] or ![>]
    - to move all of the terms, click ![<<] or ![>>]

    You can also move a term by double-clicking it.

5   Click **OK**.

Note | MINITAB represents factors and components with the letters A, B, C, ..., skipping the letter I for factors and the letter T for components. For mixture designs, process variables are represented by X1,...,Xn , and the amount variable by the letter T.

More | For more on specifying a response surface model, see *Selecting model terms* on page 20-29. For more information on specifying a mixture model, see *Selecting model terms* on page 21-41.

6   If you like, use one or more of the options listed below, then click **OK**.

Options

Select Optimal Design dialog box

- for mixture designs, you can analyze the design in proportions or pseudocomponents—see *Pseudocomponents* on page 21-36

Terms subdialog box

- for mixture designs, you can include inverse component terms, process variable terms, or an amount term in the model. You cannot include inverse terms if the lower bound for any component is zero or if you choose to analyze the design in pseudocomponents.

- include blocks in the model.

Options subdialog box

- store the selected design points in a new worksheet

- in addition to the design columns, store the rows of any non-design columns for the selected design points in a new worksheet

Results subdialog box

- display the following Session window results:
    - no results
    - a summary table for the final design only

– the default output, which includes summary tables for intermediate and final designs
– the default output, plus the final design matrix

▷ Example of evaluating a design

Suppose you want determine how reducing the model changes the optimality for the 20 point experimental design obtained in the *Example of selecting a D-optimal response surface design* on page 22-8. Remember that a model that is D-optimal for a given model only.

1 Open the worksheet OPTDES3.MTW. (The design and indicator column have been saved for you.)

2 Choose **Stat ➤ DOE ➤ Response Surface ➤ Select Optimal Design**.

3 Choose **Evaluate design** and type *OptPoint* in the box.

4 Click **Terms**.

5 From **Include the following terms**, choose **Linear**.

6 Click **OK** in each dialog box.

Session window output

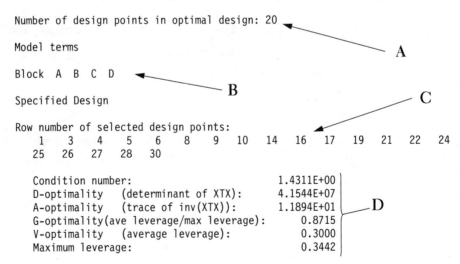

Optimal Design

Evaluation of Specified Response Surface Design

Number of design points in optimal design: 20 ⟵

Model terms   **A**

Block A B C D ⟵

Specified Design   **B**

                                                              C

Row number of selected design points:
    1   3   4   5   6   8   9   10   14   16   17   19   21   22   24
   25   26   27   28   30

    Condition number: 1.4311E+00 ⎤
    D-optimality   (determinant of XTX):   4.1544E+07 ⎥
    A-optimality   (trace of inv(XTX)):   1.1894E+01 ⎥ **D**
    G-optimality(ave leverage/max leverage):   0.8715 ⎥
    V-optimality   (average leverage):   0.3000 ⎥
    Maximum leverage: 0.3442 ⎦

Interpreting the results

The Session window output contains the following four parts:

A The number of points in the design.

B The model terms that you chose. D-optimal designs depend on the specified model. In this example, the terms include:

`Block A B C D`

These are the linear model terms that you chose in the Terms subdialog box. Remember, a design that is D-optimal for one model will most likely not be D-optimal for another model.

C The selected design points. The numbers shown identify the row of the design points in the worksheet.

D In addition to the design's D-optimality, MINITAB displays various optimality measures. You can use this information to evaluate or compare designs. If you compare the optimality of the 20 point design for a full quadratic model shown on page 22-8 with this 20 point design for a linear model, you will notice that the D-optimality increased from 1.2622E+18 to 4.1544E+07.

References

[1] A.C. Atkinson, A.N. Donev (1992). *Optimum Experimental Designs*, Oxford Press.

[2] G.E.P. Box and N.R. Draper (1987). *Empirical Model-Building and Response Surfaces*, John Wiley & Sons. p.249.

[3] A.I. Khuri and J.A. Cornell (1987). *Response Surfaces: Designs and Analyses*, Marcel Dekker, Inc.

[4] R.H Meyers and D.C. Montgomery (1995). Response Surface Methodology: Process and Product Optimization Using Designed Experiments, John Wiley & Sons.

23

Response Optimization

Response Optimization Overview

Many designed experiments involve determining optimal conditions that will produce the "best" value for the response. Depending on the design type (factorial, response surface, or mixture), the operating conditions that you can control may include one or more of the following design variables: factors, components, process variables, or amount variables.

For example, in product development, you may need to determine the input variable settings that result in a product with desirable properties (responses). Since each property is important in determining the quality of the product, you need to consider these properties simultaneously. For example, you may want to increase the yield and decrease the cost of a chemical production process. Optimal settings of the design variables for one response may be far from optimal or even physically impossible for another response. Response optimization is a method that allows for compromise among the various responses.

MINITAB provides two commands to help you identify the combination of input variable settings that jointly optimize a set of responses. These commands can be used after you have created and analyzed factorial designs, response surface designs, and mixture designs.

- **Response Optimizer** provides you with an optimal solution for the input variable combinations and an optimization plot. The optimization plot is interactive; you can adjust input variable settings on the plot to search for more desirable solutions.

- **Overlaid Contour Plot** shows how each response considered relates to two continuous design variables (factorial and response surface designs) or three continuous design variables (mixture designs), while holding the other variables in the model at specified levels. The contour plot allows you to visualize an area of compromise among the various responses.

Response Optimization

You can use MINITAB's Response Optimizer to help identify the combination of input variable settings that jointly optimize a single response or a set of responses. Joint optimization must satisfy the requirements for all the responses in the set. The overall desirability (D) is a measure of how well you have satisfied the combined goals for all the responses. Overall desirability has a range of zero to one. One represents the ideal case; zero indicates that one or more responses are outside their acceptable limits.

MINITAB calculates an optimal solution and draws a plot. The optimal solution serves as the starting point for the plot. This optimization plot allows you to interactively change the input variable settings to perform sensitivity analyses and possibly improve the initial solution.

Note | Although numerical optimization along with graphical analysis can provide useful information, it is not a substitute for subject matter expertise. Be sure to use relevant background information, theoretical principles, and knowledge gained through observation or previous experimentation when applying these methods.

Data

Before you use MINITAB's Response Optimizer, you must

1 Create and store a design using one of MINITAB's Create Design commands or create a design from data that you already have in the worksheet with Define Custom Design.

Command	on page...
Create Factorial Design	19-6, 19-24
Create Response Surface Design	20-4
Create Mixture Design	21-5
Define Custom Factorial Design	19-35
Define Custom Response Surface Design	20-19
Define Custom Mixture Design	21-28

2 Enter up to 25 numeric response columns in the worksheet.

3 Fit a model for each response using one of the following:

Command	on page...
Analyze Factorial Design	19-44
Analyze Response Surface Design	20-26
Analyze Mixture Design	21-38

Note | Response Optimization is not available for general full factorial designs.

You can fit a model with different design variables for each response. If an input variable was not included in the model for a particular response, the optimization plot for that response-input variable combination will be blank.

MINITAB automatically omits missing data from the calculations. If you optimize more than one response and there are missing data, MINITAB excludes the row with missing data from calculations for all of the responses.

▶ **To optimize responses**

1 Choose **Stat ➤ DOE ➤ Factorial, Response Surface,** or **Mixture ➤ Response Optimizer**.

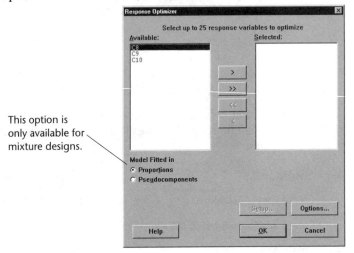

This option is only available for mixture designs.

2 Move up to 25 responses that you want to optimize from **Available** to **Selected** using the arrow buttons. (If an expected response column does not show in **Available**, fit a model to it using Analyze Factorial Design, Analyze Response Surface Design, or Analyze Mixture Design.)

- to move responses one at a time, highlight a response, then click ⬛ or ⬛
- to move all the responses at once, click ⬛ or ⬛

You can also move a response by double-clicking it.

3 Click **Setup**.

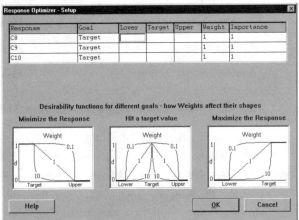

4 For each response, complete the table as follows:

- Under **Goal**, choose **Minimize**, **Target**, or **Maximize** from the drop-down list.
- Under **Lower**, **Target**, and **Upper**, enter numeric values for the target and necessary bounds as follows:

    1 If you choose **Minimize** under **Goal**, enter values in **Target** and **Upper**.

    2 If you choose **Target** under **Goal**, enter values in **Lower**, **Target**, and **Upper**.

    3 If you choose **Maximize** under **Goal**, enter values in **Target** and **Lower**.

    For guidance on choosing bounds, see *Specifying bounds* on page 23-7.

- In **Weight**, enter a number from 0.1 to 10 to define the shape of the desirability function. See *Setting the weight for the desirability function* on page 23-8.
- In **Importance**, enter a number from 0.1 to 10 to specify the relative importance of the response. See *Specifying the importance for composite desirability* on page 23-10.

4 Click **OK**.

5 If you like, use any of the options listed below, then click **OK**.

Options

Response Optimizer dialog box

- for mixture designs, refit the model in proportions or psuedocomponents.

Options subdialog box

- define a starting point for the search algorithm by providing a value for each input variable in your model. Each value must be between the minimum and maximum levels for that input variable.
- for factorial designs, define settings at which to hold any covariates that are in the model.
- suppress display of the multiple response optimization plot.
- store the composite desirability values.
- display local solutions.

Response optimization plot

- adjust input variable settings interactively. You can also
    - save new input variable settings
    - delete saved input variable settings
    - reset optimization plot to initial or optimal settings
    - view a list of all saved settings
    - for mixture designs, lock component values

    See *Using the optimization plot* on page 23-10.

Method

MINITAB's Response Optimizer searches for a combination of input variable levels that jointly optimize a set of responses by satisfying the requirements for each response in the set. The optimization is accomplished by

1 obtaining the individual desirability (d) for each response

2 combining the individual desirabilities to obtain the combined or composite desirability (D)

3 maximizing the composite desirability and identifying the optimal input variable settings

Note | If you have only one response, the overall desirability is equal to the individual desirability.

Obtaining individual desirability

First, MINITAB obtains an individual desirability (d) for each response using the goals and boundaries that you provide in the Setup subdialog box. There are three goals to choose from. You may want to:

■ minimize the response (smaller is better)

■ target the response (target is best)

■ maximize the response (larger is better)

Suppose you have a response that you want to minimize. You need to determine a target value and an allowable maximum response value. The desirability for this response below the target value is one; above the maximum acceptable value the desirability is zero. The closer the response is to the target, the closer the desirability is to one. The illustration below shows the default desirability function (also called utility transfer function) used to determine the individual desirability (d) for a "smaller is better" goal:

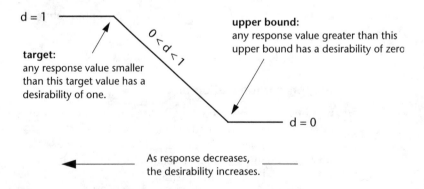

d = desirability

d = 1

target:
any response value smaller than this target value has a desirability of one.

0 < d < 1

upper bound:
any response value greater than this upper bound has a desirability of zero

d = 0

As response decreases, the desirability increases.

The shape of the desirability function between the upper bound and the target is determined by the choice of weight. The illustration above shows a function with a weight of one. To see how changing the weight affects the shape of the desirability function, see *Setting the weight for the desirability function* on page 23-8.

Obtaining the composite desirability

After MINITAB calculates an individual desirability for each response, they are combined to provide a measure of the composite, or overall, desirability of the multi-response system. This measure of composite desirability (D) is the weighted geometric mean of the individual desirabilities for the responses. The individual desirabilities are weighted according to the importance that you assign each response. For a discussion, see *Specifying the importance for composite desirability* on page 23-10.

Maximizing the composite desirability

Finally, MINITAB employs a reduced gradient algorithm with multiple starting points that maximizes the composite desirability to determine the numerical optimal solution (optimal input variable settings).

More | You may want to fine tune the solution by adjusting the input variable settings using the interactive optimization plot. See *Using the optimization plot* on page 23-10.

Specifying bounds

In order to calculate the numerical optimal solution, you need to specify a target and lower and/or upper bounds for each reponse. The boundaries needed depend on your goal:

- If your goal is to *minimize* (smaller is better) the response, you need to determine a target value and the upper bound. You may want to set the target value at the point of diminishing returns, that is, although you want to minimize the response, going below a certain value makes little or no difference. If there is no point of diminishing returns, use a very small number, one that is probably not achievable, for the target value.

- If your goal is to *target* the response, you probably have upper and lower specification limits for the response that can be used as lower and upper bounds.

- If your goal is to *maximize* (larger is better) the response, you need to determine a target value and the lower bound. Again, you may want to set the target value at the point of diminishing returns, although now you need a value on the upper end instead of the lower end of the range.

Setting the weight for the desirability function

In MINITAB's approach to optimization, each of the response values are transformed using a specific desirability function. The weight defines the shape of the desirability function for each response. For each response, you can select a weight (from 0.1 to 10) to emphasize or de-emphasize the target. A weight

- less than 1 (minimum is 0.1) places less emphasis on the target

- equal to 1 places equal importance on the target and the bounds

- greater than 1 (maximum is 10) places more emphasis on the target

The illustrations below show how the shape of the desirability function changes when the goal is to maximize the response changes depending on the weight:

Weight	Desirability function

d = desirability

0.1

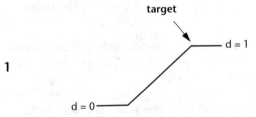

A weight less than 1 places less emphasis on the target. A response value far from the target may have a high desirability.

1

A weight equal to 1 places equal emphasis on the target and the bounds. The desirability for a response increases linearly.

10

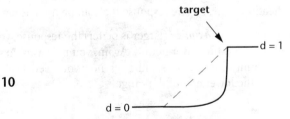

A weight greater than 1 places more emphasis on the target. A response value must be very close to the target to have a high desirability.

The illustrations below summarize the desirability functions:

When the goal is to ...

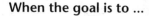

minimize the response

Below the target, the
response desirability is
1; above the upper
bound, it is 0.

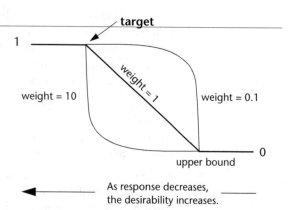

target the response

Below the lower bound,
the response desirability is 0;
at the target, it is 1; above
the upper bound, it
is 0.

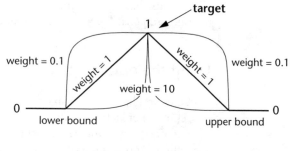

maximize the response

Below the lower bound,
the response desirability
is 0; above the target,
it is 1.

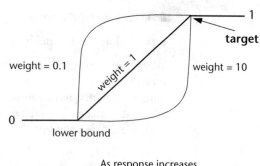

Specifying the importance for composite desirability

After MINITAB calculates individual desirabilities for the responses, they are combined to provide a measure of the composite, or overall, desirability of the multi-response system. This measure of composite desirability is the weighted geometric mean of the individual desirabilities for the responses. The optimal solution (optimal operating conditions) can then be determined by maximizing the composite desirability.

You need to assess the importance of each response in order to assign appropriate values. Importance values must be between 0.1 and 10. If all responses are equally important, use the default value of 1.0 for each response. The composite desirability is then the geometric mean of the individual desirabilities.

However, if some responses are more important than others, you can incorporate this information into the optimal solution by setting unequal importance values. Larger values correspond to more important responses, smaller values to less important responses.

You can also change the importance to determine how sensitive the solution is to the assigned values. For example, you may find that the optimal solution when one response has a greater importance is very different from the optimal solution when the same response has a lesser importance.

Using the optimization plot

Once you have created an optimization plot, you can change the input variable settings. For factorial and response surface designs, you can adjust the factor levels. For mixture designs, you can adjust component, process variable, and amount variable settings. You might want to change these input variable settings on the optimization plot for many reasons, including

- to search for input variable settings with a higher composite desirability

- to search for lower-cost input variable settings with near optimal properties

- to explore the sensitivity of response variables to changes in the design variables

- to "calculate" the predicted responses for an input variable setting of interest

- to explore input variable settings in the neighborhood of a local solution

When you change an input variable to a new level, the graphs are redrawn and the predicted responses and desirabilities are recalculated. If you discover a setting combination that has a composite desirability higher than the initial optimal setting, MINITAB replaces the initial optimal setting with the new optimal setting. You will then have the option of adding the previous optimal setting to the saved settings list.

With MINITAB's interactive Optimization Plot you can

- change input variable settings
- save new input variable settings
- delete saved input variable settings
- reset optimization plot to optimal settings
- view a list of all saved settings
- lock mixture components

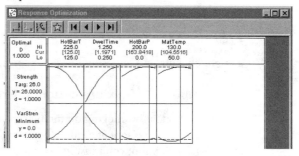

▶ To change input variable settings

1 Change input variable settings in the optimization plot by

- dragging the vertical red lines to a new position or
- clicking on the red input variable settings located at the top and entering a new value in the dialog box that appears

Note | You can return to the initial or optimal settings at any time by clicking ☆ on the Toolbar or by right-clicking and choosing **Reset to Optimal Settings**.

Note | For factorial designs with center points in the model: If you move one factor to the center on the optimization plot, then all factors will move to the center. If you move one factor away from the center, then all factors with move with it, away from the center.

Note | For a mixture design, you cannot change a component setting independently of the other component settings. If you want one or more components to stay at their current settings, you need to lock them. See *To lock components (mixture designs only)* on page 23-12.

▶ To save new input variable settings

1 Save new input variable settings in the optimization plot by

- clicking ▣ on the Optimization Plot Toolbar
- right-clicking and selecting **Save current settings** from the menu

Note | The saved settings are stored in a sequential list. You can cycle forwards and backwards through the setting list by clicking on ◀ or ▶ on the Toolbar or by right-clicking and choosing the appropriate command from the menu.

▶ **To delete saved input variable settings**

1 Choose the setting that you want to delete by cycling through the list.

2 Delete the setting by

■ clicking ▦ on the Optimization Plot Toolbar

■ right-clicking and choosing **Delete Current Setting**

▶ **To reset optimization plot to optimal settings**

1 Reset to optimal settings by

■ clicking ☆ on the Toolbar

■ right-clicking and choosing **Reset to Optimal Settings**

▶ **To lock components (mixture designs only)**

1 Lock a component by clicking on the black [ ] before the component name. You cannot lock a component at a value that would prevent any other component from changing. In addition, you must leave at least two components unlocked.

▶ **To view a list of all saved settings**

1 View the a list of all saved settings by

■ clicking ▦ on the Optimization Plot Toolbar

■ right-clicking and choosing **Display Settings List**

More | You can copy the saved setting list to the Clipboard by right-clicking and choosing Select All and then choosing Copy.

▷ **Example of a response optimization experiment for a factorial design**

You are an engineer assigned to optimize the responses from a chemical reaction experiment. You have determined that three factors—reaction time, reaction temperature, and type of catalyst—affect the yield and cost of the process. You want to find the factor settings that maximize the yield and minimize the cost of the process.

1 Open the worksheet FACTOPT.MTW. (We have saved the design, response data, and model information for you.)

2 Choose **Stat ➤ DOE ➤ Factorial ➤ Response Optimizer**.

3 Click ⟫ to move **Yield** and **Cost** to **Selected**.

4 Click **Setup**. Complete the **Goal, Lower, Target,** and **Upper** columns of the table as shown below:

Response	Goal	Lower	Target	Upper
Yield	Maximize	35	45	
Cost	Minimize		28	35

5 Click **OK** in each dialog box.

*Session
window
output*

Response Optimization

Parameters

	Goal	Lower	Target	Upper	Weight	Import
Yield	Maximum	35	45	45	1	1
Cost	Minimum	28	28	35	1	1

Global Solution

```
Time      =    46.062
Temp      =   150.000
Catalyst  =    -1.000 (A)
```

Predicted Responses

```
Yield     =   44.8077, desirability =   0.98077
Cost      =   28.9005, desirability =   0.87136
```

Composite Desirability =   0.92445

*Graph
window
output*

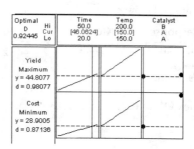

Interpreting results

The individual desirability for Yield is 0.98081; the individual desirability for Cost is 0.87132. The composite desirability for both these two variables is 0.92445.

To obtain this desirability, you would set the factor levels at the values shown under Global Solution in the Session window. That is, time would be set at 46.062, temperature at 150, and you would use catalyst A.

If you want to try to improve this initial solution, you can use the plot. Move the red vertical bars to change the factor settings and see how the individual desirability of the responses and the composite desirability change.

> ## Example of a response optimization experiment for a response surface design

You need to create a product that satisfies the criteria for both seal strength and variability in seal strength. Parts are placed inside a bag, which is then sealed with a heat-sealing machine. The seal must be strong enough so that product will not be lost in transit, yet not so strong that the consumer cannot open the bag. The lower and upper specifications for the seal strength are 24 and 28 lbs, with a target of 26 lbs. For the variability in seal strength, the goal is to minimize and the maximum acceptable value is 1.

Previous experimentation has indicated that the following are important factors for controlling the strength of the seal: hot bar temperature (HotBarT), dwell time (DwelTime), hot bar pressure (HotBarP), and material temperature (MatTemp). Hot bar temperature (HotBarT) and dwell time (DwelTime) are important for reducing the variation in seal strength.

You goal is to optimize both responses: strength of the seal (Strength) and variability in the strength of the seal (VarStrength).

1 Open the worksheet RSOPT.MTW. (The design, response data, and model information have been saved for you.)

2 Choose **Stat ➤ DOE ➤ Response Surface ➤ Response Optimizer**.

3 Click ⟫ to move **Strength** and **VarStrength** to **Selected**.

4 Click **Setup**. Complete the **Goal, Lower, Target**, and **Upper** columns of the table as shown below:

Response	Goal	Lower	Target	Upper
Strength	Target	24	26	28
VarStrength	Minimize		0	1

5 Click **OK** in each dialog box.

Response Optimization

Parameters

	Goal	Lower	Target	Upper	Weight	Import
Strength	Target	24	26	28	1	1
VarStrength	Minimum	0	0	1	1	1

Global Solution

```
HotBarT    =  125.000
DwelTime   =    1.197
HotBarP    =  163.842
MatTemp    =  104.552
```

Predicted Responses

```
Strength    = 26.0000, desirability =  1.00000
VarStrength =  0.0000, desirability =  1.00000
```

Composite Desirability = 1.00000

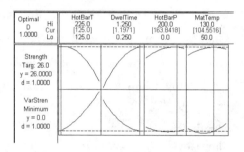

Interpreting the results

The individual desirability of both the seal strength and the variance in seal strength is 1.0. Therefore, the combined or composite desirability of these two variables is 1.0.

To obtain this desirability, you would set the factor levels at the values shown under Global Solution. That is, hot bar temperature would be set at 125.000, dwell time at 1.197, hot bar pressure at 163.842, and material temperature at 104.552.

If you want to adjust the factor settings of this initial solution, you can use the plot. Move the vertical bars to change the factor settings and see how the individual desirability of the responses and the composite desirability change. For example, you may want see if you can reduce the material temperature (which would save money) and still meet the product specifications.

Example of response optimization experiment for a mixture design

The compound normally used to make a plastic pipe is made of two materials: Material A and Material B. As a research engineer, you would like to determine whether or not a filler can be added to the existing formulation and still satisfy certain physical property requirements. You would like to include as much filler in the formulation as possible and still satisfy the response specifications. The pipe must meet the following specifications:

- impact strength must be greater than 1ft-lb / in
- deflection temperature must be greater than 190° F
- yield strength must be greater than 5000 psi

Using an augmented simplex centroid design, you collected data and are now going to optimize on three responses: impact strength (Impact), deflection temperature (Temp), and yield strength (Strength).

1 Open the worksheet MIXOPT.MTW. (The design, response data, and model information have been saved for you. The data is from [1].)

2 Choose **Stat ➤ DOE ➤ Mixture ➤ Response Optimizer**.

3 Click [>>] to move **Impact**, **Temp**, and **Strength** to **Selected**.

4 Under **Model Fitted in**, choose **Psuedocomponents**.

5 Click **Setup**. Complete the **Goal, Lower, Target**, and **Upper** columns of the table as shown below:

Response	Goal	Lower	Target	Upper
Impact	Maximize	1	3	
Temp	Maximize	190	200	
Strength	Maximize	5000	5200	

6 Click **OK** in each dialog box.

*Session
window
output*

Response Optimization

Parameters

	Goal	Lower	Target	Upper	Weight	Import
Impact	Maximum	1	3	3	1	1
Temp	Maximum	190	200	200	1	1
Strength	Maximum	5000	5200	5200	1	1

Global Solution

Components

Mat-A	=	0.575
Mat-B	=	0.425
Filler	=	0.000

Predicted Responses

Impact	=	7.26, desirability =	1
Temp	=	203.93, desirability =	1
Strength	=	5255.47, desirability =	1

Composite Desirability =   1.00000

*Graph
window
output*

Interpreting the results

In most cases, MINITAB uses the units that are displayed in the worksheet for the numerical optimization and optimization plot results. However, if you have a design that is displayed in amounts and you have multiple total amounts, the components are displayed in proportions for both the numerical optimization and the optimization plot results. In this example, the results are displayed in proportions.

Both the individual desirabilities and the combined or composite desirability of the three response variables are 1.0.

To obtain this composite desirability, you would set the mixture component proportions at the values shown under Global Solution. The proportions of the three ingredients in the formulation used to make the plastic pipe would be: 0.575 of Mat- A; 0.425 of Mat-B, and 0.0 of Filler. The predicted responses for the formulation are: impact strength = 7.26, deflection temperature = 203.93, and yield strength = 5255.47. These predicted responses indicate that the physical property specifications of the plastic pipe have been met.

However, the objective of the experiment is to include as much filler in the formulation as possible and still satisfy the response specifications. Although you have satisfied the response specifications, the resulting formulation does not include any filler. You can move the vertical bars to change the component proportions and see whether or not you can add more filler and still satisfy the specifications.

In the plot below, filler has been locked at .14 and the vertical bars have been moved to determine the proportions of a formulation with lower desirability, but one that still meets the required specifications. The specifications for impact strength and yield strength have been easily met, whereas, the specification for deflection temperature is barely satisfied. You can continue to change the formulation until you find a combination of proportions that fit your needs.

Graph window output

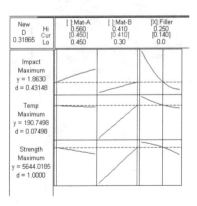

Overlaid Contour Plots

Use Overlaid Contour Plot to draw contour plots for multiple responses and to overlay multiple contour plots on top of each other in a single graph. Contour plots show how response variables relate to two continuous design variables (factorial and response surface designs) or three continuous design variables (mixture designs) while holding the rest of the variables in a model at certain settings. In a contour plot, the fitted response model is viewed as a two-dimensional surface where all points that have the same fitted value are connected to produce contour lines of constants. Contour plots are useful for establishing operating conditions that produce desirable response values.

Applications that involve multiple responses present a different challenge than single response experiments. Since each response is important in determining the quality of the product, you need to consider the responses simultaneously. Optimal input variable settings for one response may be far from optimal for another response. Overlaid contour plots allow you to visually identify an area of compromise among the various responses.

Data

Before you use Overlaid Contour Plot, you must

1 Create and store a design using one of MINITAB's Create Design commands or create a design from data that you already have in the worksheet with Define Custom Design.

Command	on page...
Create Factorial Design	19-6, 19-24
Create Response Surface Design	20-4
Create Mixture Design	21-5
Define Custom Factorial Design	19-35
Design Custom Response Surface Design	20-19
Define Custom Mixture Design	21-28

2 Enter up to ten numeric response columns in the worksheet

3 Fit a model for each response using one of the following:

Command	on page...
Analyze Factorial Design	19-44
Analyze Response Surface Design	20-26
Analyze Mixture Design	21-38

Note | Overlaid Contour Plot is not available for general full factorial designs.

▶ **To draw an overlaid contour plot**

1 Choose Stat ➤ DOE ➤ Factorial, Response Surface, or Mixture ➤ Overlaid Contour Plot.

**Factorial and
Response Surface Designs**

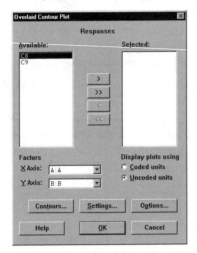

Mixture Designs

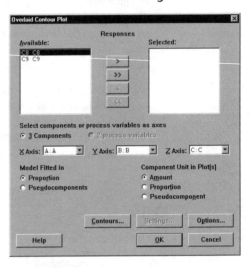

2 Under **Responses**, move up to ten responses that you want to include in the plot from **Available** to **Selected** using the arrow buttons.

■ To move the responses one at a time, highlight a response, then click ⟨ or ⟩

■ To move all of the responses, click on ⟪ or ⟫

You can also move a response by double-clicking it.

3 Do one of the following:

■ For factorial and response surface designs, under **Factors**, choose a factor from **X Axis** and a factor from **Y Axis**.

Note | Only numeric factors are valid candidates for X and Y axes.

■ For a mixture design, do one of the following:

1 To plot components, under **Select components or process variables as axes**, choose **3 Components**. Then choose a component from **X Axis**, **Y Axis**, and **Z Axis**.

Note | Only numeric process variables are valid candidates for X and Y axes.

2 To plot process variables, under **Select components or process variables as axes**, choose **2 process variables**.

3 Click **Contours**.

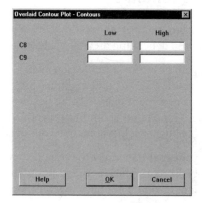

4 For each response, enter a number in **Low** and **High**. See *Defining contours* on page 23-22. Click **OK**.

5 If you like, use any of the options listed below, then click **OK**.

Options

Overlaid Contour Plot dialog box

- for factorial and response surface designs, display the plot in coded or uncoded units

- for mixture designs, refit the model using proportions or psuedocomponents

- for mixture designs, display the plot in amounts, proportions, or psuedocomponents

Settings subdialog box

- specify values for factors, components, or process variables that are not used as axes in the contour plot, instead of using the default of median (middle) values—see *Settings for extra factors, covariates, components, and process variables* on page 23-22

- for factorial designs, specify values for covariates in the design, instead of using the default of mean (middle) values—see *Settings for extra factors, covariates, components, and process variables* on page 23-22

- for mixture designs that include an amount variable, specify the hold value, instead of using the mean as the default

Options subdialog box

- for factorial and response surface designs, define minimum and maximum values for the x-axis and y-axis

- for mixture designs, define minimum values for the x-axis, y-axis, and z-axis

- replace the default title with your own title

Defining contours

For each response, you need to define a low and a high contour. These contours should be chosen depending on your goal for the responses. Here are some examples:

- If your goal is to *minimize* (smaller is better) the response, you may want to set the **Low** value at the point of diminishing returns, that is, although you want to minimize the response, going below a certain value makes little or no difference. If there is no point of diminishing returns, use a very small number, one that is probably not achievable. Use your maximum acceptable value in **High**.

- If your goal is to *target* the response, you probably have upper and lower specification limits for the response that can be used as the values for **Low** and **High**. If you do not have specification limits, you may want to use lower and upper points of diminishing returns.

- If your goal is to *maximize* (larger is better) the response, again, you may want to set the **High** value at the point of diminishing returns, although now you need a value on the upper end instead of the lower end of the range. Use your minimum acceptable value in **Low**.

In all of these cases, the goal is to have the response fall between these two values.

Settings for extra factors, covariates, components, and process variables

You can set the holding level for factors, components, and process variables that are not in the plot at their highest, lowest, or middle (calculated median) settings, or you can set specific levels to hold each. If you have a factorial design, you can also set the holding values for covariates in the model.

The hold values must be expressed in the following units:

- factorial designs—factors and covariates in *uncoded units*

- response surface designs—factors in *uncoded units*

- mixture designs—components in the *units displayed in the worksheet*; process variables in *coded units*

Note   If you have text factors/process variables in your design, you can only set their holding values at one of the text levels.

▶ **To set the holding level for variables not in the plot**

1 In the Overlaid Contour Plot dialog box, click **Settings**.

Factorial Design   ### Response Surface Design

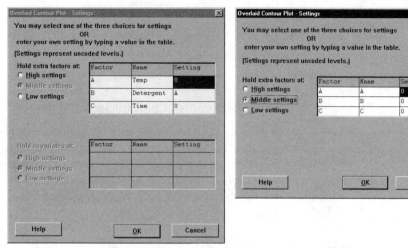

Mixture Design

2 Do one of the following to set the holding value for extra factors, components, or process variables, or covariates:

■ For factors, covariates, and process variables:
  – To use the preset values for factors, covariates, or process variables, choose **High settings**, **Middle settings**, or **Low settings**. When you use a preset value, *all* variables not in the plot will be held at their high, middle (calculated median), or low settings.
  – To specify the value at which to hold the factor, covariate, or process variable, enter a number in **Setting** for each of the design variables you want control. This option allows you to set a different holding value for each variables.

- For components:
  - To use the preset values for components, choose **Lower bound setting**, **Middle setting**, or **Upper bound setting** under **Hold components at**. When you use a preset value, *all* components not in the plot will be held at their lower bound, middle, or upper bound.
  - To specify the value at which to hold the components, enter a number in **Setting** for each component that you want control. This option allows you to set a different holding value for each components.

3 Click **OK**.

Example of an overlaid contour plot for factorial design

This contour plot is a continuation of the factorial response optimization example on page 23-12. A chemical engineer conducted a 2^3 full factorial design to examine the effects of reaction time, reaction temperature, and type of catalyst on the yield and cost of the process. The goal is to maximize yield and minimize cost. In this example, you will create contour plots using time and temperature as the two axes in the plot and holding type of catalyst at levels A and B respectively.

Step 1: Display the overlaid contour plot for Catalyst A

1 Open the worksheet FACTOPT.MTW. (The design information and response data have been saved for you.)

2 Choose **Stat ➤ DOE ➤ Factorial ➤ Overlaid Contour Plots**.

3 Click ⟩⟩ to move **Yield** and **Cost** to **Selected**.

4 Click **Contours**. Complete the **Low** and **High** columns of the table as shown below, then click **OK** in each dialog box.

Name	Low	High
Yield	35	45
Cost	28	35

Step 2: Display the overlaid contour plot for Catalyst B

5 Repeat steps 2-4, then click **Settings**. Under **Hold extra factors at**, choose **High settings**. Click **OK** in each dialog box.

*Graph
window
output*

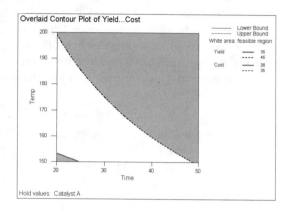

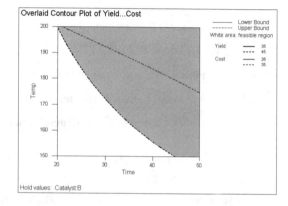

Interpreting results

Above are two overlaid contour plots. The two factors, temperature and time, are used as the two axes in the plots and the third factor, catalyst, has been held at levels A and B respectively.

The white area inside each plot shows the range of time and temperature where the criteria for both response variables are satisfied. Use this plot in combination with the optimization plot shown on page 23-12 to find the best operating conditions for maximizing yield and minimizing cost.

▷ Example of an overlaid contour plot for response surface design

This contour plot is a continuation of the analysis for the heat-sealing process experiment introduced on page 23-14. Parts are placed inside a sealable bag, which is then sealed with a heat-sealing machine. The seal must be strong enough so that product will not be lost in transit, yet not so strong that the consumer cannot open the bag. The upper and lower specifications for the seal strength are 24 and 28 lbs, with a target of 26 lbs.

Previous experimentation has indicated that the important factors for controlling the strength of the seal are: hot bar temperature (HotBarT), dwell time (DwelTime), hot bar pressure (HotBarP), and material temperature (MatTemp). Hot bar temperature (HotBarT) and dwell time (DwelTime) are important for reducing the variation in seal strength.

Your goal is to optimize both responses: strength of the seal (Strength) and variability in the strength of the seal (VarStrength). With an overlaid contour plot, you can only look at two factors at a time. You will use the optimal solution values shown on page 23-14 as the holding values for factors that are not in the plot (HotBarP and MatTemp).

1 Open the worksheet RSOPT.MTW.

2 Choose **Stat ➤ DOE ➤ Response Surface ➤ Overlaid Contour Plots**.

3 Click ⟫ to select both available responses.

4 Click **Contours**. Complete the **Low** and **High** columns of the table as shown below, then click **OK**.

Name	Low	High
Strength	24	28
VarStrength	0	1

5 Click **Settings**. In **Setting**, enter *163.842* for HotBarP and *104.552* for MatTemp.

6 Click **OK** in each dialog box.

Graph window output

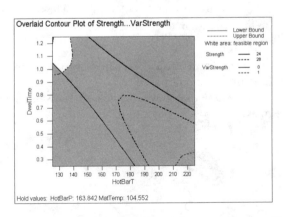

Interpreting the results

The white area in the upper left corner of the plot shows the range of HotBarT and DwellTime where the criteria for both response variables are satisfied. You may increase of decrease the holding value to see the range change. To understand the feasible region formed by the three factors, you should repeat the process to obtain plots for all pairs of factors.

You can use the plots in combination with the optimizatopm plot shown on page 23-14 to find the best operating conditions for sealing the bags.

➤ Example of an overlaid contour plot for a mixture design

This overlaid contour plot is a continuation of the analysis for the plastic pipe experiment introduced on page 23-16. The compound normally used to make a plastic pipe is made of two materials: Mat-A and Mat-B. As a research engineer, you would like to determine whether or not a filler can be added to the existing formulation and still satisfy certain physical property requirements. You would like to include as much filler in the formulation as possible and still satisfy the response specifications. The pipe must meet the following specifications:

- impact strength must be greater than 1ft-lb / in
- deflection temperature must be greater than 190° F
- yield strength must be greater than 5000 psi

Using an augmented simplex centroid design, you collected data and are now going to create an overlaid contour plot for three responses: impact strength (Impact), deflection temperature (Temp), and yield strength (Strength).

1 Open the worksheet MIXOPT.MTW. (The design, response data, and model information have been saved for you. The data is from [1].)

2 Choose **Stat ➤ DOE ➤ Mixture ➤ Overlaid Contour Plot**.

3 Click ![»] to select all available responses.

4 Click **Contours**. Complete the **Low** and **High** columns of the table as shown below.

Name	Low	High
Impact	1	7
Temp	190	205
Strength	5000	5800

5 Click **OK** in each dialog box.

*Graph
window
output*

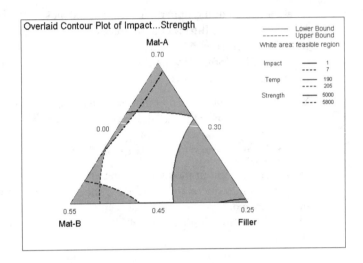

Interpreting the results

The white area in the center of the plot shows the range of the three components, Mat-A, Mat-B, and Filler, where the criteria for all three response variables are satisfied.

You can use this plot in combination with the optimization plot shown on page 23-17 to find the "best" formulation for plastic pipe.

References

[1] Koons, G.F. and Wilt, M.H. (1985). "Design and Analysis of an ABS Pipe Compound Experiment," Experiments in Industry: Design, Analysis, and Interpretation of Results. American Society for Quality Control, Milwaukee, 111-117.

[2] Derringer, G. and Suich, R. (1980). Simultaneous Optimization of Several Response Variables, Journal of Quality Technology, 12, 214-219.

[3] Myers, R.H. and Montgomery D.C. (1995). Response Surface Methodology. John Wiley & Sons, New York.

[4] Castillo, E.D., Montgomery, D.C., and McCarville, D.R. (1996). Modified Desirability Functions for Multiple Repsonse Optimization. Journal of Quality Technology, 28, 337-345.

24

Taguchi Designs

Taguchi Design Overview

Dr. Genichi Taguchi is regarded as the foremost proponent of robust parameter design, which is an engineering method for product or process design that focuses on minimizing variation and/or sensitivity to noise. When used properly, Taguchi designs provide a powerful and efficient method for designing products that operate consistently and optimally over a variety of conditions.

In robust parameter design, the primary goal is to find factor settings that minimize response variation, while adjusting (or keeping) the process on target. After you determine which factors affect variation, you can try to find settings for controllable factors that will either reduce the variation, make the product insensitive to changes in uncontrollable (noise) factors, or both. A **process** designed with this goal will produce more consistent output. A **product** designed with this goal will deliver more consistent performance regardless of the environment in which it is used.

Engineering knowledge should guide the selection of factors and responses [3]. Robust parameter design is particularly suited for energy transfer processes; for example, a car's steering wheel is designed to transfer energy from the steering wheel to the wheels of the car. You should also scale control factors and responses so that interactions are unlikely. When interactions among control factors are likely or not well understood, you should choose a design that is capable of estimating those interactions. MINITAB can help you select a Taguchi design that does not confound interactions of interest with each other or with main effects.

Noise factors for the outer array should also be carefully selected and may require preliminary experimentation. The noise levels selected should reflect the range of conditions under which the response variable should remain robust.

Robust parameter design uses Taguchi designs (orthogonal arrays), which allow you to analyze many factors with few runs. Taguchi designs are balanced, that is, no factor is weighted more or less in an experiment, thus allowing factors to be analyzed independently of each other.

MINITAB provides both static and dynamic response experiments.

- In a static response experiment, the quality characteristic of interest has a fixed level.

- In a dynamic response experiment, the quality characteristic operates over a range of values and the goal is to improve the relationship between an input signal and an output response.

An example of a dynamic response experiment is an automotive acceleration experiment where the input signal is the amount of pressure on the gas pedal and the output response is vehicle speed. You can create a dynamic response experiment by adding a signal factor to a design—see *Adding a signal factor for a dynamic response experiment* on page 24-8.

The goal of robust experimentation is to find an optimal combination of control factor settings that achieve robustness against (insensitivity to) noise factors. MINITAB calculates response tables and generates main effects and interaction plots for:

- signal-to-noise ratios (S/N ratios, which provide a measure of robustness) vs. the control factors

- means (static design) or slopes (dynamic design) vs. the control factors

- standard deviations vs. the control factors

- the natural log of the standard deviations vs. the control factors

Use these tables and plots to determine what factors and interactions are important and evaluate how they affect responses. To get a complete understanding of factor effects it is advisable to evaluate S/N ratios, means (static design), slopes (dynamic design), and standard deviations. Make sure that you choose an S/N ratio that is appropriate for the type of data you have and your goal for optimizing the response—see *Analyzing static designs* on page 24-29.

Note | If you suspect curvature in your model, select a design—such as 3-level designs—that allows you to detect curvature in the response surface.

Taguchi design experiments in MINITAB

Performing a Taguchi design experiment may consist of the following steps:

1 Before you begin using MINITAB, you need to complete all pre-experimental planning. For example, you need to choose control factors for the inner array and noise factors for the outer array. Control factors are factors you can control to optimize the process. Noise factors are factors that can influence the performance of a system but are not under control during the intended use of the product. Note that while you cannot control noise factors during the process or product use, you need to be able to control noise factors for experimentation purposes.

2 Use **Create Taguchi Design** to generate a Taguchi design (orthogonal array)—see *Creating Taguchi Designs* on page 24-4.

  Or, use **Define Custom Taguchi Design** to create a design from data that you already have in the worksheet. **Define Custom Taguchi Design** allows you to specify which columns are your factors and signal factors. You can then easily analyze the design and generate plots. See *Defining Custom Taguchi Designs* on page 24-17.

3 After you create the design, you may use **Modify Design** to rename the factors, change the factor levels, add a signal factor to a static design, ignore an existing signal factor (treat the design as static), and add new levels to an existing signal factor. See *Modifying Designs* on page 24-18.

4 After you create the design, you may use **Display Design** to change the units (coded or uncoded) in which MINITAB expresses the factors in the worksheet. See *Displaying Designs* on page 24-21.

5 Perform the experiment and collect the response data. Then, enter the data in your MINITAB worksheet. See *Collecting and Entering Data* on page 24-22.

6 Use **Analyze Taguchi Design** to analyze the experimental data. See *Analyzing Taguchi Designs* on page 24-23.

7 Use **Predict Results** to predict S/N ratios and response characteristics for selected new factor settings. See *Predicting Results* on page 24-35.

Choosing a Taguchi Design

Before you use MINITAB, you need to determine which Taguchi design is most appropriate for your experiment. In Taguchi designs, responses are measured at selected combinations of the control factor levels. Each combination of control factor levels is called a run and each measure an observation. The Taguchi design provides the specifications for each experimental test run.

A Taguchi design, also known as an orthogonal array, is a fractional factorial matrix that ensures a balanced comparison of levels of any factor. In a Taguchi design analysis, each factor can be evaluated independently of all other factors.

When choosing a design you need to

■ identify the number of control factors that are of interest

■ identify the number of levels for each factor

■ determine the number of runs you can perform

■ determine the impact of other considerations (such as cost, time, or facility availability) on your choice of design

Creating Taguchi Designs

A Taguchi design, or an orthogonal array, is a method of designing experiments that usually requires only a fraction of the full factorial combinations. In a Taguchi design, the array is orthogonal, which means the design is balanced so that factor levels are weighted equally. Because of this, an orthogonal array is one in which each factor can be evaluated independently of all the other factors.

In robust parameter design, you first choose control factors and their levels and choose an orthogonal array appropriate for these control factors. The control factors comprise the inner array. At the same time, you determine a set of noise factors, along with an experimental design for this set of factors. The noise factors comprise the outer array.

The experiment is carried out by running the complete set of noise factor settings at each combination of control factor settings (at each run). The response data from each run of the noise factors in the outer array are usually aligned in a row, next to the factors settings for that run of the control factors in the inner array. For an example, see *Data on page 24-24.*

Each column in the orthogonal array represents a specific factor with two or more levels. Each row represents a run; the cell values indicate the factor settings for the run. By default, MINITAB's orthogonal array designs use the integers 1, 2, 3... to represent factor levels. If you enter factor levels, the integers 1, 2, 3, ..., will be the coded levels for the design.

The following table displays the L8 (2^7) Taguchi design (orthogonal array). L8 means 8 runs. 2^7 means 7 factors with 2 levels each. If the full factorial design were used, it would have $2^7 = 128$ runs. The L8 (2^7) array requires only 8 runs—a fraction of the full factorial design. This array is orthogonal; factor levels are weighted equally across the entire design. The table columns represent the control factors, the table rows represent the runs (combination of factor levels), and each table cell represents the factor level for that run.

L8 (2^7) Taguchi Design

	A	B	C	D	E	F	G
1	1	1	1	1	1	1	1
2	1	1	1	2	2	2	2
3	1	2	2	1	1	2	2
4	1	2	2	2	2	1	1
5	2	1	2	1	2	1	2
6	2	1	2	2	1	2	1
7	2	2	1	1	2	2	1
8	2	2	1	2	1	1	2

In the above example, levels 1 and 2 occur 4 times in each factor in the array. If you compare the levels in factor A with the levels in factor B, you will see that B1 and B2 each occur 2 times in conjunction with A1 and 2 times in conjunction with A2. Each pair of factors is balanced in this manner, allowing factors to be evaluated independently.

Orthogonal array designs focus primarily on main effects. Some of the arrays offered in MINITAB's catalog permit a few selected interactions to be studied. See *Estimating selected interactions* on page 24-10.

You can also add a signal factor to the Taguchi design in order to create a dynamic response experiment. A dynamic response experiment is used to improve the functional relationship between an input signal and an output response. See *Adding a signal factor for a dynamic response experiment* on page 24-8.

▶ To create a Taguchi design

1 Choose **Stat ➤ DOE ➤ Taguchi ➤ Create Taguchi Design**.

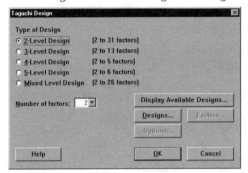

2 If you want to see a summary of the Taguchi designs available, click **Display Available Designs**. Click **OK**.

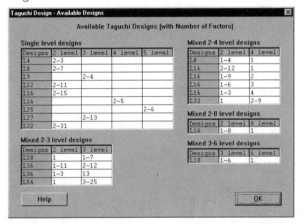

3 Under **Type of Design**, choose a design.

4 From **Number of factors**, choose a number. The choices available will vary depending on what design you have chosen.

5 Click **Designs**.

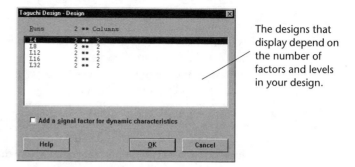

The designs that display depend on the number of factors and levels in your design.

6 In the **Designs** box, highlight the design you want to create. If you like, use the option described under *Design subdialog box* below.

7 Click **OK** even if you do not change any options. This selects the design and brings you back to the main dialog box.

8 If you like, click **Factors** or **Options** to use any of the options listed below, then click **OK** in each dialog box to create your design.

Options

Design subdialog box

- add a signal factor—see *Adding a signal factor for a dynamic response experiment* on page 24-8

Options subdialog box

- store the design in the worksheet—see *Storing the design* on page 24-9

Factors subdialog box

- select interactions to include in the design and allow Minitab to assign factors to columns of the array to allow estimation of selected interactions—see *Estimating selected interactions* on page 24-10

- assign factors to columns of the array in order to allow estimation of selected interactions—see *Estimating selected interactions* on page 24-10

- name factors—see *Naming factors* on page 24-12

- define factor levels—see *Setting factor levels* on page 24-13

- name signal factor and define signal factor levels—see *Adding a signal factor for a dynamic response experiment* on page 24-8

Adding a signal factor for a dynamic response experiment

You can add a signal factor to a Taguchi design to create a dynamic response experiment. A dynamic response experiment is used to analyze and improve the functional relationship between an input signal and an output response. Generally, you would use a signal factor when the quality characteristic operates over a range of values depending on some input to the system [3] [5]. An example is an automotive acceleration system, where the input signal is the amount of pressure on the gas pedal and the dynamic response is the speed of the vehicle. Ideally, there should be a linear relationship between the input signal and output response. Robustness requires that there is minimal variation in this relationship due to noise.

The signal factor values are repeated for every run of the Taguchi design (orthogonal array). Thus, the total number of runs (rows in the worksheet) will be the number of rows in the orthogonal array times the number of levels in the signal variable. For example, adding a signal factor with 2 levels to an L4 (2^3) design, which has 4 runs, creates a design with 8 total runs; adding a signal factor with 3 levels creates a design with 12 total runs.

Static design (No signal factor)			Dynamic design (Signal factor with 2 levels)			Dynamic design (Signal factor with 3 levels)		
A	B		A	B	Signal factor	A	B	Signal factor
1	1		1	1	1	1	1	1
1	2		1	1	2	1	1	2
2	1		1	2	1	1	1	3
2	2		1	2	2	1	2	1
			2	1	1	1	2	2
			2	1	2	1	2	3
			2	2	1	2	1	1
			2	2	2	2	1	2
						2	1	3
						2	2	1
						2	2	2
						2	2	3

Note | When you add a signal factor while creating a new Taguchi design, the run order will be different from the order that results from adding a signal factor using Modify Design—see *Adding a signal factor to an existing static design* on page 24-19. The order of the rows does not affect the Taguchi analysis.

▶ **To add a signal factor for a dynamic response experiment**

1 In the Create Taguchi Design dialog box, click **Design**.

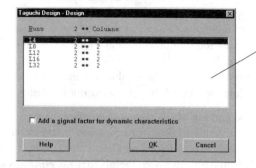

The designs that display depend on the number of factors and levels in your design.

2 Check **Add a signal factor for dynamic characteristics**. Click **OK**.

3 In the Create Taguchi Design dialog box, click **Factors**.

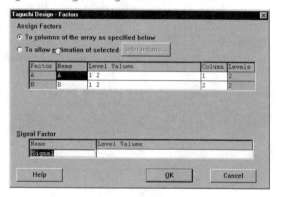

4 If you like, in the signal factor table under **Name**, click in the first row and type the name of the signal factor.

5 Under **Level Values**, click in the signal factor row and enter numeric values. You must enter at least two distinct values. Click **OK**.

Note | You can also specify signal factor levels using a range and increments. You can specify a range by typing two numbers separated by a colon. For example, 1:5 displays the numbers 1, 2, 3, 4, and 5. You can specify an increment by typing a slash "/" and a number. For example, 1:5/2 displays every other number in a range: 1, 3, and 5.

Storing the design

If you want to analyze a design or see whether or not selected interactions can be estimated from the design, you *must* store it in the worksheet. By default, MINITAB stores the design. If you want to see the properties of various designs before selecting the design you want to store, uncheck **Store design in worksheet** in the Options subdialog box.

Estimating selected interactions

Taguchi designs are primarily intended to study main effects of factors. Occasionally, you may want to study some of the two-way interactions. Some of the Taguchi designs (orthogonal arrays) allow the study of a limited number of two-way interactions. This usually requires that you leave some columns out of the array by not assigning factors to them. Some of the array columns are confounded with interactions between other array columns. Confounding means that the factor effect is blended with the interaction effect, thus they cannot be evaluated separately.

You can ask MINITAB to automatically assign factors to array columns in a way that avoids confounding—see *To select interactions* on page 24-11. Or, if you know exactly what design you want and know the columns of the full array that correspond to the design, you can assign factors to array columns yourself—see *To assign factors to columns of the array* on page 24-12.

Interaction tables show confounded columns, which can help you to assign factors to array columns. For interaction tables of MINITAB's catalog of Taguchi designs (orthogonal arrays), see Help. The interaction table for the L8 (2^7) array is shown below.

	1	2	3	4	5	6	7
1		3	2	5	4	7	6
2			1	6	7	4	5
3				7	6	5	4
4					1	2	3
5						3	2
6							1

The columns and rows represent the column numbers of the Taguchi design (orthogonal array). Each table cell contains the interactions confounded for the two columns of the orthogonal array.

For example, the entry in cell (1, 2) is 3. This means that the interaction between columns 1 and 2 is confounded with column 3. Thus, if you assigned factors A, B, and C to columns 1, 2, and 3, you could not study the AB interaction independently of factor C. If you suspect that there is a substantial interaction between A and B, you should not assign any factors to column 3. Similarly, the column 1 and 3 interaction is confounded with column 2, and the column 2 and 3 interaction is confounded with column 1.

Note | Assigning factors to columns of the array does not change how the design is displayed in the worksheet. For example, if you assigned factor A to column 3 of the array and factor B to column 2 of the array, factor A would still appear in column 1 in the worksheet and factor B would still appear in column 2 in the worksheet.

▶ To select interactions

1 In the Create Taguchi Design dialog box, click **Factors**.

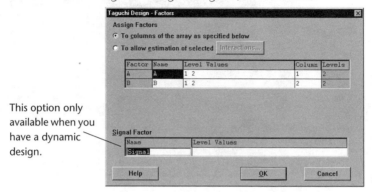

This option only available when you have a dynamic design.

2 Under **Assign Factors**, choose **To allow estimation of selected Interactions** and then click **Interactions**.

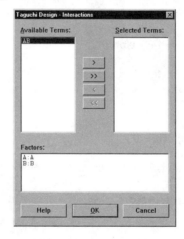

3 Move the interactions that you want to include in the design from **Available Terms** to **Selected Terms** using the arrow buttons

   ■ to move the interactions one at a time, highlight an interaction, then click `<` or `>`

   ■ to move all of the interactions, click on `<<` or `>>`

      You can also move an interaction by double-clicking it.

4 Click **OK**.

▶ **To assign factors to columns of the array**

Note | Assigning factors to columns of the array does not change how the design is displayed in the worksheet. For example, if you assigned factor A to column 3 of the array and factor B to column 2 of the array, factor A would still appear in column 1 in the worksheet and factor B would still appear in column 2 in the worksheet.

1 In the Create Taguchi Design dialog box, click **Factors**.

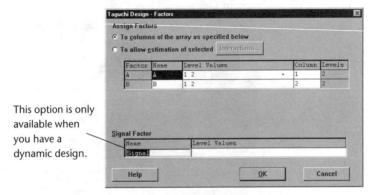

This option is only available when you have a dynamic design.

2 Under **Assign Factors**, choose **To columns of the array as specified below**.

3 In the factor table, click under **Column** in the cell that corresponds to the factor that you want to assign. From the drop-down list, choose the array column to which you want to assign the factor. Then, use the ⊡ key to move down the table and assign the factors to the remaining array columns. Click **OK**.

More | See Help for interaction tables of MINITAB's catalog of Taguchi designs (orthogonal arrays).

Naming factors

By default, MINITAB names the factors alphabetically.

▶ **To name factors**

1 In the Create Taguchi Design dialog box, click **Factors**.

2 Under **Name** in the factor table, click in the first row and type the name of the first factor. Then, use the ⊡ key to move down the column and enter the remaining factor names.

3 Click **OK**.

More | After you have created the design, you can change the factor names by typing new names in the Data window, or with Modify Design (page 24-18).

Setting factor levels

By default, Minitab sets the levels of a factor to the integers 1, 2, 3, ... You may change these to other numbers, such as the actual values of the factor level, or to text levels.

One useful technique for customizing Taguchi designs (orthogonal arrays) is the use of "dummy treatments." You can create a dummy treatment in MINITAB by repeating levels for the same factor, as long as there are at least two distinct levels. See *Creating dummy treatments* on page 24-13.

1 In the Create Taguchi Design dialog box, click **Factors**.

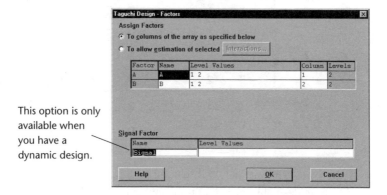

This option is only available when you have a dynamic design.

2 Under **Level Values** in the factor table, click in the first row and type the levels of the first factor. Then, use the ⬇ key to move down the column and enter the remaining levels. Click **OK**.

Creating dummy treatments

One useful technique for customizing Taguchi designs (orthogonal arrays) is the use of "dummy treatments." You can create a dummy treatment in MINITAB by repeating levels for a factor, as long as there are at least two distinct levels.

For example, if you wanted to use an L9 (3^4) array, which has four three-level factors, but had one factor with only two levels, you could use a dummy treatment to accommodate this. Here, the L9 (3^4) array is shown, both without and with a dummy treatment. In the dummy example, the factor levels for factor A are 1 2 1, where 1 is the repeated level for the dummy treatment.

L9 (3⁴) array

Run	A	B	C	D
1	1	1	1	1
2	1	2	2	2
3	1	3	3	3
4	2	1	2	3
5	2	2	3	1
6	2	3	1	2
7	3	1	3	2
8	3	2	1	3
9	3	3	2	1

L9 (3⁴) array (dummy)

Run	A	B	C	D
1	1	1	1	1
2	1	2	2	2
3	1	3	3	3
4	2	1	2	3
5	2	2	3	1
6	2	3	1	2
7	1'	1	3	2
8	1'	2	1	3
9	1'	3	2	1

Dummy treatments

In the L9 (3⁴) orthogonal array with dummy treatment above, factor A has repeated level 1, in place of level 3. This results in an L9 (3⁴) array with one factor at 2 levels and three factors at 3 levels. The array is still orthogonal, although it is not balanced.

When choosing which factor level to use as the dummy treatment, you may want to consider the amount of information about the factor level and the availability of experimental resources. For example, if you know more about level 1 than level 2, you may want to choose level 2 as your dummy treatment. Similarly, if level 2 is more expensive than level 1, requiring more resources or time to test, you may want to choose level 1 as your dummy treatment.

Summary of Available Taguchi Designs

Single-level designs

The table below summarizes the single-level Taguchi designs available. The number following the "L" indicates the number of runs in the design. For example, the L4 (2³) design has four runs. The numbers in the table indicate the minimum and maximum number of available factors for each design. For example, an L8 (2⁷) design can have from two to seven factors with two levels each; an L16 (4⁵) design can have from two to five factors with four levels each.

	Number of levels			
Designs	2	3	4	5
L4 (2^3)	2-3			
L8 (2^7)	2-7			
L9 (3^4)		2-4		
L12 (2^{11})	2-11			
L16 (2^{15})	2-15			
L16 (4^5)			2-5	
L25 (5^6)				2-6
L27 (3^{13})		2-13		
L32 (2^{31})	2-31			

Mixed 2-3 level designs

The table below summarizes the available Taguchi designs for mixed designs in which factors have 2 or 3 levels. The number in the table cells indicate the minimum and maximum number of factors available for each level. For example, an L18 ($2^1\ 3^7$) design can have one factor with two levels and from one to seven factors with three levels.

	Number of levels	
Designs	2	3
L18 ($2^1\ 3^7$)	1	1-7
L36 ($2^{11}\ 3^{12}$)	1-11	2-12
L36 ($2^3\ 3^{13}$)	1-3	13
L54 ($2^1\ 3^{25}$)	1	3-25

Mixed 2-4 level designs

The table below summarizes the available Taguchi designs for mixed designs in which factors have 2 or 4 levels. The number in the table cells indicate the minimum and maximum number of factors available for each level. For example, an L8 (2^4 4^1) design can have from one to four factors with two levels and one factor with four levels.

Designs	Number of levels	
	2	4
L8 (2^4 4^1)	1-4	1
L16 (2^{12} 4^1)	2-12	1
L16 (2^9 4^2)	1-9	2
L16 (2^6 4^3)	1-6	3
L16 (2^3 4^4)	1-3	4
L32 (2^1 4^9)	1	2-9

Mixed 2-8 level designs

The table below show the available Taguchi design for mixed designs in which factors have 2 and 8 levels. The number in the table cells indicate the minimum and maximum number of factors available for each level. An L16 (2^8 8^1) design can have from one to eight factors with two levels and one factor with eight levels.

Design	Number of levels	
	2	8
L16 (2^8 8^1)	1-8	1

Mixed 3-6 level designs

The table below shows the available Taguchi design for mixed designs in which factors have 3 and 6 levels. The number in the table cells indicate the minimum and maximum number of factors available for each level. An L18 (3^6 6^1) design can have from one to six factors with three levels and one factor with six levels.

Design	Number of levels	
	3 level	6 level
L18 (3^6 6^1)	1-6	1

Defining Custom Taguchi Designs

Use Define Custom Taguchi Design to create a design from data you already have in the worksheet. For example, you may have a design you:

- created using MINITAB session commands
- entered directly in the Data window
- imported from a data file
- created as another design type in MINITAB
- created with earlier releases of MINITAB

You can also use Define Custom Taguchi Design to redefine a design that you created with Create Taguchi Design and then modified directly in the worksheet.

Define Custom Taguchi Design allows you to specify which columns contain your factors and to include a signal factor. After you define your design, you can use Modify Design (page 24-18), Display Design (page 24-21), and Analyze Taguchi Design (page 24-23).

▶ To define a custom Taguchi design

1 Choose **Stat ➤ DOE ➤ Taguchi ➤ Define Custom Taguchi Design**.

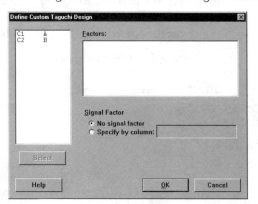

2 In **Factors**, enter the columns that contain the factor levels.

3 If you have a signal factor, choose **Specify by column** and enter the column that contains the signal factor levels. Click **OK**.

Modifying Designs

After creating a Taguchi design and storing it in the worksheet, you can use Modify Design to make the following modifications:

- rename the factors and change the factor levels for the control factors in the inner array—see *Renaming factors and changing factor levels* on page 24-18

- add a signal factor to a static design—see *Adding a signal factor to an existing static design* on page 24-19

- ignore the signal factor (treat the design as static)—see *Ignoring the signal factor* on page 24-20

- add new levels to the signal factor in an existing dynamic design—see *Adding new levels to the signal factor* on page 24-21

By default, MINITAB will replace the current design with the modified design. To store the modified design in a new worksheet, check **Put modified design in a new worksheet** in the Modify Design dialog box.

Renaming factors and changing factor levels

▶ **To rename factors or change factor levels**

1 Choose **Stat ➤ DOE ➤ Modify Design**.

Static Design	Dynamic Design

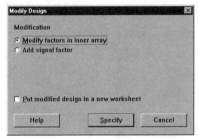 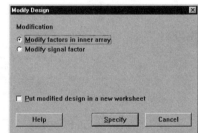

2 Choose **Modify factors in inner array**. Click **Specify**.

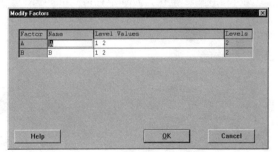

3 Under **Name**, click in the first row and type the name of the first factor. Then, use the ⬇ key to move down the column and enter the remaining factor names.

4 Under **Level Values**, click in the first row and type the levels of the first factor. Then, use the ⬇ key to move down the column and enter the remaining levels. Click **OK** in each dialog box.

Adding a signal factor to an existing static design

When you add a signal factor to an existing static design, MINITAB adds a new signal factor column after the factor columns and appends new rows (replicates) to the end of the existing worksheet. For example, if you add a signal factor with 2 levels to an existing L4 (2^3) array, 4 rows (1 replicate of 4 runs) are added to the worksheet; if you add a signal factor with 3 levels, 8 rows (2 replicates of 4 runs) are added to the worksheet. A replicate is the complete set of runs from the initial design.

Static design (No signal factor)			Dynamic design (Added signal factor with 2 levels)			Dynamic design (Added signal factor with 3 levels)		
A	B		A	B	Signal factor	A	B	Signal factor
1	1							
1	2		1	1	1	1	1	1
2	1		1	2	1	1	2	1
2	2		2	1	1	2	1	1
			2	2	1	2	2	1
			1	1	2	1	1	2
			1	2	2	1	2	2
			2	1	2	2	1	2
			2	2	2	2	2	2
						1	1	3
						1	2	3
						2	1	3
						2	2	3

Note | When you add a signal factor to an existing static design, the run order will be different from the order that results from adding a signal factor while creating a new design—see *Adding a signal factor for a dynamic response experiment* on page 24-8. The order of the rows does not affect the Taguchi analysis.

▶ **To add a signal factor**

1 Choose **Stat ➤ DOE ➤ Modify Design**.

2 Choose **Add signal factor**. Click **Specify**.

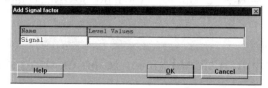

3 If you like, in the signal factor table under **Name**, click in the first row and type the name of the signal factor.

4 Under **Level Values**, enter the levels of the signal factor. You must enter at least two distinct values. Click **OK**.

Note │ You can also specify signal factor levels using a range and increments. You can specify a range by typing two numbers separated by a colon. For example, 1:5 displays the numbers 1, 2, 3, 4, and 5. You can specify an increment by typing a slash "/" and a number. For example, 1:5/2 displays every other number in a range: 1, 3, and 5.

Ignoring the signal factor

You can choose to ignore the signal factor in a dynamic design and thus treat the design as static.

▶ **To ignore the signal factor**

1 Choose **Stat ➤ DOE ➤ Modify Design**.

2 Choose **Modify signal factor**. Click **Specify**.

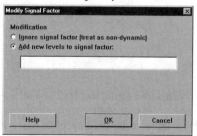

3 Select **Ignore signal factor (treat as non-dynamic)**. Click **OK** in each dialog box.

Adding new levels to the signal factor

When you add signal factor levels to an existing dynamic design, new rows (replicates) are appended to the end of the existing worksheet. For example, if you add 3 new signal factor levels to an existing L8 (2^7) design, 24 rows (3 replicates of 8 rows each) are added to the worksheet.

Note | When you add new signal factor levels to an existing dynamic design, the run order will be different from the order that results from adding a signal factor while creating a new design. The order of the rows does not affect the Taguchi analysis.

1 Choose **Stat ➤ DOE ➤ Modify Design**.

2 Choose **Modify signal factor**. Click **Specify**.

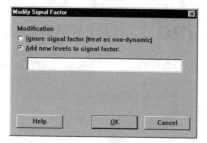

3 Choose **Add new levels to signal factor**. Enter the new signal factor levels. Click OK.

Note | You can also specify signal factor levels using a range and increments. You can specify a range by typing two numbers separated by a colon. For example, 1:5 displays the numbers 1, 2, 3, 4, and 5. You can specify an increment by typing a slash "/" and a number. For example, 1:5/2 displays every other number in a range: 1, 3, and 5.

Displaying Designs

After you create the design, you can use Display Design to change the way the design points are stored in the worksheet. You can display the factor levels in coded or uncoded form.

If you assigned factor levels in Factors subdialog box, the uncoded (actual) factor levels are initially displayed in the worksheet. If you did not assign factor levels (used the default factor levels, which are 1, 2, 3, ...), the coded and uncoded units are the same.

▶ **To change the units for the factors**

1 Choose **Stat ➤ DOE ➤ Display Design**.

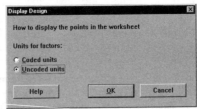

2 Choose **Coded units** or **Uncoded units**. Click **OK**.

Collecting and Entering Data

After you create your design, you need to perform the experiment and collect the response (measurement) data. To print a data collection form, follow the instructions below. After you collect the response data, enter the data in any worksheet column not used for the design.

Printing a data collection form

You can generate a data collection form in two ways. You can simply print the Data window contents, or you can use a macro. A macro can generate a "nicer" data collection form—see Help for more information. Although printing the Data window will not produce the prettiest form, it is the easiest method. Just follow these steps:

1 When you create your experimental design, MINITAB stores the factor settings in the worksheet. These columns constitute the basis of your data collection form. If you did not name factors or specify factor levels when you created the design and you want names or levels to appear on the form, see *Modifying Designs* on page 24-18.

2 In the worksheet, name the columns in which you will enter the measurement data obtained when you perform your experiment.

3 Choose **File ➤ Print Worksheet**. Make sure **Print Grid Lines** is checked, then click **OK**.

More | You can also copy the worksheet cells to the Clipboard by choosing **Edit ➤ Copy** cells. Then paste the clipboard contents into a word-processing application, such as Microsoft Word, where you can create your own form.

Analyzing Taguchi Designs

To use Analyze Taguchi Design, you must

- create and store the design using Create Taguchi Design (page 24-4), or create a design from data already in the worksheet using Define Custom Taguchi Design (page 24-17) and

- enter the response data in the worksheet — see *Data* on page 24-24

Using Analyze Taguchi Design, you can

- generate main effects and interaction plots of the S/N ratios, means (static design), slopes (dynamic design), and standard deviations vs. the control factors

- display response tables for S/N ratios, means (static design), slopes (dynamic design), and standard deviations

The response tables and main effects and interaction plots can help you determine which factors affect variation and process location. See *Two-step optimization* on page 24-23.

Two-step optimization

Two-step optimization, an important part of robust parameter design, involves first reducing variation and then adjusting the mean on target. Use two-step optimization when you are using either Nominal is Best signal-to-noise ratio. First, try to identify which factors have the greatest effect on variation and choose levels of these factors that minimize variation. Then, once you have reduced variation, the remaining factors are possible candidates for adjusting the mean on target (scaling factors).

A scaling factor is a factor in which the mean and standard deviation are proportional. You can identify scaling factors by examining the response tables for each control factor. A scaling factor has a significant effect on the mean with a relatively small effect on signal-to-noise ratio. This indicates that the mean and standard deviation scale together. Thus, you can use the scaling factor to adjust the mean on target but not affect the S/N ratio.

Use main effects plots to help you visualize the relative value of the effects of different factors.

Initial process performance

■ high variation

■ process not on target

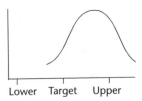

Step 1: Minimize variation

■ find factor settings that minimize the effects of noise on the response

■ variation minimized

■ process not on target

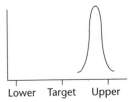

Step 2: Adjust mean on target

■ find factor settings that adjust the mean on target

■ variation minimized

■ process on target

■ robust design

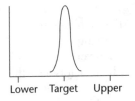

Data

Structure your data in the worksheet so that each row contains the control factors in the inner array and the response values from one complete run of the noise factors in the outer array. You must have from 2 to 50 response columns. Here is an example:

Time	Pressure	Catalyst	Temperature	Noise 1	Noise 2
1	1	1	1	50	52
1	1	1	2	44	51
1	2	2	1	56	59
1	2	2	2	65	77
2	1	2	1	47	43
2	1	2	2	42	51
2	2	1	1	68	62
2	2	1	2	51	38

This example, which is an L8 (2^4), has four factors in the inner array (Time, Pressure, Catalyst, and Temperature). Recall, the inner array represents the control factors. There are two noise conditions in the outer array (Noise 1 and Noise 2). There are two responses—one for each noise condition—in the outer array for each run in the inner array.

You can have 1 response column if you are using the Larger is Better or Smaller is Better signal-to-noise ratio and you are not going to analyze or store the standard deviation.

If you have a design and response data in your worksheet that was

- created using Minitab session commands,
- entered directly in the Data window,
- imported from a data file,
- created using as another design type in Minitab,
- or created with earlier releases in Minitab,

you can use Analyze Taguchi Design, which will prompt you to define your design— see *Defining Custom Taguchi Designs* on page 24-17.

▶ To fit a model to the data

1 Choose **Stat ➤ DOE ➤ Taguchi ➤ Analyze Taguchi Design**.

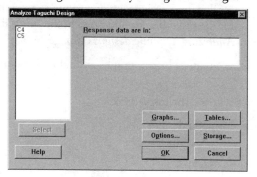

2 In **Response data are in**, enter the columns that contain the measurement data.

3 If you like, use any of the options listed below, then click **OK**.

Options

Graphs subdialog box

- for static designs, display main effects plots and selected interaction plots for the signal-to-noise (S/N) ratios, the process means, and/or the process standard deviations

- for dynamic designs, display main effects plots and selected interaction plots for the S/N ratios, the slopes, and/or the process standard deviations. Also, display scatter plots with fitted lines.

- display interaction plots for selected interactions—see *Selecting terms for the interaction plots* on page 24-28
  - display the interaction plots in a matrix on a single graph or to display each interaction plot on a separate page—see *Selecting terms for the interaction plots* on page 24-28

Tables subdialog box

- for static designs, display response tables for signal-to-noise ratios, the means, and the standard deviations—see *Displaying response tables* on page 24-29

- for dynamic designs, display response tables for signal-to-noise ratios, the slopes, and the standard deviations—see *Displaying response tables* on page 24-29

Options subdialog box

- for static designs, choose the signal-to-noise (S/N) ratio that is consistent with your goal and data—see *Analyzing static designs* on page 24-29

- for dynamic designs, enter a response reference value and a signal reference value for the fitted line or choose to fit the line with no fixed reference point—see *Analyzing dynamic designs* on page 24-30

- use natural logs in graphs and tables for standard deviations

Storage subdialog box

- for static designs, store the
  - S/N ratios
  - means
  - standard deviations
  - coefficients of variation
  - natural log of the standard deviations

- for dynamic designs, store the
  - S/N ratios
  - slopes
  - intercepts
  - standard deviations (square root of MSE)
  - natural log of the standard deviations

Displaying main effects and interaction plots

You can display main effects and selected interaction plots for signal-to-noise (S/N) ratios, means (static designs), slopes (dynamic designs), and/or standard deviations.

▶ To display main effects and interaction plots

1 In the Analyze Taguchi Design dialog box, click **Graphs**.

Static Design   **Dynamic Design**

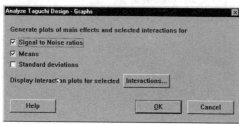 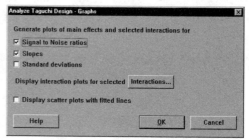

2 Under **Generate plots of main effects and selected interactions for** check **Signal-to-noise ratios**, **Means** (for static design) or **Slopes** (for dynamic design), and/or **Standard deviations**. Click **OK**.

Selecting terms for the interaction plots

You can choose which interactions to plot. You can also choose whether to display the interaction plots in a matrix on a single graph or to display each interaction plot separately on its own page.

▶ **To select which interactions to plot**

1 In the Analyze Taguchi Design dialog box, click **Graphs**.

2 In the Graphs subdialog box, click **Interactions**.

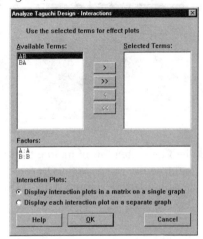

3 Move the interactions that you want to include in the plot from **Available Terms** to **Selected Terms** using the arrow buttons.

- to move the interactions one at a time, highlight an interaction, then click ⟨ or ⟩

- to move all of the interactions, click on ⟪ or ⟫

    You can also move an interaction by double-clicking it.

Note | The available terms in the Interactions subdialog box list the interactions available to plot. The second factor in the term (B in AB) is used as the horizontal scale for the plot. Thus, you can view the AB interaction both ways by selecting both AB and BA.

Displaying response tables

You can display response tables for signal-to-noise (S/N) ratios, means (static designs), slopes (dynamic designs), and/or standard deviations.

▶ **To display response tables**

1 In the Analyze Taguchi Design dialog box, click **Tables**.

Static Design

Dynamic Design

2 Under **Display response tables for** check **Signal-to-noise ratios**, **Means** (for static design) or **Slopes** (for dynamic design), and/or **Standard deviations**. Click **OK**.

Analyzing static designs

If you have a static design (no signal factor), you can choose signal-to-noise (S/N) ratios depending on the goals of your design. S/N ratios differ, therefore you should use your engineering knowledge, understanding of the process, and experience to choose the appropriate S/N ratio [3].

Choose...	Use when the goal is to...	And your data are...
Larger is better $S/N=-10(\log(\Sigma (1/Y^2)/n))$	Maximize the response	Positive
Nominal is best $S/N=-10(\log(s^2))$	Target the response and you want to base the S/N ratio on standard deviations only	Positive, zero, or negative
Nominal is best (default) $S/N=10(\log((\bar{Y}^2)/s^2))$	Target the response and you want to base the S/N ratio on means and standard deviations	Non-negative with an "absolute zero" in which the standard deviation is zero when the mean is zero
Smaller is better $S/N=-10(\log(\Sigma Y^2/n))$	Minimize the response	Non-negative with a target value of zero

Note | The Nominal is Best (default) S/N ratio is good for analyzing or identifying scaling factors, which are factors in which the mean and standard deviation vary proportionally. Scaling factors can be used to adjust the mean on target without affecting S/N ratios.

▶ **To select a signal-to-noise ratio**

1 In the Analyze Taguchi Design dialog box, click **Options**.

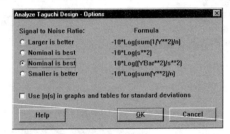

2 Under **Signal-to-Noise Ratio**, choose the S/N ratio that best fits the goals of the design. Choose from one of the following:

- Larger is better
- Nominal is best
- Nominal is best
- Smaller is better

3 Click **OK**.

Analyzing dynamic designs

Dynamic response experiments are used to improve the functional relationship between input signal and output response, in other words, to optimize tunability. The output response should be directly proportional to the input signal. The ideal functional relationship between input signal and output response is a line through the origin.

In some cases, you may wish to choose a reference point, other than the origin, through which the line should pass. For example, your results may be generated far from zero, by specifying a reference point in the range of results you can enhance the sensitivity of the analysis. Or, you can choose to fit the line with no fixed reference point. In this case, the intercept will be fitted to the data.

▶ **To specify a reference point for the response**

1 In the Analyze Taguchi Design dialog box, click **Options**.

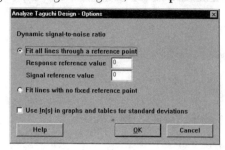

2 In **Response reference value**, enter a numeric value corresponding to the desired output (response) value.

3 In **Signal reference value**, enter a signal factor level corresponding to the response reference value. Click **OK**.

▶ **To fit a line with no fixed reference point**

1 In the Analyze Taguchi Design dialog box, click **Options**.

2 Select **Fit lines with no fixed reference point**. Click **OK**.

▷ **Example of a static Taguchi design**

Suppose you are an engineer and need to evaluate the factors that affect the seal strength of plastic bags used to ship your product. You have identified three controllable factors (Temperature, Pressure, and Thickness) and two noise conditions (Noise 1 and Noise 2) that may affect seal strength. You want to ensure that seal strength meets specifications. If the seal is too weak, it may break, contaminating the product and resulting in returns. If the seal is too strong, customers may have difficulty opening the bag. The target specification is 18.

1 Open the worksheet SEAL.MTW. The design and response data have been saved for you.

2 Choose **Stat ➤ DOE ➤ Taguchi ➤ Analyze Taguchi Design**.

3 In **Response data are in**, enter *Noise1 Noise2*.

4 Click **Graphs**. Under **Generate plots of main effects and selected interactions for**, check **Standard deviations**. Click **OK**.

5 Click **Tables**. Under **Display response tables for**, check **Standard deviations**. Click **OK** in each dialog box.

*Session
window
output*

Response Table for Signal to Noise Ratios

Nominal is best (10*Log(Ybar**2/s**2))

Level	Temperature	Pressure	Thickness
1	29.4219	21.9191	28.2568
2	27.0652	30.2117	29.0690
3	25.7842	30.1406	24.9455
Delta	3.6378	8.2926	4.1235
Rank	3	1	2

Response Table for Means

Level	Temperature	Pressure	Thickness
1	17.6500	17.5833	17.6833
2	18.3333	17.7000	17.1500
3	16.3833	17.0833	17.5333
Delta	1.9500	0.6167	0.5333
Rank	1	2	3

Response Table for Standard Deviations

Level	Temperature	Pressure	Thickness
1	0.91924	1.53206	0.96638
2	0.94281	0.75425	0.68354
3	1.01352	0.58926	1.22565
Delta	0.09428	0.94281	0.54212
Rank	3	1	2

*Graph
window
output*

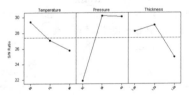

Main Effects Plot for S/N Ratios

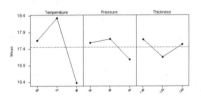

Main Effects Plot for Means

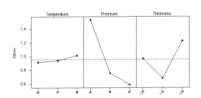

Main Effects Plot for Standard Deviations

Interpreting the results

The response tables show the average of the selected characteristic for each level of the factors. The response tables include ranks based on Delta statistics, which compare the relative magnitude of effects. The Delta statistic is the highest average for each factor minus the lowest average for each factor. Ranks are assigned based on Delta values; rank 1 is assigned to the highest Delta value, rank 2 to the second highest Delta value, and so on. The main effects plot provide a graph of the averages in the response table.

Look at the response tables and main effects plots for the signal-to-noise (S/N) ratios to see which factors have the greatest effect on S/N ratio, which in this example is nominal-is-best.

In this example, the factor with the biggest impact on the S/N ratio is Pressure (Delta = 8.29, Rank = 1). If you look at the response tables and main effects plot for S/N ratio, you can see that Pressure 36 and Pressure 40 have almost the same average S/N ratio (30.2117 and 30.1406).

Here, the response table and main effects plots for mean both show that the factor with the greatest effect on the mean is Temperature (Delta = 1.95, Rank = 1). The response table and main effects plots for standard deviation both show that the factor with the greatest effect on the standard deviation is Pressure (Delta = 0.94, Rank = 1). Next, you may want to use Predict Results to see how different factor settings affect S/N ratios and response characteristics—see *Example of predicting results* on page 24-38.

▷ Example of a dynamic Taguchi design

Suppose you are an engineer trying to increase the robustness of a measurement system. A measurement system is dynamic because as the input signal changes, the output response changes. A measurement system ideally should have a 1:1 correspondence between the value being measured (signal factor) and the measured response (system output). Similarly, zero should serve as the fixed reference point (all lines should be fit through the origin) because an input signal of zero should result in a measurement of zero.

You have identified two components of your measurement system that will serve as the control factors: Sensing and Reporting. The signal factor is the actual value of the item being measured and the output response is the measurement. You have also selected two noise conditions.

1 Open the worksheet MEASURE.MTW. The design and response data have been saved for you.

2 Choose **Stat ➤ DOE ➤ Taguchi ➤ Analyze Taguchi Design**.

3 In **Response data are in**, enter *Noise1* and *Noise2*.

4 Click **Graphs**. Under **Generate plots of main effects and selected interactions for**, check **Standard deviations**.

5 Check **Display scatter plots with fitted lines**. Click **OK**.

6 Click **Tables**. Under **Display response tables for**, check **Standard deviations**.

7 Click **OK** in each dialog box.

*Session
window
output*

Response Table for Signal to Noise Ratios

Dynamic Response

```
Level   Sensing   Reporting
1       20.3270   18.3400
2       14.2224   16.2095
Delta    6.1047    2.1305
Rank     1         2
```

Response Table for Slopes

```
Level   Sensing   Reporting
1       1.52738   1.03293
2       1.48734   1.98179
Delta   0.04004   0.94886
Rank    2         1
```

Response Table for Standard Deviations

```
Level   Sensing    Reporting
1       0.165537   0.141439
2       0.287448   0.311545
Delta   0.121911   0.170106
Rank    2          1
```

*Graph
window
output*

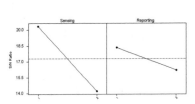

Main Effects Plot for S/N Ratios

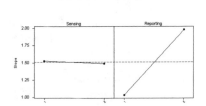

Main Effects Plot for Slopes

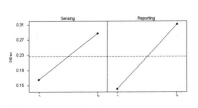

Main Effects Plot for Standard Deviations

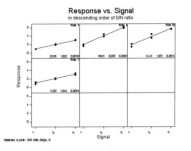

Response vs. Signal
in descending order of S/N ratio

Interpreting results

The response tables show the average of the selected characteristic for each level of the factors. The response tables include ranks based on Delta statistics, which compare the relative magnitude of effects. The Delta statistic is the highest average minus the lowest average for each factor. Ranks are assigned based on Delta values; rank 1 is assigned to the highest Delta value, rank 2 to the second highest Delta value, and so on. The main effects plot provide a graph of the averages in the response table.

Because you are trying to improve the quality of a measurement system, you want to maximize the signal-to-noise (S/N) ratio. If you examine the response table and main effects plot for S/N ratio, you can see that the Sensing (Delta = 6.1047, Rank = 1) component has a greater effect on S/N ratio than Reporting (Delta=2.1305, Rank = 2).

Here, the response table and main effects plots for slopes both show that Reporting (Delta = 0.94886, Rank = 1) has a much greater effect on slope than Sensing (Delta = 0.04004, Rank = 2). Thus, it is likely that Reporting can be used as a scaling factor to adjust the mean on target after minimizing sensitivity to noise.

The response table and main effects plot show that Reporting (Delta=0.1701, Rank=1) has a greater effect on standard deviation than sensing (Delta=0.1219, Rank=2).

Based on these results, you might first want to maximize S/N ratio using the low level of the Sensing factor and then adjust the slope on to the target of 1 using the Reporting factor.

Predicting Results

Use Predict Results after you have run a Taguchi experiment and examined the response tables and main effects plots to determine which factor settings should achieve a robust product design. Predict Results allows you to predict S/N ratios and response characteristics for selected factor settings.

For example, you might choose the best settings for the factors that have the greatest effect on the S/N, and then wish to predict the S/N and mean response for several combinations of other factors. Predict Results would provide the expected responses for those settings. You should choose the results that comes closest to the desired mean without significantly reducing the S/N ratio. You should then perform a follow-up experiment using the selected levels, to determine how well the prediction matches the observed result.

If there are minimal interactions among the factors or if the interactions have been correctly accounted for by the predictions, the observed results should be close to the prediction, and you will have succeeded in producing a robust product. On the other hand, if there is substantial disagreement between the prediction and the observed results, then there may be unaccounted for interactions or unforeseen noise effects. This would indicate that further investigation is necessary.

You can specify the terms in the model used to predict results. For example, you may decide not to include a factor in the prediction because the response table and main effects plot indicate that the factor does not have much of an effect on the response. You can also decide whether or not to include selected interactions in the model. Interactions included in the model will affect the predicted results.

Data

In order to predict results, you need to have

- created and stored the design using Create Taguchi Design (page 24-4) or created a design from data already in the worksheet with Define Custom Taguchi Design (page 24-17) and

- analyzed it using *Analyzing Taguchi Designs* on page 24-23

▶ To predict results

1 Choose **Stat ➤ DOE ➤ Taguchi ➤ Predict Results**.

<table>
<tr><th>Static Design</th><th>Dynamic Design</th></tr>
<tr><td>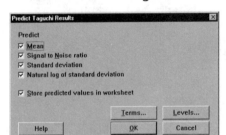</td><td>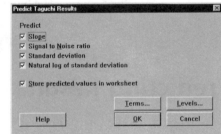</td></tr>
</table>

2 Choose to predict one or more of the following:

- mean (static design) or slope (dynamic design)

- signal-to-noise ratio

- standard deviations

- natural log of standard deviation

3 Click **Terms**.

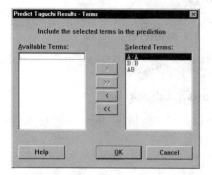

4 Move the factors that you do not want to include in the model from **Selected Terms** to **Available Terms** using the arrow buttons, then click **OK**.

- to move the terms one at a time, highlight a term, then click `<` or `>`

- to move all of the term, click on `<<` or `>>`

    You can also move a term by double-clicking it.

5 Click **Levels**.

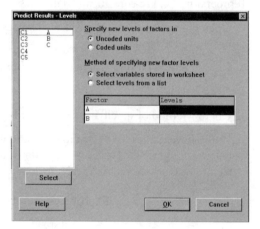

6 Do one of the following

- To specify factor levels that are already stored in a worksheet column
    - Choose **Select variables stored in worksheet**.
    - Under **Levels**, click in the first row and enter column containing the new levels of the first factor. Then, use the ↓ key to move down the column and enter the remaining factor level columns. Click **OK**.

- To select levels from a list of the existing factor levels
    - Choose **Select levels from a list**.
    - Under **Levels**, click in the first row and choose the factor level from the drop-down list. Then, use the ↓ key to move down the column and choose the remaining factor levels. Click **OK**.

Options

Predict results dialog box

■ store the predicted values in the worksheet (default)

Terms subdialog box

■ choose terms to include in the prediction model

Levels subdialog box

■ enter the new factor levels in coded or uncoded units

▷ **Example of predicting results**

We will now predict results for the seal strength experiment introduced on page 24-31. You had identified three controllable factors that you thought would influence seal strength: Temperature, Pressure, and Thickness. Because you first want to maximize the signal-to-noise (S/N) ratio, you chose factor settings that increase S/N ratios: Temperature 60, Pressure 36, and Thickness 1.25.

1 Open the worksheet SEAL2.MTW. The design and response information have been saved for you.

2 Choose **Stat ➤ DOE ➤ Taguchi ➤ Predict Results**.

3 Click **Levels**.

4 Under **Method of specifying new factor levels**, choose **Select levels from a list**.

5 Under **Levels**, click in the first row and choose the factor level according to the table below. Then, use the ⬇ key to move down the column and choose the remaining factor levels according to the table below.

Factor	Levels
Temperature	60
Pressure	36
Thickness	1.25

6 Click **OK** in each dialog box.

Session window output

Predicted values

S/N Ratio	Mean	StDev	Log(StDev)
33.8551	17.5889	0.439978	-1.03172

Interpreting results

The predicted results for the chosen factor settings are: S/N ratio of 33.8551, mean of 17.5889, and standard deviation of 0.439978. Next, you might run an experiment using these factor settings to test the accuracy of the model.

Note | The predicted values for the standard deviation and log of the standard deviation use different models of the data.

References

[1] G.S. Peace (1993). *Taguchi Methods*. Addison-Wesley Publishing Company.

[2] J.H. Lochner and J.E. Matar (1990). *Designing for Quality*. ASQC Quality Press.

[3] W. Y. Fowlkes and C.M. Creveling (1995). *Engineering Methods for Robust Product Design*. Addison-Wesley Publishing Company.

[4] S.H. Park (1996). *Robust Design and Analysis for Quality Engineering*. Chapman & Hall.

[5] M.S. Phadke (1989). *Quality Engineering Using Robust Design*. Prentice-Hall.

INDEX

multivariate analysis of variance 3-26
  balanced 3-51
  example 3-54
  general 3-57
  general, example 3-58
  general, nesting 3-57
  specify terms to test 3-53, 3-59
  tests 3-54

N

natural rate response, probit analysis 17-12

nearest neighbor cluster distance 4-24

nested factors 3-19, 3-26, 3-37, 3-51, 3-57

nesting
  in ANOVA 3-49
  in general MANOVA 3-57
  in GLM 3-37

noise factors 24-5

nominal is best, analyze Taguchi design 24-29

nominal logistic regression 2-51
  data 2-51
  example 2-55
  model 2-54
  options 2-52
  parameter estimates, interpreting 2-54
  Session window output description 2-56
  worksheet structure 2-32

nominal specification for capability analysis 14-8

non-normal data 14-6
  with control charts 12-6, 12-68

nonparametric distribution analysis 15-3, 15-52
  actuarial survival estimates 15-4, 15-58
  arbitrarily censored data 15-54
  density function 15-60

draw a hazard plot, arbitrary censoring 15-63
draw a hazard plot, right censoring 15-62
hazard function 15-57, 15-60
hazard plots 15-62
Kaplan-Meier survival estimates 15-4, 15-56
nonparametric survival plots 15-61
options 15-54
request actuarial estimates 15-60
right censored data 15-53
survival curve, comparing in 15-62
survival probabilities 15-56
Turnbull survival estimates 15-4, 15-58
uncensored/right censored data 15-53

nonparametric survival plots, nonparametric distribution analysis 15-61

nonparametrics 5-1
  overview 5-2

normal probability plot 1-43, 14-24

normality test 1-43
  example 1-44

normit link function 2-36, 2-46

NP charts 13-7

number of defectives control chart 13-7

number of defects control chart 13-9

number of defects-per-unit control chart 13-12

numeric data with a Pareto chart 10-11

O

one proportion
  confidence interval 1-26
  example 1-29
  method 1-28
  power 9-7

sample size 9-7
test 1-26

one-sample
  sign test 5-3
  Wilcoxon test 5-7

one-sample t
  confidence interval 1-15
  example 1-17
  method 1-17
  power 9-4
  sample size 9-4
  sample size example 9-6
  test 1-15

one-sample Z
  confidence interval 1-12
  example 1-14
  method 1-14
  power 9-4
  sample size 9-4
  test 1-12

one-way analysis of variance 3-5
  power 9-10
  power example 9-12
  sample size 9-10
  stacked data 3-5
  unstacked data 3-6

one-way table 6-3

optimal designs 22-2
  augmenting 22-9
  augmenting example 22-16
  D-optimal 22-6, 22-14
  distance-based 22-6, 22-14
  evaluating 22-18
  evaluating example 22-21
  overview 22-2
  selecting 22-2
  selecting example 22-8

optimization 23-2, 23-19

optimization plot 23-10

ordinal logistic regression 2-44
  data 2-44
  example 2-48
  options 2-45
  parameter estimates, interpreting 2-47
  Session window output description 2-49
  worksheet structure 2-32

U

U chart 13-12, 14-41
unequal subgroup sizes
    defectives control charts 13-3
    (R chart, Xbar-R chart, Xbar-S
    chart, S chart, Xbar chart)
    12-10
univariate analysis of variance 3-26,
    3-37
unrestricted form of mixed models
    3-28
    example 3-33
unusual observations in regression
    2-12
utility transfer function 23-6

V

V-mask 12-44
variable selection with stepwise
    regression 2-18
variables control charts 12-1
    add rows of tick labels 12-72
    between/within chart 12-24
    Box-Cox transformation for
    non-normal data 12-5
    control charts for data in
    subgroups 12-10
    control charts for individual
    observations 12-28
    control charts for short runs
    12-54
    control charts using subgroup
    combinations 12-36
    control how σ is estimated
    12-67
    customize 12-74
    customize control (sigma)
    limits 12-70
    CUSUM chart 12-44
    defining tests for special causes
    12-5
    estimate control limits and
    center line independently for
    different groups 12-61

EWMA chart 12-37
force control limits and center
    line to be constant 12-68
I (individuals) chart 12-29
I-MR chart 12-34
I-MR-R/S chart 12-24
moving average chart 12-41
moving range chart 12-32
omit subgroups from estimate
    of μ or σ 12-66
options 12-66
overview 12-2
R chart 12-14
S chart 12-17
tests for special causes 12-64
time stamp 12-72
use historical values of μ and σ
    12-64
X-bar and R chart 12-19
X-bar and S chart 12-22
X-bar chart 12-11
Z-MR chart 12-54
zone chart 12-48
variance 1-6
    inflation factor 2-7
    test 3-60
    test example 3-62
    test for equality 1-34
varimax rotation method 4-10
VIF 2-7

W

Walsh average 5-24
Ward's linkage 4-25
web site xiv
Weibull distribution
    capability analysis 14-21
    control charts 14-34
Weibull probability plot 14-34
weighted least squares regression
    2-6
Wilcoxon
    signed rank test 5-7
    test, 1-sample 5-7
Wilk's test 3-54

Winters' exponential smoothing
    7-30
    additive model 7-32
    choosing weights 7-32
    forecasting 7-33
    multiplicative model 7-32
wireframe plots 19-60, 20-34
within-subgroups variation 14-5,
    14-10, 14-17
worksheet structure
    accelerated life testing 16-3
    arbitrarily censored data 15-8
    frequency column 15-7
    multiply censored data 15-6
    probit analysis 17-2
    regression with life data 16-3,
    16-20
    right censored data 15-5
    singly censored data 15-6
    stacked vs. unstacked data 15-8
worksheet structure, logistic
    regression 2-32
WWW address xiv

X

X-bar and R chart 12-19
X-bar and S chart 12-22
X-bar chart 12-11, 14-24, 14-34

Y

Yates' order 19-17, 20-11

Z

Z and MR chart 12-54
Z-test
    one-sample confidence
    interval 1-12
    one-sample test 1-12
zone control chart 12-48
    comparing with a Shewhart
    chart 12-52

How to Order Additional Products

To order, contact Minitab Inc. between 8:00 a.m. and 5:30 p.m. Eastern time, Monday through Friday, or contact Minitab Ltd., Minitab SARL, or your distributor. If you are calling Minitab Inc. from within the USA or Canada, call 800-448-3555. Otherwise, call (+1) 814-238-3280, or contact Minitab Inc. via e-mail at sales@minitab.com. Contact information for Minitab Ltd (UK only: 0800 0929 353) and Minitab SARL (France only: 0800 608440) are provided on the back cover of this book. Or, visit our web site at http://www.minitab.com.

Additional Documentation

Minitab Inc. offers clearly-written documentation to assist MINITAB users in installing, running, and applying MINITAB functionality to statistical problem solving.

Release 13 for Windows

MINITAB User's Guide 1: Data, Graphics, and Macros

A complete and detailed manual covering data manipulation, file input and output, graphics, and macros commands, with numerous examples throughout.

MINITAB User's Guide 2: Data Analysis and Quality Tools

A complete and detailed manual covering statistics, quality control, reliability and survival analysis, and design of experimentss, with numerous examples throughout.

Meet MINITAB

A concise guide to getting started with MINITAB, including sample sessions, to get you "up and running" quickly.

Older Releases

Documentation for older releases of MINITAB is available. For details, contact Minitab Inc., Minitab Ltd., Minitab SARL, or your distributor.

Any Release

MINITAB Handbook, Third Edition

A supplementary text that teaches basic statistics using MINITAB. The Handbook features the creative use of plots, application of standard statistical methods to real data, in-depth exploration of data, and more.

Additional MINITAB Products

Please contact us if you'd like more information about these products:

- MINITAB Training, on-site and public training designed to save time and money by providing practical, useful information on how best to use MINITAB to optimize your company's performance.

- MINITAB Student, a streamlined and economical version of MINITAB, designed specially for introductory general and business statistics.

- MINITAB in French, a completely localized version of MINITAB.

Older releases of MINITAB are available in Spanish, and in English for several computer platforms including Macintosh, older Windows systems, DOS systems, and Unix workstations.

Minitab Global

Minitab products can be purchased through Minitab Inc., Minitab Ltd., Minitab SARL, or one of Minitab's authorized international partners. From Antarctica to Zimbabwe, Minitab Inc. and its partners are available world-wide to service and support Minitab customers.

For information about the international partner serving your market, please refer to the *International Partners Card* included in your software product box. For additional listings since the time of printing, please visit our web site (http://www.minitab.com), or contact

Minitab Inc. at the USA office (call +1 814.238.3280, fax +1 814.238.4383, or e-mail intlsales@minitab.com);

Minitab Ltd. at the UK office (call +44 (0) 24 7665 2777, fax +44 (0) 24 7665 2888, or e-mail sales@minitab.co.uk); or

Minitab SARL in France (call +33 (0) 1 55 33 12 36, fax +33 (0) 1 55 33 12 39, or e-mail bienvenue@minitab.fr).